T0310788

Machine Audition:
Principles, Algorithms and Systems

Wenwu Wang
University of Surrey, UK

INFORMATION SCIENCE REFERENCE

Hershey · New York

Director of Editorial Content: Kristin Klinger
Director of Book Publications: Julia Mosemann
Acquisitions Editor: Lindsay Johnston
Development Editor: Joel Gamon
Publishing Assistants: Casey Conapitski and Travis Gundrum
Typesetter: Michael Brehm
Production Editor: Jamie Snavely
Cover Design: Lisa Tosheff

Published in the United States of America by
        Information Science Reference (an imprint of IGI Global)
        701 E. Chocolate Avenue
        Hershey PA 17033
        Tel: 717-533-8845
        Fax: 717-533-8661
        E-mail: cust@igi-global.com
        Web site: http://www.igi-global.com

Library of Congress Cataloging-in-Publication Data

Machine audition : principles, algorithms, and systems / Wenwu Wang, editor.
      p. cm.
  Includes bibliographical references and index.
  Summary: "This book covers advances in algorithmic developments, theoretical frameworks, and experimental research findings to assist professionals who want an improved understanding about how to design algorithms for performing automatic analysis of audio signals, construct a computing system for understanding sound, and to learn how to build advanced human-computer interactive systems"--Provided by publisher.   ISBN 978-1-61520-919-4 (hardcover) -- ISBN 978-1-61520-920-0 (ebook) 1. Computational auditory scene analysis. 2. Signal processing. 3. Auditory perception--Computer simulation. I. Wang, Wenwu, 1974- TK7881.4.M27 2010
  006.4'5--dc22
                                     2010010161

British Cataloguing in Publication Data
A Cataloguing in Publication record for this book is available from the British Library.

All work contributed to this book is new, previously-unpublished material. The views expressed in this book are those of the authors, but not necessarily of the publisher.

Table of Contents

Section 2
Audio Signal Separation, Extraction and Localization

Detailed Table of Contents

Section 1
Audio Scene Analysis, Recognition and Modeling

Selina Chu, University of Southern California, USA
Shrikanth Narayanan, University of Southern California, USA
C.-C. Jay Kuo, University of Southern California, USA

The goal of this chapter is on the characterization of unstructured environmental sounds for understanding and predicting the context surrounding of an agent or device. Most research on audio recognition has focused primarily on speech and music. Less attention has been paid to the challenges and opportunities for using audio to characterize unstructured audio. This chapter investigates issues in characterizing unstructured environmental sounds such as the development of appropriate feature extraction algorithms and learning techniques for modeling backgrounds of the environment.

Luís Gustavo Martins, Portuguese Catholic University, Porto Portugal
Mathieu Lagrange, CNRS - Institut de Recherche et Coordination Acoustique Musique (IRCAM), France
George Tzanetakis, University of Victoria, Canada

Computational Auditory Scene Analysis (CASA) is challenging problem, to which many approaches can be broadly categorized as either model-based or grouping-based. Most existing systems either rely on prior source models or are solely based on grouping cues. In this chapter the authors argue that formulating this integration problem as clustering based on similarities between time-frequency atoms provides an expressive yet disciplined approach to building sound source characterization and separation systems and evaluating their performance. They describe the main components of the architecture, its advantages, implementation details, and related issues.

Chapter 3

Cocktail party problem is a classical and challenging scientific problem that is still unsolved. Many efforts have been attempted by researchers to address this problem using different techniques. This chapter provides a review on recent progresses in several areas, such as independent component analysis, computational auditory scene analysis, model-based approaches, non-negative matrix factorization, sparse representation and compressed sensing. As an example, a multistage approach is also provided for addressing the source separation issue within this problem.

Chapter 4

The demand to function in uncontrolled listening environments has severe implications for machine audition. The natural system has addressed this demand by adapting its function flexibly to changing task demands. This chapter addresses the functional requirements of auditory systems, both natural and artificial, to be able to deal with the complexities of uncontrolled real-world input. Signal processing methods that are needed for such scenarios are also discussed.

Section 2
Audio Signal Separation, Extraction and Localization

Machine separation of moving audio sources is a challenging problem. This chapter presents a novel multimodal solution to blind source separation (BSS) of moving sources, where the visual modality is utilized to facilitate the separation of moving sources. The movement of the sources is detected by a relatively simplistic 3-D tracker based on video cameras. The tracking process is based on particle filtering which provides robust tracking performance. Positions and velocities of the sources are obtained from the 3-D tracker and if the sources are moving, real time speech enhancement and separation of the sources are obtained by using a beamforming algorithm.

Automatic sound source localization may refer to determining only the direction of a sound source, which is known as the direction-of-arrival estimation, or also its distance in order to obtain its coordinates. Many of the methods proposed previously use the time and level differences between the signals captured by each element of a microphone array. This chapter presents an overview of these conventional array processing methods and a discussion of the factors that affect their performance. The chapter also discusses an emerging source localization method based on acoustic intensity, and addresses two well-known problems, localization of multiple sources and localization of acoustic reflections.

Chapter 7

Source separation aims to provide machine listeners with similar skills to humans by extracting the sounds of individual sources from a given audio scene. Existing separation systems operate either by emulating the human auditory system or inferring the parameters of probabilistic sound models. In this chapter, the authors focus on the latter approach and provide a joint overview of established and recent models, including independent component analysis, local time-frequency models and spectral template-based models. They show that most models are instances of one of the following two general paradigms: linear modeling or variance modeling, and they compare the merits of either paradigm, report objective performance figures and discuss promising combinations of probabilistic priors and inference algorithms.

Chapter 8

In this chapter, Tensor factorization (TF) is introduced to the problem of separation of sound particularly speech sources from their corresponding convolutive mixtures. TF is flexible and can easily incorporate all possible parameters or factors into the separation formulation. As a consequence of that fewer assumptions (such as uncorrelatedness and independency) will be required. The new formulation allows further degree of freedom to the original parallel factor analysis (PARAFAC) problem in which the scaling and permutation problems of the frequency domain blind source separation (BSS) can be resolved.

Chapter 9

Nilesh Madhu, Ruhr-Universität Bochum, Germany
André Gückel, Dolby Laboratories - Nürnberg, Germany

Machine-based multi-channel source separation in real life situations is a challenging problem, and has a wide range of applications, from medical to military. This chapter considers the specific application of a target speaker enhancement in the presence of competing speakers and background noise. It presents not only an exhaustive overview of state-of-the-art separation algorithms and the specific models they are based upon, but also the relations between these algorithms, where possible. In particular, it compares the performance difference between the mask-based techniques and the independent component analysis (ICA) techniques.

Chapter 10

Andrew Nesbit, Queen Mary University of London, UK
Maria G. Jafari, Queen Mary University of London, UK
Emmanuel Vincent, INRIA, France
Mark D. Plumbley, Queen Mary University of London, UK

The authors address the problem of audio source separation based on the sparse component analysis framework. The overriding aim of this chapter is to demonstrate how this framework can be used to solve different problems in different mixing scenarios. To address the instantaneous and underdetermined mixing model, a lapped orthogonal transform is adapted to the signal by selecting a basis from a library of predetermined bases. In considering the anechoic and determined mixing case, a greedy adaptive transform is used based on orthogonal basis functions that are learned from the observed data. The chapter also demonstrates the good signal approximations and separation performance by these methods using experiments on mixtures of speech and music signals.

Section 3
Audio Transcription, Mining and Information Retrieval

Chapter 11

Cédric Févotte, CNRS LTCI; TELECOM ParisTech, France

This chapter presents a nonnegative matrix factorization (NMF) technique for audio decomposition by considering factorization of the power spectrogram, with the Itakura-Saito (IS) divergence. The author shows that IS-NMF is connected to maximum likelihood inference of variance parameters in a well-defined statistical model of superimposed Gaussian components which is well suited to audio. The chapter further discusses the model order selection strategies and Markov regularization of the activation matrix. Extensions of NMF to the multichannel case, in both instantaneous and convolutive recordings, possibly underdetermined, together with audio source separation results of a real stereo musical excerpt are also included.

The authors provide a comprehensive introduction to the design of music onset detection algorithms. First, it introduces the general scheme and commonly-used time-frequency analysis for onset detection. Then, it reviews many methods for onset detection in detail, such as energy-based, phase-based, pitch-based and supervised learning methods. The chapter also includes commonly used performance measures, onset annotation software, public database, and evaluation methods.

This chapter presents automatic segmentation methods using different original representations of music, corresponding to rhythm, chroma, and timbre, and by calculating a shortest path through the self-similarity calculated from each time/feature representation. Each segmentation scale quality is analyzed through the use of the mean silhouette value, which permits automatic segmentation on different time scales and gives indication on the inherent segment sizes in the music analyzed. Different methods are employed to verify the quality of the inherent segment sizes, by comparing them to the literature (grouping, chunks), by comparing them among themselves, and by measuring the strength of the inherent segment sizes.

A great deal of attention has been paid recently to the automatic prediction of tags for music and audio in general. In the case of music, social tags have become an important component of ``Web 2.0'' recommender systems. In an effort to better understand the task and also to help new researchers bring their insights to bear on this problem, this chapter provides a review of the state-of-the-art methods for addressing automatic tagging of audio. It is divided in the following sections: goal, framework, audio representation, labeled data, classification, evaluation, and future directions.

Non-negative matrix factorization (NMF) has been shown recently to be a useful technique for audio decomposition. However, the instantaneous NMF model has difficulty in dealing with the audio signals whose frequencies change dramatically over time, which is nevertheless in practice a case for many real signals. This chapter intends to provide a brief overview of the models and algorithms for both instantaneous and convolutive NMF, with a focus on the theoretical analysis and performance evaluation of the convolutive NMF algorithms, and their applications to audio pattern separation problems.

Section 4
Audio Cognition, Modeling and Affective Computing

This chapter investigates the modeling methods for musical cognition. The author explores possible relations between cognitive measures of musical structure and statistical signal properties that are revealed through information dynamics analysis. The addressed questions include: (1) description of music as an information source, (2) modeling of music–listener relations in terms of communication channel, (3) choice of musical features and dealing with their dependencies, (4) survey of different information measures for description of musical structure and measures of shared information between listener and the music, and (5) suggestion of new approach to characterization of listening experience in terms of different combinations of musical surface and structure expectancies.

This chapter provides a survey of research efforts in emotion recognition using different modalities: audio, visual and audio-visual combined. It also describes fifteen audio, visual and audio-visual data sets, and the types of feature that researchers have used to represent the emotional content. Several important issues, such as feature selection and reduction, emotion classification, and methods for fusing information from multiple modalities are also discussed. The chapter concludes by pointing out interesting areas in this field for future investigation.

Propagation of sound from a source to a receiver in an enclosure can be modeled as an acoustic transmission channel. Objective room acoustic parameters are routinely used to quantify properties of such channels in the design and assessment of acoustically critical spaces. This chapter discusses a number of new methods and algorithms for determining room acoustic parameters using machine audition of naturally occurring sound sources, i.e. speech and music. In particular, reverberation time, early decay time and speech transmission index can be estimated from received speech or music signals using statistical machine learning or maximum likelihood estimation in a semi-blind or blind fashion.

Chapter 19

    Pedro Gómez-Vilda, Universidad Politécnica de Madrid, Spain
    José Manuel Ferrández-Vicente, Universidad Politécnica de Madrid, Spain
    Victoria Rodellar-Biarge, Universidad Politécnica de Madrid, Spain
    Roberto Fernández-Baíllo, Universidad Politécnica de Madrid, Spain
    Agustín Álvarez-Marquina, Universidad Politécnica de Madrid, Spain
    Rafael Martínez-Olalla, Universidad Politécnica de Madrid, Spain
    Víctor Nieto-Lluis, Universidad Politécnica de Madrid, Spain
    Luis Miguel Mazaira-Fernández, Universidad Politécnica de Madrid, Spain
    Cristina Muñoz-Mulas, Universidad Politécnica de Madrid, Spain

In speech perception and recognition, many hidden phenomena are not well understood yet, including the semantic gap going from spectral time-frequency representations to the symbolic translation into phonemes and words, and the construction of morpho-syntactic and semantic structures. This chapter is intended to explore some of these facts at a simplifying level under two points of view: that of top-down analysis provided from speech perception, and the symmetric from bottom-up synthesis provided by the biological architecture of auditory pathways. It also includes an application-driven design of a neuromorphic speech processing architecture and the simulation details provided by a parallel implementation of the architecture in a supercomputer.

Preface

OUTLINE AND SUBJECT OF THIS BOOK

Machine audition is the field of the study of algorithms and systems for the automatic analysis and understanding of sound by machine. It plays an important role in many applications, such as automatic audio indexing for internet searching, robust speech recognition in un-controlled natural environment, untethered audio communication within an intelligent office scenario, and speech enhancement for hearing aids and cochlear implants, etc. It has recently attracted increasing interest within several research communities, such as signal processing, machine learning, auditory modelling, perception and cognition, psychology, pattern recognition, and artificial intelligence. However, the developments made so far are fragmented within these disciplines, lacking connections and incurring potentially overlapping research activities in this subject area. The proposed book intends to bring together the advances in recent algorithmic developments, bridge the gaps between the methodologies adopted by the various disciplines, and overlook future directions in this subject.

OBJECTIVES, MISSIONS AND THE SCHOLARLY VALUE

This book aims to provide algorithmic developments, theoretical frameworks and empirical and experimental research findings in the area of machine audition. It could be useful for professionals who want to improve their understanding about how to design algorithms for performing automatic analysis of audio signals, how to construct a computing system that could understand sound sources around us, and how to build advanced human-computer interactive systems. The book covers the existing and the emerging algorithms and frameworks for processing sound mixtures, the practical approaches for implementing machine audition systems, as well as the relationship between human and machine audition. It will provide professionals, academic researchers, students, consultants and practitioners with a good overview of how the sound might be understood by a machine based on algorithmic operation, and how the machine audition approaches might be useful for solving practical engineering problems in daily life.

The book is the first of its kind that describes the theoretical, algorithmic and systematic results from the area of machine audition. It intends to promote "machine audition" as a subject area that is equally attractive to the popular subject of "computer vision". The book treats audition in the context of general audio, rather than for specific data, such as speech in some existing literature. It contains many new approaches and algorithms, most recent numerical and experimental results, which could foster a better understanding of the state of the art of the subject and ultimately motivate novel ideas and thinking in the research communities. A unique characteristic about the book is that it brings together the fragments of the research findings in machine audition research across several disciplines, which could potentially promote cutting-edge research in this subject area.

TARGET AUDIENCE

The contents of this book are expected to be attractive to professionals, researchers, students and practitioners working in the fields of machine audition, audio engineering and signal processing. Researchers from the field of computer sciences, information technology and psychology will also be the audience of the book. The proposed book will be a precious reference for these audience who wish to have better understanding about the subject, to contribute to research of the subject, and to implement their new ideas and to provide technical consultancy in the field.

The potential uses of the book include library reference, upper-level course supplement, resource for instructors, reference for researchers, reference book for policy makers, reference book for businessman, studying material for undergraduate or postgraduate students, resource for practitioners, resource for consultants, etc.

ORGANIZATION OF THE BOOK

This book has nineteen chapters divided into four broader areas as follows:

- Audio Scene Analysis, Recognition and Modeling
- Audio Signal Separation, Extraction and Localization
- Audio Transcription, Mining and Information Retrieval
- Audio Cognition, Modeling and Affective Computing

We briefly summarize the contents of each section and the main contributions of each chapter, based on the abstracts and details of the chapters provided by the authors. To be as much consistent with the original contributions as possible, the following summaries for each chapter are direct quotations of the descriptions provided by the authors, with some moderations.

Section 1: Audio Scene Analysis, Recognition and Modeling

This section focuses on the computational principles and algorithms for audio scene analysis, recognition and modeling. It includes four chapters in several aspects of audio scene analysis, such as environmental audio recognition, computational auditory scene analysis, cocktail party problem, and the functional requirements of auditory systems for uncontrolled natural environments. The key issue that machine audition attempts to address is on the automatic analysis (understanding by computers) of the audio scenes using algorithm-based operations. From this aspect, progresses in this area are likely to have significant impact on this subject.

Chapter 1, "*Unstructured Environmental Audio: Representation, Classification and Modeling*" by Chu, Narayanan, and Jay Kuo, discusses the characterization of unstructured environmental sounds for understanding and predicting the context surrounding of an agent or device. Most research on audio recognition has focused primarily on speech and music. Less attention has been paid to the challenges and opportunities for using audio to characterize unstructured audio. This chapter investigates issues in characterizing unstructured environmental sounds such as the development of appropriate feature extraction algorithms and learning techniques for modeling backgrounds of the environment.

Chapter 2, "*Modeling Grouping Cues for Auditory Scene Analysis using a Spectral Clustering Formulation*" by Martins, Lagrange, and Tzanetakis, proposes to formulate the integration problem in scene analysis as clustering based on similarities between time-frequency atoms and this provides an expressive yet disciplined approach to building sound source characterization and separation systems and evaluating their performance. The authors describe the main components of the architecture, its advantages, implementation details, and related issues.

Chapter 3, "*Cocktail Party Problem: Source Separation Issues and Computational Methods*" by Jan and Wang, provides a review on recent progresses for cocktail party problem in several areas, such as independent component analysis, computational auditory scene analysis, model-based approaches, non-negative matrix factorization, sparse representation and compressed sensing. As an example, a multistage approach is also provided for addressing the source separation issue within this problem. The chapter also discusses the applications of cocktail party processing and its potential research directions for the future.

Chapter 4, "*Audition: From Sound to Sounds*" by Andringa, addresses the functional requirements of auditory systems, both natural and artificial, to be able to deal with the complexities of uncontrolled real-world input. Signal processing methods that are needed for such scenarios are also discussed. The discussions are based on the demand to function in uncontrolled listening environments and their implications for machine audition.

Section 2: Audio Signal Separation, Extraction and Localization

Source separation, extraction and localization play a central role in automatic auditory scene analysis. This section collects six recent contributions in this area, such as a multimodal approach for moving source separation, source separation based on probabilistic modeling or sparse representation, tensor factorization for source separation, multichannel source separation, and sound source localization based on intensity vector directions. Source separation problems have been studied extensively in the past two decades. It has widespread applications in, for example, robust speech recognition, teleconferencing, human-computer interaction and so on.

Chapter 5, "*A Multimodal Solution to Blind Source Separation of Moving Sources*" by Naqvi, Zhang, Yu, and Chambers, proposes a novel multimodal solution to blind source separation (BSS) of moving sources, where the visual modality is utilized to facilitate the separation of moving sources. The movement of the sources is detected by a relatively simplistic 3-D tracker based on video cameras. The tracking process is based on particle filtering which provides robust tracking performance. Positions and velocities of the sources are obtained from the 3-D tracker and if the sources are moving, real time speech enhancement and separation of the sources are obtained by using a beamforming algorithm.

Chapter 6, "*Sound Source Localization: Conventional Methods and Intensity Vector Direction Exploitation*" by Günel and Hacıhabiboğlu, presents an overview of the conventional array processing methods for sound source localization and a discussion of the factors that affect their performance. The chapter then discusses an emerging source localization method based on acoustic intensity, and addresses two well-known problems, localization of multiple sources and localization of acoustic reflections.

Chapter 7, "*Probabilistic Modeling Paradigms for Audio Source Separation*" by Vincent, Jafari, Abdallah, Plumbley, and Davies, focuses on the audio source separation methods by inferring the parameters of probabilistic sound models. The authors provide a joint overview of established and recent models, including independent component analysis, local time-frequency models and spectral template-based models. They show that most models are instances of one of the following two general paradigms: linear modeling or variance modeling, and they compare the merits of either paradigm, report objective performance figures and discuss promising combinations of probabilistic priors and inference algorithms.

Chapter 8, "*Tensor Factorization with Application to Convolutive Blind Source Separation of Speech*" by Sanei and Makkiabadi, introduces the Tensor factorization (TF) technique for the separation of sound particularly speech sources from their corresponding convolutive mixtures. TF is flexible and can easily incorporate all possible parameters or factors into the separation formulation. As a consequence of that fewer assumptions (such as uncorrelatedness and independency) will be required. The new formulation allows further degree of freedom to the original parallel factor analysis (PARAFAC) problem in which the scaling and permutation problems of the frequency domain blind source separation (BSS) can be resolved.

Chapter 9, "*Multi-Channel Source Separation: Overview and Comparison of Mask-Based and Linear Separation Algorithms*" by Madhu and Gückel, considers the specific application of a target speaker enhancement in the presence of competing speakers and background noise. It presents not only an exhaustive overview of state-of-the-art separation algorithms and the specific models they are based upon, but also the relations between these algorithms, where possible. In particular, it compares the performance difference between the mask-based techniques and the independent component analysis (ICA) techniques.

Chapter 10, "*Audio Source Separation using Sparse Representations*" by Nesbit, Jafari, Vincent, and Plumbley, addresses the problem of audio source separation based on the sparse component analysis framework. The overriding aim is to demonstrate how this framework can be used to solve different problems in different mixing scenarios. To address the instantaneous and underdetermined mixing model, a lapped orthogonal transform is adapted to the signal by selecting a basis from a library of predetermined bases. In considering the anechoic and determined mixing case, a greedy adaptive transform is used based on orthogonal basis functions that are learned from the observed data. The chapter also demonstrates the good signal approximations and separation performance by these methods using experiments on mixtures of speech and music signals.

Section 3: Audio Transcription, Mining and Information Retrieval

This section includes five contributions on different aspects of audio transcription, mining and information retrieval, such as music decomposition based on machine learning techniques, music onset detection, music segmentation, and automatic tagging of audio. All these are important topics in machine audition and they attract increasing research interests recently. Research outputs in this area are likely to have strong impact in audio coding, compression, and indexing.

Chapter 11, "*Itakura-Saito Nonnegative Factorizations of the Power Spectrogram for Music Signal Decomposition*" by Févotte, presents a nonnegative matrix factorization (NMF) technique for audio decomposition by considering factorization of the power spectrogram, with the Itakura-Saito (IS) divergence. The author shows that IS-NMF is connected to maximum likelihood inference of variance parameters in a well-defined statistical model of superimposed Gaussian components which is well suited to audio. The chapter further discusses the model order selection strategies and Markov regularization of the activation matrix. Extensions of NMF to the multichannel case, in both instantaneous and convolutive recordings, possibly underdetermined, together with audio source separation results of a real stereo musical excerpt are also included.

Chapter 12, "*Music Onset Detection*" by Zhou and Reiss, provides a comprehensive introduction to the design of music onset detection algorithms. First, it introduces the general scheme and commonly-used time-frequency analysis for onset detection. Then, it reviews many methods for onset detection in detail, such as energy-based, phase-based, pitch-based and supervised learning methods. The chapter also includes commonly used performance measures, onset annotation software, public database, and evaluation methods.

Chapter 13, "*On the Inherent Segment Length in Music*" by Jensen, presents automatic segmentation methods using different original representations of music, corresponding to rhythm, chroma, and timbre, and by calculating a shortest path through the self-similarity calculated from each time/feature representation. Each segmentation scale quality is analyzed through the use of the mean silhouette value, which permits automatic segmentation on different time scales and gives indication on the inherent segment sizes in the music analyzed. Different methods are employed to verify the quality of the inherent segment sizes, by comparing them to the literature (grouping, chunks), by comparing them among themselves, and by measuring the strength of the inherent segment sizes.

Chapter 14, "*Automatic Tagging of Audio: The State-of-the-Art*" by Bertin-Mahieux, Eck, and Mandel, provides a review of the state-of-the-art methods for addressing automatic tagging of audio. A great deal of attention has been paid recently to the automatic prediction of tags for music and audio in general. In the case of music, social tags have become an important component of ``Web 2.0'' recommender systems. The chapter is devoted as an effort to better understand the task and also to help new researchers bring their insights to bear on this problem. It is divided in the following sections: goal, framework, audio representation, labeled data, classification, evaluation, and future directions.

Chapter 15, "*Instantaneous vs. Convolutive Non-Negative Matrix Factorization: Models, Algorithms and Applications to Audio Pattern Separation*" by Wang, presents an overview of the models and algorithms for instantaneous and convolutive non-negative matrix factorization (NMF), with a focus on the convolutive NMF algorithms and their performance. The chapter discusses the limitations of the instantaneous model and the advantages of the convolutive model in addressing such limitations. The chapter also provides application examples of both models and algorithms in audio pattern separation and onset detection. A theoretical analysis of the convolutive NMF algorithms is also included.

Section 4: Audio Cognition, Modeling and Affective Computing

This section is a collection of four contributions in the area of audio cognition, modeling and affective computing, such as the modeling methods for music cognition, in particular, music anticipation, emotion recognition from audio, video, or audio-visual data, acoustic channel modeling and parameter estimation from speech or music signals recorded in a room, and using semantic and symbolic information from speech perception for the design of speech processing systems. The topics in this section bring together knowledge from several subjects including signal processing, psychology, computer science, and statistics. Many of these topics are emerging areas in the field.

Chapter 16, "*Musical Information Dynamics as Models of Auditory Anticipation*" by Dubnov, investigates the modeling methods for musical cognition. The author explores possible relations between cognitive measures of musical structure and statistical signal properties that are revealed through information dynamics analysis. The addressed questions include: 1) description of music as an information source, 2) modeling of music–listener relations in terms of communication channel, 3) choice of musical features and dealing with their dependencies, 4) survey of different information measures for description of musical structure and measures of shared information between listener and the music, and 5) suggestion of new approach to characterization of listening experience in terms of different combinations of musical surface and structure expectancies.

Chapter 17, "*Multimodal Emotion Recognition*" by Haq and Jackson, provides a survey of research efforts in emotion recognition using different modalities: audio, visual and audio-visual combined. It also describes fifteen audio, visual and audio-visual data sets, and the types of feature that researchers have used to represent the emotional content. Several important issues, such as feature selection and reduction, emotion classification, and methods for fusing information from multiple modalities are also discussed. The chapter concludes by pointing out interesting areas in this field for future investigation.

Chapter 18, "*Machine Audition of Acoustics: Acoustic Channel Modeling and Room Acoustic Parameter Estimation*" by Li, Kendrick, and Cox, discusses a number of new methods and algorithms for determining room acoustic parameters using machine audition of naturally occurring sound sources, i.e. speech and music. In particular, reverberation time, early decay time and speech transmission index can be estimated from received speech or music signals using statistical machine learning or maximum likelihood estimation in a semi-blind or blind fashion.

Chapter 19, "*Neuromorphic Speech Processing: Objectives and Methods*" by Gómez-Vilda, Ferrández-Vicente, Rodellar-Biarge, Fernández-Baíllo, Álvarez-Marquina, Martínez-Olalla, Nieto-Lluis, Mazaira-Fernández, and Muñoz-Mulas, is intended to explore some of the hidden phenomena in speech perception and recognition, including the semantic gap going from spectral time-frequency representations to the symbolic translation into phonemes and words, and the construction of morpho-syntactic and semantic structures, for the design of a neuromorphic speech processing architecture. These facts are considered in a simplifying level under two points of view: that of top-down analysis provided from speech perception, and the symmetric from bottom-up synthesis provided by the biological architecture of auditory pathways. It also includes an application-driven design of a neuromorphic speech processing architecture and the simulation details provided by a parallel implementation of the architecture in a supercomputer

Wenwu Wang
University of Surrey, UK

Acknowledgment

I wish to thank all the people who were involved in different phases during the preparation of this book, including all the authors who have submitted their important contributions to this book and also provided assistance in reviewing the submitted chapters, all the advisory editorial board members who have helped in the review of the submissions and given useful suggestions on the structure of the book, and the executive editors at IGI Global, in particular, Mr. Joel A. Gamon, who has provided many helpful suggestions and answered each question that I raised when preparing this book. My thanks also go to Clive Cheong Took and Hector Perez-Meana for their assistance in the review process. Finally, I would like to take this opportunity to thank my wife and lovely daughter for their consistent support and love. Without the unselfish assistance of all these people, the successful publication of the book would not have been possible.

Wenwu Wang
University of Surrey, UK

Section 1
Audio Scene Analysis, Recognition and Modeling

Chapter 1
Unstructured Environmental Audio:
Representation, Classification and Modeling

Selina Chu
University of Southern California, USA

Shrikanth Narayanan
University of Southern California, USA

C.-C. Jay Kuo
University of Southern California, USA

ABSTRACT

Recognizing environmental sounds is a basic audio signal processing problem. The goal of the authors' work is on the characterization of unstructured environmental sounds for understanding and predicting the context surrounding of an agent or device. Most research on audio recognition has focused primarily on speech and music. Less attention has been paid to the challenges and opportunities for using audio to characterize unstructured audio. The authors' research investigates issues in characterizing unstructured environmental sounds such as the development of appropriate feature extraction algorithm and learning techniques for modeling backgrounds of the environment.

INTRODUCTION

Unstructured audio is an important aspect in building systems that are capable of understanding their surrounding environment through the use of audio and other modalities of information, i.e. visual, sonar, global positioning, etc. Consider, for example, applications in robotic navigation, assistive robotics, and other mobile device-based services, where context aware processing is often desired. Human beings utilize both vision and hearing to navigate and respond to their surroundings, a capability still quite limited in machine processing. The first step toward achieving recognition of multi-modality is the ability to process unstructured audio and recognize audio scenes (or environments).

DOI: 10.4018/978-1-61520-919-4.ch001

By audio scenes, we refer to a location with different acoustic characteristics such as a coffee shop, park, or quiet hallway. Differences in acoustic characteristics could be caused by the physical environment or activities of humans and nature. To enhance a system's context awareness, we need to incorporate and adequately utilize such audio information. A stream of audio data contains a significant wealth of information, enabling the system to capture a semantically richer environment. Moreover, to capture a more complete description of a scene, the fusion of audio and other sensory information can be advantageous, say, for disambiguation of environment and object types. To use any of these capabilities, we have to determine the current ambient context first.

Most research in environmental sounds has centered mostly on recognition of specific events or sounds. To date, only a few systems have been proposed to model raw environment audio without pre-extracting specific events or sounds. In this work, our focus is not in the analysis and recognition of discrete sound events, but rather on characterizing the general unstructured acoustic environment as a whole. Unstructured environment characterization is still in its infancy. Current algorithms still have difficulty in handling such situations, and a number of issues and challenges remain. We briefly describe some of the issues that we think make learning in unstructured audio particularly challenging:

- One of the main issues arises from the lack of proper audio features for environmental sounds. Audio signals have been traditionally characterized by Mel-frequency cepstral coefficients (MFCCs) or some other time-frequency representations such as the short-time Fourier transform and the wavelet transform, etc. We found from our study that traditional features do not perform well with environmental sounds. MFCCs have been shown to work relatively well

for structured sounds, such as speech and music, but their performance degrades in the presence of noise. Environmental sounds, for example, contain a large variety of sounds, which may include components with strong temporal domain signatures, such as chirpings of insects and sounds of rain. These sounds are in fact noise-like with a broad spectrum and are not effectively modeled by MFCCs.

- Modeling the background audio of complex environments is a challenging problem as the audio, in most cases, are constantly changing. Therefore the question is what is considered the background and how do we model it. We can define the background in an ambient auditory scene as something recurring, and noise-like, which is made up of various sound sources, but changing over time, i.e., traffic and passers-by on a street. In contrast, the foreground can be viewed as something unanticipated or as a deviation from the background model, i.e., passing ambulance with siren. The problem arises when identifying foreground existence in the presence of background noise, given the background also changes with a varying rate, depending on different environments. If we create fixed models with too much prior knowledge, these models could be too specific and might not do well with new sounds.

In this chapter, we will try to answer these problems. The remainder of the chapter will be organized as follows: We will review some related and previous work. The next section afterwards, the MP algorithm is described and MP-based features are presented. The following section reports on a listening test for studying human abilities recognizing acoustic environments. In the background modeling section, we present a framework that utilizes semi-supervised learning to model the background and detect foreground events. Concluding remarks are drawn in the last section.

BACKGROUND

Research in general audio environment recognition has received some interest in the last few years (Ellis, 1996, Eronen, 2006, Malkin, 2005, Peltonen, 2001, Aucouturier, 2007), but the activity is considerably less compared to that for speech or music. Some areas of non-speech sound recognition that have been studied to various degrees are those pertaining to recognition of specific events using audio from carefully produced movies or television tracks (Cai, 2006). Others include the discrimination between musical instruments (Cano, 2004), musical genres (Tzanetakis, 2002), and between variations of speech, nonspeech and music (Carey, 1999, Zhang, 2001).

As compared to other areas in audio such as speech or music, research on general unstructured audio-based scene recognition has received little attention. To the best of our knowledge, only a few systems (and frameworks) have been proposed to investigate environmental classification with raw audio. Sound-based situation analysis has been studied in (Eronen, 2006, Peltonen, 2001) and in (Clarkson, 1998, Ellis, 2004), for wearables and context-aware applications. Because of randomness, high variance, and other difficulties in working with environmental sounds, the recognition rates fall rapidly with increasing number of classes; representative results show recognition accuracy limited to around 92% for 5 classes (Chu, 2006), 77% for 11 classes (Malkin, 2005) and approximately 60% for 13 or more classes (Eronen, 2006, Peltonen, 2001).

The first step in building a recognition system for auditory environment was to investigate on techniques for developing a scene classification system using audio features. In our previous work, we performed the study by first collecting real world audio with a robot and then building a classifier to discriminate different environments, which allows us to explore and investigate on suitable features and the feasibility of designing an automatic environment recognition system using audio information. Details can be found in (Chu et al, 2006). We showed that we could predict with fairly accurate results the environment in which the robot is positioned (92% accuracy for 5 types of environments). We also surveyed the current features that were being used for audio recognition in general, which include features such as Mel-frequency cepstrum coefficient analysis (MFCC), statistical moments from the audio signal's spectrum (e.g. spectral centroid, spectral bandwidth, etc.) and temporal features (e.g. zero-crossing rate, energy range) (Chu et al, 2009). What we found was that many previous efforts would utilize a combination of these features and their derivatives, resulting in a high dimension feature vector (i.e. 40-50 dimensions) to represent audio signals (Eronen et al., 2006). We showed that a high dimension feature set for classification does not always produce good performance. This in turn leads to the issue of selecting an optimal subset of features from a larger set of possible features to yield the most effective subset. In the same work, we utilized a simple forward feature selection algorithm to obtain a smaller feature set to reduce the computational cost and running time and achieve a higher classification rate. Although the results showed improvements, the features found after the feature selection process were more specific to each classifier and environment type. It is with these findings that motivated us to look for a more effective approach for representing environmental sounds. Toward this goal, our next step was to investigate in ways of extracting features and introduce a novel idea of using matching pursuit as a way to extract features for unstructured sounds.

Recognition with Time Frequency Audio Features

Desirable types of features should be robust, stable and straightforward, with the representation being sparse and physically interpretable. Environmental sounds, such as chirpings of insects and sounds of rain which are typically noiselike with a broad flat spectrum, may include strong temporal domain signatures.

However, only few temporal-domain features have been developed to characterize such diverse audio signals previously.

As with most pattern recognition systems, selecting proper features is key to effective system performance. Audio signals have been tradition- ally characterized by MFCCs or some other time- frequency representations such as the short-time Fourier transform and the wavelet transform. The filterbanks used for MFCC computation approxi- mates some important properties of the human auditory system. MFCCs have been shown to work well for structured sounds such as speech and music, but their performance degrades in the presence of noise. MFCCs are also not effective in analyzing noise-like signals that have a flat spectrum. Environmental audio contain a large and diverse variety of sounds, including those with strong temporal domain signatures, such as chirpings of insects and sounds of rain that are typically noise-like with a broad flat spectrum that may not be effectively modeled by MFCCs.

In this work, we propose to use the matching pursuit (MP) algorithm to analyze environmental sounds. MP provides a way to extract time-fre- quency domain features that can classify sounds where using frequency-domain only features (e.g., MFCCs) fails. The process includes finding the decomposition of a signal from a dictionary of atoms, which would yield the best set of func- tions to form an approximate representation. The advantages of this representation are the ability to capture the inherent structure within each type of signal and to map from a large, complex signal onto a small, simple feature space. More importantly, it is conceivably more invariant to background noise and could capture characteristics in the signal where MFCCs tend to fail.

The MP algorithm has been used in a variety of applications, such as video coding (Neff, 1997) and music note detection (Gribonval, 2003). MP has also been used in music genre classification (Umapathy, 2005) and classification of acoustic emissions from a monitoring system (Ebenezer, 2004). In our proposed technique, MP is used for feature extraction in the context of environmental sound.

Signal Representation with MP

The intuition behind our strategy is that there are underlying structures that lie within signals of each type of environment, and we could use MP to discover them. Different types of environmental sounds have their own unique characteristics, mak- ing the decomposition into sets of basis vectors to be noticeably different from one another. By using a dictionary that consists of a wide variety of functions, MP provides an efficient way of selecting a small set of basis vectors that produces meaningful features as well as flexible represen- tation for characterizing an audio environment.

To achieve an efficient representation, we would like to obtain the minimum number of basis vectors to represent a signal, resulting in a sparse approximation. However, this is an NP-complete problem. Various adaptive approximation tech- niques to obtain such a signal representation in an efficient manner have been proposed in the literature, including basis pursuit (BP) (Chen, 1998) and matching pursuit (MP) (Mallat, 1993), These methods utilize the notion of a dictionary that capacitates the decomposition of a signal by selecting basis vectors from a given dictionary to find the best subset.

By using a dictionary that consists of a wide variety of elementary waveforms, MP aims at finding a sparse linear expansion of waveforms

Figure 1. Matching pursuit algorithm (© 2009 IEEE. Used with permission.)

Algorithm matching pursuit

Input: signal s, dictionary D
Return: List of coefficients α for $(\alpha_k, \phi_{\gamma_k})$ with $\phi_{\gamma_k} \in D$
Initialize: $s^{(0)} \leftarrow s$
Repeat
    Find ϕ_{γ_k} with maximum inner product $\langle s^{(k)}, \phi_{\gamma_k} \rangle$
    $\alpha_k \leftarrow \langle s^{(k)}, \phi_{\gamma_k} \rangle$
    $s^{(k+1)} \leftarrow s^{(k)} - \alpha_k \phi_{\gamma_k}$
    $k \leftarrow k + 1$
until either $\|s^{(k)}\| < threshold$ or certain k is reached

---

efficiently in a greedy manner. MP is sub-optimal in the sense that it may not achieve the sparsest solution. However, even with just a few steps, the algorithm can yield a reasonable approximation with a few atoms. Therefore, we adopt the classic MP approach to generate audio features in our study. The MP algorithm is given in Figure 1. Details of the MP algorithm can be found in (Mallat, 1993)

Extracting MP-Features

The strategy for feature extraction is based on the assumption that the most important information of a signal lies in leading synthesizing atoms with the highest energy, yielding a simple representation of the underlying structure. Since MP selects atoms in order by eliminating the largest residual energy, it lends itself in providing the most useful atoms, even just after a few iterations.

The MP algorithm selects atoms in a stepwise manner among the set of waveforms in the dictionary that best correlate the signal structures. The iteration can be stopped when the coefficient associated with the atom selection falls below a threshold or when a certain number of atoms selected overall have been reached. Another common stopping criterion is to use the signal to residual energy ratio. In this work, we chose n atoms as the stopping criterion for the iteration. MP-features are selected by the following process.

Based on our experimental setup, explained in Sec. 3.5 we use a rectangular window of 256 points with a 50% overlap. This corresponds to the window size used for all feature extraction. We decompose each 256-point segment using MP with a dictionary of Gabor atoms that are also 256 points in length. We stop the MP process after obtaining n atoms, where n is the number of atoms used in the MP-feature extraction process. Afterwards, we record the frequency and scale parameters for each of these n atoms and find the mean and the standard deviation corresponding to each parameter separately, resulting in 4 feature values.

To select parameter n in the stopping criterion, we perform a classification experiment that analyzes the performance as a function of n. We found that an initial rise in performance as the number of features increases due to their discriminatory, but levels off around 4 or 5 atoms. Thus, we chose $n = 5$ atoms in our experiments and use the same process to extract features for both training and test data. The decomposition of different signals from the same environmental class might not be composed of exactly the same atoms or order. However, since we are taking the average of their parameters as features, the sequencing order of atoms is neglected and the robustness of these features is enhanced by averaging. Using these atom parameters as features abstracts away finer details and forces the concentration on the most pronounced characteristics.

MP Dictionary Selection

A combination of both time and frequency functions can be demonstrated in the Gabor dictionary. Gabor functions are sine-modulated Gaussian functions that are scaled and translated, providing joint time-frequency localization. The Gabor representation is formed by a band-limited signal of finite duration, thus making it more suitable for time-frequency localized signals. Due to the non-homogeneous nature of environmental sounds, using features with these Gabor properties would benefit a classification system. Based on the above observation, we choose to use the Gabor function in this work.

Mathematically, the discrete Gabor time-frequency atom is written as

$$g_{s,u,\omega,\theta}\left(n\right) = \frac{K_{s,u,\omega,\theta}}{\sqrt{s}} e^{-\pi\left(n-u\right)^2/s^2} \cos\left[2\pi\omega\left(n-u\right)+\theta\right],$$

where $s \in R+$; $u, \omega \in R$; $\theta \in [0, 2\pi]$. $K_{s,u,\omega,\theta}$ is a normalization factor such that $\|g_{s,u,\omega,\theta}\|^2 = 1$. We use $g_{s,u,\omega,\theta}$ to denote parameters of the Gabor function, where s, u, ω, and θ correspond to an atom's position in scale, time, frequency and phase, respectively. The Gabor dictionary in (Mallat, 1993) was implemented with atom parameters chosen from dyadic sequences of integers. The scale s, which corresponds to the atom width in time, is derived from dyadic sequence $s = 2p$, $1 \le p \le m$, and the atom size is equal to $N = 2^m$. We chose the Gabor function with the following parameters in this work: $s = 2p$ ($1 \le p \le 8$), $u = \{0, 64, 128, 192\}$, $\omega = Ki^{2.6}$ (with $1 \le i \le 35$, $K = 0.5 \times 35^{-2.6}$ so that the range of ω is normalized between K and 0.5), $\theta = 0$ and the atom length is truncated to $N = 256$. Thus, the dictionary consists of $1120 = 8 \times 35 \times 4$ Gabor atoms that were generated using scales of $2p$ and translation by quarters of atom length N.

We attempt to keep the dictionary size small since a large dictionary demands higher complexity. For example, we choose a fixed phase term since its variation does not help much. By shifting the phase, *i.e.* $\theta = \left\{0, \frac{\pi}{4}, \frac{\pi}{2}, \dots\right\}$, each basis vector only varies slightly. Since we are using the top few atoms for creating the MP-features, it was found not necessary to incorporate the phase-shifted basis vectors.

A logarithmic frequency scale is used to permit a higher resolution in the lower frequency region and a lower resolution in the higher frequency region. We found the exponent 2.6 in ω experimentally given the parameter setting of the frequency interval. We wanted to have a finer granularity below 1000Hz as well as enough descriptive power in the higher frequency. The reason for finer granularity in lower frequencies is because more audio object types occur in this range, and we want to capture finer differences between them. The decomposition of signals from six sound classes using Gabor atoms is shown in Figure 2 where the top five atoms are shown.

We can observe differences in synthesizing atoms for different environments, which demonstrate that different environments exhibit different characteristics, and each set of decompositions encapsulates the inherent structures within each type of signal. For example, because the two classes, *On boat* and *running water*, contain ocean sounds, the decompositions are very similar to each other. Another example is between *Nature-daytime* and *Street with traffic*. Both were recorded outdoors; therefore there are some similarities in the subset of their decomposition but because the *Street with traffic* class has the presence of traffic noise, this has led to distinctively different atoms with higher frequency components, compared to *Nature-daytime*. When we compared them with differing classes, e.g., *Nature-nighttime* and *Street with traffic*, the decompositions are noticeably different from one another. Therefore, we utilize these set of atoms as a simple representation to these structures.

Computational Cost of MP-Features

For each input audio signal, we divide into k overlapping windows of length N, and MP is performed on each of these k windows. At each iteration, the MP algorithm computes the inner product of the window of signals (or residuals) with all D atoms in the dictionary. The cost of computing all inner products would be $O(kND)$. During this process, we need to record the highest correlation value and the corresponding atom. We terminate the MP algorithm after n iterations, yielding a total cost of $O(nkND)$. By keeping the dictionary

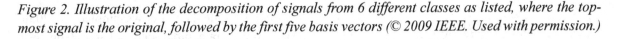

Figure 2. Illustration of the decomposition of signals from 6 different classes as listed, where the topmost signal is the original, followed by the first five basis vectors (© 2009 IEEE. Used with permission.)

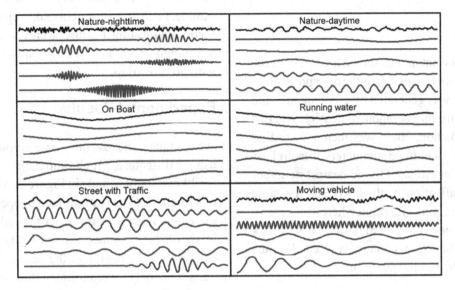

size small with constant iteration number, n, and window size, N, the computational cost is a linear function of the total length of the signal. Thus, it can be done in real time.

Experimental Evaluation

We investigated the performance of a variety of audio features and provide an empirical evaluation on fourteen different types of environmental sounds commonly encountered. We used recordings of natural (unsynthesized) sound clips obtained from (Sound Ideas, n.d., Freesound, n.d.). We used recordings that are available in WAV formats to avoid introducing artifacts in our data (e.g., from the MP3 format). Our auditory environment types were chosen so that they are made up of non-speech and non-music sounds. It was essentially background noise of a particular environment, composed of many sound events. We do not consider each constituent sound event individually, but as many properties of each environment. Naturally, there could be infinitely many possible combinations. To simplify the problem,

we restricted the number of environment types examined and enforced each type of sound to be distinctively different from one another, which minimized overlaps as much as possible. The fourteen environment types considered were: *Inside restaurants, Playground, Street with traffic and pedestrians, Train passing, Inside moving vehicles, Inside casinos, Street with police car siren, Street with ambulance siren, Nature-daytime, Nature-nighttime, Ocean waves, Running water/stream/river, Raining/shower, and Thundering.*

We examined the performance of the MP-features, MFCCs, and a concatenation of the MP-features and MFCCs to form a longer feature vector MP+MFCC (16). We adopted the Gaussian Mixture Model (GMM) classification method in the feature space for our work. With GMMs, each data class was modeled as a mixture of several Gaussian clusters. Each mixture component is a Gaussian represented by the mean and the covariance matrix of the data. Once the model was generated, conditional probabilities were computed using

$$p\left(x \mid X_{k}\right) = \sum_{j=1}^{m_{k}} p\left(x \mid j\right) P\left(j\right),$$

where X_k is the datapoints for each class, m_k is the number of components, $P(j)$ is the prior probability that datum x was generated by component j, and $p(x|j)$ is the mixture component density. The EM algorithm (Bishop, 2003) was then used to find the maximum likelihood parameters of each class.

We also investigated the K-nearest neighbor (kNN) classification method. kNN is a simple supervised learning algorithm where a new query is classified based on the majority class of its k nearest neighbors. A commonly used distance measure is the Euclidean distance

$$d\left(x,y\right) = \sqrt{\sum_{i=1}^{n} \left(x_i - y_i\right)^2}.$$

In our experiments, we utilized separate source files for training and test sets. We kept the 4-sec segments that were originated from the same source file separate from one another. Each source file for each environment was obtained at different locations. For instance, the Street with traffic class contains four source files which were labeled as taken from various cities. We required that each environment contained at least four separate source recordings, and segments from the same source file were considered a set. We used three sets for training and one set for testing. Finally, we performed a 4-fold cross validation for the MP-features and all commonly-used features individually for performance comparison. In this setup, none of the training and test items originated from the same source. Since the recordings were taken from a wide variety of locations, the ambient sound might have a very high variance. Results were averaged over 100 trials. These sound clips were of varying lengths (1-3 minutes long), and were later processed by dividing up into

4-second segments and downsampled to 22050 Hz sampling rate, mono-channel and 16 bits per sample. Each 4-sec segment makes up an instance for training/testing. Features were calculated from a rectangular window of 256 points (11.6 msec) with 50% overlap.

Experimental Results

We compare the overall recognition accuracy using MP-feature, MFCC and their combination for 14 classes of sounds in Figure 3. As shown in this figure, MFCC features tend to operate on the extremes. They perform better than MP-features in six of the examined classes while producing extremely poor results in the case of five other classes; namely, a recognition rate of 0% for four classes, *Casino, Nature-nighttime, Train passing*, and *Street with ambulance* and less than 10% for *Thundering*. MP-features perform better overall, with the exception of two classes (Restaurant and Thundering) having the lowest recognition rate at 35%. One illustrative example is the Nature-nighttime class, which contains many insect sounds of higher frequencies. Unlike MFCCs that recognized 0% of this category, MP-features were able to yield a correct recognition rate of 100%. Some of these sounds are best characterized by narrow spectral peaks, like chirps of insects. MFCC is unable to encode such narrow-band structure, but MP-features are effective in doing so. By combining MP and MFCC features, we were able to achieve an averaged accuracy rate of 83.9% in discriminating fourteen classes. There are seven classes that have a classification rate higher than 90%. We see that MFCC and MP-features complement each other to give the best overall performance.

For completeness, we compared the results from the two different classifiers, namely GMM and kNN. We examine the results from varying the number of neighbors k and using the same k for each environment type. The highest recognition rate was obtained using $k = 32$, with an accuracy

Figure 3. Overall recognition rate (GMM) comparing 14 classes using MFCC only, MP only, and MP+MFCC as features. 0% recognition rate for four classes using MFCC only: Casino, Nature-nighttime, Train passing, and Street with ambulance. (© 2009 IEEE. Used with permission.)

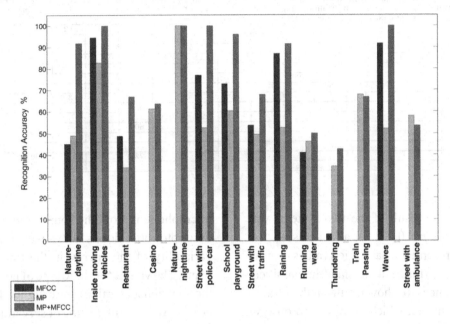

of 77.3%. We could observe the performance slowly flattens out and further degrades as we increase the number of neighbors. By increasing k, we are in fact expanding the radius of its neighbors. Extending this space makes it more likely the classes would overlap. In general, the results from GMM outperform those from using kNN. Therefore, we will concentrate on GMM for the rest of our experiments. Using GMM allows for better generalization. kNN would perform well if the data samples are very similar to each other. However, since we are using different sources for testing and training, they might be similar in their overall structure but not finer details.

To determine the model order of GMM, we examine the results by varying the number of mixtures. Using the same settings as the rest of the experiments, we examined mixtures of 1-10, 15, and 20 and used the same number of mixtures for each environment type. We see that the classification performance peaks around 5 mixtures and the performance slowly degrades

as the number of mixtures increases. The highest recognition rate for each class across the number of mixtures was obtained with 4-6 mixtures. They were equal to 4, 5, 5, 5, 5, 5, 6, 5, 4, 4, 5, 6, 5, 5 for the corresponding classes: Nature-daytime, Inside moving vehicles, Inside restaurants, Inside casinos, Nature-nighttime, Street with police car siren, Playground, Street with traffic, Thundering, Train passing, Raining/shower, Running water/ stream, Ocean waves, and Street with ambulance. We also experimented with this combination of mixtures numbers, and resulted in an accuracy rate of 83.4%. Since the latter requires tailoring to each class, we decided to just use 5 mixtures throughout all of our experiments to avoid making the classifier too specialized to the data.

We performed an analysis of variance (ANOVA) on the classification results. Specifically, we used the t-test, which is a special case of ANOVA for comparing two groups. The t-test was run on each of the 14 classes individually. The t-tests

Figure 4. Confusion matrix for 14 class classification using MP-features and MFCC with GMM (© 2009 IEEE. Used with permission.)

14 classes: 1) Nature-daytime, 2) Inside vehicle, 3) Restaurant, 4) Casino, 5) Nature-nighttime, 6) Street - police, 7) Playground, 8) Street - traffic, 9) Thundering, 10), Train passing, 11) Rain / shower, 12) River / stream, 13) Waves, 14) Traffic - ambulance. All values are in percentages. Blank cells equates to less than 1%.

	1	2	3	4	5	6	7	8	9	10	11	12	13	14
1	92.2													
2		100												
3			66.8				2.5	12.8	8.6					
4			23.0	62.2										
5					100									
6			1.8	33.7		97.5								4.4
7			2.9				94.6					13.5		
8			1.2					74.8		5.9				3.5
9	7.6						1.3	12.1	91.1	11.2		7.1		
10										60.7				
11											46.5			
12			3.8	3.5			1.2				53.3	78.3		37.1
13										22.0			100.0	
14			2.2											54.6

showed that the result of the two systems was significant with $p < 0.001$ for all 14 classes.

Results presented are averaged values from all trials together. To further understand the classification performance, we show results in the form of a confusion matrix, which allows us to observe the degree of confusion among different classes. The confusion matrix given in Figure 4 is built from a single arbitrary trial, constructed by applying the classifier to the test set and displaying the number of correctly/incorrectly classified items. The rows of the matrix denote the environment classes we attempt to classify, and the columns depict classified results. We see from Figure 4 that *Restaurant, Casino,*

Train, Rain, and *Street with ambulance* were more often misclassified than the rest. We could further point out that the misclassification overlaps between pairs, such as those of *Inside restaurant* and *Inside casino* and of *Rain* and *Steam* (*Running River*). Interestingly, there exists a one-sided confusion between *Train* and *Waves*, where samples of *Train* were misclassified as *Waves*, but not vice versa.

We use *mean-F* and *std-F* to denote the mean and standard deviation for the frequency indices and likewise, *mean-S* and *std-S* for the scale indices. The *mean-S* can be viewed as an indication of the overall amplitude of the signal. It depends on the loudness of the signal or how far away the microphone is from the sound source. The *std-S* descriptor provides us with a way to disclose the variability of the energy in the time-frequency plane. The values for static type of noises, such as those of constant raining, are higher than diverse noises. Another interesting observation is that out of the four descriptors, *std-S* was the only one that separates out much of the *Nature-daytime* class from the others, which was the most difficult to do with the other descriptors. The *mean-F* might be similar to that of the centroid as it represents where the energy on the frequency axis. Although, the *mean-F* only describes the frequency, but it still proved to be useful when combined with MFCC. One of the reasons is that MFCCs model the human auditory system and do poorly when modeling non-speech type noise. *Mean-F* furnishes us with a description of the basic frequency without being modeled based on any auditory system. *Std-F* expresses the frequency range. If the sound frequency is narrow, *std-F* is low, i.e. *running stream*. For readers interested in the MP-feature, a more detailed treatment is provided in (Chu, in press).

Listening Tests

A listening test was conducted to study human recognition capability of these environmental sounds. Our motivation was to find another human-centric performance benchmark for our automatic recognition system. Our test consisted of 140 audio clips from 14 categories, with 10 clips from each of the classes described in Section Experimental Evaluation. Audio clips were randomly picked from the test and training sets, and the duration varied between 2, 4, and 6 seconds. A total of 18 subjects participated in the test. They were volunteers and had no prior experience in analyzing environmental sounds. Participants consisted of both male and female subjects with their ages between 24-40. About half of the subjects were from academia while the rest were from non-related fields. Four of the subjects were involved in speech and audio research.

Each subject was asked to complete 140 classification tasks (the number of audio clips) in the course of this experiment. In each task, subjects were asked to evaluate the sound clip presented to them by assigning a label of one of 15 choices, which includes the 14 possible scenes and the others category. In addition to class labeling, we also obtained the confidence level for each of the tasks. The confidence levels were between 1 and 5, with 5 being the most confident. The order in which sound clips were presented was randomized to minimize any bias. The test was set up so that the first 14 clips were samples of each of the classes and was not included in calculating the final results. They were used to introduce subjects to the variety of sounds to be examined and to accustom them to different categories.

The user interface was a webpage accessible via a browser with internet connection. Users were asked to use headphones so as to reduce the amount of possible background noise. The test was performed without any time limit, and users were able to break and return at any time. For each task, the results are expressed as an entry consisting of 4 data items: 1) the original environment type, 2) the audio clip duration, 3) user labeled environment type, and 4) user confidence level.

The results from the listening test are shown in Figure 5. The overall recognition rate was 82.3%,

and the recognition accuracy for each individual environment ranged from 50% to 100%. The three best recognized scenes were *Nature-daytime* (98%), *Playground* (95%), and *Thundering* (95%). On the other hand, the four most difficult scenes were *Ocean waves* (65%), *Inside Casino* (70%), *Inside moving vehicles* (73%), and *Street with traffic* (74%). The listening test showed that humans are able to recognize everyday auditory scenes in 82% of the cases. The confusions were mainly between scenes that had similar types of prominent sound events. We can also examine the performance of each sound class as an effect of the duration in Figure 5. The overall average recognition rates were 77%, 82%, and 85% for an audio clip duration of 2, 4 and 6 seconds, respectively. There is a larger difference in the rates between 2 and 4 seconds, but less between 4 and 6 seconds. A longer duration permits the listener more opportunities to pick up prominent sounds within each clip. However, the duration effect becomes less important as it passes a certain threshold.

One of the main reasons for misclassification was due to misleading sound events. For example, the scene *Street with traffic* was recorded with different types of traffic, which was frequently recognized as *Inside moving vehicles*, and vice versa. The recordings from Inside moving vehicles consist of different vehicles passing, which included a variety of vehicles like passenger sedans, trucks, and buses. Another reason for misclassification arises from the similarity between two different sounds and the inability of human ears to separate them. For example, *Ocean waves* actually sounds very similar to that of *Train passing*. Another problem comes from subjects' unfamiliarity of a particular scene. For example, some users reported that they have never set foot inside a casino. Thus, the sound event *Inside casino* was mislabeled by them as *Inside restaurant* due to the crowd type of the ambient sound.

The confusion matrix for the test is given in Figure 6. The rows of the matrix are the presented environmental scenes while the columns describe

Figure 5. Recognition accuracy of 14 classes from the listening test (© 2009 IEEE. Used with permission.)

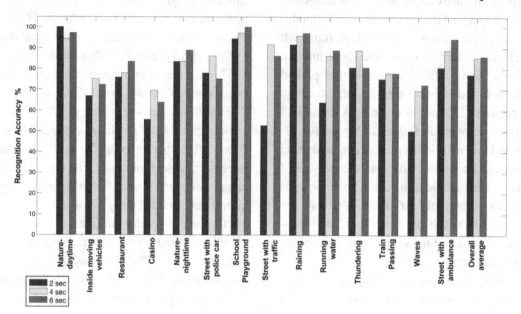

the subject responses. All values are given in percentages. Confusion between scenes was most noticeably high between *Street with police car* and *Streets with ambulance*, between *Raining* and *Running water*, and between *Street with traffic* and *Inside moving vehicles*.

The highest off-diagonal value occurs when *Streets with police car* is recognized as *Street with ambulance}*. Confusion between sirens from police cars and ambulance was not due to the actual discrimination between the two sound classes but rather some people were semantically confused between the two sirens. In other words, the discrimination between the two classes requires background knowledge of subjects. Many users reported afterwards that they were second guessing the type of emergency vehicles that sirens were originating from. Confusion also occurred between scenes that are filled with crowded people, such as *Inside restaurant* and *Inside casino*.

The listening test shows that human listeners were able to correctly recognize 82% of ambient environment sounds for a duration of 4 seconds. Under the condition of 4 second clips, our auto-

matic recognition system achieved a rate of 83%, which demonstrates that our recognition system has comparable performance to that of human listeners.

The results of our listening test and those in (Eronen, 2006) are dissimilar. As indicated in the studies in (Eronen, 2006), their results were higher for humans than that obtained from the computer system.

Whereas in our case, the results were fairly similar between human and computer recognition. One possible reason for the differences is that their experimental setup was different than the one presented here, most notably in the length of the data presented to the subjects. The data presented to the users in our setup are the same segments as used in our automatic classification system, which was 4 seconds long, while the samples in Eronen's experiments were 30 seconds to 1 minute long. Given that humans may have prior knowledge to different situations that can be advantageously used in classification, allowing them a much longer time to listen to the audio sample increases the likelihood that they would

Figure 6. Confusion matrix of human performance from the listening test (© 2009 IEEE. Used with permission.)

14 classes: 1) Nature-daytime, 2) Inside vehicle, 3) Restaurant, 4) Casino, 5) Nature-nighttime, 6) Street - police, 7) Playground, 8) Street - traffic, 9) Thundering, 10), Train passing, 11) Rain / shower, 12) River / stream, 13) Waves, 14) Traffic - ambulance.

	1	2	3	4	5	6	7	8	9	10	11	12	13	14	Others
1	98.5				1.5										
2		73.1						10.0		1.5			3.1		12.3
3			86.9	3.0				4.8							5.4
4			14.8	70.0			3.1								11.5
5	6.2				88.5			1.5							4.0
6		6.2				76.2							17.9		
7							95.0		3.1						2.0
8		15.6						73.8			5.6				3.8
9									94.6	2.3	3.1				
10								8.5		80.8		3.1			4.8
11											82.3	15.6			2.3
12											16.9	83.9			
13								13.1	2.3		4.6	2.3	65.4		2.3
14						16.4								83.1	

All values are in percentages. Blank cells equates to less than 1%.

find some audio cue within each segment as to the environmental context in question.

ONLINE AUDIO BACKGROUND MODELING AND EVENT DETECTION USING SEMI-SUPERVISED LEARNING

The ultimate goal of our research is to characterize an environment. What we would like to achieve is to have a general model of an environment. The first step in this direction is being able to model the background sound. Once we have a general notion of the background, we can then identify foreground events even if we have not previously encountered them. The background in an ambient auditory scene can be considered as something recurring, and noise-like, which is made up of various sound sources, but changing over time, i.e., traffic and passers-by on a street. In contrast, the foreground can be viewed as something unanticipated or as a deviation from the background model, i.e., passing ambulance with siren.

In this work, we consider modeling and detecting background and foreground sounds by incorporating explicit knowledge of data into the process. We propose to include audio prediction models as a procedure to learn the background and foreground sounds. Our framework is comprised of two modules, each addressing a separate issue. First, we use a semi-supervised method to train classifiers to learn models for the foreground and background of an environment. Then, we use the learned models as a way to bootstrap the overall system. A separate model is constructed to detect the changes in the background. It is then integrated together with audio prediction models to decide on the final background/foreground (BG/FG) determination.

Background Modeling

Various approaches have been proposed to model the background. The problem in modeling the background arises when identifying foreground existence in the presence of background noise, given the background also changes with a varying rate, depending on different environments. If we create fixed models with too much prior knowledge, these models could be too specific and might not do well with new sounds. On the other hand, models that do not consider prior knowledge, such as unsupervised techniques, typically use simple methods of thresholding (Harma, 2005). However, this would lead to the problem of threshold determination. This is impractical in unstructured environments since there are no clear boundaries between different types of sounds. Other systems employ learning techniques, such as in (Ellis,

2001), build models explicitly for specific audio events, making it inflexible to new events.

The state-of-the-art approaches in background modeling (Moncrieff, 2007) do not make any assumptions about the prior knowledge of the location and operate with ephemeral memory of the data. Their proposed method models the persistency of features by defining the background as changing slowly over time and assuming foreground events to be short and terse, e.g., breaking glass. The problem arises when the foreground is also gradual and longer lasting, e.g., plane passing overhead. In this case, it would adapt the foreground sound as background, since there is no knowledge of the background or foreground. It would be difficult to verify whether the background model is indeed correct or models some persistent foreground sound as well.

Semi-Supervised Learning with Audio

We begin our study by building prediction models to classify the environment into foreground and background. To obtain classifiers with high generalization ability, a large amount of training samples are typically required. However, labeled samples are fairly expensive to obtain while unlabeled natural recordings consisting of environmental sounds are easy to come by. Thus, we investigate ways to automatically label them using self-training (Nigam, 2000) to increase the training example size. In self-training, a classifier for each class is trained on a labeled data set. Then, it labels these unlabeled examples automatically. The newly labeled data are added to the original labeled training set, and the classifier is refined with the augmented data set.

After the above steps, we train a multivariate probability density model to recognize the background and a separate one for the foreground, where the expectation maximization (EM) approach is used to estimate the parameters of the model. We use the augmented EM approach

(EM-λ) in (Nigam, 2000), where parameters are estimated using both labeled and unlabeled samples. The contribution of unlabeled samples are weighted by a factor $0 \leq \lambda \leq 1$, which provides a way to reduce the influence of the use of a large amount of unlabeled data (as compared to the labeled data). It also makes the algorithm less sensitive to the newly labeled data. With the standard EM, we maximize the M-step using:

$$l_c\left(\theta \mid X\right) = \log\left(P\left(\theta\right)\right) + \sum_{x_i \in X} \log \sum_{i=1}^{K} \alpha_j P\left(X_i \mid \theta_j\right),$$

(1)

where there are N training data, X, α is the prior, θ is the set of parameters, with class labels $y_i \in K$.

When unlabeled data $x_i \in X_u$ are incorporated into the labeled data $x_i \in X_l$, the new training set becomes $X = X_l \cup X_u$. Then to maximize the M-step in EM-λ, we have

$$l_c\left(\theta \mid X\right) = \log\left(P\left(\theta\right)\right) + \sum_{x_i \in X^l} \log \sum_{i=1}^{K} \alpha_j P\left(X_i \mid \theta_j\right) + \sum_{x_i \in X^u} \log \sum_{i=1}^{K} \alpha_j P\left(X_i \mid \theta_j\right),$$

(2)

which results in the following parameter estimation:

$$P\left(X \mid k_j; \theta\right) = \frac{1 + \sum_{i=1}^{|X|} P\left(y_i = k_j \mid x_i\right)}{\sum_{i=1}^{|X|} \Lambda\left(i\right) P\left(y_i = k_j \mid d_i\right)}$$

(3)

with the prior as

$$P\left(k_j \mid \theta\right) = \frac{1 + \sum_{i=1}^{|X|} \Lambda\left(i\right) P\left(y_i = k_j \mid x_i\right)}{\left|K\right| + \left|X^l\right| + \lambda\left|X^u\right|},$$

(4)

and a weighting factor $\Lambda(i)$, defined as

$$\Lambda\left(i\right) = \begin{cases} \lambda, & if \quad x_i \in D^u, \\ 1, & if \quad x_i \in D^l. \end{cases} \quad (5)$$

If none of the classifiers found the unlabeled sample to be probable (e.g., probabilities are low, say, less than 15%), we assign the unlabeled data to the foreground classifier since it is more likely that the unseen data sample is part of the foreground model.

Online Adaptive Background Detection

Once prediction models, P_{fg} and P_{bg}, are learned for foreground (FG) and background (BG) classification, we utilize these models in the online adaptive background detection process. The initial background modeling work was done for video (CStauffer, 1999), which uses the mixture of Gaussians for each pixel. Instead of modeling the pixel process, Moncrieff et al. (SMoncrieff, 2007) proposed to model the audio feature vector as Gaussians mixture densities. Our adaptation is based on the latter. The resultant algorithm is summarized below.

The history of feature vector X_t can be viewed as $\{x_1, x_2, ..., x_t\}$, each x_t is modeled by a mixture of K Gaussian distributions. The probability of observing current x_t is given by

$$P_{online}\left(x_t\right) = \sum_{i=1}^{K} \alpha_{i,t} P\left(x_t \mid \theta_{i,t}\right)$$

That is, x_t is represented by the components of the mixture model. Since x_t varies over time, the mixture models need to be re-trained at every time t to maximize the likelihood of X. Instead, we use an online K-means approximation algorithm. Every x_t is checked against the existing K Gaussian distributions to determine if a match is found. The Kth component is viewed as a match

if x_t is within 2.5 standard deviations from the mean of a distribution, as done in (Moncrieff, 2007; Stauffer, 1999). If none of the distributions qualify, the least probable distribution is replaced by the current observation x_t as the mean value with an initial high variance and a low prior. The parameters are adjusted with the prior weights of each component as

$$\alpha_{k,t} = \left(1 - \beta_\omega * M_{k,t}\right) \omega_{k,t-1} + \beta_\omega \left(M_{k,t}\right),$$

$$(6)$$

where $M_{k,t}$ is 1 for matched models and 0 for mismatched ones and β_ω is the learning rate, which determines the rate of adaptation of the background model. After the approximation, priors are re-normalized (summing to 1) and used to decrease the weight of the models that are not matched. The parameters for unmatched models remain the same, while matched models update their parameters with new observation x_t as

$$\mu_{k,t} = \left(1 - \rho\right) \mu_{t-1} + \rho X,$$

where $M_{k,t}$ is 1 for matched models and 0 for mismatched ones and β_ω is the learning rate, which determines the rate of adaptation of the background model. After the approximation, priors are re-normalized (summing to 1) and used to decrease the weight of the models that are not matched. The parameters for unmatched models remain the same, while matched models update their parameters with new observation x_t as

$$\mu_{k,t} = \left(1 - \rho\right) \mu_{t-1} + \rho X$$

$$\sum_{t}^{i,j} = \left(1 - \rho\right) \sum_{t-1}^{i,j} + \rho \left(X_t^i X_t^j\right),$$

where

$$\rho = \beta_g e^{-\frac{1}{2d}\left(X_t - \mu_{t-1}\right)^T \sum_{t-1}^{-1}\left(X_t - \mu_{t-1}\right)}$$

is the second learning rate that is dependent on the data and β_g determines the update rate of model parameters. Using this method to update does not destroy the existing models with new incoming data, but remains in the overall system (while having their prior weights α decrease). The model with the lowest α becomes the least probable model, which will then be replaced by the new observation.

From here on, we deviate from that of (Moncrieff, 2007) by including both P_{fg} and P_{bg} into the system. For updating P_{fg} and P_{bg}, we continue to use Equations (2)-(4), but in a sliding windows approach. As the system runs online, if we permit an increasing amount of unlabeled data to be included in the model, it would allow errors from the self-training process to propagate. To regulate possible concept drifts (as trends and patterns tend to change over time), we use a simple sliding window method, where only unlabeled data within the window of size m is utilized in the self-training process. Any unlabeled data outside the window is not used. Furthermore, to avoid re-training models at every second, we perform the self-training process at every $\frac{m}{4}$ interval. This

means that we remove the oldest $\frac{m}{4}$ of the data from the window to include newly arrived unlabeled data. For example if m = 120 samples, then we perform self-training at every 30 samples interval.

In addition, we attempt to maintain P_{fg} to reflect the current concept by placing more emphasis on the current data sample and using a new Λ_{fg} for

P_{fg} defined as $\Lambda_{fg}\left(i\right) = \begin{cases} \frac{m - z_m}{m} & if \quad x_i \in D^u, \\ \lambda, & if \quad x_i \in D^l, \end{cases}$

where $z = \{z1, z2, ..., z_t\}$, and where z_1 and z_m are the beginning and the end of window m, respectively.

For BG/FG classification, we rank their distributions by prior weights $\overline{\alpha}_{online}$ and α_{bg}, α_{fg} (from P_{bg}, P_{fg}, respectively, depending on $P(k|x_t ;\theta)$). Since we use separate models for the foreground and background, we normalize their priors to 1. For classification, we ordered the Gaussians by their values of $\alpha_{online} + \alpha_s$, where $\alpha_s = \alpha_{bg}$ if $P_{bg}(\mu_t)$ $\geq P_{fg}(\mu_t)$ and 0 otherwise. The distributions chosen as the foreground model are obtained via

$$FG = \left\lceil \sum_{k=1}^{k_{highest}} \alpha_{online_k +} \alpha_{s_k} \right\rceil \leq T, \text{where } k_{highest} \text{ is the}$$

highest rank model and $k = 1$ the lowest ranked. T is the tolerance threshold for background classification. A lower T will result in more distributions being classified as background. Models not chosen as foreground are considered background models.

We use a heuristic to perform the final classification. We utilize a queue to keep track of results at each time t from either a background or foreground classification of $P_{bg|fg}(x_t, x_{t-1}, ...)$. If there is no change between classifications of previous distribution P_{online}^{t-1} and the current one, P_{online}^t, we append the result $P_{bg|fg}(x_t)$ into the queue and make the classification at t by taking a majority vote of the result queue at $t, t-1, ...,$ $t-q$, where q is the queue size. Using a queue to remember the results allows for some misclassification in the prediction process. When there is change between P_{online}^{t-1} and P_{online}^t, we examine $P_{bg|fg}(x_t)$ and $P_{bg|fg}(x_{t-1})$. If they are consistent, we also take a majority vote. Otherwise, we take on the classification $P_{bg|fg}(x_t)$ at t. Whenever there is a change in classification, we clear the queue of results from $t-1, ..., t-q$.

Data and Experiments

To demonstrate the effectiveness of the proposed online background modeling algorithm, the following three environment sounds are used in the experiments:

1. *Coffee room*: Background includes footsteps, shuffling of things, people coming in and out. Foreground includes coffee grinding and brewing, printing sound (since a printer is located in the coffee room), etc.;
2. *Courtyard*: Background includes water fountain, distant talking from passers-by and traffic from nearby streets. Foreground includes plane passing overhead, cell phone ringing, loud talking, footsteps, etc.;
3. *Subway station platform*: Background includes passers-by noise and talking, trains in the distant. Foreground includes train arrival/departure, trains breaking, announcements, etc.

They are made up of ambient noise of a particular environment, composed of many sound events. We do not consider each constituent sound event individually, but as the different properties of each environment. We use continuous, unedited audio streams as the training and testing data. The first two data sets were collected and recorded in mono-channel, 16 bits per sample with a sampling rate of 44.1 KHz and of varying lengths in the Electrical Engineering building of the University of Southern California. They were taken at various times over a period of two weeks, with a duration averaging around 15 minutes each. The *subway station* set is also recordings of natural (unsynthesized) sound clips, which were obtained from (Freesound) and down-sampled to a 22.050 KHz sampling rate.

The incoming audio signal was segmented into fixed duration 1-second clips. Every second of the data sets was manually labeled. Features were computed for every 1-second window by averaging those from a 30-msec rectangular sampling window with 5 msec overlap. They were calculated for each clip and combined to form those of current clip x_t. We use two types of features: 1) Mel-frequency cepstrum coefficient analysis (MFCC), widely popular in speech and audio processing, and 2) MP-features. MP-features utilize the matching pursuit (MP) algorithm and a dictionary of Gabor atoms to learn the inherent structure of each type of sounds and select a small set of joint time frequency features. This method has shown to be robust for classifying sounds where the pure frequency-domain features fail and can be advantageous in combining with MFCC to improve the overall performance. Examples of MP-features are given in Figure 2. The feature vector used in this work contains a combination of MFCC and MP-features. For details of feature extraction and extensive experiments, we refer to the Section Extracting MP-Features.

For evaluation, the BG/FG classification was compared with labeled testing sets. We had 40 minutes of data for *Coffee room* and *Courtyard*. We were only able to obtain 15 minutes for the Subway station. The data were divided into 4 sets for each class. We used 2 sets as unlabeled data and 1 set as labeled in the self-training process. The last subset was used for testing in the final online BG/FG determination. Results were taken from the average of six trials (from different permutations of the 4 sets). The data were segmented into 1-second segments, but analyzed in sequence, where each segment was considered a sample. Therefore for each time frame, we determine whether it is predominantly background or foreground sound and then label it as such. The accuracy of the detection is calculated by

$$BG_{accuracy} = \frac{N_{y=bg}}{N_{total} - N_{fg}},$$

where $N_{y=bg}$ is the number of samples classified as BG, N_{fg} is the number of FG samples that are correctly classified, and N_{total} is the total number of samples.

Figure 7. Background detection accuracy (in %) (© 2009 IEEE. Used with permission.)

Data	CM		PSM	
	FG	BG	FG	BG
Coffee room	75.9	82.5	27.4	56.8
Courtyard	63.5	92.1	36.7	89.9
Subway platform	74.8	79.2	46.5	58.9

We calibrated the parameter values for each dataset to produce better overall results. The weighting factor, $\lambda = 0.5$, was set to reduce the sensitivity to unlabeled data. The threshold, $T = 0.5$, was the tolerance for determining distributions that were considered as BG. α_g and α_ω were set to 0.01 in the experiments. The sliding window size m was set to 120 samples. Based on the observation from (SChu, 2008), the setting for the MP-features was chosen for the Gabor function with parameters to be same as Section Experimental Evaluation.

Results and Discussion

We compared the performance accuracy between the proposed method and the one from (SMoncrieff, 2007) as a baseline. We refer to our approach as combination models (CM) and (SMoncrieff, 2007) as persistency only models (PSM). The experimental results are summarized in Figure 7. We see that both methods produce better accuracy for the background than foreground since the background is more constant than the foreground, and therefore is easier to learn. The PSM method performs poorly on Coffee room data since it cannot classify the long-persistent sound of a printer as the foreground. At one time, the printing sound continuously ran for 49 seconds and these segments were misclassified as background.

We examine a small segment of data (as shown in Figure 8) in more detail. In this example, the delay from PSM was about 7 seconds, while CM results in a 2-3 second delay. We also note that, after about 10 seconds of considering the current sound clip as foreground, the foreground

distributions were soon considered to part of the background process. With a quick change in the BG/FG events, PSM takes about 10-15 seconds to stabilize depending on the update rates.

We observe that it is more difficult to detect the foreground segments in the *Courtyard* class. When a plane passed over for 16 seconds, PSM only detected 4 seconds of it, while CM detected about 10 seconds. The Subway set provides an example comprised of many short events. There were very few moments when there is a constant background. In this case, we observe that it was difficult for both systems to achieve high performances. However, CM still outperforms PSM. For the CM method, class determination is based on the combined effort of both online models and prediction models, making it less sensitive to changes in parameters. The PSM method is more sensitive to parameter changes since its classification only depends on one model. More details of this work can be found in (Chu, 2009)

CONCLUSION

Unstructured environmental audio is extensively studied in this chapter. We investigated in terms of classification, feature extraction, modeling, and characterization by introducing a novel feature extraction method that utilizes matching pursuit (MP) to select a small set of time-frequency features, which is flexible, intuitive and physically interpretable. MP-features can classify sounds where the pure frequency-domain features fail and can be advantageous combining with them to improve the overall performance. Extensive experiments were conducted to demonstrate the advantages of MP-features as well as joint MFCC and MP-features in environmental sound classification. The experimental results show promising performance in classifying fourteen different audio environments, and shows comparable performance to human classification results on a similar task.

Figure 8.

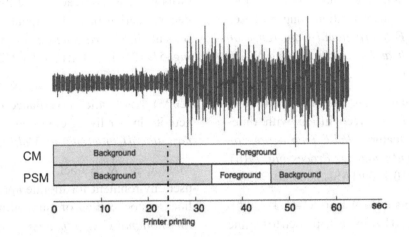

As our ultimate goal is to characterize an environment, we would like to achieve is a general model of the environment. The first step in that direction is to determine if we can model the background. Once we have a general notion of the background, we can identify foreground events even if we have not previously encountered them. Therefore, we proposed a framework for audio background modeling, which includes prediction, data knowledge and persistent characteristics of the environment, leading to a more robust audio background detection algorithm. This framework has the ability to model the background and detect foreground events as well as the ability to verify whether the predicted background is indeed the background or a foreground event that protracts for a longer period of time. Experimental results demonstrated promising performance in improving the state-of-the-art in background modeling of audio environments. We also investigated the use of a semi-supervised learning technique to exploit unlabeled audio data. It is encouraging that we could utilize more unlabeled data to improve generalization as they are usually cheap to acquire but expensive to label. And more than often, we are forced to work with relatively small amount of labeled data due to this limitation.

REFERENCES

Aucouturier, J.-J., Defreville, B., & Pachet, F. (2007). The bag-of-frames approach to audio pattern recognition: A sufficient model for urban soundscapes but not for polyphonic music. *The Journal of the Acoustical Society of America, 122,* 881–891. doi:10.1121/1.2750160

Bishop, C. (2003). *Neural networks for pattern recognition.* Oxford, UK: Oxford University Press.

Cai, R., Lu, L., Hanjalic, A., Zhang, H., & Cai, L.-H. (2006). A flexible framework for key audio effects detection and auditory context inference. *IEEE Transactions on Audio. Speech and Language Processing, 14*(3), 1026–1039. doi:10.1109/TSA.2005.857575

Cano, P., Koppenberger, M., Groux, S., Ricard, J., Wack, N., & Herrera, P. (2004). Nearest-neighbor generic sound classification with a wordnet-based taxonomy. In *116th Convention of the Audio Engineering Society.*

Chen, S., Donoho, D., & Saunders, M. (1998). Atomic decomposition by basis pursuit. *SIAM Journal on Scientific Computing, 20,* 33–61. doi:10.1137/S1064827596304010

Chu, S., Narayanan, S., & Kuo, C.-C. J. (2008). Environmental sound recognition using mp-based features. In *IEEE International Conference on Acoustics, Speech, and Signal Processing*. Washington, DC: IEEE.

Chu, S., Narayanan, S., & Kuo, C.-C. J. (2009). Environmental sound recognition with time-frequency audio features. *IEEE Transactions on Audio. Speech and Language Processing, 17*(6), 1142–1158. doi:10.1109/TASL.2009.2017438

Chu, S., Narayanan, S., & Kuo, C.-C. J. (2009) A Semi-Supervised Learning Approach to Online Audio Background Detection. In *IEEE International Conference on Acoustics, Speech, and Signal Processing*. Washington, DC: IEEE.

Chu, S., Narayanan, S., Kuo, C.-C. J., & Mataric, M. (2006). Where am I? scene recognition for mobile robots using audio features. In *IEEE International Conference on Multimedia and Expo*. Washington, DC: IEEE.

Ebenezer, S., Papandreou-Suppappola, A., & Suppappola, S. (2004). Classification of acoustic emissions using modified matching pursuit. *EURASIP Journal on Applied Signal Processing*, 347–357. doi:10.1155/S1110865704311029

Ellis, D. (1996). *Prediction-driven computational auditory scene analysis*. Unpublished doctoral dissertation, MIT Department of Electrical Engineering and Computer Science, MIT, Cambridge.

Ellis, D. (2001). Detecting alarm sounds. In *Workshop Consistent and Reliable Acoustic Cues*.

Ellis, D., & Lee, K. (2004). Minimal-impact audio-based personal archives. In *Workshop on Continuous Archival and Retrieval of Personal Experiences*.

Eronen, A., Peltonen, V., Tuomi, J., Klapuri, A., Fagerlund, S., & Sorsa, T. (2006). Audio-based context recognition. *IEEE Transactions on Audio. Speech and Language Processing, 14*, 321–329. doi:10.1109/TSA.2005.854103

Gribonval, R., & Bacry, E. (2003). Harmonic decomposition of audio signals with matching pursuit. *IEEE Transactions on Signal Processing, 51*, 101–111. doi:10.1109/TSP.2002.806592

Härmä, A., McKinney, M., & Skowronek, J. (2005). Automatic surveillance of the acoustic activity in our living environment. In *IEEE International Conference on Multimedia and Expo*.

Malkin, R., & Waibel, A. (2005). Classifying user environment for mobile applications using linear autoencoding of ambient audio. In *IEEE International Conference on Acoustics, Speech, and Signal Processing*.

Mallat, S., & Zhang, Z. (1993). Matching pursuits with time-frequency dictionaries. *IEEE Transactions on Signal Processing, 41*, 3397–3415. doi:10.1109/78.258082

Moncrieff, S., Venkatesh, S., & West, G. (2007). On-line audio background determination on-line audio background determination for complex audio environments. *ACM Transactions on Multimedia Computing, Communications, and Applications, 3*, 1–30.

Neff, R., & Zakhor, A. (1997). Very low bit rate video coding based on matching pursuits. *IEEE Transactions on Circuits and Systems for Video Technology, 7*, 158–171. doi:10.1109/76.554427

Nigam, K., McCallum, A., Thrun, S., & Mitchell, T. (2000). Text classification from labeled and unlabeled documents using EM. *Machine Learning, 39*, 103–134. doi:10.1023/A:1007692713085

Peltonen, V. (2001). *Computational auditory scene recognition*. Master's thesis, Tampere University of Technology, Finland.

Sound Ideas. (n.d.). *The BBC sound effects library - original series*. Retrieved from http://www.sound-ideas.com/bbc.html

Stauffer, C., & Grimson, W. (1999). *Adaptive background mixture models for real-time tracking*. IEEE Computer Vision and Pattern Recognition.

The Freesound Project. (n.d.). *The freesound project*. Retrieved from http://freesound.iua.upf.edu/index.php

Tzanetakis, G., & Cook, P. (2002). Musical genre classification of audio signals. *IEEE Transactions on Speech and Audio Processing, 10*, 293–302. doi:10.1109/TSA.2002.800560

Umapathy, K., Krishnan, S., & Jimaa, S. (2005). Multigroup classification of audio signals using time-frequency parameters. *IEEE Transactions on Multimedia, 7*, 308–315. doi:10.1109/TMM.2005.843363

Zhang, T., & Kuo, C.-C. J. (2001). Audio content analysis for online audiovisual data segmentation and classification. *IEEE Transactions on Speech and Audio Processing, 9*, 441–457. doi:10.1109/89.917689

Chapter 2
Modeling Grouping Cues for Auditory Scene Analysis Using a Spectral Clustering Formulation

Luís Gustavo Martins
Portuguese Catholic University, Portugal

Mathieu Lagrange
CNRS - Institut de Recherche et Coordination Acoustique Musique (IRCAM), France

George Tzanetakis
University of Victoria, Canada

ABSTRACT

Computational Auditory Scene Analysis (CASA) is challenging problem for which many different approaches have been proposed. These approaches can be based on statistical and signal processing methods such as Independent Component Analysis or can be based on our current knowledge about human auditory perception. Learning happens at the boundary interactions between prior knowledge and incoming data. Separating complex mixtures of sound sources such as music requires a complex interplay between prior knowledge and analysis of incoming data. Many approaches to CASA can also be broadly categorized as either model-based or grouping-based. Although it is known that our perceptual-system utilizes both of these types of processing, building such systems computationally has been challenging. As a result most existing systems either rely on prior source models or are solely based on grouping cues. In this chapter the authors argue that formulating this integration problem as clustering based on similarities between time-frequency atoms provides an expressive yet disciplined approach to building sound source characterization and separation systems and evaluating their performance. After describing the main components of such an architecture, the authors describe a concrete realization that is based on spectral clustering of a sinusoidal representation. They show how this approach can be used to model both traditional grouping cues such as frequency and amplitude continuity as well as other types of information and prior knowledge such as onsets, harmonicity and timbre-models for specific instruments.

DOI: 10.4018/978-1-61520-919-4.ch002

Experiments supporting their approach to integration are also described. The description also covers issues of software architecture, implementation and efficiency, which are frequently not analyzed in depth for many existing algorithms. The resulting system exhibits practical performance (approximately real-time) with consistent results without requiring example-specific parameter optimization and is available as part of the Marsyas open source audio processing framework.

INTRODUCTION

Inspired by the classic book by Bregman on Auditory Scene Analysis (ASA) (Bregman, 1990) a variety of systems for Computational Auditory Scene Analysis (CASA) have been proposed (Wang and Brown, 2006). They can be broadly classified as bottom-up systems (or data-driven) where the flow of information is from the incoming audio signal to higher level representations or top-down systems (or model-based) where prior-knowledge about the characteristics of a particular type of sound source in the form of a model is utilized to assist the analysis. The human auditory system utilizes both of these types of processing. Although it has been argued that computational CASA systems should also utilize both types (Slaney, 1998) most existing systems fall into only one of the two categories. Another related challenge is the integration of several grouping cues that operate simultaneously into a single system. We believe that this integration becomes particularly challenging when the CASA system has a multiple stage architecture where each stage corresponds to a particular grouping cue or type of processing. In such architectures any errors in one stage propagate to the following stages and it is hard to decide what the ordering of stages should be. An alternative, which we advocate in this chapter, is to formulate the entire sound source formation problem from a complex sound mixture as a clustering based on similarities of time-frequency atoms across both time and frequency. That way all cues are taken into account simultaneously and new sources of information such as source models or other types

of prior-knowledge can easily be taken into consideration using one unifying formulation.

Humans, even without any kind of formal music training, are typically able to extract, almost unconsciously, a great amount of relevant information from a musical signal. Features such as the beat of a musical piece, the main melody of a complex musical arrangement, the sound sources and events occurring in a complex musical mixture, the song structure (e.g. verse, chorus, bridge) and the musical genre of a piece, are just some examples of the level of knowledge that a naive listener is commonly able to extract just from listening to a musical piece. In order to do so, the human auditory system uses a variety of cues for perceptual grouping such as similarity, proximity, harmonicity, common fate, among others.

In the past few years interest in the emerging research area of Music Information Retrieval (MIR) has been steadily growing. It encompasses a wide variety of ideas, algorithms, tools, and systems that have been proposed to handle the increasingly large and varied amounts of musical data available digitally. Typical MIR systems for music signals in audio format represent statistically the entire polyphonic sound mixture (Tzanetakis and Cook, 2002). There is some evidence that this approach has reached a "glass ceiling" (Aucouturier and Pachet, 2004) in terms of retrieval performance. One obvious direction for further progress is to attempt to individually characterize the different sound sources comprising the polyphonic mixture. The predominant melodic voice (typically the singer in western popular music) is arguably the most important sound source and its separation and has a large number of applications in Music Information Retrieval.

The proposed system is based on a sinusoidal modeling from which spectral components are segregated into sound events using perceptually inspired grouping cues. An important characteristic of clustering based on similarities rather than points is that it can utilize more generalized context-dependent similarities that can not easily be expressed as distances between points. We propose such a context-dependent similarity cue based on harmonicity (termed "Harmonically-Wrapped Peak Similarity" or HWPS). The segregation process is based on spectral clustering methods, a technique originally proposed to model perceptual grouping tasks in the computer vision field (Shi and Malik, 2000). One of the main advantages of this approach is the ability to incorporate various perceptually-inspired grouping criteria into a single framework without requiring multiple processing stages. Another important property, especially for MIR applications that require analysis of large music collections, is the running time of the algorithm which is approximately real-time, as well as the independence of the algorithm from recording-specific parameter tuning.

RELATED WORK

Auditory Scene Analysis and Perceptual Organization of Sound

The psychologist Albert Bregman was the first to systematically explore the principles underlying the perception of complex acoustic mixtures, whereby all the auditory evidence coming over time from a single environmental source is put together as a perceptual unit. He coined this process Auditory Scene Analysis (ASA) (Bregman, 1990).

This cognitive approach to perception implies that the information contained in the stimuli that reach the sensory organs must be interpreted at some higher level processes, since by itself, sensory information is not always sufficient to form a consistent image of the surrounding sound environment (Bregman, 1990, McAdams and Bigand, 1993). One of the reasons for this is the temporal nature of sound, where sound events succeed one another in time (a typical example would be music sounds). The perception of the structure of these events requires the construction of a mental representation where the relations among events (which may be separated in time by arbitrarily long intervals) can be established. Furthermore, at the presence of insufficient sensory information, the perceptual system tries to take into consideration knowledge that it has previously acquired of the surrounding sound world. This prior knowledge interacts with the current sensory data to interpret the auditory stimulation.

Although the early stages of the human auditory system are an important part of the human ability to solve the ASA problem from eardrum vibrations, relatively little is known at the physiological level about how higher order mechanisms participate in the perception processes. It is intrinsically difficult to measure something as abstract and unobservable as the internal perception of sounds that belong together. Taking on the results from carefully prepared perceptual experiments using simple stimuli, Bregman brought some light to these questions and proposed an attractive conceptual framework for ASA where he assumes an important distinction between the actual acoustic sources in a mixture and the corresponding mental representations (Bregman, 1990). A number of auditory cues and principles exploited by the auditory system when performing ASA have been proposed. They can be divided into a two-stage organization process, namely simultaneous grouping and sequential grouping.

Simultaneous vs. Sequential Grouping

Bregman suggested the division of the ASA problem as a two-stage organization process. In the first stage, called simultaneous grouping, acoustic energy occurring concurrently in different frequency regions are fused into a single percept, which takes place in a specific time-frequency region known as a segment. Fusion of harmonically related sinusoid components (in the Fourier sense) into a single "rich" tone is a good example of this process. This grouping principle is usually based on auditory cues as the ones summarized next.

Simultaneous Grouping Cues

- **Harmonicity.** When a body vibrates with a periodic movement, its vibrations create an acoustic pattern whose frequency components are multiples of a common fundamental (i.e. harmonics of a fundamental frequency). Interestingly, the auditory system tends to group a set of harmonically related acoustic components into a single event.

- **Common onset and offset.** Sound components with the same onset time and, to a lesser extent, the same offset time, tend to be grouped into the same unit by the auditory system. Since unrelated sounds seldom start or stop at exactly the same time, the auditory system assumes that components exhibiting a "common fate" are likely to have origin in a common single source.

- **Common modulation.** Another example of the sensibility of the auditory system to "common fate" is the segregation of components of a mixture exhibiting a common amplitude or frequency modulation. If a sound source exhibits amplitude or frequency modulation, it is expected that all of its components exhibit similar modulation manifestations.

- **Spatial proximity.** One of the best generalizations that can be made about independent sound sources is that they normally occupy distinct positions in space. As a consequence, sound source location could provide the strongest cue in the construction of an ecological representation of the

surrounding sound environment. However, spatial location of sound sources is, accordingly to some authors, taken as an auxiliary cue by the human auditory system (Bregman, 1990). In fact, humans can still segregate sound mixtures when listening to monaural acoustic signals (i.e. no spatial information is included for the different sources comprising the mixture).

In the second stage, known as sequential grouping, the series of segments from the first stage are built up into one or more streams. Each stream is a sequence of events assumed as coming from a single source (e.g. a human listener can easily assign the notes of two melody lines played concurrently by two different instruments to the correct source). The following list presents some of the auditory cues possibly involved in sequential grouping.

Sequential Grouping Cues

- **Time and frequency proximity.** Acoustic components close in frequency tend to be interpreted by the auditory system as coming from the same sound source. Additionally, components close in time tend to be perceptually grouped into a same stream. Consequently, the closer in time and frequency components are, the stronger the tendency of being grouped into a same auditory stream.

- **Loudness proximity.** Sources with different energy levels consist of acoustic components with correspondingly distinct sound intensities. The auditory organization of physical stimuli also resorts to loudness similarity to group components into the same acoustic event.

- **Timbral similarity.** Sound elements that sound alike (i.e. have similar spectral properties or similar timbres) tend to be grouped into the same auditory stream (Bregman, 1990, pp.19; 92-127). This similarity grouping is increased by the temporal closeness of similar auditory components.

- **Smoothness of change.** A single sound tends to change its properties smoothly over time. Consequently, a sequence of sounds from a same source also tends to change its properties gradually over time. The auditory system favors the sequential grouping of sound components whose properties are stable. Abrupt discontinuities are perceived as new and unrelated events, probably with origin in a distinct source. Smooth changes in pitch contour, intensity, spatial location and spectral characteristics of a sound are usually interpreted as a continuation of an existing sound.

Sound Source Separation and CASA

A fundamental characteristic of the human hearing system is the ability to selectively focus on different sound elements and events in complex mixtures of sounds such music. The goal of computational auditory scene analysis (Rosenthal and Okuno, 1998, Wang and Brown, 2006) is to create computer systems that can take as input a mixture of sounds and form units of acoustic evidence such that each unit most likely has arisen from a single sound entity.

Humans use a variety of cues for perceptual grouping in hearing such as similarity, proximity, harmonicity and common fate. However, many of the computational issues of perceptual grouping for hearing are still unsolved. In particular, considering the several perceptual cues altogether is still an open issue (Roweis, 2000, Vincent, 2006), and the definition of what a sound entity should sound like when segregated is an ill-posed problem.

Accordingly, this chapter will propose and discuss a flexible and extensible CASA framework for modeling the perceptual grouping problem in music listening. The goal of the proposed approach is to partition the acoustical mixture into a perceptually motivated topological description of the sound scene (similar to the way a naive listener would perceive it) instead of attempting to accurately separate the mixture into its original constituent "sources". Thus, the term "sound source" will be used in the remaining of this text to mainly refer to "perceptual" sound events or "objects" in complex audio mixtures instead of limiting its meaning to the actual "physical" sources active at each time instant. The resulting topological representation leverages subsequent feature analysis, sound resynthesis and further transformations and manipulation of the segregated sound elements.

SPECTRAL CLUSTERING IN AUDIO ANALYSIS

Many of the computational issues of perceptual grouping for hearing are still unsolved. In particular, considering the several perceptual cues altogether is still an open issue (Vincent, 2006, Roweis, 2000). We propose in this work to cast this problem into a graph cut formulation using the normalized cut criterion. This global criterion for graph partitioning has been proposed for solving similar grouping problems in computer vision (Shi and Malik, 2000).

The normalized cut is a representative example of spectral clustering techniques which use an affinity matrix to encode topological knowledge about a problem. Spectral clustering approaches have been used in a variety of applications including high performance computing, web mining, biological data, image segmentation and motion tracking.

To the best of our knowledge there are few applications of spectral clustering to audio processing. It has been used for the unsupervised clustering of similar sounding segments of audio (Ellis and Lee, 2004, Cai et al., 2005). In these approaches, each audio frame is characterized by a feature vector and a self-similarity matrix across frames is constructed and used for clustering. This approach has also been linked to the singular value decomposition of feature matrices to form audio basis vectors (Dubnov and Appel, 2004). These approaches characterize the overall audio mixture without using spectral clustering to form and track individual sound sources.

Spectral clustering has also been used for blind one-microphone speech separation (Bach and Jordan, 2004, Bach and Jordan, 2006). Rather than building specific speech models, the authors show how the system can separate mixtures of two speech signals by learning the parameters of affinity matrices based on various harmonic and non-harmonic cues. The entire STFT magnitude spectrum is used as the underlying representation.

Closer to our approach, harmonicity relationships and common fate cues underlie a short-term spectra-based similarity measure presented by Srinivasan (Srinivasan and Kankanhalli, 2003). To integrate time constraints, it is alternatively proposed in (Srinivasan, 2004) to cluster previously tracked partials to form auditory «blobs» according to onset cues. Normalized cut clustering is then carried out on these blobs. In contrast, a short-term sinusoidal modeling framework is used in our approach. It results in more accurate and robust similarity relations as well as significantly smaller affinity matrices that are computationally more tractable. The idea of simultaneous clustering/tracking across both time and frequency has been explored with a difference formulation using the EM-algorithm (Kameoke et al, 2007).

This chapter integrates work presented in several conference, a journal publication and a PhD thesis by the authors (Lagrange et al., 2006, Lagrange and Tzanetakis, 2007, Martins et al., 2007, Martins, 2009).

System Overview

An overview of the main analysis and processing blocks that constitute the proposed sound segregation system is presented in Figure 1. The system uses sinusoidal modeling as the underlying representation for the acoustic signals. Sinusoidal modeling is a technique for analysis and synthesis whereby sound is modeled as the summation of sine waves parameterized by time-varying amplitudes, frequencies and phases. In the classic McAulay and Quatieri method (McAulay and Quatieri, 1986), these time varying quantities are estimated by performing a short-time Fourier transform (STFT), and locating the peaks of the magnitude spectrum. Partial tracking algorithms track the sinusoidal parameters from frame to frame, and determine when new partials begin and existing ones terminate (Lagrange et al., 2007).

If the goal is to identify potential sound sources then a separate stage of partial grouping is needed. Typically grouping cues such as common onsets and spectral proximity are used. These two processes of connecting peaks over time to form partials (i.e. tracking) and grouping them to form potential sound sources (i.e. formation) roughly correspond to the sequential and simultaneous aspects of organization proposed by Bregman (Bregman, 1990). Although frequently implemented as separate stages (e.g. (Srinivasan, 2004)) these two organizational principles directly influence one another. For example, if one has knowledge that a set of peaks belongs to the same source, then their correspondence with the next frame is easier to find. Similarly, the formation of sound sources is easier if peaks can be tracked perfectly over time. However, methods that apply these two stages in a fixed order tend to be brittle as they are sensitive to errors and ambiguity.

To cope with this "circular cause and consequence" problem, the following sections try to show how both sound source tracking and formation can be jointly optimized within a unified framework using spectral clustering, and in particular the Normalized Cut criterion (Ncut) (Shi and Malik, 2000, von Luxburg, 2007).

Correspondingly, for each audio analysis frame at the input (set to have a length of about 46 ms) the system starts by computing the STFT (with

Figure 1. Block diagram of the proposed sound segregation framework

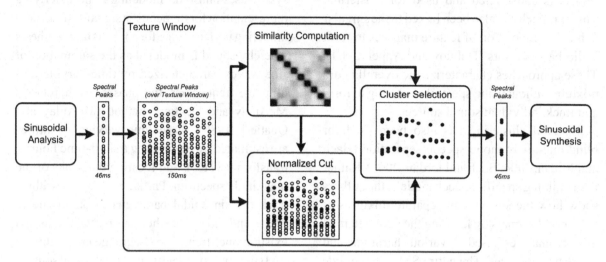

a hop size of about 11 ms), where at each frame the local maxima of the magnitude spectrum are selected and stored as peaks characterized by their precise amplitude, frequency and phase. The current system selects the 20 highest amplitude peaks at each STFT frame, but ignores peaks whose frequencies are above 2500 Hz (empirical experiments have shown that components above 2500 Hz are often unstable, hurting the final segregation performance).

The challenge is then to express perceptual cues in terms of similarity between these time-frequency components in the signal. The peaks are therefore accumulated over a "texture" window (amounting to approximately 150 ms, although this value can be user or dynamically adjusted and the problem is modeled as a weighted undirected graph (Balakrishnan, 1997, Shneiderman and Aris, 2006), where the nodes of the graph are the peaks of the magnitude spectrum and an undirected edge is formed between each pair of nodes. The edge weight is a function of the similarity between nodes and utilizes various grouping cues such as frequency and amplitude proximity, as well as a novel harmonicity criterion, termed Harmonically Wrapped Peak Similarity. The system is nevertheless flexible enough to accommodate new similarity cues allowing to model an increasing

number of perceptual mechanisms involved in human hearing. Based on these grouping cues, and as depicted in Figure 2, the similarity across all the peaks is calculated and stored in similarity matrices, which are subsequently combined into an overall similarity matrix.

Peak clustering is then performed on this overall similarity matrix and each peak is assigned to a particular cluster, ideally grouping together components which are close in the similarity space, and therefore have a higher chance of coming from a same sound source or event. Clustering is performed in the same way for all peaks within the «texture window» independently of whether they belong to the same frame or not, implementing some degree of time integration in the process. The peak clustering procedure, hereby formulated as a graph partitioning problem, can be efficiently solved using a spectral clustering approach, a technique used in a variety of applications including high performance computing, web mining, biological data and computer vision (Shi and Malik, 2000, von Luxburg, 2007). Spectral clustering conveniently makes use of the computed similarity matrix to encode topological knowledge about a problem (von Luxburg, 2007) and to subsequently group together similar components, all in an unsupervised manner. In particular, the Ncut

Figure 2. Similarity cues currently implemented in the proposed sound segregation framework (black boxes). The system is flexible enough to accommodate new similarity cues (gray blocks) allowing to model an increasing number of perceptual mechanisms involved in human hearing. The individual similarity matrices from each grouping cue are combined into an overall similarity matrix that can be subsequently used by the clustering algorithm for sound event segregation (i.e. Normalized Cut).

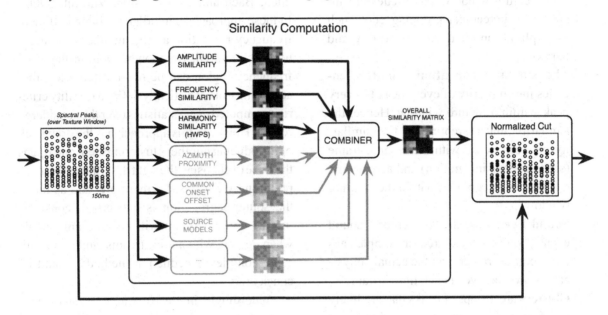

(Shi and Malik, 2000), a representative example of spectral clustering techniques, is employed in the system proposed in this chapter. The Ncut algorithm is computationally efficient and causal, eventually executing in real-time.

Once identified, the resulting clusters should ideally have a close perceptual correspondence to the sound events or «objects» as perceived by a human listener (at least a naive one). As a result, the clusters that most likely represent the different sound events or «objects» in the mixture can be selected and resynthesized for further sound processing or evaluation.

Concepts and Terminology

For the sake of clarity, some of the parameters and terminology used when describing the audio segregation approach proposed in the remaining of this chapter are summarized next.

- **Frames or analysis windows** are sequences of audio samples used to estimate sinusoidal peaks from the complex spectrum computed using a Short Time Fourier Transform. For the experiments described later in the chapter a frame size corresponding to 46 ms and a hop size of 11 ms are used.

- **Peaks** are the output of the sinusoidal modeling stage. For each frame, a variable number of peaks corresponding to the local maxima of the spectrum are estimated. Each peak is characterized by its amplitude, frequency and phase.

- **Texture windows** correspond to an integer number of frames. Clustering of peaks across both frequency and time is performed for each texture window rather than per frame. For the experiments described in this chapter a texture window corresponding to 10 frames (approximately 150 ms) is used, but this value can be user or dynamically adjusted.

- **Similarity cues** express the similarity between spectral peaks belonging to the same texture window. These cues are inspired by perceptual grouping cues such as amplitude and frequency proximity, and harmonicity.
- **The similarity or affinity matrix** encodes the similarity of every peak to every peak within a texture window. Hence, the similarity matrix represents the similarity between peaks within the same frame (simultaneous integration) and across time (sequential integration) within the "texture window".
- **Sound Events** are the "perceptual" sound events, "objects" or sources in complex audio mixtures, rather than the actual "physical" sources active at each time instant.
- **Clusters** are groups of peaks that are likely to originate from the same sound event or source. By optimizing the Normalized Cut criterion (Ncut), the overall peak similarity within a cluster is maximized and the similarity between clusters is minimized. The audio corresponding to any set of peaks (one or more clusters) can be conveniently resynthesized using a bank of sinusoidal oscillators.
- **Sound Segregation**, also known as sound separation or sound source formation in the scope of this chapter, is the process of approximately reconstructing a particular sound event from a decomposition of the polyphonic mixture.

Sinusoidal Modeling of Music Signals

Several CASA approaches consider auditory filterbanks and correlograms as their analysis front-end (Wang and Brown, 2006). In these approaches the number of time-frequency components is rela-

tively small. However closely-spaced components within the same critical band are hard to separate.

Other authors consider the Fourier spectrum as their front-end (Srinivasan and Kankanhalli, 2003, Bach and Jordan, 2004, Vincent, 2006). In these approaches, in order to obtain sufficient frequency resolution a large number of components is required. Components within the same frequency region can be pre–clustered together according to a heuristically defined stability criterion computed using statistics over the considered region. However, this approach has the drawback of introducing another clustering step, and opens the issue of choosing the right descriptors for those preliminary clusters. Furthermore, and as far as the sound segregation is concerned, considering the entire mixture will become untractable when dealing with audio streams, and as a result some complexity reduction methods should be considered.

Accordingly, in this work an alternative sinusoidal front-end is used. The sinusoidal model fulfills most of the desirable properties of a mid-level representation, namely:

- it allows to provide a meaningful and precise representation of the auditory scene while considering only a limited number of components;
- it is invertible, allowing to reconstruct an approximation of the segregated sound components and it is efficient and intuitive to compute;
- it is particularly suited for sustained sounds with a well defined pitch and harmonic structure such as the vowels of a singing voice or the notes from pitched music instrument (e.g. trumpet, piano or violin);
- it easily enables to use prior information about the harmonic spectral structure, making it suitable for the separation of pitched musical instruments and voiced speech and singing.

Because in traditional Western music pitched sounds tend to dominate and last for longer periods when compared to transient signals (usually originated at the attacks or onsets of notes and events, or resulting from percussion instruments such as drums), a sinusoidal model can, in practice, capture most of the pitched information that is useful for MIR applications. This includes the ability to detect musical events in a complex mixture, such as the melodic line or the timbral characteristics of the instruments playing or the main singing voice in the signal.

The following sections summarize the method used in this work for the precise estimation of the frequency and amplitude of the most prominent spectral peaks in an audio frame. The interested reader can find more detailed information about the presented technique in (Marchand and Lagrange, 2006, Lagrange and Marchand, 2007, Lagrange et al., 2007).

Short Term Sinusoidal Analysis

Sinusoidal modeling represents a sound signal as a sum of sinusoids characterized by their main parameters: amplitudes, frequencies, and phases. It is rooted in Fourier's theorem, which states that any periodic function can be modeled as a sum of sinusoids at various amplitudes and harmonic frequencies. Since considering these parameters as constant through the whole signal duration is not perceptually relevant, a common approach is to segment the signal into successive frames of small duration. The length of each frame (N samples), and the hop size (H samples) between successive frames should be set so that the parameters can be considered constant within the frame (for a sampling frequency of 44100 Hz, N is set to 2048 samples and H is set to 512 samples, corresponding to a frame length of about 46 ms and a hop size of about 11 ms these are typically used values in music analysis).

The discrete signal $x^k(n)$ at frame index k is then modeled as follows:

$$x^k(n) = \sum_{l=1}^{L^k} a_l^k \, \cos\left(\frac{2\pi}{F_s} f_l^k \cdot n + \phi_l^k\right)$$

where n is the sample index, F_s is the sampling frequency, ϕ_l^k is the phase at the beginning of the frame of the l-th component of L^k sinusoids, and f_l^k and a_l^k are respectively the frequency and the amplitude. Both are considered as constant within the frame.

Peak Parameters Estimation

For each frame k, a set of sinusoidal parameters $S^k = \{p_1^k, \cdots, p_{L^k}^k\}$ is estimated. The system parameters of this Short-Term Sinusoidal (STS) model S^k are the L^k triplets $p_l^k = \{f_l^k, a_l^k, \phi_l^k\}$, often called *peaks*. These parameters can be efficiently estimated by picking some local maxima from a Short-Term Fourier Transform.

To estimate each set of peaks S^k, the spectrum X^k is computed using a discrete Fourier transform (DFT) applied to the windowed samples of frame k. The samples are weighted by a Hann window with an even lenght N, and subsequently circularly shifted by $N/2$ samples prior to the DFT computation. This results in zero-phase windowing, a procedure that allows to obtain a robust estimation of the phase (Serra, 1989).

The precision of these estimates is further improved by using phase-based frequency estimators which utilize the relationship between phases of successive frames (Puckette and Brown, 1998, Marchand and Lagrange, 2006, Lagrange and Marchand, 2007).

Time Segmentation of Music Signals

In order to introduce some degree of temporal integration and simultaneously optimize partial tracking and source formation, peaks should be grouped along time and frequency, into what is known in this work as a texture window. This allows to compute the proximity between peaks both within a frame as well as across frames belonging to a same texture window, resulting in the construction of a similarity graph. Unlike approaches based on local information (McAulay and Quatieri, 1986), such a similarity graph enables the use of the global Normalized Cut criterion to partition the graph over an entire texture window. Thus, peaks are grouped over texture windows rather than per frame.

Two approaches for defining texture windows have been implemented: the first based on fixed length texture windows, and a second one based on the use of an onset detector to automatically define the texture window lengths.

Fixed Length Texture Windows

Texture windows can be obtained by simply accumulating a fixed number of frames over time (which in this work is set to correspond to a length of about 150 ms). In such a case, if L^k is the number of peaks in frame k, then the number of peaks in a texture window is T:

$$T = \sum_{k=1}^{N} L^k$$

where N is the texture window length (in frames). This will later allow to compute the pairwise similarity between all peaks p_l^k and p_m^{k+n} in the texture window, where l, m are the peak indices, $n \in \{0 \dots N\text{-}1\}$ is the frame offset between the peaks and $n = 0$ is used for peaks of the same frame.

Although simple and computationally efficient, this fixed length approach does not take into consideration the perceptual organization of sound as performed by the human ear. The human auditory system is highly sensitive to the time structure of a sound stream, and onsets seem to be particularly important to the segregation

of complex mixtures of sounds (Scheirer, 2000, Srinivasan, 2004). The human ear tries to lock on onset events as a way to perform a first low-level time segmentation of the acoustic stimuli, dividing the sound into perceptually coherent time regions, where sources assume a clear presence and additional grouping principles become into play (e.g. harmonicity grouping). This fact is even more evident in the case of music signals, where in most cases a regular time structure exists, mainly resulting from the onset of the notes and events in the musical piece (Gouyon, 2005). As a result, a more perceptually motivated way to adjust the length of the texture windows could be based on the use of an onset detector.

Dynamic Length Texture Windows

Fixed length texture windows blindly chop an audio signal into segments without taking into consideration the various sound events occurring over time. Additionally, by not following a perceptually inspired approach, such a method will often result in texture windows where only parts of the sound events in a signal are present - be it their attack regions (i.e. onsets), sustained sections (i.e. usually the steady-state part of the sound event) or the release sections (i.e. the offsets).

One way to address this problem is to use an onset detector in order to identify the occurrence of new sound events in an audio signal, and to adjust texture windows to the corresponding inter-onset audio segments. As an example, Figure 3 depicts the time domain and the corresponding spectrogram representations of a fragment of a jazz recording, below which are plotted the onsets automatically identified using the algorithm described below. As it is clearly visible from this example, the audio segments between consecutive onsets present a high correlation to the occurrence of sound events in the signal (visible in the spectrogram representation), be them pitched events such as musical notes, or unpitched and noisy events such as percussion hits. As a result, taking

Figure 3. Dynamic adjustment of the length of the texture windows based on the detection of onsets in the audio signal. The top panel depicts the time domain representation of a fragment of a polyphonic jazz recording, below which is displayed its corresponding spectrogram. The bottom panel plots both the onset detection function SF(n) (grayline), as well as its filtered version (blackline). The automatically identified onsets are represented as vertical dotted lines.

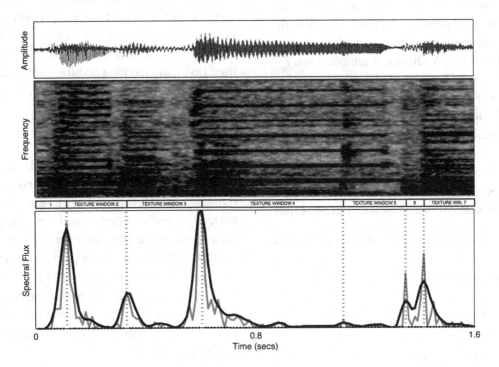

this onset information into account tends to result in more perceptually and musically meaningful texture windows.

The following section presents a summarized description of the implemented onset detector algorithm.

Onset Detection Algorithm

Onset detection aims at finding the starting time of musical events (e.g. notes, chords, drum events) in an audio signal. However, polyphonic music poses an increased challenge since nominally simultaneous notes might be spread over tens of milliseconds, turning the definition of onsets ambiguous. Similarly, it is hard to define a precise onset time for sounds with slow attacks.

In a recent tutorial article, Simon Dixon revisited the problem of onset detection (Dixon, 2006), where a number of onset detection algorithms were reviewed and compared on two datasets. This study was itself based on a previous article by Bello et al. (Bello et al., 2005) where a theoretical and empirical comparison of several state-of-the-art onset detection approaches is presented. Dixon concluded that the use of a spectral flux detection function for onset detection resulted in the best performance versus complexity ratio.

Hence, and following the findings and results in (Dixon, 2006), the approach used in this work is based on the use of the spectral flux as the onset detection function, defined as:

$$SF(n) = \sum_{k=0}^{N/2} H(\mid X(n,k)\mid - \mid X(n-1,k)\mid)$$

where $H(x) = \dfrac{x + |x|}{2}$ is the half-wave rectifier function, $X(n,k)$ represents the k-th frequency bin of the n-th frame of the power magnitude (in dB) of the short time Fourier Transform, and N is the corresponding Hamming window size. For the experiments performed in this work a window size of 46 ms (i.e. N=2048 at a sampling rate f_s = 44100 Hz) and a hop size of about 11ms (i.e. 512 samples at f_s = 44100 Hz) are used.

The bottom panel of Figure 3 plots the values over time of the onset detection function $SF(n)$ for a jazz excerpt example. The onsets are subsequently detected from the spectral flux values by a causal peak picking algorithm, where it attempts to find local maxima as follows. A peak at time $t = \dfrac{nH}{f_s}$ is selected as an onset if it satisfies the following conditions:

$$SF(n) \geq SF(k) \; \forall k : n - w \leq k \leq n + w$$

$$SF(n) > \frac{\sum\limits_{k=n-mw}^{n+w} SF(k)}{mw + w + 1} \times thres + \delta$$

where $w = 6$ is the size of the window used to find a local maximum, $m = 4$ is a multiplier so that the mean is calculated over a larger range before the peak, $thres = 2.0$ is a threshold relative to the local mean that a peak must reach in order to be sufficiently prominent to be selected as an onset, and $\delta = 10^{-20}$ is a residual value to avoid false detections on silence regions of the signal. All these parameter values were derived from preliminary experiments using a collection of music signals with varying onset characteristics.

As a way to reduce the false detection rate, the onset detection function $SF(n)$ is smoothed using a Butterworth filter (see bottom panel of Figure 3), defined as:

$$H(z) = \frac{0.1173 + 0.2347z^{-1} + 0.1174z^{-2}}{1 - 0.8252z^{-1} + 0.2946z^{-2}}.$$

Additionally, a minimum and maximum texture window length was defined, so that onsets detected inside a 50 ms range from the previous one are discarded (avoiding too short texture windows) and a maximum inter-onset interval of 300 ms is used (avoiding too long texture windows, a limitation mainly due to computational constraints).

Spectral Clustering

Spectral clustering, an alternative clustering approach that goes back to Donath and Hoffman (Donath and Hoffman, 1973), was shown to correctly handle complex and structured data. As a result, in the machine learning community, spectral clustering has been made popular by the works of Shi and Malik (Shi and Malik, 2000), Ng et al. (Ng et al., 2002) and Meila and Shi (Meila and Shi, 2001). A recent and comprehensive tutorial on spectral clustering can be found in (von Luxburg, 2007).

Instead of estimating an explicit model of data distribution, spectral clustering rather performs a spectral analysis of the matrix of point-to-point similarities (i.e. the similarity or affinity matrix). The success of spectral clustering mainly results from the fact that it does not make strong assumptions on the shape of the clusters. Differently from k-means, where data is assumed to follow a convex shaped distribution, or opposed to Expectation Maximization (EM), which assumes a Gaussian distribution of the data, spectral clustering can solve very general problems.

Being based on the eigen-structure of the computed similarity matrix, spectral clustering simply needs to solve a linear problem. This avoids risks of getting stuck in local minima and consequently having to restart the algorithm for several times with different initializations (as happens with k-means). On the other hand, spectral clustering allows to extract a global impression of the data structure (e.g. the components of a sound mixture) rather than focusing on local features and their consistencies in the data.

Moreover, compared to point based clustering algorithms such as k-means, the use of a similarity matrix as the underlying representation enables expression of similarities that are context-dependent and therefore cannot be computed as a distance function of independently calculated feature vectors. The Harmonically Wrapped Peak Similarity (HWPS) measure, which is described below, is an example of such as a similarity measure.

Finally, spectral clustering can be computationally efficiently even for large data sets, as long as the similarity matrix is made sparse. However computing a suitable similarity matrix depends on the choice of a good similarity graph, an operation, which is not trivial, and spectral clustering can become quite unstable under different choices of the parameters for the neighborhood graphs. Like in all machine learning approaches, the main issue is in the definition of the feature or similarity functions (i.e. the way data is abstracted) and not so much in the classifier or clustering algorithms. As a result, and as argued in (von Luxburg, 2007), spectral clustering should not be taken as a "black box algorithm" which is able to automatically detect the correct clusters in any arbitrary data set. It can, nevertheless, be used as a powerful tool, which can produce interesting results if applied diligently.

Grouping Cues as Similarities between Time-Frequency Peaks

The specification of grouping criteria should attempt to capture the perceptual proximity between sound components (i.e. spectral peaks) in accordance to the perceptual grouping principles. These include frequency and amplitude proximity and a novel harmonicity criterion, termed Harmonically Wrapped Peak Similarity (HWPS). Such a harmonicity criterion is of upmost importance since amplitude and frequency cues are not enough for

segregating multiple overlapping harmonic sound sources. Still, the proposed framework is able to easily accommodate future similarity functions such as frequency or time masking (Lagrange et al., 2006), common fate, stereo location, or other grouping principles, allowing to model an increasing number of perceptual mechanisms involved in human hearing.

Amplitude and Frequency Similarity

Two of the most basic similarities explored by the auditory system are related to the frequency and amplitude features of the sound components in a sound mixture.

Accordingly, the edge weight connecting two peaks p_l^k and p_m^{k+n} will depend on their frequency and amplitude proximities. Amplitude and frequency similarities, W_a and W_f respectively, are defined as follows:

$$W_a(p_l^k, p_m^{k+n}) = e^{-\left(\frac{a_l^k - a_m^{k+n}}{\sigma_a}\right)^2}$$

$$W_f(p_l^k, p_m^{k+n}) = e^{-\left(\frac{f_l^k - f_m^{k+n}}{\sigma_f}\right)^2}$$

where the Euclidean distances are modeled as two Gaussian functions. The amplitudes are measured in deciBels (dB) and the frequencies are measured in Barks (a frequency scale approximately linear below 500 Hz and logarithmic above), since these scales have shown to better model the sensitivity response of the human ear (Hartmann, 1998).

Harmonically Wrapped Peak Similarity (HWPS)

A wide variety of sounds produced by humans are harmonic, from singing voice and speech vowels, to musical sounds. As stated by Alain de Cheveigné: "Harmonicity is the most powerful among ASA cues. It is also the cue most often exploited in computational ASA systems and voice-separation systems" (Wang and Brown, 2006). It is therefore a critical cue for separating harmonic sounds, which are particularly important for musical signals. Accordingly, some of the source separation and multiple fundamental frequency estimation algorithms iteratively estimate the dominant fundamental frequency f0, and then remove the spectral components that are most likely to belong to the source attached to the corresponding f0 (e.g. (Klapuri, 2004)). Few studies have focused on the identification of harmonic relations between peaks without any prior fundamental frequency estimation. By contrast, in this work the focus is on the definition of a similarity function between time-frequency components, of the same frame or of different frames, that considers the harmonicity cue without fully relying on the prior knowledge of the f0 's (although such prior information can be easily embedded and improve the grouping capability of the proposed similarity function). The challenge is therefore to define a similarity measure between two frequency components (i.e. peaks) that is high for harmonically related peaks and low for peaks that are not harmonically related.

Existing Harmonicity Cues

Most existing approaches use the mathematical properties of the harmonically related frequencies to build a harmonicity similarity measure for a single frame (Virtanen and Klapuri, 2000, Srinivasan and Kankanhalli, 2003). For example, Virtanen and Klapuri (Virtanen and Klapuri, 2000) consider whether the ratio of the frequencies of the components is a ratio of small positive integers. Srinivasan and Kankanhallli consider a harmonicity map that can be precomputed to estimate the harmonic similarity between two spectral bins (Srinivasan and Kankanhalli, 2003).

There are several issues concerning these approaches, both from the technical and perceptual points of view. First, this type of measures

cannot be safely considered for peaks belonging to different frames, which is a strong handicap when trying to simultaneously optimize partial tracking and source formation. The reason of this restriction is that the fundamental frequency of the source can change across frames. Secondly, these mathematical conditions are not sufficient to determine whether two peaks are part of a harmonic source. From a perceptual point of view, the fact that two components have harmonic frequencies is not directly linked to the fact that an audible pitch is perceived. And inversely, the fact that there is an audible pitch does not imply that all of the frequencies of the spectral components of the pitched source will be in perfect harmonic relation. Thus, two peaks should be close on the "harmonic" axis if these peaks belong to a perceptible compound of harmonically-related peaks in the spectrum and not simply because their frequencies happen to have a harmonic relation (probably caused by noise or spurious spectral components from the analysis front-end). This fact perhaps explains why some sound separation algorithms first attempt to identify the pitch of the sounds within the mixture by considering the spectral information globally, and then assign frequency components to each estimated pitch (e.g. (Li and Wang, 2007)). In contrast, a novel similarity measure termed Harmonically Wrapped Peak Similarity (HWPS) is proposed and shown to work reasonably well without estimating the underlying pitch. HWPS tries to take a global view when defining harmonic relations between time-frequency components in the signal.

The HWPS Algorithm

The Harmonically Wrapped Peak Similarity (HWPS) is a novel criterion for computing similarity between sinusoidal peaks that are potentially harmonically related. The main goal of the HWPS measure is to take advantage of the flexibility of a harmonically-related similarity between peaks which not only considers each peak in isolation, but also takes into consideration the entire spectral information associated with the remaining peaks. This measure can be used both for peaks within the same frame and among peaks of different frames (although with slightly different properties, as will be discussed later).

The basic mechanism behind the HWPS measure is to assign each peak a spectral pattern. The pattern captures information about the spectrum in relation to the specific peak. The degree of matching between two spectral patterns is used as a similarity measure between the two peaks thus utilizing more spectral information than just frequency of the two peaks. Additionally, HWPS takes into account the relative amplitudes of all the peaks involved in the computation, implicitly assigning more importance to the stronger peaks and reducing the impact of weak peaks usually resulting from noise or spurious components in the signal. As the spectral pattern of a peak might shift when changing frames and contains peaks belonging to multiple harmonic sources, a harmonically wrapped frequency space is used to align the two spectral patterns corresponding to the peaks. The goal is that the similarity between peaks belonging to the «same» harmonic series is higher than the similarity of peaks belonging to different harmonic series. In the following, a formal description about the three steps involved in the HWPS algorithm is introduced, after which a more motivational discussion is presented.

STEP 1. Shifted Spectral Pattern

The HWPS approach relies on a description of the spectral content using estimates of the frequency and amplitude of local maxima of the power spectrum, i.e. the peaks. Therefore, a given spectral pattern F_l^k is assigned to each peak p_l^k (recall that l is the peak index, and k is the frame index), defined as the set of frequencies (in Hz):

$$F_l^k = \{f_i^k, \forall i \in [1, L^k]\}$$

where L^k is the number of peaks in frame k. Although the F_l^k definition in the above equation does not depend on the peak index l (i.e. according to the current spectral pattern definition, peaks in a same frame will all have a similar spectral pattern; $F_l^k = F_m^k, \forall l, m \in [1, L^k]$), it was nevertheless chosen, for the sake of generality, to keep the l index in the expression. A shifted version of this spectral pattern $\tilde{F}_l^k$ can be defined as follows:

$$\tilde{F}_l^k = \{\tilde{f}_i^k \mid \tilde{f}_i^k = f_i^k - f_l^k, \forall i \in [1, L^k]\}.$$

This shifted spectral pattern is essentially a shift of the set of peak frequencies such that the frequency of the peak corresponding to the pattern maps to 0 (when i is equal to l). One can easily see that two peaks of different frames modeling the same partial will have roughly similar spectral patterns under the assumption that the spectral parameters evolve slowly with time. This spectral pattern forms a peak-specific view of the spectral content which is used to calculate a pitch invariant representation using a wrapped frequency space as described in the following step. The top graphs of Figures 6 and 8 show overlaid peak-specific spectral patterns for two pairs of peaks from the harmonic mixture depicted in Figure 4 and defined as in Figure 7.

STEP 2. Wrapped Frequency Space

To estimate whether two peaks p_l^k and p_m^{k+n} belong to the same harmonic source, the proposal is to measure the correlation between the two shifted spectral patterns corresponding to the peaks. To achieve this, it would be helpful to find a way to transform the peak-specific shifted spectral patterns in such a way that when the peaks under consideration belong to the same harmonic series the correlation is higher than when they belong to different harmonic sources. In order to achieve this the following operations are performed: the

Figure 4. Two sets A and B of harmonically related peaks, following the values specified in Figure 7

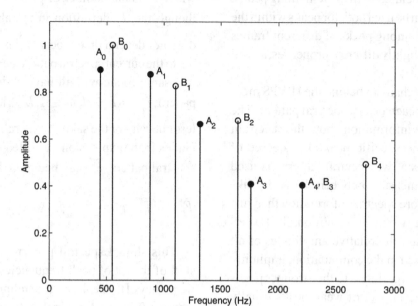

*Figure 5. HWPS calculation for peaks A0 ♦ and A1 *, from Figure 4. From top to bottom: Shifted Spectral Pattern, Harmonically-Wrapped Frequency and Histogram of Harmonically-Wrapped Frequency. Notice the high correlation between the two histograms at the bottom of the Figure.*

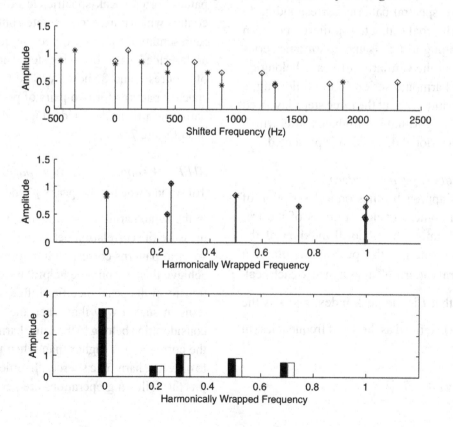

Figure 6. HWPS calculation for peaks A1 ♦ and B1 ∗, from Figure 4. From top to bottom: Shifted Spectral Pattern, Harmonically-Wrapped Frequency and Histogram of Harmonically-Wrapped Frequency. Notice the lack of correlation between the two histograms at the bottom of the Figure.

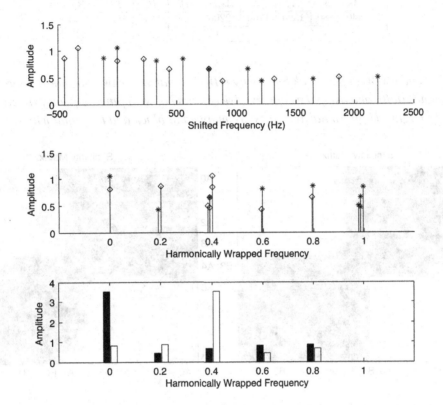

energy distribution of a harmonic source along the frequency axis can be seen as a cyclic unfolding with periodicity equal to the fundamental frequency of the «source». To concentrate these energies as much as possible before correlating them, it is proposed to wrap the frequencies of each spectral pattern as follows:

$$\hat{f}_i^k = \mathrm{mod}\left(\frac{\tilde{f}_i^k}{h}, 1\right)$$

where h is the wrapping frequency function and mod is the real modulo function.[1]

This wrapping operation would be perfect with the prior knowledge of the fundamental frequency. With this knowledge it would be possible to parameterize the wrapping operation h as:

$$h = \min(f_{0_l}^k, f_{0_m}^{k+n})$$

where $f_{0_l}^k$ is the fundamental frequency of the source of the peak p_l^k. Without such prior, a conservative approach h' is considered instead, although it will tend to over estimate the fundamental frequency (as will be discussed later in this text):

$$h' = \min(f_l^k, f_m^{k+n}).$$

Notice that the value of the wrapping frequency function h is the same for both patterns corresponding to the peaks under consideration. Therefore the resulting shifted and wrapped frequency pattern

Figure 7. Frequencies and amplitudes of the peaks from two harmonic series A and B, as depicted in Figure 4

	A_0	A_1	A_2	A_3	A_4, B_3	B_0	B_1	B_2	B_4
f	440	880	1320	1760	2200	550	1100	1650	2750
a	.8	.8	.6	.4	.4	1	.8	.6	.4

Figure 8. Harmonically-Wrapped Peak Similarity (HWPS) matrix for two harmonic sources using the correct f_0 estimates (left), and using the conservative estimate of wrapping frequency (likely a harmonic of the «true» f_0) (right). High similarity values are mapped to black and low similarity values to white.

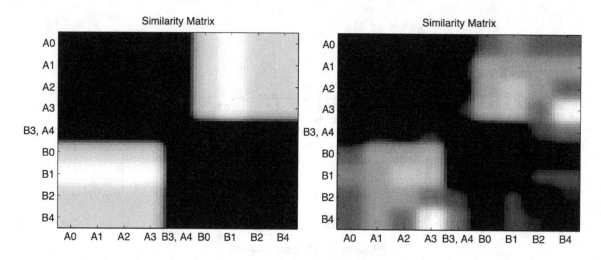

will be more similar if the peaks belong to the same harmonic «source». The resulting shifted and wrapped patterns are pitch invariant and can be seen in the middle plot of Figures 6 and 8.

STEP 3. Discrete Cosine Similarity

The last step is now to correlate the two shifted and harmonically wrapped spectral patterns ($\hat{F}_l^k$ and $\hat{F}_m^{k+n}$) to obtain the HWPS measure between the two corresponding peaks. The proposal is to discretize each shifted and harmonically wrapped spectral pattern into an amplitude weighted histogram, H_l^k, corresponding to each spectral pattern $\hat{F}_l^k$. The contribution of each peak to the histogram is equal to its amplitude and the range

between 0 and 1 of the Harmonically-Wrapped Frequency is divided into 20 equal-size bins.

In addition, the harmonically wrapped spectral patterns are also folded into a pitch-invariant profile. For example, in Figure 5, the energy of the spectral pattern in wrapped frequency 1 (all integer multiples of the wrapping frequency) is mapped to histogram bin 0.

The HWPS similarity between the peaks p_l^k and p_m^{k+n} is then defined based on the cosine distance between the two corresponding discretized histograms as follows:

$$W_h(p_l^k, p_m^{k+n}) = \text{HWPS}(p_l^k, p_m^{k+n}) = e^{-\left(1 - \frac{c(H_l^k, H_m^{k+n})}{\sqrt{c(H_l^k, H_l^k) \times c(H_m^{k+n}, H_m^{k+n})}}\right)^2}$$

where c is the dot product between two vectors (which correspond to the histograms in this particular case) and is defined as:

$$c(H_a^b, H_c^d) = \sum_i H_a^b(i) \times H_c^d(i).$$

The use of the cosine distance (which is bounded to the interval [0,1]) allows to put the emphasis on the alignment of the two histograms while reducing the impact of any existing scale differences (i.e. if the two histograms have a similar shape, their distance will be small, regardless of the absolute occurrence values at each bin). A Gaussian function is then once again used to convert the cosine distance into a similarity value, where the neighborhood width of the harmonicity similarity cue can be controlled by means of its σ_h parameter.

Similarly to the cases of amplitude and frequency similarity functions, peaks with a low HWPS distance will have a high HWPS value, while peaks far apart in the harmonicity distance space will end up with a low HWPS value. One may also notice that due to the wrapping operation, the size of the histograms can be relatively small (e.g. 20 bins), thus being computationally inexpensive.

The interested reader may find a more detailed and intuitive view on HWPS at (Martins, 2009).

Use of Estimated Fundamental Frequencies in the HWPS Computation

In what regards the impact of the use of estimated fundamental frequencies instead of the true ones in the HWPS computation, consider the case of the mixture of two pitched sound sources, A and B, each consisting of four harmonics with fundamental frequencies of 440 Hz and 550 Hz respectively, as presented in Figure 7 and depicted in Figure 4. For these experiments, random frequency deviations of a maximum of 5 Hz are added to test the resilience of the algorithm to frequency estimation

errors. Once again, if considering two peaks of the same source A_0 and A_1, the discrete version of the harmonically-wrapped sets of peaks are highly correlated, as can be seen in the histograms at the bottom of Figure 5. On the other hand, if two peaks of different sources, A_1 and B_0, are considered, the correlation between the two discretized histograms is low (see Figure 6).

However, if instead of using the true fundamental f_0, any harmonic of it is used as the wrapping frequency (as proposed for the conservative wrapping function h'), the correlation between two histograms of harmonically related peaks will still work, though to a lesser extent. Figure 8 (left) shows a HWPS similarity matrix computed among the peaks of two overlapping harmonic sounds within a frame (as shown in Figure 4 with perfect knowledge of the fundamental frequency for each peak respectively. As can be seen clearly from the figure, the similarity is high for pairs of peaks belonging to the same source and low for pairs belonging to different sources. Figure 8 (right) shows the HWPS similarity matrix computed among the peaks of the same two overlapping harmonic sounds within a frame using the conservative approach to estimate the wrapping frequency (i.e. h', where basically the lower peak is considered as the «wrapping» frequency). As can be seen from the figure, although the similarity matrix on the right is not as clearly defined as the one on the left, it still clearly shows higher values for pairs of peaks belonging to the same sound source.

Combining Similarity Functions

The use of a single similarity cue for sound segregation has been presented in the previous sections and the results have shown that each cue allows to obtain a different representation of the complex audio mixture. As a result, each cue by itself only provides a limited ability to represent the different sound events in a complex mixture. Therefore, the combination of different similarity cues could allow to make the best use of their isolated grouping abilities towards a more meaningful segregation of a sound mixture.

Following the work of Shi and Malik (Shi and Malik, 2000), who proposed to compute the overall similarity function as the product of the individual similarity cues used for image segmentation, the current system combines the amplitude, frequency and HWPS grouping cues presented in the previous sections into a combined similarity function W as follows:

$$W(p_l, p_m) = W_{afh}(p_l, p_m) = W_a(p_l, p_m) \times W_f(p_l, p_m) \times W_h(p_l, p_m).$$

EXPERIMENTAL VALIDATION AND APPLICATIONS

Typical audio content analysis systems for music signals represent statistically the entire polyphonic sound mixture (Pachet and Cazaly, 2000, Tzanetakis, 2002). There is some evidence that this approach has reached a «glass ceiling» (Aucouturier and Pachet, 2004) in terms of analysis and retrieval performance. One obvious direction for further progress is to attempt to individually characterize the different sound events or sources comprising the polyphonic mixture.

The overall goal of the sound segregation framework proposed in the previous sections is to extract structural information from a complex sound scene consisting of simultaneously occurring sound events, mainly produced by musical sources (although in principle nothing prevents environmental sources from also being considered). Still, the main objective of this work is not to achieve an actual separation of all the physical sources in a sound mixture. Instead, the aim is to provide a perceptually motivated topological description of the sound scene similar to the way a naive listener would perceive it.

Unless stated otherwise, all experiments whose results are presented and discussed in this chapter

use the following parameters 46 ms analysis windows using a hop size of 11 ms, 20 spectral peaks are selected from the highest amplitude peaks in each analysis frame, and texture windows are set to a fixed length of about 150 ms.

Preliminary Evaluation of Perceptual Grouping Cues

The grouping cues play a determinant role on the performance of the sound segregation framework proposed in this text. As a result, it is of upmost importance to start by objectively validating their influence on the segregation ability of the system. In particular, the novel HWPS cue will be shown to have an important impact on the system capacity to identify harmonic sources in complex audio signals.

Evaluation of the HWPS Cue

In this section, the properties of the HWPS cue will be studied and compared to existing state-of-the art harmonicity cues using a generic evaluation methodology. The experiments show the improvement in segregation performance achieved by using the HWPS similarity cue compared to two existing cues proposed in Srinivasan (Srinivasan and Kankanhalli, 2003) and Virtanen (Virtanen and Klapuri, 2000). To evaluate the capabilities of the presented harmonic cues, two synthetic sets of peaks with harmonically related frequencies and exponentially decaying amplitude envelope were considered. The first set of peaks has a fundamental frequency of 440 Hz, whereas the f_0 of the second set is iteratively changed to values from 10 to 5000 Hz, using a 10 Hz step (both sets of peaks follow harmonic distributions similar to the ones presented in Figure 7).

It is then possible to define a Fisher criterion F (loosely based on the Fisher discriminant commonly used in statistical analysis (Duda et al., 2000, pp. 117) as the sum of the inter-class scatter divided by the sum of the intra-class scatter. Since the Fisher criterion is not scale invariant, it may not be the best choice to compare the performance of distinct cues. Nevertheless, it is still an interesting way of evaluating the performance of a metric with respect to different scenarios.

Given so, a Density criterion D, computed as the number of peaks that have the closest neighboring peak in the feature space belonging to the same set, is also defined. This criterion is scale invariant and closer to the one considered by clustering algorithms.

The partitioning of a set of elements X is represented using an indicator function, as follows:

$$E : X \to \mathbb{N}$$
$$x \mapsto i$$

where i is the partition index x belongs to. The closest neighbor of a peak $a \in X$, $V(a)$, can be represented as:

$$V(a) = b \mid b \in X \setminus \{a\} \wedge d(a,b) = min_{c \in X \setminus \{a\}} d(a,c).$$

The Density criterion can then be defined as:

$$\mathcal{D}(X) = \frac{1}{(\# \tilde{X})^2}$$

where $\tilde{X}$ is defined as:

$$\tilde{X} = \{c \mid c \in X \wedge E(c) = E(V(c))\}.$$

This Density criterion will result higher when peaks belonging to a same harmonic set end up close together in the similarity space (and hence, there is a higher chance of being the nearest neighbors of each other), as desired. Figure 9 presents the average performance of the evaluated harmonic cues in the [100, 5000] Hz range, using the Fisher and Density criteria. The last column shows the performance of the HWPS with prior knowledge of the f_0's of the two sets of peaks.

Figure 10 (a) shows the evolution of the Fisher criterion with respect to the f_0 of the second set for the three harmonic cues. The Srinivasan cue shows the expected behavior, with minimal performance when the two sources have close f_0's (around 440 Hz). Another local minima is found around 880 Hz and the performance globally increases with the second f_0. Since the Virtanen and HPWS cues consider more precise frequency estimates, a finer behavior can be noticed around frequencies multiple of the first peak f_0. Differently from the cue proposed by Virtanen, the HWPS performance increases with the frequency difference between the two f_0's, as desired. As shown in Figure 10 (b), the HWPS performs well as far as the Density criterion is concerned, except at frequency locations multiple of 440 Hz, the f_0 of the reference set.

Combined Use of Grouping Cues

For the evaluation of the combination of the different grouping cues an experimental setup inspired by the «old+new» heuristic described by Bregman (Bregman, 1990, pp. 261) is used. The dataset consists of synthetically-created mixtures of isolated instrument sounds, voice, harmonic

Figure 9. Results for the separation of two harmonics sets of peaks. Mean and standard deviation values of the Fisher and Density criteria are computed for the Srinivasan (W_s), Virtanen (W_v), HWPS (W_h), and HWPS with prior knowledge of the two f_0's (W_h (f_0)).

	W_s	W_v	W_h	$W_h(f_0)$
$\mathcal{F}$	1.44 (0.31)	1.00 (0.01)	1.22 (0.05)	2.27 (0.37)
$\mathcal{D}$	0.50 (0.01)	0.55 (0.11)	0.80 (0.12)	0.94 (0.16)

Figure 10. Fisher (a) and Density (b) criteria versus the f_0 of the second source for the Srinivasan cue (dotted line), the Virtanen cue (dashed line) and the HPWS cue (solid line). The f_0 of the first source is set to 440 Hz.

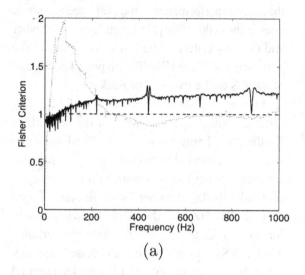

(a)

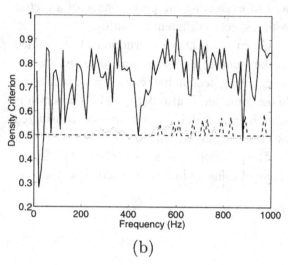

(b)

sweeps and noise. Each clip is approximately 1 second long and is created by mixing two sound sources in the following way: for the first part of the sound only the «old» sound source is played followed by the addition of the «new» sound source (i.e. «old+new») in the second part of the sample.

Ncut clustering is then performed over the entire duration of the clip. The clusters that contain peaks in the initial «old»-only part are selected as the ones forming the separated source. The remaining peaks are considered to be part of the «new» sound source. The Signal-to-Distortion ratio (SDR) is used to measure the distortion/interference caused by this «new» sound source to the separation algorithm. Similar experiments were presented in (Lagrange and Tzanetakis, 2007).

Figure 11 compares different mixtures of isolated sounds separated using only frequency and amplitude similarities, and also separated with the additional use of the HWPS similarity. As can be seen from the table, in almost all cases the use of the HWPS improves the SDR measure of separation performance.

A second set of experiments where the «old+new» mixtures are separated directly by selecting the most dominant sound source (see a detailed description of in (Martins, 2009, pp. 111)) were conducted. Unlike the previous experiments, the spectral clustering is performed separately for each «texture window» and the highest density cluster is selected as the separated voice. This is a more realistic scenario as no knowledge of the individual sound sources is utilized.

The results are presented in Figure 12 and, as expected, the SDR values are lower than the ones in Figure 11, but once again the use of the HWPS improves separation performance in most cases.

Timbre Identification in Polyphonic Music Signals

The increasing quantity of music titles available in digital format added to the huge amount of personal music storage capacity available today has resulted in a growing demand for more efficient and automatic means of indexing, searching and retrieving music content. The computer identifica-

Figure 11. SDR values (in dB) for experiments using different «old+new» mixtures. The following conventions are used: X is saxophone, N is noise, V is violin, S is harmonic sweep, and C is voice. A, F, H correspond to using amplitude, frequency and HWPS similarities, respectively.

	XN	XS	VN	VS	CN	CS
A+F	12.87	9.33	10.11	7.67	2.94	1.52
A+F+H	13.05	9.13	11.54	7.69	3.01	2.09

Figure 12. SDR values (in dB) using «texture windows» for experiments with different «old+new» mixtures. The same experimental setup and conventions described in Figure 11 are used.

	XN	XS	VN	VS	CN	CS
A+F	9.79	3.09	3.29	6.50	3.01	3.01
A+F+H	7.33	5.03	4.73	5.35	3.08	3.07

tion of the instruments playing in a music signal can assist the automatic labeling and retrieval of music.

Several studies have been made on the recognition of musical instruments on isolated notes or in melodies played by a single instrument. A comprehensive review of those techniques can be found in (Herrera et al., 2003). However, the recognition of musical instruments in multi-instrumental, polyphonic music is much more complex and presents additional challenges. The main challenge stands from the fact that tones from performing instruments can overlap in time and frequency. Therefore, most of the isolated note recognition techniques that have been proposed in the literature are inappropriate for polyphonic music signals. Some of the proposed techniques for the instrument recognition on polyphonic signals consider the entire audio mixture, avoiding any prior source separation (Essid et al., 2005, Livshin and Rodet, 2004). Other approaches are based on the separation of the playing sources, requiring the prior knowledge or estimation of the pitches of the different notes (Kashino and Murase, 1999, Kostek, 2004). However, robustly extracting the fundamental frequencies in such multiple pitch scenarios is difficult.

In this section, the segregation framework proposed in this work is used and evaluated for the task of timbre classification of polyphonic, multi-instrumental music signals. This work and the corresponding results have also been published in (Martins et al., 2007). A work on source separation based on the use of the same timbre models, originally proposed in (Burred et al., 2006), can be found in (Burred and Sikora, 2007).

System Overview

Figure 13 presents a block-diagram of the complete timbre identification system. After grouping the spectral peaks into separated sound events each identified cluster is matched to a collection of six timbre models, namely piano, oboe, clarinet, trumpet, violin and alto sax. These models are a compact description of the spectral envelope and its evolution in time, and were previously trained using isolated note audio recordings. The design of the models, as well as their application to isolated note classification, were originally proposed in (Burred et al., 2006).

In this evaluation the system was configured to extract a maximum of 20 sinusoids per frame which are 46 ms long, using a hop size of 11 ms.

Figure 13. Block diagram of the timbre recognition system

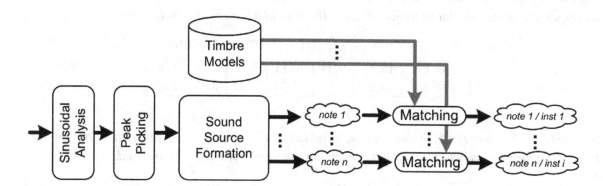

However, texture windows were now set to the duration of the audio signals (i.e. the duration of the notes being played).

However, the number of clusters to be segregated and selected for resynthesis was in this case set manually to correspond to the known number of notes playing in each audio signal.

As an example of the output of the sound source formation block, Figure 14 depicts the result of the sound segregation for a single-channel audio signal with mixture of two notes (E4 and B4, same onset, played by a piano and an oboe, respectively). Each dot corresponds to a peak in the time-frequency space and the different coloring reflects the cluster to which it belongs (i.e. its source). Each cluster is then matched to a set of pre-trained timbre models, described in the following section.

Once each single-note cluster of sinusoidal parameters has been extracted, it is classified into an instrument from a predefined set of six: piano (p), oboe (o), clarinet (c), trumpet (t), violin (v) and alto sax (s). The method, originally described in (Burred et al., 2006), models each instrument as a set of time-frequency templates, one for each instrument. The template describes the typical evolution in time of the spectral envelope of a note. The spectral envelope is an appropriate representation to generate features to analyze sounds described by sinu-

soidal modeling, since it matches the salient peaks of the spectrum, i.e., the amplitudes a_l^k of the partials.

Training the Timbre Models

The training process consists of arranging the training dataset as a time-frequency matrix $X(g, k)$ of size $G \times K$, where g is the frequency bin index and k is the frame index, and performing spectral basis decomposition upon it using Principal Component Analysis (PCA). This yields a factorization of the form X =BC, where the columns of the $G \times G$ matrix B are a set of spectral basis sorted in decreasing order of contribution to the total variance, and C is the $G \times K$ matrix of projected coefficients. By keeping a reduced set of $R < G$ basis, a reduction of the data needed for a reasonable approximation is obtained and, more importantly for the purpose of this application, a representation is also obtained that is based only on the most essential spectral shapes. Having as goal a pitch-independent classification, the time-frequency templates should be representative for a wide range of notes. In the training process, notes from several pitches must be considered to give rise to a single model. The training samples are subjected to sinusoidal modeling, and arranged in the data matrix X by linearly interpolating the am-

Figure 14. Resulting sound source formation clusters for two notes played by a piano and an oboe (E4 and B4, respectively)

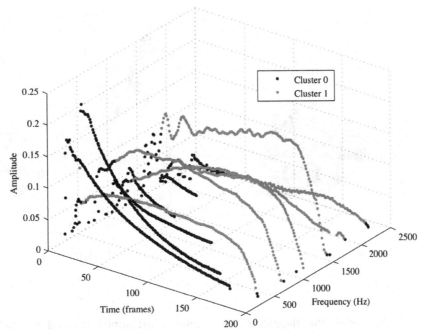

plitude values to a regular frequency grid defined at the locations of the G bins. This is important for appropriately describing formants, which are mostly independent of the fundamental frequency.

The projected coefficients of each instrument in the R-dimensional PCA space are summarized as a prototype curve by interpolating the trajectories corresponding to the individual training samples at common time points and point-wise averaging them. When projecting back into the time-frequency domain by a truncated inverse PCA, each P^i-point prototype curve will correspond to a $G \times P^i$ prototype envelope $M^i(g, k)$ for instrument i. The same number of time frames $P = P^i$ are considered for all instrument models. Figure 15 shows the obtained prototype envelopes for the fourth octave of a piano and of an oboe.

Timbre Matching

Each one of the clusters obtained by the sound source separation step is matched against each one of the prototype envelopes. Let a particular cluster of K frames be represented as an ordered set of amplitude and frequency vectors $A = (a^1, \ldots, a^K)$, $F = (f^1, \ldots, f^K)$ of possibly differing lengths $L^1, \ldots, L^K$.

It becomes now necessary to evaluate the prototype envelope of model i at the frequency support of the input cluster j. This operation is denoted by $\widetilde{\mathbf{M}}(i, j) = \mathbf{M}_i(\mathbf{F}(j))$. To that end, the time scales of both input and model are first normalized. Then, the model frames closest to each one of the input frames in the normalized time scale are selected. Finally, each new amplitude value $\tilde{m}_l^k(i, j)$ is linearly interpolated from the neighboring amplitude values of the selected model frame.

Figure 15. Examples of prototype envelopes for a range of one octave

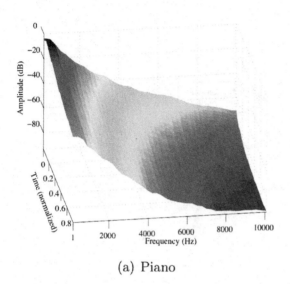

(a) Piano

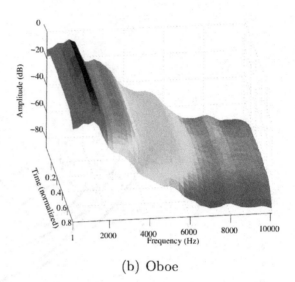

(b) Oboe

It is then possible to define the distance between a cluster j and an interpolated prototype envelope i as

$$d(\mathbf{A}(j), \widetilde{\mathbf{M}}(i,j)) = \frac{1}{K(j)} \sum_{k=1}^{K(j)} \sqrt{\sum_{l=1}^{L^k(j)} (a_l^k(j) - \tilde{m}_l^k(i,j))^2}$$

i.e., the average of the Euclidean distances between frames of the input clusters and interpolated prototype envelope at the normalized time scale.

The model $\widetilde{\mathbf{M}}(i,j)$ minimizing this distance is chosen as the predicted instrument for classification. Figure 16 shows an attempt to match a cluster extracted from an alto sax note and the corresponding section of the piano prototype envelope. As it is clearly visible, this weak match results in a high distance value.

Corpus Description and Experimental Setup

The evaluation procedure will be limited to the separation and classification of concurrent notes sharing the same onset and played from different instruments.

The evaluation dataset was artificially created mixing audio samples of isolated notes of piano, oboe, clarinet, trumpet, violin and alto sax, all from the RWC Music Database (Goto et al., 2003). The training dataset used to derive the timbre models for each instrument is composed of audio samples of isolated notes, also from the RWC Music Database. However, in order to get meaningful timbre recognition results, independent instances of each instrument for the evaluation dataset and for the training dataset were used. Ground-truth data was also created for each mixture and includes information about the notes played and the corresponding instrument. Given that the timbre models used in this work have shown good results for a range of about two octaves (Burred et al., 2006), the notes used for evaluation were constrained to the range C4 to B4. Furthermore, for simplicity's sake, only notes with a fixed intensity were considered for this evaluation.

Figure 16. Weak matching of an alto sax cluster and a portion of the piano prototype envelope

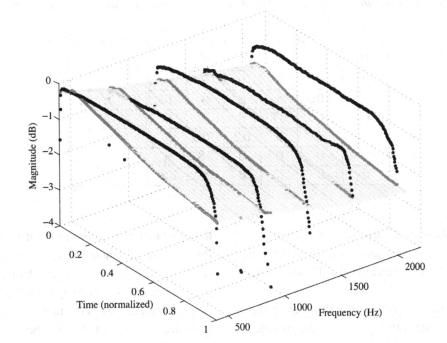

Experimental Results

Several experiments were conducted for evaluating the system ability to identify sound events produced by specific instruments in a sound mixture. These evaluations range from a simple single-note instrument identification problem (as a way to define a baseline evaluation of the sinusoidal model and subsequent matching algorithm), go through the evaluation of the ability to detect the presence of a specific timbre in a sound mixture, to the final test where the system tries to perform event segregation and subsequent timbre recognition in signals with a varying number of notes playing simultaneously.

Timbre Identification for Single Note Signals

The first evaluation tested the performance of the timbre matching block for the case of isolated notes coming from each of the six instruments modeled. This provides a base-ground with which it will be possible to compare the ability of the framework to classify notes separated from mixtures. For the case of isolated notes, the sound source separation block reduces its action to just performing sinusoidal analysis, since there are no other sources to be separated. This basically only results in the loss of the non-harmonic residual, which although not irrelevant to timbre identification, has been demonstrated to have a small impact in the classification performance (Livshin and Rodet, 2006).

Figure 17 presents the confusion matrix for the instrument classification for a dataset of 72 isolated notes, ranging from C4 to B4, from each one of the six considered instruments. The system presents an overall classification accuracy of 83.3%, being violin and clarinet the instruments causing the biggest difficulties.

Instrument Presence Detection in Mixtures of Notes

In the next experiment the objective was to evaluate the ability of the system to separate and classify the notes from audio signals with up to 4

Figure 17. Confusion matrix for single--note instrument identification. Six different instruments from the RWC database were considered: piano (p), oboe (o), clarinet (c), trumpet (t), violin (v), alto sax (s).

| True instruments | | | | | | classified |
p	o	c	t	v	s	as
100	0	0	0	0	0	p
0	**100**	8	8	0	0	o
0	0	**67**	0	33	0	c
0	0	0	**92**	0	8	t
0	0	0	0	**58**	8	v
0	0	25	0	8	**83**	s

simultaneously sounding instruments. A combination of 54 different instruments and mixtures of 2-, 3- and 4-notes was created (i.e. 18 audio files for each case).

The first and simplest evaluation performed was to test the system ability to detect the presence of an instrument in a mixture of up to 4 notes. In this case it was just a matter of matching each one of the six timbre models with all the separated clusters and counting the true and false positives for each instrument.

A true positive (TP) is here defined as the number of separated clusters correctly matched to an instrument playing in the original mixture (such information is available in the dataset ground-truth). A false positive (FP) can be defined as the number of clusters classified as an instrument not present in the original audio mixture. Given these two values, it is then possible to define three performance measures for each instrument Recall (RCL), Precision (PRC) and F-Measure (F1):

$$RCL = \frac{TP}{COUNT}, \quad PRC = \frac{TP}{TP + FP}, \quad F1 = \frac{2 \times RCL \times PRC}{RCL + PRC},$$

where *COUNT* is the total number of instances of an instrument over the entire dataset (i.e. the total number of notes it plays). As shown in Figure 18, the system was able to correctly detect 56% of the occurrences of instruments in mixtures of up to 4 notes, with a precision of 64%. Piano appears as the most difficult timbre to identify, specifically for the case of 4-note mixtures, where from the existing 15 notes playing in the dataset, none was correctly detected as coming from that instrument. As anticipated, the system performance degrades with the increase of the number of concurrent notes. Nevertheless, it was still possible to retrieve 46% of the present instruments in 4-note mixtures, with a precision of 56%.

Note Separation and Timbre Identification in Mixtures of Notes

Although informative, the previous evaluation has a caveat it does not allow to precisely verify if a separated and classified cluster does in fact correspond to a note played with the same instrument in the original audio mixture. In order to fully assess the separation and classification performance of the framework, an attempt to make a correspondence between each separated cluster and the notes played in the mix (available in the ground-truth) was conducted.

A possible way to obtain such a correspondence is by estimating the pitch of each one of the detected clusters, using the following simple technique. For each cluster the histogram of peak frequencies was calculated. Since the audio recordings of the instruments used in this evaluation are from notes with steady pitch over time (i.e. no vibrato, glissandos or other articulations), the

Figure 18. Recall and precision values for instrument presence detection in multiple-note mixtures

	2-note			3-note			4-note			total		
	RCL	PRC	F1	RCL	PRC	F1	RCL	PRC	F1	RCL	PRC	F1
p	83	100	91	22	100	36	0	0	0	23	100	38
o	100	75	86	100	46	63	67	40	50	86	50	63
c	33	100	50	33	100	50	40	86	55	36	93	52
t	89	100	94	58	100	74	58	64	61	67	85	75
v	67	67	67	83	45	59	83	36	50	80	43	56
s	100	43	60	67	60	63	60	75	67	67	62	64
total	75	79	77	56	64	59	46	56	50	56	64	60

peaks on the histogram provide a good indication of the frequencies of the strongest partials. Having the set of the strongest partial frequencies, another histogram of the differences among all partials was computed, and the highest mode as the best f_0 candidate for that cluster was selected. Given these pitch correspondences, it is now possible to check the significance of each separated cluster as a good note candidate, as initially hypothesized. For the entire dataset, which includes a total of 162 notes from all the 2-, 3- and 4-note audio mixtures, the system was able to correctly establish a pitch correspondence for 55% of the cases (67%, 57% and 49% for the 2-, 3- and 4-note mixtures, respectively). These results can not however be taken as an accurate evaluation of the sound source separation performance, as they are influenced by the accuracy of the used pitch estimation technique.

The results in Figure 19 show the correct classification rate for all modeled instruments and multiple-note scenarios, excluding the clusters whose correspondence was not possible to establish. This allows decoupling the source separation/pitch estimation performance from the timbre identification accuracy. Figure 19 shows a correct identification rate of 47% of the separated notes overall, diminishing sharply its accuracy with the increase of concurrent notes in the signal. This shows the difficulties posed by the overlap of spectral components from different notes/instruments into a single detected cluster.

Figure 20 presents the overall confusion matrix for the instrument classification.

SOFTWARE IMPLEMENTATION

Attempting to do research on the topic of audio analysis and processing poses challenging demands on the development of software modules and tools so that any proposed hypothesis and algorithms can be objectively implemented and evaluated. The following sections will briefly discuss the implementation of the computational analysis of sound signals approach proposed in the previous sections, which is based on the open source sofware framework MARSYAS.

MARSYAS

MARSYAS (**M**usic **A**nalysis **R**etrieval and **SY**nthesis for **A**udio **S**ignals) is a free and open source software (FOSS) framework with specific emphasis on building music information retrieval (MIR) and sound analysis and processing systems. Originally created in 1998 by George Tzanetakis (Tzanetakis and Cook, 2000, Tzanetakis, 2002), it has been under steady development and is used for a variety of projects, both in academia and industry. The guiding principle behind the design of MARSYAS has always been to provide a flexible, efficient and extensible framework without sacrificing computational efficiency.

Figure 19. Instrument classification performance for 2-, 3- and 4-note mixtures

	Instrument Detection Rate			
	2-note	**3-note**	**4-note**	**overall**
p	67	67	0	55
o	100	86	60	81
c	33	29	19	26
t	75	33	22	43
v	67	100	50	75
s	75	36	42	44
total	65	50	33	**47**

Figure 20. Instrument classification confusion matrix for 2-, 3- and 4-note mixtures

True instruments						classified
p	**o**	**c**	**t**	**v**	**s**	*as*
55	0	0	4	0	0	**p**
27	**81**	21	30	8	15	**o**
9	0	**26**	0	8	3	**c**
0	6	5	**43**	0	32	**t**
0	6	28	4	**75**	6	**v**
9	6	21	17	8	**44**	**s**

MARSYAS provides a general, extensible and flexible framework that enables experimentation with algorithms and provides the fast performance necessary for developing efficient and real-time and audio analysis and synthesis tools. A variety of existing building blocks that form the basis of many published algorithms are provided as dataflow components that can be combined to form more complicated algorithms (black-box functionality). In addition, it is straightforward to extend the framework with new building blocks (white-box functionality). These blocks can be combined into data flow networks that can be modified and controlled dynamically while they process data in soft real-time.

Dataflow Programming

Marsyas follows a dataflow programming paradigm, which is based on the idea of expressing computation as a network of processing nodes/components connected by a number arcs/com-munication channels. Expressing audio processing systems as dataflow networks has several advantages (Tzanetakis, 2008). The programmer can provide a declarative specification of what needs to be computed without having to worry about the low level implementation details of how it is computed. The resulting code can be very efficient and have a small memory footprint as data just "flows" through the network without having complicated dependencies. In addition, dataflow approaches are particularly suited for visual programming. One of the initial motivations for dataflow ideas was the exploitation of parallel hardware and therefore dataflow systems are particularly good for parallel and distributed computation.

Implicit Patching and Composition

The basic idea behind Implicit Patching is to use object composition rather than explicitly specifying connections between input and output ports in order to construct the dataflow network. It evolved from the integration of different ideas that were developed independently in previous versions of MARSYAS (Tzanetakis, 2008). Combined with Implicit Patching, the expressive power of composition is increased and a large variety of complex dataflow networks can be expressed only using object composition, and therefore no Explicit Patching. Another side benefit of Implicit Patching is that it enforces the creation of trees and therefore avoids problems with cycles in the dataflow graph.

Basic Processing Units and Networks

Systems in Marsyas are expressed as interconnected dataflow networks of processing modules. Each processing module performs a specific task that always consists of a matrix transformation.

Audio and other types of data are represented by matrices with some semantics associated with them: rows represent *observations* (over time) and columns represent *samples* in time. For instance, a stereo audio signal might be processed in chunks of 2 observations (i.e. two channels) and 512 samples in time. This clean data structure, although quite specific, suits well audio processing applications. All modules process one input matrix (known as a *slice*) and store the result on another matrix so it can be shared with the next processing module. Hence, each module accepts only one input and produces one output. Processing is performed on defined chunks of data and is executed whenever the **tick()** function of the module is called.

All processing blocks in MARSYAS are called **MarSystems** and provide the basic components out of which more complicated networks can be constructed. Essentially any audio processing algorithm can be expressed as a large **composite MarSystem** which is assembled by appropriately connected basic **MarSystems**.

Some representative examples of **MarSystems** include sound file reading and writing (e.g. wav, au, mp3 and ogg audio file formats), real-time audio

input and output (i.e. from and to a soundcard), signal processing algorithms (e.g. filters, STFT, DWT), feature extraction (e.g. MFCC, centroid, rolloff, flux) and machine learning modules (e.g. KNN, GMM, SVM, PCA, SVM).

To assemble multimedia processing systems, modules are *implicitly connected* using hierarchical *composition*. Special composite modules such as **Series**, **Fanout**, **Parallel** are used for this purpose. The basic idea behind *Implicit Patching* is to use object composition rather than explicitly specifying connections between input and output ports in order to construct the dataflow network.

For instance, modules added to a **Series** composite will be connected in series, following the order they were added - the first module's output is shared with the second module's input and so on. Moreover, the **tick()** method is called sequentially following the same order.

Dataflow in MARSYAS is synchronous which means that at every **tick()** call, a specific slice of data is propagated across the entire dataflow network. This eliminates the need for queues between processing nodes and enables the use of shared buffers which improves performance. This is similar to the way UNIX pipes are implemented but with audio specific semantics.

Implementing the Sound Segregation Framework in MARSYAS

Figure 21 shows the overall MARSYAS network that implements the system proposed in this chapter. Each dark box in the figure represents a basic **MarSystem**, while the white boxes represent *composite* **MarSystem**'s. Optional **MarSystem**'s are represented as light gray boxes, and their existence is not mandatory for the base purpose of the system, being used for added functionality. For the sake of clarity, Figures 23, 24, and 25 present detailed views of some of the more complex composite **MarSystem**'s, using numbers inside black circles to cross-reference the different views of a same composite along the different figures. In all

Figure 21. Overview of the MARSYAS network used for the sound segregation framework proposed in this chapter. Detailed views of the blocks signaled with numbered dark circles and the data structures signaled with letters inside gray squares are presented in Figures 23, 24 and 25.

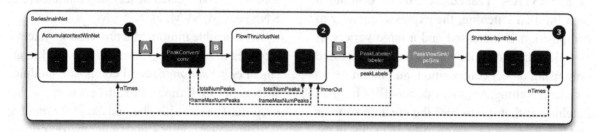

figures, a *link* between two controls is represented by dashed directed lines (whose orientation represents the original linking direction).

As described in (Tzanetakis, 2008, Tzanetakis et al., 2008), MARSYAS uses two-dimensional real valued matrices (known as **realvec**'s) for expressing data flowing in a network. However, the data at each point in the network can be very different, depending on the particular **MarSystem** producing it (e.g. it can be used to represent time domain audio samples at the output of an audio file source, or a complex spectrum data at the output of an FFT block). As a result, Figure 22 presents schematic views on how data is expressed using **realvec**'s at some relevant points in the network. Capital letters inside dark and bracketed squares are used as cross-references between all the figures.

The sound segregation system implemented using MARSYAS is available as a command line application known as **peakClustering**, whose source code can be found in the MARSYAS distribution. After building MARSYAS (instructions for building MARSYAS in several platforms are provided in detail in the documentation), it is possible to experiment with the current system implementation by running **peakClustering**, as follows:

$ peakClustering myAudioFile.wavwhere «$» is the command prompt. After completing

execution, the program returns two files: an audio file (in this example, named **myAudioFileSep. wav**) which is the result of the segregation and resynthesis process and a text file (named for this example, **myAudioFile.peak**) which lists all the peaks in the signal and their corresponding features (i.e. time frame, frequency, amplitude, phase, group - see Figure 22/**B**) in a table format.

By running **peakClustering** without any options, the default parameters are used (e.g. maximum number of peaks per frame is set to 20; number of clusters k is set to 5, from which the 2 «denser» clusters are selected at each texture window for resynthesis; texture windows are set to have a fixed length and equal to 10 frames). Several other options exist and they can be consulted by calling **peakClustering** with the **-h** option.

SUMMARY

Computational Auditory Scene Analysis and more specifically predominant melodic sound source separation is a challenging problem with a number of potential applications in music information retrieval. In this chapter we argue that expressing grouping cues as clustering based on similarities between time-frequency atoms is an effective and expressive way of formulating this problem. We describe a specific incarnation of this

Figure 22. Graphic representation of the data structures used at different points of the data flow of the MARSYAS networks depicted in Figures 21, 23, 24, and 25

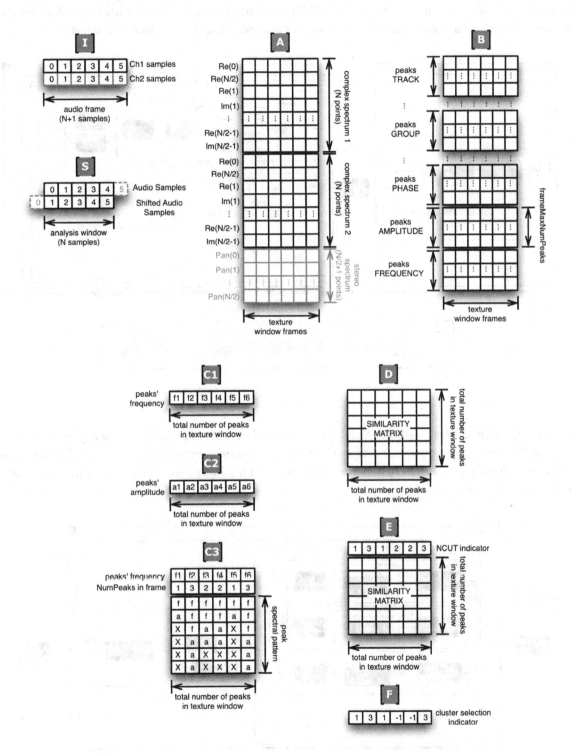

Figure 23. Detailed view of the MARSYAS network used for the computation of the texture windows and the corresponding spectral representations used as the base for the sinusoidal modeling of the audio signals. A detailed view of the optional MARSYAS network which implements the onset detector used for the dynamic adjustment of the texture windows is depicted at the bottom of the figure.

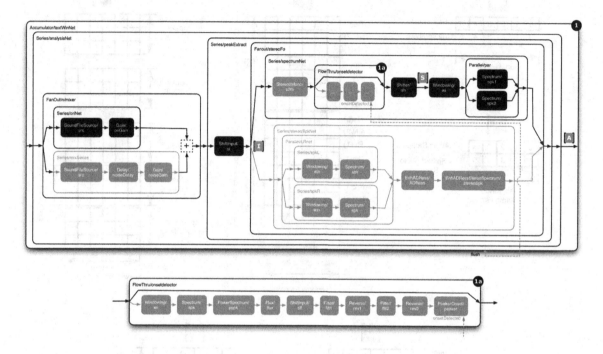

Figure 24. Detailed view of the MARSYAS network used for the computation of the different similarity cues and the subsequent grouping process. This composite and hierarchical architecture is flexible enough to support the future inclusion of new similarity cues and the expression of more complex combination schemes of similarity cues.

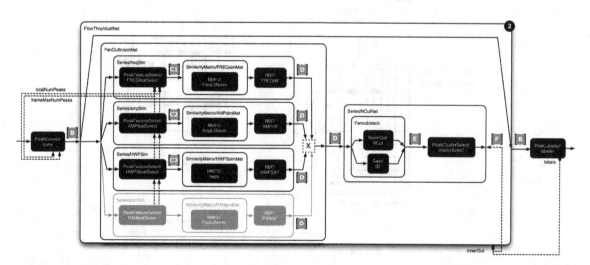

Figure 25. Sound event resynthesis MARSYAS network, based on an additive synthesis approach and implemented as a bank of sinusoidal oscillators using an overlap-add scheme

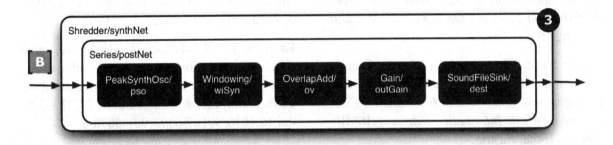

formulation using a sinusoidal modeling analysis front-end followed by spectral clustering using the Normalized Cut criterion. The proposed system integrates different grouping cues including a novel harmonicity criterion termed the Harmonically Wrapped Peak Similarity. Some experimental results supporting the proposed approach as well as a short discussion of implementation issues are provided.

ACKNOWLEDGMENT

Jennifer Murdock and Juan José Burred made important contributions to the presented work, and were co-authors of some of the publications that resulted from this work. Luis Filipe Teixeira helped a lot with solving various coding problems related to the use of Marsyas. The authors would like to thank the National Science and Research Council of Canada (NSERC), the Portuguese Science and Technology Foundation (FCT), the Calouste Gulbenkian Foundation, the European Commission under the IST research network of excellence VISNET and VISNET II of the 6th Framework Programme, the COST IC0601 Action on Sonic Interaction Design (SID), as well as INESC Porto for partially funding this work.

REFERENCES

Aucouturier, J.-J., & Pachet, F. (2004). Improving timbre similarity: How high is the sky? *Journal of Negative Results in Speech and Audio Sciences, 1*(1).

Bach, F., & Jordan, M. I. (2004). Blind one-microphone speech separation: A spectral learning approach. In *Proc. Neural Information Processing Systems* (NIPS), Vancouver, Canada.

Balakrishnan, V. K. (1997). *Graph Theory* (1st ed.). New York: McGraw-Hill.

Bello, J., Daudet, L., Abdallah, S., Duxbury, C., Davies, M., & Sandler, M. (2005). A tutorial on onset detection in music signals. *IEEE Transactions on Speech and Audio Processing, 13*(5), 1035–1047. doi:10.1109/TSA.2005.851998

Bello, J., Daudet, L., Abdallah, S., Duxbury, C., Davies, M., & Sandler, M. (2005). A tutorial on onset detection in music signals. *IEEE Transactions on Speech and Audio Processing, 13*(5), 1035–1047. doi:10.1109/TSA.2005.851998

Bregman, A. (1990). *Auditory Scene Analysis: The Perceptual Organization of Sound*. Cambridge, MA: MIT Press.

Burred, J. J., Röbel, A., & Rodet, X. (2006). An accurate timbre model for musical instruments and its application to classification. In *Proc. Workshop on Learning the Semantics of Audio Signals*, Athens, Greece.

Burred, J. J., & Sikora, T. (2007). Monaural source separation from musical mixtures based on time-frequency timbre models. In *International Conference on Music Information Retrieval* (ISMIR 2007), Vienna, Austria.

Cai, R., Lu, L., & Hanjalic, A. (2005). Unsupervised content discovery in composite audio. In *Proc. ACM Multimedia*.

Dixon, S. (2006). Onset detection revisited. In *Proc. International Conference on Digital Audio Effects* (DAFx), Montreal, Canada.

Dubnov, S., & Appel, T. (2004). Audio segmentation by singular value clustering. In *Proc. International Computer Music Conference* (ICMC).

Duda, R. O., Hart, P. E., & Stork, D. G. (2000). *Pattern Classification* (2nd ed.). New York: Wiley-Interscience.

Essid, S., Richard, G., & David, B. (2005). Instrument recognition in polyphonic music. In *Proc. IEEE International Conference on Acoustics, Speech, and Signal Processing* (ICASSP), Philadelphia, USA.

Goto, M., Hashiguchi, H., Nishimura, T., & Oka, R. (2003). RWC music database: Music genre database and musical instrument sound database. In *Proc. International Conference on Music Information Retrieval* (ISMIR) (pp. 229–230).

Gouyon, F. (2005). A computational approach to rhythm description — Audio features for the computation of rhythm periodicity functions and their use in tempo induction and music content processing. *Phd thesis*, Universitat Pompeu Fabra, Barcelona, Spain.

Hartmann, W. M. (1998). *Signals, Sound, and Sensation*. AIP Press - Springer.

Herrera, P., Peeters, P., & Dubnov, S. G. (2003). Automatic classification of musical instrument sounds. *Journal of New Music Research, 32*(1), 3–22. doi:10.1076/jnmr.32.1.3.16798

Kashino, K., & Murase, H. (1999). A sound source identification system for ensemble music based on template adaptation and music stream extraction. *Speech Communication, 27,* 337–349. doi:10.1016/S0167-6393(98)00078-8

Klapuri, A. P. (2004). Automatic music transcription as we know it today. *Journal of New Music Research, 33*(3), 269–282. doi:10.1080/0929821042000317840

Kostek, B. (2004). Musical instrument classification and duet analysis employing music information retrieval techniques. *Proceedings of the IEEE, 92*(4), 712–729. doi:10.1109/JPROC.2004.825903

Lagrange, M., & Marchand, S. (2007). Estimating the instantaneous frequency of sinusoidal components using phase-based methods. *Journal of the Audio Engineering Society. Audio Engineering Society, 55*(5), 385–399.

Lagrange, M., Marchand, S., & Rault, J. (2007). *Enhancing the tracking of partials for the sinusoidal modeling of polyphonic sounds*. IEEE Transactions on Acoustics, Speech and Signal Processing.

Lagrange, M., Murdoch, J., & Tzanetakis, G. (2006). Temporal constraints for sound source formation using the normalized cut. In Proc. *Neural Information Processing Systems Workshop* (NIPS), Whistler, BC, Canada.

Lagrange, M., & Tzanetakis, G. (2007). Sound source tracking and formation using normalized cuts. In *Proc. IEEE International Conference on Acoustics, Speech, and Signal Processing* (ICASSP), Honolulu, USA.

Li, Y., & Wang, D. (2007). Separation of singing voice from music accompaniement for monaural recordings. *IEEE Transactions on Audio, Speech, and Language Processing, 15*(4), 1475–1487. doi:10.1109/TASL.2006.889789

Livshin, A., & Rodet, X. (2004). Musical instrument identification in continuous recordings. In *Proc. International Conference on Digital Audio Effects* (DAFx), Naples, Italy.

Livshin, A., & Rodet, X. (2006). The importance of the non-harmonic residual for automatic musical instrument recognition of pitched instruments. In *Proc. 120th Convention of the Audio Engineering Society*, Paris.

Marchand, S., & Lagrange, M. (2006). On the equivalence of phase-based methods for the estimation of instantaneous frequency. In *Proc. European Conference on Signal Processing* (EUSIPCO).

Martins, L. G. (2009). A Computational Framework For Sound Segregation in Music Signals. *PhD. thesis*, Faculdade de Engenharia da Universidade do Porto (FEUP).

Martins, L. G., Burred, J. J., Tzanetakis, G., & Lagrange, M. (2007). Polyphonic instrument recognition using spectral clustering. In *Proc. International Conference on Music Information Retrieval* (ISMIR), Vienna, Austria.

McAdams, S., & Bigand, E. (Eds.). (1993). *Thinking in Sound*. Oxford University Press.

McAulay, R., & Quatieri, T. (1986). Speech analysis/synthesis based on a sinusoidal representation. *IEEE Transactions on Acoustics, Speech, and Signal Processing, 34*(4), 744–754. doi:10.1109/TASSP.1986.1164910

Pachet, F., & Cazaly, D. (2000). A classification of musical genre. In *Proc. RIAO Content-Based Multimedia Information Access Conference.*

Puckette, M. S., & Brown, J. C. (1998). Accuracy of frequency estimates using the phase vocoder. *IEEE Transactions on Audio and Speech Processing,* 6(2).

Rosenthal, D. F., & Okuno, H. G. (Eds.). (1998). *Computational auditory scene analysis.* Lawrence Erlbaum Associates, Inc.

Roweis, S. T. (2000). One microphone source separation. In *Proc. Neural Information Processing Systems* (NIPS), pages 793–799.

Scheirer, E. D. (2000). Music-Listening Systems. *Phd thesis*, Massachusetts Institute of Technology (MIT).

Serra, X. (1989). A System for Sound Analysis/Transformation/Synthesis based on a Deterministic plus Stochastic Decomposition. *Phd thesis*, Stanford University.

Shi, J., & Malik, J. (2000). Normalized cuts and image segmentation. *IEEE Transactions on Pattern Analysis and Machine Intelligence, 22*(8), 888–905. doi:10.1109/34.868688

Shneiderman, B., & Aris, A. (2006). Network visualization by semantic substrates. *IEEE Transactions on Visualization and Computer Graphics, 12*(5). doi:10.1109/TVCG.2006.166

Slaney, M. (1998). A Critique of Pure Audition, Chapter 3. *Computational Auditory Scene Analysis.* Lawrence Erlbaum Associates, Inc.

Srinivasan, S. H. (2004). Auditory blobs. In *Proc. IEEE International Conference on Acoustics, Speech, and Signal Processing* (ICASSP), Montreal, Canada (Vol. 4, pp. 313–316).

Srinivasan, S. H., & Kankanhalli, M. S. (2003). Harmonicity and dynamics based audio separation. In *Proc. IEEE International Conference on Acoustics, Speech, and Signal Processing* (ICASSP), volume 5, pages v–640–v–643, Hong Kong, China.

Tzanetakis, G. (2002). Manipulation, Analysis and Retrieval Systems for Audio Signals. *Phd thesis*, Princeton University.

Tzanetakis, G., & Cook. P. Musical Genre Classification of Audio Signals *IEEE Transactions on Acoustics, Speech and Signal Processing, 10*(5), pp. 293-302, 2002.

Tzanetakis, G. (2008). Marsyas: a case study in implementing Music Information Retrieval Systems, pages 31–49. *Intelligent Music Information Systems: Tools and Methodologies. Information Science Reference*. ISBN 978-1-59904-663-1.

Tzanetakis, G., Castillo, C., Jones, R., Martins, L. G., Teixeira, L. F., & Lagrange, M. (2008). Interoperability and the marsyas 0.2 runtime. In *Proc. International Computer Music Conference* (ICMC), Belfast, Northern Ireland.

Tzanetakis, G., & Cook, P. (2000). Marsyas: a framework for audio analysis. *Organized Sound, 4*(3).

Vincent, E. (2006). Musical source separation using time-frequency source priors. *IEEE Transactions on Audio. Speech and Language Processing, 14*(1), 91–98. doi:10.1109/TSA.2005.860342

Virtanen, T., & Klapuri, A. (2000). Separation of harmonic sound sources using sinusoidal modeling. In *Proc. IEEE International Conference on Acoustics, Speech, and Signal Processing* (ICASSP), Istanbul, Turkey.

von Luxburg, U. (2007). A tutorial on spectral clustering. *Statistics and Computing, 17*(4), 395–416. doi:10.1007/s11222-007-9033-z

Wang, D., & Brown, G. J. (Eds.). (2006). *Computational Auditory Scene Analysis: Principles, Algorithms and Applications*. Wiley-IEEE Press.

ENDNOTE

[1] The real modulo function is inhere defined as a modulo operation according to the following conditions: if taking $D = q \times d + r$, where D is the dividend, d is the divisor $q \in \cdot$ is the quotient, and the returned remainder $r \in^{\circ}$ is in the range $0 < r < d$. E.g. mod(5.3, 2) = 1.3 or mod(5.3, 1) = 0.3.u

Chapter 3
Cocktail Party Problem:
Source Separation Issues and Computational Methods

Tariqullah Jan
University of Surrey, UK

Wenwu Wang
University of Surrey, UK

ABSTRACT

Cocktail party problem is a classical scientific problem that has been studied for decades. Humans have remarkable skills in segregating target speech from a complex auditory mixture obtained in a cocktail party environment. Computational modeling for such a mechanism is however extremely challenging. This chapter presents an overview of several recent techniques for the source separation issues associated with this problem, including independent component analysis/blind source separation, computational auditory scene analysis, model-based approaches, non-negative matrix factorization and sparse coding. As an example, a multistage approach for source separation is included. The application areas of cocktail party processing are explored. Potential future research directions are also discussed.

INTRODUCTION

The concept of the cocktail party problem (CPP) was coined by Cherry (1953). It was proposed to address the phenomenon associated with human auditory system that, in a cocktail party environment, humans have the ability to focus their listening attention on a single speaker when multiple conversations and background interferences and noise are presented simultaneously. Many researchers and scientists from a variety of research areas attempt to tackle this problem (Bregman, 1990; Arons, 1992; Yost, 1997; Feng et al., 2000; Bronkhorst, 2000). Despite of all these works, the CPP remains an open problem and demands further research effort. Figure 1 illustrates the cocktail party effect using a simplified scenario with two simultaneous conversations in the room environment.

As the solution to the CPP offers many practical applications, engineers and scientists have spent their efforts in understanding the mechanism of the human auditory system, and hoping to design a machine which can work similarly to the human

DOI: 10.4018/978-1-61520-919-4.ch003

Figure 1. A simplified scenario of the cocktail party problem with two speakers and two listeners (microphones)

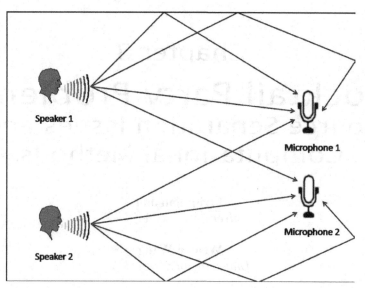

auditory system. However, there are no machines produced so far that can perform as humans in a real cocktail party environment. Studies on the human auditory system could help understand the cocktail party phenomenon, and offer hopes of designing a machine that could approach a normal human's listening ability.

It has been observed that people with the perceptive hearing loss suffer from insufficient speech intelligibility (Kocinski, 2008). It is difficult for them to pick up the target speech, in particular, when there exist some interfering sounds nearby. However, amplification of the signal is not sufficient to increase the intelligibility of the target speech as all the signals (both target and interference) are amplified. For this application scenario, it is highly desirable to produce a machine that can offer clean target speech to these hearing impaired people.

Scientists have attempted to analyze and simplify the complicated CPP problem, see, for example, a recent overview in (Haykin, 2005). A variety of methods have been proposed for this problem. For example, computational auditory scene analyses (CASA) approach attempts to

transform the human auditory system into mathematical modeling using computational means (Wang & Brown, 2006; Wang, 2005). Blind source separation (BSS) is also used by many people to address this problem (Wang et al., 2005; Araki et al., 2003; Olsson et al., 2006; Makino et al., 2005). BSS approaches are based on the independent component analysis (ICA) technique assuming that the source signals coming from different speakers are statistically independent (Hyvarinen et al., 2001; Lee, 1998). Non-negative matrix factorization (NMF) and its extension non-negative tensor factorization (NTF) have also been applied to speech and music separation problems (Smaragdis, 2004, Virtanen, 2007; Schmidt & Olsson, 2006, Schmidt & Laurberg, 2008, Wang, 2009). Another interesting approach is the sparse representation of the sources in which the source signals are assumed to be sparse and hence only one of the source signals in the mixture is active while others are relatively insignificant for a given time instant (Pearlmutter et al., 2004; Bofill et al., 2001; Zibulevsky & Pearlmutter, 2001). Some model based approaches have also been employed to address this problem (Todros et al., 2004; Radfar et al., 2007). The following sections provide a detailed review of these techniques for addressing the cocktail party problem, in particular, for audio source separation which is a key issue for creating an artificial cocktail party machine.

BACKGROUND FOR AUDIO SOURCES

Audio sources are usually classified as speech, music or natural sounds. Each of the categories has its own specific characteristics which can be exploited during its processing. Speech sounds are basically composed of discrete phonetic units called phonemes (O'Shaughnessy, 2000; Deng & O'Shaughnessy, 2003). Due to the co-articulation of successive phonemes, each signal that corresponds to a specific phoneme exhibits time varying properties. The resultant signal is composed of periodic harmonic pulses which are produced due to the periodic vibration of the vocal folds, a noise part which is generated because of the air passing via lips and teeth, or a transient part due to the release of pressure behind lips or teeth. Harmonics within the generated signal has periodic frequency components which are the multiples of a fundamental frequency component. In real speech signals the fundamental frequency component of the periodic phonemes varies due to the articulation, but typically for male speech is 140 Hz, and 200 Hz for female speech with variation of 40 Hz for each.

Music sources (Hall, 2001) generally constitute of sequences of notes or tones produced by musical instruments, singers and synthetic instruments. Each note is composed of a signal which further can be made of a periodic part containing harmonic sinusoids produced by blowing into pipe or bowing a string, or a transient part generated due to hitting a drum or plucking a string, or a wideband noise produced by blowing the wind instruments. For example, in western music the periodic frequencies of the notes generated typically remain constant or varying slowly. Musical instruments usually produce musical phrases which are composed of successive notes without any silence between the notes. Unlike monophonic music, polyphonic sounds are composed of several simultaneous notes that are generated by multiple musical instruments.

The third source comes from the environment, called natural sounds (Gygi et al., 2004). Their characteristic varies depending on the origin of the natural sound. Similar to the speech and music signals it can also be classified as periodic, transient and noise. For example, a car horn produces the natural periodic sound signal, a hammer thrashing the hardwood generates the transient signal and raining results in a wideband noise signal. The discrete structure of natural sound is simpler as compared with the organization of notes and phonemes. In this chapter, we will mainly focus on the first type of the audio source signal i.e. speech signals. The methods for the CPP discussed in this chapter are mainly applied in context of the speech signals.

COMPUTATIONAL AUDITORY SCENE ANALYSIS

The ear is mainly composed of three parts: the outer ear, the middle ear and the inner ear. The outer ear constitutes of a flap of tissue which is visible and called pinna, and the auditory canal (Mango, 1991). The combination of pinna and auditory canal helps in sound source localization. Sound moving through the auditory canal results in the vibration of eardrum within the middle ear. The middle ear transmits these vibrations to the inner ear. The middle ear, which is composed of three small bones i.e., the malleus, incus, and strapes, plays an important role in the transmission of vibrations. The middle ear is an impedance matching device between the air and fluid-filled inner ear. Inside the inner ear there is an organ called cochlea containing fluid. The vibrations transferred into the inner part of the ear press the cochlear fluid and hence stimulate the hair cells in the cochlea. Hair cells have a role of converting physical vibrations into a set of nerve responses (i.e. electrical signals), and they are frequency-selective, which means that different regions of the cochlea, more precisely different areas of basilar membrane, response to different frequencies (hair cells at the end near the oval window correspond to high frequency up to 20 kHz, and those in a narrow part to low frequency). Therefore the cochlea performs a kind of spectral analysis and can be modeled as a bank of band-pass filters (Auditory scene analysis: listening to several things at once, 2007). Electrical signals from the cochlea are transferred as neural impulses along the auditory nerve towards the brain. The central parts of the auditory system are relatively complex and less understood in comparison to periphery.

CASA is the study of auditory scene analysis (ASA) by computational means (Wang & Brown, 2006). ASA is the process by which the human auditory system organizes sound into perceptually meaningful elements. The concept of ASA was coined by Bregman (1990). The human auditory system is complicated and constitutes of two ears and auditory routes (Haykin et al., 2005). Specifically it is a refined system which has the ability to distinguish the frequency components coming from different sources and also can find the exact location for the source signals. This ability of the human auditory system is very unique because of the fact that the frequency component arrangement inside the signal and the combination of signals is very perplexing. Generally speaking, the human auditory system performs sound localization and recognition in order to pick up the target signal from the cocktail party environment. In literatures we can find different approaches for the localization of sound signal, for example (Blauert, 1983; Yost, 2000). Time difference, level difference and spectral difference are the important acoustic cues used for the localization of sound sources. The recognition can be well explained from the

work presented by Bregman (1990). According to his analysis recognition can be done in two major steps called sound segregation and sound determination. Segregation of sound sources can be achieved using feature selection and feature grouping. Feature selection consists of some very important features like pitch. Feature grouping basically combines the incoming sound components in such a way that a stream of similar components corresponding to a single sound source is grouped together. Sound determination is then performed to identify the elements within the sound stream rather than just segregation.

Hence CASA systems are machine listening systems that aim to separate mixtures of sound sources in the way that the human auditory system does. The fundamental steps required in order to segregate the speech signal by CASA systems are: First, to analyze the signals in such a way that the interfering speech signals can be neglected. In the second step, a recognition process is involved where the speech signals mixed in a stream are analyzed according to their statistical property that is important for recognizing the target signal. The last step called synthesis involves reorganizing the target signals from the separated sound stream. CASA approaches have been employed to investigate the cocktail party problem (Wang et al., 2006; Wang, 2005; Cooke et al., 2001, Cooke, 2002). The architecture of a typical CASA system is shown in Figure 2.

In general, there are two types of approaches for the separation of the target signal in the cocktail party environment in the context of CASA. The first one is called "signal-driven" approach which is used for the segregation of the auditory scene into the different components belonging to the different sound streams (Bregman, 1990). The second one called "knowledge-driven" approach uses the prior knowledge of the unknown speech sources, so that the target signal can be separated from the interference. In 1994, Brown and Cooke investigated some of the key issues related to the early CASA methods (Brown & Cooke, 1994).

Figure 2. Schematic diagram of a typical CASA system

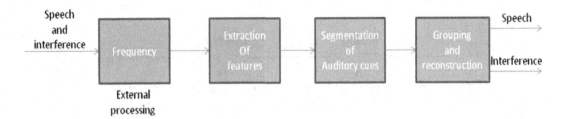

Specifically they avoid the assumptions made about the type and number of sources. They proposed to model the human auditory system into separate parts. The key parts are ear filtering, cochlear filtering and central processing (combination of different auditory maps which shows onset, offset, periodicities and frequency transitions). Wang and Brown (1999) extended the work of Brown and Cooke by replacing the central processing with a double layer oscillator network and applied simple computational methods for auditory feature extraction.

A technique called ideal binary masking (IBM) has been recently used in CASA to segregate the target signal from the interference (Wang et al., 2006). Consider a microphone signal recorded in a cocktail party problem: $x(t) = s_1(t) + s_2(t)$, where $s_1(t)$ is the target speech signal and $s_2(t)$ is the interference speech signal and t is the discrete time instant. Denote X, S_1 and S_2 as the time-frequency (T-F) representation of $x(t)$, $s_1(t)$ and $s_2(t)$, obtained from some T-F transformation respectively. Then the ideal binary mask (IBM) for $s_1(t)$ with respect to $s_2(t)$, is defined as follows,

$$M_1(t,f) = \begin{cases} 1 & \text{if } |S_1(t,f)| > |S_2(t,f)| \\ 0 & \text{otherwise} \end{cases} \quad (1)$$

The target speech $s_1(t)$ can then be extracted by applying the IBM to X, followed by an inverse T-F transform. The decision is binary, and hence the intelligibility of the segregated speech signal is high. But on the other hand the resultant mask M_1 entirely depends on the availability of the target and interference speech signals. In practice, the target and interference signals are usually unknown, and the mask has to be estimated from the mixtures.

BLIND SOURCE SEPARATION

Another technique to address the cocktail party problem is BSS, where the mixing process is usually described as a linear convolutive model and convolutive ICA algorithms can then be applied to segregate the source signals from their mixtures assuming the sources are statistically independent (Araki et al., 2003; Olsson & Hansen, 2006; Makino et al., 2005; Mitianondis & Davies, 2002; Nickel & Iyer, 2006; Pedersen et al., 2008). BSS is an approach used for the estimation of the source signals having only the information of the mixed signals observed at each input channel, without prior information about sources and the mixing channels. Its potential applications include speech segregation in cocktail party environment, teleconferences and hearing aids. In such applications, the mixture signals are reverberant, due to the surface reflections of the rooms. ICA is a major statistical tool for the BSS problem, for which the statistical independence between the sources is assumed (Hyvarinen et al., 2001; Lee, 1998). The mathematical model (Ainhoren, 2008) used to describe the ICA is given as,

Figure 3. Schematic diagram for a typical BSS system with two sources and two mixtures. Unknown source signals: s, observed signals: x, estimated signals: y

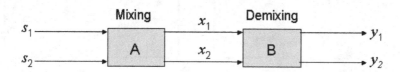

$$x_1(t) = a_{11}s_1(t) + a_{12}s_2(t) + \dots + a_{1N}s_N(t)$$
$$\vdots$$
$$\vdots$$
$$x_M(t) = a_{M1}s_1(t) + a_{M2}s_2(t) + \dots + a_{MN}s_N(t)$$
$$(2)$$

where $s_1(t),\dots,s_N(t)$ representing unknown source signals in the cocktail party environment, $x_1(t),\dots,$ $x_M(t)$ denote the mixture signals (e.g. microphone recordings). If the coefficients a_{ij} ($i = 1,\dots,M$ and $j = 1,\dots,N$) are scalars, the resultant mixtures are referred to as instantaneous mixtures, and if they are filters, the mixtures are referred to as convolutive mixtures. If $N = M$, i.e., the number of sources equals to the number of mixtures, it is called exactly determined BSS problem. If $N > M$, it is the under-determined case, and $N < M$ the over-determined BSS problem. A schematic diagram of a typical two input two output BSS system is given in Figure 3, in which A represents the unknown mixing system and B is the demixing system used for the estimation of the unknown source signals.

The BSS approach using ICA can be applied either in the time domain (Pedersen at al., 2008; Cichocki & Amari, 2002) or in the frequency domain (Wang et al., 2005; Araki et al., 2003; Olsson & Hansen, 2006; Makino et al., 2005) or their hybrid (Lee et al., 1997; Lambert & Bell, 1997), assuming that the source signals are statistically independent. The time-domain approaches attempt to extend the instantaneous ICA model to the convolutive case. They can achieve good separation performance once the algorithms converge, as the independence of segregated signals is measured accurately (Makino et al., 2005). However the computational cost for the estimation of the filter coefficients in the convolutive operation can be very demanding, especially when dealing with reverberant mixtures using long time delay filters (Amari et al., 1997; Matsuoka & Nakashima, 2001; Buchner et al., 2004; Douglas & Sun, 2002; Douglas et al., 2005).

To improve the computational efficiency, the frequency domain BSS approaches transform the mixtures into the frequency domain, and then apply an instantaneous but complex ICA algorithm to each frequency bin (Wang et al., 2005; Araki et al., 2003; Parra & Spence, 2000; Schobben & Sommen, 2002; Sawada et al., 2003; Mukai et al., 2004). As a result, many complex valued and instantaneous ICA algorithms that have already been developed can be directly applied to the frequency domain BSS. However an important issue associated with this approach is the permutation problem, i.e., the permutation in each frequency bin may not be consistent with each other so that the separated speech signal in the time domain contains the frequency components from the other sources. Different methods have been developed to solve this problem. By reducing the length of the filter in the time domain (Buchner et al., 2004; Parra & Spence, 2000) the permutation problem can be overcome to some extent. Source localization approach has also been employed to mitigate the permutation inconsistency (Soon et al., 1993; Sawada et al., 2004). Another technique for the alignment of the permutations across the frequency bands is based on correlation between separated source components at each frequency bin using the envelope similarity between the neighboring frequencies (Murata et al., 2001).

The third approach is the combination of both time and frequency domain approaches. In some methods (Lee et al., 1997; Back & Tosi, 1994), the coefficients of the FIR filter are updated in the frequency domain and the non-linear functions are employed in the time domain for evaluating the independence of the source signals. Hence no permutation problem exists any more, as the independence of the source signals is evaluated in the time domain. Nevertheless, the limitation of this hybrid approach is the frequent switch between two different domains at each step and thereby consuming extra time on these inverse transformation operations.

The separation performance of many developed algorithms is however still limited, and leaves a large room for improvement. This is especially true when dealing with reverberant and noisy mixtures. For example in the frequency-domain BSS framework, if the frame length of the DFT is long and the number of samples in each frequency bin is small, the independence assumption may not be satisfied. Similarly, if the short length DFT frame is used, the long reverberations cannot be covered and hence the segregation performance is limited (Araki et al., 2003).

Apart from the above discussed methods, some authors consider the assumption of W-disjoint orthogonality for speech signals in order to separate the source signals from the observe data. For example in (Jourjine et al., 2000), for a given windowing function $W(t)$, two sources, $s_i(t)$ and $s_j(t)$ are called W-disjoint orthogonal if the supports of the short-time Fourier Transform of $s_i(t)$ and $s_j(t)$ are disjoint (Jourjine et al., 2000). The windowed Fourier Transform of $s_i(t)$ is defined as,

$$F^w\left[s_i\right](\tau, w) = \int_{-\infty}^{\infty} W(t - \tau)s_i(t)e^{-iwt}dt \qquad (3)$$

which can be denoted as $s_i^w(\tau, w)$. The W-disjoint orthogonality assumption can be expressed as below (Jourjine et al., 2000).

$$s_i^w(\tau, w) * s_j^w(\tau, w) = 0, \forall i \neq j, \forall w, \tau \qquad (4)$$

This equation implies that either of the sources is zero for any w and τ as long as two sources do not come from the same source. If $w(t) = 1$, then $s_i^w(\tau, w)$ can be interpreted as the Fourier Transform of $s_i(t)$, which can be referred to as $s_i(w)$. Therefore, W-disjoint orthogonality can be written as,

$$s_i(w) * s_j(w) = 0, \forall i \neq j, \forall w \qquad (5)$$

which represents the property of disjoint orthogonality (Jourjine et al., 2000).

Another challenging problem is to separate moving sources rather than stationary in a cocktail party environment. A recent work by (Naqvi et al., 2009) is devoted to the blind separation of moving sources. Here a multimodal approach is proposed for the segregation of moving speech sources. The key issue in blind estimation of moving sources is the time varying nature of the mixing and unmixing filters, which is hard to track in real world. In this work the authors applied the visual modality for the separation of moving sources as well as stationary sources. The 3-D tracker based on particle filtering is used to detect the movement of the sources. This method performs well for the blind separation of moving sources in a low reverberant environment.

So far, two important techniques for the CPP were discussed in detail. It is interesting to make a comparison between these two techniques. In the case of BSS, the unknown sources are assumed to be statistically independent. However, no such assumption is required for CASA. On the other hand, the IBM technique used in the CASA domain needs to estimate the binary mask from the target and interference signals which should be obtained from the mixture in practice. Another difference is in the way how the echoes within the mixture are dealt with by these two techniques. In BSS algorithms (Wang et al., 2005; Araki et al., 2003; Olsson & Hansen, 2006; Makino et al., 2005), such a situation is modeled as a convolutive process. On the other hand CASA approaches deal with echoes based on some intrinsic properties of audio signals, such as, pitch, which are usually preserved (with distortions) under reverberant conditions. However, the human auditory system has a remarkable ability of concentrating on one speaker by ignoring others in a cocktail party environment. Some of the CASA approaches (Wang & Brown, 1999) work in a similar manner i.e. extracting a target signal by treating other signals as a background sound. In contrast, BSS approaches attempt to separate every source signal simultaneously from the mixture. Motivated by the complementary advantages of the CASA and BSS approaches, we have developed a multistage approach in (Jan et al., 2009, 2010) where a convolutive BSS algorithm is combined with the IBM technique followed by cepstral smoothing. The details of this method (Jan et al., 2009) will be discussed later in this chapter as an example.

MODEL BASED APPROACHES

Another method to address the cocktail party problem is based on the statistical modeling of signals and the parameters of the model are estimated from the training data. Some model based approaches have been used for the blind separation of speech signals e.g., (Todros & Tabrikian, 2004; Radfar & Dansereau, 2007; Ichir & Djafari, 2006; Radfar et al., 2006). In (Todros & Tabrikian, 2004) Gaussian mixture model (GMM) which is widely used for the modeling of the highly complex probability density functions (pdf), is employed for the modeling of the joint pdf of the sources by exploiting

the non-gaussianity and/or non-stationarity of the sources and hence the statistical properties of the sources can vary from sample to sample.

In (Radfar & Dansereau, 2007) the model-based approach is used for single channel speech separation. The authors considered the problem as speech enhancement problem in which both the target and interference signals are non-stationary sources with same characteristics in terms of pdf. Firstly, in the training phase, the patterns of the sources are obtained using the Gaussian composite source modeling. Then the patterns representing the same sources are selected. Finally, the estimation of the sources can be achieved using these selected patterns. Alternatively, a filter can be built on the basis of these patterns and then applied to the observed signals in order to estimate the sources.

Source separation in the wavelet domain by model-based approaches has been considered in (Ichir & Djafari, 2006). This method consists of a Bayesian estimation framework for the BSS problem where different models for the wavelet coefficients have been presented. However there are some limitations with the model based approach. The trained model can only be used for the segregation process of the speech signals with the same probability distribution, i.e., the pdf of the trained model must be similar to that of the observation data. In addition, the model based algorithms can perform well only for a limited number of speech signals.

NON NEGATIVE MATRIX/ TENSOR FACTORIZATION

NMF was proposed by Lee & Seung in 1999. Using the constraint of non-negativity, NMF decomposes a non-negative matrix V into the product of two non-negative matrices W and H, given as:

$$V_{mxn} = W_{mxr}H_{rxn} \qquad (6)$$

where $(n + m) r < mn$. Unlike other matrix factorizations, NMF allows only additive operations i.e. no subtractions (Lee & Seung, 1999, Lee & Seung, 2001, Laurberg et al., 2008). As NMF does not depend on the mutual statistical independence of the source components, it has a potential to segregate the correlated sources. NMF has been applied to a variety of signals including image, speech or music audio. In (Cichocki et al., 2006) the authors attempted to separate the general form of signals from the observe data i.e. both positive and negative signals using the constraints of sparsity and smoothness. For machine audition of audio scenes, NMF has also found some applications. For example, it has been applied to music transcription (Smaragdis & Brown, 2003, Wang et al, 2006) and audio source separation (Smaragdis, 2004, Smaragdis, 2007, Wang & Plumbley, 2005, Parry & Essa, 2007, FitzGerald et al, 2005, FitzGerald et al, 2006, Morup et al, 2007, Schmidt & Morup, 2006, Wang, 2007, Virtanen, 2007, Wang et al, 2008, Wang et al, 2009). In these applications, the audio data are usually transformed to non-negative parameters, such as spectrogram, which are then used as the input to the algorithms. The application of the NMF technique to the CPP problem is still an emerging area which attracts increasing interests in the research community. For an overview of recent progress on NMF for audio and speech applications, readers may refer to another chapter by Wang in this book.

SPARSE REPRESENTATION AND COMPRESSED SENSING

Separation of signals blindly from their underdetermined mixtures has attracted a great deal of attention over the past few years. It is a challenging source separation problem. One of the most common methods adopted for this problem is based on the sparse representation of signals (Zibulevsky & Bofill, 2001; Davies & Mitianoudis, 2004; Fevotte & Godsill, 2005; Zibulevsky & Pearlmutter, 2001).

Closely related to sparse representation, there is an emerging technique called compressed sensing, which suggests that a signal can be perfectly recovered based on information rate, instead of the Nyquist rate, and random sampling, instead of uniform sampling, under certain conditions. It has been observed that compressed sensing exploits two important properties (Candès, 2006, Candès & Wakin, 2008; Donoho, 2006; Candès & Romberg, 2007). The first one is sparsity, which means that many natural signals can be represented in some proper basis in sparse (compressible) form. The second property is incoherence, i.e. the signal which is represented in some proper basis in sparse form should be dense as compared to the original representation of the signal. It is basically the extension of duality property between time and frequency domain.

There are similarities between the compressed sensing and source separation and their connections have been explored by (Blumensath & Davies, 2007), and further investigated by (Xu & Wang, 2008, Xu & Wang, 2009). It was found that the compressed sensing based signal recovery methods can be applied to the source reconstructions provided that the unmixing matrix is available or has been estimated (Zibulevsky & Bofill, 2001; Davies & Mitianoudis, 2004; Fevotte & Godsill, 2005; Zibulevsky & Pearlmutter, 2001; Blumensath & Davies, 2007).

A MULTISTAGE APPROACH

As mentioned above, both ICA and IBM have some limitations, i.e., the performance of the ICA is limited under the reverberant and noisy conditions and for the IBM technique, both the target speech and interference signal should be known *a priori*. In order to improve their performance, we have recently proposed a novel algorithm for the separation of convolutive speech mixtures based on the combination of ICA and IBM (Jan et al, 2009, Jan et al, 2010). The proposed method consists of three steps. First, a constrained convolutive ICA algorithm (Wang et al., 2005) is applied to the binaural recordings to obtain the source signals. As is common to many other existing ICA algorithms, the separated target speech from this step still contains a considerable amount of interference from other sources. The performance steadily degrades with the increase of reverberation time (RT). To further reduce the interference, we use IBM to process the outputs from the previous step. Specifically, we estimate the ideal binary mask by comparing the energy of corresponding T-F units from the binaural outputs of the convolutive ICA algorithm. The estimated binary masks are then applied to the original mixtures for obtaining the target speech and interfering sources. The third step in our algorithm is to reduce musical noise using cepstral smoothing, where the noise was introduced by the errors in the estimation of the binary masks (Madhu et al., 2008; Araki et al., 2005). More specifically, we transform the binary mask into the cepstral domain, and smooth the transformed mask over time frames using the overlap-and-add technique. The benefit of doing this is that it is easier to distinguish the unwanted isolated random peaks from the mask patterns resulting from the spectral structure of the segregated speech in the cepstrum domain. As a result, we can apply different levels of smoothing to the binary T-F mask based on their various frequency ranges. The smoothed mask is transformed back into the T-F plane, which is then applied to the binaural outputs of the previous step in order to reduce the musical noise. Our multistage algorithm was first presented in (Jan et al., 2009), and the implementation details and systematic evaluations were provided in (Jan et al., 2010). Here, we briefly review this algorithm.

Stage 1. BSS of Convolutive Mixtures in the Frequency Domain

In a cocktail party environment, N speech signals are recorded by M microphones, and this can be described mathematically by a linear convolutive model,

$$x_i(n) = \sum_{i=1}^{n} \sum_{p=1}^{P} h_{ji}(p)s_i(n-p+1) \quad (j=1,...,M)$$

(8)

where s_i and x_j are the source and mixture signals respectively, h_{ji} is a P-point room impulse response. This time-domain convolutive source separation problem can be converted to multiple instantaneous problems in the frequency domain (Wang et al., 2005; Araki et al., 2003) by applying short time Fourier transform (STFT). Using matrix notations, we have

$$X(k,m) = H(k)S(k,m)$$

(9)

where k represents the frequency index and m is the discrete time index. The mixing matrix H(k) is assumed to be invertible and time invariant. The sources are then estimated by apply an unmixing filter W(k) to the mixtures,

$$Y(k,m) = W(k)X(k,m)$$

(10)

where Y(k, m) represents the estimated source signals, and W(k) is estimated based on the assumption of independence. There are many algorithms that are suitable for this, e.g. (Araki et al., 2003; Parra & Spence, 2000; Sawada et al., 2007; Araki et al., 2007; Araki et al., 2004; Cichocki & Amari, 2002). In our multistage algorithm, we have used the constrained convolutive ICA approach in (Wang et al., 2005) for the separation in this stage. To further improve the separation quality, we apply the IBM technique to process the separated signal.

Stage 2. Combining Convolutive ICA and Binary Masking

Applying an inverse Fourier transform, Y(k, m) obtained above can be converted back to the time domain denoted as,

$$Y(n) = [Y_1(n)Y_2(n)]^T \qquad (11)$$

Scaling is further applied to $Y_1(N)$ and $Y_2(N)$ for obtaining the normalized outputs $\tilde{Y}_1(n)$ and $\tilde{Y}_2(n)$. After this we transform the two normalized outputs and into the T-F domain using STFT,

$$\tilde{Y}_i(k,m) = STFT(\tilde{Y}_i(n)) \qquad (12)$$

By comparing the energy of each T-F unit of the above two spectrograms, the two binary masks are estimated as,

$$M_1^f(k,m) = \begin{cases} 1 & \text{if } \left|\tilde{Y}_1(k,m)\right| > \tau \left|\tilde{Y}_2(k,m)\right|, \\ 0 & \text{otherwise} \quad \forall \text{ k,m} \end{cases}$$

$$(13)$$

$$M_2^f(k,m) = \begin{cases} 1 & \text{if } \left|\tilde{Y}_2(k,m)\right| > \tau \left|\tilde{Y}_1(k,m)\right|, \\ 0 & \text{otherwise} \quad \forall \text{ k,m} \end{cases}$$

$$(14)$$

where τ is a threshold for controlling the sparseness of the mask, and typically $\tau = 1$ was used in our work (Jan et al, 2009, Jan et al, 2010). The masks are then applied to the T-F representation of the original two microphone recordings as follows

$$Y_i^f(k,m) = M_i^f(k,m).X_i(k,m) \quad i = 1,2$$

$$(15)$$

The source signals in the time domain are recovered using the inverse STFT (ISTFT).

$$Y_i^t(n) = ISTFT(Y_i^f(k,m)) \quad i = 1,2 \qquad (16)$$

As found in (Jan et al, 2009, Jan et al, 2010), this masking technique considerably improves the separation performance over that achieved by the convolutive ICA algorithm. However, a typical problem associated with the binary T-F masking is the so-called musical noise problem due to the the errors in mask estimation (Madhu et al., 2008; Araki et al., 2005). To address this issue, we employ a cepstral smoothing technique (Madhu et al., 2008) as detailed in the next subsection.

Stage 3. Cepstral Smoothing of the Binary Mask

The idea of using cepstral smoothing to reduce the musical artifacts was motivated by the speech production mechanism (Madhu et al., 2008; Oppenheim & Schafer, 1975). That is, for different frequency bands, different levels of smoothing are applied. By doing this, not only the broadband structure and pitch information in the speech signal are preserved, but also the musical artifacts can be reduced. Representing the binary masks of equation (6) and (7) in the cepstrum domain we have,

$$M_i^c(l,m) = DFT^{-1}\{ln(M_i^f(k,m))\} \quad \{k = 0,...,K-1\}$$

$$(17)$$

where l and k are the quefrency bin index and the frequency bin index respectively (Madhu et al., 2008). *DFT* represents the discrete Fourier transform and K is the length of the DFT. After applying smoothing the resultant smoothed mask is given as,

$$\bar{M}_i^s(l,m) = \gamma_l \bar{M}_i^s(l,m-1) + (1-\gamma_l)M_i^c(l,m) \quad i = 1,2$$

$$(18)$$

where γ_l is a parameter for controlling the smoothing level, and is selected as follows,

$$\gamma_l = \begin{cases} \gamma_{env} & \text{if } l \in \{0,...,l_{env}\} \\ \gamma_{pitch} & \text{if } l = l_{pitch} \\ \gamma_{peak} & \text{if } l \in \{(l_{env}+1),...,K\}\backslash l_{pitch} \end{cases}$$

$$(19)$$

71

where $0 \leq \gamma_{env} < \gamma_{pitch} < \gamma_{peak} \leq 1$, l_{env} is the quefrency bin index that represents the spectral envelope of the mask and l_{pitch} is the quefrency bin index for the pitch. The underlying principle for the choice of γ_l is the illustrated as follows. M^c (l,m), $l \in \{0,...,l_{env}\}$, basically represents the spectral envelop of the mask M^f (k,m). In this region the relatively low value is selected for γ_l to avoid the distortion in the envelope. Also, low smoothing is applied if l is equal to l_{pitch} so that the harmonic structure of the speech signal is maintained. High smoothing is applied in the last range to reduce the artifacts. Different from (Madhu ET Al., 2008) We calculate the pitch frequency by using the segregated speech signal obtained in the previous subsection, as follows,

$$l_{pitch} = argmax_l\{sig^c(l,m) \mid l_{low} \leq l \leq l_{high}\}$$

(20)

where $sig^c(l,m)$ is the cepstrum domain representation of the segregated speech signal y^t (n). The range l_{low}, l_{high} is chosen so that it can accommodate pitch frequencies of human speech in the range of 50 to 500 HZ. The final smoothed version of the spectral mask is given as,

$$M_i^f(k,m) = \exp(DFT\{M_i^s(l,m) \mid l = 0,....,K-1\})$$

(21)

This smoothed mask is then applied to the output segregated speech signals of the previous subsection to get the signals with reduced musical noise, as follows,

$$\overline{Y}_i^f(k,m) = M_i^f(k,m).Y_i^f(k,m)$$

(22)

RELATIONS TO OTHER METHODS

We have evaluated substantially the multistage approach discussed above using the audio mixtures generated by the simulated room model (Allen & Berkley, 1979), and the real recorded room impulse responses in (Pedersen et al., 2008). More details about the evaluations can be found in (Jan et al., 2009, Jan et al., 2010). Here, we only briefly discuss the separation performance that can be achieved with the multistage algorithm, as compared with two recent methods. Clean speech signals from a pool of 12 sources (Pedersen et al., 2008) were randomly selected to generate the reverberant mixture. In (Wang et al., 2005), the authors proposed a method for the segregation of speech signals using the frequency domain convolutive ICA approach. The results in terms of signal to noise ratio (SNR) for separated speech signals in (Wang et al., 2005) shows that the segregated signal contains a considerable amount of interference from other sources. In contrast to the method in (Wang et al., 2005), our proposed approach has better separation performance in terms of SNR measurements. Our results show that the multistage algorithm offers 3-4 dB gain in comparison to the method in (Wang et al., 2005). Listening tests also shows that our proposed method considerably improves the separation performance by suppressing the interference to a much lower level as compare to the method in (Wang et al., 2005). In the multistage algorithm, the complementary advantages of both techniques i.e. ICA and IBM are exploited to improve the performance of the separation system in contrast to the method in (Wang et al., 2005), and the musical noise is further reduced by cepstral smoothing.

The authors of (Pedersen et al., 2008) proposed a method in which ICA is also combined with IBM to improve the segregation performance in terms of interference suppression. However, our multistage method employed cepstral smoothing which can reduce the artifacts (musical noise) introduced due to the estimation of the binary masks. Also a constrained convolutive ICA (Wang et al., 2005) is used in the multistage algorithm, while the instantaneous ICA algorithm is used in (Pedersen et al., 2008). It was also shown in (Jan et al., 2009, Jan et al., 2010) that the multistage approach is 18 times faster than the method in (Pedersen et al., 2008) in extracting the target speech signal from the convolutive mixture. Readers can find more details about the experimental set up and results including subjective listening test results of the multistage approach in (Jan et al., 2009, Jan et al., 2010).

APPLICATION AREAS

There are many applications that can benefit from the solution of the cocktail party problem, such as teleconferencing, speech recognition, bio-inspired systems, hearing aid, and reverberant environments, see e.g., (Yegnanarayana & Murthy, 2000, Wu & Wang, 2006). For example, in teleconferencing systems there might be multiple speakers talking at the same time, and echoes might also be a problem. To distinguish one speaker from another and the original speech from its echoes is necessary in this application. Progress in the cocktail party problem can facilitate the development of high quality teleconferencing systems with fewer practical constraints.

Speech recognition is another promising application area. Although the area of speech recognition has been developed for several decades and many successful systems have been implemented (John & Wendy, 2001; Junqua & Haton, 1995), the performance of these systems for uncontrolled natural environments is still limited. Any major progress in the cocktail party problem will prove to be crucial for the development of robust speech recognition systems that can deal with general auditory scenes within an uncontrolled natural environment.

As we have discussed, CASA is one of the most active areas of research for the cocktail party problem. In CASA, much effort has been devoted to the implementation (simulation) of the mechanism of the human auditory system. Similar ideas have evolved to the auditory scene analysis of non-human animals (Barker, 2006; Lippmann, 1997). Study of the cocktail party problem will facilitate our understanding of the designing techniques for the biologically inspired artificial scene analysis systems.

Research progress in cocktail party problem can be beneficial for other related applications in, for example, interference cancellation, deconvolution, and inverse problems. The common feature with these applications is that the propagation channels that the signals are transmitted are in multi path, and not known *a priori*, and is similar to what we have seen in a cocktail party environment. From this sense, the methods developed for the cocktail party problem are applicable for a broader area of applications.

CONCLUSION AND FUTURE RESEARCH

We have discussed the concept of the cocktail party problem, and in particular, the source separation issues in the cocktail party problem. We have presented several recent methods for speech source separation and auditory scene analysis, which are enabling techniques for addressing the cocktail party problem, including blind source separation, computational auditory scene analysis, non-negative matrix factorization, sparse representation, and model based techniques. Each method has its own advantages. As shown in the example, combinations of these techniques may achieve better separation performance. We have also briefly discussed the application areas of the cocktail party processing. Future research may include reducing the room effect on an auditory mixture, dealing with the unknown number of sources and unknown type of sources, handling dynamic listening environment for multiple moving speakers, and analyzing the multimodal auditory data.

REFERENCES

Ainhoren, Y., Engelberg, S., & Friedman, S. (2008). *The cocktail party problem*. IEEE Instrumentation and Measurement Magazine.

Allen, J. & Berkley, D. (1979). Image method for efficiently simulating small-room acoustics, *J. of the Acoustical Soc. Am.* (pp. 943-950), 65(4).

Amari, S., Douglas, S. C., Cichocki, A., & Wang, H. H. (1997). Multichannel blind deconvolution and equalization using the natural gradient, *in Proc. IEEE Workshop Signal Process* (pp. 101–104).

Araki, S., Makino, S., Sawada, H., & Mukai, R. (2004). Underdetermined blind separation of convolutive mixtures of speech with directivity pattern based mask and ICA. *In Proc. 5th International Conference Independent Component Anal. Blind Signal Separation* (pp. 898–905).

Araki, S., Makino, S., Sawada, H., & Mukai, R. (2005). Reducing musical noise by a fine-shift overlap-add method applied to source separation using a time-frequency mask. *In Proc. IEEE International Conference Acoustics, Speech. Signal Processing, 3*, 81–84.

Araki, S., Mukai, R., Makino, S., & Saruwatari, H. (2003). The fundamental limitation of frequency domain blind source separation for convolutive mixture of speech. *IEEE Transactions on Speech and Audio Processing, 11*, 109–116. doi:10.1109/TSA.2003.809193

Araki, S., Sawada, H., Mukai, R., & Makino, S. (2007). Underdetermined blind sparse source separation for arbitrarily arranged multiple sources. In *EURASIP Journal App (Vol. 87*, pp. 1833–1847). Signal Process.

Arons, B. (1992). A review of the cocktail party effect. *Journal of the American Voice I/O Society, 12*, 35-50

Back, A. D., & Tosi, A. C. (1994). Blind deconvolution of signals using a complex recurrent network. In *Proc. IEEE Workshop Neural Networks Signal Process.* (pp. 565–574).

Barker, J. (2006). Robust automatic speech recognition. In Wang, D., & Brown, G. J. (Eds.), *Computational auditory scene analysis: Principles, algorithms, and applications* (pp. 297–350). Hoboken, NJ: Wiley-IEEE Press.

Blauert, J. (1983). *Spatial hearing: The psychophysics of human sound localization* (rev. Ed.). Cambridge, MA: MIT Press.

Blumensath, T., & Davies, M. (2007). Compressed sensing and source separation. In *International Conference on Independent Component Anal and Blind Source Separation.*

Bofill, P., & Zibulevsky, M. (2001). Underdetermined blind source separation using sparse representations. *Signal Processing*, 2353–2362. doi:10.1016/S0165-1684(01)00120-7

Bregman, A. S. (1990). *Auditory Scene Analysis.* Cambridge, MA: MIT Press.

Bronkhorst, A. (2000). The cocktail party phenomenon: A review of research on speech intelligibility in multiple talker condition. *Acoustica, 86*, 117–128.

Brown, G. J., & Cooke, M. (1994). Computational auditory scene analysis. *Computer Speech & Language, 8*(4), 297–336. doi:10.1006/csla.1994.1016

Buchner, H., Aichner, R., & Kellermann, W. (2004). Blind source separation for convolutive mixtures: A unified treatment. In Huang, Y., & Benesty, J. (Eds.), *Audio Signal Process. for Next-Generation Multimedia Communication Systems* (pp. 255–293). Boston, Dordrecht, London: Kluwer Academic Publishers. doi:10.1007/1-4020-7769-6_10

Candès, E. (2006). Compressive sampling. In *Proceedings of the International Congress of Mathematics*. Madrid, Spain. Candès, E. & Romberg, J. Sparsity and incoherence in compressive sampling. *Inverse Prob. 23*(3), 969–985

Candès, E. J., & Wakin, M. B. (2008). An introduction to compressive sampling. In *IEEE Signal Process Magazine*. (21).

Cherry, E. C. (1953). Some experiments on the recognition of speech, with one and with two ears. *The Journal of the Acoustical Society of America, 25*, 975–979. doi:10.1121/1.1907229

Cichocki, A., & Amari, S. (2002). *Adaptive Blind Signal and Image Processing*. New York: Wiley Press. doi:10.1002/0470845899

Cichocki, A., Zdunek, R., & Amari, S. (2006). New algorithms for non-negative matrix factorization in applications to blind source separation. In *Proc. ICASSP* (Vol. 5, pp. 621–624) Toulouse, France.

Cooke, M., & Ellis, D. (2001). The auditory organization of speech and other sources in listeners and computational models. *Speech Communication, 35*, 141–177. doi:10.1016/S0167-6393(00)00078-9

Cooke, M. P. (Dec 2002). Computational Auditory Scene Analysis in Listeners and Machines, *Tutorial at NIPS2002*, Vancouver, Canada.

Davies, M., & Mitianoudis, N. (2004, Aug). A simple mixture model for sparse overcomplete ICA. *IEE Proceedings. Vision Image and Signal Processing, 151*(1), 35–43. doi:10.1049/ip-vis:20040304

Deng, L., & O'Shaughnessy, D. (2003). *Speech processing: A dynamic and optimization-oriented approach, ser. signal processing and communications*. London: Marcel Dekker, Taylor & Francis.

Donoho, D. (2006). Compressed sensing. *IEEE Transactions on Information Theory, 52*(4), 1289–1306. doi:10.1109/TIT.2006.871582

Douglas, S., Sawada, H., & Makino, S. (2005, Jan). Natural gradient multichannel blind deconvolution and speech separation using causal FIR filters. *IEEE Transactions on Speech and Audio Processing, 13*(1), 92–104. doi:10.1109/TSA.2004.838538

Douglas, S. C., & Sun, X. (2002). Convolutive blind separation of speech mixtures using the natural gradient. *Speech Communication, 39*, 65–78. doi:10.1016/S0167-6393(02)00059-6

Feng, A. S., & Ratnam, R. (2000). Neural basis of hearing in real-world situations. *Annual Review of Psychology, 51*, 699–725. doi:10.1146/annurev.psych.51.1.699

Fevotte, C., & Godsill, S. (2005). A bayesian approach for blind separation of sparse sources, In *IEEE Transactions on Speech and Audio Processing*. Washington D.C.

FitzGerald, D., Cranitch, M., & Coyle, E. (2005). Shifted non-negative matrix factorization for sound source separation. In *Proc. IEEE Int. Workshop on Statistical Signal Process*. Bordeaux, France (pp.1132-1137).

FitzGerald, D., Cranitch, M., & Coyle, E. (2006) Sound source separation using shifted non-negative tensor factorization. In *Proc. IEEE Int. Conf. on Acoust., Speech, and Signal Process., 5*, 653-656.

Gygi, B., Kidd, G. R., & Watson, C. S. (2004). Spectral-temporal factors in the identification of environmental sounds. *The Journal of the Acoustical Society of America, 115*(3), 1252–1265. doi:10.1121/1.1635840

Hall, D. E. (2001). *Musical Acoustics* (3rd ed.). Florence, Kentucky: Brooks Cole.

Haykin, S., & Chen, Z. (2005). The Cocktail Party Problem. *Journal Paper* [Cambridge, MA: MIT Press.]. *Neural Computation, 17,* 1875–1902. doi:10.1162/0899766054322964

Hyvarinen, A., Karhunen, J., & Oja, E. (2001). *Independent Component Analysis.* John Wiley and Sons. doi:10.1002/0471221317

Ichir, M. H. & Djafari, A. M. (Jul 2006). Hidden markov models for wavelet based blind source separation, *IEEE Transaction on Image Process.* (pp. 1887–1899), vol. 15.

Jan, T. U., Wang, W., & Wang, D. L. (2009). A multistage approach for blind separation of convolutive speech mixtures. In *Proc ICASSP* (pp. 1713-1716). Taiwan.

Jan, T. U., Wang, W., & Wang, D. L. (2010). A multistage approach to blind separation of convolutive speech mixtures. In *IEEE Trans.* Audio Speech and Language Processing.

John, H., & Wendy, H. (2001). *Speech synthesis and recognition* (2nd ed.). London: Taylor & Francis.

Jourjine, A., Rickard, S., & Yılmaz, O˝. (2000). Blind separation of disjoint orthogonal signals: demixing N sources from 2 mixtures. In *Proc. ICASSP* (Vol. 5, pp. 2985–8). Turkey.

Junqua, J. C., & Haton, J. P. (1995). *Robustness in Automatic Speech Recognition: Fundamentals and Applications.* London: Kluwer Academic Publishers.

Kocinski, J. (2008). Speech intelligibility improvement using convolutive blind source separation assisted by denoising algorithms. In *EURASIP Journal. Speech Communication, 50,* 29–37. doi:10.1016/j.specom.2007.06.003

Lambert, R. H., & Bell, A. J. (1997). Blind separation of multiple speakers in a multipath environment. In *Proc. IEEE International Conference Acoustics, Speech Signal Process.* (pp. 423–426).

Laurberg, H., Christensen, M. G., Plumbley, M. D., Hansen, L. K., & Jensen, S. H. (2008). *Theorems on positive data: on the uniqueness of NMF.* Computational Intelligence and Neuroscience.

Lee, D. D. & Seung, H. S. (1999). *Learning of the parts of object by non-negative matrix factorization, nature, 401*(10), 788-791.

Lee, D. D., & Seung, H. S. (2001). *Algorithms for non-negative matrix factorization. Advances in neural information processing* (pp. 556–562). Cambridge, MA: MIT Press.

Lee, T. W. (1998). *Independent Component Anal: Theory and Applications.* London: Kluwer Academic Publishers.

Lee, T. W., Bell, A. J., & Orglmeister, R. (1997). Blind source separation of real world signals. In *Proc. IEEE International Conference Neural Networks* (pp. 2129–2135).

Lippmann, R. P. (1997). Speech recognition by machines and humans. *Speech Communication, 22,* 1–15. doi:10.1016/S0167-6393(97)00021-6

Madhu, N., Breithaupt, C., & Martin, R. (2008). Temporal smoothing of spectral masks in the cepstral domain for speech separation. In *Proc. ICASSP* (pp. 45–48).

Makino, S., Sawada, H., Mukai, R., & Araki, S. (2005). Blind source separation of convolutive mixtures of speech in frequency domain. In *IEICE Trans. Fundamentals. E (Norwalk, Conn.), 88-A*(7), 1640–1655.

Mango, K. N. (1991). *Hearing loss.* New York: Franklin Watts.

Matsuoka, K., & Nakashima, S. (2001). Minimal distortion principle for blind source separation. In *Proc. International Conference Independent Component Anal* (pp. 722–727), San Diego, CA, USA.

Mitianondis, N. & Davies, M. (2002). Audio source separation: solutions and problems. *International Journal of Adaptive Control and Signal Process.* (pp. 1–6).

Mukai, R., Sawada, H., Araki, S., & Makino, S. (2004) Frequency domain blind source separation for many speech signals. In *Proc. International Conference Independent Component Anal* (pp. 461-469).

Murata, N., Ikeda, S., & Ziehe, A. (2001, Oct). An approach to blind source separation based on temporal structure of speech signals. *Neuro Comput, 41*(1-4), 1–24.

Naqvi, S. M., Zhang, Y., & Chambers, J. A. (2009). Multimodal blind source separation for moving sources. In *Proc ICASSP* (pp. 125-128), Taiwan.

Nickel, R. M., & Iyer, A. N. (2006). A novel approach to automated source separation in multispeaker environments. In *Proc. IEEE ICASSP* (pp. 629–632).

O'Shaughnessy, D. (2000). Speech communications-human and machin (2nd Ed.) In *Institute of electrical and electronic engineers.* New York.

Olsson, R. K., & Hansen, L. K. (2006). Blind separation of more sources than sensors in convolutive mixtures. In *Proc. IEEE ICASSP* (pp. 657–660).

Oppenheim, A. V., & Schafer, R. W. (1975). *Digital Signal Processing.* New Jersey: Prentice Hall.

Parra, L., & Spence, C. (2000). Convolutive blind separation of non stationary sources. *IEEE Transactions on Speech and Audio Processing, 8,* 320–327. doi:10.1109/89.841214

Parry, R. M., & Essa, I. (2007). Incorporating phase information for source separation via spectrogram factorization. In *Proc. IEEE Int. Conf. on Acoust., Speech, and Signal Process, 2,* 661-664. Honolulu, Hawaii.

Pearlmutter, B. A., & Zador, A. M. (2004). Monaural source separation using spectral cues. In *Proc. ICA 2004* (pp. 478–485).

Pedersen, M. S., Wang, D. L., Larsen, J., & Kjems, U. (2008). Two-microphone separation of speech mixtures. *IEEE Transactions on Neural Networks, 19,* 475–492. doi:10.1109/TNN.2007.911740

Radfar, M. H., & Dansereau, R. M. (2007). Single channel speech separation using soft mask filtering. In *IEEE Trans. on Audio* (*Vol. 15,* pp. 2299–2310). Speech and Language Process.

Radfar, M. H., Dansereau, R. M., & Sayadiyan, A. (2006). Performance evaluation of three features for model-based single channel speech separation problem. In *Interspeech 2006, International Conference Spoken Language Process.* (ICSLP06), Pittsburgh, PA, (pp. 2610–2613).

Sawada, H., Araki, S., Mukai, R., & Makino, S. (2007). Grouping separated frequency components by estimating propagation model parameters in frequency domain blind source separation. In *IEEE Transaction Speech Audio Language Process.* (Vol. 15, pp. 1592–1604).

Sawada, H., Mukai, R., Araki, S., & Makino, S. (2003). Polar coordinate based nonlinear function for frequency-domain blind source separation. In *IEICE Transactions Fundamentals,* E86 (3), 590–596.

Sawada, H., Mukai, R., Araki, S., & Makino, S. (2004). A robust and precise method for solving the permutation problem of frequency domain blind source separation. *IEEE Transactions on Speech and Audio Processing, 12,* 530–538. doi:10.1109/TSA.2004.832994

Schmidt, M. N., & Laurberg, H. (2008). *Non-negative matrix factorization with Gaussian process priors*. Computational Intelligence and Neuroscience.

Schmidt, M. N., & Morup, M. (2006). Nonnegative matrix factor 2D deconvolution for blind single channel source separation. In *Proc. 6th Int. Conf. on Independent Component Analysis and Blind Signal Separation*. Charleston, SC, USA, (pp. 700-707).

Schmidt, M. N., & Olsson, R. K. (2006). *Single-channel speech separation using sparse non-negative matrix factorization*. Interspeech.

Schobben, L., & Sommen, W. (2002). A frequency domain blind signal separation method based on decorrelation. *IEEE Transactions on Signal Processing, 50*(8), 1855–1865. doi:10.1109/TSP.2002.800417

Smaragdis, P. (2004). Non-negative matrix factor deconvolution, extraction of multiple sound sources from monophonic inputs. In *Proc. 5th Int. Conf. on Independent Component Analysis and Blind Signal Separation*. Granada, Spain, (LNCS 3195, pp.494-499).

Smaragdis, P. (2007). Convolutive speech bases and their application to supervised speech separation. In *IEEE Trans. Audio Speech and Language Processing, 15*(1), 1-12.

Smaragdis, P., & Brown, J. C. (2003). Nonnegative matrix factorization for polyphonic music transcription. In *IEEE Int. Workshop on Applications of Signal Process. to Audio and Acoustics*, New Paltz, NY. (pp. 177-180).

Soon, V. C., Tong, L., Huang, Y. F., & Liu, R. (1993). A robust method for wideband signal separation. In *Proc. IEEE International Symposium Circuits Systems* (Vol.1, pp. 703–706).

Todros, K., & Tabrikian, J. (2004) Blind separation of non stationary and non gaussian independent sources. In *Proc. IEEE Convention of Electrical and Electronics in Israel.*

University of Sheffield, Department of Computer Science. (2007). *Auditory scene analysis: Listening to several things at once*. Retrieved on June 27, 2009 from http://www.dcs.shef.ac.uk/spandh/research/asa.html

Virtanen, T. (2007). Monaural sound source separation by nonnegative matrix factorization with temporal continuity and sparseness criteria. In *IEEE Trans. Audio, Speech, and Language Process, 15,* (3).

Wang, B., & Plumbley, M. D. (2005). Musical audio stream separation by non-negative matrix factorization. In *Proc. DMRN Summer Conference*. Glasgow, UK.

Wang, D. L. (2005). On ideal binary mask as the computational goal of auditory scene analysis. In Divenyi, P. (Ed.), *Speech Separation by Humans and Machines* (pp. 181–197). Norwell, MA: Kluwer Academic. doi:10.1007/0-387-22794-6_12

Wang, D. L., & Brown, G. J. (1999, May). Separation of speech from interfering sounds based on oscillatory correlation. *IEEE Transactions on Neural Networks, 10,* 684–697. doi:10.1109/72.761727

Wang, D. L., & Brown, G. J. (2006). *Computational Auditory Scene Analysis: Principles, Algorithms, and Applications*. Hoboken, NJ: Wiley/IEEE Press.

Wang, W. (2007). Squared Euclidean distance based convolutive non-negative matrix factorization with multiplicative learning rules for audio pattern separation. In *Proc. IEEE Int. Symp. on Signal Proces. and Info. Tech.* Cairo, Egypt.

Wang, W., Cichocki, A., & Chambers, J. A. (2009). A multiplicative algorithm for convolutive non-negative matrix factorization based on squared Euclidean distance. In *IEEE Trans* (pp. 447–452). On Signal Processing.

Wang, W., Luo, Y., Sanei, S., & Chambers, J. A. (2008). Note onset detection via non-negative factorization of magnitude spectrum, In *EURASIP Journal on Advances in Signal Processing* (pp. 447-452).

Wang, W., Sanei, S., & Chambers, J. A. (2005). Penalty function-based joint diagnolization approach for convolutive blind separation of nonstationary sources. *IEEE Transactions on Signal Processing, 53*, 1654–1669. doi:10.1109/TSP.2005.845433

Wu, M., & Wang, D. L. (2006). A two-stage algorithm for one-microphone reverberant speech enhancement. In *IEEE Transaction on Audio, Speech, and Language Process, 14*.

Xu, T., & Wang, W. (2009). A compressed sensing approach for underdetermined blind audio source separation with sparse representations. In *Proc. IEEE Int. Workshop on Statistical Signal Processing*. (pp. 493-496). Cardiff, UK.

Xu, T., & Wang, W. (2010). A block-based compressed sensing method for underdetermined blind speech separation incorporating binary mask. In *Proc. IEEE Int. Conf. on Acoustics, Speech and Signal Processing*. Texas, USA.

Yegnanarayana, B., & Murthy, P. S. (2000, May). Enhancement of reverberant speech using LP residual signal. *IEEE Transactions on Speech and Audio Processing, 8*(3), 267–281. doi:10.1109/89.841209

Yost, W. A. (1997). The cocktail party problem: Forty years later. In Gilkey, R., & Anderson, T. (Eds.), *Binaural and spatial hearing in real and virtual environments* (pp. 329–348). Ahwah, NJ: Erlbaum.

Yost, W. A. (2000). *Fundamentals of hearing: An introduction* (4th ed.). San Diego: Academic Press.

Zibulevsky, M., & Bofill, P. (2001). Underdetermined blind source separation using sparse representations. *Signal Processing, 81*(11), 2353–2362. doi:10.1016/S0165-1684(01)00120-7

Zibulevsky, M., & Pearlmutter, B. A. (2001). Blind source separation by sparse decomposition in a signal dictionary. *Neural Computation, 13*(4), 863–882. doi:10.1162/089976601300014385

Chapter 4
Audition:
From Sound to Sounds

Tjeerd C. Andringa
University of Groningen, Netherlands

ABSTRACT

This chapter addresses the functional requirements of auditory systems, both natural and artificial, to be able to deal with the complexities of uncontrolled real-world input. The demand to function in uncontrolled environments has severe implications for machine audition. The natural system has addressed this demand by adapting its function flexibly to changing task demands. Intentional processes and the concept of perceptual gist play an important role in this. Hearing and listening are seen as complementary processes. The process of hearing detects the existence and general character of the environment and its main and most salient sources. In combination with task demands these processes allow the pre-activation of knowledge about expected sources and their properties. Consecutive listening phases, in which the relevant subsets of the signal are analyzed, allow the level of detail required by task and system-demands. This form of processing requires a signal representation that can be reasoned about. A representation based on source physics is suitable and has the advantage of being situation independent. The demand to determine physical source properties from the signal imposes restrictions on the signal processing. When these restrictions are not met, systems are limited to controlled domains. Novel signal representations are needed to couple the information in the signal to knowledge about the sources in the signal.

INTRODUCTION

This chapter addresses machine audition and natural audition by carefully analyzing the difficulties

and roles of audition in real-world conditions. The reason for this focus is my experience with the development of a verbal aggression detection system (van Hengel and Andringa, 2007). This system was first deployed in 2004 and 2005 in the inner city of Groningen (the Netherlands), by the

DOI: 10.4018/978-1-61520-919-4.ch004

company Sound Intelligence, and helps the police to prioritize camera feeds. It is the first commercial sound recognition application for a complex target in uncontrolled (city) environments.

Furthermore, the system is a prototypical and a rather idiosyncratic example of machine audition. It is prototypical because it must function, like its natural counter part, in realistic and therefore complex social environments. Inner cities are complex because they are full of people who speak, shout, play, laugh, tease, murmur, sell, run, fall, kick, break, whistle, sing, and cry. The same environment contains birds that sing, dogs that bark, cars that pass or slam with doors, police and ambulances that pass with wailing sirens and screeching tires, pubs that play music, wind that whines, rain that clatters, builders who build, and many, many other rare or common sound events.

What makes the system idiosyncratic is simple: *it must ignore all these sounds*. The simplest way of doing this is to make it deaf. However, there is one type of sound that should not be ignored: verbal aggression. Of the 2,678,400 seconds each week, the system is interested in about 10 seconds of verbal aggression and has to ignore the other 2.6 million seconds. Fortunately the situation is not as bleak as it seems. The police observers may graciously allow the system some false alarms, as long as the majority of them are informative and justifiable. This means that the system is allowed to select no more than about 50 seconds per month, which corresponds to 0.002% of the time. Ignoring almost everything, while remaining vigilant for the occasional relevant event, is an essential property of the natural auditory system. It requires the (subconscious) processing of perceptual information up to the point of estimated irrelevancy. That is exactly what the system aims to do.

After a considerable period of optimization the system worked (and works) adequately. However it has one major restriction: the system is not easily extended or adapted to other tasks and environments. Every migration to a new city

or new operating environment requires some expert-time to readjust the system. Although this is a restriction the system has in common with other applications of machine learning and pattern recognition, it is qualitatively different from the performance of human audition. In general, the comparison between a natural and an artificial system is not favorable for the artificial system. In fact, it is quite a stretch to refer to the function of the verbal aggression detection system as similar to audition: I consider the comparison degrading for the richness, versatility, robustness, and helpfulness of the natural auditory system.

My experiences with the development of the verbal aggression detection system have led me to reconsider my approach to machine audition. This chapter aims at the functional demands of audition, both natural and artificial, because I consider the functional level the level where most progress can be made. The functional level is both beneficial for theories about the natural system and for the design of technology that can function on par with its natural counter-part.

Working with police-observers, who are not at all interested in the technology itself, but only in whether or not it actually helps them, was also revealing. Expectation management was essential to ensure a favorable evaluation and the eventual definitive deployment of the first system. This is why I use a common sense definition of audition as starting point and why I aim to develop systems that comply with common-sense expectations. Only these systems will be truly impressive for the end-user.

The chapter addresses four connected topics. The next section addresses the demands that operating in the real world poses on a system. It is followed by an investigation into the special options that sounds offer as source of information about the environments. This forms the basis for the longest section, which addresses how the natural system detects the relevance in the signal and can analyze it up to the desired degree. The flexible and knowledge intensive analysis requires signal representations that are situation independent. The properties of these representations form the topic of the next section that suggests that sonic knowledge should represent source physics to some degree. The chapter is concluded with a short vision on the possible future of machine audition applications.

The chapter will not provide definite answers, nor ready to implement algorithms, but it will provide a number of design constraints that help to design and build systems that approach the performance of that of a human listener, and that, in my opinion, truly deserve the term machine audition.

REAL WORLD DEMANDS

Scientific Challenges

Research that is aimed at building systems endowed with cognitive functions normally associated with people or animals is becoming increasingly important to our information society. Such cognitive systems should exhibit a high degree of robustness and flexibility in coping with unpredictable situations and to handle simple everyday situations with common sense and without detailed pre-programming (http://cordis.europa.eu/fp7/ict/ cognition/home_en.html). True cognitive systems prove their value in open-ended environments. A EU program manager stated this bluntly as: "Stop making toy-systems! We know you can do that. Impress us outside the lab!" (Roberto Cencioni at SAMT2006). This statement refers to an important limitation of current technology that becomes apparent whenever scientists and engineers attempt to scale-up laboratory demonstrators of intelligent systems to actual applications that can deal with real-world conditions.

For example, despite considerable technological progress, exponentially increasing computational power, and massive training databases,

automatic speech recognition (ASR) has been a promising technology for more than 30 years (O'Shaughnessy, 2008). During all these years ASR-systems have never been able to impress a majority of potential users (the observation that many pc-users do not know or care that their computers has preinstalled ASR-software is testimony of this). It is likely that these ASR-systems constrain the majority of users more than they prefer. Although the performance in terms of recognition accuracy on benchmark tests has improved immensely, the basic probabilistic architecture and robustness of ASR systems has remained the same. It is possible this approach suffers from the fundamental limitations characteristic of modern intelligent systems. Since natural audition can deal with the complexities of the real world it is instructive to contrast the two types of systems.

Natural Intelligence

A natural intelligent system, such as a human listener, is extremely versatile; both in terms of function and operating environment. A single auditory system can perform a multitude of different functions that vary from detecting an animal rustling between leaves, determining the temperature of tea being poured in a cup, identifying a problem with a car, recognizing a similar melody when played on different instruments, to recognizing speech. In addition, the operating environment of a natural auditory system can be very complex in the sense that it may contain many different objects and processes. It may also be partially or largely unknown and variable. And finally it is unlimited in the sense that novel events can be introduced at any time and that the sonic world may be extended indefinitely. Basically, a natural intelligent system can dynamically adapt to the demands that complex, unknown, variable, and unlimited environments pose. Humans, therefore, only need a single auditory system for all sonic tasks and environments.

Artificial Intelligence

Although system designers aim to make systems as versatile as possible, the operating environment of engineering systems is fundamentally limited by the definition of the task to be executed: a dictation system is not a keyword-spotting device. The seemingly innocent choice to build a single-function system limits engineering to a different domain than natural systems. The rational is that dictation systems pose different demands than keyword spotting devices, and music genre detection poses different demands than verbal aggression detection. By focusing on task-specific demands it is assumed that effective technology can be developed more efficiently, because irrelevant functionality does not have to be developed. This is a very dangerous assumption because the existence of (natural) multipurpose systems that can perform these tasks is no proof that single purpose systems can perform individual tasks. It is quite possible that some level of "multi-purposeness" is essential for the robust execution of single tasks in real-world environments.

For current technology to function optimally, or even adequately, it is important to impose limitations on the operating environment. Typically, the operation environment must be simplified to one source that must be known in advance and of which the properties are assumed to be constant and representative of the training data. For modern ASR-systems one can even conclude that they have been designed for input of which everything except the word order is known. Essentially, the operating environment must be limited to conditions the system can handle. All additional uncertainty will reduce the reliability of the results. In other words, these systems require the user to keep the operating environment under control. Without the user's essential role in controlling the environment, the output of the system is unspecified. At best it withholds output (which might be erroneous as well), at worst it produces random results, i.e. results with no apparent relation to

the input. All in all, the current approaches lead to a large number of task and domain specific systems in combination with an essential role for a human user to prevent nonsense output. Figure 1 depicts the scope of human and artificial tasks and operating environments. Modern technology is clearly limited to a subset of the human scope.

Each new prototype shows that scientists and engineers can develop task and domain specific systems and applications. Although the intellectual challenge of adding advanced new example systems and applications might be considerable, the true scientific challenge is to develop new strategies for intelligent systems that, by design, remove the limits of modern technology. A good starting point is to study the demands of functioning in a world without simplifications: the real world if you like.

We will describe the flexibility of the natural perceptive system to change its tasks and to rely on a smart interplay between bottom-up and top-down processing. But we will start with a study of the functional role of the auditory system. This role will be approached from a common sense definition that reflects how non-experts think and talk about audition and secondly from an exploratory perspective on the opportunities offered by modern perception research.

THE FUNCTIONAL ROLE OF THE AUDITORY SYSTEM

Common Sense Definitions

Experts often use different and typically more constrained terminology than non-experts. This may be confusing in cases where expert terminology utilizes common words for a specific domain-dependent purpose. The term "machine audition" might have this confusing aspect because it suggests a strong relation between a class of applications and a highly developed, intimately familiar but partially understood natural ability.

Figure 1. The typical scope of human task operating environments extends from complex tasks in uncontrolled environments to simple tasks in controlled environments. Modern applications are limited to simple tasks in controlled environments. The dashed gray bar denotes the likely scope limitation of modern technology.

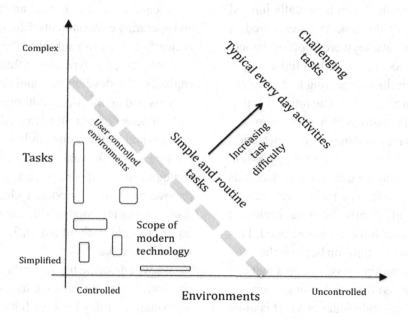

Researchers in the field of machine audition will always be confronted with user-expectations based on common sense notions of audition. Therefore, it is instructive to study common-sense definitions of audition and related words to make the expectations of the users of the technology explicit. Because the definitions within a single dictionary show often a high degree of circularity (a=b=a), the definitions selected below here have been derived from a range of (online) dictionaries. All selected definitions are quoted verbatim.

For the word "audition" one might find for example:

- **Audition (noun):** the act, sense, or power of hearing.

Audition therefore refers either to the activity of hearing like in the case of "involving an act of hearing", or secondly "the sense of hearing as similar to the sense of vision", and thirdly "the

enabling capacity to hear". Because dictionaries define words using other words this leads to the problem of defining the word "hearing". Of this word there are two relevant variants:

- **To hear (verb):** perceive with the ear the sound made by someone or something.
- **Hearing (noun):** the faculty of perceiving sounds.

Of the two definitions the first refers to "the act of hearing", while the second refers to "the enabling capacity to hear". Both definitions combine variants of sound and perception that require a definition as well. Two different concepts of sound are introduced: 1) "a" or "the" sound and 2) sound (without article):

- **Sound (uncountable noun):** vibrations that travel through the air or other media and can be heard when they reach a person's or animal's ear.

- **A sound (countable noun):** audible sound stemming from someone or something.

The uncountable noun refers to the physical phenomenon. The countable noun uses the uncountable noun with the adjective audible. With a focus on "sound" it refers to the audible subset of the physical phenomenon that originated from a single source, but with the focus on "audible" it refers to the role of the sound source in audition.

For the verb to perceive and its noun perception one can find:

- **To perceive (verb):** become aware or conscious of something [through the senses].
- **Perception (noun):** the ability to become aware of something through the senses.

Perception refers to more senses than hearing alone. However, when applied to hearing, the first definition specifies the "act of hearing", while the second specifies "the enabling capacity to hear". These definitions refer to the adjectives aware and conscious.

- **Aware (adjective):** noticing or realizing something, knowing that something exists because you notice it or realize that it is happening.
- **Conscious (adjective):** keenly aware, fully appreciating the importance of something.

Apparently "being aware" and "being conscious" differ in degree, but both refer to being able to include the existence of something in a reasoning process. "Being aware of something" refers to knowledge of its existence, while "conscious of something" refers to fully appreciating its consequences. The difference between the two degrees is reflected in the words hearing and listening. Hearing in the sense of "can you hear the boy?" may be a question directed at whether or not the boy was audible. The question "did you listen to the boy" presupposes a more detailed analysis of what you heard. Consequently, the difference between hearing and listening seems to correspond to the difference between a passive and a more active process. In fact listening and listener can be defined as:

- **Listening (verb):** making an effort to hear something
- **Listening to (verb):** to give one's attention to a sound
- **Listener (noun):** someone who listens, especially someone who does so in an attentive manner

These definitions introduce the term "attention" of which one dictionary definition reads:

- **Attention (noun):** concentration of mental powers, especially on a particular object

The "concentration of mental powers" in this definition involves memory and reasoning. When memory and reasoning are focused on a particular object we can use the memories we have stored about it to reason about the object and its consequences, In other words, we can determine its meaning:

- **Meaning (noun):** inner importance, psychological or moral sense, purpose, or significance

While the users of a language negotiate the meaning of a word, the meaning of something for someone is the individual importance one gives to a thing.

Elaborated Common Sense Definition of Audition

Most dictionary definitions so far have used words like object, something, and someone to denote an event, thing, object, or person in the world. The perception process makes these available for the perceiver. It is now possible to formulate an elaborated common sense definition of audition based on the previous dictionary definitions.

Audition (noun): the capacity for, or act of sound-based processing in which the existence of something or someone becomes mentally available (in the case of awareness), this availability can be used in a reasoning process to discover the consequences of what has been perceived (in the case of consciousness).

Someone who is limited to the passive form of audition can be called "a hearer", but this term is rarely used in this context. Furthermore future systems for machine audition will typically be required to assist content based reasoning and automated decision-making, the active process is consequently very relevant for machine audition. If (human, animal, or natural) audition is to be contrasted to machine audition it is reasonable to contrast a listener to a system for machine audition.

The elaborated common sense definition is consistent with modern insights in perception (see section Audition = hearing + listening). It will be argued that the sound induced processes that lead to awareness, correspond to hearing and that the more detailed conscious analysis is typical of listening (Harding et al., 2007). The "problem" with the elaborated common sense definition of audition is that there are no easy short cuts to understand the phenomenon of audition. Awareness and conscious processing are intimately involved in audition. The design of systems that approach the common sense expectations of most users requires some engineering equivalent of these phenomena. This does not imply that we have to wait until computers are conscious. It only indicates that some of the essential functional consequences of both awareness and consciousness cannot be ignored. The properties of attention will be a guideline to formulate these ingredients.

Another apparent complication is the requirement that audition has to work reliably in the real world. However it will be argued that real-world constraints pose a number of very helpful restrictions to guide the development of models of audition. The next sections make a first step in that direction by addressing the special possibilities that sound affords as a channel to derive information from the environment.

The Specialties of Audition

Each sense has unique strength and limitations. Sound for example is caused by mechanically interacting objects and carries detailed information about the objects and their interaction (Gaver, 1993). A direct consequence of this is that it makes sense to ask the question "What caused the sound?" In the case of vision, light-sources like the sun or lamps produce or cause the light that we see. But in the visual domain the most relevant question is not "What caused the light?" but "Which objects reflected the light last?" The related question "What reflected the sound last?" is generally less important, but it is of particular relevance for echolocating animals and blind people.

The answer to the question "What caused the sound?" requires a transformation from sound as a physical phenomenon to sounds as an interpreted sound. The interpreted sound refers either to an interpretation as a real-world cause (an explanation like "I hear a car") or to the subsets of the signal that belong to the sources that the sounds refer to ("This part of the sound is caused by a car"). The answer to "What caused the sound" can be used as further specification of the common sense definition of audition. Audition may even be defined as the process that makes sounds from sound, hence the subtitle of this chapter.

Compared to light, sound carries less far, which limits sonic information to the proximal environment. Furthermore, visual processing is spatially oriented while auditory processing is spectrally oriented. Both the visual and the auditory system are computationally limited and the whole system needs to make choices concerning what to process superficially and what to process in detail. The visual field covers only a subset of all spatial directions and only a tiny fraction with a cross-section of 3° can be analyzed in detail. Consequently, it is not trivial to aim detailed visual analysis at the most relevant region of space. Because auditory information is spectrally oriented, spectral information from all directions is pooled, which makes auditory sensitivity omnidirectional. This omnidirectionality, in combination with sounds being informative of mechanical interactions in the proximal environment, implies that audition has properties that make it very suitable to monitor the proximal environment.

A special and highly relevant aspect of the interaction with an unpredictable environment is the ability to detect and analyze unexpected but potentially important events. The combination with the directional sensitivity of binaural integration allows audition to guide visual attention to the correct spatial region. Responding to unexpected events requires audition to interrupt ongoing mental activities in favor of analyzing the unexpected event. This has a negative consequence when the unexpected event is not worth the interruption. Irrelevant sonic events that interrupt mental activities and interfere with the tasks and goals of the individual are annoying. The prominence of noise annoyance in our society forms strong support for audition's role in detecting unexpected and potentially relevant events.

Masking and Reverberation

While listeners move around, they are exposed to a wealth of different sound sources in a wealth of acoustically different spaces. Some of the sources may be intimately familiar, others completely novel. Some may be proximal and with a favorable signal-to-noise ratio, others are partially masked by louder or more proximal sources. As a consequence much of the information of a source is masked by other sources. Whatever is still avail-able as reliable source information is distributed in varied ways over the time-frequency plane.

There is an important additional complication. Close to the source within the reverberation radius, direct sounds such as smoothly developing harmonics may be much more prominent than the sum of the indirect reflections of objects and walls. Outside reverberation radius the indirect sound dominates. Because the indirect sound consists of delayed copies of the direct sounds that recombine with random phase, the resulting signal shows fluctuations and temporal and spectral smearing that changes smoothly developing harmonics in fluctuating narrow-band noise. Consequently, the indirect contributions are quite different from direct sounds.

Hence reverberation will ensure that even when the relevant ranges of the time-frequency plane have been found the information it represents will appear quite different depending on the ratio between direct and indirect sounds. However, it takes a trained ear, or paired comparisons of speech samples recorded without and with reverberation, to detect these prominent effects on the signal (Nábělek & Robinson, 1982). The same amount of indirect sound poses ASR-systems with serious fluctuations on the input parameterization that impair the recognition process. This is the reason that most ASR-systems require the use of a close-talking microphone.

Everyday vs. Musical Listening

The qualitative difference in sensitivity to reverberation is indicative of the relevance of the question "What caused the sound?" Human auditory processing seems to focus on the cause of the sounds, while modern ASR-systems seem to focus on the detailed properties of the sound and not its probable cause. The difference between cause and signal properties is reflected in Gaver's (Gaver, 1993) distinction between everyday listening and musical listening. Everyday listening refers to a description of the sounds (as countable noun) in terms of the processes or events that produced them. For example, we do not hear a noisy harmonic complex in combination with a burst of noise; instead we hear a passing car. Likewise we do not hear a double pulse with prominent energy around 2.4 and 6 kHz, but we hear a closing door. In contrast, musical listening focuses on the properties of sound (as uncountable noun) and couples sensations like pitch and loudness to physical properties like frequency and amplitude. A typical aspect of musical listening is that we can focus on melodies, hear differences in the timbre of different instruments, and determine that someone sings at the wrong pitch.

Controlled vs. Uncontrolled Sounds

Considering all sources of variability in acoustic environments and the problems they pose to modern engineering systems, it makes sense to introduce the term uncontrolled sound as a sound of which no a priori knowledge is available: uncontrolled sounds can be any sound out of the set of all possible sound combinations. All knowledge about its contents must be derived from the signal itself. Arbitrary sounds can be contrasted to controlled sounds, in which some essential intervention has ensured that some of the problems of arbitrary sounds have been defined away. Recording with a close-talking microphone or telephone constrains the signal in a similar way as careful recording by a researcher does. In both cases it results in a limitation to a (convenient) subset of all possible sounds. For machine audition, it is important to distinguish approaches for controlled and uncontrolled sounds. In the case of controlled input the type of control needs to be defined as precise as possible. For example, the results reported by Cowling & Sitte (2003) on environmental sound recognition presuppose one typical instance of a sound source per recording. This constraint is quite severe for signals described as environmental sounds.

The Role of Meaning

The answer to the question "What caused the sound?" is only part of the task of a listener. According to the elaborated common sense definition of audition, the possible consequences of the sound producing events should be investigated in a reasoning process. Each audible sound contributes information. If this information is not included, behavioral options may be suboptimal and sometimes dangerously inadequate. Therefore, the auditory system should predict the consequences of the events in a proper context and in doing so give meaning to the event.

The term meaning is still ill defined, but the "meaning of something to someone" denotes the personal importance of something. The importance of something is of course personal and highly situation dependent. Hence the importance is defined through the interactions of the individual with its environment. The meaning of something for someone can be therefore defined as the difference between mental and behavioral states with and without it. If something affords strict behavioral options it is obviously meaningful. However if not including it does not change behavioral options, it is meaningless. Audition, and especially the process of listening, is about figuring out the most effective behavioral options afforded by the sounds. This process, which can be described as maximizing the meaning of sound, requires an intimate interaction between (auditory) perception, the rest of cognition, and the environment.

Note that the *meaning of something*, without a direct reference to a person, refers typically to the linguistic meaning of a thing. Linguistic meaning is a common denominator of personal meanings and is, as all words, the result of a negotiation between the users of a language to ensure that the use of the word leads to a predictable interpretation by a listener or reader. This form of meaning is not referred to in this chapter.

Maximizing the meaning of sound in terms of the effective behavior it affords can be considered the goal of machine audition as well. Take the example of a verbal aggression detection system that guides the attention of police observers to the most informative surveillance camera feeds (van Hengel & Andringa, 2007). Commercial systems like this wait for very rare, but highly significant, events by computing a moving average of signal evidence indicative of verbal aggression. The moment a threshold is exceeded, a possible aggressive event is indicated to the police observer for more detailed inspection. Because observers do not want to be bothered with a large number of "meaningless" events, the improvement of systems like these is aimed at making the output of the system as meaningful as possible. Ideally the systems should indicate, with explicit justification, why they considered this event as more relevant than all ignored events. Something similar is the case in dictation systems: meaningless or bizarre recognition results are less appreciated than an equal number of word-errors that do not change the meaning of the dictated message.

Summarizing the Role of Audition

The analysis of the functional role of audition in this section was based on the special properties of sound in combination with the demands a complex and uncontrolled operating environment pose. This led to a number of conclusions about the role of audition that are equally valid for human and machine audition. These can be summarized as follows:

- From sound to sounds: one purpose of audition is to separate sound in a way that explains the causes of the sounds that constitute it.
- Uncontrolled input: nothing is known in advance from the signal, consequently the signal itself (including its full history) must inform the system how it should be analyzed

- Work everywhere and always: internal representation must be based on knowledge that is always and everywhere applicable.
- Detect the unexpected: compare expectations with the actual signal and detect mismatches.
- Listening: the search for the most meaningful interpretation of the signal.

These conclusions will be elaborated in the course of this chapter. The next section focuses on the way attention helps to estimate task relevance.

ESTIMATING TASK-RELEVANCE

In uncontrolled environments the input is unconstrained. Therefore, an unknown fraction of the input will be relevant for the system's task. When the response of a system is based on either a random selection of evidence or on an arbitrary mixture of sources, it has no relation to the information in the signal and is extremely unlikely to be correct. Therefore, determining the relevant part of the signal is a prerequisite to correct task performance. One strategy to deal with the clutter of task-irrelevant contributions is to process each part of the input up to the moment it can be ignored without the risk of discarding essential information.

Attentive Listening

This leads to a central design guideline, namely that all input needs to be processed up to the point of estimated task-irrelevance. The naive approach is to hope that the target is much louder than the background so that the background can be easily ignored or discarded. This approach is helpful in many situations and in particular in situations in which the noise can be assumed to be stationary or known. However, extensive research on human audition in noise, called the cocktail-party effect (Cherry, 1953, Bronkhorst, 2000), has shown that listeners reliably detect and recognize speech (and other sources) in situations where the target speech is neither louder nor otherwise different from a "background" of babble sounds. In other words listeners can detect and recognize the target whenever there is a minimum of reliable evidence unmasked by the background (Allen, 1994). However, listeners must focus more and more attention on the task if the sonic environment becomes more challenging.

Attention is a core cognitive process that allows animals to selectively focus on one aspect of the environment while ignoring the rest. Attention is intimately related with the solution to dealing with uncontrolled environments because it ensures the efficient allocation and application of the brain's algorithmic and knowledge resources. For these reasons it is very useful to study the algorithmic properties of attentional processes in some detail.

Bottom-Up Attention

Attention has been a target of research for many decades, which has led to a consensus on a number of its key aspects. For example, it is possible to differentiate signal driven (bottom-up) and knowledge driven (top-down) attentional processes (Koch & Tsuchiya, 2007, Knudsen, 2007). In the first form, attention is captured by salient parts of the input, which can suspend the current mental task in favor of the analysis of the salience sound. Attention can be captured involuntarily by either sudden and/or unexpected changes in the situation or by well-trained stimuli (Gopher & Iani, 2003). The saliency of sudden or unexpected stimuli allows attention to be captured by mismatches between expected and actual input. Alternatively, the saliency of well-trained and personally relevant stimuli makes a conversation more difficult when you hear your own name mentioned in the background. Moreover, emotional stimuli like angry faces are easier to respond to than neutral faces in the same conditions (Whalen et al., 1998). Your name and emotional individuals are both of high

potential relevance for you as a system, which justifies a strong effect towards involuntarily suspending the current mental task or activity in favor of analyzing the unexpected or otherwise relevant stimulus.

Top-Down Attention and Consciousness

The top-down variant of attention is a prerequisite for advanced cognitive processes like reasoning, language, and the (strategic) analysis of complex input (Dehaene et al., 2006). Top-down attention is said to govern task execution through the flow of internal and external information. Consequently, it governs the planning and selection of responses (Gopher & Iani, 2003). As such it is also involved in the algorithmic processing of sound. Top-down attention is intimately related to conscious processing. Consciousness can be interpreted as our current best summary of the knowledge pertaining to the mental current state of the organism, its environment, and the behavioral options it affords (Koch & Tsuchiya, 2007). Top-down attention is a process that actively structures the input by applying stored knowledge in memory.

The result of this attentive structuring is, at least in part, a configuration of interacting discrete entities (objects, concepts) that describes the state-of-the-world in so far it is relevant for the individual and its goals. For example, during the analysis of a picture, observers have constant access to the best current interpretation, while attentional processes ensure that suitable knowledge is made available to improve the current interpretation more and more. The analysis continues up to the point that the individual's goals and task demands do not benefit further. Generally, the estimation of the relevance in the input is adequate, but errors, accidents, and misunderstandings do occur when relevance has been judged inadequately. For example while writing it is easy to miss a typo, especially when you know what the text should be. While driving it is quite possible to miss an important sign with far reaching consequences.

And when you fail to pick up the irony in a voice it is easy to misunderstand each other.

Inattentional Blindness

Structuring novel and complex input and formulating verbal reports are only possible when the perceptual input is 1) sufficiently strong and informative, and 2) if task specific top-down attention is present (Dehaene et al., 2006). The combination of demands is important for the phenomenon of inattentional blindness (Mack, 2003). This phenomenon suggests that when top-down attention is engaged in a sufficiently demanding task we are blind for task-irrelevant information, even when it is very strong and informative. Inattentional blindness is typically demonstrated with a visual task where two teams pass balls and the subject has to count the number of times the ball is passed within each team. Most task-engaged subjects fail to "see" clearly visible task-irrelevant objects like a woman with an open umbrella or a man in a gorilla suit. A recent study (Cartwright-Finch & Lavie, 2007) shows that more participants fail to notice the presence of task-irrelevant stimuli when the perceptual load is increased through increasing the number of items or by requiring more subtle perceptual discriminations. Cartwright-Finch concludes that stimulus complexity and not task-complexity, is the main limiting factor of attentional blindness.

Inattentional Deafness?

Similar effects are well known in audition: it is usually easy to focus on one perceptual stream while being completely unaware of the contents of other streams. In early work on the 'cocktail party effect', Cherry (1953) found that, when listeners attend to one of two talkers, they might not be aware of the meaning or even the language of the unattended speech. But they are aware of its presence and basic properties such as pitch range and the end of the message. Similarly, it is possible that novel details in music and soundscapes only become noticeable after multiple exposures. And from that moment on it is difficult to understand how these details could be missed. Hence, it is often impossible to analyze a signal fully in a single presentation, because task demands and the complexity of the signal will lead to a partial analysis. The more information and knowledge a listener has about the situation and the signal, the more detailed analysis is possible. Which demonstrates that activating task-relevant knowledge through attentional processes allows us to select matching evidence from the signal that can be missed without knowledge preactivation.

Perceiving Task-Relevant Information

The results in vision and audition substantiate the conclusion that perceptual systems process input up to the point of estimated task-irrelevance. For example, in the case of the demanding visual task, irrelevant information did not become consciously available even though the balls passed frequently behind the gorilla or the woman with the umbrella. The task-irrelevant persons were treated as 3-D objects behind which balls can pass, so they were clearly represented at some fairly advanced level of visual processing. However, the task-irrelevant object was not consciously accessible for most participants, although information about it was available. In the auditory example the situation is similar. Task-relevant speech can be tracked and understood, while only the existence and basic properties of task-irrelevant speech can be estimated. The existence and basic properties of the interfering speech are task-relevant for the auditory system because we use pitch-based grouping (Bregman, 1990) to separate speakers. The awareness of only these task-relevant properties is a particular convincing example that processing up to the point of task-irrelevance is performed. Note that this is only the case in demanding tasks. Less demanding tasks leave processing capacity for task irrelevant, but possibly system relevant, processing (Cartwright-Finch & Lavie, 2007).

Connect Signal Subsets to Interpretations and Vice Versa

Attention and estimating task-relevance in the input are closely related. Signal-driven attention capturing occurs through salient subsets of the input. It corresponds to either a mismatch between expected and actual input or to well-trained stimuli with system relevance. Salient stimuli forces the system to process the salient subset up to the conscious interpretation of the stimulus at the cost of other mental tasks. In task-driven attention, attentional processes lead to the selection of task-relevant subsets of the input by task-relevant interpretations. Hence bottom-up attentional processes connect subsets of the stimulus to (potentially conscious) interpretations, while top-down attention connects conscious interpretations to subsets of the stimulus. The combination forms a very flexible process because it can, to good approximation at least, be assumed that whatever is relevant in the input can be coupled to the correct interpretation. This process is depicted in Figure 2.

The bottom-up processes are qualitatively different from the top-down processes. The bottom-up processes lead to possible interpretation hypotheses, while the top-down processes capture the signal evidence consistent with generated interpretation hypotheses. The interpretation hypotheses that are able to capture sufficient and consistent evidence remain active and can become conscious. A similar combination of bottom-up hypothesis generation and top-down checking, but exclusively based on functional arguments, was described for speech recognition in Andringa (2002). This proposed a system that leads only to recognition results that are sufficiently supported by a combination of signal evidence and the state of the recognition system.

This section addressed the need for a task-optimized analysis of the signal. Since task-opti-

mization requires task-related knowledge, the next sections will address how suitable knowledge can be made serviceable to capture relevant information from the output. However, the first question is if and how suitable knowledge can be activated at all. A suitable form of knowledge activation has been extensively studied in vision research as the gist of a scene, a notion that seems extendable to the auditory domain.

VISUAL AND AUDITORY GIST

Visual Gist

A study performed more than 30 years ago (Potter, 1976) has shown that a preliminary meaningful interpretation of a complex scene occurs within only 100 ms after stimulus onset. This preliminary semantic interpretation is independent on whether or not the scene is expected and occurs independently of the clutter and the variety of details in the scene. This fast and preliminary interpretation is called the 'gist' of a scene (Oliva, 2005). The gist includes all levels of visual information, among which low-level features such as color and contours, intermediate-level features as shapes and texture regions, and high-level information such as the activation of a meaningful interpretation. The gist estimation process is strongly related to bottom-up attention. The gist is also related to top-down attention, because it connects, like top-down attention, perceptual input to interpretations.

The gist can be separated in a perceptual gist, which refers to the structural representation of a scene built during perception, and a conceptual gist, which includes the semantic information that is inferred during or shortly after the scene has disappeared from view. Conceptual gist is enriched and modified as the perceptual information bubbles up from early stages of visual processing (Oliva, 2005) and develops from a fast initial indicative interpretation to a fully reliable interpretation.

Figure 2. Hearing and Listening. A schematic representation of the attentional processes associated with an event sequence involving footsteps, someone saying "Hello", and a passing car. The clouds in the upper part reflect the flow of consciousness and the situation dependent tasks. The lower part depicts a time-frequency plane with pulse-like, tonal and noise-like events. Unexpected sounds (like the onset of the footsteps) or highly trained sound (like the word "hello") can be salient so that attention is directed to subsets of the input. This attentional change leads to task changes and top-down attentional processes that capture task-relevant subsets of signal evidence and that connect it to the explanation the listener becomes conscious of. The listener's state and task changes from determining the presence of a passer-by, to whether or not one is greeted, and to the question if a passing car is relevant. Together these form a meaningful narrative describing real-world events.

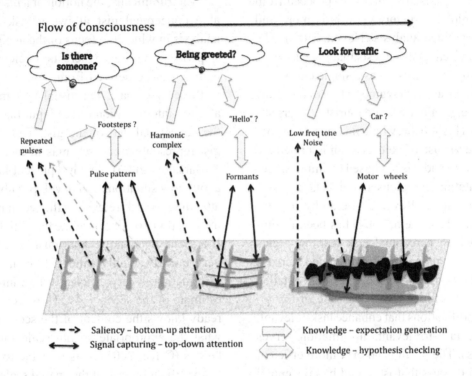

In general, speed and accuracy in scene (gist) recognition are not affected by the quantity of objects in a scene when these objects are grouped (Ariely, 2001). While gist information about the type and position of individual items is minimal, the gist represents accurate statistical information about groups of items. Additionally, scene information outside the focus of (top-down) attention becomes consciously accessible in the form of ensemble representations that lack local detail. Nevertheless they carry a reliable statistical summary of the visual scene in the form of group centroids of similar objects (Alvarez and Oliva,

2008). Without specific expectations of the scene, the gist is based on an analysis of the low spatial frequencies in the image that describe the scene only in coarse terms (Oliva, 2005) and that may even be insufficient for a reliable interpretation after prolonged visual analysis.

Gist and Scene Recognition

The rapid activation of the conceptual gist is in marked contrast with prominent views of scene recognition that are based on the idea that a scene is built as a collection of objects. This notion has been influenced by seminal approaches in computational vision, which have treated visual processing as a strictly bottom-up hierarchical organization of modules of increasing complexity (edges, surfaces, objects), with at the highest level, object identification, and scene schema activation (Marr, 1982).

However, modern empirical results seem more consistent with perceptual processes that are temporally organized so that they proceed from an initial global structuring towards more and more fine-grained analysis (Navon, 1977). The role of the visual gist suggests that visual scenes may initially be processed as a single entity, e.g. a sunny beach, and that segmentation of the scene in objects, e.g. palm trees and tourists, occurs at a later stage. This holistic, whole first, approach does not require the use of objects as an intermediate representation and it is not based on initial stages of segmentation in regions and objects.

Additionally a Reverse Hierarchy Theory (Ahissar and Hochstein, 2004) has been formulated, in which perceptual task learning stems largely from a gradual top-down-guided increase in the usability of first coarse, then more detailed task-relevant information. A cascade of top-to-bottom modifications that enhance task-relevant, and prune task-irrelevant, information serves this process. The result is an ever more efficient perceptual process that is guided by conceptual gist based expectations about input signal detail.

Task Optimized Analysis

The success of a top-down and task-adapted approach depends crucially on the relation between the gist contents and the actual content of a scene. The process of visual gist content activation was modeled by Torralba and Oliva (2003), who reported that eight perceptual dimensions capture most of the three-dimensional structures of real-world scenes (naturalness, openness, perspective or expansion, size or roughness, ruggedness, mean depth, symmetry, and complexity). They observed

that scenes with similar perceptual dimensions shared the same semantic category. In particular, scenes given the same base-level name, e.g., street, beach, (Rosch et al., 1976) tend to cluster within the same region of a multidimensional space in which the axes are the perceptual properties. Torralba's and Oliva's results show that (simple) signal properties are able to activate the correct semantic evaluation.

Algorithmically, the notion of a rapidly available conceptual gist allows a task-optimized analysis in which the focus of the analysis shifts stepwise to regions where task-relevant information can be derived from. By first attending to the coarse scale, the visual system acquires a rough interpretation of the input that activates the conceptual part of the gist. The conceptual gist represents scene schemas in memory (Yeh & Barsalou, 2006), which represent knowledge about how situations can develop. Subsequently attending to task relevant salience may provide information to refine or refute the initial estimate. If a scene is unknown and must be categorized very quickly, highly salient, though uncertain, information is very efficient for an initial rough estimate of the scene's gist. However, if one already knows the content of the scene or knows what the appropriate spatial scale for a visual task is (Oliva, 2005), it is possible to initiate a fast verification task at the spatial scale that may lead to a selection of expected details (Schyns & Oliva, 1994)

Is There an Auditory Gist?

The perceptual gist has the algorithmic properties required to make task-relevant information available to the system and as such it is ideal for audition. In contrast to visual gist, the concept of auditory gist has not yet had much scientific attention. Nevertheless Harding et al. (2007) concluded there is ample evidence that auditory processing complies with the ideas proposed for vision. Their paper addresses a number of proposals for an auditory gist, but due to the lack of focused research the auditory gist has not been defined and described in scientifically satisfying terms. In particular they found auditory (and visual) domain evidence that:

- Only the gist of the scene or object is initially processed;
- Processing of the gist is rapid;
- The focus of attention is deployed according to prior knowledge and the perception of the gist;
- Conscious detailed analysis is possible on the part of the scene within the focus of attention;
- Only limited processing of the unattended parts of the scene occurs.

These are all properties consistent with gist-guided expectation-based processing. Completely in line with this evidence is the hierarchical decomposition model (Cusack et al., 2004). In this model of sound perception, basic streaming is performed on the whole input, but only a single stream can be attended and subdivided further. Unattended streams cannot be fragmented further. Because the studies were conducted on (meaningless) tones instead of complex real-world sounds, the effects of task-specific knowledge might not be maximally prominent. Nevertheless it was concluded that if a general idea about the whole signal is obtained, the unattended parts of the signal do not need to be subdivided. For example, during a conversation at a street corner café with speech, music, and traffic noise, it is not necessary that the auditory system segregates music into instruments or speech into individual words if the listener is interested in the sound of people entering in a bus. This is depicted in Figure 3.

Audition = Hearing + Listening

Harding et al. (Harding, Cooke, & Konig, 2007) suggest a 'hearing' stage as an initial bottom-up gist processing stage which provides an overview of the whole auditory scene suitable for higher level processes. The initial processing indicates the likely number of sources and the source categories. Additional, task-specific top-down processes can focus on the attended source and analyze its detail, which they suggest is the 'listening' stage. This stage determines the features of the attended stream. Details of the signal outside the focus of attention will not be consciously perceived, although some limited processing of these regions might occur, typically in ways consistent with processing capabilities of the hearing-stage. Note that these suggestions dovetail nicely with the differences between hearing and listening in the elaborated common sense definition of audition as formulated earlier:

Audition (noun): the capacity for, or act of sound-based processing in which the existence of something or someone becomes mentally available (in the case of awareness), this availability can be used in a reasoning process to discover the consequences of what has been perceived (in the case of consciousness).

In this interpretation, hearing and listening are complementary processes. Hearing detects the existence and general character of the environment and its main and salient sources. In combination with task demands this allows the pre-activation of knowledge about expected sources and their properties. Consecutive listening phases, in which the task-relevant subsets of the signal are analyzed, allow the level of detail required by task- and system-demands.

As was outlined in the section addressing the estimation of relevance, one of the functions of top-down attention is to capture relevant subsets of the output by connecting it to suitable knowledge. This poses several demands on the way the signal is processed, the way information about sounds is stored and accessible, and the way the interpretation is connected to the signal. These will be addressed in the next sections, of which the first subsection focuses on knowledge and

Figure 3. The focus of attention. Not all sonic events are analyzed in similar detail. The gist of the scene with a general analysis of the content is always available. In this case the gist represents the sounds of a street-corner café. Only a single stream, in this case the one belonging to a stopping bus with a focus on the door, is analyzed in detail. Especially when the door-events are partially masked by the other sounds, attentive listening is required to detect them. This reduces the awareness of other sounds in the environment, which might lead to the conscious accessibility of only the events in bold. (Conform Cusack et al., 2004).

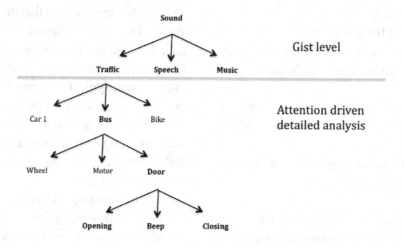

signal representations suitable for audition in uncontrolled environments.

THE PHYSICAL CHARACTER OF AUDITORY KNOWLEDGE

Physical Realizability

There is an often ignored but very important and useful constraint on real-world input that makes the task of interaction in the real world considerably less daunting by constraining both top-down expectations and bottom-up signal representations. This constraint follows from the acknowledgement that all input stems from a physically realizable world. Gaver (Gaver, 1993), who studied everyday listening from an ecological perspective, used this constraint implicitly when he stressed the relation between source physics and perception as follows:

"Taking an ecological approach implies analyses of the mechanical physics of source events, the acoustics describing the propagation of sound through an environment, and the properties of the auditory system that enable us to pick up such information. The result of such analyses will be a characterization of acoustic information about sources, environments, and locations, which can be empirically verified. This information will often take the form of complex, constrained patterns of frequency and amplitude which change over time: These patterns, not their supposedly primitive components, are likely to provide listeners with information about the world" (Gaver, 1993, p. 8)

Gaver argues that sonic input, if suitably processed, leads to complex but constrained patterns that are informative of the sources that produced the sounds. Top-down attentional processes should be aimed at the detection and capturing of these patterns.

If individual sources are subject to physical constraints, by extension a natural sonic environment consisting of individual sources is also subject to physical constraints. In fact the whole sonic environment is physically realizable in the sense that the sounds it produces stem from a physically allowed configuration. This is an extremely important property because it entails that the system can limit the set of possible signal interpretations to those that might actually describe a real-world situation and as such does not violate the physical laws that shape reality. Although this set is still huge, it is at least not contaminated with a majority of physically impossible, and therefore certainly incorrect, signal interpretations. Recognition systems that are based on computationally convenient manipulations that do not use this constraint have no way to decide which of a number of possible interpretations is an allowed state of reality. Without methods to limit the output of engineering systems to the physically probable, these systems cannot be extended from limited and controlled domains to uncontrolled domains.

Physics and Knowledge

The strong relation between physics and knowledge can be demonstrated by a thought experiment, adapted from Andringa (2002), in the form of the question: "Which sound source cannot be recognized?" We might perform an actual experiment by hiding the sound source in question behind an opaque screen. First you hear a sound and you say "a violin". "That is correct" we say. Then you hear another sound. You hear again a violin and you report that. "Wrong" we say. But you definitely heard the violin. We remove the screen and you see both a violin player and a HiFi-set with very good loudspeakers. The loudspeakers are definitely sound sources and they tricked you the second time. This might not seem particular informative because this is exactly what loudspeakers are used for. However, the point is that the violin will always produce 'the sound of a violin'; it is the only sound that physics allows it to produce and that our auditory system allows us to interpret. The same hold for all other "normal" sound sources. The (ideal) HiFi-set in contrast can reproduce any sound at will. It has no audible physical limitations and as a consequence it has no sound of itself. It will always be interpreted as another sound source as long as the listener is naïve about the true origin of the sound. And even then it is effortless to interpret the sounds it produces as the sound sources it reproduces.

Gaver's argument, generalized to arbitrary modalities, is that the sources (e.g. the sun, sound sources, and surfaces with evaporating odor molecules) and the transmission properties (e.g. reflecting surfaces, decay with distance, wind) do not lead to arbitrary structures, but on the contrary, lead to highly structured patterns that can be estimated by a perceptive system. These patterns can be stored and used as top-down expectations.

This argument leads to the relations in Figure 4 that couples physical representations via two routes to the patterns refered to in Gaver (1993). The counter-clockwise route is via knowledge and expectations; the clockwise route is via a real-world signal and a suitable form of signal processing. For example a guitar sound stems from a physical process involving a string being plucked that can be modeled as a differential equation of which the solutions correspond to a number of modes that can be summarized in a formula. The formula corresponds to the expectation of a pattern of damped sinusoidal contributions. The brain computes something functionally similar, but it uses generalized memories of previous exposures to expect the pattern of damped sinusoidal contributions. The clockwise route is via the real world in which a guitar sound is mixed with other sounds and transmitted through a reverberant environment. The resulting sound can be analyzed and compared with the generalized and idealized expectation. The mismatches can be used to refine the knowledge driven expectation; in this case for example by including the guitar's resonances around 1000-1500 Hz.

This example was idealized in the sense that it was trivial to assign signal evidence to the correct source. Competing sounds makes this more

Figure 4. Two different routes to connect a physical process to a pattern. The counter clockwise route is via knowledge; the clockwise route is via a real world signal and suitable preprocessing.

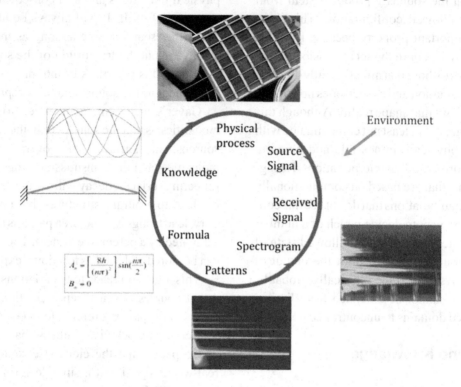

difficult in normal situations. The signal processing should therefore be optimized to form units of evidence that are highly likely to stem from a single source and that capture the information needed for the counter-clockwise route. The next section addresses this problem.

Representing Sounds Physically

Suppose you are presented with a test sound consisting of a tone that starts low and ends at a high pitch: a signal that can be visualized as in Figure 5. The question you are asked is "How many sounds did you hear?"

You are likely to report that you heard a single sound. But why is it a *single* sound? During the interval with sonic energy there was obviously sound, but how many sounds? The justification to call this a single sound is that the signal does not provide any evidence that somewhere during

its development it stopped and one or more other sounds took over. While this is not impossible, the probability is vanishingly small that one sound stopped and was smoothly extended by an *uncorrelated* new sound that had exactly the correct phase and energy to ensure no discontinuity whatsoever. This suggests that that our auditory system uses a continuous source development to form a single, and continuous, representation of the sound. This basic assumption formed the basis for Continuity Preserving Signal Processing (Andringa, 2002).

Continuity Preserving Signal Processing (CPSP) is a form of Computational Auditory Scene Analysis (CASA) (Rosenthal and Okuno, 1998) that aims to track the development of sound sources as reliable as possible. CPSP was developed to allow recognition systems to function as often as possible in varying and uncontrollable acoustic environments. CPSP aims to start from the weak-

Figure 5. A single sound in the form of a log-sweep represented as cochleogram according to Andringa, 2002. The signal starts at 100 Hz and ends at 2000 Hz two seconds later. The cochleogram was computed with a transmission line model of the basilar membrane that does not bias special frequencies or points in time like frame-based approaches like an FFT do. As a consequence the development of the sweep is, like its representations in the human cochlea, localized and very smooth.

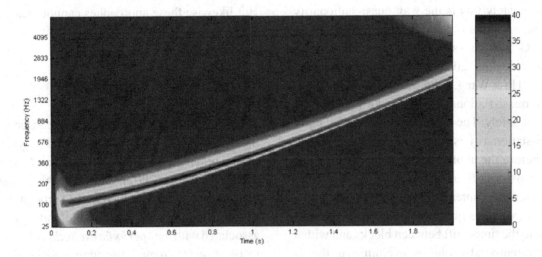

est (most general) possible basic assumptions. For sounds, the weakest possible basic assumption is that sounds consist of signal components that each shows an onset, an optional continuous development and an offset. The sine-sweep in Figure 5 is an example of a signal component.

Quasi-Stationarity

The inertia of sound sources entails that they cannot change infinitely fast. This entails that sound sources can be approximated with a quasi-stationarity assumption that assumes that the source can be modeled as originating from a process that is assumed to be stationary over short intervals. This is similar to the sample-and-hold process used to transform continuous signals into discrete signals that are suitable for computerized analysis and storage. For speech a quasi-stationarity period of 10 ms is often assumed (Young and Bloothooft, 1997). Quasi-stationarity is a perfectly reasonable assumption, but because it depends on a source dependent stationarity interval, it holds exclusively

for the signal of a single and (partially) known source type. If, however, a signal is produced by two speakers, it will change more rapidly and certainly differently than is allowed by the physics of a single vocal tract. Consequently, a form of quasi-stationarity that is only valid for a single source is not justified for mixtures of sources and should be avoided. The same holds for sources outside the reverberation radius.

In uncontrolled environments, the situation is even worse, since a suitable stationarity interval may be impossible to choose. If quasi-stationarity is nevertheless applied, the induced approximation errors will degrade the combined signal irreparably and therefore reduce the probability to reach a correct recognition result. This leads to the conclusion that quasi-stationarity, with a proper time-constant must either be applied to individual signal components or to complex signals, like the speech of a single speaker, for which it holds. As long as the signal, or some selection of it, is not positively identified as suitable for the quasi-stationarity assumption, the application of quasi-stationarity is not justified and may lead to suboptimal or incorrect results.

The Danger of Frame Blocking

Unfortunately this is the way quasi-stationarity is usually applied. All common approaches to ASR (O' Shaughnessy, 2008), sound recognition (Cowlin & Sitte, 2003), and most approaches to CASA (Hu & Wang, 2006, Wang & Brown, 2006) apply quasi-stationarity, but make no effort to apply it safely. The most common way to apply quasi-stationarity is frame-blocking as essential step before the application of a short term Fourier Transform. Frame-blocking determines that whatever the contents of the resulting window is, it is treated as quasi-stationary with a period equal to the time-shift between blocks and with a spectro-temporal resolution determined by the effective window size. Since this may or may not be appropriate for physical information in the signal, it limits these approaches to controlled domains in which the user can ensure that the detrimental effects are not dominant.

The Safe Application of Quasi-Stationarity

It is possible that the auditory system takes great care to apply quasi-stationarity safely. At least there are no known violations during cochlear processing. In auditory modeling is possible to preserve continuity as long as possible and to postpone the application of quasi-stationarity to the moment it can be justified. The use of a transmission line model of the basilar membrane (or suitable approximation as for example the gammachirp filterbank (Irino and Patterson, 1997) can lead to *cochleogram* as spectrogram variant in which it is possible to apply quasi-stationarity in some subsets of the time-frequency plane when transmission effects are not too prominent. (Andringa, 2002). In general the problems associated with the safe application of quasi-stationarity,

and therefore of signal component estimation, are not yet solved. Note that work on adaptive sparse coding (Smith & Lewicki, 2006) or sinusoidal modeling approaches (Daudet, 2006, Davies & Daudet, 2006) avoid frame-blocking altogether. But likewise these approaches cannot guarantee the formation of representation consisting of single source evidence.

Tones, Pulses, and Noises

The two-dimensional cochleogram can be augmented with periodicity information to yield a three dimensional *Time Normalized Correlogram* (Andringa, 2002). The Time Normalized Correlogram reflects always a superposition of two qualitatively different stable patterns: one associated with the *aperiodic excitation* of the corresponding BM region, the other associated with a *periodic excitation*. Furthermore the aperiodic excitation has two variants, one associated with a pulse-like excitation and one associated with broadband noise stimulation. This results in three qualitatively different excitations of the basilar membrane: tonal, pulse-like, and noise-like.

Interestingly these three patterns reflect the different sound production mechanisms, and as such the source production physics described by (Gaver, 1993). Recently it was shown (Gygi & Watson, 2007) that environmental sounds appear to be grouped perceptually in harmonic sounds with predominantly periodic contributions, impact sounds with predominantly pulse-like contributions, and "continuous sounds" with prominent aperiodic contributions. This entails that signal-processing, source physics, and perceptual experiments all suggest that tone, pulses, and noises should be treated as qualitatively different types of signals that are represented by different types of signal components.

Initial experiments to measure the fractions of tonal, pulse-like and aperiodic contributions indicate that the distribution of these contributions correlates with the perceptual results of Gygi

(Andringa, 2008). Additionally, the perceptual evaluation of a highly reverberant bouncing ball, which was strongly aperiodic in terms of signal content, was scored as a typical impact sound by the listeners. This perceptual insensitivity to transmission effects suggests, again, that listeners use sound production physics to represent the sound and ignore, in the source evaluation at least, much of the signal if it is the result of transmission effects.

CONCLUSION

This chapter argued that machine audition, as the rest of intelligent systems, is currently trapped in application domains in which a human user must ensure that the system is exposed to input it can process correctly. Apparently something essential is missing in modern systems, which is provided by the human user. Since a human listener is a multi-purpose system, it is able to assign its computational resources very flexibly to the ever-changing demands of real world environments. By processing all input only up to the point of estimated irrelevance, human audition processes only a relevant subset of all input in detail. This efficiency is the result of interplaying bottom-up hearing and top-down listening. The hearing stage keeps track of the general properties of the physical environment. The listening stage leads to a knowledge guided strategic analysis of subsets of the signal. The strategic analysis requires a signal representation that is closely related to the physical limitations imposed on the signal by sources and environments that lead to the demand to interpret the signal as a physically realizable configuration. This demand poses restrictions on the form of signal processing that are not met by most modern signal processing approaches, but that seem to be realized in the human auditory system.

THE FUTURE OF MACHINE AUDITION

The moment machine audition is able to make the transition from simplified tasks in controlled domains to uncontrolled real-world input (Andringa & Niessen, 2006, Krijnders, Niessen & Andringa, 2010), it extends its application scope considerably. First, it will no longer be necessary to develop a large number of different single-purpose applications. A single, but flexible, multi-purpose system will suffice. This system will, like the natural auditory system, not be able to analyze every sound in detail, but if it happens to have the knowledge required for the task, it can produce a reliable and well-founded result, which it can justify to the user. While the recognition of unconstrained sonic environments might be well outside our current reach, due to the huge amount of knowledge required, it will be possible to implement all kinds of expert knowledge domains into, for example, a mobile phone. Devices like this can be used as a singing coach to give feedback on pitch and singing style. The next day they might download the knowledge required to analyze irregular sounds of a car from the web. In the evening they can be used as a smart baby phone, and during the night they function as a device that detects and diagnoses apnea (prolonged suspension of breathing during sleep with serious medical consequences).

A second range of novel applications is related to environmental monitoring and especially noise monitoring. Current noise regulations rely exclusively on noise levels, which have only a strong correlation with annoyance above 70 dB(A). Listeners are exquisitely sensitive to the source composition of signals, while being bad dB-meters. An approach that mimics human perception well can be used to detect the sounds that attract attention and as such demand processing time. Typically, sounds that attract attention but do not contribute to the tasks and goals of the listener are not appreciated, because they steal time from higher valued activities. Systems that are able to measure, and even better, are able to predict, level independent noise disturbance can be used in urban planning procedures to design and monitor regions where the combination of sound and human activities are least likely to disturb.

Both examples share a vision of the ubiquitous application of the next generation of machine audition and are by no means exhaustive. The imminent technological transition from controlled domains to uncontrolled domains is a major technological breakthrough that is likely to lead to applications and new generations of technology that cannot yet be foreseen. This makes the future of machine audition seem bright indeed.

ACKNOWLEDGMENT

I thank Maria Niessen, Dirkjan Krijnders, Ronald van Elburg for helpful comments. I thank INCAS3 for supporting this work.

REFERENCES

Ahissar, M., & Hochstein, S. (2004). The reverse hierarchy theory of visual perceptual learning. *Trends in Cognitive Sciences*, 8(10), 457–464. doi:10.1016/j.tics.2004.08.011

Allen, J. (1994). How do humans process and recognize speech? *Speech and Audio Processing*, 2(4), 567–577. doi:10.1109/89.326615

Alvarez, G., & Oliva, A. (2008). The representation of simple ensemble visual features outside the focus of attention. *Psychological Science*, 19(4), 392–398. doi:10.1111/j.1467-9280.2008.02098.x

Andringa, T. C. (2002). Continuity Preserving Signal Processing. *Dissertations University of Groningen,* http://dissertations.ub.rug.nl/FILES/faculties/science/2001/t.c.andringa/thesis.pdf.

Andringa, T. C. (2008). The texture of natural sounds. *Proceedings of Acoustics'08, Paris* (pp. 3141-3146).

Andringa, T. C., & Niessen, M. E. (2006). *Real World Sound Recognition, a Recipe. Learning the Semantics of Audio Signals*. Athens, Greece: LSAS.

Ariely, D. (2001). Seeing Sets: Representation by Statistical Properties. *Psychological Science*, 12(2), 157–162. doi:10.1111/1467-9280.00327

Bregman, A. S. (1990). *Auditory Scene Analysis*. Cambridge, MA: MIT Press.

Bronkhorst, A. (2000). The Cocktail Party Phenomenon: A Review of Research on Speech Intelligibility in Multiple-Talker Conditions. *Acoustica – acta acoustica, 86*, 117-128.

Cartwright-Finch, U., & Lavie, N. (2007). The role of perceptual load in inattentional blindness. *Cognition, 102*, 321–340. doi:10.1016/j.cognition.2006.01.002

Cherry, E. (1953). Some Experiments on the Recognition of Speech, with One and with Two Ears. *The Journal of the Acoustical Society of America, 25*(5), 975–979. doi:10.1121/1.1907229

Cowling, M., & Sitte, R. (2003). Comparison of techniques for environmental sound recognition. *Pattern Recognition Letters, 24*, 2895–2907. doi:10.1016/S0167-8655(03)00147-8

Cusack, R., Deeks, J., Aikman, G., & Carlyon, R. (2004). Effects of location, frequency region, and time course of selective attention on auditory scene analysis. *Journal of Experimental Psychology. Human Perception and Performance, 30*(4), 643–656. doi:10.1037/0096-1523.30.4.643

Daudet, L. (2006). A review on techniques for the extraction of transients in musical signals (LNCS). In Kronland-Martinet, R., Voinier, T., & Ystad, S. (Eds.), *Springer-Verlag Berlin Heidelberg, Jan 2006*.

Davies, M., & Daudet, L. (2006). Sparse audio representations using the mclt. *Signal Processing, 86*(3), 457–470. doi:10.1016/j.sigpro.2005.05.024

Dehaene, S., Changeux, J., Naccache, L., & Sackur, J. (2006). Conscious, preconscious, and subliminal processing: a testable taxonomy. *Trends in Cognitive Sciences, 10*(5), 204–211. doi:10.1016/j.tics.2006.03.007

Gaver, W. (1993). What in the World Do We Hear?: An Ecological Approach to Auditory Event Perception. *Ecological Psychology, 5*(1), 1–29. doi:10.1207/s15326969eco0501_1

Gopher and Iani. (2002). Attention. Encyclopedia of Cognitive Science L. Nadel (Ed). (pp. 220-226).

Gygi, B., Kidd, G., & Watson, C. (2007). *Similarity and categorization of environmental sounds.* Perception & Psychophysics.

Harding, S., Cooke, M., & Konig, P. (2007). Auditory gist perception: an alternative to attentional selection of auditory streams? *In Lecture Notes in Computer Science: Attention in Cognitive Systems.* [Springer-Verlag Berlin Heidelberg.]. *Theories and Systems from an Interdisciplinary Viewpoint, 4840,* 399–416. doi:10.1007/978-3-540-77343-6_26

Haykin, S., & Chen, Z. (2005). The Cocktail Party Problem. *Neural Computation, 17,* 1875–1902. doi:10.1162/0899766054322964

Hu, G., & Wang, D. (2006). An auditory scene analysis approach to monaural speech segregation. *Topics in acoustic echo and noise control* (pp. 485-515).

Irino, T., & Patterson, R. D. (1997). A time-domain, level-dependent auditory filter: The gammachirp. *The Journal of the Acoustical Society of America, 101*(1), 412–419. doi:10.1121/1.417975

Knudsen, E. (2007). Fundamental Components of Attention. *Annual Review of Neuroscience, 30,* 57–78. doi:10.1146/annurev.neuro.30.051606.094256

Koch, C., & Tsuchiya, N. (2007). Attention and consciousness: two distinct brain processes. *Trends in Cognitive Sciences, 11*(1), 16–22. doi:10.1016/j.tics.2006.10.012

Krijnders, J.D., Niessen, M.E. & Andringa, T.C. (2010). Sound event identification through expectancy-based evaluation of signal-driven hypotheses. Accepted for publication in Pattern Recognition Letters.

Mack, A. (2003). Inattentional blindness: Looking without seeing. *Current Directions in Psychological Science, 12*(5), 180–184. doi:10.1111/1467-8721.01256

Marr, D. (1982). *Vision.* New York: Henry Holt and Co., Inc.

Nábělek, A. K., & Robinson, P. K. (1982). Monaural and binaural speech perception in reverberation for listeners of various ages. *The Journal of the Acoustical Society of America, 71*(5), 1242–1248. doi:10.1121/1.387773

Navon, D. (1977). Forest before trees: The precedence of global features in visual perception. *Cognitive Psychology, 9,* 353–383. doi:10.1016/0010-0285(77)90012-3

O'Shaughnessy, D. (2008). Invited paper: Automatic speech recognition: History, methods and challenges. *Pattern Recognition, 41,* 2965–2979. doi:10.1016/j.patcog.2008.05.008

Oliva, A. (2005). *Gist of a scene* (pp. 251–256). Neurobiology of Attention.

Potter, M. (1976). Short-term conceptual memory for pictures. *Journal of Experimental Psychology. Human Learning and Memory, 2*(5), 509–522. doi:10.1037/0278-7393.2.5.509

Rosch, E., Mervis, C., Gray, W., Johnson, D., & Boyes-Braem, P. (1976). Basic objects in natural categories. *Cognitive Psychology, 8*(3), 382–439. doi:10.1016/0010-0285(76)90013-X

Rosenthal, D. F., & Okuno, H. G. (1998). *Computational Auditory Scene Analysis.* Mahwah, NJ: Lawrence Erlbaum.

Schyns, P., & Oliva, A. (1994). Evidence for Time-and Spatial-Scale-Dependent Scene Recognition. *Psychological Science, 5*(4), 195–200. doi:10.1111/j.1467-9280.1994.tb00500.x

Smith, E., & Lewicki, M. (2006). Efficient auditory coding. *Nature, 439*(23), 978–982. doi:10.1038/nature04485

Torralba, A., & Oliva, A. (2003). Statistics of natural image categories. *Network (Bristol, England), 14*, 391–412. doi:10.1088/0954-898X/14/3/302

Van Hengel, P. W. J., & Andringa, T. C. (2007). Verbal aggression detection in complex social environments. In *IEEE Conference on Advanced Video and Signal Based Surveillance* (pp. 15-20).

Wang, D., & Brown, G. J. (2006). *Computational auditory scene analysis: Principles, Algorithms, and Applications*. New York: IEEE Press/Wiley-Interscience.

Whalen, P. J., Rauch, S. L., & Etcoff, N. L. (1998). Masked presentations of emotional facial expressions modulate amygdala activity without explicit knowledge. *The Journal of Neuroscience, 18*(1), 411–418.

Yeh, W., & Barsalou, L. (2006). The situated nature of concepts. *The American Journal of Psychology, 119*(3), 349–384. doi:10.2307/20445349

Young, S., & Bloothooft, G. (Eds.). (1997). *Corpus-Based Methods in Language and Speech Processing. Text, Speech and Language Technology*. Dordrecht, Netherlands: Kluwer.

ADDITIONAL READING

Alain, C., & Izenberg, A. (2003). Effects of attentional load on auditory scene analysis. *Journal of Cognitive Neuroscience, 15*(7), 1063–1073. doi:10.1162/089892903770007443

Aucouturier, J., Defreville, B., & Pachet, F. (2007). The bag-of-frames approach to audio pattern recognition: A sufficient model for urban soundscapes but not for polyphonic msic. *The Journal of the Acoustical Society of America, 122*(2), 881–891. doi:10.1121/1.2750160

Chu, S., Narayanan, S., & Kuo, C. (2008). *Environmental sound recognition using MP-based features*. Acoustics.

Cooke, M. (2006). A glimpsing model of speech perception in noise. *The Journal of the Acoustical Society of America, 34*, 267–285.

Guastavino, C. (2007). Categorization of environmental sounds. *Canadian Journal of Experimental Psychology, 61*(1), 54–65. doi:10.1037/cjep2007006

Guastavino, C., Katz, B., Polack, J., Levitin, D., & Dubois, D. (2005). Ecological validity of soundscape reproduction. *Acta Acustica united with Acustica, 91* (2), 333-341.

Nahum, M., Nelken, I., & Ahissar, M. (2008). Low-level information and high-level perception: The case of speech in noise. *PLoS Biology, 6*(5), 978–991. doi:10.1371/journal.pbio.0060126

Niessen, M. E., van Maanen, L., & Andringa, T. C. (2009). Disambiguating Sounds through Context. *International Journal of Semantic Computing, 2*(3), 327–341. doi:10.1142/S1793351X08000506

Oliva, A., & Torralba, A. (2006). Building the gist of a scene: The role of global image features in recognition. *Progress in Brain Research, 155*, 23–36. doi:10.1016/S0079-6123(06)55002-2

Recanzone, G., & Sutter, M. (2008). The Biological Basis of Audition. *Annual Review of Psychology, 56*, 119–142. doi:10.1146/annurev.psych.59.103006.093544

Shinn-Cunningham, B. (2008). Object-based auditory and visual attention. *Trends in Cognitive Sciences*, *12*(5), 182–186. doi:10.1016/j.tics.2008.02.003

KEY TERMS AND DEFINITIONS

Attention: the mental processes that allocates algorithmic and knowledge resources perception or other mental tasks.

Audition: the capacity for, or act of sound-based processing in which the existence of something or someone becomes mentally available (in the case of hearing), this availability can be used in a reasoning process to discover the consequences of what has been perceived (in the case of listening).

Bottom-Up Attention: a subprocess of attention that allows unexpected and well-trained stimuli to interrupt ongoing mental tasks in favor of a more detailed analysis.

Every Day Listening: a form of listening aimed at discovering the events, objects, and processes that caused the sound

Gist: the representation of a scene and its possible meaning that results from even a short stimulation, the gist can be refined to a reliable interpretation with subsequent analysis.

Hearing: the bottom-up, gist activation stage of audition aimed at discovering the existence of sound sources and their possible behavioral significance

Listening: the top-down, task and knowledge specific detailed analysis of sound and sound sources.

Meaning of Something for Someone: the difference in behavioral options for someone with and without the inclusion of something

Musical Listening: a form of listening aimed at listening to the properties of the sound as a physical signal

Physical Realizability: a property indicating whether or not an interpretation corresponds to a physically allowed configuration

Quasi-Stationarity: the assumption, valid for a single source, that the development of a source can be described as a set of discrete steps

Reverberation Radius: the distance around a source where the energy of the direct sound is equal to the energy of the summed indirect reflections

Sound: vibration that travel through the air or other media and can be heard when they reach a person's or animal's ear.

A/The Sound: audible sound stemming from someone or something

Top-Down Attention: a subprocess of attention that uses knowledge-based expectations to capture subsets of the input and connect these to an interpretation

Section 2
Audio Signal Separation, Extraction and Localization

Chapter 5
A Multimodal Solution to Blind Source Separation of Moving Sources

Syed Mohsen Naqvi
Loughborough University, UK

Yonggang Zhang
Harbin Engineering University, China

Miao Yu
Loughborough University, UK

Jonathon A. Chambers
Loughborough University, UK

ABSTRACT

A novel multimodal solution is proposed to solve the problem of blind source separation (BSS) of moving sources. Since for moving sources the mixing filters are time varying, therefore, the unmixing filters should also be time varying and can be difficult to track in real time. In this solution the visual modality is utilized to facilitate the separation of moving sources. The movement of the sources is detected by a relatively simplistic 3-D tracker based on video cameras. The tracking process is based on particle filtering which provides robust tracking performance. Positions and velocities of the sources are obtained from the 3-D tracker and if the sources are moving, a beamforming algorithm is used to perform real time speech enhancement and provide separation of the sources. Experimental results show that by utilizing the visual modality, a good BSS performance for moving sources in a low reverberant environment can be achieved.

INTRODUCTION

Professor Colin Cherry in 1953 first asked the question: "How do we [humans] recognise what one person is saying when others are speaking at the same time?" (Cherry, 1953). This was the genesis of the so-called machine **cocktail party problem**, i.e. mimicing the ability of a human to separate sound sources within a machine, and

DOI: 10.4018/978-1-61520-919-4.ch005

attempts to solve it have evolved from the signal processing community in the form of convolutive blind source separation (CBSS), which is a topic of considerable active research due to its potential applications (Haykin, Eds., 2000). CBSS consists of estimating sources from observed audio mixtures with only limited information and the associated algorithms have been conventionally developed in either the time or frequency domains (Bregman, 1990; Cichocki & Amari, 1990; Yilmaz & Rickard, 2004; Wang et al., 2005; Parra & Spence, 2000; Bingham et al. 2000; Makino et al., 2005; Sanei et al., 2007; Naqvi et.al., 2008, 2009). Frequency domain convolutive blind source separation (FDCBSS) has however been a more popular approach as the time-domain convolutive mixing is converted into a number of independent complex instantaneous mixing operations. The permutation problem inherent to FDCBSS presents itself when reconstructing the separated sources from the separated outputs of these instantaneous mixtures and grows geometrically with the number of instantaneous mixtures (Wang et al., 2005).

Most existing BSS algorithms assume that the sources are physically stationary and based on statistical information extracted from the received mixed audio data (Cichocki & Amari, 1990; Wang et al., 2005; Parra & Spence, 2000). However, in many real applications, the sources may be moving. In such applications, there will generally be insufficient data length available over which the sources are physically stationary, which limits the application of these algorithms. Only a few papers have been presented in this area (Mukai et al., 2003; Koutras et al., 2000; Naqvi et al., 2008; Prieto & Jinachitra 2005; Hild-II et al., 2002). In (Mukai et al., 2003), sources are separated by employing frequency domain ICA using a block-wise batch algorithm in the first stage, and the separated signals are refined by postprocessing in the second stage which constitutes crosstalk component estimation and spectral subtraction. In the case of (Koutras et al., 2000), they used a

framewise on-line algorithm in the time domain. However, both these two algorithms potentially assume that in a short period the sources are physically stationary, or the change of the mixing filters is very slow, which are very strong constraints. In (Prieto & Jinachitra, 2005), BSS for time-variant mixing systems is performed by piecewise linear approximations. In (Hild-II et al., 2002), they used an online PCA algorithm to calculate the whitening matrix and another online algorithm to calculate the rotation matrix. However, both algorithms are designed only for instantaneous source separation, and can not separate convolutive mixed signals. Fundamentally, it is very difficult to separate convolutively mixed signals by utilizing the statistical information only extracted from audio signals, and this is not the manner in which humans solve the problem (Haykin, Eds., 2007) since they use both their ears and eyes.

In this chapter, a multimodal approach is therefore proposed by utilizing not only received linearly mixed audio signals, but also the video information obtained from cameras. A video system can capture the approximate positions and velocities of the speakers, from which we can identify the directions and motions, i.e., stationary or moving, of the speakers. A source is identified as moving if the velocity is larger than an upper bound value. In this case, a beamforming method is used to enhance the signal from one source direction and reduce the energy received from another source direction, so that source separation can be obtained. Although the beamforming approach can only reduce the signal from a certain direction and the reverberance of the interference still exists, which are also limitations in the BSS approach, it can obtain a good separation performance in a low reverberation environment. To obtain an online real time source separation, the beamforming approach used in this work only depends on the angle of arrival information to the sensor array, and no received audio data are required (Veen & Buckley, 1988).

A key component in the proposed approach is the tracking of speakers. Tracking speakers based only on audio is difficult because human speech is an intermittent signal and it contains much of its energy in the low-frequency bins where spatial discrimination is imprecise, and locations estimated only by audio are also affected by noise and room reverberations (Maganti et al., 2007). We therefore track the speakers by using visual information motivated by Colin Cherry's observation that the human approach to solve the cocktail party problem exploits visual cues (Cherry, 1953) and (Cherry & Taylor, 1954). The face area is identified based on a skin model and template matching, and tracked by using a particle filter framework (Back & Tosi, 1994) and (Gatica-Perez et al., 2007) from color video cameras. We do not claim that these techniques represent the state-of-the-art in terms of face detection and tracking but they are sufficient to demonstrate the source separation concept. More future research will be performed in the future to improve the stages of the proposed approach. The output of the tracking is position and velocity information, on the basis of which we decide either whether the sources are physically stationary or moving. As will be shown in later simulations, the proposed approach can provide a reasonable BSS performance for moving sources in a low reverberant environment in which the reverberation time (RT) is 130ms. Performing BSS in rooms with large RT typically >130ms remains as a research challenge.

This book chapter is therefore organized as follows: Section-the system model, presents the block diagram of the system. Section-source direction and velocity extraction, explains the localization and tracking process. Section-source separation, describes the source separation by beamforming. Experimental results are provided in Section-experiments and results, based on real room recordings. Finally, in Section-conclusion, we conclude the paper.

THE SYSTEM MODEL

The schematic diagram of the system is shown in Figure 1. The proposed approach can be divided into two stages: human tracking to obtain position and velocity information; and source separation by utilizing the position and velocity information based on beamforming. The first stage of the system is discussed in Section-source direction and velocity extraction and the second stage of the system is presented in Section-source separation.

Source Direction and Velocity Extraction

Face Extraction

We use two color video cameras to determine the approximate positions of the speakers. Both cameras are synchronized by the external hardware trigger module and frames are captured at the rate of $f_v = 25\ frames\ /\ sec$, which means $T_v = 1/25\ sec$. We extract the face of each speaker in the images of both cameras to find the position of each speaker at each state (time). In each image frame, the face is extracted on the basis of a skin pixel model and a face model, briefly we can explain this procedure as (for further detail see (Lee & Yoo, 2002) and (Fisher et al., 2003))

1. **Off line formulation of the skin pixel model:**
   - A training set of skin regions for different people with varying skin tones is obtained by manual extraction of the facial regions within a number of measured frames.
   - Each skin region is converted from the RGB color space into the normalized r-g color space $r, g = R, G /(R + G + B)$, and a corresponding pixel in r-g color space, i.e. a two-dimensional vector, is denoted by D.

Figure 1. System block diagram: Sources are localized based on skin model and template matching with the human face, this 2-D image information of the video cameras is converted to 3-D world co-ordinates through the calibration parameters. The 3-D estimates are fed to the visual-tracker, and on the basis of position and velocity information from the tracking, the sources are separated by beamforming.

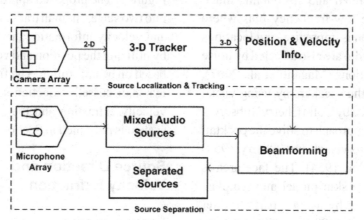

A two-dimensional histogram of all the D vectors from the training set of skin regions is produced. Parameters a_i are calculated which correspond to the relative occurrence of each vector D_i within the training set.

° Vectors which have a value of a_i less than some threshold are considered to correspond to noisy pixels. Such pixels are removed from the training set.

° The remaining unique vectors $D_1, \ldots, D_l$ with their respective a_i where $i = 1, \ldots, l$ are next used to formulate a skin pixel model.

° Skin pixel model: A skin pixel model $\Phi = (D; \Psi, \Lambda)$ is defined as

$$\Phi(D) = [D - \Psi]^T \Lambda^{-1} [D - \Psi] \tag{1}$$

where $(\cdot)^T$ denotes vector transpose and the parameters Ψ and Λ can be calculated as

$$\Psi = \frac{1}{l} \sum_{i=1}^{l} D_i \tag{2}$$

$$\Lambda = \frac{1}{l} \sum_{i=1}^{l} a_i (D_i - \mu)(D_i - \mu)^T \tag{3}$$

$$\mu = \frac{1}{l} \sum_{i=1}^{l} a_i D_i \tag{4}$$

Given threshold θ_{thresh} and r-g vector D of a pixel, D is classified as skin chrominance if $\Phi(D) < \theta_{thresh}$ and as non-skin chrominance otherwise.

2. **Face extraction:** Given a measured frame converted to normalized r-g color space all candidate face pixels are extracted according to the above skin pixel model on the basis of a threshold θ_{thresh}.

° Each significant cluster of candidate face pixels is cross-correlated with a standard face (which is an averaging of front views of 16 male and female faces wearing no glasses and having no facial hair), appropriate processing is used to align the relative sizes of the two images.

○ The cross-correlation value between the standard face template and every skin region is calculated. The region that yields maximum cross-correlation is chosen as the desired face.

The center of the resultant face region is determined as the approximate position of the lips of the speaker in image coordinates. These image coordinates of each speaker i are passed to the next section to calculate the position of the speakers in 3-D world coordinates.

Source Position in the Real World

Both static video cameras are calibrated off line by the Tsai calibration (non-coplanar) technique (R. Tsai, 1987). The method for camera calibration recovers the interior orientation (principle distance f), the exterior orientation (relationship between a scene-centered coordinate system and a camera-centered coordinate system, the transformation from scene to camera consists of a rotation matrix R and translation vector t, the power series coefficients for distortion k, and image scale factor p (for more detail see (Tsai, 1987)). So the off line calibration parameters for each camera are f_c, R_c, t_c, k_c and p_c, where $c = 1$, 2 is the index of cameras.

With the help of the above calibration parameters we transform the image coordinates to undistorted sensor plane coordinates. Then we calculate distorted sensor plane coordinates and finally these distorted sensor plane coordinates of the approximate 2-D image information of the same speaker in two different camera views are transformed to 3-D world coordinates. In 3-D space each point in each camera frame defines a ray. Intersection of both rays is found by optimization methods, which finally help in calculation of the positions of the speakers in 3-D real world coordinates (Hartley & Zisserman, 2001). In the following section we will discuss the tracker. The calculated position of the lips z^i of each speaker

is then used in a particle filter based algorithm, and the position and velocity obtained from the tracker will be used in the source separation. For simplicity we will discuss the tracker for one speaker and therefore here after we omit i from z^i unless mentioned otherwise. The tracking process will be formulated in the next section.

Tracking the Source Position and Velocity

We divide this section into two parts. Initially, we will discuss the basis of the 3-D tracker and finally we will discuss the output of the tracker, i.e. position and velocity information.

3-D visual tracker: Before we introduce the recursive update of the particle filter based tracking, the state-measurement model is formulated first. The state and measurement configurations are $\mathbf{x}_{0:k}, \mathbf{z}_{0:k} = \{\mathbf{x}_j, \mathbf{z}_j, j = 0, \cdots k\}$, where $\mathbf{x}_{0:k}$ formulates the state sequence of the target which we want to obtain, and $\mathbf{z}_{0:k}$ is the observation sequence, both in R^3. For each iteration, the target state evolves according to the following discrete-time stochastic model:

$$\mathbf{x}_k = f_k(\mathbf{x}_{k-1,k-2}, k) + \mathbf{v}_{k-1} \qquad (5)$$

where $f_k(\mathbf{x}_{k-1,k-2}, k) = 2\mathbf{x}_{k-1} - \mathbf{x}_{k-2}$ represents a simple random walk model for the state $\mathbf{x}_k$ and is used for the approach and k is the discrete time index. This model could be enhanced by incorporating velocity components within the state variables, but in this book chapter we are only demonstrating the concept. Process noise $\mathbf{v}_{k-1}$ is white noise and caters for undermodeling effects and unforeseen disturbances in the state model, and its covariance matrix is Q_v.

The objective of the filter is to estimate recursively state x_k from the measurement z_k and the measurement equation is:

$$\mathbf{z}_k = h_k(\mathbf{x}_k, k) + \mathbf{r}_k \qquad (6)$$

where $h_k(\mathbf{x}_k, k) = \mathbf{x}_k$ and r_k is a vector of Gaussian random variables with covariance matrix Q_r which caters for the measurement errors. The basic idea of particle filtering is to estimate recursively the posterior distribution of the state $x_{o:k}$ based on the observations $z_{1:k}$. The posterior distribution of the state can be represented in a nonparametric way, by using particles drawn from the distribution $p(\mathbf{x}_{0:k}|\mathbf{z}_{1:k})$, as formulated below:

$$p(\mathbf{x}_{0:k}|\mathbf{z}_{1:k}) \approx \frac{1}{N_p}\sum_{n=1}^{N_p}\delta(\mathbf{x}_{0:k} - \mathbf{x}_{0:k}^n) \qquad (7)$$

where $(\cdot)^n$ refers to the n_{th} particle, $\delta(\cdot)$ is the Dirac delta function, N_p is the number of particles, and we have a discrete approximation of the true posterior. As N_p approaches to infinity, this discrete formulation will converge to the true posterior distribution. However, practically this is impossible, since the posterior distribution $p(\mathbf{x}_{0:k}|\mathbf{z}_{1:k})$ is to be estimated and hence is unknown. In practice, we sample the particles from a known proposal distribution $q(\mathbf{x}_{0:k}|\mathbf{z}_{1:k})$ called the importance density and the concept is known as importance sampling (Ristic, Eds., 2004). The distribution $p(\mathbf{x}_{0:k}|\mathbf{z}_{1:k})$ can then be formulated as

$$p(\mathbf{x}_{0:k}|\mathbf{z}_{1:k}) \approx \sum_{n=1}^{N_p}\omega_k^n\delta(\mathbf{x}_{0:k} - \mathbf{x}_{0:k}^n) \qquad (8)$$

where

$$\omega_k^n \propto \frac{p(\mathbf{x}_{0:k}^n|\mathbf{z}_{1:k})}{q(\mathbf{x}_{0:k}^n|\mathbf{z}_{1:k})} \qquad (9)$$

and is normalized so that $\sum_i \omega_k^i = 1$.

Before state k if we can approximate $p(\mathbf{x}_{0:k-1}^n|\mathbf{z}_{1:k-1})$ from the samples $\mathbf{z}_{1:k-1}^n$ we have, then with the arrival of measurement z_k at state k, we can approximate $p(\mathbf{x}_{0:k}^n|\mathbf{z}_{1:k})$ with a new set of samples. We can factorize the importance density by

$$q(\mathbf{x}_{0:k}^n|\mathbf{z}_{1:k}) = q(\mathbf{x}_k^n|\mathbf{x}_{0:k-1}^n, \mathbf{z}_{1:k})q(\mathbf{x}_{0:k-1}^n|\mathbf{z}_{1:k-1}) \qquad (10)$$

then we can obtain new samples $\mathbf{x}_{0:k}^n$ from $q(\mathbf{x}_{0:k}^n|\mathbf{z}_{1:k})$ by augmenting each of the old samples $\mathbf{x}_{0:k-1}^n$ from $q(\mathbf{x}_{0:k-1}^n|\mathbf{z}_{1:k-1})$ with the new state $\mathbf{x}_k^n$ from $q(\mathbf{x}_k^n|\mathbf{x}_{0:k-1}^n, \mathbf{z}_{1:k})$.

The pdf $p(\mathbf{x}_{0:k}^n|\mathbf{z}_{1:k})$ can be simplified (Ristic, Eds., 2004) to

$$p(\mathbf{x}_{0:k}^n|\mathbf{z}_{1:k}) \propto p(\mathbf{z}_k|\mathbf{x}_k^n)p(\mathbf{x}_k^n|\mathbf{x}_{k-1}^n)p(\mathbf{x}_{0:k-1}^n|\mathbf{z}_{1:k-1}) \qquad (11)$$

By placing (10) and (11) in (9) and if $q(\mathbf{x}_k^n|\mathbf{x}_{k-1}^n, \mathbf{z}_k) = q(\mathbf{x}_k^n|\mathbf{x}_{0:k-1}^n, \mathbf{z}_{1:k})$, the weight update equation can be written as

$$\omega_k^n = \omega_{k-1}^n \frac{p(\mathbf{z}_k|\mathbf{x}_k^n)p(\mathbf{x}_k^n|\mathbf{x}_{k-1}^n)}{q(\mathbf{x}_k^n|\mathbf{x}_{k-1}^n, \mathbf{z}_k)} \qquad (12)$$

The choice of importance density function is one of the critical issues in the design of a particle filter and plays a critical role in the performance

(Ristic, Eds., 2004). The function should have the same support as the probability distribution to be approximated, and the approximation will be better if the importance function is closer to the distribution. The assumption $q(\mathbf{x}_k^n | \mathbf{x}_{k-1}^n, \mathbf{z}_k) = q(\mathbf{x}_k^n | \mathbf{x}_{0:k-1}^n, \mathbf{z}_{1:k})$ mentioned above, means that the importance density depends only on the previous state $\mathbf{x}_{k-1}^n$ and current measurement $\mathbf{z}_k$, and the path $\mathbf{x}_{0:k-2}^n$ and history of observations $\mathbf{z}_{1:k-1}$ will be discarded. The most popular choice for the prior importance function which is also used in the proposed algorithm, is given by

$$q(\mathbf{x}_k^n | \mathbf{x}_{k-1}^n, \mathbf{z}_k) = p(\mathbf{x}_k^n | \mathbf{x}_{k-1}^n) \qquad (13)$$

and this particular importance density is applied at every time index which simplifies the weight update equation to:

$$\omega_k^n \propto \omega_{k-1}^n p(\mathbf{z}_k | \mathbf{x}_k^n) \qquad (14)$$

The importance sampling weight indicates the level of importance of the corresponding particle. In the above mentioned sequence importance sampling algorithm, after a few iterations, all but one particle will have very small weight, this is known as the degeneracy phenomenon. A relatively small weight means the particle is ineffective in calculation of the posterior distribution. To overcome the degeneracy we use residual resampling, a scheme that eliminates the particles with small weights and replicates those with large weights accordingly (Ristic, Eds., 2004).

The implement of the particle filter can then be divided into two steps:

1. Sampling step: N particles are sampled from the proposal density formulated by (13) according to (5).

2. Computing the particle weights according to (14), and resampling the particles if necessary.

Based on the weights the conditional mean of $\mathbf{x}_k$ can then be calculated. The output of the 3-D tracker is position $\mathbf{x}_j$ at each state j and on the basis of this information we calculate the velocity information elaborated below. Further enhancements to the particle filtering, such as exploiting a **Markov Chain Monte Carlo** (MCMC) approach are possible as described in (Ristic, Eds., 2004).

Position and Velocity Information: As we already mentioned that the output of the 3-D visual tracker is position $\mathbf{x}_k = [x_k^x, x_k^y, x_k^z]^T$ and velocity s_k of a speaker at each state k. The distance between consecutive states is calculated as $d_k = \|\mathbf{x}_k - \mathbf{x}_{k-1}\|_2$ where $\|\cdot\|_2$ denotes Euclidean norm, and velocity at state k is calculated as $s_k = d_k / T_v$. The change in the position of a speaker with respect to the previous state plays a critical role in source separation by using beamforming.

SOURCE SEPARATION

The audio mixtures from the microphone sensor array are separated with the help of visual information from the 3-D tracker. On the basis of the above visual information we decide either the sources are moving or stationary. The pseudo code to issue the command for selecting the source separation method for moving sources is as follows.

Pseudo Code: Command for selecting the beamforming method for separation

```
Reset the counter and set the thresh-
old
FOR i = 2: k
     -Find  d_i = ||x_i - x_{i-1}||_2

   IF d_i < threshold
     -Update the counter
```

```
     ELSE
          -Reset the counter
   END IF
   IF counter < T_k / T_v
      -Command for moving sources.
          ELSE
             - Command for physically
stationary sources.
      END IF
END FOR
```

Where T_k represent the expected stationary period for the sources, $T_v = 1 / f_v$ and *threshold* is the minimum distance between source positions of consecutive states.

When the sources are moving we can separate the sources by beamforming, otherwise, if the sources are physically stationary for certain period T_k we can separate the sources by using geometrical information of the sources in our works (Sanei et al., 2007, Naqvi et al., 2008). By changing the value of T_k we can change the expected required stationary period for the sources.

The other important parameter to be calculated before starting the source separation is the angle of arrival of each speaker to the sensor array. By having the position information of the microphones and the speakers at each state from the 3-D visual tracker we can easily calculate the angle of arrival $\theta_{0:k}$ of speakers to the microphone sensor array. The angle of arrival information will be used in beamforming for separation of moving sources.

A simple two set beamforming system configuration is shown in Figure 2. The equivalence between frequency domain blind source separation and frequency domain adaptive beamforming is already studied in (Araki et al., 2003). In the case of a two microphone sensor array an ABF creates only one null towards the jammer. Since the aim is to separate two source signals s_1 and s_2 therefore two sets of ABFs are presented in Figure 2. An ABF by using filter coefficients w_{21} and w_{22} forms a null directive patterns towards source s_1 and by using filter coefficients w_{11} and w_{12} forms

a null directive patterns towards source s_2. If two speakers are located at the same direction with different distances, it is not possible to separate the sources by phase difference. One of the other limitation for the blind source separation is acoustic environment with the long reverberations, in this work the reverberation time in the intelligent office is 130msec which will be considered as a fairly moderate reverberant environment.

We used unidirectional microphones in the intelligent office where our recordings are taken. By using a short-time discrete Fourier transform (DFT) the mixing process can be formulated as follows: having M statistically independent real sources $s(\omega) = [s_1(\omega), \cdots s_M(\omega)]^H$ where ω denotes discrete normalized frequency, a multichannel FIR filter $H(\omega)$ producing N observed mixed signals $u(\omega) = [u_1(\omega), \cdots, u_N(\omega)]^H$, where $(\cdot)^H$ is Hermitian transpose, can be described as (we assume there is no noise or noise can be deemed as a source signal in the model for simplicity)

$$\mathbf{u}(\omega) = \mathbf{H}(\omega)s(\omega) \tag{15}$$

where

Figure 2. Two set beamforming system configuration: (a) Beamformer for target s_2 and jammer s_1 (b) Beamformer for target s_1 and jammer s_2

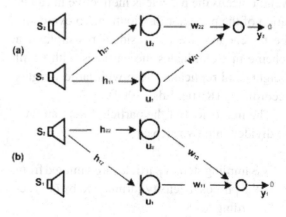

$$\mathbf{H}(\omega) = \begin{bmatrix} h_{11}(\omega) & \cdots & h_{1M}(\omega) \\ \vdots & & \vdots \\ h_{N1}(\omega) & \cdots & h_{NM}(\omega) \end{bmatrix} \qquad (16)$$

The system model can be seen in Figure 3. The source separation can be described as

$$\mathbf{y}(\omega) = \mathbf{W}(\omega)\mathbf{u}(\omega) \qquad (17)$$

where

$$\mathbf{W}(\omega) = \begin{bmatrix} w_{11}(\omega) & \cdots & w_{1N}(\omega) \\ \vdots & & \vdots \\ w_{M1}(\omega) & \cdots & wMN(\omega) \end{bmatrix} \qquad (18)$$

$\mathbf{y}(\omega) = [y_1(\omega), \cdots y_N(\omega)]^H$ contains the estimated sources, and $W(\omega)$ is the unmixing filter matrix. An inverse short time Fourier transform is then used to find the estimated sources $\hat{s}(t) = y(t)$. To demonstrate the proposed approach we consider

Figure 3. Microphone and source layout

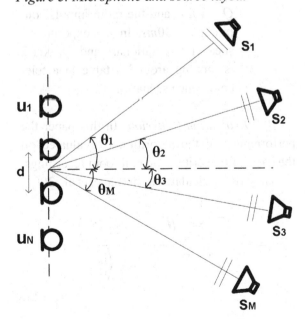

the exactly determined convolutive BSS problem i.e. $N = M = 2$, without loss of generality, and additive noise is not considered in (15).

The unmixing matrix $W(\omega)$ for each frequency bin is formulated as

$$\mathbf{W}(\omega) = inv(H(\omega)^H) \qquad (19)$$

where $\mathbf{W}(\omega) = [\mathbf{w}_1(\omega), \cdots, \mathbf{w}_N(\omega)]^H$, $\mathbf{H}(\omega) = [\mathbf{h}_1(\omega), \cdots, \mathbf{h}_M(\omega)]^H$ and $inv(\cdot)$ is inverse of the matrix. We assume in this work that the inverse exists and no further source or noise statistics are available, as is convention in blind source separation, so more sophisticated beamforming methods can not be used.

The delay element between source l and sensor k i.e. $h_{kl}(\omega)$ is calculated as

$$h_{kl}(\omega) = e^{j(k-l)d\cos(\theta_l)\omega/c} \\ k = 1, \cdots, N \qquad l = 1, \cdots, M \qquad (20)$$

where d is the distance between the sensors and c is the speed of sound in air.

Ideally, $h_{kl}(\omega)$ should be the sum of all echo paths, which are not possible to be tracked, therefore it is approximated by neglecting the room reverberations.

Finally, by placing $W(\omega)$ in (17) we estimate the sources. Since the scaling is not a major issue (Sanei et al., 2007) and there is no permutation problem, therefore we can align the estimated sources for reconstruction in the time domain. (see Table 1).

EXPERIMENTS AND RESULTS

A.   **Setup and Evaluation Criterion**
   ◦   **Data Collection:** The simulations are performed on real recorded audio-visual signals generated from a room

Table 1. Implementation steps for the proposed approach

Calibrate the video cameras and calculate calibration parameters.
Detect the face region in the synchronized frames of both cameras.
Find the positions of the lips from the face regions in synchronized video frames and calculate the position of speakers z_k in 3-D world coordinates.
Implement the 3-D visual tracker and find the actual position of the speakers. Output of the 3-D tracker is actual position of the speaker x_k and velocity information s_k.
Calculate angle of arrivals 0_k to the sensor array and check the sources are stationary or moving.
Incorporate the visual information in (20) and separate the sources.

Figure 4. A two-speaker two-microphone layout for recording within a reverberant (room) environment. Source 1 was stationary and Source 2 was moving. Room impulse response length is 130 ms.

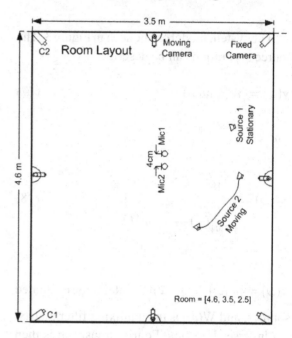

geometry as illustrated in Figure 4. Data are collected in a 4.6 x 3.5 x 2.5 m^3 intelligent office. Two out of eight calibrated color video cameras ($C1$ and $C2$ shown in Figure 4) are utilized to collect the video data. Video cameras are fully synchronized with external hardware trigger module and frames are captured at $f_v = 25$ Hz with an image size of 640x480 pixels, frames were down-scaled if it was necessary, and we found that reducing the resolution by half was a good tradeoff between accuracy and resolution. Both video cameras have overlapping field of view. The duration between consecutive states is $T_v = 1/25$ sec. Audio recordings are taken at $f_a = 8$ Hz and are synchronized manually with video recordings. Distance between the audio-sensors is $d = 4cm$. Skin models for the people in recordings were developed off line. The other important variables are selected as: number of sensors and speakers $N = M = 2$, number of particles $N_p = 600$, the number of im-

ages is $k = 525$ which indicates 21 sec data, $\theta_{thresh} = 100$, $T_k = 5$sec, $Q_v = 10^{-4}I$, $Q_r = 10^{-2}I$, $threshold = 0.04m$, FFT length $T = 2048$ and filter length $Q = 1024$, and the room impulse duration is $130ms$. In the experiments speaker 1 is stationary and speaker 2 is moving around a table in a tele-conference scenario.

BSS Evaluation Criterion: In this paper the performance of the algorithm is evaluated on the basis of two criteria on real room recordings. The SIR is calculated as in (Sanei et al., 2007)

$$SIR = \frac{\sum_i \sum_\omega |H_{ii}(\omega)|^2 \left\langle |s_i(\omega)|^2 \right\rangle}{\sum_i \sum_{i \neq j} \sum_\omega |H_{ij}(\omega)|^2 \left\langle |s_j(\omega)|^2 \right\rangle}$$

(25)

where H_{ii} and H_{ij} represent respectively, the diagonal and off-diagonal elements of the frequency domain mixing filter, and s_i is the frequency domain representation of the source of interest.

Secondly, in order to evaluate the source separation with solution to permutation by integrating audio-visual information, we use Performance Index (PI) measurement which provides results at each frequency bin level. The PI as a function of the overall system matrix G = WH is given as

$$PI(G) = [\frac{1}{n}\sum_{i=1}^{n}(\sum_{k=1}^{m}\frac{abs(G_{ik})}{\max_k abs(G_{ik})} - 1)] + [\frac{1}{m}\sum_{k=1}^{m}(\sum_{i=1}^{n}\frac{abs(G_{ik})}{\max_i abs(G_{ik})} - 1)]$$

(26)

where G_{ik} is the *ikth* element of G.

As we know the above PI based on (Cichocki and Amari, 2002) is insensitive to permutation. We therefore introduce a criterion for the two sources case which is sensitive to permutation and shown for the real case for convenience, i.e. in the case of no permutation, H = W = *I* or *H = W* = [0, 1; 1, 0] then *G = I* and in the case of permutation if *H* = [0, 1; 1, 0] then *W = I* and vice versa; therefore *G* = [0, 1; 1, 0]. Hence for a permutation free FDCBSS $[abs(G_{11}G_{22}) - abs(G_{12}G_{21})] > 0$.

B. Results and Discussion

1. **3-D Tracking and Angle of Arrival results:** In this section we will discuss the results obtained from tracking. Since speaker 2 is moving around the table so we will discuss the tracking results of the speaker 2 in detail. Since we have color video cameras therefore the face detection of the speakers is possible by using the skin model as discussed in Section-source direction and velocity extraction. The limitation of the skin model (other parts of the body, such as hands or neck and also when color of the items in background

is similar) is covered by the standard face template matching. In Figure 5 the color blob indicates that the faces are detected well. Since in the dense environment as shown in Figure 5 it is very hard to detect the lips directly, we approximate the center of the detected face region as the position of the lips in each sequence.

The approximate 2-D position of the lips of the speaker in both synchronized camera frames at each state is converted to 3-D world coordinates as discussed in Subsection-source position in the real world. With this measurement we update the particle filter. The number of particles was N_p = 600 and results were obtained using 4 runs. The gait of the speaker is not smooth and the speaker is also stationary for a while at some points during walking around the table which provides a good test for the evaluation of 3-D tracker as well as for source separation method.

In order to view the tracking results in more detail and to decide the effective change, we plotted the tracking results in xy and z axes separately. Figure 6 clearly shows that the error in detection and conversion (measurement error) is almost corrected by the particle filter. Actually, the height of the speaker is fixed and during walking only the movement in the head will produce the minor change which is clear in Figure 7. Figure 7 also helps us to decide that the mouth level is approximately fixed in the z-axis. Since the speakers and microphones are approximately at the same level therefore we can assume that effective movement is in the xy plane. Figure 8 provides the view of change in each axis at each state.

The calculated position of the center of the microphones is [-8.01, -22.06, 155.44]^T cm, position of the speaker1 is [94.23, 59.85, 155.82]^T cm (the reference point in the room is under the table, just near to the microphones). In the results of tracking we find that the effective movement of the speaker 2 was in the x and y-axis therefore the

Figure 5. 3-D Tracking results: frames of synchronized recordings, (a) frames of first camera and (b) frames of second camera; face detection based on skin model and template matching efficiently detected the faces in the frames

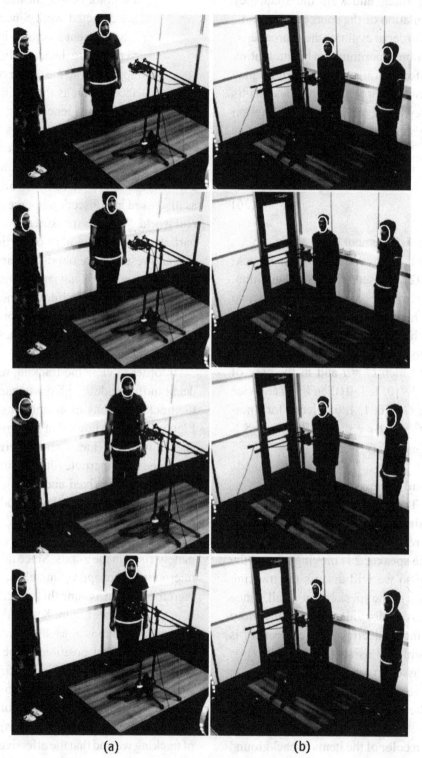

(a)   (b)

Figure 6. 3-D Tracking results: PF based tracking of the speaker in the x and y-axis, while walking around the table in the intelligent office. The result provides more in depth view in the x and y-axis.

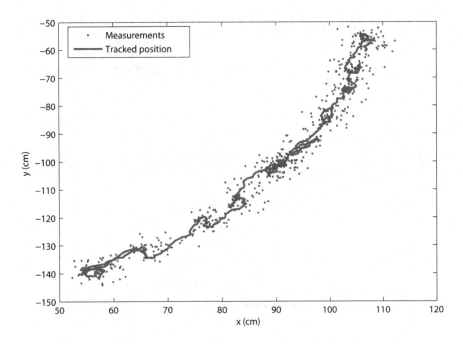

Figure 7. 3-D Tracking results: PF based tracking of the speaker in the z-axis, while walking around the table in the intelligent office. The result confirms that there is very small change in the z-axis with respect to the x and y-axis.

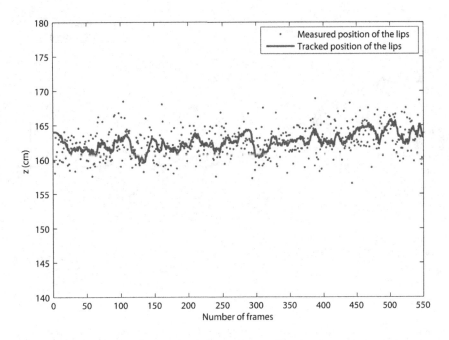

Figure 8. 3-D Tracking results: PF based tracking of the speaker. The result provides the information which helps in deciding the method to separate the sources by beamforming.

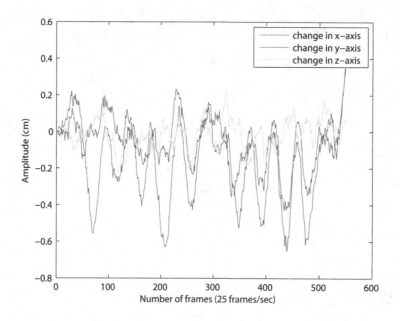

Figure 9. Angle of arrival results: Angle of arrival of the speaker 2 to the sensor array. The estimated angle before tracking and corrected angle by PF are shown. The change in angle is not smooth because of the gait of the speaker.

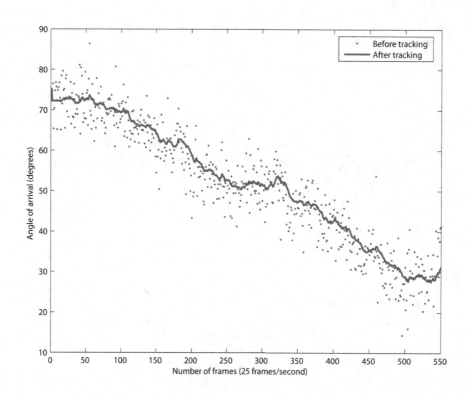

Figure 10. BSS Results: performance index at each frequency bin for 3-D tracking based angle of arrival information used in beamforming at the top and evaluation of permutation at the bottom, on the recorded signals of known room impulse response, beamforming based separation is independent of length of the signals. A lower PI refers to a superior method and $[abs(G_{11}G_{22}) - abs(G_{12}G_{21})] > 0$ *means no permutation.*

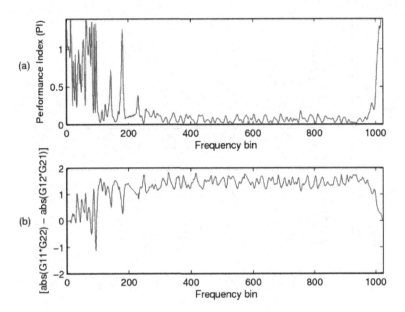

effective change in the angle of arrival was only in the xy plane. The angle of arrival of speaker 1 is 51.3 *degrees* and the angles of arrivals of the speaker 2 are shown in Figure 9.

In order to evaluate the performance of the 3-D visual tracking we provide the experiment which covers stationary, step wise moving and continuously moving sources. On the basis of the criterion mention in Section-source separation, if the sources are moving we separate the sources by the beamformer.

BSS Results: In the first simulation the angles of arrival of the both speakers obtained from the 3-D tracker are passed to (20) and the sources are separated by using beamforming (discussed in Section-source separation) and the results are shown in Figure 10. The resulting performance indices are shown in Figure 10(a) and confirm good performance i.e. close to zero across majority of the frequency bins at lower frequencies spatial dis-

crimination is a problem. Figure 10(b) also shows that the beamforming mitigates the permutation because [abs(G11G22) - abs(G12G21)] > 0 means no permutation. Since there is no permutation problem therefore we can align the sources in the time domain. For comparison the data length of the mixtures used in this simulation is 0.4sec and SIR in the case is 9.7dB. Note the data length of the signal (0.4sec) is used for comparison because it is near to moving case otherwise beamforming is independent of the length of the signal.

In the second simulation we separated the sources when speaker 2 is physically close to speaker 1 and results are shown in Figure 11. In this case, the performance reduces because of the limitations of the beamformer i.e. it is unable to discriminate spatially one speaker from another due to the width of its main lobe being greater than the separation of the speakers. In conclusion we can say that beamforming provides the solution for

Figure 11. BSS Results: performance index at each frequency bin for 3-D tracking based angle of arrival information used in beamforming at the top and evaluation of permutation at the bottom, on the recorded signals of known room impulse response, beamforming based separation is independent of length of the signals. A lower PI refers to a superior method and $[abs(G_{11}G_{22}) - abs(G_{12}G_{21})] > 0$ means no permutation.

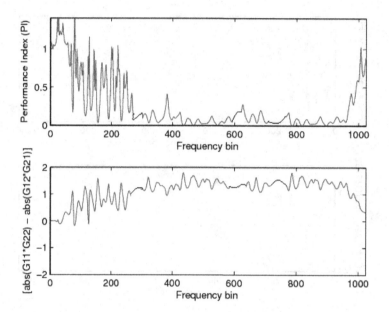

source separation of moving sources at acceptable level because beamforming is independent of the data length requirement unlike second or fourth order statistics based batch-wise BSS algorithms. The data length used in this simulation is 0.4sec and SIR in the case is 8.3dB. As we know that the ideal condition for beamforming is when there is no reverberation in the room (instantaneous case) which is not possible in real environment but beamforming still works in moderate reverberant environment like our case (room impulse response length is 130 ms).

Finally, separation of real room recordings was evaluated subjectively by listening tests, six people participated in the listening tests and mean opinion score is provided in Table 3 (MOS tests for voice are specified by ITU-T recommendation P.800 and listening-quality scale is shown in Table 2).

Table 2. Listening-quality scale

Quality of the speech	Mean opinion score
Excellent	5
Good	4
Fair	3
Poor	2
Bad	1

Table 3. Subjective evaluation MOS for separation of real room recording by beamforming when sources are moving

Algorithm	Mean opinion score
Multimodal BSS of Moving Sources	3.9

CONCLUSION

In this chapter a new multimodal BSS approach to solve the moving source separation is presented. Video information is utilized which provides velocity and direction information of sources. Based on the velocity of the source it is decided that either the sources are physically stationary or moving. The direction information is utilized to facilitate the beamforming based source separation. As shown by the simulation results, the proposed approach has a good performance for moving sources, which is not previously possible. This work provides an important step forward towards the solution of the real cocktail party problem. On-going work is considering enhancing the face-tracking, process and evaluating the scheme when the source motion is more complex.

ACKNOWLEDGMENT

Some of the material in this chapter and further research is presented in, Naqvi, S. M., Yu. M. and Chambers, J. A. (2010), A multimodal approach to blind source separation of moving sources, *accepted for publication in IEEE Journal of Selected Topics in Signal Processing, 2010.*

REFERENCES

Araki, S., Makino, S,, Hinamoto, Y., Mukai, R., Nishikawa, T., & Saruwatari, H. (2003). Equivalence between frequency domain blind source separation and frequency domain adaptive beamforming for convolutive mixtures. *EURASIP Journal on Applied Signal Processing*, (11): 1157–1166. doi:10.1155/S1110865703305074

Back, A. D., & Tsoi, A. C. (1994). *Blind deconvolution of signals using a complex recurrent network*, Proc. IEEE Workshop, Neural Networks for Signal Processing 4, pp. 565–574.

Bregman, A. S. (1990). *Auditory scence analysis*. Cambridge, MA: MIT Press.

Cherry, C. (1953). Some experiments on the recognition of speech, with one and with two ears. *The Journal of the Acoustical Society of America, 25*(9), 975–979. doi:10.1121/1.1907229

Cherry, C., & Taylor, W. (1954). Some further experiments upon the recognition of speech, with one and with two ears. *The Journal of the Acoustical Society of America, 26,* 554–559. doi:10.1121/1.1907373

Cichocki, A., & Amari, S. (2002). *Adaptive Blind Signal and Image Processing: Learning Algorithms and Applications*. John Wiley. doi:10.1002/0470845899

Fisher, R., Perkins, S., Walker, A., & Wolfart, E. (2003). *Roberts cross edge detector*. Image Processing Learning Resources.

Gatica-Perez, D., Lathoud, G., Odobez, J. & McCowan, I. (2007). Audiovisual probabilistic tracking of multiple speakers in meetings. *IEEE Trans. On Audio, Speech and Language processing, 15(2),* 601-616.

Hartley, R., & Zisserman, A. (2001). *Multiple View Geometry in Computer Vision*. Cambridge University Press.

Haykin, S., Principe, J. C., Sejnowski, T. J., & McWhirter, J. (2007). *New Directions in Statistical Signal Processing: From Systems to Brain,* Cambridge, Massachusetts London: The MIT Press.

Hild-II. K. E., Erdogmus, D. & Principe, J. C. (2002). *Blind source extraction of time-varying, instantaneous mixtures using an on-line algorithm.* Proc. IEEE ICASSP, Orlando, Florida, USA.

Hyvarinen. A., Karhunen, J. & Oja, E. (2001). *Independent Component Analysis.* New York: Wiley.

Koutras, A., Dermatas, E., & Kokkinakis, G. (2000). *Blind source separation of moving speakers in real reverberant environment.* Proc. IEEE ICASSP, 1133–1136.

Lee,. Y. & Yoo, S. I. (2002). *An elliptical boundary modal for skin color detection.* Proc. Imaging Science, Systems, and Technology.

Maganti, H. K., Gatica-Perez, D. & McCowan, I. (2007). Speech enhancement and recognition in meetings with an audio-visual sensor array. *IEEE Trans. on Audio, Speech and Language processing, 15(8),* 2257–2269.

Makino, S., Sawada, H., Mukai, R., & Araki, S. (2005). Blind separation of convolved mixtures of speech in frequency domain. *IEICE Trans. Fundamentals. E (Norwalk, Conn.), 88-A,* 1640–1655.

Mukai, R., Sawada, H., Araki, S., & Makino, S. (2003). *Robust real-time blind source separation for moving speakers in a room.* Proc. IEEE ICASSP, Hong Kong.

Naqvi, S. M., Zhang, Y., & Chambers, J. A. (2008). *A multimodal approach for frequency domain blind source separation for moving sources in a room.* Proc. IAPR CIP2008, Santorini, Greece.

Naqvi, S. M., Zhang, Y., & Chambers, J. A. (2009). *Multimodal blind source separation for moving sources.* Proc. IEEE ICASSP, Taipei, Taiwan.

Naqvi, S. M., Zhang, Y., Tsalaile, T., Sanei, S., & Chambers, J. A. (2008). *A multimodal approach for frequency domain independent component analysis with geometrically-based initialization.* Proc. EUSIPCO, Lausanne, Switzerland.

Parra, L., & Spence, C. (2000). Convolutive blind separation of non-stationary sources. *IEEE Transactions on Speech and Audio Processing, 8(3),* 320–327. doi:10.1109/89.841214

Prieto, R. E., & Jinachitra, P. (2005). *Blind source separation for time-variant mixing systems using piecewise linear approximations.* Proc. IEEE ICASSP, 301–304.

Ristic, B., Arulampalam, S., & Gordon, N. (2004). *Beyond the Kalman Filter: Particle Filter for Tracking Applications.* Boston, London: Artech House Publishers.

Roberts, S., & Everson, R. (2001). *Independent Component Analysis.* Cambridge, England: Cambridge University Press.

Sanei, S., Naqvi, S. M., Chambers, J. A., & Hicks, Y. (2007). *A geometrically constrained multimodal approach for convolutive blind source separation.* Proc. IEEE ICASSP, 969–972.

Saruwatari, H., Kawamura, T., Nishikawa, T., Lee, A., & Shikano, K. (2006). Blind source separation based on a fast-convergence algorithm combining ICA and beamforming. *IEEE Trans on Audio. Speech and Language Processing, 14,* 666–678. doi:10.1109/TSA.2005.855832

Tsai, R. Y. (1987). A versatile camera calibration technique for high-accuracy 3d machine vision metrology using off-the-shelf tv cameras and lenses. *IEEE Journal on Robotics and Automation, RA-3*(4), 323–344. doi:10.1109/JRA.1987.1087109

Tsalaile, T., Naqvi, S. M., Nazarpour, K., Sanei, S., & Chambers, J. A. (2008). *Blind source extraction of heart sound signals from lung sound recordings exploiting periodicity of the heart sound.* Proc. IEEE ICASSP, Las Vegas, USA.

Veen, B. D. V., & Buckley, K. M. (1988). Beamforming: A versatile approach to spatial filtering. *IEEE ASSP Magazine,* 4–21. doi:10.1109/53.665

Wang, W., Sanei, S., & Chambers, J. A. (2003). *A joint diagonalization method for convolutive blind separation of nonstationary sources in the frequency domain.* Proc. ICA, Nara, Japan.

Wang, W., Sanei, S., & Chambers, J. A. (2005). Penalty function based joint diagonalization approach for convolutive blind separation of nonstationary sources. *IEEE Transactions on Signal Processing, 53*(5), 1654–1669. doi:10.1109/TSP.2005.845433

Yilmaz, O., & Rickard, S. (2004). Blind separation of speech mixtures via time-frequency masking. *IEEE Transactions on Signal Processing, 52*(7), 1830–1847. doi:10.1109/TSP.2004.828896

Chapter 6
Sound Source Localization:
Conventional Methods and Intensity Vector Direction Exploitation

Banu Günel
University of Surrey, UK

Hüseyin Hacıhabiboğlu
King's College London, UK

ABSTRACT

Automatic sound source localization has recently gained interest due to its various applications that range from surveillance to hearing aids, and teleconferencing to human computer interaction. Automatic sound source localization may refer to the process of determining only the direction of a sound source, which is known as the direction-of-arrival estimation, or also its distance in order to obtain its coordinates. Various methods have previously been proposed for this purpose. Many of these methods use the time and level differences between the signals captured by each element of a microphone array. An overview of these conventional array processing methods is given and the factors that affect their performance are discussed. The limitations of these methods affecting real-time implementation are highlighted. An emerging source localization method based on acoustic intensity is explained. A theoretical evaluation of different microphone array geometries is given. Two well-known problems, localization of multiple sources and localization of acoustic reflections, are addressed.

INTRODUCTION

Sound source localization aims to determine the location of a target sound source with respect to a reference point. When only the direction of the sound source is important, sound source localization may be reduced to the estimation of the direction-of-arrival (DOA) of a sound wave.

Detection of the location of a sound source automatically is essential for many machine audition systems due to its broad application areas. These include automatic camera aiming for teleconferencing (Ito, Maruyoshi, Kawamoto, Mukai, & Ohnishi, 2002; Sturim, Brandstein, & Silverman, 1997; Brandstein & Silverman, 1997), locating a gunshot or another sound of interest for surveillance (Cowling & Sitte, 2000; Valenzise, Gerosa, Tagliasacchi, Antonacci, & Sarti, 2007), hear-

DOI: 10.4018/978-1-61520-919-4.ch006

ing aids (Desloge, Rabinowitz, & Zurek, 1997; Welker, Greenberg, Desloge, & Zurek, 1997; Kates, 1998; Widrow, 2001) and human-computer interaction (HCI).

Sound source localization is impossible using a single sensor. Considering a fixed sensor structure, it is a natural conclusion that there should be at least two sensors. Various methods using an array of microphones have previously been proposed for sound source localization. These include, but are not limited to, steered response power (SRP) localization, high-resolution spectral-estimation, and time-delay-of-arrival (TDOA) estimation. There are also different variations and combinations of these methods. However, all of these methods use the time and level differences between the signals captured by each sensor in a microphone array.

Steered response power localizers carry out beamforming at all directions by digitally steering the array and look for the direction that maximizes the signal power. A simple version of this type of locator is known as the steered-beamforming based localizer.

High-resolution spectral estimation based localizers, such as the **MU**ltiple **SI**gnal **C**lassification (MUSIC) algorithm, compute a spatio-spectral correlation matrix using the signals recorded by each microphone and decompose it into signal and noise subspaces. A search is then carried out in these subspaces to detect the possible direction of arrivals.

TDOA-based localizers use the time delays between pairs of microphones and the array position information. For a plane wave, the observed time delay between a pair of microphones is constant on a hyperboloid. A direction estimate can be obtained from several microphone pairs by finding the optimal solution of this system of hyperboloids. TDOA estimation is usually made by the generalized cross-correlation (GCC) method. GCC involves a weighting operation to improve the performance of the TDOA based localizers under reverberant conditions.

In addition to these conventional methods, there are other approaches proposed for sound source localization, such as biologically inspired methods that mimic binaural hearing mechanism as well as methods that mimic cognitive aspects of hearing by using artificial intelligence. The auditory system provides an efficient means of sound source localization. The mammalian auditory systems consist of two ears and the central processing in the brain to determine the DOA exploiting the time and level differences between the sounds arriving at the two ears. Positions of ears can be changed by head/body movements to allow optimal and adaptive localization when combined with visual cues. In addition, the auditory cognitive system uses other cues, such as the loudness, and direct-to-reverberant sound energy ratio in order to determine the source distance.

There are several real-life requirements that should be met by a successful sound source localization system. Most important of these requirements are good localization accuracy, high speed, low cost, small array size, small number of channels for ease of data interfacing and 3D symmetry of operation. Conventional array processing methods do not satisfy most of these requirements due to real-life considerations. For example, cosmetic constraints may limit the number of microphones for hearing aid applications.

This chapter provides an overview of conventional microphone array processing methods including the recent developments based on these methods. The factors that affect the performance of sound source localization algorithms are classified and discussed. The limitations of conventional localizers are highlighted within the context of real-life design considerations. An emerging method based on sound intensity, which was proposed as a solution to these limitations, is explained. Special microphone array geometries required for calculating the intensity vector directions and the directional accuracy achieved by these geometries are discussed in detail. Solutions to some well-known practical problems, more specifically, the localization of multiple sound sources and the localization of dominant reflections in a reverberant environment, are provided.

PROBLEM DEFINITION USING A SIMPLE MICROPHONE ARRAY

Sound waves emanating from isotropic sources are spherical and travel outwards. In the acoustical far-field, i.e., sufficiently away from the sound source, the wave starts to appear as a plane wave. Most source localization algorithms assume that the source to be localized is situated in the acoustical far field and that the resulting plane waves arrive with uniform time-delays to pairs of microphones. Spherical waves, on the other hand, result in non-uniform delays which make localization difficult. Far-field assumption is valid for most application environments, and even at very close distances if the size of the microphone array is comparatively small.

The acoustic pressure due to a complex monochromatic plane wave propagating along the $+x$ axis can be written as

$$p(t) = A e^{jk(x-ct)}, \tag{1}$$

where t is the time, j is the imaginary unit, A is the amplitude, $k = 2\pi / \lambda$ is the wavenumber for the wavelength λ, x is the displacement and c is the speed of sound. Equation 1 can also be written as

$$p(t) = A e^{j(\omega t - kx)}, \tag{2}$$

where $\omega = 2\pi f$ is the angular frequency. The frequency, f and the wavelength, λ of a sound wave is also related as $f = c / \lambda$.

The pressure values due to a plane wave recorded by a pair of microphones separated by a distance d as shown in Figure 1, can be expressed as

Figure 1. Plane wave arriving at a pair microphone positions

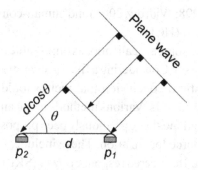

$$p_1(t) = A e^{j(\omega t - kx)} \tag{3}$$

$$p_2(t) = A e^{j(\omega t - kx - kd\cos\theta)} \tag{4}$$

The aim of DOA estimation is to detect the arrival direction, θ, of this plane wave, while source localization may also imply the detection of the source distance as well.

In order to detect the arrival direction of a single plane wave, the cross-correlation of small segments of the microphone signals can be calculated:

$$R(\tau) = \int_{-T}^{T} p_1^*(t) p_2(t+\tau) dt$$

$$= A^2 \int_{-T}^{T} e^{-j(\omega t - kx)} e^{j(\omega t + \omega\tau - kx - kd\cos\theta)} dt$$

$$= A^2 \int_{-T}^{T} e^{j(\omega\tau - kd\cos\theta)} dt$$

$$= 2TA^2 e^{j(\omega\tau - kd\cos\theta)}. \tag{5}$$

The real part of the cross correlation, which equals to $2TA^2 \cos(\omega\tau - kd\cos\theta)$ takes its maximum value when. The direction of the plane wave can then be estimated using this relationship.

When there are multiple sound sources, noise and reflections, several peaks are observed in the cross-correlation function, which makes it very hard, if not impossible, to determine the source direction. More microphones and more complex algorithms are then employed for localising sound sources, which are explained in the following sections.

Using two very closely placed omnidirectional microphones, the projection of the pressure gradient along their look direction can also be approximated taking the pressure difference between the two microphones:

$$p_1(t) - p_2(t) = ae^{j(\omega t - kx)}(1 - e^{-jkd\cos\theta})$$

$$= p_1(t)(1 - e^{-jkd\cos\theta})$$

$$= p_1(t)(1 - \cos(kd\cos\theta) + j\sin(kd\cos\theta)). \tag{6}$$

If the microphones are very closely placed, i.e., $kd << 1$, then $\cos(kd\cos\theta) \approx 1$ and $\sin(kd\cos\theta) \approx kd\cos\theta$. Then, the pressure difference in Equation 6 becomes

$$p_1(t) - p_2(t) \approx jp_1(t)kd\cos\theta. \tag{7}$$

While it is not possible to determine the source direction from Equation 7, it is useful to show the relationship between the pressure, pressure gradients and the source direction. If pressure is defined as a continuous function of space, then the pressure gradient indicates the direction and the rate of change of pressure.

By using more microphones in a spherical geometry, these relationships can be exploited for source localization. This approach will be explained in the following sections.

DOA estimation is seen as the initial step for full sound source localization, i.e., determining the source distance as well as its direction. Basically, different DOA estimates obtained using clusters

of microphones are combined together with the knowledge of the microphone array geometry to find the optimum source position. The simplest of these techniques is known as triangulation. Triangulation requires DOA estimates at different positions. The optimum intersecting point of these directions is calculated to estimate the source position. Since, DOA estimation can be exploited for source distance estimation in this way, source localization term is frequently used in place of DOA estimation term.

CONVENTIONAL SOURCE LOCALIZATION METHODS

Steered-Response Power Localizers

Steered-response power (SRP) localizers have steerable pointing directions making it possible to scan all the directions and search for a peak in the output power (DiBiase, Silverman, & Brandstein, 2001). The simplest implementation of these localizers is achieved by using the delay-and-sum beamformer. Figure 2 shows this beamformer with an incident wavefront.

Output of this beamformer can be expressed as:

$$b(t) = \sum_{i=1}^{N} w_i m_i(t - \tau_i), \tag{8}$$

where w_i is the weight and τ_i is the time delay applied to the ith sensor signal $m_i(t)$.

Planar wavefronts arrive at the array microphones with different time delays depending on the relative direction of the sound source with respect to the array. For example, in Figure 2, the time delay between the two adjacent sensors is $d\cos(\theta)/c$, where d is the microphone spacing and c is the speed of sound. This time delay can be compensated for prior to summing so that the signals can be added constructively increasing the power output of the array. As this is the sim-

Figure 2. Delay and sum beamformer with far field sound source

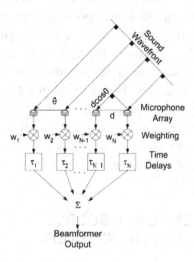

plest beamformer implementation, it is also known as the conventional beamformer (CBF).

For sound source localization, the array is steered in all directions by adjusting the time delays accordingly. If the steered direction coincides with a sound source direction, a peak is observed at the array output.

Computational load of these localizers is usually very high as the steering needs to be done for all directions. Another issue regarding the implementation of a beamformer is the microphone spacing. Depending on the frequency range of the source signal, the spacing affects the quality of the output. At low frequencies (i.e. large wavelength) the spacing between the microphones appears to be small, and at high frequencies (i.e. small wavelength) the spacing appears to be large. This leads to low pass filtering of sounds coming from directions other than the look direction of the array, which is the direction of the highest signal gain.

In the discrete-time implementation of steered-beamforming, the delay elements are integer multiples of a unit delay. Therefore, the temporal sampling period determines the steering-angle intervals, hence the spatial resolution. In order to alleviate this limitation on the spatial resolution,

fractional-delay filters can be used (Pridham & Mucci, 1979). Hierarchical searching (Zotkin & Duraiswami, 2004) and inverse mapping that maps relative delays to candidate locations (Dmochowski, Benesty, & Affes, 2007b) were proposed to improve the speed of these algorithms.

High-Resolution Spectral-Estimation Based Localizers

High-resolution spectral-estimation based localizers are based on the computation of a spatio-spectral correlation matrix using the signals recorded at each microphone in the array and decomposing this matrix into signal and noise subspaces by eigenvalue decomposition. A search is then made in either subspace to locate the sources. A commonly applied algorithm for high-resolution spectral-estimation is the MUltiple SIgnal Classification (MUSIC) algorithm (Schmidt, 1986).

Let us assume there are M microphones and D incident wavefronts corresponding to D sources. L samples captured by the microphones constituting an $L \times M$ matrix, X. A covariance matrix is calculated by $R = X^* X$ which results in an $M \times M$ matrix, where X^* is the conjugate transpose of the matrix X. This square matrix has M eigenvalues.

Since this matrix has rank D, there are $M - D$ small eigenvalues. The eigenvectors of these eigenvalues form the $M - D$ - dimensional noise subspace. The rest of the eigenvectors form the D-dimensional signal subspace.

A column vector r that belongs to the signal subspace minimizes the Euclidean distance from this vector to the noise subspace $d^2 = \mathbf{r}^* \mathbf{S}_N \mathbf{S}_N^* \mathbf{r}$, where $\mathbf{S}_N$ is the $M \times (M - D)$ matrix whose columns are made up of the noise eigenvectors.

The vector r can be varied as a function of direction θ and the Euclidean distances can be calculated for each direction. Denoting these distances as $P(\theta)$, the MUSIC algorithm looks for peak in the $1/P(\theta)$ in order to determine the direction of incidence.

High-resolution spectral estimation is used mainly for localizing narrowband signals and is based on the assumption that the source and noise signals are stationary and their locations are fixed. Narrowband processing can be applied to broadband signals after dividing the waveforms into narrowband segments (Lorenzelli, Wang, & Yo, 1996). High-resolution spectral estimation is also suitable for detecting multiple sources. However this localizer requires exhaustive search similar to steered-beamforming based localizers. In order to reduce the computational complexity of the MUSIC algorithm, the root-MUSIC algorithm that uses a simple root-finding approach was proposed (Barabell, 1983; Rao & Hari, 1989).

Both MUSIC and root-MUSIC algorithms are suitable for use with uniform linear arrays (ULAs) consisting of equally spaced microphones in a linear configuration. In order to overcome this restriction on the array geometry while retaining search-free processing, other methods were proposed such as estimation of signal parameters using rotational invariance technique (ESPRIT) that exploits the rotational invariance between signal subspaces (Roy & Kailath, 1989), manifold separation technique (MST) that carries out the orthogonal expansion of the wavefield (Belloni, Richter, & Koivunen, 2007) and Fourier domain root-MUSIC that is based on the Fourier series expansion of the MUSIC function (Rubsamen & Gershman, 2009).

Time-Delay-of-Arrival (TDOA) Based Localizers

Time-delay-of-arrival (TDOA) based localizers exploit the calculated time delays and the array position information to determine a set of hyperboloids denoting possible source positions. Solution of the system of these hyperboloids leads to an estimate of the source location (Rabinkin et al., 1996). Therefore, these localizers carry out a two-stage process: time delay estimation (TDE) and mapping according to array geometry.

The signal received by each microphone in the array can be expressed as:

$$m_i(t) = a_i x(t - t_i) + n_i(t) \qquad (9)$$

where a_i is the attenuation, $x(t)$ is the source signal, t_i is the source propagation time and $n_i(t)$ is the noise captured by the ith microphone.

Let us define $D_{ik} = t_i - t_k$ as the time-delay-of-arrival between the microphones i and k. D_{ik} can be computed from $m_i(t)$ and $m_k(t)$ using the cross-correlation, R_{ik}, of these signals which has a peak at $\tau = D_{ik}$:

$$R_{ik}(\tau) = \int_{-\infty}^{\infty} m_i(t) m_k(t - \tau) dt. \qquad (10)$$

The TDOA estimate for each pair $m_i(t)$ and $m_k(t)$ determines the distance difference $r_i - r_k = c(t_i - t_k)$, where r_i and r_k are the distances between the sound source and the microphones, i and k, respectively. These define a hyperboloid.

Since all points on a single hyperboloid are potential source locations, an optimal solution of the system of these hyperboloids is searched for. The least mean square (LMS) solution can be used for this purpose (Haykin, 1996). For the horizontal plane, a linear intersection estimation algorithm that has a closed-form solution was also proposed (Brandstein, Adcock, & Silverman, 1997).

The estimation of the TDOA can be made in different ways. The simplest way is by calculating the phase difference. However, in order to avoid errors due to aliasing, the phase difference between a pair of microphones should be less than π. In other words, this requires that $2\pi f_{max} \tau \leq \pi$, where τ is the time delay and f_{max} is the maximum frequency of operation. The time delay τ is maximum when the sound source is in line with the array and so $\tau = d / c$, where d is the microphone spacing and c is the speed of sound. Therefore, $d \leq \lambda_{min} / 2$, which puts the limit on the microphone spacing to be no greater than half the minimum wavelength present in the signal to be localized. This limit is not suitable for most applications and therefore cross-correlation methods are essential (Varma, 2002).

For cross-correlation based TDOA calculations, the reflections cause errors as they create undesired local maxima. Therefore, pre-filtering is applied before cross-correlation to reduce these errors. This method is called the generalized cross-correlation (GCC) method (Knapp & Carter, 1976). GCC can be calculated as:

$$\hat{R}_{GCC}(\tau) = \int_{-\infty}^{\infty} |G(\omega)|^2 \, \hat{P}_{12}(\omega) e^{j\omega\tau} d\omega \qquad (11)$$

where $|G(\omega)|^2$ is the weighting function, $\hat{P}_{12}(\omega) = X_1^*(\omega)X_2(\omega)$ is the cross-power spectrum calculated using the Fourier transforms of $x_1(t)$ and $x_2(t)$ and ω is the angular frequency. The time delay can be calculated as:

$$\hat{\tau} = \arg\max_{\tau} \hat{R}_{GCC}(\tau) \qquad (12)$$

One of the design issues is the selection of the weighting function, $G(\omega)$. It was shown that the phase transform (PHAT) weighting, which is also known as the cross-power spectrum phase (CSP), performs better than the others under reverberant conditions (Gustafsson, Rao, & Trivedi, 2003; Omologo & Svaizer, 1994; Svaizer, Matassoni, & Omologo, 1997). The weighting function can be found using this method as:

$$|G(\omega)|^2 = \frac{1}{|X_1(\omega)X_2^*(\omega)|} \qquad (13)$$

TDOA-based localizers do not require exhaustive search algorithms like the other two localizer types and can also localize broadband signals. TDOA-based localizers can easily be implemented on embedded hardware as the processing is based on the Fourier transform and the cross-correlation computations (Rabinkin et al., 1996) for which fast algorithms exist. Localization accuracy is difficult to estimate as it depends on the position of the sound source relative to the array. In general, reverberation decreases localization accuracy (Champagne, Bedard, & Stephenne, 1996). In order to estimate the direct paths in the presence of reverberation, a variation of the GCC-based TDOA estimation method has been proposed that is known as adaptive eigenvalue decomposition (Huang, Benestry, & Elko, 1999; Benesty, 2000). An algorithm based on multichannel cross-correlation coefficient (MCCC) calculation was also proposed to improve the accuracy of time delay estimation under adverse conditions with noise and reverberation (Chen, Benesty, & Huang, 2003; Benesty, Huang, & Chen, 2007; Dmochowski, Benesty, & Affes, 2007a).

A direct comparison of the localization accuracies for different techniques is not possible due to different test conditions present in each work. However, in moderately reverberant rooms, the accuracy of TDOA-based localizers is usually better than the others, achieving a DOA estimation error between 2°- 7°. This accuracy is usually sufficient for most applications. The implementation of TDOA-based localizers is also easier than the others. Therefore, TDOA-based techniques are preferred over other conventional techniques unless other design considerations, such as the size of the microphone array, prevent their application.

Biologically Inspired Methods

Human auditory system performs localization extraordinarily well even in the presence of noise, reverberation and interfering sounds, despite the fact that it processes only two channels of information from the ears. Therefore, apart from the conventional methods explained above, several other source localization strategies inspired by psychoacoustics research and learning were also proposed. These methods, which are within the domain of the general research area called computational auditory scene analysis (CASA) (Bregman, 1990), mostly exploit psychoacoustical and perceptual models making use of the time and level differences between the ears, the precedence effect, auditory onset detection mechanisms, and familiarity with the sound source and the acoustical environment.

Human sound source localization and related methods

Interaural time differences (ITD) and interaural level differences (ILD) are the two main mechanisms allowing human sound source localization on the horizontal plane. Rayleigh's duplex theory states that this localization mechanism depends on ITD cues for frequencies lower than approximately 1500 Hz and ILDs for higher frequencies (Rayleigh, 1907; Blauert, 1997). The frequency limit of 1500 Hz is due to the fact that around 1500 Hz, the distance between the eardrums becomes comparable to half of the wavelength of the sound wave and results in a phase ambiguity. Therefore, for frequencies higher than this limit, ILD becomes the main direction cue.

Another reason for the human auditory system using two different cues for low and high frequencies is related to the psychophysical properties of the auditory system. The neurons fire in synchrony with the phase of the sound signal, which is known as the phase locking. However, this occurs up to 5 kHz. Above this limit, the firing times of the neurons vary and make it difficult to detect the phase information (Crow, Rupert, & Moushegian, 1978).

ITD and ILD change according to the size and shape of the head. A simple formula for approximating the ITD values by calculating the path difference between the signals arriving at the two ears is given by:

$$ITD = \frac{r_{head}}{c}(\theta + \sin(\theta)) \qquad (14)$$

where r_{head} is the radius of the head, c is the speed of sound and θ is the azimuth angle of source direction as shown in Figure 3.

It should be noted that ITD and ILD provide cues for localizing the sound source only on the horizontal plane. However localization on the horizontal plane is not perfect as there exist surfaces of constant ITD and ILD. Due to the subjective confusion regarding front-back ambiguity, these surfaces are called cones-of-confusion. Another mechanism exists for the perception of the elevation information and also for front-back discrimination. This mechanism uses the spectral coloration imposed on the sound wave by the pinnæ, head and torso when the sound travels from source to the listener's eardrums. The transfer function characterizing all of these cues is known as the head-related transfer function (HRTF). Pinnæ, head and torso of a listener apply acoustic filtering to the sounds, depending on the direction of the sound source. This shaping is specific to each listener due to the unique shape of pinnæ, head and torso each listener has (Cheng & Wakefield, 1999).

Binaural cues discussed above have been used to design source localization methods. These methods use interaural coherence in complex listening situations (Faller & Merimaa, 2004). A filter-bank based source localization and separation algorithm was also explained (Hu & Liu, 2009). Several similar methods were also proposed for robot audition (J. Huang, Ohnishi, & Sugie, 1997; Nakadai, Okuno, & Kitano, 2002; Liu & Meng, 2007).

The perception of the sound source location in the presence of an acoustical reflection is governed by the precedence effect (Hartmann, 1983; Rakerd & Hartmann, 1985). Precedence effect occurs when the time delay between the direct sound and a simulated reflection at the

Figure 3. Occurrence of interaural time difference (ITD) and interaural level difference (ILD)

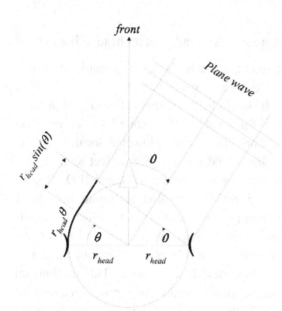

same level is below a certain threshold (around 5 ms for broadband clicks and 20 ms for speech). Under the precedence effect, the auditory event is perceived between the direct sound and its reflection and closer to the direct sound (Blauert, 1997). A source localization method that exploits the precedence effect was proposed in (Wilson & Darrell, 2006). Precedence effect is particularly prominent at signal onsets and offsets (Rakerd & Hartmann, 1986; Hartmann & Rakerd, 1989a). Onset detection was also exploited in conjunction with a model of the precedence effect for source localization (Supper, Brookes, & Rumsey, 2006).

Apart from the factors like familiarity with the sound source and its loudness, the reflections are also important factors for sound source localization performance. Reflections provide important cues for distance perception, but decrease the accuracy of direction estimation as they smear the available localization cues. However, in familiar environments, learning the acoustical characteristics help localization (Shinn-Cunningham, 2000). A localization method that learns source positions

using a set of training recordings was proposed in (Smaragdis & Boufounos, 2007). Neural networks were also used to learn the directional filtering properties of the pinnæ and exploit this information for source localization (Neti, Young, & Schneider, 1992).

Human Sound Source Localization Acuity

The localization performance of humans can be assessed by subjective listening tests. In these tests, the minimum perceivable change in the direction of a sound source is obtained by psychoacoustical means (Mills, 1958; Hartmann & Rakerd, 1989b).

Localization blur is the smallest change in direction and distance of the sound source that is sufficient to produce a change in the perceived mean location of the auditory event (Blauert, 1997). Localization is most accurate in the front direction. Minimum detectable horizontal displacement of a sinusoidal source incident from the front direction was found to be about 2°. For a sound source facing one of the ears, localization blur is about 10° and for sources behind the listener it is about 5° (Zwicker & Fastl, 1999). A source in the median plane must be displaced by about 15° to perceive the change of its elevation (Shilling & Shinn-Cunningham, 2000). The localization blur for distance was found as 13%-15%. It should be noted that localization blur depends on the methods and signal types used in the tests. The reader is referred to (Blauert, 1997) for details of the localization blur experiments.

Despite its wide usage, localization blur is not sufficient to explain the mean absolute error of detected sound source locations. Localization blur experiments depend on detecting the displacement of a sound source when a reference signal is present at the original location. When such a reference is not present, the error of estimated sound source locations can increase up to 20° for short broadband sounds (Makous & Middlebrooks, 1990).

FACTORS AFFECTING AUTOMATIC LOCALIZATION

The performance of source localization methods depends on several factors, which can be grouped into three: environmental, microphone array related and source related.

Environmental factors include the reverberation, presence of major reflecting surfaces, and the relative positioning of the sources and the microphone array. Increasing reverberation and major reflecting surfaces decrease the accuracy of localization, in general. The effect of geometric positioning however is more complicated. In general, when the spatial separation between the sound sources is small, their localization becomes more difficult. Sound source distance may also affect the localization accuracy. Sources closer to the microphone array can be localized more accurately as the direct path dominates over reflections. However, if the source is too close to the microphone array, this may violate the far-field assumption, which is essential for some algorithms. The relative position of the source with respect to the microphone array may also affect the localization accuracy as most arrays perform better for certain directions.

Microphone array related factors include the geometry of the array, the size of the array and the number of sensors in the array. The geometry of array depends on the dimensions of localization problem. For example, for localizing in the horizontal and the vertical planes only, linear or planar arrays are usually employed. In contrast, 3D array topologies are needed for localization of sound sources in three dimensions. As the microphone array geometry and size are closely related to the source localization algorithm and its application field, it is not possible to generalise their effect on the localization performance. However, as a general rule it may be stated that localization accuracy increases with the number of microphones in the array.

Source related factors include the spectro-temporal content of the sources, their durations, levels, number, directional properties and the observed apertures. Broadband impulsive sounds, which have a short duration such as gun-shots, can be localized better with time-delay estimation based methods. Localization becomes easier if the target and interfering sources do not significantly overlap in time-frequency bins. While the lengths of the sound segments used in localization is an algorithm design parameter, a persistent sound source is usually better than an impulsive or a short-duration source as the localization accuracy can be improved by using earlier estimates obtained from the previous segments.

When the level of a target signal increases, it becomes easier to detect and localize it since it dominates over interferences. When there are several sound sources, it becomes more difficult to localize them. The directivity of a sound source, when combined with geometric positioning, also has an effect on the localization accuracy. When a directional sound source is positioned towards a reflecting surface, the detected DOA may be wrong as the reflection may dominate over the direct sound. Sound sources are never point-like and have a finite aperture. However, they are usually treated as such for the sake of simplicity while evaluating the localization accuracy.

All of the above listed factors relate to the operating conditions rather than the algorithms themselves. Therefore, in order to evaluate the performance of a localization algorithm formally for comparison purposes, the algorithm has to be tested under as many different conditions as possible and these factors have to be reported as in greater detail as possible.

It should be noted that while the localization accuracy of a localizer is important, application areas and operating conditions may have additional requirements. Ideally, the microphone array should be small and should have 3D symmetry for easy integration and installation. This is especially important for applications on wearable devices.

The number of sensors in the array should also be limited to avoid complex data acquisition and interfacing circuitry. The algorithms should be able to work in real-time and under real-life operating conditions such as in noisy and/or reverberant environments. The computational complexity of the algorithms should also be low to decrease the power consumption, which is especially important for applications on mobile devices. Unfortunately, there are trade-offs between these desirable features. Therefore, successful implementations are usually driven by the requirements of the application areas, rather than the localization accuracy alone.

INTENSITY MEASUREMENT FOR SOURCE LOCALIZATION

Time-averaged energy flux in an acoustic field is called the acoustic intensity. For sound source localization, one is usually interested in the time-varying process of this energy transfer, which is called the instantaneous acoustic intensity. In a time-stationary plane wave field, the instantaneous intensity can be divided into active and reactive components. At a single frequency, these are in phase and in quadrature with the particle velocity, respectively (Fahy, 1995). Wavefronts lie perpendicular to the direction of the in phase component and therefore the active component of the instantaneous intensity at a single frequency is valuable in estimating the sound source direction.

The acoustic particle velocity, $v(\omega, t)$, which is the velocity of an air molecule due to the small displacements caused by the sound wave, is defined in two dimensions for a time-frequency bin as

$$\mathbf{v}(\omega, t) = \frac{1}{\rho_0 c} \left[p_X\left(\omega, t\right) \mathbf{u_x} + p_Y\left(\omega, t\right) \mathbf{u_y} \right],$$

(15)

where p_0 is the ambient density, c is the speed of sound, $p_x(\omega, t)$ and $p_y(\omega, t)$ are the components of the pressure gradient along the x and y axes, and u_x and u_y are unit vectors in these directions.

Instantaneous intensity is the product of the sound pressure, $p_W(\omega, t)$ and the particle velocity. The active intensity can be expressed as,

$$\mathbf{I}(\omega, t) = \frac{1}{\rho_0 c} \left[Re\{p_W^*(\omega, t) p_X(\omega, t)\} \mathbf{u_x} + Re\{p_W^*(\omega, t) p_Y(\omega, t)\} \mathbf{u_y} \right],$$

(16)

where * denotes conjugation and $Re\{\bullet\}$ denotes taking the real part of the argument.

Then, the direction of the active intensity vector, $\gamma(\omega, t)$ can be calculated as

$$\gamma(\omega, t) = \arctan\left[\frac{Re\{p_W^*(\omega, t) p_Y(\omega, t)\}}{Re\{p_W^*(\omega, t) p_X(\omega, t)\}} \right].$$

(17)

Therefore, in order to determine the direction of the active intensity vector and hence the source direction, measurements of the pressure and pressure gradients are needed. The following subsection explains some microphone array geometries for these measurements.

Spherical Microphone Arrays for Calculation of Pressure Gradients

A spherical microphone array consists of microphones placed on a spherical surface. Usually, spherical microphone arrays employ several microphones such as the 24-element array placed on a sphere of 37.5 mm radius (Meyer & Agnello, 2003). There is not a generic way of processing the recordings. While some methods combine the microphone signals to simulate different directional patterns (Okubo, Otani, Ikezawa, Komiyama, & Nakabayashi, 2001), some other implementations use the measured energies together with the posi-

Figure 4. Spherically symmetric microphone arrays on the vertices of regular convex polyhedra: (a) cubic, (b) tetrahedral, (c) octahedral, (d) dodecahedral, and (e) icosahedral. The microphone positions on the sphere are denoted as filled circles, the centre of the polyhedron is denoted as an empty circle. The radius of the sphere is d.

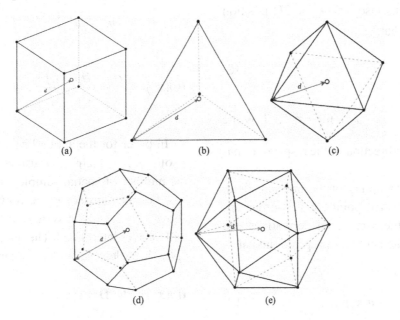

tions of the microphones to create 3-D surface plots of the sound energy at a time instant (Gover, Ryan, & Stinson, 2002). Spherical microphone arrays can also be used to calculate the pressure gradients and intensity vector directions.

A first-order approximation to pressure gradients can be calculated using pressure values sampled on an open spherical shell and the pressure at the centre of that shell. The calculation involves the projection of first-order difference approximations of the directional derivatives of the sound field to Cartesian coordinates. The spatial sampling on the sphere will cause errors to be direction dependent. Therefore, sampling on the sphere should be regular to obtain a uniform error distribution. Vertices of convex regular polyhedra (also known as Platonic solids) satisfy this condition (Huggett & Jordan, 2001). There is only a limited set of such polyhedra. These are cube, tetrahedron, octahedron, dodecahedron, and the icosahedron, having, 8, 4, 6, 20, and 12 vertices, respectively. Figure 4 shows these polyhedra. Due

to the small number of microphones in the tetrahedron geometry, this is the most commonly used structure (Gerzon, 1975; Sekiguchi, Kimura, & Hanyuu, 1992; Merimaa & Pulkki, 2005) and such microphone arrays are commercially available.

In the remainder of this section we assume that pressure values at the vertices of these polyhedra are available. In practice, this means that the sound field is recorded using omnidirectional microphones positioned at the vertices of these polyhedra.

Calculation of Pressure Gradients

This section provides a method for the calculation of a first-order approximation to pressure gradients. A similar approach was used for calculating numerical gradients in multidimensional numerical acoustic models (Hacıhabiboğlu, Günel, & Kondoz, 2008) including models of room acoustics (Hacıhabiboğlu, Günel, & Cvetković, 2010).

Let us denote the centre of the spherical microphone as $x_0 \in R^3$ with V spatial samples positioned at $\{ \mathbf{x}_i \in R^3 : i = 1 \cdots V \}$ on an open sphere of radius d. Let us also define the 3D position vectors, $\overline{\mathbf{d}}_i$ such that:

$$\overline{\mathbf{d}}_i = \mathbf{x}_i - \mathbf{x}_0 = d\,\hat{\mathbf{u}}_i, \tag{18}$$

where $\hat{\mathbf{u}}_i = [u_{i,x} \ \ u_{i,y} \ \ u_{i,z}]$ for $i = 1 \ldots V$ is the unit vector in the direction of the respective spatial sample.

For a spatial sampling of the pressure field, $p(\mathbf{x})$, at the described points, a first-order approximation of the directional derivatives can be obtained for the centre point positioned at x_0 such that:

$$D_{\hat{u}_i} p(\mathbf{x}_0) = \left[p(\mathbf{x}_i) - p(\mathbf{x}_0) \right] / d, \tag{19}$$

where $D_{\hat{u}_i}$ denotes the directional derivative of the pressure field $p(\mathbf{x})$ along the direction of the vector from x_0 to x_i. This is a first-order approximation of the pressure gradient, $\nabla p(\mathbf{x})$ projected in the direction of $\hat{\mathbf{u}}_i$ such that:

$$\nabla p(\mathbf{x}) \big|_{\mathbf{x}=\mathbf{x}_0} \cdot \ \ \hat{\mathbf{u}}_i \simeq D_{\hat{u}_i} p(\mathbf{x}_0). \tag{20}$$

There will be an ensemble of V approximations, which can be expressed as a set of linear equations by:

$$\mathbf{D}p(\mathbf{x}_0) \simeq \mathbf{U}\mathbf{d}p(\mathbf{x}_0), \tag{21}$$

where

$$\mathbf{D}p(\mathbf{x}_0) = [D_{\hat{u}_1} p(\mathbf{x}_0)\ D_{\hat{u}_2} p(\mathbf{x}_0) \cdots D_{\hat{u}_V} p(\mathbf{x}_0)]^T, \tag{22}$$

$$\mathbf{U} = \begin{bmatrix} u_{1,x} & u_{1,y} & u_{1,z} \\ u_{2,x} & u_{2,y} & u_{2,z} \\ \vdots & \vdots & \vdots \\ u_{V,x} & u_{V,y} & u_{V,z} \end{bmatrix}, \tag{23}$$

$$\mathbf{d}p(\mathbf{x}_0) = \begin{bmatrix} \dfrac{\partial p}{\partial x} & \dfrac{\partial p}{\partial y} & \dfrac{\partial p}{\partial z} \end{bmatrix}^T. \tag{24}$$

In order for the above linear system to have a solution, the matrix U must be of full rank and the number of spatial samples on the sphere, $V \geq 3$. For the convex regular polygons described above, $V > 3$ and the system of linear equations will be overdetermined. The optimal solution for $dp(\mathbf{x}_0)$ in the least squares sense can be obtained by:

$$\mathbf{d}p(\mathbf{x}_0) = \mathbf{U}^+ \mathbf{D}p(\mathbf{x}_0), \tag{25}$$

where the inverse projection matrix, $\mathbf{U}^+ = (\mathbf{U}^T\mathbf{U})^{-1}\mathbf{U}^T$, is the left pseudoinverse of the matrix U such that $\mathbf{U}^+\mathbf{U} = \mathbf{I}$.

A simplification is possible if the directional derivative vector in Equation *22* is expressed as:

$$\mathbf{D}p(\mathbf{x}_0) = \left[\mathbf{p}_i - p(\mathbf{x}_0)\mathbf{J}_{V\times 1} \right] / d \tag{26}$$

where $\mathbf{p}_i(\mathbf{x}) = [p(\mathbf{x}_1)\ p(\mathbf{x}_2) \cdots p(\mathbf{x}_V)]^T$ is a column vector of vertex pressures and $\mathbf{J}_{V\times 1}$ is a column matrix. The gradient can then be expressed as:

$$\mathbf{d}p(\mathbf{x}_0) = \mathbf{U}^+ \left[\mathbf{p}_i(\mathbf{x}) - p(\mathbf{x}_0)\mathbf{J}_{V\times 1} \right] / d, \tag{27}$$

Each spherical microphone array geometry has a different inverse projection matrix. However, due to the symmetric positioning of the microphones on the open sphere all the inverse projection matrices will have column sums of zero. Therefore, the central pressure term in Equation *27* vanishes, decreasing the number of necessary channels to *V* such that:

$$\mathbf{d}p(\mathbf{x}_0) = d^{-1}\mathbf{U}^+\mathbf{p}_i(\mathbf{x}). \tag{28}$$

In other words, the pressure gradient can be calculated as a linear combination of the pressure values at the vertices only.

Directional Accuracy of Pressure Gradients

The directional accuracy of pressure gradients will be frequency-dependent. Therefore, the analysis of different topologies for their accuracy of direction estimation is carried out in the spatial frequency-domain.

Let us express the pressure field as $p(\mathbf{x})$ and the spatial Fourier transform of the given plane wave as $P(\bar{\xi})$ where $\bar{\xi} = [\xi_x \ \xi_y \ \xi_z]$ is the spatial frequency vector. This is equivalent to expressing the sound field as superposition of plane waves of the form $p(t) = Ae^{j\omega t}$. The spatial frequency components are related to the normalized temporal frequency vector $\bar{\omega} = [\omega_x \ \omega_y \ \omega_z]$ as $\omega_x = 2\pi c\xi_x$, $\omega_y = 2\pi c\xi_y$, and $\omega_z = 2\pi c\xi_z$. The norm of this vector $\|\bar{\omega}\|$ is equal to the frequency of the corresponding plane wave component. The angle $\angle(\xi_x, \xi_y, \xi_z)$ is coincident with the propagation direction of the wave. The frequency vector is related to the wave vector $\mathbf{k} = [k_x \ k_y \ k_z]$ as $\mathbf{k} = 2\pi\bar{\xi}$ and the wave number $k = \omega / c$ as $|k| = 2\pi\|\bar{\xi}\|$.

For the given pressure field, the pressure sampled at the vertex microphones can be expressed using the shift theorem as:

$$P_i(\bar{\xi}) = e^{-jd2\pi\bar{\xi}\cdot\hat{u}_i}P(\bar{\xi}) \tag{29}$$

If the pressure vector $p_i(\mathbf{x})$ is expressed in the spatial frequency domain as $\mathbf{P}_i(\xi) = \mathbf{E}(\bar{\xi})P(\bar{\xi})$, where

$$\mathbf{E}(\bar{\xi}) = [e^{-jd2\pi\bar{\xi}\cdot\hat{u}_1} \ e^{-jd2\pi\bar{\xi}\cdot\hat{u}_2} \cdots e^{-jd2\pi\bar{\xi}\cdot\hat{u}_V}]^T \tag{30}$$

Then, the numerical gradient expressed in the spatial frequency domain becomes

$$\mathbf{d}P(\bar{\xi}) = d^{-1}\mathbf{U}^+\mathbf{E}(\bar{\xi})P(\bar{\xi}). \tag{31}$$

The actual gradient expressed in the frequency domain is:

$$\nabla p(\mathbf{x}) \xrightarrow{F_{3D}} j2\pi\bar{\xi}P(\bar{\xi}). \tag{32}$$

The accuracy of direction estimation can be quantified by the angle between the actual and numerical gradients in the spatial frequency domain. The angle between two real valued vectors in $\mathbb{R}^N$ can be obtained using the scalar product of the vectors. However, frequency-domain vectors representing gradients are in $\mathbb{C}^N$. The angle between two complex vectors, $\mathbf{a}, \mathbf{b} \in \mathbb{C}^N$ is defined as the Hermitian angle $\Theta_H\{\mathbf{a}, \mathbf{b}\}$ (Scharnhorst, 2001):

$$\Theta_H\{\mathbf{a}, \mathbf{b}\} = \arccos\left|\frac{(\mathbf{a}, \mathbf{b})_C}{|\mathbf{a}||\mathbf{b}|}\right|, \tag{33}$$

where $(\mathbf{a}, \mathbf{b})_C = \sum_{k=1}^N a_k^* b_k$ is the Hermitian product, and $|\mathbf{a}| = \sqrt{(\mathbf{a}, \mathbf{a})_C}$. The Hermitian angle is limited to the first quadrant such that $0 \leq \Theta_H \leq \pi / 2$. The directional estimation error in spatial frequency domain, $\varepsilon_\theta(\bar{\omega})$, can then be expressed as the Hermitian angle between the real and approximate gradients such as:

$$\varepsilon_\theta(\bar{\xi}) = \Theta_{\mathbf{H}}\left\{j2\pi\bar{\xi},\ d^{-1}\mathbf{U}^+\mathbf{E}(\bar{\xi})\right\}. \qquad (34)$$

Directional accuracy of different spherically symmetric microphone array structures can be analysed using the exposition presented above. Figure 5 shows the directional accuracy of tetrahedral, cubic, octahedral, dodecahedral, and icosahedral microphone arrays for an array radius of $d = 2$ cm and a plane wave with a frequency of 4 kHz. It may be observed that increasing the number of microphones decreases the angular error significantly. The directional properties and the error ranges of octahedral and cubic, and dodecahedral and icosahedral arrays are similar to each other. This may be due to the fact that cube and octahedron; as well as dodecahedron and icosahedron are dual polyhedra. This similarity also suggests that, octahedral and icosahedral arrays provide a better trade-off between the number of input channels and accuracy compared to cubic and dodecahedral arrays, respectively.

Figure 6 shows the frequency-dependence of the angular error for horizontal incidence. The plots show the temporal frequencies 1, 2, and 4 kHz as circles. It may be observed that pressure gradient is more accurately calculated for lower frequencies regardless of direction. As the number of microphones increases, the directional accuracy of the pressure gradient also increases. In addition, the error is more homogenous when the number of microphones is increased.

As with differential microphones the dimensions of the array plays an important role in determining the directional accuracy of the array. Figure 7 shows the mean error across all frequencies up to 4 kHz and all directions for different spherical array topologies with respect to array radius. Mean angular errors for the array radii of $d = 1$ cm to $d =$

4 cm are shown for all array topologies. It may be observed that more accurate results are obtained if the number of microphones in the array is higher. However, the differences between dual topologies (cubic/octahedral and dodecahedral/icosahedral) are small, and it makes practical sense to use the topology with a smaller number of microphones. Icosahedral and dodecahedral topologies provide very accurate pressure gradients regardless of the array diameter. However, it is not easy in practice to have many microphones with closely matched acoustical characteristics, and calibration gets more complicated as the number of microphones is increased.

ANALYSIS OF INTENSITY VECTOR DIRECTIONS FOR SOURCE LOCALIZATION

The previous section provided an accuracy analysis of the intensity vector directions calculated from signals acquired using different microphone array geometries. Calculated intensity vector directions also deviate from the actual sound source directions in the presence of noise and reverberation. The following section explains the vectorial analysis of the intensity vector directions in time-frequency bins, which implies the use of short-time Fourier transform (STFT).

Vectorial Analysis

Let us assume that the signal and interference components are arriving simultaneously in a time-frequency bin with pressure values $p_s(\omega,t)$ and $p_n(\omega,t)$, respectively. Let us also assume that $\vec{v}_s(\omega,t)$ and $\vec{v}_n(\omega,t)$ are the particle velocity vectors with directions $\theta_s(\omega,t)$ and $\theta_n(\omega,t)$, respectively for these components.

Particle velocity vectors are summed vectorially, resulting in $\vec{v}_r$ as shown in Figure 8. The

Figure 5. Direction dependence of angular errors for the calculation of pressure gradient for (a) tetrahedral, (b) octahedral, (c) cubic, (d) icosahedral, and (e) dodecahedral arrays at 4 kHz. The array radius is d = 2 cm.

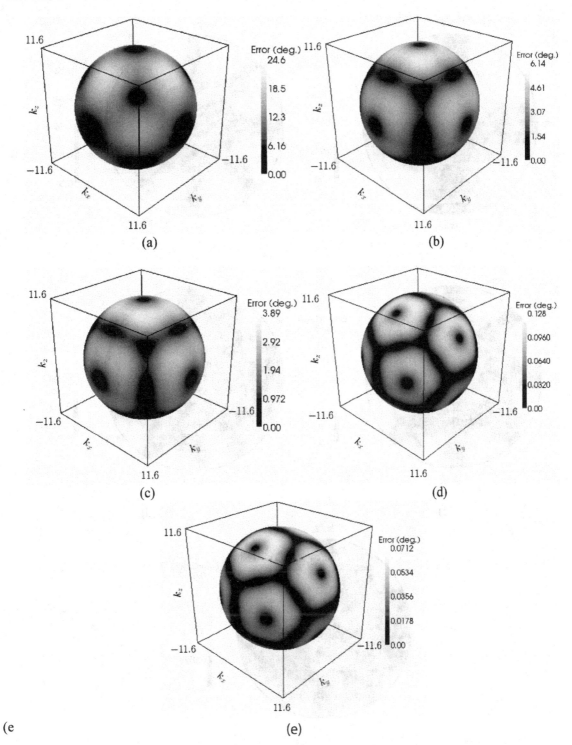

(a)

(b)

(c)

(d)

(e

(e)

Figure 6. Frequency and direction dependence of angular errors for the calculation of pressure gradient for (a) tetrahedral, (b) octahedral, (c) cubic, (d) icosahedral, and (e) dodecahedral arrays. The temporal frequencies of 1, 2, and 4 kHz are denoted as circles on the plots. The array radius is d d = 2 cm.

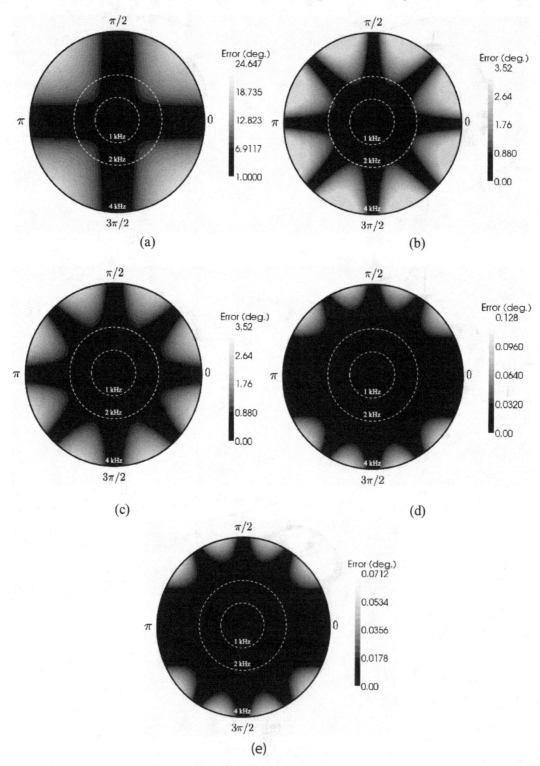

Figure 7. Effect of microphone array radius on the accuracy of pressure gradients

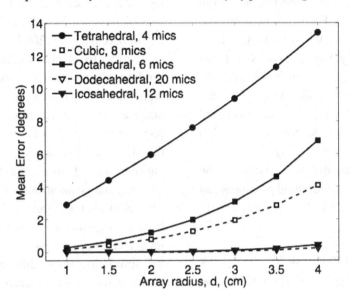

Figure 8. Signal and interference particle velocity vectors with directions θ_s and θ_n for a time-frequency bin

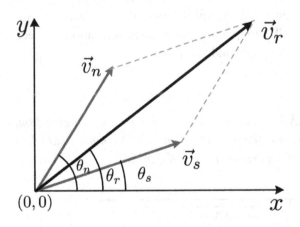

pressure values are summed arithmetically, resulting in $p_s(\omega, t) + p_n(\omega_n, t)$.

Then, the resultant active intensity vector is written as:

$$\vec{I}_r(\omega, t) = (p_s(\omega, t) + p_n(\omega, t))\vec{v}_r(\omega, t). \quad (35)$$

The direction of the active intensity vector is calculated as:

$$\gamma(\omega, t) = \begin{cases} \theta_r & \text{if } (p_s(\omega,t) + p_n(\omega_n)) > 0 \\ \theta_r + \pi & \text{if } (p_s(\omega,t) + p_n(\omega_n)) < 0 \\ \text{undefined} & \text{otherwise} \end{cases}$$

$$(36)$$

where θ_r is the direction of the particle velocity vector as shown in Figure 8, which can be approximated as

$$\theta_r \approx \arctan\left(\frac{p_s(\omega, t)\sin\theta_s + p_n(\omega, t)\sin\theta_n}{p_s(\omega, t)\cos\theta_s + p_n(\omega, t)\cos\theta_n}\right)$$

$$(37)$$

It can be seen that when the magnitude of the interference component is zero, the calculated direction equals to the direction of the target signal. However, in the presence of an interference, the direction shifts away from the source direction towards the interference direction.

The interference component represents the combined effect of all the noise and reflections that are present in the same time-frequency bin of the signal component. For isotropic noise and reverberant environments, where all arrival directions are equally likely, the vectorial sum tends to be small due to cancellation. In fact, in a diffuse field, the magnitude of any directed component will dominate over the level of space-averaged sound pressure. For example, for a room with a reverberation time of T excited by noise with a bandwidth of B Hz, the difference between the directed and space-averaged sound pressures can be formulated as $\log\left(3\pi\left(1 + BT / 3\ln 10\right)\right)$

(Fahy, 1995).

According to the Equations *36* and *37*, the error between the target source direction and the calculated intensity vector direction depends both on the relative magnitudes of the pressures and the directions of the signal and interference components.

Although a target signal and an interference signal can be quite similar in terms of their waveforms and spectral content, they usually do not overlap significantly in a single time-frequency bin. This is also called as W-disjoint orthogonal-

ity and is frequently exploited by time-frequency masking based blind source separation algorithms (Yılmaz & Rickard, 2004).

In order to quantify the localization accuracy, random signals can be generated representing signal and noise components. The overall levels and the arrival directions of the signal and noise components can then be varied. Figure 9 shows the simulated localization errors in degrees for various levels of input signal-to-noise ratio (SNR) and angular separations of 0°, 60°, 120° and 180° between the target and interference sources. Random signals were generated and their overall levels were adjusted to yield varying SNR values for simulating these different conditions. The figure also shows the localization error when the direction of the interference component is equally likely in all directions, i.e. isotropic noise or ideal diffuse field.

When input SNR is very high, the localization error is as small as 1°. However, when the SNR decreases, the localization error increases, eventually approaching the angular separation between the target and the noise.

Figure 9. Localization error in degrees for various SNR values and angular separations ranging from 0° to 180°. The localization error shown with the marker is for the case of an isotropic noise field when the direction of the interference component is uniformly distributed over all angles.

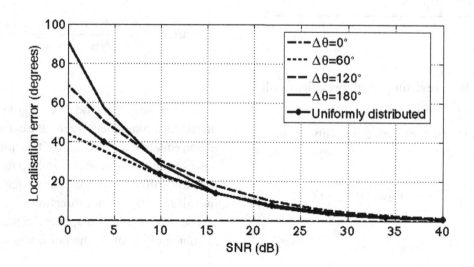

Statistical Analysis

It was shown in the previous section that the calculated intensity vector directions shift away from the target source direction in the presence of noise and reverberation. If the level and arrival directions of the interferences are known or can reliably be predicted, the error can be compensated for accurate sound source localization using the vectorial analysis method. However, if this infor-mation is not available, statistical analysis can be carried out to observe the effect of the target and interference signals.

Figure 10 shows the directional distribution of calculated intensity vectors for a sound source at 180° and an isotropic interference component simulated to yield SNR values of 5 dB, 10 dB and 20 dB. As the SNR increases, the variance of the directional distribution decreases.

Figure 10. Histograms of calculated intensity vector directions obtained from the simulations for input SNR values of (a) 5 dB, (b) 10 dB and (c) 20 dB

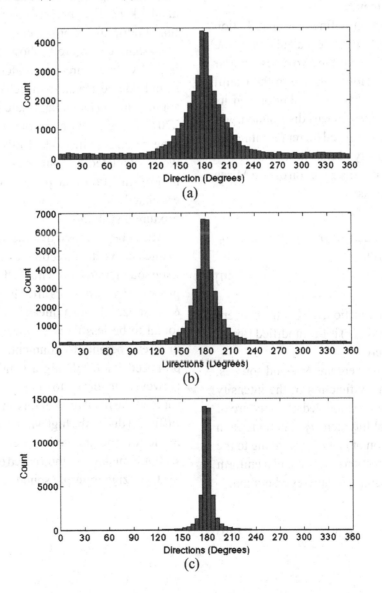

Since the calculated directions are periodic with 2π, circular or directional statistics are required for analysing this data. The distributions shown in Figure 10 are similar to a wrapped Cauchy distribution. Wrapped Cauchy distribution is a 2π-periodic version of the Cauchy distribution defined on a circle (Mardia & Jupp, 1999).

$$f_C(\theta;\mu,\rho) = \frac{1}{2\pi}\frac{1-\rho^2}{1+\rho^2-2\rho\cos(\theta-\mu)}, \qquad 0 \le \theta < 2\pi,$$

(38)

where μ is the mean direction and $0 \le \rho \le 1$ is the concentration parameter.

Cauchy distribution defines the distribution of an angle for a right triangle, calculated by the arctangent of the ratios of the two sides, similar to the Equation *17*. However, due to the useful properties of the von Mises distribution and its similarity to the wrapped Cauchy distribution, von Mises distribution can be used for representing the distribution of intensity vector directions.

The probability density function of von Mises distribution is given as:

$$f_{vM}(\theta;\mu,\kappa) = \frac{e^{\kappa\cos(\theta-\mu)}}{2\pi I_0(\kappa)},0<\theta\le 2\pi,0\le\mu<2\pi$$

(39)

where μ is the mean direction, $\kappa>0$ is the concentration parameter and $I_0(\kappa)$ is the modified Bessel function of order zero.

In the case where there are N sound sources, the probability density function of the intensity vector directions can be modeled as a mixture of N von Mises probability density functions each with a mean direction of μ_n, corresponding to the respective source directions, and a circular uniform density due to the isotropic late reverberation.

$$g(\theta) = \sum_{n=1}^{N}\alpha_n f_{vM}(\theta;\mu_n,\kappa_n) + \frac{\alpha_0}{2\pi},$$

(40)

where, $0 \le \alpha_i \le 1$ are the component weights, and $\sum_i \alpha_i = 1$.

Once the intensity vector directions are calculated, the contribution of each component can be estimated by numerical maximum likelihood estimation since analytical methods do not exist.

In order to demonstrate the agreement between actual sound fields and the statistical exposition given above, intensity vector directions were calculated from recordings made by using a commercially available tetrahedral microphone array. The recordings consisted of 2 s of audio captured at 44.1 kHz. The analysis was made using short-time Fourier transform with a window length of 1024 samples. Figure 11 shows the histograms of intensity vector directions calculated for a single sound source (female speech) at 60° and two sound sources (female and male speech) at 45° and 270°, respectively in a room with reverberation time of 0.83 s. Individual mixture components were calculated by numerical maximum likelihood estimation and plotted together with the estimated probability density function for the mixture distribution.

It can be observed that the statistical analysis of intensity vector directions can be used for localizing sound sources. Such a method was originally proposed by the authors in (Günel, Hacıhabiboğlu, & Kondoz, 2007). The mean localization error was found to be less than 7° after extensive testing in a reverberant environment. The method was proposed for localizing a single sound source. However, in order to localize multiple sound sources, the resolution of this analysis may not be sufficient due to the high variance value observed in the reverberant environments. The following section explains a method based on spatial filtering for localizing multiple sound sources.

Figure 11. Histograms of intensity vector directions, individual mixture components and estimated probability density function for the mixture distribution (a) for a single source at 60° and (b) for two sources at 45° and 270°

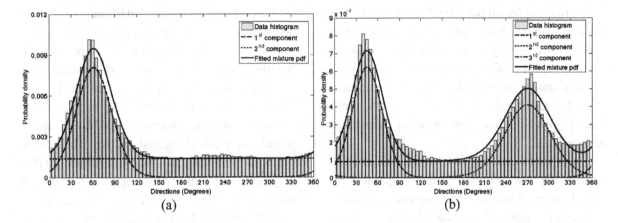

(a)   (b)

Spatial Filtering For Multiple Sound Source Localization

Various methods have previously been proposed for multiple source localization, such as the root-MUSIC algorithm based on TDOA estimation and clustering (Di Claudio, Parisi, & Orlandi, 2000), adaptive multiple-input multiple-output filtering based on adaptive eigenvalue decomposition (Buchner, Aichner, Stenglein, Teutsch, & Kellennann, 2005), cross-power spectrum phase analysis (Nishiura, Yamada, Nakamura, & Shikano, 2000), and histogram mapping (Huang, Ohnishi, & Sugie, 1995). All of these methods exploit the time delay differences between the elements of a microphone array.

Typically source localization is employed to improve the performance of blind source separation (BSS) algorithms (Parra & Alvino, 2002; Saruwatari, Kawamura, Nishikawa, Lee, & Shikano, 2006) or solve the permutation problem of BSS (Wang, Chambers, & Sanei, 2004; Mitianoudis & Davies, 2004). However, it is also possible to use the results of source separation to localize multiple sound sources.

Exhaustive Blind Source Separation

Intensity vector directions calculated for each time-frequency bin (using short-time Fourier transform or similar) can be used for spatial filtering of the recordings in any arbitrary direction. As the directional distribution of instantaneous intensity vectors can be modeled as a von Mises function, a natural conclusion is to use the same distribution also for spatial filtering. A separated signal s_μ in the direction μ can be calculated by spatial filtering an omnidirectional pressure signal P_W as:

$$s_\mu(\omega, t) = p_W(\omega, t) f_{vM}\big(\gamma(\omega, t); \mu, \kappa\big), \qquad (41)$$

where $f_{vM}\big(\gamma(\omega, t); \mu, \kappa\big)$ is the value of the von

Mises function at the direction of the intensity vector $\gamma(\omega, t)$ and this function is generated as shown in Equation *39*.

This way, the time-frequency components that are around the selected look direction μ are enhanced, while the other directions are suppressed (Günel, Hacıhabiboğlu, & Kondoz, 2008). Conventional BSS algorithms usually produce a fixed number of separated signals as many as the number of microphones or sound sources due to the formulation of the problem. However, separation based on the intensity vector directions can be carried out for all possible directions creating several channels. In this way the number of output channels exceeds by far both the number of sound sources and the microphones, although most of these channels would effectively be redundant. This process of decomposing the sound field into all possible directions is called exhaustive separation.

In order to generate N channels, N different spatial filters with look directions separated by $2\pi / N$ intervals can be generated and applied on the same P_W signal. This spatial filtering separates signals to yield a column vector of size N for each time-frequency component:

$$\begin{bmatrix} s_0 \\ s_{\frac{2\pi}{N}} \\ s_{\frac{4\pi}{N}} \\ \vdots \\ s_{2\pi} \end{bmatrix} = \begin{bmatrix} f_{vM}(\gamma;0,\kappa) & 0 & \cdots & 0 & 0 \\ 0 & f_{vM}(\gamma;\frac{2\pi}{N},\kappa) & \cdots & 0 & 0 \\ 0 & 0 & f_{vM}(\gamma;\frac{4\pi}{N},\kappa) & \cdots & 0 \\ \vdots & \vdots & & \ddots & 0 & 0 \\ 0 & 0 & 0 & \cdots & f_{vM}(\gamma;2\pi,\kappa) \end{bmatrix} \begin{bmatrix} p_W \\ p_W \\ p_W \\ \vdots \\ p_W \end{bmatrix}$$

$$(42)$$

Localization Using Exhaustively Separated Channels

Once the pressure signal is separated into several channels corresponding to different directions, a search can be carried out for sound activity in these channels. In order to eliminate the dependencies between the channels, dimensionality reduction methods can also be applied. Such a method based on singular value decomposition (SVD) was proposed before (Günel, Hacıhabiboğlu, & Kondoz, 2009). SVD factorizes the exhaustively separated signal matrix and enables selecting the highest singular values to decrease the dimension of the data (Golub & Loan, 1996). In this way, the rank of the matrix can be selected to be equal to the number of sound sources or maximum number of allowed sound sources in the application domain.

After SVD, the root-mean square (RMS) energies of the channels can be used for determining the locations of sound sources.

This method was evaluated for simultaneously active 2, 3 and 4 sound sources in a room with a reverberation time of 0.32 s. Male speech (M), female speech (F), cello music (C) and trumpet music (T) were used as sound sources. For the 2-source case, M and F, for the 3-source case, M, F and C, and for the 4-source case M, F, C and T sounds were simultaneously active. The source positions were varied as shown in Table 1, so that the angular separation between the sound sources was varying in the 2-source case, but were fixed as 120° and 90° for the 3-source and 4-source cases, respectively.

Localization errors obtained in this testing are shown in Figure 12. The localization errors were found to be larger for source directions of 150°, 180° and 210° than for other directions, possibly due to gain mismatches of microphones in the array. The average localization error for all cases was found to be 14.8°.

Alternatively, in order to determine the channels with audio activity, spatial, spectral and temporal differences between the channels can also be used. This type of analysis is based on cross-dissimilarity and exploits the fact that those channels with sound activity will differ from each other more significantly than the channels with no sound activity. For this, mel-frequency cepstrum coefficients (MFCC) of the signals are calculated and their cross-correlations are calculated to reveal the inherent similarity in the data. Figure 13 shows the cross-dissimilarity matrices between the separated channels for two sound sources at directions 30° and 130°, and three sound sources at directions 30°, 130° and 270°, respectively. The sound sources were all 3 s-long speech sounds recorded in a room with reverberation time of 0.32 s using a tetrahedral microphone array described above. The signals were separated using von Mises functions with 30° beamwidths. MFCC coefficients of the separated signals at 44.1 kHz

Table 1. Directions and type of sound sources for multiple sound source localization tests

Number of sound sources	Source directions (degrees)											
	0	30	60	90	120	150	180	210	240	270	300	330
2	M	F	F	F	F	F	F	F	F	F	F	F
3	M	M	M	M	F	F	F	F	C	C	C	C
4	M	M	M	F	F	F	C	C	C	T	T	T

Figure 12. Localization errors for various source positions for 2, 3 and 4 simultaneously active sound sources

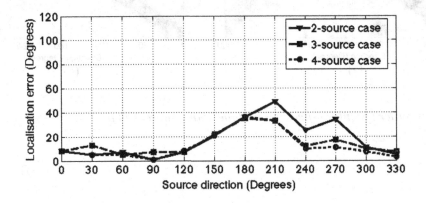

were calculated using 25 ms frame rate and an FFT size of 512.

As may be observed, the channels or directions that contain actual sound sources are quite different from each other, as may be observed from the peaks (darker regions) in the cross-dissimilarity plots. This method can be used to localize multiple sound sources as long as their short-time spectra do not overlap. It should also be noted that when the number of sound sources increases, it becomes more difficult to locate the peaks as they tend to overlap. For such cases, clustering algorithms may be useful.

Reflection Localization

Reflections are usually seen as unwanted interferences that decrease the accuracy of a localizer. However, intensity processing-based technique also enables localising the specular reflections of a sound source in addition to the source itself. Specular reflections are mirror-like reflections of the sound waves where the angle of incidence equals the angle of reflection. These reflections can be attributed to secondary sources as shown in Figure 14. Localizing specular reflections, or these secondary sources, is useful for the acoustical analysis of rooms and also for improving the performance of other machine audition algorithms such as source separation or echo cancellation by exploiting the extracted knowledge of the room geometry.

Reflection localization is usually investigated by impulse response measurements using microphone arrays. In order to obtain the arrival directions of reflections, microphone arrays of various geometries have previously been proposed (Sekiguchi et al., 1992; Merimaa, Lokki, Peltonen, & Karjalainen, 2001; Gover et al., 2002). However, all of these techniques require the use

Figure 13. Cross-dissimilarity values between the separated channels for (a) two sound sources at directions 30° and 130°, and (b) three sound sources at directions 30°,130° and 270°. Darker regions represent higher dissimilarity.

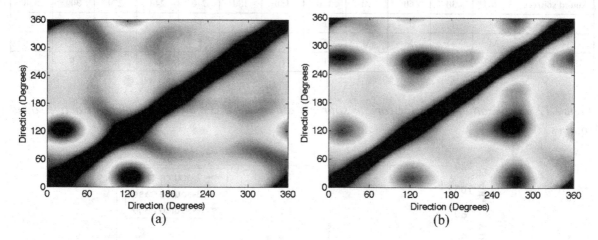

(a)   (b)

Figure 14. First order specular reflections and the image sources in a room

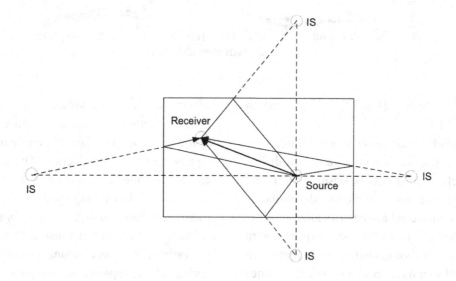

of a known sound source for deconvolution or a maximum length sequence (MLS) which is a pseudorandom signal used for impulse response calculations (Schroeder, 1979). A passive analysis method based on plane wave decomposition was also proposed (Berkhout, Vries, & Sonke, 1997). Although this method can be used to discriminate between simultaneously arriving waves, localising specular reflections still required the calculation of impulse responses.

This section explains a passive reflection localization method that carries out blind estimation of the direct sound with the help of directional wavelet packet decomposition and reconstruction (Günel, Hacıhabiboğlu, & Kondoz, 2007).

Directional Recordings

Based on plane wave decomposition, any sound field can be represented as the superposition of plane waves. The pressure signal $P_W[n]$, and the pressure gradients $P_X[n]$, $P_Y[n]$, and $P_Z[n]$ along the x, y and z axes, respectively captured due to a source signal $s[n]$ arriving from horizontal direction θ_0 and vertical direction φ_0 in a reverberant environment can be expressed in discrete-time domain as

$$p_W[n] = \sum_{k=0}^{L} a_k s[n - \tau_k], \qquad (43)$$

$$p_X[n] = \sum_{k=0}^{L} a_k s[n - \tau_k] \cos \theta_k, \qquad (44)$$

$$p_Y[n] = \sum_{k=0}^{L} a_k s[n - \tau_k] \sin \theta_k, \qquad (45)$$

$$p_Z[n] = \sum_{k=0}^{L} a_k s[n - \tau_k] \sin \varphi_k, \qquad (46)$$

where, L is the number of plane waves, and a_k, τ_k, θ_k and φ_k are the amplitude, delay time, horizontal and vertical arrival angles of the kth plane wave component, respectively. It is assumed that $k = 0$ for the direct sound that arrives without any reflections and $k = 1,...,L$ for the reflections.

Using these signals, a cardioid microphone signal $C[\mu, n]$ facing the pointing direction μ on the horizontal plane can be simulated:

$$C[\mu, n] = p_W[n] + p_X[n] \cos \mu + p_Y[n] \sin \mu$$

$$= \sum_{k=0}^{L} a_k s[n - \tau_k](1 + \cos(\theta_k - \mu)). \qquad (47)$$

A cardioid microphone is a directional microphone whose sensitivity presents a cardioid polar pattern, i.e., its sensitivity is highest in the forward direction, gradually decreasing towards the back down to zero at $\theta = \pi$. By using the pressure and pressure gradient signals, the forward direction,

or the pointing direction of the microphone can be altered without physically rotating the microphone. This process yields various directional recordings.

It is also possible to simulate a cardioid microphone signal pointing both an azimuth and an elevation angle. However, for the sake of simplicity only the horizontal plane will be considered for the remainder of this section.

Processing with Directional Wavelet Packets

For a time-varying signal, temporal and spectral characteristics change in time. Therefore, the direct sound, early reflections and the late reflections arriving at the recording location at the same instance belong to different temporal sections of the input signal due to different travel times.

Wavelet packet decomposition is a useful tool for examining signal variation through time by a flexible division of the time-frequency space (Mallat, 1998). Wavelet packet decomposition caries out filtering and subsampling operations at each scale, similar to wavelet decomposition. However, unlike the discrete wavelet transform, both the approximation and the detail coefficients are decomposed at each level, resulting in what is called a wavelet packet tree.

At each node of the wavelet packet tree, the amount of the reflections will be limited since the direct sound and reflections that arrive simultaneously are not fully coherent. Let us assume that the directional wavelet packet coefficients at a terminating node are $d_j^p \{C[\mu, n]\}$, where d_j^p represents the wavelet packet coefficients at the node of scale j and position p. At each node and for each sample, an intensity vector direction $\gamma_j^p[n]$ can be found, which satisfies

$$\gamma_j^p[n] = \arg \max_{\mu} d_j^p(C[\mu, n]).$$

An estimate of the source signal, $D[n]$ can be obtained by selecting only the coefficients of nodes that take their maximum value around the vicinity of the source direction, θ_0, which is assumed to be known or detected prior to this analysis. Then, the new wavelet packet coefficients for the direct sound, $\hat{d}_j^p\{D[n]\}$ are found as:

$$\hat{d}_j^p\{D[n]\} = \begin{cases} d_j^p\{C[\gamma_j^p[n],n]\}, & \text{if } \theta_0 - 10 < \gamma_j^{\ p}[n] < \theta_0 + 10, \\ 0, & \text{otherwise.} \end{cases}$$

(48)

where

$$d_j^p(C[\mu,n]) = d_j^p(p_W[n]) + d_j^p(p_X[n])\cos\mu + d_j^p(p_Y[n])\sin\mu.$$

(49)

This is equivalent to eliminating the coefficients corresponding to reflections and reconstructing the remaining samples using wavelet packet reconstruction. The samples of the coefficients affected by a strong reflection take their maximum value at other directions. Therefore

the effect of early reflections is alleviated by discarding them.

The time-domain estimate of the direct sound, $D[n]$ can be calculated by reconstructing the wavelet packet coefficients $\hat{d}_j^p\{D[n]\}$. Then, it is used for deconvolving the cardioid recordings $C[\mu, n]$ to yield the directional room responses, $M[\mu, n]$ such that:

$$M[\mu,n] \approx \sum_{k=0}^{L} a_k \delta[n - \tau_k]\left(1 + \cos\left(\theta_k - \mu\right)\right).$$

(50)

It may be observed that at the arrival time τ_k of the kth reflection, a peak occurs when the pointing direction μ is equal to the arrival direction of the reflection, θ_k. The level of the detected peak indicates the arrival amplitude of the reflection as well. In this way, the arrival time, amplitude and direction of the major reflections can be found.

Figure 15 shows the first 1500 samples of the original and the approximate directional room responses for a sound source at 40° in a room with reverberation time of 0.32 s. Note that the arrival

Figure 15. (a) Original and (b) approximate directional room responses showing the arrival amplitude, direction and time delays of the reflections for a sound source at 40° in a room with reverberation time of 0.32 s. Figure adapted from (Günel, Hacıhabiboğlu, & Kondoz, 2007).

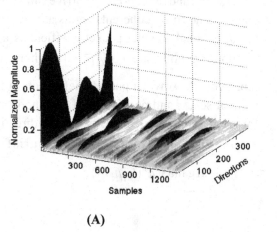

(A)

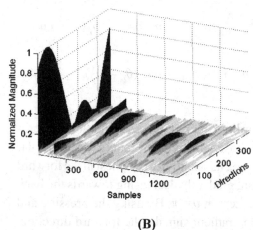

(B)

times and directions of the reflections match well, while their amplitudes differ slightly.

Figure 16 shows example results of tests made when the source was at 200° in a room with reverberation time of 0.83 s.

As can be observed from these figures, exploiting the intensity vector directions for directional wavelet packet decomposition provides information on the reflections. For this purpose, making 2s-long recordings passively with a spherical microphone array is sufficient.

FUTURE RESEARCH DIRECTIONS

Current technology trends in intelligent environments, and machine audition is moving towards the integration of data fusion and multimodal data analysis with sensor array processing. Sound source localization has also started moving in this direction as joint audio/visual processing algorithms are being developed for object localization and tracking (Beal, Attias, & Jojic, 2002; Gatica-Perez, Lathoud, Odobez, & McCowan, 2007).

Recent developments in the microphone manufacturing process are also realising new opportunities for sound source localization. Silicon-based MEMS (Micro Electro Mechanical Systems) microphones are decreasing both the size and the cost of the microphone arrays (Wu, Ren, & Liu, 2004). MEMS microphones are printed on silicon, rather than assembled from various components. This increases the precision of the manufacturing process, and it becomes easier to produce microphones with matching frequency responses. This is an important consideration for most microphone array processing algorithms (Naumann, 2003; Elko, Pardo, Lopez, Bishop, & Gammel, 2003). It is foreseen that most microphones in use today will be replaced by MEMS microphones in the future and intensity-based microphone array processing techniques will benefit greatly from this development. Decreased size and cost of the microphones will enable the use of spherical arrays with a higher number of matching sensors allowing improved accuracy.

Localizing moving sound sources, such as moving human speakers, is one of the remaining challenges in sound source localization. Most con-

Figure 16. (a) Original and (b) approximate directional room responses showing the arrival amplitude, direction and time delays of the reflections for a sound source at 200° in a room with reverberation time of 0.83s. Figure adapted from (Günel, Hacıhabiboğlu, & Kondoz, 2007).

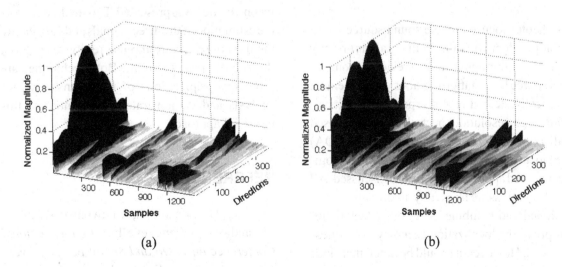

(a)   (b)

ventional techniques assume that sound sources do not move. This is not a valid assumption in most practical situations. While particle filtering (Ward, Lehmann, & Williamson, 2003) techniques have been proposed for tracking a source by estimating its trajectory, tracking multiple sources still continues to be an unsolved problem.

Among the applications of sound source localization, surveillance and robotics are expected to be the leading application areas in the future. The current state of the art does not exploit acoustic information as much as video for surveillance applications. However, there is an increasing acceptance of the importance of audio as an additional modality for automatically detecting threats, localizing events, and aiming surveillance cameras towards these events (Alghassi, Tafazoli, & Lawrence, 2006; Valenzise et al., 2007). Robotics is itself a quickly evolving field and there are many emerging applications of source localization for robots that can hear (J. Huang et al., 1997; Liu & Meng, 2007; Nakadai et al., 2002).

These developments in the manufacturing and applications of microphone arrays as well as the decreasing cost, increasing speed and capabilities of signal processors are creating new challenges and opportunities.

CONCLUSION

This chapter focused on the sound source localization problem which is an integral part of any machine audition application. A review of conventional source localization methods was presented. Specifically, steered-response power (SRP) localization, high-resolution spectral-estimation based localization and time-delay-of-arrival (TDOA) based localization were reviewed. Some biologically inspired approaches were also discussed. All of these solutions are frequently used, continuously developed and combined with other techniques to improve the localization accuracy, robustness and speed. However, it should be noted that since

the time-delay exploitation lies at the core of these algorithms, the ambiguities in time-delay estimation caused by the reflections, noise and other interfering sounds continue to be an issue.

Factors that affect the performance of localization algorithms were also discussed. It is not possible to objectively evaluate the performance of an algorithm without considering the microphone array topology, the environmental conditions under which the algorithm was tested, and the sound sources used during the tests. There are trade-offs between the desirable features of a microphone-array based solution such as high accuracy, small size, ease of interfacing, high speed, and low computational complexity.

A new source localization method based on intensity processing was explained. A theoretical analysis of the accuracy of the intensity vector direction estimation for various spherical array geometries was given. The effect of noise and interferences on the accuracy of the method was analyzed. Theoretical and experimental analyses of localization accuracy were then provided.

Two important sound source localization problems were addressed: localization of multiple sound sources and localization of reflections. For the former, an exhaustive blind source separation technique that uses the intensity vector directions for spatial filtering was explained. For the latter, directional wavelet packet decomposition and reconstruction was presented. This method enables the estimation of the direct signals and calculating the directional room impulse responses without the use of special stimuli. Both techniques are promising applications of the intensity vector analysis and demonstrate the potential of this powerful approach.

REFERENCES

Alghassi, H., Tafazoli, S., & Lawrence, P. (2006). The audio surveillance eye. In *IEEE International Conference on Video and Signal Based Surveillance*. Washington, DC, USA.

Barabell, A. (1983). *Improving* the resolution performance of eigenstructure-based direction-finding algorithms (Vol. 8*). Paper presented at the IEEE International Conference on Acoustics, Speech, and Signal Processing.* Boston, USA.

Beal, M. J., Attias, H., & Jojic, N. (2002). Audio-video sensor fusion with probabilistic graphical models. *In Proceedings of the 7th European conference on computer vision (pp. 736–752).* London, UK: Springer-Verlag.

Belloni, F., Richter, A., & Koivunen, V. (2007). DoA estimation via manifold separation for arbitrary array structures. *IEEE Transactions on Signal Processing, 55*(10), 4800–4810. doi:10.1109/TSP.2007.896115

Benesty, J. (2000). *Adaptive* eigenvalue decomposition algorithm for passive acoustic source localization. *The Journal of the Acoustical Society of America, 107*(1), 384–391. doi:10.1121/1.428310

Benesty, J., Huang, Y., & Chen, J. (2007). Time delay estimation via minimum entropy. *Signal Processing Letters, IEEE, 14*(3), 157–160. doi:10.1109/LSP.2006.884038

Berkhout, A. J., de Vries, D., & Sonke, J. J. (1997). Array technology for acoustic wave field analysis in enclosures. *The Journal of the Acoustical Society of America, 102*(5), 2757–2770. doi:10.1121/1.420330

Blauert, J. (1997). *Spatial hearing: The psychophysics of human sound localization.* Cambridge, MA: MIT Press.

Brandstein, M. S., Adcock, J. E., & Silverman, H. F. (1997, January). A closed-form location estimator for use with room environment microphone arrays. *IEEE Transactions on Speech and Audio Processing, 5*(1), 45–50. doi:10.1109/89.554268

Brandstein, M. S., & Silverman, H. F. (1997, April). A practical methodology for speech source localization with microphone arrays. Journal of Computer. *Speech and Language, 11*(2), 91–126. doi:10.1006/csla.1996.0024

Bregman, A. S. (1990). *Auditory scene analysis: The perceptual organization of sound.* Cambridge, MA: The MIT Press.

Buchner, H., Aichner, R., Stenglein, J., Teutsch, H., & Kellennann, W. (2005). Simultaneous localization of multiple sound sources using blind adaptive MIMO filtering (Vol. 3). *Paper presented at the IEEE International Conference on Acoustics, Speech and Signal Processing.*

Champagne, B., Bedard, S., & Stephenne, A. (1996). Performance of time-delay estimation in the presence of room reverberation. *IEEE Transactions on Speech and Audio Processing, 4*(2), 148–152. doi:10.1109/89.486067

Chen, J., Benesty, J., & Huang, Y. (2003). Robust time delay estimation exploiting redundancy among multiple microphones. *IEEE Transactions on Speech and Audio Processing, 11*(6), 549–557. doi:10.1109/TSA.2003.818025

Cheng, C., & Wakefield, G. (1999). Introduction to head-related transfer functions (HRTFs): Representations of HRTF's in time, frequency, and space. *Presented at the 107th AES Convention,* preprint 5026. New York.

Cowling, M., & Sitte, R. (2000). Sound identification and direction detection in Matlab for surveillance applications. *Paper presented at the Matlab Users Conference.* Melbourne, Australia.

Crow, G., Rupert, A. L., & Moushegian, G. (1978). Phase locking in monaural and binaural medullary neurons: Implications for binaural phenomena. *The Journal of the Acoustical Society of America, 64*(2), 493–501. doi:10.1121/1.381999

Desloge, J. G., Rabinowitz, W. M., & Zurek, P. M. (1997). Microphone-array hearing aids with binaural output - Part I: Fixed-processing systems. *IEEE Transactions on Speech and Audio Processing, 5*(5), 529–542. doi:10.1109/89.641298

Di Claudio, E., Parisi, R., & Orlandi, G. (2000). Multi-source localization in reverberant environments by root-MUSIC and clustering (Vol. 2). *Paper presented at the IEEE International Conference on Acoustics, Speech and Signal Processing.*

DiBiase, J. H., Silverman, H. F., & Brandstein, M. S. (2001). Robust localization in reverberant rooms. In Brandstein, M. S., & Ward, D. (Eds.), *Microphone arrays signal processing techniques and applications* (pp. 159–160). Berlin: Springer-Verlag.

Dmochowski, J., Benesty, J., & Affes, S. (2007a). Direction of arrival estimation using the parameterized spatial correlation matrix. *IEEE Transactions on Audio, Speech, and Language Processing, 15*(4), 1327–1339. doi:10.1109/TASL.2006.889795

Dmochowski, J., Benesty, J., & Affes, S. (2007b). A generalized steered response power method for computationally viable source localization. *IEEE Transactions on Audio, Speech, and Language Processing, 15*(8), 2510–2526. doi:10.1109/TASL.2007.906694

Elko, G. W., Pardo, F., Lopez, D., Bishop, D., & Gammel, P. (2003, October). Surface-micromachined MEMS microphone. *Paper presented at the AES 115th Convention.* New York.

Fahy, F. J. (1995). *Sound intensity* (2nd ed.). London: E&FN SPON.

Faller, C., & Merimaa, J. (2004). Source localization in complex listening situations: Selection of binaural cues based on interaural coherence. *The Journal of the Acoustical Society of America, 116*(5), 3075–3089. doi:10.1121/1.1791872

Gatica-Perez, D., Lathoud, G., Odobez, J.-M., & McCowan, I. (2007). Audiovisual probabilistic tracking of multiple speakers in meetings. *IEEE Transactions on Audio, Speech, and Language Processing, 15*(2), 601–616. doi:10.1109/TASL.2006.881678

Gerzon, M. (1975). *The* design of precisely coincident microphone arrays for stereo and surround sound. *Presented at the 50th AES Convention.* London, UK.

Golub, G., & Loan, C. (1996). *Matrix computations* (3rd ed.). Baltimore, MD: John Hopkins University Press.

Gover, B. N., Ryan, J. G., & Stinson, M. R. (2002). Microphone array measurement system for analysis of directional and spatial variations of sound fields. *The Journal of the Acoustical Society of America, 112*(5), 1980–1991. doi:10.1121/1.1508782

Günel, B., Hacıhabiboğlu, H., & Kondoz, A. M. (2007, July). Wavelet-packet based passive analysis of sound fields using a coincident microphone array. *Applied Acoustics, 68*(7), 778–796. doi:10.1016/j.apacoust.2006.04.008

Günel, B., Hacıhabiboğlu, H., & Kondoz, A. M. (2008, May). Acoustic source separation of convolutive mixtures based on intensity vector statistics. *IEEE Transactions on Audio, Speech, and Language Processing, 16*(4), 748–756. doi:10.1109/TASL.2008.918967

Günel, B., Hacıhabiboğlu, H., & Kondoz, A. M. (2009, April). Intensity vector direction exploitation for exhaustive blind source separation of convolutive mixtures. *Paper presented at the IEEE International Conference on Acoustics.* Taipei, Taiwan.

Gustafsson, T., Rao, B. D., & Trivedi, M. (2003, November). *Source* localization in reverberant environments: Modeling and statistical analysis. *IEEE Transactions on Speech and Audio Processing, 11*(6), 791–803. doi:10.1109/TSA.2003.818027

Hacıhabiboğlu, H., Günel, B., & Cvetković, Z. (2010, February). Simulation of directional microphones in digital waveguide mesh-based models of room acoustics. *IEEE Transactions on Audio. Speech and Language Processing, 18*(2), 213–223. doi:10.1109/TASL.2009.2025100

Hacıhabiboğlu, H., Günel, B., & Kondoz, A. M. (2008). On the accuracy of first-order numerical derivatives in multidimensional digital waveguide mesh topologies. *IEEE Signal Processing Letters, 15*, 9–12. doi:10.1109/LSP.2007.911162

Hartmann, W. M. (1983). Localization of sound in rooms. *The Journal of the Acoustical Society of America, 74*(5), 1380–1391. Retrieved from http://link.aip.org/link/?JAS/74/1380/1. doi:10.1121/1.390163

Hartmann, W. M., & Rakerd, B. (1989a). Localization of sound in rooms IV: The Franssen effect. *The Journal of the Acoustical Society of America, 86*(4), 1366–1373. doi:10.1121/1.398696

Hartmann, W. M., & Rakerd, B. (1989b). On the minimum audible angle – A decision theory approach. *The Journal of the Acoustical Society of America, 85*(5), 2031–2041. doi:10.1121/1.397855

Haykin, S. (1996). *Adaptive filter theory* (3rd ed.). Englewood Cliffs, NJ, USA: Prentice Hall.

Hu, J.-S., & Liu, W.-H. (2009). Location classification of nonstationary sound sources using binaural room distribution patterns. *IEEE Transactions on Audio, Speech, and Language Processing, 17*(4), 682–692. doi:10.1109/TASL.2008.2011528

Huang, J., Ohnishi, N., & Sugie, N. (1995). A biomimetic system for localization and separation of multiple sound sources. *IEEE Transactions on Instrumentation and Measurement, 44*(3), 733–738. doi:10.1109/19.387320

Huang, J., Ohnishi, N., & Sugie, N. (1997). Building ears for robots: Sound localization and separation. *Artificial Life and Robotics, 1*(4), 157–163. doi:10.1007/BF02471133

Huang, Y., Benestry, J., & Elko, G. W. (1999, March). Adaptive eigenvalue decomposition algorithm for realtime acoustic source localization system. *Paper presented at the IEEE International Conference on Acoustics.* Phoenix, Arizona.

Huggett, S., & Jordan, D. (2001). *A topological aperitif.* London, UK: Springer-Verlag.

Ito, M., Maruyoshi, M., Kawamoto, M., Mukai, T., & Ohnishi, N. (2002). Effectiveness of directional microphones and utilization of source arriving directions in source separation. *Paper presented at 9th International Conference on Neural Information Processing. Singapore.*

Kates, J. M. (1998). Signal processing for hearing aids. In Kahrs, M., & Brandenburg, K. (Eds.), *Applications of digital signal processing to audio and acoustics* (pp. 235–277). Norwell, MA: Kluwer.

Knapp, C. H., & Carter, G. C. (1976). The generalized correlation method for the estimation of time delay. *IEEE Transactions on Acoustics, Speech, and Signal Processing, 24*(4), 320–327. doi:10.1109/TASSP.1976.1162830

Liu, P., & Meng, M.-H. (2007). A bio-inspired robotic sound localization method. *Paper presented at IEEE/ASME International Conference on Advanced Intelligent Mechatronics.*

Lorenzelli, F., Wang, A., & Yo, K. (1996). Broadband array processing using subband techniques. *Paper presented at the IEEE International Conference on Acoustics, Speech and Signal Processing.* Atlanta, GA USA.

Makous, J. C., & Middlebrooks, J. C. (1990). Two-dimensional sound localization by human listeners. *The Journal of the Acoustical Society of America, 87*(5), 2188–2200. doi:10.1121/1.399186

Mallat, S. (1998). *A wavelet tour of signal processing.* London, UK: Academic Press.

Mardia, K. V., & Jupp, P. (1999). *Directional statistics.* London, New York: Wiley. doi:10.1002/9780470316979

Merimaa, J., Lokki, T., Peltonen, T., & Karjalainen, M. (2001). Measurement, analysis, and visualisation of directional room responses. *Presented at the 111th AES Convention, preprint 5449.* New York, NY, USA.

Merimaa, J., & Pulkki, V. (2005). Spatial impulse response rendering I: Analysis and synthesis. *Journal of the Audio Engineering Society. Audio Engineering Society, 53*(12), 1115–1127.

Meyer, J., & Agnello, T. (2003). Spherical microphone array for spatial sound recording. *Presented at the 115th AES Convention, preprint 5975. New York.*

Mills, A. W. (1958). On the minimum audible angle. *The Journal of the Acoustical Society of America, 30*, 237–246. doi:10.1121/1.1909553

Mitianoudis, N., & Davies, M. (2004*)*. Permutation alignment for frequency domain ICA using subspace beamforming method. *Paper presented at the International Conference on Independent Component Analysis and Blind Signal Separation.* Granada, Spain.

Nakadai, K., Okuno, H. G., & Kitano, H. (2002). Real-time sound source localization and separation for robot audition. *Paper presented at the IEEE International Conference on Spoken Language Processing.*

Naumann, J. J. (2003). MEMS (Microelectromechanical systems) audio devices - dreams and realities. *Paper presented at the AES 115th Convention.* New York, USA.

Neti, C., Young, E. D., & Schneider, M. H. (1992). Neural network models of sound localization based on directional filtering by the pinna. *The Journal of the Acoustical Society of America, 92*(6), 3140–3156. doi:10.1121/1.404210

Nishiura, T., Yamada, T., Nakamura, S., & Shikano, K. (2000). Localization of multiple sound sources based on a CSP analysis with a microphone array (Vol. 2). *Paper presented at the IEEE International Conference on Acoustics, Speech and Signal Processing.*

Okubo, H., Otani, M., Ikezawa, R., Komiyama, S., & Nakabayashi, K. (2001). A system for measuring the directional room acoustical parameters. *Applied Acoustics, 62*, 203–215. doi:10.1016/S0003-682X(00)00056-6

Omologo, M., & Svaizer, P. (1994). Acoustic event localization using a crosspower-spectrum phase based technique. *Paper presented at the IEEE International Conference on Acoustics, Speech and Signal Processing. Adelaide, Australia.*

Parra, L. C., & Alvino, C. V. (2002). Geometric source separation: Merging convolutive source separation with geometric beamforming. *IEEE Transactions on Speech and Audio Processing, 10*(6), 352–362. doi:10.1109/TSA.2002.803443

Pridham, R. G., & Mucci, R. A. (1979). Digital interpolation beamforming for lowpass and bandpass signals. *Proceedings of the IEEE, 67*(6), 904–919. doi:10.1109/PROC.1979.11354

Rabinkin, D. V., Renomeron, R. J., Dahl, A., French, J. C., Flanagan, J. L., & Bianch, M. H. (1996). A DSP implementation of source location using microphone arrays. In *Advanced signal processing algorithms, architectures, and implementations VI* (*Vol. 2846*, pp. 88–99). Denver, Colorado: SPIE.

Rakerd, B., & Hartmann, W. M. (1985). Localization of sound in rooms II: The effects of a single reflecting surface. *The Journal of the Acoustical Society of America, 78*(2), 524–533. doi:10.1121/1.392474

Rakerd, B., & Hartmann, W. M. (1986). Localization of sound in rooms, III: Onset and duration effects. *The Journal of the Acoustical Society of America, 80*(6), 1695–1706. doi:10.1121/1.394282

Rao, B., & Hari, K. (1989). Performance analysis of root-music. *IEEE Transactions on Acoustics, Speech, and Signal Processing, 37*(12), 1939–1949. doi:10.1109/29.45540

Rayleigh, L. (1907). On our perception of sound direction. *Philosophical Magazine, 13*, 214–232.

Roy, R., & Kailath, T. (1989). *ESPRIT*-estimation of signal parameters via rotational invariance techniques. *IEEE Transactions on Acoustics, Speech, and Signal Processing, 37*(7), 984–995. doi:10.1109/29.32276

Rubsamen, M., & Gershman, A. (2009). Direction-of-arrival estimation for nonuniform sensor arrays: From manifold separation to Fourier domain music methods. *IEEE Transactions on Signal Processing, 57*(2), 588–599. doi:10.1109/TSP.2008.2008560

Saruwatari, H., Kawamura, T., Nishikawa, T., Lee, A., & Shikano, K. (2006). Blind source separation based on a fast-convergence algorithm combining ICA and beamforming. *IEEE Transactions on Speech and Audio Processing, 14*(2), 666–678. doi:10.1109/TSA.2005.855832

Scharnhorst, K. (2001). Angles in complex vector spaces. *Acta Applicandae Mathematicae, 69*(1), 95–103. doi:10.1023/A:1012692601098

Schmidt, R. O. (1986, March). Multiple emitter location and signal parameter estimation. *IEEE Transactions on Antennas and Propagation, 34*(3), 276–280. doi:10.1109/TAP.1986.1143830

Schroeder, M. R. (1979, August). Integrated-impulse method measuring sound decay without using impulses. *The Journal of the Acoustical Society of America, 66*(2), 497–500. doi:10.1121/1.383103

Sekiguchi, K., Kimura, S., & Hanyuu, T. (1992). Analysis of sound field on spatial information using a four-channel microphone system based on regular tetrahedron peak point method. *Applied Acoustics, 37*(4), 305–323. doi:10.1016/0003-682X(92)90017-M

Shilling, R. D., & Shinn-Cunningham, B. (2000). *Virtual auditory displays. In virtual environments handbook*. New York: Lawrence Erlbaum, Associates.

Shinn-Cunningham, B. G. (2000). Learning reverberation: Considerations for spatial auditory displays. *Presented at the International Conference on Auditory Display*. Atlanta, GA.

Smaragdis, P., & Boufounos, P. (2007). Position and trajectory learning for microphone arrays. *IEEE Transactions on Audio. Speech and Language Processing, 15*(1), 358–368. doi:10.1109/TASL.2006.876758

Sturim, D. E., Brandstein, M. S., & Silverman, H. F. (1997). Tracking multiple talkers using microphone-array measurements. *Paper presented at the IEEE International Conference on Acoustics, Speech and Signal Processing*. Munich, Germany.

Supper, B., Brookes, T., & Rumsey, F. (2006). An auditory onset detection algorithm for improved automatic source localization. *IEEE Transactions on Audio, Speech, and Language Processing, 14*(3), 1008–1017. doi:10.1109/TSA.2005.857787

Svaizer, P., Matassoni, M., & Omologo, M. (1997). Acoustic source location in a three-dimensional space using crosspower spectrum phase. *Paper presented at the IEEE International Conference on Acoustics, Speech and Signal Processing.* Munich, Germany.

Valenzise, G., Gerosa, L., Tagliasacchi, M., Antonacci, F., & Sarti, A. (2007,). Scream and gunshot detection and localization for audio-surveillance systems. *Paper presented at the IEEE Conference on Advanced Video and Signal Based Surveillance.*

Varma, K. (2002). Time-delay-estimate based direction-of-arrival estimation for speech in reverberant environments. *Unpublished doctoral dissertation, Department of Electrical and Computer Engineering, Virginia Polytechnic Institute and State University.* Blacksburg, VA.

Wang, W., Chambers, J. A., & Sanei, S. (2004). A novel hybrid approach to the permutation problem of frequency domain blind source separation. *Paper presented at the International Conference on Independent Component Analysis and Blind Signal Separation.* Granada, Spain.

Ward, D., Lehmann, E., & Williamson, R. (2003). Particle filtering algorithms for tracking an acoustic source in a reverberant environment. *IEEE Transactions on Speech and Audio Processing, 11*(6), 826–836. doi:10.1109/TSA.2003.818112

Welker, D. P., Greenberg, J. E., Desloge, J. G., & Zurek, P. M. (1997). Microphone-array hearing aids with binaural output Part II: A two-microphone adaptive system. *IEEE Transactions on Speech and Audio Processing, 5*(6), 543–551. doi:10.1109/89.641299

Widrow, B. (2001). A microphone array for hearing aids. *IEEE Circuits and Systems Magazine, 1*(2), 26–32. doi:10.1109/7384.938976

Wilson, K., & Darrell, T. (2006). Learning a precedence effect-like weighting function for the generalized cross-correlation framework. *IEEE Transactions on Audio, Speech, and Language Processing, 14*(6), 2156–2164. doi:10.1109/TASL.2006.872601

Wu, X., Ren, T., & Liu, L. (2004). Sound source localization based on directivity of MEMS microphones (Vol. 3). *Paper presented at the 7th International Conference on Solid-State and Integrated Circuits Technology.*

Yılmaz, O., & Rickard, S. (2004). Blind separation of speech mixtures via time-frequency masking. *IEEE Transactions on Signal Processing, 52*(7), 1830–1847. doi:10.1109/TSP.2004.828896

Zotkin, D., & Duraiswami, R. (2004, September). Accelerated speech source localization via a hierarchical search of steered response power. *IEEE Transactions on Speech and Audio Processing, 12*(5), 499–508. doi:10.1109/TSA.2004.832990

Zwicker, E., & Fastl, H. (1999). *Psychoacoustics: Facts and models* (2nd ed.). Berlin, Germany: Springer.

KEY TERMS AND DEFINITIONS

Sound Source Localisation: The process of determining the direction and/or distance of a sound source.

Direction-of-Arrival Estimation: Determining the direction of a sound source with respect to a reference coordinate system usually defined by the geometry and orientation of the microphone array.

Microphone Array: A sensor structure that is made up of a number of individual microphones arranged in a known geometry.

Platonic Solid: A solid geometric structure with many plane faces whose vertices are regularly spaced.

Intensity: Time-averaged energy flux in an acoustic field.

Instantaneous Acoustic Intensity: Time-varying process of energy transfer through a point in space.

Particle Velocity: Velocity of an infinitesimal particle due to the small displacements caused by the sound wave.

Spatial Filtering: Filtering of sound signal according to its direction, also known as directional filtering.

Exhaustive Separation: Process of decomposing the sound field into all possible directions, thereby obtaining multiple channels of separated sounds whose number exceeds both the number of microphones and the active sound sources.

Specular Reflection: Mirror-like reflection of a sound wave where the angle of incidence equals the angle of reflection.

Chapter 7
Probabilistic Modeling Paradigms for Audio Source Separation

Emmanuel Vincent
INRIA, France

Maria G. Jafari
Queen Mary University of London, UK

Samer A. Abdallah
Queen Mary University of London, UK

Mark D. Plumbley
Queen Mary University of London, UK

Mike E. Davies
University of Edinburgh, UK

ABSTRACT

Most sound scenes result from the superposition of several sources, which can be separately perceived and analyzed by human listeners. Source separation aims to provide machine listeners with similar skills by extracting the sounds of individual sources from a given scene. Existing separation systems operate either by emulating the human auditory system or by inferring the parameters of probabilistic sound models. In this chapter, the authors focus on the latter approach and provide a joint overview of established and recent models, including independent component analysis, local time-frequency models and spectral template-based models. They show that most models are instances of one of the following two general paradigms: linear modeling or variance modeling. They compare the merits of either paradigm and report objective performance figures. They also, conclude by discussing promising combinations of probabilistic priors and inference algorithms that could form the basis of future state-of-the-art systems.

DOI: 10.4018/978-1-61520-919-4.ch007

INTRODUCTION

Many everyday sound scenes are produced by several concurrent sound sources: spoken communications are often obscured by background talkers, outdoor recordings feature a variety of environmental sounds, and most music recordings involve a group of several instruments. When facing such scenes, humans are able to perceive and listen to individual sources so as to communicate with other speakers, navigate in a crowded street or memorize the melody of a song (Wang and Brown, 2006). Source separation aims to provide machine listeners with similar skills by extracting the signals of individual sources from a given mixture signal. The estimated source signals may then be either listened to or further processed, giving rise to many potential applications such as speech enhancement for hearing aids, automatic speech and speaker recognition in adverse conditions, automatic indexing of large audio databases, 5.1 rendering of stereo recordings and music post-production.

Depending on the application, the notion of "source" may differ. For instance, musical instruments accompanying a singer may be considered as multiple sources or fused into a single source (Ozerov, Philippe, Bimbot, & Gribonval, 2007). Hence some minimal prior knowledge about the sources is always needed to address the separation task. In certain situations, information such as source positions, speaker identities or musical score may he known and exploited by *informed source separation* systems. In many situations however, only the mixture signal is available and *blind source separation* systems must be employed that do not rely on specific characteristics of the processed scene.

A first approach to audio source separation called computational auditory scene analysis (CASA) is to emulate the human auditory source formation process (Wang and Brown, 2006). Typical CASA systems consist of four processing stages. The signal is first transformed into a time-frequency-lag representation. Individual time-frequency bins are then clustered into small clusters, each associated with one source, by applying primitive auditory grouping and streaming rules. These rules state for example that sinusoidal sounds should be clustered together when they have harmonic frequencies, a smooth spectral envelope, similar onset and offset times, correlated amplitude and frequency modulations, and similar interchannel time and intensity differences. The resulting clusters are further processed using schema-based grouping rules implementing knowledge acquired by learning, such as the timbre of a known speaker or the syntax of a particular language, until a single cluster per source is obtained. The source signals are eventually extracted by associating each time-frequency bin with a single source and inverting the time-frequency transform, an operation known as *binary time-frequency masking*. Although some processing rules may explicitly or implicitly derive from probabilistic priors (Ellis, 2006), the overall process is deterministic: predefined rules implementing complementary knowledge are applied in a fixed precedence order. This bottom-up strategy allows fast processing, but relies on the assumption that each time-frequency bin is dominated by a single source. When this assumption is not satisfied, clustering errors might occur during early processing stages and propagate through subsequent stages.

An alternative approach to source separation is to rely on top-down generative models of the mixture signal that incorporate knowledge about the sound production process. The theory of Bayesian signal processing (Gelman, Carlin, Stern, & Rubin, 2003) provides an appropriate framework to build and exploit such models. The probabilistic distribution of a class of mixture signals is specified by a set of latent variables, including the source signals, and conditional prior distributions between these variables, that are either fixed or learned from training data. For a given mixture signal, the value of any variable may be estimated according to some criterion via standard algorithms such as expectation-maximization (EM) (Dempster, Laird, & Rubin, 1977) or convex or nonconvex optimization (Nocedal & Wright, 2006). Because the auditory system is the product of natural selection based on exposure to natural sounds, the knowledge about the sources exploited by model-based separation systems turns out to be similar to that exploited by CASA (Ellis, 2006). However, contrary to CASA, model-based systems exploit all available knowledge at once and can account for multiple sources per time-frequency bin, hence increasing robustness and maximum potential separation quality. Another advantage of model-based systems is that feedback between high-level and low-level variables allow unsupervised training and adaptation of the systems to unknown data. As a counterpart, computation is generally more intensive.

A large number of model-based audio source separation systems have been presented in the literature in the last twenty years, some of which were individually reviewed elsewhere (Makino, Lee, & Sawada, 2007; Ellis, 2006). Presentations have often focused on historical differences between systems suited to *e.g.* specific numbers of sources and channels, instead of similarities between the underlying models and estimation criteria. In this chapter, we provide an overview of state-of-the-art systems amenable to fully probabilistic generative models and Bayesian estimation criteria, with particular emphasis on recent systems. We identify six classes of models and interpret them as instances of two general paradigms: linear modeling or variance modeling. For each class, we present some popular prior distributions and estimation criteria. We also report typical performance figures and discuss the outcomes of a recent evaluation campaign. We conclude by summarizing the common principles behind most models and the merits of either paradigm and by discussing promising combinations of probabilistic priors and inference algorithms

that could form the basis of future source separation systems.

The following notations are employed throughout the chapter. In the general case when the mixture may consist of several channels, multichannel variables are denoted by bold letters and single-channel variables by regular letters. Subscripts represent nested subsets of entries of multidimensional variables, for instance $\mathbf{C}=(\mathbf{C}_1,\ldots,\mathbf{C}_j,\ldots,\mathbf{C}_J)$ and $\mathbf{C}_j=(\mathbf{C}_{j1},\ldots,\mathbf{C}_{jt},\ldots,\mathbf{C}_{jT})$. Calligraphic letters denote standard parametric probability distributions, whose definitions are recalled in appendix.

SOURCE SEPARATION VIA LINEAR MODELING

General Principles

The general Bayesian approach to signal processing is to build a generative model of the observed signal based on the available knowledge about its production process. In the context of audio, mixture signals may result from different acquisition techniques. Hearing aid recordings and noisy phone conversations are obtained by simultaneously recording all sources with one or more microphones. Due to the linearity of air propagation, the signal recorded at each microphone is equal to the sum of individual *mixture components*, which would have been recorded if each source alone was present. Pop music CDs and movie soundtracks are often made not from such live recordings but by synthetic mixing of source signals separately recorded in a studio. The mixing process then consists of applying sound effects to each source signal and adding the resulting multichannel components. In the following, we denote by I the number of channels and by J the number of sources. Regardless of the acquisition technique, the mixture signal $\mathbf{x}_t$ at time t is given by the linear model (Cardoso, 1998)

$$\mathbf{x}_t = \sum_{j=1}^{J} \mathbf{c}_{jt} + \mathbf{\mu}_t. \qquad (1.1)$$

$$\mathbf{X}_{nf} = \sum_{j=1}^{J} \mathbf{C}_{jnf} + \mathbf{E}_{nf}. \qquad (1.2)$$

where $\mathbf{c}_{jt}$ is the *j*th mixture component at that time and ε_t some residual measurement or background noise.

In order to complete the above model, the mixture components and noise must be characterized by prior distributions. A general principle behind the choice of these priors is that they should provide sufficient knowledge to solve the problem, but not too much. When the chosen priors are too weak, they may *underfit* the characteristics of audio sources and result in poor discrimination. This would happen for instance if all mixture components and noise followed a uniform prior, in which case any set of mixture components would be a solution. When the priors are too strong, they may *overfit* the characteristics of the source signals for which they have been designed but badly generalize to other sources.

In the framework of linear modeling, all sources are generally assumed to be *point sources* localized at well-defined, possibly moving, spatial positions. This assumption is valid for speakers and small musical instruments, but not for diffuse or semi-diffuse sources. The effects of air propagation between all sources and microphones or the applied sound effects are then modeled as linear time-varying mixing filters, whose length depends on the amount of reverberation. This filtering process is typically represented by transforming the signals into the time-frequency domain using the short time Fourier transform (STFT), although auditory-motivated or adaptive time-frequency transforms are also applicable (Roman & Wang, 2008; Nesbit, Vincent, & Plumbley, 2009).

Denoting by $\mathbf{X}_{nf}$, $\mathbf{C}_{jnf}$ and $\mathbf{E}_{nf}$ the vectors of complex-valued STFT coefficients of the mixture, the *j*th source and the residual over all channels in time frame *n* and frequency bin *f*, the model becomes

Assuming that the residual noise is Gaussian with covariance $\mathbf{\Sigma}^{\mathbf{E}}$, the likelihood of the mixture STFT coefficients $\mathbf{X}$ given the STFT coefficients of the mixture components $\mathbf{C}$ is equal to

$$P\left(\mathbf{X} \mid \mathbf{C}, \mathbf{\Sigma}^{\mathrm{E}}\right) = \prod_{nf} \mathcal{N}\left(\mathbf{X}_{nf}; \sum_{j=1}^{J} \mathbf{C}_{jnf}, \mathbf{\Sigma}^{\mathrm{E}}\right).$$

$$(1.3)$$

Furthermore, under low reverberation conditions, filtering translates approximately into complex-valued multiplication in the Fourier domain, so that each mixture component is equal to the product of single-channel source STFT coefficients S_{jnf} by some *mixing vectors* $\mathbf{A}_{jnf}$ encoding interchannel intensity and phase differences

$$\mathbf{C}_{jnf} = S_{jnf} \mathbf{A}_{jnf}. \qquad (1.4)$$

The $I \times J$ matrix $\mathbf{A}_{nf}$ whose *j*th column is given by the mixing vector $\mathbf{A}_{jnf}$ is called the *mixing matrix*. Both the source coefficients and the mixing vectors are generally unknown and possibly depend on a set of additional latent variables *z*. The choice of a model consists of identifying relevant variables and setting suitable priors $P(\mathbf{A}|z)$, $P(S|z)$ and $P(z)$. When the same priors are set over all sources, source separation is feasible at best up to permutation indeterminacy.

For a given mixture signal, the STFT coefficients of the mixture components[1] can be inferred using one of several alternative Bayesian estimation criteria (Gelman et al., 2003) such as minimum mean square error (MMSE)

$$\widehat{\mathbf{C}}_{\mathrm{MMSE}} = \int \mathbf{C} P\left(\mathbf{C} \mid \mathbf{X}\right) d\mathbf{C} \qquad (1.5)$$

or maximum a posteriori (MAP)

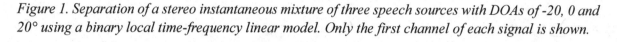

Figure 1. Separation of a stereo instantaneous mixture of three speech sources with DOAs of -20, 0 and 20° using a binary local time-frequency linear model. Only the first channel of each signal is shown.

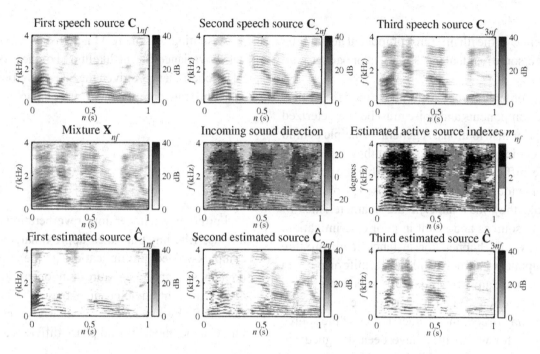

$$\widehat{C}_{MAP} = \arg\max_{C} P\left(C \mid X\right) \qquad (1.6)$$

where the posterior distribution of the mixture components is defined up to a multiplicative constant as

$$P\left(C \mid X\right) \propto$$
$$\iint P\left(X \mid C, \pounds^{E}\right) P\left(A \mid z\right) P\left(S \mid z\right) P\left(z\right) P\left(\pounds^{E}\right) d\pounds^{E} dz.$$

$$(1.7)$$

Time-domain mixture components are then computed by inverting the STFT. The MAP criterion is also called maximum likelihood (ML) when the priors are deterministic or uniform. The choice of a criterion depends on the target tradeoff between robustness and accuracy and on computational constraints. In practice, the above integrals are often intractable and approximate inference criteria such as joint MAP estimation of several variables are employed instead.

Binary Local Time-Frequency Linear Models

The simplest approach to source separation is perhaps to assume that the sources have arbitrary spectro-temporal characteristics but that they are located at different spatial positions. Under this assumption, the source coefficients S_{jnf} in different time-frequency bins can be modeled as independent. Looking at the STFT coefficients of speech signals in Figure 1, it appears that these are *sparse*: few coefficients have significant values and most are close to zero. Moreover, the most significant coefficients of each source are often in different time-frequency bins than for other sources. In the limit where the coefficients are very sparse, it can be assumed that a single source indexed by m_{nf} is active in each time-frequency bin (Yılmaz & Rickard, 2004). With a uniform prior over the coefficient of the active source, the STFT coefficients S_{jnf} of all sources follow the binary local time-frequency model

$$P(m_{nf}) = \mathcal{U}(m_{nf}) \text{ and } \begin{cases} P(S_{jnf} \mid m_{nf}) = \mathcal{U}(S_{jnf}) \text{ if } j = m_{nf} \\ S_{jnf} = 0 \text{ otherwise.} \end{cases}$$

$$(1.8)$$

In order to achieve source separation with this model, dependencies between the mixing vectors of a given source in different time-frequency bins must be introduced via some prior $P(\mathbf{A}_j)$ (Sawada, Araki, Mukai, & Makino, 2007). For instance, $\mathbf{A}_{jnf}$ is constant over time for nonmoving sources and over both time and frequency for *instantaneous* mixtures generated via amplitude panning. For *anechoic* mixtures recorded in an environment without sound reflections or simulating such an environment, $\mathbf{A}_{jnf}$ is given by

$$\mathbf{A}_{jnf} = \begin{pmatrix} g_{1jn} e^{-2i\pi f \tau_{1jn}} \\ \vdots \\ g_{Ijn} e^{-2i\pi f \tau_{Ijn}} \end{pmatrix} \qquad (1.9)$$

where g_{ijn} and τ_{ijn} denote respectively the attenuations and the delays associated with direct propagation from source j to all microphones i, which can be determined up to an overall attenuation and delay given the source direction of arrival (DOA) θ_{jn} (Yılmaz & Rickard, 2004). In *echoic* mixtures, reflected sounds result in smearing of the mixing vectors around the above anechoic model. This smearing effect may be either considered as part of the residual noise (Izumi, Ono, & Sagayama, 2007) or modeled via some prior $P(\mathbf{A}_{jnf} \mid \theta_{jn})$ (Mandel, Ellis, & Jebara, 2007; Sawada et al., 2007; Roman & Wang, 2008). Parametric priors $P(\theta_j)$ modeling source movements were also studied in (Roman & Wang, 2008).

Under a noiseless echoic model, joint MAP estimation of the source DOAs and the mixture components amounts to alternating optimization of the source DOAs and the active source indexes and results in a form of binary time-frequency masking: the STFT coefficients of the active mixture component in each time-frequency bin are set to

those of the mixture, while the coefficients of other sources are set to zero. This is the principle behind the popular degenerate unmixing estimation technique (DUET) (Yılmaz & Rickard, 2004). MMSE estimation of the mixture components results in *soft time-frequency masking* instead (Mandel et al., 2007): the estimated STFT coefficients of each mixture component are equal to the mixture STFT coefficients scaled by the posterior probability of activity of the corresponding source, which is a scalar between 0 and 1 determined via EM. Similar estimates are obtained under the noisy anechoic model, except that each mixture component is projected over the corresponding mixing vector (Izumi et al., 2007). Figure 1 illustrates the application of the latter model to a stereo instantaneous mixture of three speech sources. The clustering of incoming sound directions around the source DOAs is clearly visible. Although the estimated mixture components exhibit similar features to the original ones, sinusoidal partial tracks are often interrupted and zeroed out.

Source separation systems based binary local time-frequency linear models have been applied to various speech and music mixtures, including instantaneous and anechoic mixtures of nonmoving sources (O'Grady & Pearlmutter, 2008; Yılmaz & Rickard, 2004), live recordings of nonmoving sources (Izumi et al., 2007; Mandel et al., 2007; Sawada et al., 2007) and, more rarely, live recordings of moving sources (Roman & Wang, 2008). Although these systems can recover the mixture components with a typical signal-to-distortion ratio (SDR) (Vincent, Araki, & Bofill, 2009a) around 10 decibels (dB) for stereo instantaneous or anechoic mixtures of three sources, they generally produce *musical noise* artifacts due to discontinuities introduced between neighboring time-frequency bins. Moreover, performance degrades with additional sources or reverberation, since the number of significant sources per time-frequency bin and the smearing of the mixing vectors around the source DOAs increase.

Figure 2. Separation of the stereo instantaneous mixture of Figure 1 using a continuous time-frequency linear model. The distributions of the source magnitude STFT coefficients (plain) are compared to the generalized Gaussian distribution with constant prior scale parameter β and shape parameter p=0.4 (dashed). Only the first channel of each estimated mixture component is shown.

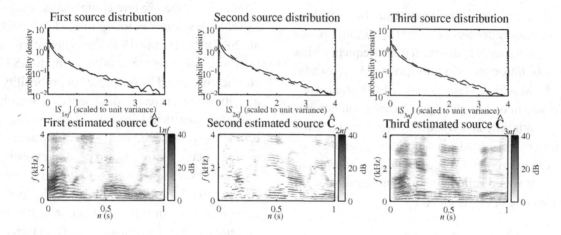

Continuous Local Time-Frequency Linear Models

A common critique of the above binary time-frequency models is that they assume a priori dependency between the STFT coefficients of all sources within each time-frequency bin, while several experiments have shown that these coefficients can be considered as independent in most situations (Puigt, Vincent, & Deville, 2009). These coefficients can therefore be modeled in a more principled fashion as independent continuous nongaussian variables (Cardoso, 2001). The sparsity property of audio signals suggests the use of a sparse distribution $P(S_{jnf})$ characterized by a peak at zero and heavy tails with respect to a Gaussian. A common choice is the circular *generalized exponential distribution*

$$P(S_{jnf}) = \mathcal{G}(S_{jnf}; \beta, p) \qquad (1.10)$$

where β is a variance-related parameter and p a shape parameter. Circularity means that the distribution has zero mean and is phase-invariant. The shape parameter encodes prior knowledge about

sparsity: the smaller p, the sparser the distribution. Figure 2 shows that the generalized exponential closely follows the empirical distribution of $|S_{jnf}|$ for speech sources and that $p\approx0.4$ for all sources in this example. A range of values of p were explored in (Vincent, 2007). The value $p=1$ yielding the *Laplacian distribution* is often assumed (Winter, Kellermann, Sawada, & Makino, 2007). Alternative circular and non-circular sparse distributions, some of which were implicitly specified by their score function $\Phi(S_{jnf})=\partial \log P(S_{jnf})/\partial S_{jnf}$, were used in (Smaragdis, 1998; Zibulevsky, Pearlmutter, Bofill, & Kisilev, 2001; Cemgil, Févotte, & Godsill, 2007). The priors over the mixing vectors $\mathbf{A}_{jnf}$ employed in this context are similar to above and based either on instantaneous mixing assumptions (Zibulevsky et al., 2001), on latent source DOAs (Sawada et al., 2007) or on continuity over frequency (Nesta, Omologo, & Svaizer, 2008).

In general, joint MAP estimation of the mixture components and other model parameters is achieved via nonlinear optimization. A case of particular interest is when the number of sources is equal to the number of mixture channels and no measurement noise is assumed. In that case, it is sufficient to estimate the mixing vectors $\mathbf{A}_{jnf}$

since the vector of source coefficients can be derived as the inverse of the mixing matrix $\mathbf{A}_{nf}$ multiplied by the vector of mixture coefficients $\mathbf{X}_{nf}$. The inverse mixing matrix acts as a linear spatial filter or *beamformer* that attenuates sounds from certain directions (Trees, 2002). A range of nonlinear optimization algorithms suited to that case were proposed under the name of nongaussianity- based *frequency-domain independent component analysis* (FDICA). Most FDICA algorithms achieve approximate MAP inference by dropping across-frequency dependencies between mixing vectors in a first stage so as to estimate the mixture components up to an arbitrary permutation within each frequency bin and finding the optimal permutations in a second stage by exploiting these dependencies (Sawada et al., 2007). In the case when the number of sources is larger than the number of mixture channels, *sparse component analysis* (SCA) algorithms may be used instead. Most SCA algorithms also adopt approximate inference strategies, such as deriving the MAP source coefficients given fixed mixing vectors estimated via a binary model (Zibulevsky et al., 2001; Winter et al., 2007). When p is small, MAP inference under a generalized Gaussian prior splits the mixture in each time-frequency bin between I sources and sets the other mixture components to zero (Vincent, 2007). Figure 2 depicts an example of application of SCA with a Laplacian prior to the stereo mixture of three speech sources considered in Figure 1. Comparison between the figures shows that the estimated mixture components are more accurate with SCA than with binary masking.

FDICA-based systems have been applied to the separation of live recordings of nonmoving sources (Smaragdis, 1998; Sawada et al., 2007; Nesta, Omologo, & Svaizer, 2008) and moving sources (Mukai, Sawada, Araki, & Makino, 2004), and SCA-based systems to the separation of instantaneous or echoic mixtures (Zibulevsky et al., 2001; Peterson & Kadambe, 2003; Cemgil et al., 2007; Vincent, 2007; Nesbit et al., 2009) and live recordings of nonmoving sources (Winter et al.,

2007). These systems generally outperform binary or soft masking-based systems. For instance, they achieve a typical SDR around 15 dB for stereo live recordings of two speech sources in a room with moderate reverberation time or for stereo instantaneous mixtures of three speech sources. An objective comparison conducted in (Winter et al., 2007) showed that SCA improved the SDR by an average 1 dB compared to binary masking on stereo live recordings of three or four speech sources in a room with moderate reverberation time. In addition, FDICA does not generate musical noise. Nevertheless, performance decreases in reverberant conditions for the same reason as above, namely that the smearing of the mixing vectors around the source DOAs increases.

Linear Models over Arbitrary Basis Signals

One approach to improve separation performance is to exploit the spectral characteristics of each source in addition to its spatial characteristics. This approach also makes it feasible to separate single-channel signals. Speech and music involve wideband periodic, near-periodic, noisy or transient sounds. The sounds produced by each source exhibit resonances at specific frequencies. Also, male and female speakers or instruments from the same family usually have different fundamental frequency ranges. Assuming that a given source can produce a few such sounds at a time, each source signal can be modeled in the time domain as the linear combination of a set of wideband basis signals b_{jkt} multiplied by scale factors α_{jk} following independent continuous sparse priors. This model can be equivalently written in the time-frequency domain as

$$S_{jnf} = \sum_{k=1}^{K} \alpha_{jk} B_{jknf}. \qquad (1.11)$$

Since a given sound may be produced at any time instant, the set of basis signals must be translation-invariant, *i.e.* any delayed basis signal must also be a basis signal (Blumensath & Davies, 2006). This implies that the number K of basis signals be much larger than the number of samples of the mixture signal. Due to computational constraints, approximate translation invariance is generally assumed instead by constraining each basis signal to be nonzero over a single time frame and restricting the set of possible delays to an integer number of time frames (Jang & Lee, 2004).

This approach has led to a few different inference strategies. In (Jang & Lee, 2004), single-channel mixtures are separated by MAP estimation of the scale factors given fixed basis signals learned in the MAP sense from a different set of training signals for each source. In (Gowreesunker & Tewfik, 2007), the separation of synthetic instantaneous mixtures is achieved by first estimating the mixing vectors using a binary time-frequency model, then deriving the MAP scale factors associated with basis signals learned from a different set of training signals for each source. These two strategies rely on prior knowledge that the sources to be separated are similar to those in the training set. By contrast, in (Blumensath & Davies, 2006), both the basis signals and the scale factors are blindly inferred from the observed single-channel mixture and partitioned into sources using prior dependencies between the scale factors of each source.

The source separation system in (Gowreesunker & Tewfik, 2007) has been reported to provide modest SDR improvement on the order of 1 dB compared to SCA on stereo instantaneous mixtures of three speech sources using a few thousand basis signals per time frame. This limited improvement may be explained by the fact that the representation of spectral characteristics via linear modeling is efficient only for a few sound sources such as electronic musical instruments which generate reproducible waveforms. Most sound sources, in particular near-periodic or noise sources, generate sounds whose relative phase across frequency varies almost randomly from one instance to another.

In order to accurately represent such sources, the set of basis signals must be phase-invariant, which greatly increases the number of basis signals and makes inference even less tractable.

SOURCE SEPARATION VIA VARIANCE MODELING

General Principles

The search for efficient ways of representing spectral sound characteristics has led to the investigation of an alternative paradigm consisting of modeling the STFT coefficients of each mixture component by a circular distribution whose parameters vary over time and frequency, thus exploiting nonstationarity and nonwhiteness instead of or in addition to nongaussianity (Cardoso, 2001). In a single-channel context, this distribution is often parameterized in terms of a single parameter related to its variance, hence we call this paradigm variance modeling.

The Gaussian distribution is a popular choice. Assuming that the STFT coefficients of different mixture components are independent and Gaussian and considering noise as an additional (diffuse) component, the mixture STFT coefficients follow a Gaussian distribution whose covariance matrix Σ^X_{nf} in time-frequency bin (n, f) is given by

$$\Sigma^X_{nf} = \sum_{j=1}^{J} \Sigma^C_{jnf} \tag{2.1}$$

where Σ^C_{jnf} is the covariance matrix of the jth mixture component in that bin. This results in the following expression of the likelihood

$$P\left(X \mid \Sigma^C\right) = \prod_{nf} \mathcal{N}\left(X_{nf}; 0, \sum_{j=1}^{J} \Sigma^C_{jnf}\right). \tag{2.2}$$

This model is identical to that used by classical beamforming approaches for the enhancement of a target source (Trees, 2002), except that interfering sources are now modeled as individual sources instead of a global background noise. The covariance matrix of each mixture component can be factored as the product of a scalar nonnegative variance V_{jnf} and a *mixing covariance* matrix $\mathbf{R}_{jnf}$

$$\Sigma_{jnf}^{C} = V_{jnf}\mathbf{R}_{jnf} \tag{2.3}$$

which may depend on additional latent variables z via some priors $P(V|z)$, $P(\mathbf{R}|z)$ and $P(z)$. In addition to interchannel intensity and phase differences, mixing covariances encode correlation between channels known as interchannel coherence. As a consequence, the model is not anymore restricted to point sources in low reverberation conditions with high interchannel coherence but becomes valid for diffuse or semi-diffuse sources with lower coherence (Duong, Vincent, & Gribonval, 2009). Under this model, exact MMSE or MAP inference of the mixture components is often intractable. A common approximation consists of estimating the covariance matrices of the mixture components in a first stage as

$$\widehat{\Sigma}_{\text{MAP}}^{C} = \arg\max_{\Sigma^{C}} P\left(\Sigma^{C} \mid \mathbf{X}\right) \tag{2.4}$$

with

$$P(\Sigma^{C} \mid \mathbf{X}) \propto \int P\left(\mathbf{X} \mid \Sigma^{C}\right) P\left(\mathbf{R} \mid z\right) P\left(V \mid z\right) P\left(z\right) dz. \tag{2.5}$$

and derive the MMSE STFT coefficients of the mixture components in a second stage by Wiener filtering

$$\widehat{\mathbf{C}}_{jnf} = \widehat{\Sigma}_{jnf}^{C} \left(\widehat{\Sigma}_{nf}^{X}\right)^{-1} \mathbf{X}_{nf}. \tag{2.6}$$

This multichannel nonlinear filtering attenuates interfering sounds based both on their spatial direction and their variance (Trees, 2002).

Besides the Gaussian model, another popular model is to assume that the magnitude STFT coefficients of all sources follow a log-Gaussian distribution with tied covariance. Although the likelihood does not admit a closed-form expression, various approximate expressions were proposed in (Roweis, 2001; Kristjánsson, Hershey, Olsen, Rennie, & Gopinath, 2006; Vincent, 2006). In the specific case of single-channel mixtures, Gaussian and Poisson distributions over the magnitude STFT coefficients were also investigated in (Rennie, Hershey, & Olsen, 2008; Virtanen & Cemgil, 2009). Sparse distributions were more rarely considered (Mitianoudis & Davies, 2003; Lee, Kim, & Lee, 2007). In the following, we focus on distributions that can be equivalently defined in terms of a single variance parameter V_{jnf} in the single-channel case and one or more entries of $\mathbf{R}_{jnf}$ in the multichannel case.

Local Time-Frequency Variance Models and Vector Models

Once more, the simplest approach is to assume that the mixture components have potentially arbitrary spectro-temporal characteristics but distinct spatial distributions. The resulting local time-frequency variance models behave similarly to the local time-frequency linear models presented above. For a point source in low reverberation conditions, the source variances V_{jnf} are equal to the squared magnitude $|S_{jnf}|^2$ of the source signals and the mixing covariances $\mathbf{R}_{jnf}$ are rank-1 matrices equal to the outer product of the mixing vectors $\mathbf{A}_{jnf}$ with themselves

$$\mathbf{R}_{jnf} = \mathbf{A}_{jnf}\mathbf{A}_{jnf}^{H}. \tag{2.7}$$

Some of the priors previously designed for S_{jnf} and $\mathbf{A}_{jnf}$ translate into priors over V_{jnf} and $\mathbf{R}_{jnf}$. For instance, $\mathbf{R}_{jnf}$ was modeled as constant over time and frequency for synthetic instantaneous mixtures in (Févotte & Cardoso, 2005; Vincent, Arberet, & Gribonval, 2009b) and V_{jnf} was modeled by independent binary or sparse discrete priors in (El Chami, Pham, Servière, & Guerin, 2008; Vincent et al., 2009b). Another way of modeling V_{jnf} is to assume that it is constant over small time-frequency regions (Pham, Servière, & Boumaraf, 2003; Févotte & Cardoso, 2005). The parameterization of $\mathbf{R}_{jnf}$ as a rank-1 matrix is not valid for diffuse sources or reverberated point sources, which are better modeled via a full-rank mixing covariance (El Chami et al., 2008; Duong et al., 2009). As an extension of the above local time-frequency models, vector models have been proposed that account for across-frequency correlation between the source variances. For instance, V_{jnf} was assumed to be constant over all frequency bins in each time frame in (Mitianoudis & Davies, 2003) and implicit across-frequency variance dependencies were defined using multivariate sparse distributions in (Lee et al., 2007; Lee, 2009).

Approximate MMSE or MAP inference is performed via similar algorithms to those used for local time-frequency linear models. In the case where the number of sources is equal to the number of mixture channels and all sources are point sources, the mixture components can again be derived from the mixing vectors. ML estimation of the mixing vectors can then be achieved by approximate joint diagonalization of the mixture empirical covariance matrices using a nonstationarity-based FDICA algorithm for local time-frequency models (Pham et al., 2003) or by some *independent vector analysis* (IVA) algorithm for vector models. In the case where the number of sources is larger than the number of mixture channels, MMSE estimation of the mixture components under a binary variance prior can be addressed via EM and results in soft time-frequency masking (El Chami et al., 2008). Finally, ML estimation of the source covariance matrices with a uniform variance prior is feasible either via EM or nonconvex optimization (Févotte & Cardoso, 2005; Vincent et al., 2009b). Figure 3 illustrates the discrimination potential of variance models with respect to linear models for the

separation of a stereo mixture of three sources. As an example, two sets of mixture components yielding the same mixture STFT coefficients are considered. While the mixture STFT coefficients do not suffice to discriminate these two possible solutions via linear modeling, the additional information carried by the correlation between the mixture channels suffices to discriminate them without any additional prior via variance modeling.

A few systems based on local time-frequency variance models and vector models have been applied to the separation of audio mixtures, focusing on synthetic instantaneous mixtures (Févotte & Cardoso, 2005; Vincent et al., 2009b) and live recordings of nonmoving sources (Mitianoudis & Davies, 2003; Pham et al., 2003; Lee et al., 2007; El Chami et al., 2008; Lee, 2009; Duong et al., 2009). Objective comparisons conducted over stereo speech and music mixtures in (Puigt et al., 2009; Vincent et al., 2009b; Duong et al., 2009) concluded in an average SDR improvement compared to nongaussianity-based FDICA and SCA of about 6 dB for instantaneous mixtures of two sources, 1 dB for instantaneous mixtures of three sources and 2 dB for reverberant mixtures of three sources.

Monophonic Spectral Models

While vector models account for certain variance dependencies across the time-frequency plane, the dependencies exhibited by audio signals are much more complex. Prior distributions commonly used in the field of speech processing rely on the fact that speech is monophonic, *i.e.* it is the result of a single excitation process. The power spectrum V_{jnf} of a given speech source at a given time is assumed to be one of K template spectra w_{jkf} indexed by some discrete state k, which may represent for example a certain phoneme pronounced with a particular intonation. This model extends to music sources which may be considered as a sequence of states representing a certain note or chord played with a particular timbre. The template spectra define

Figure 3. Illustration of the discrimination between two possible solutions (left and right) to the separation of a stereo mixture of three sources via local time-frequency linear modeling (top) vs. local time-frequency variance modeling (bottom) in a given time-frequency bin. Covariance matrices are represented as ellipses whose axes and axe lengths represent their eigenvectors and the square roots of their eigenvalues. All variables are represented as real-valued and time-frequency indices are dropped for the sake of legibility.

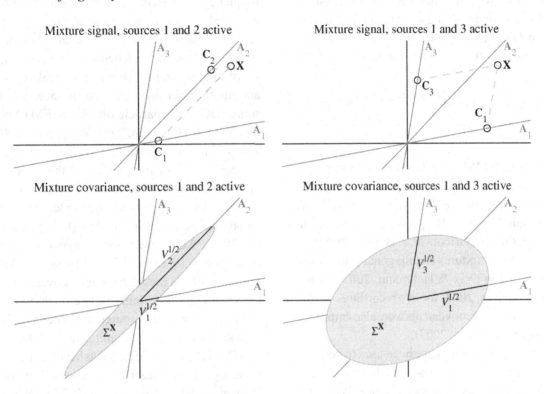

the mean power spectrum of each state, which typically involves a set of spectral peaks with characteristic frequencies and intensities. Smooth template spectra parameterizing the coarse spectral structure via an autoregressive (AR) model were also considered in (Srinivasan, Samuelsson, & Kleijn, 2006). The states underlying different sources are modeled as independent and the J-uplet $(q_{1n}, \ldots, q_{Jn})$ of states of all sources at a given time is called the factorial state of the mixture. The simplest way of modeling the sequence of states of a single source is to assume that they are independent. Denoting by q_{jn} the state of source j in time frame n and by π_{jk} the prior probability of state k, this yields the mixture model (Attias, 2003; Benaroya, Bimbot, & Gribonval, 2006)

$$V_{jnf} = w_{jq_{jn}f} \text{ with } P(q_{jn} = k) = \pi_{jk}. \qquad (2.8)$$

This model is also called *Gaussian mixture model* (GMM) when V_{jnf} is the parameter of a Gaussian or a log-Gaussian distribution. *Hidden Markov models* (HMM) generalize this concept by assuming that each state of a sequence depends on the previous state via a set of transition probabilities ω_{kl} (Roweis, 2001; Kristjánsson et al., 2006)

$$V_{jnf} = w_{jq_{jn}f} \text{ with } \begin{cases} P(q_{j1} = k) = \pi_k \\ P(q_{jn} = l \mid q_{j,n-1} = k) = \omega_{kl} \text{ for } n > 1. \end{cases}$$

$$(2.9)$$

The transition probabilities may encode both short-term continuity priors and long-term language priors. In the case when the sounds produced by a given source have recurring spectra but variable intensities, its power spectrum may be represented by multiplying each template spectrum by an arbitrary time-varying scale factor h_{jn}. Starting from a GMM, this yields the *Gaussian scaled mixture model* (GSMM) (Benaroya et al., 2006)

$$V_{jnf} = h_{jn} w_{jq_{jn}f} \text{ with } \begin{cases} P(q_{jn} = k) = \pi_{jk} \\ P(h_{jn}) = \mathcal{U}(h_{jn}). \end{cases} \quad (2.10)$$

GMMs, HMMs and GSMMs can apply to multichannel mixtures by specifying a prior over the mixing covariance $\mathbf{R}_{jnf}$ given the source DOA θ_{jn}. A rank-1 prior $P(\mathbf{R}_{jnf} \mid \theta_{jn})$ was employed in (Arberet, Ozerov, Gribonval, & Bimbot, 2009) for instantaneous mixtures and diagonal priors were investigated in (Nix & Hohmann, 2007; Weiss, Mandel, & Ellis, 2008) for live recordings. Priors $P(\theta_j)$ about source movements were also employed in (Nix & Hohmann, 2007).

Different strategies have been used to perform source separation using these models. One strategy employed for single-channel mixtures is to learn via EM the template spectra w_{jkf} and the prior state probabilities π_{jk} or ω_{kl} associated with each source from a set of training signals containing that source alone, then to estimate the MAP scale factors for each possible factorial state on each time frame and either select the optimal factorial state on each frame or find the optimal sequence of factorial states by the Viterbi algorithm (Roweis, 2001; Benaroya et al., 2006; Srinivasan et al., 2006). This necessitates that the identity of the speakers or the musical instruments in the mixture be known and that sufficient training data is available. Approximate inference techniques based on probability bounds or beam search are used in practice to avoid testing all possible factorial states. Figure 4 illustrates the application of this strategy to a single-channel mixture of piano and violin. The template spectra represent each a single note for violin and a chord consisting of several notes for the piano, where each note translates into a set of peaks at harmonic or near-harmonic frequencies. Although GMMs do not account for frequency or intensity variations within a given note or chord, satisfactory separation is achieved. Another strategy suited to multichannel mixtures is to learn speaker-independent models from a set of training signals covering several speakers and jointly infer the source covariances and the source DOAs via particle filtering or EM (Attias, 2003; Nix & Hohmann, 2007; Weiss et al., 2008). The last and perhaps most promising strategy is to adapt the template spectra and the prior state probabilities to the mixture. Adaptation schemes include MAP selection of one model per source among alternative prior models (Kristjánsson et al., 2006), MAP interpolation between several prior models (Weiss & Ellis, in press) and MAP inference of the model parameters over time intervals involving a single source (Ozerov et al., 2007) or from coarse source estimates provided by a simpler system (Arberet et al., 2009).

GMMs, HMMs and GSMMs have been applied to the separation of single-channel speech mixtures (Roweis, 2001; Kristjánsson et al., 2006; Weiss & Ellis, in press), single-channel music (Benaroya et al., 2006; Ozerov et al., 2007), stereo echoic mixtures of moving or nonmoving speech sources (Attias, 2003; Nix & Hohmann, 2007; Weiss et al., 2008) and stereo instantaneous music mixtures (Arberet et al., 2009). The separation quality achieved over single-channel speech mixtures has not been reported, since most systems focus on estimating the word sequence pronounced by each speaker instead. This typically requires on the order of ten thousand or more template spectra per source and strong language priors, in line with conventional speech recognition systems (Kristjánsson et al., 2006). In (Ozerov et al., 2007), a SDR of 10 dB was achieved on single-channel mixtures of singing voice and accompaniment music using a few tens of states per source only. Multichan-

Figure 4. Separation of a single-channel mixture of two music sources using GMMs

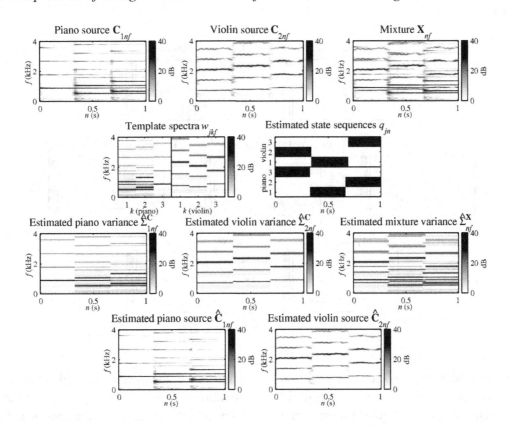

nel GMMs have been reported to improve SDR by about 2 dB compared to soft time-frequency masking or SCA over stereo echoic mixtures of three speech sources and stereo instantaneous mixtures of three music sources (Weiss et al., 2008; Arberet et al., 2009).

Polyphonic Spectral Models

Although monophonic spectral models provide a meaningful representation of speech and most musical instruments, they appear less suited to polyphonic musical instruments, which can play chords made of several notes at a time. When the number of concurrent notes increases, the number of states needed to represent all combinations of notes with different relative intensities quickly becomes huge, which favors overfitting. A more principled model consists of representing the

power spectrum V_{jnf} of a given source as the linear combination of K basis spectra w_{jkf} multiplied by time-varying scale factors h_{jkn}

$$V_{jnf} = \sum_{k=1}^{K} h_{jkn} w_{jkf} \qquad (2.11)$$

where each basis spectrum may represent for example a single note with a certain timbre. The scale factors are often assumed to be independent and follow either uniform priors (Benaroya, Mc-Donagh, Bimbot, & Gribonval, 2003) or sparse priors modeling the fact that only a few basis spectra may be active at the same time (Rennie et al., 2008; Virtanen & Cemgil, 2009). In (Vincent, 2006), dependencies between the scale factors of a given basis spectrum in adjacent time frames were exploited via a binary Markov model. In (Smaragdis, 2007), the basis spectra were replaced

Figure 5. Separation of the single-channel mixture of two music sources in Figure 4 using a polyphonic spectral model

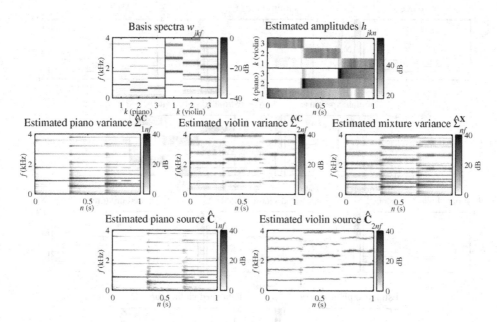

by basis spectral patches spanning a few time frames, which is equivalent to setting a constraint over the scale factors of different basis spectra in successive time frames. Priors over the source variances were combined with rank-1 priors over the mixing covariance in (Vincent, 2006; Ozerov & Févotte, 2009).

The Bayesian inference strategies employed in the literature for polyphonic spectral models resemble those for monophonic models. The simplest strategy is again to learn the basis spectra w_{jkf} from separate training data for each source and estimate the scale factors h_{jkn} and additional variables from the mixture (Benaroya et al., 2003; Vincent, 2006; Schmidt & Olsson, 2007; Smaragdis, 2007). For single-channel mixtures, MAP learning and inference consist of approximating an observed matrix of power STFT coefficients as the product of two nonnegative matrices: a matrix of spectra and a matrix of scale factors. This *nonnegative matrix factorization* (NMF) objective is typically addressed via nonlinear optimization algorithms or via EM. Figure 5 represents the results of this

strategy when applied to the single-channel music mixture of Figure 4. The spectrum of the piano is now better modeled as the sum of individual note spectra whose intensities decay over time. However, comparison between the two figures indicates that this increased modeling accuracy does not significantly affect separation performance. Another strategy is to adapt the basis spectra to the mixture by joint MAP inference of all variables. With a single-channel mixture, this requires that priors learned from separate training data be set over the basis spectra of each source (Rennie et al., 2008; Virtanen & Cemgil, 2009). With a multichannel mixture, such priors are not needed provided that the sources have different spatial positions (Ozerov & Févotte, 2009).

Polyphonic spectral models have been applied to the separation of single-channel music mixtures (Benaroya et al., 2003; Vincent, 2006) and multichannel instantaneous and echoic music mixtures of nonmoving sources (Vincent, 2006; Ozerov & Févotte, 2009). In (Vincent, 2006), a SDR of 14 dB was achieved on a highly reverberant stereo mixture of two music sources using knowledge of the instruments and the source DOAs, improving over FDICA and SCA by more than 10 dB. Although polyphonic models are less appropriate for speech than monophonic models, they have also been used for the separation of single-channel speech mixtures since the associated inference algorithms are much faster (Schmidt & Olsson, 2007; Smaragdis, 2007; Rennie et al., 2008; Virtanen & Cemgil, 2009). The resulting SDR over mixtures of two speech sources is typically around 7 dB.

OBJECTIVE PERFORMANCE EVALUATION

While the SDR figures previously reported in this chapter provide an idea of average performance of each class of models, they are not always comparable due to the use of different datasets. More importantly, the performance of a given source separation system does not only depend on the underlying model or class of models but also on the selection of appropriate parameter values or priors and on the choice of a parameter

initialization and optimization algorithm avoiding local maxima of the criterion. In the absence of a generic way of addressing these issues such as the Bayesian evidence maximization framework discussed below, objective comparison appears feasible only between individual systems.

Figure 6 presents the results achieved by fourteen model-based blind source separation systems on four different types of ten-second speech or music mixtures in the framework of the 2008 Signal Separation Evaluation Campaign (Vincent et al., 2009a). Performance is evaluated not only in terms of SDR, but also in terms of signal-to-interference ratio (SIR) and signal-to-artifacts ratio (SAR), which measure the amount of residual crosstalk and musical noise artifacts.

In low reverberation conditions, the best achieved SDR equals 12 dB on four-channel near-anechoic recordings of three sources and 9 dB on stereo instantaneous mixtures of four sources. The SIR is always larger than the SAR, which indicates satisfactory rejection of interfering sources but linear or nonlinear distortion of the target source. Apart from the lower performance of the system in (Lee et al., 2007) due to convergence issues, the most noticeable difference between

Figure 6. Average source separation performance achieved by model-based systems in the framework of the 2008 Signal Separation Evaluation Campaign

Paradigm	Model class	Systems	Average separation quality		
			SDR (dB)	SIR (dB)	SAR (dB)
Four-channel recordings of three music sources in a room with cushioned walls					
Linear	Continuous local models	(Nagain et al., 2008)	11.7	23.0	12.3
Variance	Vector models	(Lee et al., 2007)	0.7	6.1	4.1
		(Lee, 2009)	9.8	18.8	10.5
Binaural recordings of two speech sources in an office room					
Linear	Binary local models	(Mandel et al., 2007)	4.4	5.9	11.2
Variance	Monophonic models	(Weiss et al., 2008)	3.7	6.1	10.7
Stereo recordings of four speech sources in an office room					
Linear	Binary local models	(Izumi et al., 2007)	1.6	1.4	6.6
		(Mandel et al., 2007)	0.9	-3.3	12.5
		(Sawada et al., 2007)	2.3	4.2	5.0
Variance	Binary local models	(El Chami et al., 2008)	1.9	1.4	7.4
Stereo instantaneous mixtures of four speech sources					
Linear	Continuous local models	(Nesbit et al., 2009)	6.4	11.5	7.3
		(Vincent, 2007)	8.3	14.6	9.1
	Arbitrary basis models	(Gowreesunker & Tewfik, 2007)	3.6	12.6	4.8
Variance	Binary local models	(El Chami et al., 2008)	3.9	10.8	7.4
	Continuous local models	(Vincent et al., 2009b)	8.0	13.8	8.9
	Monophonic models	(Arberet et al., 2009)	8.1	14.5	8.8
	Polyphonic models	(Ozerov & Févotte, 2009)	8.6	14.8	9.7

systems is that the SDRs achieved by the binary local time-frequency model in (El Chami et al., 2008) and the linear model over a learned signal basis in (Gowreesunker & Tewfik, 2007) are 5 dB lower than those achieved by most other systems. This illustrates the limitations of binary local time-frequency models with respect to continuous models and linear signal bases with respect to spectral variance bases. Interestingly, systems based on monophonic or polyphonic spectral models (Arberet el al., 2009; Ozerov & Févotte, 2009) do not significantly improve performance compared to those based on continuous local time-frequency models (Vincent, 2007). We believe that this may be due to the difficulty of blindly learning spectral models with many parameters from a short mixture without incurring overfitting and to convergence to local maxima of the MAP criterion.

In medium reverberation conditions, the best achieved SDR drops to 4 dB on stereo recordings of two sources and 2 dB on stereo recordings of two sources. The SIR is now always smaller than the SAR, which reveals a lack of discrimination between the sources, and most systems provide almost the same SDR up to 1 dB. Again, the system in (Weiss et al., 2008) based on a spectral model of speech does not improve performance compared to the system in (Mandel et al., 2007) using the same mixing vector priors within a local time-frequency model.

DISCUSSION AND FUTURE RESEARCH DIRECTIONS

General Principles and Merits of Variance Modeling vs. Linear Modeling

The overview of model-based source separation systems conducted in this chapter indicates that most models ultimately follow the same general principle, whereby the mixture STFT coefficients

in each time-frequency bin depend on a scalar variable (S_{jnf} or V_{jnf}) encoding spectro-temporal characteristics and a vector or matrix-valued variable ($\mathbf{A}_{jnf}$ or $\mathbf{R}_{jnf}$) encoding spatio-temporal characteristics. This principle defines a link between single-channel and multichannel models. A range of priors have been proposed, relating for example S_{jnf} or V_{jnf} to discrete or continuous latent states and $\mathbf{A}_{jnf}$ or $\mathbf{R}_{jnf}$ to the source DOAs. Intuitively, informative priors over both variables are needed to achieve robust source separation. Indeed, spectral cues alone rarely suffice to discriminate sources with similar pitch range and timbre, while spatial cues alone do not suffice to discriminate sources with the same DOA. Even in situations when either cues suffice to discriminate the sources to a certain extent, combining both cues often increases separation performance (Attias, 2003; Vincent, 2006; Weiss et al., 2008; Arberet et al., 2009).

Two alternative modeling paradigms following the above general principle have been investigated. Linear modeling relies on the assumption that all sources are point sources and appears inappropriate for the encoding of spectral cues. By contrast, variance modeling allows better modeling of reverberant and diffuse sources and efficient encoding of spectral cues. Even when exploiting spatial cues only, variance modeling yields better separation performance than linear modeling on a wide variety of mixtures (Puigt et al., 2009; Vincent et al., 2009b; Duong et al., 2009). Therefore we believe that variance modeling is a stronger candidate paradigm for the building of future model-based source separation systems.

Towards Higher Level Spatial And Spectral Priors

One of the greatest challenges for future research is to address the separation of difficult mixtures involving a large number of sources, reverberation or source movements. Together with Ellis (2006), we believe that a promising approach is to design stronger priors based on higher-level variables encoding sound features possibly exploited by the auditory system. For instance, mixing covariances could be described via a library of priors relating to distinct mixture acquisition techniques and parameterized as functions of room reverberation time and source directivity in addition to the source DOAs. Priors over the source DOAs themselves could account for typical long-term movements in addition to short-term acceleration. Similarly, the source variances could be represented by separate libraries of priors over the coarse and fine spectral structure providing different parameterizations of periodic and noisy sounds. The variables underlying these priors, including the fundamental frequencies of periodic sounds, would themselves follow different priors for speech and music. Recent advances in this area have been made in the fields of source localization on the one hand (Gustafsson, Rao, & Trivedi, 2003; Fallon, Godsill, & Blake, 2006) and CASA and NMF on the other hand (Ellis, 1996; FitzGerald, Cranitch, & Coyle, 2008).

Towards Modular Blind Source Separation Systems

Another great challenge for research is to build fully blind systems able to process all kinds of mixtures without any prior information. Many existing systems are designed for a specific number of channels, a specific kind of mixing or a specific kind of sources. Even the systems considered as blind today often rely on prior knowledge of the number of sources, which is rarely available in real-world applications. We believe that modularity and model selection are keys to overcome these limitations. Indeed, a blind system relying on the same spatial and spectral priors over *e.g.* a periodic point source and a noisy diffuse source would likely achieve poor results due to underfitting. Better results might be obtained by providing the system with a library of priors suited to each possible situation and enabling it to select and combine suitable priors depending on the actual

situation. The Bayesian framework provides a principled approach to the design of such modular systems (Gelman et al., 2003).

The combination of source models within the linear modeling or the Gaussian variance modeling paradigm is particularly attractive since the resulting likelihood exhibits a closed-form expression. A step in this direction was taken in (Blouet, Rapaport, Cohen, & Févotte, 2008), where GSMMs, AR models and polyphonic spectral models were combined into a single system achieving MAP inference via a generalized EM algorithm. Experiments conducted on a single-channel mixture of piano and speech showed good performance with manual selection of a polyphonic spectral model for the piano and an AR model for speech. Additional mixing covariance models and Gaussian variance models, including binary or continuous local time-frequency models, GMMs and HMMs, could also be incorporated into this system using generalized EM inference. Soft masking, FDICA, IVA and spectral model-based Wiener filtering could then all be used at the same time to separate different sources within a given mixture.

In order for such a system to be usable, the most appropriate models should be automatically selected. Advanced Bayesian inference algorithms such as Gibbs sampling and variational Bayes may address this problem by deriving the probabilistic evidence for a particular model (Gelman et al., 2003). These algorithms have already been employed by a few systems for parameter inference within fixed models (Attias, 2003; Cemgil et al., 2007), but not for model selection. Complete evidence maximization could result in a fully blind source separation system, addressing automatic estimation of the number of sources, the most appropriate spatial and spectral model for each source, the number of latent parameters of this model and the best parameter values. Statistical-symbolic languages have recently been proposed that would allow efficient partial implementation of such a system via a sequence of programming constructs (Winn & Bishop, 2005).

CONCLUSION

To sum up, although model-based systems have already achieved very promising separation results, most systems are not entirely blind and fail to separate certain difficult mixtures. The theory of Bayesian signal processing provides a principled research track to address these issues by combination of advanced probabilistic priors and inference criteria. We believe that gradual emergence of the Bayesian modeling paradigms identified in this chapter will result in a major breakthrough in the way source separation systems are developed, with future systems being built from several modules developed by different researchers and selected automatically on the basis of separation quality and computational constraints.

ACKNOWLEDGMENT

Part of this work was supported by EPSRC grants GR/S82213/01, GR/S85900/01, EP/D000246/1, EP/E045235/1 and EP/G007144/1, and EU FET-Open project FP7-ICT-225913 "SMALL". Mike E. Davies acknowledges support of his position from the Scottish Funding Council.

REFERENCES

Arberet, S., Ozerov, A., Gribonval, R., & Bimbot, F. (2009). Blind spectral-GMM estimation for underdetermined instantaneous audio source separation. In *Proceedings of the 8th International Conference on Independent Component Analysis and Signal Separation* (p. 751-758).

Attias, H. (2003). New EM algorithms for source separation and deconvolution with a microphone array. In *Proceedings of the 2003 IEEE International Conference on Acoustics, Speech and Signal Processing* (p. V-297-300).

Benaroya, L., Bimbot, F., & Gribonval, R. (2006). Audio source separation with a single sensor. *IEEE Transactions on Audio. Speech and Language Processing, 14*(1), 191–199. doi:10.1109/TSA.2005.854110

Benaroya, L., McDonagh, L., Bimbot, F., & Gribonval, R. (2003). Non negative sparse representation for Wiener based source separation with a single sensor. In *Proceedings of the 2003 IEEE International Conference on Acoustics, Speech and Signal Processing* (p. VI-613-616).

Blouet, R., Rapaport, G., Cohen, I., & Févotte, C. (2008). Evaluation of several strategies for single sensor speech/music separation. In *Proceedings of the 2008 IEEE International Conference on Acoustics, Speech and Signal Processing* (p. 37–40).

Blumensath, T., & Davies, M. E. (2006). Sparse and shift-invariant representations of music. *IEEE Transactions on Audio. Speech and Language Processing, 14*(1), 50–57. doi:10.1109/TSA.2005.860346

Cardoso, J.-F. (1998). Multidimensional independent component analysis. In *Proceedings of the 1998 IEEE International Conference on Acoustics, Speech and Signal Processing* (p. IV-1941-1944).

Cardoso, J.-F. (2001). The three easy routes to independent component analysis; contrasts and geometry. In *Proceedings of the 3rd International Conference on Independent Component Analysis and Blind Signal Separation* (p. 1-6).

Cemgil, A. T., Févotte, C., & Godsill, S. J. (2007). Variational and stochastic inference for Bayesian source separation. *Digital Signal Processing, 17*(5), 891–913. doi:10.1016/j.dsp.2007.03.008

Dempster, A. P., Laird, N. M., & Rubin, D. B. (1977). Maximum-likelihood from incomplete data via the EM algorithm. *Journal of the Royal Statistical Society. Series B. Methodological, 39*(1), 1–38.

Duong, N. Q. K., Vincent, E., & Gribonval, R. (2009). Spatial covariance models for under-determined reverberant audio source separation. In *Proceedings of the 2009 IEEE Workshop on Applications of Signal Processing to Audio and Acoustics* (p. 129-132).

El Chami, Z., Pham, D. T., Servière, C., & Guerin, A. (2008). A new model-based underdetermined source separation. In *Proceedings of the 11ᵗʰ International Workshop on Acoustic Echo and Noise Control* (paper ID 9061).

Ellis, D. P. W. (1996). *Prediction-driven computational auditory scene analysis.* Unpublished doctoral dissertation, Dept. of Electrical Engineering and Computer Science, MIT. Cambridge, MA.

Ellis, D. P. W. (2006). Model-based scene analysis. In *Computational Auditory Scene Analysis: Principles, Algorithms, and Applications* (p. 115–146). Wiley/IEEE Press.

Fallon, M. F., Godsill, S. J., & Blake, A. (2006). Joint acoustic source location and orientation estimation using sequential Monte Carlo. In *Proceedings of the 9ᵗʰ International Conference on Digital Audio Effects* (p. 203-208).

Févotte, C., & Cardoso, J.-F. (2005). Maximum likelihood approach for blind audio source separation using time-frequency Gaussian models. In *Proceedings of the 2005 IEEE Workshop on Applications of Signal Processing to Audio and Acoustics* (p. 78–81).

FitzGerald, D., Cranitch, M., & Coyle, E. (2008). Extended nonnegative tensor factorisation models for musical sound source separation. *Computational Intelligence and Neuroscience*, 872425.

Gelman, A., Carlin, J. B., Stern, H. S., & Rubin, D. B. (2003). *Bayesian Data Analysis* (2nd ed.). Chapman & Hall/CRC.

Gowreesunker, B. V., & Tewfik, A. H. (2007). Two improved sparse decomposition methods for blind source separation. In *Proceedings of the 7ᵗʰ International Conference on Independent Component Analysis and Signal Separation* (p. 365-372).

Gustafsson, T., Rao, B. D., & Trivedi, M. (2003). Source localization in reverberant environments: modeling and statistical analysis. *IEEE Transactions on Speech and Audio Processing*, *11*(6), 791–803. doi:10.1109/TSA.2003.818027

Izumi, Y., Ono, N., & Sagayama, S. (2007). Sparseness-based 2ch BSS using the EM algorithm in reverberant environment. In *Proceedings of the 2007 IEEE Workshop on Applications of Signal Processing to Audio and Acoustics* (p. 147-150).

Jang, G.-J., & Lee, T.-W. (2004). A maximum likelihood approach to single-channel source separation. *Journal of Machine Learning Research*, *4*(7-8), 1365–1392. doi:10.1162/jmlr.2003.4.7-8.1365

Kristjánsson, T. T., Hershey, J. R., Olsen, P. A., Rennie, S. J., & Gopinath, R. A. (2006). Superhuman multi-talker speech recognition: The IBM 2006 speech separation challenge system. In *Proceedings of the 9ᵗʰ International Conference on Spoken Language Processing* (p. 97-100).

Lee, I. (2009). Permutation correction in blind source separation using sliding subband likelihood function. In *Proceedings of the 8ᵗʰ International Conference on Independent Component Analysis and Signal Separation* (p. 767-774).

Lee, I., Kim, T., & Lee, T.-W. (2007). Independent vector analysis for convolutive blind speech separation. In *Blind speech separation* (pp. 169–192). New York: Springer. doi:10.1007/978-1-4020-6479-1_6

Makino, S., Lee, T.-W., & Sawada, H. (Eds.). (2007). *Blind Speech Separation*. New York: Springer.

Mandel, M. I., Ellis, D. P. W., & Jebara, T. (2007). An EM algorithm for localizing multiple sound sources in reverberant environments. *Advances in Neural Information Processing Systems*, *19*, 953–960.

Mitianoudis, N., & Davies, M. E. (2003). Audio source separation of convolutive mixtures. *IEEE Transactions on Speech and Audio Processing*, *11*(5), 489–497. doi:10.1109/TSA.2003.815820

Mukai, R., Sawada, H., Araki, S., & Makino, S. (2004). Blind source separation for moving speech signals using blockwise ICA and residual crosstalk subtraction. *IEICE Transactions on Fundamentals of Electronics, Communications and Computer Sciences. E (Norwalk, Conn.)*, *87-A*(8), 1941–1948.

Nesbit, A., Vincent, E., & Plumbley, M. D. (2009). Extension of sparse, adaptive signal decompositions to semi-blind audio source separation. In *Proceedings of the 8th International Conference on Independent Component Analysis and Signal Separation* (p. 605-612).

Nesta, F., Omologo, M., & Svaizer, P. (2008). Separating short signals in highly reverberant environment by a recursive frequency-domain BSS. In *Proceedings of the 2008 IEEE Joint Workshop on Hands-free Speech Communication and Microphone Arrays* (p. 232-235).

Nix, J., & Hohmann, V. (2007). Combined estimation of spectral envelopes and sound source direction of concurrent voices by multidimensional statistical filtering. *IEEE Transactions on Audio. Speech and Language Processing*, *15*(3), 995–1008. doi:10.1109/TASL.2006.889788

Nocedal, J., & Wright, S. J. (2006). *Numerical Optimization* (2nd ed.). New York: Springer.

O'Grady, P. D., & Pearlmutter, B. A. (2008). The LOST algorithm: finding lines and separating speech mixtures. *EURASIP Journal on Advances in Signal Processing*, *2008*, 784296. doi:10.1155/2008/784296

Ozerov, A., & Févotte, C. (2009). Multichannel nonnegative matrix factorization in convolutive mixtures. With application to blind audio source separation. In *Proceedings of the 2009 IEEE International Conference on Acoustics, Speech and Signal Processing* (p. 3137-3140).

Ozerov, A., Philippe, P., Bimbot, F., & Gribonval, R. (2007). Adaptation of Bayesian models for single-channel source separation and its application to voice/music separation in popular songs. *IEEE Transactions on Audio. Speech and Language Processing*, *15*(5), 1564–1578. doi:10.1109/TASL.2007.899291

Peterson, J. M., & Kadambe, S. (2003). A probabilistic approach for blind source separation of underdetermined convolutive mixtures. In *Proceedings of the 2003 IEEE International Conference on Acoustics, Speech and Signal Processing* (p. VI-581-584).

Pham, D.-T., Servière, C., & Boumaraf, H. (2003). Blind separation of speech mixtures based on nonstationarity. In *Proceedings of the 7th International Symposium on Signal Processing and its Applications* (p. II–73–76).

Puigt, M., Vincent, E., & Deville, Y. (2009). Validity of the independence assumption for the separation of instantaneous and convolutive mixtures of speech and music sources. In *Proceedings of the 8th International Conference on Independent Component Analysis and Signal Separation* (p. 613-620).

Rennie, S. J., Hershey, J. R., & Olsen, P. A. (2008). Efficient model-based speech separation and denoising using non-negative subspace analysis. In *Proceedings of the 2008 IEEE International Conference on Acoustics, Speech and Signal Processing* (p. 1833-1836).

Roman, N., & Wang, D. L. (2008). Binaural tracking of multiple moving sources. *IEEE Transactions on Audio. Speech and Language Processing*, *16*(4), 728–739. doi:10.1109/TASL.2008.918978

Roweis, S. T. (2001). One microphone source separation. *Advances in Neural Information Processing Systems, 13*, 793–799.

Sawada, H., Araki, S., Mukai, R., & Makino, S. (2007). Grouping separated frequency components with estimating propagation model parameters in frequency-domain blind source separation. *IEEE Transactions on Audio. Speech and Language Processing, 15*(5), 1592–1604. doi:10.1109/TASL.2007.899218

Schmidt, M. N., & Olsson, R. K. (2007). Linear regression on sparse features for single-channel speech separation. In *Proceedings of the 2007 IEEE Workshop on Applications of Signal Processing to Audio and Acoustics* (p. 26-29).

Smaragdis, P. (1998). Blind separation of convolved mixtures in the frequency domain. *Neurocomputing, 22*(1-3), 21–34. doi:10.1016/S0925-2312(98)00047-2

Smaragdis, P. (2007). Convolutive speech bases and their application to supervised speech separation. *IEEE Transactions on Audio. Speech and Language Processing, 15*(1), 1–12. doi:10.1109/TASL.2006.876726

Srinivasan, S., Samuelsson, J., & Kleijn, W. B. (2006). Codebook driven short-term predictor parameter estimation for speech enhancement. *IEEE Transactions on Audio. Speech and Language Processing, 14*(1), 163–176. doi:10.1109/TSA.2005.854113

van Trees, H. L. (2002). *Optimum array processing*. Hoboken, NJ: Wiley. doi:10.1002/0471221104

Vincent, E. (2006). Musical source separation using time-frequency source priors. *IEEE Transactions on Audio. Speech and Language Processing, 14*(1), 91–98. doi:10.1109/TSA.2005.860342

Vincent, E. (2007). Complex nonconvex lp norm minimization for underdetermined source separation. In *Proceedings of the 7th International Conference on Independent Component Analysis and Signal Separation* (p. 430–437).

Vincent, E., Araki, S., & Bofill, P. (2009a). The 2008 Signal Separation Evaluation Campaign: A community-based approach to large-scale evaluation. In *Proceedings of the 8th International Conference on Independent Component Analysis and Signal Separation* (p. 734-741).

Vincent, E., Arberet, S., & Gribonval, R. (2009b). Underdetermined instantaneous audio source separation via local Gaussian modeling. In *Proceedings of the 8th International Conference on Independent Component Analysis and Signal Separation* (p. 775-782).

Virtanen, T., & Cemgil, A. T. (2009). Mixtures of gamma priors for non-negative matrix factorization based speech separation. In *Proceedings of the 8th International Conference on Independent Component Analysis and Signal Separation* (p. 646-653).

Wang, D. L., & Brown, G. J. (Eds.). (2006). *Computational Auditory Scene Analysis: Principles, Algorithms and Applications*. Hoboken, NJ: Wiley/IEEE Press.

Weiss, R. J., & Ellis, D. P. W. (in press). Speech separation using speaker-adapted eigenvoice speech models. *Computer Speech & Language*.

Weiss, R. J., Mandel, M. M., & Ellis, D. P. W. (2008). Source separation based on binaural cues and source model constraints. In *Proceedings of the 10th ISCA Interspeech Conference* (pp. 419–422).

Winn, J., & Bishop, C. M. (2005). Variational message passing. *Journal of Machine Learning Research, 6*, 661–694.

Winter, S., Kellermann, W., Sawada, H., & Makino, S. (2007). MAP-based underdetermined blind source separation of convolutive mixtures by hierarchical clustering and l1-norm minimization. *EURASIP Journal on Advances in Signal Processing, 2007*, 24717. doi:10.1155/2007/24717

Yılmaz, Ö., & Rickard, S. T. (2004). Blind separation of speech mixtures via time-frequency masking. *IEEE Transactions on Signal Processing, 52*(7), 1830–1847. doi:10.1109/TSP.2004.828896

Zibulevsky, M., Pearlmutter, B. A., Bofill, P., & Kisilev, P. (2001). Blind source separation by sparse decomposition in a signal dictionary. In *Independent Component Analysis: Principles and Practice* (p. 181-208). Cambridge, MA: Cambridge Press.

ENDNOTE

[1] In the particular case when all the sources are point sources, the source separation problem is often defined as that of recovering the single-channel source signals emitted by individual sources. Strictly speaking, this involves not only separation, but also dereverberation. Moreover, these source signals can be estimated at best up to a filtering indeterminacy in the absence of information about *e.g.* preamplifier transfer functions or global sound effects. The chosen definition of the source separation problem in terms of mixture components, taken from (Cardoso, 1998), is more general, since it is valid for diffuse sources and it is not subject to the above indeterminacy.

APPENDIX: STANDARD PARAMETRIC PROBABILITY DISTRIBUTIONS

$\mathcal{G}$: circular generalized Gaussian distribution over

$$\mathbb{C} \quad \mathcal{G}(y; \beta, p) = \frac{p}{2\pi\beta\Gamma(1/p)\,|y|} \exp\left(-\left|\frac{y}{\beta}\right|^p\right)$$

with Γ denoting the gamma function.

$\mathcal{N}$: multivariate Gaussian distribution over $\mathbb{C}^I$

$$\mathcal{N}(\mathbf{y}; \mu, \Sigma) = \frac{1}{\pi^{I/2}\,|\det \pounds\,|^{1/2}} \exp\left(-(\mathbf{y}-\mu)^H \Sigma^{-1}(\mathbf{y}-\mu)\right)$$

$\mathcal{U}$: uniform distribution

$\mathcal{U}(\mathbf{y})$ is equal to one over the volume of the space over which $\mathbf{y}$ is defined.

Chapter 8
Tensor Factorization with Application to Convolutive Blind Source Separation of Speech

Saeid Sanei
Cardiff University, UK

Bahador Makkiabadi
Cardiff University, UK

ABSTRACT

Tensor factorization (TF) is introduced as a powerful tool for solving multi-way problems. As an effective and major application of this technique, separation of sound particularly speech signal sources from their corresponding convolutive mixtures is described and the results are demonstrated. The method is flexible and can easily incorporate all possible parameters or factors into the separation formulation. As a consequence of that fewer assumptions (such as uncorrelatedness and independency) will be required. The new formulation allows further degree of freedom to the original parallel factor analysis (PARAFAC) problem in which the scaling and permutation problems of the frequency domain blind source separation (BSS) can be resolved. Based on the results of experiments using real data in a simulated medium, it has been concluded that compared to conventional frequency domain BSS methods, both objective and subjective results are improved when the proposed algorithm is used.

INTRODUCTION

Decomposition of mixed information into its constituent components has been very useful in many applications such as acoustics, communications, and biomedicine. Eigenvalue decomposition (EVD), singular value decomposition (SVD), and independent component analysis (ICA) based on various criteria such as uncorrelatedness, inde-pendency, minimizing mutual information, and differences in distributions, have been widely used for this purpose before. In the case of convolutive mixtures however, further processing to handle multiple time lags of the signals has to be undertaken. Although many researchers have worked on convolutive blind source separation, as comprehensively reported by Pederson et al. in (Pederson et al., 2007) no robust solution, as given for linear instantaneous cases, has been reported. Moreover, generally, the uncorrelated-

DOI: 10.4018/978-1-61520-919-4.ch008

ness or independency assumption may not be true for many applications. In this chapter the fundamental techniques on convolutive BSS are reviewed and a new method has been developed for separation of convolutive sources. The method is based on tensor assumption (or tensorization) of the convolutive mixtures.

TF and multi-way array factorisation and decomposition have become very popular for multi-way signal processing recently. Using this approach generally, there won't be any need for any strong assumptions about mutual statistical properties of the sources such as uncorrelatedness or independence but a mild assumption about the disjointedness in some domain often helps.

This revolutionary technique circumvents many problems in the way of traditional and current convolutive source separation techniques such as the above limiting assumptions, scaling, permutation, causality, circularity (of the convolution), and ill-posedness problems, and provides a unique solution directly.

In the following sections, first the problem of convolutive BSS is stated. Then, TF is discussed in detail and some examples for both overdetermined and underdetermined cases (where the number of sources are more than the number of sensors) are demonstrated.

CONVOLUTIVE BLIND SOURCE SEPARATION

The problem of convolutive BSS has been under research over the past two decades. A number of papers and reviews on convolutive BSS as addressed in (Pederson et al., 2007) have been published recently. In many practical situations the signals reach the sensors with different time delays. The corresponding delay between source j and sensor i, in terms of number of samples, is directly proportional to the sampling frequency and conversely to the speed of sound in the medium, i.e. $\delta_{ij} \propto d_{ij} \times f_s / c$, where $d_{ij}, f_s,$ and c

are respectively, the distance between source j and sensor i, the sampling frequency, and the speed of sound. For speech and music in the air as an example we may have d_{ij} in terms of meters, f_s between 8 to 44 KHz, and c=330 m/sec. Also, in an acoustic environment the sound signals can reach the sensors through multi-paths after reflections by obstacles (such as walls). A general matrix formulation of the **CBSS** for mixing and separating the source signals can be given as:

$$\mathbf{x}(t) = \mathbf{H}(t) * \mathbf{s}(t) + \mathbf{v}(t) \qquad (1)$$

and

$$\mathbf{y}(t) = \mathbf{W}(t) * \mathbf{x}(t) \qquad (2)$$

where $M \times 1$ $\mathbf{s}(t)$, $N \times 1$ $\mathbf{x}(t)$, and $N \times 1$ $\mathbf{v}(t)$ denote respectively the vector of source signals, observed signals, and noise at discrete time t. $\mathbf{H}$ is the mixing matrix of size $N \times M$ and * denotes convolution operator. The separation is performed by means of a separating $M \times N$ matrix, $\mathbf{W}$, which uses only the information about $\mathbf{x}(t)$ to reconstruct the original source signals denoted as $\mathbf{y}(t)$.

Equation (1) and (2) are the general forms of both anechoic and echoic BSS models. In an anechoic model, however, the expansion of the mixing process may be given as:

$$x_i(t) = \sum_{j=1}^{M} h_{ij} s_j(t - \delta_{ij}) + v_i(t), \quad \text{for } i = 1, \cdots, N \qquad (3)$$

where the attenuation, h_{ij}, and delay, δ_{ij}, of source j to sensor i would be determined by the physical position of the source relative to the sensors. Then, the unmixing process is given as:

$$y_j(t) = \sum_{i=1}^{N} w_{ji} x_i(t - \delta_{ji}), \quad \text{for } j = 1, \cdots, M \qquad (4)$$

where w_{ji} are the elements of $\mathbf{W}$. In an echoic mixing environment it is expected that the signals from the same sources reach to the sensors through multiple paths. Therefore, the expansion of the mixing model is changed to

$$x_i(t) = \sum_{j=1}^{M} \sum_{k=1}^{K} h_{ijk} s_j(t - \delta_{ijk}) + v_i(t), \quad \text{for } i = 1, \cdots, N$$

$$(5)$$

where K denotes the number of paths, δ_{ijk} is the delay from source j to sensor i through the kth path, and $v_i(t)$ is the accumulated noise at sensor i. The unmixing process maybe formulated similarly to the anechoic one. Obviously, for a known number of sources an accurate result may be expected if the number of paths is known.

The aim of BSS using ICA is to estimate an unmixing matrix $\mathbf{W}$ such that $\mathbf{Y}$ best approximates the independent sources $\mathbf{S}$, where $\mathbf{Y}$ and $\mathbf{X}$ are respectively the matrices with columns

$$\mathbf{y}(t) = \left[y_1(t), y_2(t), \cdots y_M(t) \right]^T \text{ and}$$

$$\mathbf{x}(t) = \left[x_1(t), x_2(t), \cdots x_N(t) \right]^T.$$

There are three major approaches in using ICA for BSS:

1. factorising the joint pdf of the reconstructed signals into its marginal pdfs. Under the assumption that the source signals are stationary and non-Gaussian, the independence of the reconstructed signals can be measured by a statistical distance between the joint distribution and the product of its marginal pdfs. Kullback-Laibler (KL) divergence (distance) is an example. For non-stationary cases and for the short-length data, there will be poor estimation of the pdfs. Therefore, in such cases, this approach may not lead to good results. On the other hand, such methods are not robust for noisy data since

in this situation the pdf of the signal will be distorted.

2. decorrelating the reconstructed signals through time, that is, diagonalizing the covariance matrices at every time instant. If the signals are mutually independent, the off-diagonal elements of the covariance matrix vanish. Although the reverse of this statement is not always true. If the signals are nonstationary we can utilise the time-varying covariance structure to estimate the unmixing matrix. An advantage of this method is that it only uses second order statistics, which implies that it is likely to perform better in noisy and short data length conditions than higher order statistics.

3. eliminating the temporal cross-correlation functions of the reconstructed signals as much as possible. In order to perform this, the correlation matrix of observations can be diagonalized at different time lags simultaneously. Here, second order statistics are also normally used. As another advantage, it can be applied in the presence of white noise since such noise can be avoided by using the cross correlation only for $\tau \neq 0$. Such a method is appropriate for stationary and weakly stationary sources (i.e when the stationarity condition holds within a short segment of data).

Mutual information (MI) may be considered as a measure of independence and maximizing the non-Gaussianity of the source signals is equivalent to minimizing the mutual information between them.

In the majority of cases the number of sources is known. The assumption about number of sources avoids any ambiguity caused by false estimation of the number of sources. In exactly-determined cases the number of sources is equal to the number of mixtures. In over-determined situations however, the number of mixtures is more than the number of sources.

Generally, the solution to echoic cases is more difficult and it normally involves some approximations to the actual system. As an example, in the cocktail party problem the source signals propagate through a dynamic medium with many parasitic effects such as multiple echoes and reverberation. So, the received signals are a weighted sum of mixed and delayed components. In other words, the received signals at each microphone are the convolutivemixtures of speech signals.

Due to the propagation delays involved in the convolutive mixtures, the developed algorithms for instantaneous BSS may not be used directly for their separation. Two major approaches have been followed for both anechoic and echoic cases; the first approach is to solve the problem in the time domain. In such methods in order to have accurate results both the weights of the unmixing matrix and the delays have to be estimated. However, in the second approach, the problem is transformed into the frequency domain as $\mathbf{h}(n) * \mathbf{s}(n) \xrightarrow{F} \mathbf{H}(\omega) \cdot \mathbf{S}(\omega)$ and instantaneous BSS applied to each frequency bin mixed signal. In the instantaneous separation of frequency domain mixtures the separation is subject to permutation and scaling ambiguities in the output independent components, i.e. when the numbers of sources and sensors are the same $\mathbf{W} = \mathbf{PDH}^{-1}$, where $\mathbf{P}$ and $\mathbf{D}$ are, respectively, the permutation and scaling matrices. The separated signals at different frequency bins are then combined and transformed to the time domain to reconstruct the estimated sources. The short-term Fourier transform is often used for this purpose. In the latter scheme the inherent permutation problem of BSS severely deteriorates the results since the order of the separated sources in different frequency bins can vary from segment-to-segment of the signals.

An early work in convolutive BSS is by Platt and Faggin (Platt and Faggin, 1992) who applied adaptive noise cancellation network to the BSS model of Herault and Jutten (Herault and Jutten,

1986). Their network has delays in the feedback path, and the method is based on the minimum output power principle. This scheme exploits the fact that the signal corrupted by noise has more power than the clean signal. The feedback path cancels out the interferences as the result of delayed versions of the other sources. This circuit was also used later to extend the Infomax BSS to convolutive cases (Torkkola, 1996a). The combined network maximises the entropy at the output of the network with respect to the weights and delays. Torkkola (Torkkola, 1996b) extended this algorithm to the echoic cases too. In order to achieve a reasonable convergence, some prior knowledge of the recording situation is necessary.

In another work an extension of the second order blind identification (SOBI) algorithm has been used for anechoic BSS (Wang et al., 2005); the problem has been transformed to the frequency domain and joint diagonalization of spectral matrices has been utilised to estimate the mixing coefficients as well as the delays. In attempts by Parra (Parra et al., 2000), Ikram (Ikram and Morgan, 2000), and Cherkani (Cherkani and Deville, 1999) second order statistics have been used to ensure that the estimated sources, $\mathbf{Y}(\omega, m)$, are uncorrelated at each frequency bin. $\mathbf{W}(\omega)$ is estimated in such a way that it diagonalizes the covariance matrices $\mathbf{R}_Y(\omega, k)$ simultaneously for all time blocks k; $k = 0, 1, ..., K-1$, i.e.

$$= \mathbf{W}(\omega)\mathbf{H}(\omega)\Lambda_S(\omega, k)\mathbf{H}^H(\omega)\mathbf{W}^H(\omega) = \Lambda_c(\omega, k)$$

(6)

where $\Lambda_S(\omega, k)$ is the covariance matrix of the source signals, which changes with k, $\Lambda_c(\omega, k)$ is an arbitrary diagonal matrix, and $\mathbf{R}_X(\omega, k)$ is the covariance matrix of $\mathbf{X}(\omega)$, estimated by

$$\hat{\mathbf{R}}_X(\omega, k) = \frac{1}{N}\sum_{n=0}^{N-1}\mathbf{X}(\omega, N_k + n)\mathbf{X}^H(\omega, N_k + n)$$

(7)

where N is the number of mixtures and the unmixing filter $\mathbf{W}(\omega)$ for each frequency bin ω that simultaneously satisfies the K decorrelation equations can then be obtained using an over-determined least squares solution. Since the output covariance matrix $\mathbf{R}_Y(\omega, k)$ has to be diagonalized the update equation for estimation of the unmixing matrix $\mathbf{W}$ can be found by minimizing the off-diagonal elements of $\mathbf{R}_Y(\omega, k)$, which leads to

$$\mathbf{W}_{\rho+1}(\omega) = \mathbf{W}_\rho(\omega) - \mu(\omega) \cdot \frac{\partial}{\partial \mathbf{W}_\rho^H(\omega)} \left\{ \left\| \mathbf{V}_\rho(\omega, k) \right\|_F^2 \right\}$$
(8)

where ρ is the iteration index, $\left\| \, . \, \right\|_F^2$ is the squared Frobenius norm,

$$\mu(\omega) = \frac{\alpha}{\sum_k \left\| \mathbf{R}_X(\omega, k) \right\|^2},$$
(9)

and

$$\mathbf{V}(\omega, k) = \mathbf{W}(\omega)\mathbf{R}_X(\omega, k)\mathbf{W}^H(\omega) - diag\left[\mathbf{W}(\omega)\mathbf{R}_X(\omega, k)\mathbf{W}^H(\omega) \right]$$
(10)

and α is a constant which is adjusted practically.

Time–frequency approaches are also common for when the sources are approximately cyclostationary and nonstationary, the auto-terms and cross-terms of the covariance matrix of the mixtures are first separated and BSS is applied to both terms (Belouchrani et al., 2004; Cirillo and Zoubir, 2005). The sources are then estimated by combining the above two separated terms.

To mitigate the permutation problem a number of techniques have been suggested. The readers can refer to (Smaragdis, 1998) and (Murata et al., 2001). The most straightforward methods are based on the spectrum uniformity (or continuity) assumption or by using a beamformer to locate the source of interest.

To circumvent the above problems and as new ways of tackling the convolutive BSS problem tensor factorization using PARAFAC is discussed.

PARALLEL FACTOR ANALYSIS

PARAFAC also called canonical decomposition (CANDECOMP) is a special case of TF approach (Mørup et al., 2006; Cohen, 1995). Also, it is considered as generalization of PCA to the cases where a set of data matrices is to be analysed simultaneously. In this approach generally the events are considered sparse in the space-time-frequency domain and no assumption is made on either independency or uncorrelatedness of the sources. Therefore, the main advantage of PARAFAC over PCA or ICA is that the uniqeness is ensured under mild conditions, making it unnecessary to impose orthogonality or statistical independence constraints. Harshman (Harshman, 1970) was the first researcher who suggested the use of PARAFAC for EEG decomposition. Harshman, Carol, and Chang (Carol and Chang, 1970) independently proposed PARAFAC in 1970.

Möcks reinvented the model, naming it topographic component analysis, to analyze the ERP of channel × time × subjects (Möcks, 1988). The model was further developed by Field and Graupe (Field and Graupe, 1991). Miwakeichi et al. eventually used PARAFAC to decompose the EEG data to its constituent space-time-frequency components (Miwakeichi et al., 2004). Figures 1 and 2 show respectively the space-time-frequency decomposition of 15 channel EEG signals recorded during left and right index finger movement imagination in a brain-computer interfacing context. Spectral contents, temporal profiles of the two identified factors, and the topographic mapping of EEG for the two factors are shown in these images (Sanei and Chambers 2007).

PARAFAC models are divided into two categories of PARAFAC1 and PARAFAC2. In PARAFAC1 the data matrix has the same row and

Figure 1. Sample space-time-frequency decomposition of the EEG signals recorded during left index movement imagination. The factor demonstrated with the solid line indicates a clear desynchronization (ERD) in the contralateral hemisphere: (a) spectral contents of the two identified factors, (b) temporal signatures of the factors, the onset of preparation and execution cues are shown in light and dark patches, respectively, (c) and (d) represent topographic mapping of EEG for the two factors. "Figure adapted from (Sanei and Chambers, 2009)".

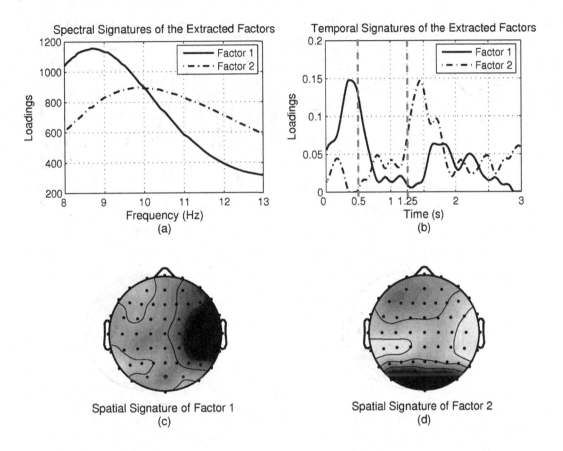

column units and the resulting data are three-way data. If each data matrix has the same column units but different number of row units, the PARAFAC2 model can be used. A schematic concept of PARAFAC1 has been depicted in Figure 3.

Let the $I \times J$ matrix $\mathbf{X}_k$, $=1, \ldots, K$, represent the kth slab of a three-way data array $\underline{\mathbf{X}}$, for example, consisting of scores of I observation units on J variables at K occasions. According to the PARAFAC1 model, the kth slab of three-way model $\mathbf{X}_k$ be expressed as (Kiers et al., 1999)

$$\mathbf{X}_k = \mathbf{SD}_k\mathbf{A}^T + \mathbf{E}_k \qquad (11)$$

where $\mathbf{A}$ is $J \times F$, $\mathbf{S}$ is $I \times F$, $\mathbf{E}_k$ is $I \times J$, and $\mathbf{D}_k$ is an $F \times F$ diagonal matrix. It is seen that by replacing $\mathbf{S}_k = \mathbf{SD}_k$, the model resembles the PCA model with the same factor score matrix for all slabs, and loading matrices that are column wise proportional across slabs. The factors can be estimated by minimising the following cost function:

191

Figure 2. Sample space-time-frequency decomposition of the EEG signals recorded during right index movement imagination. The factor demonstrated with the solid line indicates a clear event-related desynchronization (ERD) in the contralateral hemisphere: (a) spectral contents of the two identified factors, (b) temporal signatures of the factors, the onset of preparation and execution cues are shown in light and dark patches, respectively, (c) and (d) show topographic mapping of EEG for the two factors. "Figure adapted from (Sanei and Chambers, 2009)".

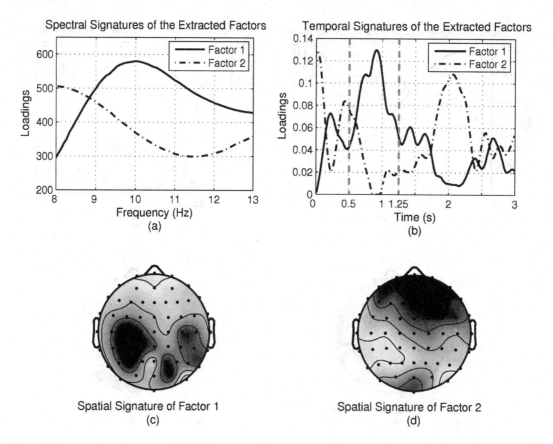

$$J_1(\mathbf{A},\mathbf{S},\mathbf{D}_1,...,\mathbf{D}_K) = \sum_{k=1}^{K} \| \mathbf{X}_k - \mathbf{SD}_k\mathbf{A}^T \|^2 \tag{12}$$

There has been shown that under some mild conditions there are unique solutions for **A**, **S**, and $\mathbf{D}_k$s (Harshman, 1972a). The algorithm can be initialised in several ways, i.e. by randomly defining all parameters and stopping when they all have converged.

However, the assumption of equality of the factor scores is too strong and often the observa-tion units are not comparable. In such cases the parallel proportional profile principle may be used in an adjusted way in which the observations $\mathbf{X}_k$, $I\times J$, are modelled as

$$\mathbf{X}_k = \mathbf{S}_k\mathbf{D}_k\mathbf{A}^T + \mathbf{E}_k \tag{13}$$

In this case for each data matrix we have a different factor score matrix. The major problem with this new model is that the factors won't be unique any more. This is because the factor scores can no longer be constrained to be equal for the

Figure 3. Decomposition of multi-way array **X** *using PARAFAC1 "Figure adapted from (Cichocki et al., 2009)"*

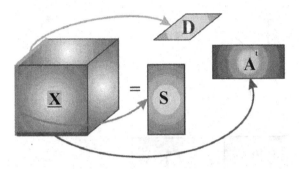

different data matrices. To develop a unique model, Harshman (Harshman, 1972a; Harshman, 1972b) imposed a particular invariance constraint on the factor scores as $\mathbf{S}_k^T\mathbf{S}_k$ remaining constant over k. This constrained problem is referred to PARAFAC2. Such a model can be useful in many cases where the data can be described in three different domains respectively or in places where the PCA model varies from sample to sample. In the latter case the idea is to represent the shift variable as a dimension in PARAFAC2. A schematic diagram of the concept can be seen in Figure 4.

As another alternative to the above constrained model, Harshman (Harshman, 1972b) proposed to fit the cross-product version of the above model to the observed cross product. Assuming $\mathbf{C}_k$, $k=1,...,K$ is the cross-product matrix associated with $\mathbf{x}_k$, then the following model can be fitted:

$$\mathbf{C}_k = \mathbf{A}\mathbf{D}_k\Phi\mathbf{D}_k\mathbf{A}^T + \mathbf{E}_k^{(c)} \qquad (14)$$

where Φ denotes the invariant matrix $\mathbf{S}_k^T\mathbf{S}_k$ and $\mathbf{E}_k^{(c)}$ denotes the error matrix for $\mathbf{C}_k$. This however, is not applied here. This (minimisation of the residual in (14)) refers to *indirect fitting* method.

The PARAFAC2 components can be estimated by *direct fitting* through minimising

$$J_2(\mathbf{S}_1,...,\mathbf{S}_K,\mathbf{A},\mathbf{D}_1,...,\mathbf{D}_K) = \sum_{k=1}^{K} \| \mathbf{X}_k - \mathbf{S}_k\mathbf{D}_k\mathbf{A}^T \|^2 \qquad (15)$$

Subject to the equality constraint $\mathbf{S}_k^T\mathbf{S}_k = \mathbf{S}_l^T\mathbf{S}_l$ for all pairs $k,l = 1,..., K$ and $\mathbf{D}_k$ diagonal. This minimisation depends on $\mathbf{X}_k^T\mathbf{X}_k$ only. Establishing a direct fitting method is important since in this scheme the actual data rather than derived entities, are fitted and, as a consequence, factor scores (for the row units) are estimated, whereas, these are not obtained by the indirect fitting procedure.

In order to solve the direct fitting problem using PARAFAC2 the effect of the above equality constraint should be considered. To enforce the constraint, it is necessary and sufficient to have $\mathbf{S}_k = \mathbf{P}_k\mathbf{H}$ for a column-wise orthonormal ($I \times F$) matrix $\mathbf{P}_k$ and an $F \times F$ matrix $\mathbf{H}$ where F is the number of sources. This is sufficient since $\mathbf{S}_k^T\mathbf{S}_k = \mathbf{H}^T\mathbf{P}_k^T\mathbf{P}_k\mathbf{H} = \mathbf{H}^T\mathbf{H}$ is constant for all k. Based on the fact that $\mathbf{S}_k^T\mathbf{S}_k = \mathbf{S}_l^T\mathbf{S}_l$ for all k and l, and the constraint $\mathbf{S}_k = \mathbf{P}_k\mathbf{H}$, this can be substituted in (15) to have

$$J_3(\mathbf{P}_1,...,\mathbf{P}_K,\mathbf{H},\mathbf{A},\mathbf{D}_1,...,\mathbf{D}_K) = \sum_{k=1}^{K} \| \mathbf{X}_k - \mathbf{P}_k\mathbf{H}\mathbf{D}_k\mathbf{A}^T \|^2 \qquad (16)$$

This has to minimized over all its arguments subject to the constraints of $\mathbf{P}_k^T\mathbf{P}_k = \mathbf{I}_F$ and $\mathbf{D}_k$ diagonal, where $\mathbf{I}_F$ is an $F \times F$ identity matrix. As a minimization option for the above cost function alternating least squares (ALS) is proposed. The ALS minimizes (16) iteratively with respect to $\mathbf{P}_k$, $\mathbf{A}$, H, and $\mathbf{D}_k$ for all k. Minimizing (16) over $\mathbf{P}_k$ subject to $\mathbf{P}_k^T\mathbf{P}_k = \mathbf{I}_F$ leads to maximizing

$$J_{P_k} = tr\{\mathbf{H}\mathbf{D}_k\mathbf{A}^T\mathbf{X}_k^T\mathbf{P}_k\} \qquad (17)$$

The solution is found by singular value decomposition of $\mathbf{H}\mathbf{D}_k\mathbf{A}^T\mathbf{X}_k^T$, i.e.

Figure 4. Schematic diagrams of (a) tensor and (b) slab-wise decomposition of multi-way array **X** *using PARAFAC 2. Each matrix* **X**$_k$ *is decomposed separately. Figure adapted from (Cichocki et al., 2009).*

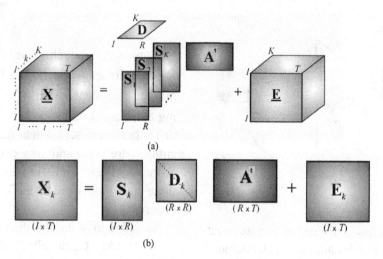

$$\mathbf{HD}_k\mathbf{A}^T\mathbf{X}_k^T = \mathbf{U}_k{''}_k\mathbf{V}_k^T .$$ Then, $\mathbf{P}_k = \mathbf{V}_k\mathbf{U}_k^T$ for all k. On the other hand, the problem of minimizing (21) with respect to **H**, **D**$_k$, and **A** reduces to minimizing

$$J_4(\mathbf{S}_k,\mathbf{A},\mathbf{D}_1,...,\mathbf{D}_k\,|\,\mathbf{P}_k) = \sum_{k=1}^{K} \|\,\mathbf{P}_k^T\mathbf{X}_k - \mathbf{A}_k\mathbf{D}_k\mathbf{A}^T\,\|^2 \tag{18}$$

This minimization is equivalent to that of PARAFAC1 when $\mathbf{X}_k$ is replaced by $\mathbf{P}_k^T\mathbf{X}_k$.

In some applications such as image analysis it may be useful to constrain some of the parameters to have, for example, non-negative values only. PARAFAC2 algorithm uses the steps from PARA-FAC1. Therefore, this is clear since the parameter matrices **H**, **D**$_k$, and **A** can be constrained in the same way as they can be constrained in PARA-FAC1 model despite the fact that the use of these constraints may frequently lead to zero values in some of the matrices **D**$_k$ and hence violate one of the uniqueness assumptions.

As the second extension, complex data structures consisting of sets of three- or higher-way arrays can be easily handled by the present PARAFAC2 approach. For clarity, consider the following case with a set of three-way arrays.

Given a set of K three-way arrays $\underline{\mathbf{X}}_k$ of orders $I \times J_1 \times J_2$, $k = 1,...\ K$, and each of these to be modelled by a PARAFAC1 model with parameter matrix $\mathbf{G}_k$, **A** and **B**. Defining $\mathbf{X}_k$ as the $I \times J_1J_2$ supermatrix with frontal planes of $\underline{\mathbf{X}}_k$ next to each other, then the PARAFAC1 model for $\mathbf{X}_k$ as (Kiers et al., 1999):

$$\mathbf{X}_k = \mathbf{G}_k(\mathbf{B}\otimes\mathbf{A})^T + \mathbf{E}_k \tag{19}$$

where $\otimes$ denotes Khatri-Rao product. Furthermore, let the models be related to each other by the constraint $\mathbf{G}_k = \mathbf{S}_k\mathbf{D}_k$, with $\mathbf{D}_k$ diagonal and $\mathbf{S}_k^T\mathbf{S}_k$ invariant over k. In this case there will be a direct four-way generalization of the original PARAFAC2 model that can be written as:

$$\mathbf{X}_k = \mathbf{P}_k\mathbf{HD}_k(\mathbf{B}\otimes\mathbf{A})^T + \mathbf{E}_k \tag{20}$$

The problem can be solved by fitting the model in the least squares sense by using an ALS algorithm where $\mathbf{P}_k$ is updated by maximizing

$$J_{P_k} = tr\{\mathbf{HD}_k(\mathbf{B} \otimes \mathbf{A})^T \mathbf{X}_k^T \mathbf{P}_k\} \qquad (21)$$

where *tr* denotes trace of a matrix. This is by using the SVD $\mathbf{HD}_k(\mathbf{B} \otimes \mathbf{A})^T \mathbf{X}_k^T = \mathbf{U}_k "_k \mathbf{V}_k^T$ and updating $\mathbf{P}_k = \mathbf{V}_k \mathbf{U}_k^T$. In order to find the other parameters, as before, we need to minimise the function

$$J_s(\mathbf{A}, \mathbf{B}, \mathbf{H}, \mathbf{D}_1, ..., \mathbf{D}_K) = \sum_{k=1}^{K} \| \mathbf{P}_k^T \mathbf{X}_k - \mathbf{HD}_k(\mathbf{B} \otimes \mathbf{A})^T \|^2$$
$$(22)$$

with respect to **H**, **A**, **B**, and **D**$_k$s. This may be recognized as a four-way PARAFAC problem which is solved in exactly the same way as three-way problems. This refers to the generalization of PARAFAC2 to more than three ways. This solution is significantly important since the multi-way arrays of different size and number of dimensions can be solved through this method.

Due to the multi-way nature of TF it can be used not only for separation but for localization of the multiple sources.

APPLICATION OF PARAFAC TO CONVOLUTIVE MIXTURES

In this application the objective is to separate the signal sources from their anechoic mixtures. Also, it will be useful to examine the technique for echoic cases. The three-way array is established by considering the dimensions as the time samples, the channel number, and the delays. The delays reflect the shifted versions of the mixed signals. Generally, as far as the sources don't overlap in the multi-way domain they can be separated. There have been some attempts in application of PARAFAC1 in separation of convolutive mixtures (Mokios et al., 2006; Olsson et al., 2006; Mokios et al., 2008). In (Mokios et al., 2006) and (Mokios et al., 2008) a two-step frequency domain BSS algorithm with unknown channel order using

PARAFAC for separation of convolutive speech mixtures has been developed. The method is subject to permutation of the bin frequencies. Therefore, it has been supported by an integer-least-squares (ILS) based method for matching the arbitrary permutations in the frequency domain. To build up the multi-way PARAFAC model the whole data block of N snapshots is divided into P subblocks, with each sub-block corresponding to a time interval over which the source signals are assumed stationary, the measured snapshots within any pth sub-block correspond to the following autocorrelation matrix:

$$\mathbf{R}_x(f, t_p) = \mathbf{A}(f)\mathbf{R}_s(f, t_p)\mathbf{A}^H(f) + \mathbf{R}_n(f, t_p)$$
$$(23)$$

Therefore, ignoring the noise, the element-wise representation of the above equation can be given as:

$$r_{jlp}^x = [\underline{\mathbf{R}}_x(f)] = \sum_{i=1}^{I} \alpha_{ji}(f) r_i^s(f, p) \alpha_{li}^* \qquad (24)$$

Where $r_i^s(f, p)$ is the power density of the sources for sub-block p, $(.)^*$ is conjugate operation and $\underline{\mathbf{R}}_x(f)$ is the tensor representation of autocorrelation matrices in all frequency bins. To move to PARAFAC model matrix $\mathbf{P}(f) \in C^{P \times P}$ is defined as:

$$\mathbf{P}(f) \overset{\Delta}{=} \begin{bmatrix} r_1^s(f,1) & \cdots & r_I^s(f,1) \\ \vdots & & \vdots \\ r_1^s(f,P) & \cdots & r_I^s(f,P) \end{bmatrix} \qquad (25)$$

Where $\mathbf{P}(f)$ and $\mathbf{R}_s(f, t_p)$ can be related to each other using $\mathbf{R}_s(f, t_p) = D_P(\mathbf{P}(f)) = \Lambda(f, t_p)$ for all sub-blocks and all frequency bins $f = 1, ..., T$. $D_p(.)$ is the operator which makes a diagonal matrix by selecting the pth row and putting it on the main diagonal while putting zeros elsewhere. Equation (24) implies that r_{jlp} is a sum of rank-1 triple products; this equation is known as (conjugate-symmetric) PARAFAC analysis of r_{jlp} (Rong et al., 2005). If I is sufficiently small then Equation (24) represents a low-rank decomposition of $\underline{\mathbf{R}}_x(f)$. Therefore, the problem of estimating matrix $\mathbf{A}(f)$ for a specific frequency f can be re-formulated as the problem of low-rank decomposition of the three-way autocorrelation array $\underline{\mathbf{R}}_x(f)$. By solving a similar problem separately for every frequency we obtain the entire collection of the frequency-domain mixing matrices $\mathbf{A}(f), f = 0,..., T - 1$. The uniqueness (up to inherently unresolvable source permutation and scale ambiguities) of all source spatial signatures, given the exact frequency-domain autocorrelation data is an issue known as the identifiability of the model. Identifiability conditions i.e., conditions under which the trilinear decomposition of $\underline{\mathbf{R}}_x(f)$ is unique, are discussed in (Rong et al., 2005). In (Mokios et al., 2006) PARAFAC fitting at each frequency has been based on implementation of trilinear alternating least squares (TALS) tech-nique (Rong et al., 2005), which is used to estimate the matrices $\mathbf{A}(f)$, up to a frequency-dependent permutation and scaling ambiguities. The same methods often used for solving these ambiguities in the ICA context may be used to solve these problems here. One straightforward approach, as attempted in the ICA context (Pesquet et al., 2001) is by measuring the similarity in the spectrums in different frequency bins. The method was applied to the mixtures when two sources were mixed at four microphones located in distances from the sources. The results have been compared with those of Parra's frequency domain convolutive BSS method (Parra and Spence, 2000) and has been shown that PARAFAC outperforms Parra's considerably (Mokios et al., 2006).

On the other hand, underdetermined systems of instantaneous mixtures have been discussed

by different researchers and some solutions to that have been reported (Luo et al., 2006; Li et al., 2006; Jurjine et al., 2000; Vielva et al., 2002; Takigawa et al., 2004). These solutions mainly rely on the sparseness of the source signals. Li's and DUET algorithms are the most popular ones. In these methods the dimensionality of the data remains the same. Therefore, for natural data these solutions are not feasible since the sparsity may not be verified. On the other hand, for the convolutive case such models are not valid.

In (Olsson et al., 2006) the underdetermined separation system using PARAFAC has been examined. In this work it has been assumed that the sources are non-stationary and sparsely dis-tributed in the time-frequency plane. The mixture model is convolutive, i.e. acoustic setups such as the cocktail party problem are contained. In this study the limits of identifiability in the PARA-FAC framework are determined. The general PARAFAC model in this work is similar to that in Equation (22). Similarly, it can be denoted as

$$\mathbf{R}_x(f, t_p) = (\mathbf{A}(f) \otimes \mathbf{A}^*(f))\Lambda^T(f, t_p) \qquad (26)$$

The standard ALS method can also be used in this case to minimise the Frobenius norm to esti-mate the diagonal matrix $\Lambda(f, t_p)$ for all the frequency bins. The solution takes the form

$$\hat{\mathbf{A}}^T(f) = (\mathbf{A}(f) \otimes \mathbf{A}^*(f)) \qquad (27)$$

where $(.)^\dagger$ represents pseudo-inverse of a matrix. After $\mathbf{R}_s(f, t_p) = \Lambda(f, t_p)$ and $\mathbf{A}(f)$ are esti-mated, the sources can be estimated (recon-structed) in each frequency bin through

$$\hat{S}(f) = \mathbf{R}_s(f, t_p)\mathbf{A}(f)\left(\mathbf{A}(f)\mathbf{R}_s(f, t_p)\mathbf{A}^H(f)\right)^{-1}\mathbf{X}(f) \qquad (28)$$

In an experiment three speech sources and two microphones have been considered which is an underdetermined system. The results for the cases of different sex subjects have been shown to be better than those of known underdetermined BSS systems (Olsson et al., 2006).

In (Mokios et al., 2008) the solutions to scaling and permutation ambiguities and consequently the identifiability of the PARAFAC system have been discussed.

In this model the autocorrelation matrices of the sub-blocks are taken into account for further processing. Although this makes the process easy but it requires the data to be stationary and suffers the problem of replacing sample autocorrelation estimates for the statistical autocorrelation $\mathbf{R}_x(f, t_p)$. Moreover, diagonality of $\mathbf{R}_s(f, t_p)$ implies uncorrelatedness of the sources. In a new development a solution to this shortcoming has been attempted. In this scheme, the separation is performed directly and there is no need to compute the autocorrelation of each block of the signals.

In this method instead of having a small rectangular matrix on each sub block there is a measurement matrix with many more columns than rows, $\mathbf{X}(f, t_p)$, as:

$$\mathbf{X}(f, t_p) = \mathbf{A}(f)\mathbf{S}(f, t_p) + \mathbf{E}(f, t_p) \quad (29)$$

Then, PARAFAC2 tensor factorization is applied. To build up the multi-way PARAFAC2 model the whole data block of N snapshots is divided into T hyper subblocks and each subblock is further divided into P subblocks, each corresponding to a time interval over which the source signals can be assumed stationary, the measured snapshots within any pth sub-block can be fitted in

$$\mathbf{X}(f, t_p, t_t) = \mathbf{A}(f)\mathbf{S}(f, t_p, t_t) + \mathbf{E}(f, t_p, t_t) \quad (30)$$

In the proposed PARAFAC2 model considering $\bar{\mathbf{X}} = \mathbf{X}^T(f, :, :)$, as a tensor, at each frequency bin. Then, each transposed frontal slab of $\bar{\mathbf{X}}$ can be written as

$$\mathbf{X}_{t_t} = \mathbf{S}_{t_t}\mathbf{D}_{t_t}\mathbf{A}^T + \mathbf{E}_{t_t} \quad (31)$$

Like in conventional PARAFAC2 model here there is a fixed $\mathbf{A}^T$ for all slabs and each $\mathbf{S}_{t_t}$ can be considered as $\mathbf{S}_{t_t} = \mathbf{P}_{t_t}\mathbf{H}$ where $\mathbf{P}_{t_t}^T\mathbf{P}_{t_t} = \mathbf{I}$. It is worth mentioning that after applying PARAFAC2-BSS in each frequency bin $\mathbf{A}(f) \in \mathbb{R}^{M \times N}, \mathbf{P}(f) \in \mathbb{R}^{L \times N}$, and $\mathbf{H}(f) \in \mathbb{R}^{N \times N}$ will be estimated/factorized. $\mathbf{A}(f)$ represents the mixing matrix and $\mathbf{P}(f)$ is the separated signals up to some scaling and permutation.

For solving the scaling ambiguity a sensor normalization may be adopted. The normalization is carried out in two steps: in the first step each column of $\mathbf{A}(f)$ i.e. $\mathbf{a}_{:,i}(f)$, is divided by one of its elements $a_{r,i}(f)$ where r is related to the number of reference electrode;

$$\tilde{\mathbf{a}}_{:,i}(f) \overset{\Delta}{=} \frac{\mathbf{a}_{:,i}(f)}{a_{r,i}(f)} \quad (32)$$

In this case $d_i(f)$ is defined as:

$$d_i(f) - a_{r,i}(f)\left\|\tilde{\mathbf{a}}_{:,i}(f)\right\| \quad (33)$$

where $i = 1, \ldots, N$ and $d_i(f)$ is a scaling factor applied to each column of $\mathbf{A}$. Second step for the normalization is done by dividing each column of $\tilde{\mathbf{a}}_{:,i}(f)$ by its norm i.e.

$$\tilde{\mathbf{a}}_{:,i}(f) \leftarrow \frac{\tilde{\mathbf{a}}_{:,i}(f)}{\left\|\mathbf{a}_{:,i}(f)\right\|} \quad (34)$$

There are many possible solutions for solving the permutation problem similar to those related to frequency domain BSS problems. These methods mainly exploit either spatial information of the sources (such as beamforming approaches) or continuity of the spectrum for the adjacent frequency bands. In multimodal cases such as combined audio-video processing the spatial information of the sources is estimated from the video data. There are some methods which exploit both above properties. As an example, after normalization, a clustering method such as in (Mokios et al., 2006) can be used to solve the permutation problem. The method is simple and tries to introduce a number of clusters equal to the number of sources. In this approach a two-step frequency domain algorithm for BSS when the channel order is unknown has been presented which employs PARAFAC to separate the speech signals and a clustering algorithm such as vector quantization followed by an ILS-based method for mitigating the inherent permutations in the frequency domain (Mokios et al. 2006). In this method, the spatial signatures of the sources are first normalized with respect to an arbitrary reference microphone. Then, after each separation the estimated signal are clustered into say J clusters equivalent to the number of sources. The centroids of the clusters $C = \{c_1, c_2, ..., c_J\}$ are identified and a coupled ILS algorithm is applied to align the permuted sources. The proposed ILS cost function consists of two terms; the first term minimises the distance from the cluster centres and the second term minimises the distance between consecutive frequency bin spectrums by exploiting the continuity of the spectrum. The optimization algorithm has been detailed in (Mokios et al. 2006). The ILS minimization criterion is satisfactory for resolving the permutation problem that arises in the majority of real world BSS problems.

EXPERIMENTAL RESULTS

To evaluate the developed PARAFAC technique firstly a number of source signals are located within a room of size 5m × 4m × 6m have been simulated. Multichannel recordings were then performed by convolving the impulse responses generated using the Roomsim toolbox (http://media.paisley.ac.uk/ ~campbell/Roomsim/). The sampling rate was selected as $f_s = 8$kHz. The maximum reverberation time was considered as 20 samples.

The speakers and their location coordinates are as follows:

S1: male sound at location (x,y,z) = (0.5, 0.68, 0.38)

S2: female sound at location (x,y,z) = (0.6,0.76,0.51)

Accordingly, there are 4 microphones at locations with coordinates

M1: the microphone at location (x,y,z) = (1.00,0.80,0.44)

M2: the microphone at location (x,y,z) = (0.81, 0.71,0.41)

M3: the microphone at location (x,y,z) = (0.22,0.62,0.38)

M4: the microphone at location (x,y,z) = (0.43,0.53,0.35)

The sources and sensors are all located in one corner of the room for a better assessment of the reverberation without changing the model. Figure 5 shows the original sounds and also the measurement signal from the fourth sensor.

Figure 6 shows the impulse response from both sources to M4. The powerspectrum of the impulse response is shown in the second subplot and finally in the third subplot the normalized-powerspectrum of M4 with respect to M1 as in Equation (32) where $r = 1$, is shown. We can compare this normalized spectrum with the estimated spectrum from PARAFAC2-BSS method.

Figure 5. Original sounds and the 4th sensor signal

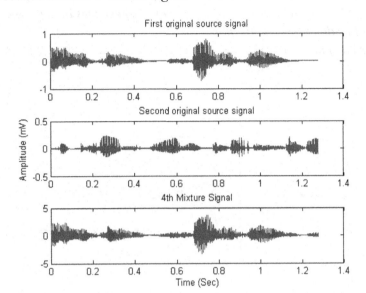

As it can be seen from the impulse responses, there is a weak echo in dashed line (dashed signal) at the 19th tap, which requires the medium to be mildly echoic.

Using PARAFAC2-BSS to each frequency bin signal separately, the estimated spectrum is subject to the scaling and permutation ambiguities. In Figure 7 (for the simulated signals) the estimated spectrum is compared with the original spectrum.

In the estimated spectrum we can see that due to scaling and permutation problems the spectrums are subject to random change in each frequency bin. After the normalization process based on Equations (32) to (34) the inherent scaling problem is mitigated but the permutation ambiguity still remains. In Figure 8 both the original and the estimated normalized spectrums are shown for comparison purpose. In Figure 8(b) the signal scales are more consistent with the original signal scales.

It is clear that the samples of the permuted spectrums can be clustered into two categories belonging to the two signal spectrums. In general, in a multi-channel problem a clustering technique can be employed for the alignment of

the estimated bin frequency spectrums. In the experiments followed herein however, the ILS was applied to estimate the alignment matrices. This results in the signals in Figure 9(b). From this figure it is clearly seen that the samples belonged to each signal (in frequency domain) are well separated.

These estimated spectrums are close to the original ones. This fact can be clearly viewed from the results of separation using the proposed PARAFAC method depicted in Figure 10.

To compare the results with the well-known Parra's algorithm for frequency domain blind source separation, we used the default parameters in his algorithm and separated the above two simulated signals. The *SNR* is defined as

$$SNR = 10\log\frac{\sum_{i=1}^{2}\left\|\mathbf{s}_i\right\|^2}{\sum_{i=1}^{2}\left\|\mathbf{s}_i-\hat{\mathbf{s}}_i\right\|^2} \qquad (35)$$

The total *SNR* values for Parra's and the new PARAFAC methods are depicted in the following Table 1.

Figure 6. The impulse response of the medium between microphone M4 and both speakers (a), the power spectrum of medium (b), and the normalized power spectrum of medium (c)

Figure 7. The original (a) and the estimated (b) power spectrums of the two sources

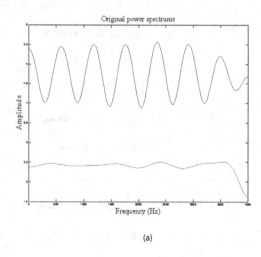

(a)

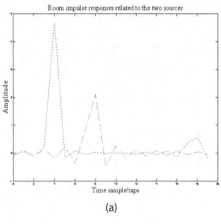

(a)

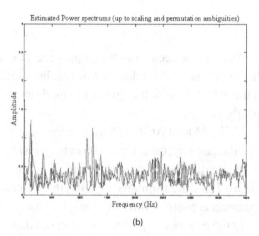

(b)

Using Parra's method the estimated sources (together with the original sources) are depicted in Figure 11. Based on these results, it has been verified that both objective and subjective results have been improved when the new PARAFAC algorithm has been used.

Most importantly, the separation algorithms based on TF can work for underdetermined cases where the number of sources is more than the number of sensors as in (Olsson et al. 2006). This is mainly because the rank of a tensor can be larger than the rank of the slabs.

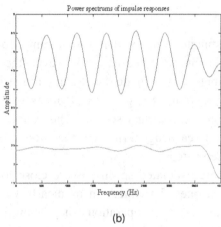

(b)

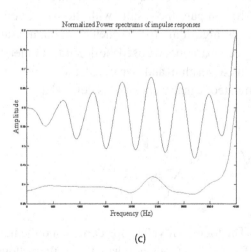

(c)

Figure 8. The original (a) and the estimated (b) power spectrums after mitigating the scaling problem. Using Equations (32) to (34) the permutation problem however still exists

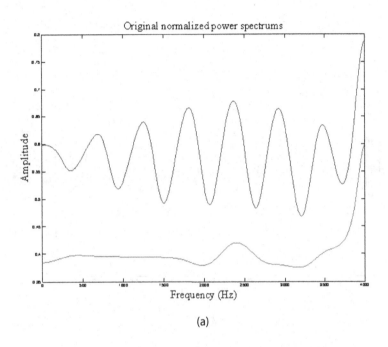

(a)

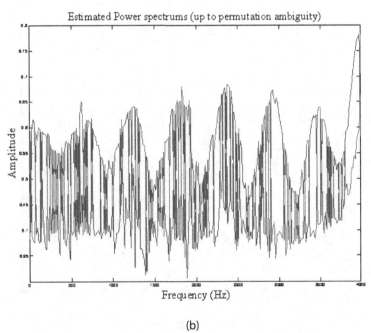

(b)

Figure 9. The original (top) and the estimated (bottom) power spectrums after both scaling and permutation problems are mitigated

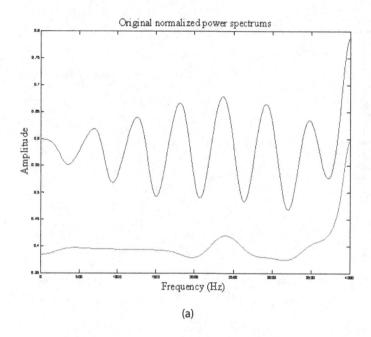

(a)

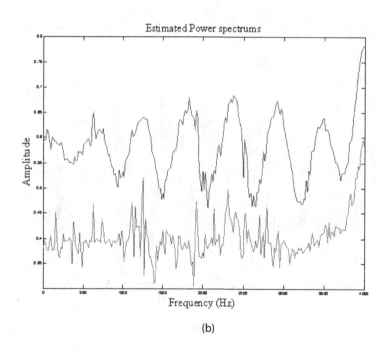

(b)

Figure 10. Both original (first and third from top) and estimated (second and forth) sources using the proposed PARAFAC decomposition method

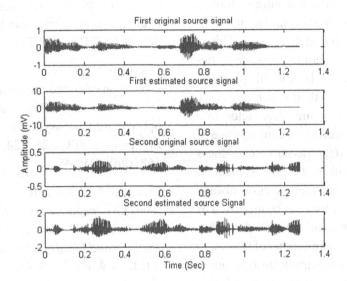

Figure 11. Both original (first and third from top) and estimated (second and forth) sources using Parra's convolutive BSS method

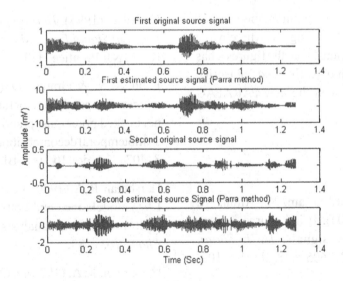

Table 1. The SNRs for the new PARAFAC compared to traditional Parra's method

Parra's convolutive BSS	New PARAFAC2 method
18.23 dB	27.18 dB

DISCUSSION AND CONCLUSION

Although BSS is becoming a mature technique in multichannel signal processing but the convolutive scenario is still under research. This is mainly because various parameters such as delays and multipath are involved in this problem. PARAFAC is a flexible method which can easily incorporate all possible parameters or factors into the separation formulation. As a consequence of that fewer assumptions (such as uncorrelatedness and independency) will be needed. Generally, the main assumption of disjointedness is always valid if the number of factors can be increased or a sparse domain can be selected for the data. This allows identification of more number of factors. In the BSS context a potential application is source localization as well as separation. Although in this chapter this hasn't been delivered but as a conclusion of PARAFAC application, both forward and inverse problems in source localization can be solved. Despite separation of time convolutive mixtures the tensor factorization method can be applied to space convoluitve signals whereby the sources change in location. From the figures it has been verified that both objective and subjective results are improved when the new PARAFAC algorithm is used.

REFERENCES

Belouchrani, A., Abed-Mariam, K., Amin, M. G., & Zoubir, A. (2004). Blind source separation of nonstationary signals. *IEEE Signal Processing Letters*, (7): 605–608. doi:10.1109/LSP.2004.830119

Bro, R. (1997). Multi-way analysis in the food industry: Models, algorithms and applications. *PhD thesis, University of Amsterdam, and Royal Veterinary and Agricultural University.*

Carol, J. D., & Chang, J. (1970). Analysis of individual differences in multidimensional scaling via an N-way generalization of 'Eckart-Young' decomposition. *Psychometrika, 35,* 283–319. doi:10.1007/BF02310791

Cherkani, N., & Deville, Y. (1999). Self adaptive separation of convolutively mixed signals with a recursive structure, Part 1: stability analysis and optimisation of asymptotic behaviour. *Signal Processing, 73*(3), 225–254. doi:10.1016/S0165-1684(98)00195-9

Cichocki, A., Zdunek, R., Phan, A. H., & Amari, S. (2009). *Nonnegative Matrix and Tensor Factorizations: Applications to Exploratory Multi-way Data Analysis and Blind Source Separation.* Hoboken, NJ: John Wiley & Sons.

Cirillo, L., & Zoubir, A. (2005). On blind separation of nonstationary signals. *Proc. of the 8th Symp. On Signal Processing and its Applications (ISSPA).* Sydney, Australia.

Cohen, L. (1995). *Time frequency analysis, Prentice Hall Signal Processing Series.* Upper Saddle River, NJ: Prentice Hall.

Field, A. S., & Graupe, D. (1991). Topographic component (parallel factor) analysis of multichannel evoked potentials: practical issues in trilinear spatiotemporal decomposition. *Brain Topography, 3,* 407–423. doi:10.1007/BF01129000

Harshman, R. A. (1970). Foundation of the PARAFAC: models and conditions for an 'explanatory' multi-modal factor analysis. *UCLA Work. Pap. Phon., 16,* 1–84.

Harshman, R. A. (1972). *UCLA Working Papers. Phonet, 22,* 111.

Harshman, R. A. (1972). *UCLA Working Papers. Phonet, 22,* 33.

Herault, J., & Jutten, C. (1986). Space or time adaptive signal processing by neural models. *Proc. AIP Conf., Neural Network for Computing, American Institute of physics*(pp. 206-211).

Ikram, M., & Morgan, D. (2000). Exploring permutation inconstancy in blind separation of speech signals in a reverberant environment. *Proc. of IEEE Conf. on Acoustic, Speech, and Signal Processing (ICASSP)*. Turkey.

Jurjine, A. Rickard, S. & Yilmaz, O. (2000). Blind separation of disjoint orthogonal signals: demixing N sources from 2 mixtures. *Proc. of IEEE Conf. on Acoustic, Speech, and Signal Processing (ICASSP)*, 4, 2985-2988.

Kiers, H. A. L., Ten Berge, J. M. F., & Bro, R. (1999). PARAFAC2 – Part 1. A direct fitting algorithm for PARAFAC2 model. *Journal of Chemometrics*, *13*, 275–294. doi:10.1002/(SICI)1099-128X(199905/08)13:3/4<275::AID-CEM543>3.0.CO;2-B

Li, Y., Amari, S., Cichocki, A., Ho, D. W. C., & Shengli, X. (2006). Underdetermined blind source separation based on sparse representation. *IEEE Transactions on Signal Processing, 54*(2), 423–437. doi:10.1109/TSP.2005.861743

Luo, Y., Chambers, J., Lambotharan, S., & Proudler, I. (2006). Exploitation of source non-stationarity in underdetermined blind source separation with advanced clustering techniques. *IEEE Transactions on Signal Processing, 54*(6), 2198–2212. doi:10.1109/TSP.2006.873367

Miwakeichi, F., Martinez-Montes, E., Valdes-Sosa, P. A., Nishiyama, N., Mizuhara, H., & Yamaguchi, Y. (2004). Decomposing EEG data into space-time-frequency components using parallel factor analysis. *NeuroImage, 22*, 1035–1045. doi:10.1016/j.neuroimage.2004.03.039

Möcks, J. (1988). Decomposing event-related potentials: a new topographic components model. *Biological Psychology, 26*, 199–215. doi:10.1016/0301-0511(88)90020-8

Mokios, K. N., Potamianos, A., & Sidiropoulos, N. D. (2008). On the effectiveness of PARAFAC-based estimation for blind speech separation. *Proc. of IEEE Conf. on Acoustic, Speech, and Signal Processing (ICASSP)*(pp. 153-156).

Mokios, K. N., Sidiropoulos, N. D., & Potamianos, A. (2006). Blind speech separation using PARAFAC analysis and integer least squares. *Proc. of IEEE Conf. on Acoustic, Speech, and Signal Processing (ICASSP)* (Vol. 4, pp73-76).

Mørup, M., Hansen, L. K., Herrmann, C. S., Parnas, J., & Arnfred, S. M. (2006). Parallel factor analysis as an exploratory tool for wavelet transformed event-related EEG. *NeuroImage, 29*(3), 938–947. doi:10.1016/j.neuroimage.2005.08.005

Murata, N., Ikeda, S., & Ziehe, A. (2001). An approach to blind source separation based on temporal structure of speech signals. *Neurocomputing, 41*, 1–4. doi:10.1016/S0925-2312(00)00345-3

Olsson, R. K., & Hansen, L. K. (2006). Blind separation of more sources than sources in convolutive mixtures. *Proc. of IEEE Conf. on Acoustic, Speech, and Signal Processing (ICASSP)*(Vol. 4, pp. 657 – 660).

Parra, L., & Spence, C. (2000). Convolutive blind separation of non-stationary sources. *IEEE Transactions on Speech and Audio Processing, 5*, 320–327. doi:10.1109/89.841214

Parra, L., Spence, C., Sajda, P., Ziehe, A., & Muller, K. R. (2000). Unmixing hyperspectral data. *Advances in Neural Information Processing*, 13, 942-948.Boston: MIT Press.

Pederson, M. S., Larsen, J., Kjems, U., & Parra, L. (C:\Program Files\Canon\ZoomBrowser EX\Image Library One\2009_11_242007). A survey of convolutive blind source separation methods. Springer Handbook on Speech Processing and Speech Communication.

Pesquet, J. Chen, B. & Petropulu, A. P. (2001). Frequency-domain contrast functions for separation of convolutive mixtures. *Proc. of the IEEE International Conference on Acoustics, Speech, and Signal Processing (ICASSP)*(pp. 2765-2768).

Platt, C., & Faggin, F. (1992). Networks for the separation of sources that are superimposed and delayed. *Advances in Neural Information Processing*, 4, 730-737. San Francisco: Morgan Kaufmann.

Rong, Y., Vorobyov, S. A., Gershman, A. B., & Sidiropoulos, N. D. (2005). Blind Spatial Signature Estimation via Time-Varying User Power Loading and Parallel Factor Analysis. *IEEE Transactions on Signal Processing*, 53, 1697–1710. doi:10.1109/TSP.2005.845441

Sanei, S., & Chambers, J. (2007). *EEG Signal Processing*. Hoboken, NJ: John Wiley & Sons.

Smaragdis, P. (1998). Blind separation of convolved mixtures in the frequency domain. *Neurocomputing*, 22, 21–34. doi:10.1016/S0925-2312(98)00047-2

Takigawa, I., Kudo, M., Nakamura, A., & Toyama, J. (2004). On the minimum l_1-norm signal recovery in underdetermined source separation. *Proc. of 5th Int. Conf. on Independent Component Analysis*(pp. 22-24).

Torkkola, K. (1996). Blind separation of delayed sources based on information maximization. *Proc. IEEE Conf. on Acoustic, Speech, and Signal Processing (ICASSP)*(pp. 3509-3512) Atlanta, Georgia.

Torkkola, K. (1996). Blind separation of convolved sources based on information maximization. *Proc. IEEE workshop on Neural Networks and Signal Processing (NNSP)*(pp. 315-323).

Vielva, L., Erdogmus, D., Pantaleon, C., Santamaria, I., Pereda, J., & Principe, J. C. (2002). Underdetermined blind source separation in a time-varying environment. *Proc. of IEEE Conf. On Acoustic, Speech, and Signal Processing (ICASSP)*(Vol. 3, pp. 3049-3052).

Wang, W., Sanei, S., & Chambers, J. A. (2005). Penalty function based joint diagonalization approach for convolutive blind separation of nonstationary sources. *IEEE Transactions on Signal Processing*, 53(5), 1654–1669. doi:10.1109/TSP.2005.845433

Chapter 9

Multi–Channel Source Separation:
Overview and Comparison of Mask–Based and Linear Separation Algorithms

Nilesh Madhu
Ruhr-Universität Bochum, Germany

André Gückel
Dolby Laboratories - Nürnberg, Germany

ABSTRACT

Machine-based multi-channel source separation in real life situations is a challenging problem, and has a wide range of applications, from medical to military. With the increase in computational power available to everyday devices, source separation in real-time has become more feasible, contributing to the boost in the research in this field in the recent past. Algorithms for source separation are based on specific assumptions regarding the source and signal model – which depends upon the application. In this chapter, the specific application considered is that of a target speaker enhancement in the presence of competing speakers and background noise. It is the aim of this contribution to present not only an exhaustive overview of state-of-the-art separation algorithms and the specific models they are based upon, but also to highlight the relations between these algorithms, where possible. Given this wide scope of the chapter, we expect it will benefit both, the student beginning his studies in the field of machine audition, and those already working in a related field and wishing to obtain an overview or insights into the field of multi-channel source separation.

INTRODUCTION

Separation of speech signals in noisy multi-speaker environments – as exemplified by the cocktail party problem – is a feasible task for a human listener, even under rather severe conditions such as many interfering speakers and loud background noise. Algorithms that help machines perform a similar task are currently the hotbed of research due to their wide range of applications, such as in human-machine interfaces, digital hearing aids, intelligent robots and so on.

DOI: 10.4018/978-1-61520-919-4.ch009

In this contribution we shall discuss multi-channel separation and enhancement algorithms for acoustic sources, specifically speech, in a noisy environment with competing (multiple, simultaneously active sources) and non-competing source scenarios. We aim to provide the reader with an overview of the state of the art approaches for this purpose, illustrating where possible the relations between the algorithms. We shall further present a taxonomy for the classification of the separation algorithms, examine representative algorithms from each class and compare their performance. It will be shown that while it is possible to tune these algorithms to obtain similar performance on objective measures, listening tests illustrate the gulf that still exists between the algorithms of the different classes. It will also be shown that currently there exists no algorithm in any class that makes use of all the degrees of freedom available to the separation system. To this end we present a post-processor scheme, piggybacked onto the existing approaches. This is perceptually motivated and combines the advantages of each class of algorithms, performing better than the individual algorithms in each class.

We begin with the classification taxonomy before introducing the signal model used subsequently. Then we proceed to give an overview of the basic principles of each class of algorithms before presenting the comparison between representative algorithms of each class. Finally we outline the details of the post-processor scheme and present the results using this algorithm.

SEPARATION TAXONOMY

Multi-channel source separation algorithms rely on the spatial diversity afforded by microphone *arrays* to accomplish the goal of suppressing all sources other than the target source. They can be, broadly speaking, divided into two major categories: linear and non-linear.

Linear approaches to source separation attain target signal *enhancement* or interference *cancellation* by steering a spatial null in the direction of the interfering sources. The algorithms are based on a linear generative mixing model (the observed mixtures are assumed to be linear combinations of the individual source signals), whereupon null steering is obtained through a linear combination of the mixtures. Additional constraints may be placed on these algorithms to ensure that no target signal *degradation* takes place during the process. This process is also known as *beamforming*, and the corresponding spatial filters are termed as *beamformers*. Beamforming algorithms may further be sub-divided into two categories: those based explicitly on a spatial model and corresponding constraints, and those that depend upon specific long term statistical characteristics of the source signals. Examples of the former kind of approaches include the generalized sidelobe canceller (GSC) (Griffiths & Jim, 1982) and its variants, and are primarily based on the second order statistics (SOS) of the microphone signals. The independent component analysis (ICA) based algorithms of e.g. (Hyvärinen *et al*, 2001; Smaragdis, 1998; Saruwatari *et al*, 2006; Sawada *et al*, 2004) which use higher order statistics (HOS) of the signals, and the simultaneous-decorrelation based algorithms of e.g. (Fancourt & Parra, 2001; Buchner *et al*, 2004; Diamantaras, 2001; Ikram & Morgan, 2002) which are based on SOS are examples of the latter class of linear separation algorithms. Note that while these algorithms do not explicitly impose any spatial constraints, the separation filters form spatial exclusion regions along the interference directions – in effect functioning as beamformers. This aspect is examined in some more detail in (Araki *et al*, 2003; Parra & Fancourt, 2002).

Non-linear separation algorithms (Bofill & Zibulevski, 2000; Rickard *et al*, 2001, Roman *et al*, 2003; Rosca *et al*, 2004; Wang, 2008; Yilmaz *et al*, 2000) are realized based on specific properties of the source signals. In a very general sense, the aim of such algorithms is to partition a set of data points (sensor signals in their time or frequency domain representations) into clusters, with the data points in each cluster belonging to a specific source. The clustering may be *hard* or *binary* (non-overlapping clusters, each data point can belong only to one cluster) or *soft* (overlapping clusters, many sources may share a data point, albeit to different degrees). In effect this corresponds to generating a *mask* for each source, which has a high value (≈ 1) for the data points judged as belonging to that source and low values (≈ 0) for the data points belonging to the other sources. The individual source signals are then obtained by resynthesizing the masked signal representation. In this case we refer to the improvement obtained as interference *suppression*. While spatial diversity is not a requirement for the non-linear approaches (indeed, single-channel noise suppression algorithms may be seen as a class of non-linear algorithms), it is usually required to extract the features required for generating the masks.

Note that while the term *interferer* is used to represent a source (generally directive) other than the source of interest, in signal separation where the goal is to resynthesize individual source signals from a mixture, this term may be misleading as, depending upon the context, a source may function as an interferer or a target. As an example, in the two source scenario with signals $s_1(n)$ and $s_2(n)$, the latter is the interferer when $s_1(n)$ is to be extracted and vice-versa. The role of a source will be explicitly disambiguated where required in the following discussion.

SIGNAL MODEL

The signal model we consider is that of an array consisting of M microphones at positions $\mathbf{r}_m = (x_m, y_m, z_m)^T$ capturing the signals[1] emitted from Q sources at positions $\mathbf{r}_q = (x_q, y_q, z_q)^T$. The

signals recorded by any microphone m may be written as:

$$x_m(n) = \sum_{q=1}^{Q} a_{0,mq}(n) * s_{0,q}(n) + v_m(n), \qquad (1)$$

where $s_{0,q}(n)$ represents the (sampled) source waveform; $a_{0,q}(n)$, the room impulse response from $\mathbf{r}_q$ to $\mathbf{r}_m$; *, the convolution operator; $v_m(n)$, the noise at microphone m; and n, the sample index. We use the additional subscript 0 in the definitions of the source waveform and room impulse response in (1) to stress their representation in an absolute sense (i.e., not relative to a reference position or microphone). Where we consider a relative representation, this subscript will be dropped.

In general, the $a_{0,q}(n)$ are very long, of many thousands of taps in length. For practical, real-time realizations of the separation algorithms, they are approximated by finite impulse response (FIR) filters of order $L - 1$, i.e.,

$$\mathbf{a}_{0,mq} = (a_{0,mq}(0), a_{0,mq}(1), \dots, a_{0,mq}(L-1))^T,$$

whereby we may write the signal at microphone m as

$$x_m(n) = \sum_{q=1}^{Q} \mathbf{a}_{0,mq}^T \mathbf{s}_{0,q}(n) + v_m(n), \qquad (2)$$

with

$$\mathbf{s}_{0,q}(n) = (s_{0,q}(n), s_{0,q}(n-1), \dots, s_{0,q}(n-L+1))^T.$$

FREQUENCY DOMAIN REPRESENTATION

Consider, now, the frame-wise spectral representation of the signal as obtained from the K-point discrete Fourier transform (DFT) on overlapped, windowed segments of the discrete time domain signal. We shall denote this operation as the short-time Fourier transform (STFT), and the corresponding domain as the STFT domain. The STFT representation $X(k,b)$ of a discrete time signal $x(n)$ is obtained as

$$X(k,b) = \sum_{n=1}^{K} \mathsf{W}(n)\, x\left(bO + n\right) e^{-j2\pi n\frac{k}{K}}, \quad k = 0,1,...,K$$

(3)

Where k is the discrete frequency bin index, O indicates the frame shift (in samples) between the frames, b is the frame index, and $\mathsf{W}(n)$ is the window function. With respect to (3), we obtain the following STFT domain representation of (2):

$$
\begin{aligned}
\mathbf{X}(k,b) &\approx
\begin{pmatrix}
|A'_{0,11}(k)|\, e^{-j\Omega_k \tau_{11}} & \cdots & |A'_{0,1Q}(k)|\, e^{-j\Omega_k \tau_{1Q}} \\
\vdots & \ddots & \vdots \\
|A'_{0,M1}(k)|\, e^{-j\Omega_k \tau_{M1}} & \cdots & |A'_{0,MQ}(k)|\, e^{-j\Omega_k \tau_{MQ}}
\end{pmatrix}
\mathbf{S}_0(k,b) \\
&+
\begin{pmatrix}
A''_{0,11}(k) & \cdots & A''_{0,1Q}(k) \\
\vdots & \ddots & \vdots \\
A''_{0,M1}(k) & \cdots & A''_{0,MQ}(k)
\end{pmatrix}
\mathbf{S}_0(k,b) + \mathbf{V}(k,b) \\
&= \mathbf{A}'_0(k)\,\mathbf{S}_0(k,b) + \mathbf{A}''_0(k)\,\mathbf{S}_0(k,b) + \mathbf{V}(k,b).
\end{aligned}
$$

(4)

where $\Omega_k = 2\pi k f_s / K$ is the kth discrete frequency and f_s is the sampling frequency. $\mathbf{S}_0(k,b) = \left(S_{0,1}(k,b),...,S_{0,Q}(k,b)\right)^T$ is the vector of source signals. $\left|A'_{0,mq}\right|$ represents the gain along the direct path and $A''_{0,mq} \in \mathbb{C}$ indicates the net gain and phase smearing caused by the reflections along the indirect paths. τ_{mq} represents the *absolute* time delay of the signal from source q to the microphone m along the direct path. The approximation is a result of truncating the support of the signals to finite length. Despite this approximation, we shall use this model subsequently to good effect.

The *propagation* matrix $A'_0(k)$ is directly related to the geometric arrangement of the sources and the sensors and is key to the source local-

ization and separation problem. The vectors $\mathbf{A}''_0(k)\mathbf{S}_0(k,b)$ and $\mathbf{V}(k,b)$ constitute disturbances. While the former term is obviously correlated with the source signals, the latter is typically modeled as being statistically independent of the source signals.

To further simplify the model in (4), we consider the signals received at the first microphone through the direct path as the reference:

$$S_q(k,b) = |A'_{0,1q}(\Omega)|\, e^{-j\Omega_k \tau_{1q}} S_{0,q}(k),$$

(5)

and rewrite in terms of the source signal vector $\mathbf{S}(k,b) = \left(S_1(k,b),...,S_Q(k,b)\right)^T$ as

$$
\begin{aligned}
\mathbf{X}(k,b) &=
\begin{pmatrix}
1 & \cdots & 1 \\
\vdots & \ddots & \vdots \\
\left|\frac{A'_{0,M1}(k)}{A'_{0,11}(k)}\right| e^{j\Omega_k \Delta\tau_{M1}} & \cdots & \left|\frac{A'_{0,MQ}(k)}{A'_{0,1Q}(k)}\right| e^{j\Omega_k \Delta\tau_{MQ}}
\end{pmatrix}
\mathbf{S}(k,b) \\
&+
\begin{pmatrix}
\breve{A}_{11}(k) & \cdots & \breve{A}_{1Q}(k) \\
\vdots & \ddots & \vdots \\
\breve{A}_{M1}(k) & \cdots & \breve{A}_{MQ}(k)
\end{pmatrix}
\mathbf{S}(k,b) + \mathbf{V}(k,b), \\
&\overset{\Delta}{=} \mathbf{A}(k)\,\mathbf{S}(k,b) + \breve{\mathbf{A}}(k)\,\mathbf{S}(k,b) + \mathbf{V}(k,b)
\end{aligned}
$$

(6)

where $\Delta\tau_{mq} = \tau_{1q} - \tau_{mq}$ is the relative time delay or time delay of arrival (TDOA) with respect to the reference point, and

$$\breve{A}_{mq}(k) = \frac{A''_{0,mq}(k)}{|A'_{0,1q}(k)|}\, e^{j\Omega_k \tau_{1q}}$$

represents the normalized indirect components. If the array is well calibrated (i.e., the microphones do not exhibit significantly deviant amplitude and phase characteristics), and the array is in the farfield of the sources, we may further simplify (6) and obtain (Vary & Martin, 2006):

$$\mathbf{X}(k,b) = \begin{pmatrix} 1 & \cdots & 1 \\ \vdots & \ddots & \vdots \\ e^{j\Omega_k \Delta \tau_{M1}} & \cdots & e^{j\Omega_k \Delta \tau_{MQ}} \end{pmatrix} \mathbf{S}(k,b)$$
$$+ \begin{pmatrix} \breve{A}_{11}(k) & \cdots & \breve{A}_{1Q}(k) \\ \vdots & \ddots & \vdots \\ \breve{A}_{M1}(k) & \cdots & \breve{A}_{MQ}(k) \end{pmatrix} \mathbf{S}(k,b) + \mathbf{V}(k,b).$$

$$(7)$$

For the development of the separation algorithms we shall assume dominance of the direct path, which implies that $\left| A_{mq} \right| >> \left| \breve{A}_{mq} \right|$. Indeed, for diffuse target sources spatial diversity does not yield much of an advantage in terms of beamforming or masking, and algorithms for the extraction of the corresponding source signals in such scenarios is out of the scope of this work.

In addition to the spatial diversity, a property of speech signals used frequently in enhancement algorithms is their sparsity[2], both in their time and their frequency representations. Consequently, speech signals show evidence of a strongly super-Gaussian distribution of their amplitudes in the time domain, and of the real and imaginary parts of their corresponding DFT coefficients in the STFT domain, on a long-term basis (O'Shaughnessy, 2000; Porter & Boll, 1984; Martin, 2004) In conjunction with sparsity, another property that is exploited, especially by masking approaches, is the *approximate disjointness* (Rickard & Yilmaz, 2002) of speech signals in the STFT domain. This means that if the STFT spectra $S_1(k,b)$ and $S_2(k,b)$ of two sources are overlaid, there are very few time-frequency (T-F) atoms (k,b) at which the spectra overlap. Mathematically this may be expressed as:

$$S_q(k,b) S_{q'}(k,b) \approx 0 \qquad \forall q' \neq q. \qquad (8)$$

Consequently for a T-F atom occupied by the source q, the signal model of (6) may be approximated as:

$$\mathbf{X}(k,b) \approx \mathbf{A}_q(k) S_q(k,b) + \breve{\mathbf{A}}_q(k) S_q(k,b) + \mathbf{V}(k,b).$$

$$(9)$$

For a given sampling frequency, the disjointness is dependent upon the resolution K of the DFT, the number of simultaneously active speakers Q, and the amount of reverberation (quantified by the reverberation time T_{60}) present. As an example, if the number of sources Q increases, the amount of T-F atoms concurrently occupied by more than one source will increase, causing disjointness to *decrease*, and vice-versa. We may extend this line of thought to the other parameters affecting disjointness and we may summarize their effect as in Table 1.

This influence of the parameters on the disjointness assumption has been evaluated in more detail in (Yilmaz *et al*, 2004).

MASK-BASED, NON-LINEAR APPROACHES

Masks are usually generated in the STFT domain for each time-frequency (T-F) atom. *Ideal binary masks* $\Xi_{q,b}$ (note the use of the additional subscript b to distinguish the binary mask from the other masks that will subsequently be derived) may be defined for a source q as:

$$\Xi_{q,b}(k,b) = \begin{cases} 1 & |S_q(k,b)| > |S_{q'}(k,b)| \qquad \forall q' \neq q \\ 0 & \text{otherwise,} \end{cases}$$

$$(10)$$

and the target source spectrum obtained by applying the mask either to the spectrum of any microphone signal m:

$$\hat{S}(k,b) = \Xi_{q,b}(k,b) X_m(k,b), \qquad (11)$$

or to a *beamformed* signal in the direction of the target source:

$$\hat{S}(k,b) = \Xi_{q,b}(k,b)\Big(\mathbf{W}_q^H(k)\,\mathbf{X}_m(k,b)\Big), \qquad (12)$$

where $\mathbf{W}_q(k)$ is the corresponding beamforming filter. This beamformer may be realized using either the simple delay-and-sum approach (Vary & Martin, 2006, Chapter 12), or more sophisticated, data-independently optimized approaches (Tashev & Acero, 2006; Yoon *et al*, 2007). The time domain signal can then be resynthesized from the masked representation using standard techniques such as the overlap-and-add.

Where the knowledge of the source signals or their locations is not directly available, as is usually the case, we require a data-driven classifier to segregate the T-F atoms belonging to the various sources. With respect to the signal model of (9) the classification may be accomplished by clustering each T-F atom according to the estimated $\mathbf{A}_q(k)$ obtained for that atom. For an $M = 2$ case and the model of (6), estimating the $\mathbf{A}_q(k)$ corresponds to estimating the inter-sensor signal delay and attenuation. Consider then, the following estimates of attenuation and delay:

$$\widehat{|A_2(k,b)|} = \left|\frac{X_2(k,b)}{X_1(k,b)}\right|,$$
$$\widehat{\Delta\tau_2(k,b)} = -\Omega_k^{-1}\arg\left(\frac{X_2(k,b)}{X_1(k,b)}\right). \qquad (13)$$

If source disjointness holds, and under the assumption of dominant direct path, the estimated values for attenuation and delay for each (k,b) should correspond to only one source. Subsequently, if the features so estimated are grouped into Q clusters in the two dimensional plane defined by $|A_2(k)|$ and $\Delta\tau_2(k)$, the centroid $(\Delta\tau_{2q}(k), |A_{2q}(k)|)^T$ of each cluster q may be taken as an estimate for the true parameters for each source. Note that these parameters may, in general, be frequency variant, which fact is indicated by expressing them as a function of the respective frequency bin. Using this knowledge,

Table 1. Effect of mixing system properties on the approximate disjointness. The symbols $\Downarrow$ / $\Uparrow$ indicate an increase/decrease in the respective quantity.

Parameter	Change	Disjointness
K	$\Uparrow$	$\Uparrow$
	$\Downarrow$	$\Downarrow$
Q	$\Uparrow$	$\Downarrow$
	$\Downarrow$	$\Uparrow$
T_{60}	$\Uparrow$	$\Downarrow$
	$\Downarrow$	$\Uparrow$

we may then estimate the binary mask for the source q as:

$$\mathcal{M}_{q,b}(k,b) = \begin{cases} 1 & q = \underset{q'}{\arg\min}\left\|\left(\widehat{\Delta\tau_2(k,b)},\,\widehat{|A_2(k,b)|}\right)^T - \left(\Delta\tau_{2q'}(k),\,|A_{2q'}(k)|\right)^T\right\| \\ 0 & \text{otherwise.} \end{cases}$$
$$(14)$$

Similar estimation may be done in the case of $M > 2$ (see e.g. Araki *et al*, 2005). When the arrays are well calibrated and the sources are in the far-field, a computationally less expensive approach would be to cluster the T-F atoms according to the direction of arrival θ, which may be estimated using, e.g., the SRP-PHAT (DiBiase *et al*, 2001; Madhu & Martin, 2008).

To avoid random triggering of the masks in noisy conditions, we may additionally impose a threshold on the distance to the cluster centroids, in which case the masks are estimated as:

$$\mathcal{M}_{q,b}(k,b) = \begin{cases} 1 & \begin{aligned} & q = \arg\min\left\|\left(\widehat{\Delta\tau_2(k,b)},\,\widehat{|A_2(k,b)|}\right)^T - \left(\Delta\tau_{2q'}(k),\,|A_{2q'}(k)|\right)^T\right\| \\ & \left\|\left(\widehat{\Delta\tau_2(k,b)},\,\widehat{|A_2(k,b)|}\right)^T - \left(\Delta\tau_{2q'}(k),\,|A_{2q'}(k)|\right)^T\right\| \le \Upsilon_b \end{aligned} \\ 0 & \text{otherwise} \end{cases}$$
$$(15)$$

where γ_b is the maximum allowable distance threshold.

An improvement over the binary mask is the so-called soft mask, $\Xi_s \in [0,1]$, which makes allowances for case where more than one source occupies a T-F atom. The corresponding advantage is that of lower target signal distortion in the presence of closely-spaced interferers, reverberation and errors in the estimates of the cluster parameters.

SOFT MASKS

Assuming that we have estimates $\hat{\mathbf{A}}_q(k)$ of the propagation vector $\mathbf{A}_q(k)$ for each source q (the cluster centroids as obtained in the previous section), we may approximate the source signals (when $M \geq Q$) as:

$$\hat{\mathbf{S}}(k,b) = \hat{\mathbf{A}}^\dagger(k)\mathbf{X}(k,b), \tag{16}$$

where † represents the Moore-Penrose pseudo-inverse (Strang, 1988) operator. We may then compute the soft mask $\Xi_{q,s}$ for the target source q as:

$$\Xi_{q,s}(k,b) = \frac{1}{1+\left(\mathrm{SIR}_q^\xi(k,b)\right)^{-1}}, \tag{17}$$

Where $\mathrm{SIR}_q^\xi(k,b)$ is defined as:

$$\mathrm{SIR}_q^\xi(k,b) = \frac{|\hat{S}_q(k,b)|^\xi}{\sum_{q' \neq q}|\hat{S}_{q'}(k,b)|^\xi}. \tag{18}$$

As $\mathrm{SIR}_q^\xi(k,b) > 0$, Ξ_s is guaranteed to be less than 1. It is easy to see that, given perfect disjointness, the proposed soft mask reduces to the ideal binary mask. For time-frequency atoms where the disjointness is imperfect, an appropriately attenuated weight is obtained. The parameter ξ controls the 'intensity' of the weighting, with $\xi = 2$ being reminiscent of the Wiener rule.

The use of a soft mask leads, in general, to less target signal distortion than the binary masks, especially in reverberant environments where the degree of disjointness is lower. However, it also leads to more cross-talk, especially when the sources are spatially close. One countermeasure against the higher level of cross-talk in the soft masking algorithms is to introduce a threshold γ_s, such that

$$\Xi_{q,s}(k,b) = \begin{cases} \dfrac{1}{1+(\mathrm{SIR}_q^\xi(k,b))^{-1}}, & \mathrm{SIR}_q^\xi(k,b) > \Upsilon_s \\ 0 & \text{otherwise} \end{cases} \tag{19}$$

The soft mask of (19) works well in the over- and well-determined cases $M \geq Q$. An alternative soft mask can be defined for the more general case of M-sensors and Q-sources by introducing a spatial window that allows for tolerances in the estimation of the parameters. Considering, here, only the delay, we may then pose the soft mask gain as:

$$\Xi_{q,s}(k,b) = \exp\left(-\left|\frac{\mathrm{Im}(\log(\varepsilon(k,b)))}{\Omega_k \mathcal{T}}\right|^\xi\right), \tag{20}$$

where

$$\varepsilon(k,b) = \frac{e^{j\Omega_k \Delta\tau_{2q}}}{\left(\dfrac{X_2(k,b)}{X_1(k,b)}\right)},$$

with the ratio of the microphone signals yielding the time delay of arrival for the particular source dominant at that T-F atom. The delays τ_{2q} for the sources are obtained by clustering as in the previous section. Note, additionally, that the estimation as above is less sensitive to *spatial aliasing*, even for larger microphone spacings. $\mathbf{T}$ represents the tolerance window. A large **T** implies a larger spatial tolerance (T-F atoms that lie further out from a cluster centroid are still allocated to the corresponding cluster, but to a degree that depends upon their separation from the centroid). Lower values of **T** impose narrower spatial selectivity. This parameter may need tuning according to the amount of reverberation and noise present. A plot of the selectivity is presented in Figure 1, over the azimuth range of the sources, with the desired source located along an angle of 90° with respect to the array axis (this is also known as the broadside orientation).

Note that in this case, the threshold setting is implicit.

LINEAR APPROACHES

As mentioned previously, this class of separation algorithms utilizes the spatial diversity to steer nulls in the direction of the interfering sources, with the realization of the spatial filter being dependent upon the null-steering philosophy (optimality criterion) considered.

GSC based approaches and their variants estimate the optimal filter by placing a non-zero constraint on signals coming from the spatial region associated with the *target* and minimize the power of the signals coming from all the other directions. If the interferences are directive and $M \geq Q$, this minimization leads to the formation of nulls along the direction of the interferers. If the location of the target is not known, it must be estimated prior to separation.

ICA and simultaneous-decorrelation based algorithms, on the other hand, do not explicitly impose spatial constraints. Rather, they use the long time statistical properties inherent to speech, i.e., statistical independence between two speaker signals, non-whiteness, non-Gaussianity, and non-stationarity to estimate the optimal spatial filters. Such algorithms explicitly require concurrent speaker activity, with $M \geq Q$. Knowledge of

the target source location is not required in this case – indeed, the source positions are estimated implicitly during the *demixing*.

We shall examine both the above classes of algorithms in some detail, based on their realization in the STFT domain.

Linear Approaches ICA

With respect to the model of (6), the separation problem is posed as the search for a so-called demixing *matrix* W(k) for each frequency bin k such that:

$$\mathbf{Y}(k,b) = \mathbf{W}(k)\mathbf{X}(k,b) \approx \mathbf{S}(k,b), \qquad (21)$$

where $\mathbf{S}(k,b)$ is the vector of individual source signals as received at a *reference* microphone. In order to obtain an insight into the state-of-the-art of ICA-based separation algorithms, we shall first briefly describe the general idea of ICA. The interested reader is referred to (Hyvärinen & Oja, 2000) for an excellent introduction or to (Hyvärinen *et al*, 2001) for more detail.

ICA based separation approaches assume a generative mixing model of the kind in equation (6), and treat the source signals as realizations of Q independent (but not necessarily identical) random processes with an underlying *non-Gaussian* distribution. The aim is to find a transformation $\mathbf{X} \xrightarrow{\text{w}} \mathbf{Y}$ on the input signals $\mathbf{X}$, such that the elements Y_q of $\mathbf{Y}$ are 'as statistically independent of each other as possible'. The logic is intuitive: if the underlying signals are statistically independent, obtaining independent variables at the output of the demixing system can only mean that the sources have been separated.

The search for any such **W** lies in the generation and optimization of a **W**-parameterized cost function that penalizes the dependence between the variables Y_q. Examples of popular cost functions are:

Figure 1. Effect of the soft mask based on the spatial window of (20) $\mathbf{T}_1 < \mathbf{T}_2 < \mathbf{T}_3 < \mathbf{T}_4$

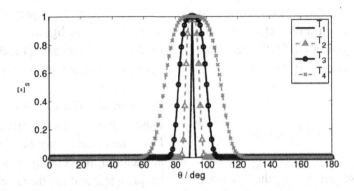

- the absolute value of the kurtosis,
- the Kullback-Leibler divergence, and
- mutual information.

The approaches based on the Kullback-Leibler divergence and mutual information approximate the required entropies using non-polynomial moments of the corresponding signals. Due to the non-linearity utilized, such approaches are less sensitive to outliers in the data than the kurtosis-based approaches. Further, the selection of the particular non-polynomial form is based on the underlying empirical distribution of the source signals. For speech, a super-Gaussian density is the template on which the non-linearity selection is based.

Usually ICA is carried out in two steps. In the first step the signals are pre-processed by (a) centering, which consists of mean removal (the means may be re-introduced post-separation); and (b) sphering or principle component analysis (PCA), which mutually decorrelates the sources and normalizes each source to unit variance. Dimension reduction may also be done here when the system is overdetermined $(M > Q)$.

The advantage of such pre-processing is that it reduces the resulting search in the next step to that over the space of orthonormal matrices, $\breve{\mathbf{W}}$ (see (Hyvärinen *et al*, 2001), (Madhu, 2002)). This allows for the implementation of the FastICA (Hyvärinen & Oja, 1997), (Hyvärinen, 1999)

principle. FastICA is a fixed-point algorithm with approximately cubic convergence and which, further, does not require any step-size tuning as in other optimization algorithms based on gradient descent. We may express the results of the above steps as:

$$\mathbf{W}(k) = \breve{\mathbf{W}}(k)\overset{o}{\mathbf{W}}(k), \qquad (22)$$

with $\overset{o}{\mathbf{W}}(k)$ being the sphering stage estimated from the correlation matrix of the input signals and $\breve{\mathbf{W}}(k)$ being the orthonormal matrix to be estimated using FastICA.

In the absence of any further *a priori* knowledge regarding the elements $A_{mq}(k)$ of A(k) or the underlying processes, the solution for W(k) contains two inherent ambiguities: *scale* and *permutation*. Any W(k) that fulfills:

$$\mathbf{W}(k) = \mathbf{J}(k)\mathbf{D}(k)\mathbf{A}^{-1}(k), \qquad (23)$$

with J(k) being a *permutation* matrix and D(k) being a diagonal *scaling* matrix, is a valid solution to the optimization problem. Such ambiguities are, in themselves, not critical. The problem arises because J(k) and D(k) are, in general, different in different frequency bins. We shall term a permutation and scaling as *local*, if it is for a particular frequency bin, and as *global*, if it is common to all bins. Obviously, source reconstruction from the spectral domain is only successful if the permutation and scaling matrices are global, i.e.

$$\mathbf{J}(k) = \mathbf{J}(k') \quad \text{and}$$
$$\mathbf{D}(k) = \mathbf{D}(k') \quad \forall\, k, k' \in \{0, \dots, K\}. \tag{24}$$

We note here consequently, that the key issue with ICA-based approaches is *not* in the selection of the optimal *core* algorithm. Rather, it lies in finding a practical solution to the permutation and scaling problem. While the scaling problem is rather reliably solved by the minimal distortion principle (Matsuoka & Nakashima, 2001), inter-frequency permutation remains a rather formidable issue, especially due to its combinatorial nature. It is to this aspect of the ICA solution that much research has been devoted in the recent past.

Some of the work in this regard is the inter-frequency amplitude envelope correlation (AmDeCor) approach of (Anemüller & Kollmeier, 2000), where the spectral amplitude envelopes for a given source are assumed to be similar over frequencies, and this similarity is exploited for permutation resolution; the inter-frequency transfer function correlation approaches of (Obradovic, Madhu, Szabo, & Wong, 2004), which assume that the transfer functions across neighbouring bins are correlated and use the estimate of the demixing system of a previous frequency bin to initialize the search for the current bin; and that of (Guddeti & Mulgrew, 2005), which utilizes both the spectral envelopes and the smoothness of the transfer function across frequencies for solving the permutation problem. However, the basic assumptions of these methods – similar spectral envelopes and correlation of the transfer functions – might not hold in general. Therefore, (Servière & Pham, 2009) proposes a two-pronged method that utilizes the frequency continuity of the spatial filters to initialize the demixing, and

further uses the smoothness of speech sources in their time-frequency representations to correct any permutation misalignments remaining. However, the danger with serial approaches – the propagation of errors made at a frequency through successive bins – remains.

Approaches based on localization cues obtained either explicitly or implicitly (estimated within the ICA framework) may be applied *independently* at each bin, preventing error propagation across frequencies, and are therefore quite popular (c.f. (Ikram & Morgan, 2002 ; Mitianoudis & Davies, 2004; Mukai *et al.*, 2005 ; Saruwatari *et al.*, 2006)). In (Ikram & Morgan, 2002), the beampattern of the demixing matrix is used to generate direction of arrival (DOA) information subsequently used for permutation resolution; an essentially similar approach is followed in (Mitianoudis & Davies, 2004), where the narrowband direction information is obtained by first generating the separated signal components at each microphone, for each frequency, followed by a DOA estimation using the multiple signal classification (MUSIC) (c.f. (Schmidt, 1981)) approach. In (Saruwatari *et al.*, 2006) the demixing matrices are selected for each frequency bin as the best option from a null-beam solution and an ICA solution, using source localization estimates and a quality criterion that is based upon the coherence function; (Baumann *et al.*, 2003) uses an anechoic approximation to the mixing model and forms a cumulant based cost function for optimizing the null-beamformers for the considered model, again using the DOA estimates for permutation resolution; (Parra & Alvino, 2002) argues that proper initialization of the demixing matrices – using geometric constraints based on beamformers – obviates the need for permutation correction in the proposed algorithm. The DOA-based approach of (Mukai *et al.*, 2005) or the clustering approach of (Araki *et al.*, 2005) for permutation solution are similar to the beampattern approach of (Ikram & Morgan, 2002).

Combinations of the above philosophies also exist. The approach of (W. Wang *et al.*, 2004) combines the spectral envelope correlation with robust DOA estimation as in (Mitianoudis & Davies, 2004). This is followed by a psychoacoustic post-filtering, in order to suppress the effects of remaining permutation inconsistencies. Another, more recent, robust algorithm that iteratively applies the amplitude correlation approach and the DOA based approach was proposed in (Sawada et al., 2004). However these algorithms are computationally very expensive. A recent algorithm, proposed in (Madhu *et al.,* 2006) for the 2×2 case, combines the DOA and the amplitude correlation approach in a single step, using the DOA information to initialize the demixing matrices and the amplitude correlation to resolve the permutation independently at each bin. Note, that simply initializing the demixing matrices properly as in (Parra & Alvino, 2002) does not suffice. The approach of (Madhu *et al.,* 2006) is, however, restricted to the specific case of $M = Q = 2$. We shall present a variant of this algorithm that is applicable to a general $M \times Q$ system. We term this the beam-initialized ICA (BI-ICA) approach.

Beam-Initialized ICA

The approach we examine here may be seen as an amalgamation of the AmDeCor and DOA-based approaches to permutation resolution. For the core *ICA* itself, any algorithm may be selected, from the profusion of algorithms in the literature.

We begin with a spatial pre-filtering of the microphone signals. For the pre-filtering matrix, we first make an anechoic, far-field approximation to the mixing model of (7), with the assumption that only the direct path is present. The estimation of the corresponding propagation matrix parameters may be obtained by clustering either the DOA or the time-delay estimates, as discussed previously for the mask-based approaches. Denote this estimate as $\hat{\mathbf{A}}(k)$, which should correspond to the approximation:

$$\hat{\mathbf{A}}(k) = \begin{pmatrix} 1 & \cdots & 1 \\ \vdots & \ddots & \vdots \\ e^{\jmath \Omega_k \widehat{\Delta\tau_{M1}}} & \cdots & e^{\jmath \Omega_k \widehat{\Delta\tau_{MQ}}[MQ]} \end{pmatrix} \qquad (25)$$

Now, form the spatially pre-filtered signals $Z(k,b)$ as:

$$\mathbf{Z}(k, b) = \mathbf{W}_{sp}(k)\mathbf{X}(k, b), \qquad (26)$$

with $\mathbf{W}_{sp}(k) = \det(\hat{\mathbf{A}}(k))\hat{\mathbf{A}}^{-1}(k)$ being the spatial pre-filter. Thus, we now have an *approximation* to the separated signals. This approximation alone is not sufficient due to the rather simple model it is based upon, consisting only of the direct path, and this spatially pre-filtered signal is input to the ICA system. For the ICA itself, we proceed by centering $\mathbf{Z}$ and sphering it. The moments required for centering and sphering are obtained by a temporal average over the B frames of the signal available. Denote by $\overset{\circ}{\mathbf{Z}}(k, b)$ the centered and sphered vector of input signals, where the sphering is done as:

$$\overset{\circ}{\mathbf{Z}}(k, b) = \overset{\circ}{\mathbf{W}}(k)\mathbf{Z}(k, b), \qquad (27)$$

and $\overset{\circ}{\mathbf{W}}(k) = {}^{\cdots}{}_{zz}(k)^{-1/2}$ is the whitening (sphering) matrix.

In the next step, we search for an orthogonal matrix $\breve{\mathbf{W}}(k)$ that decomposes $\overset{\circ}{\mathbf{Z}}(k, b)$ into mutually independent components $\mathbf{Y}(k, b) = \breve{\mathbf{W}}(k) \overset{\circ}{\mathbf{Z}}(k, b)$. The estimation of $\breve{\mathbf{W}}(k)$ is done by the FastICA iterative update, the general form of which is:

$$\nabla_{\breve{\mathbf{W}}(k)}\Theta(\hat{\mathbf{W}}(k)) = \left[\mathbf{I} - \mathrm{E}\left\{K(\overset{\circ}{\mathbf{Y}}(k,b))\overset{\circ}{\mathbf{Y}}{}^H(k,b)\right\}\right]\breve{\mathbf{W}}(k),$$

$$\breve{\mathbf{W}}(k) \leftarrow \nabla_{\breve{\mathbf{W}}(k)}\Theta(\breve{\mathbf{W}}(k)), \tag{28}$$

where $E\{.\}$ stands for the expectation operator, replaced in practice by the temporal average and $\nabla_{\breve{\mathbf{W}}(k)}$ represents the complex matrix gradient operator with respect to $\breve{\mathbf{W}} = [\breve{\mathbf{W}}_1,...,\breve{\mathbf{W}}_Q]^H$. $K(x)$ is the derivative of the particular non-polynomial approximation to the entropy[3]. A function that converges the quickest (among the non-linearities proposed in (Hyvärinen *et al*, 2001; Sawada *et al*, 2001; Smaragdis, 1998)) is the polar co-ordinate non-linearity (Sawada *et al*, 2001) $K(x) = \tanh(|x|)e^{j\arg(x)}$.

The update is followed by the orthonormalization of the updated matrix $\breve{\mathbf{W}}(k)$:

$$\breve{\mathbf{W}}(k) \leftarrow \left(\breve{\mathbf{W}}(k)\breve{\mathbf{W}}^H(k)\right)^{-1/2}\breve{\mathbf{W}}(k). \tag{29}$$

Permutation and Scaling Resolution

The result of the sphering and ICA steps is a scaled and permuted estimate of the underlying source components:

$$\overset{\circ}{\mathbf{Y}}(k,b) \approx \mathbf{J}(k)\mathbf{D}(k)\mathbf{S}(k,b). \tag{30}$$

These ambiguities must be resolved before source reconstruction can take place. Noting that the Z_q from (26) are approximations of the source signals, with better separation being yielded by the ICA, if we compute the *magnitude squared coherence* between any such $\overset{\circ}{Y}_q$ and the elements $Z_{q'}$ of $\mathbf{Z}$, we may expect that this is *maximum* for that q' which corresponds to the ICA separated

source estimate in Y_q. In other words, we seek the optimal permutation matrix $\mathbf{J}_\Pi(k)$ as:

$$\mathbf{J}_\Pi(k) = \underset{\mathbf{J}}{\arg\max}\ \mathrm{trace}(\mathrm{abs}(\Psi_{\mathbf{Z}(\mathbf{J}\overset{\circ}{\mathbf{Y}})}(k))), \tag{31}$$

where $\Psi_{\mathbf{XY}} = \mathrm{E}\{\mathbf{XY}^H\}$ is the coherence between the vectors $\mathbf{X}$ and $\mathbf{Y}$, and the abs($\bullet$) is the element-wise magnitude operator. The idea is illustrated in Figure 2 for a 2 x 2 mixing system. In practice, instead of computing the permutation matrix in one step, it might be advisable to solve for this by *iteratively* finding the optimal permutation for each separated source.

Once the permutation has been resolved, the minimum distortion principle is used to obtain an estimate of the scaling matrix $\hat{\mathbf{D}}(k)$ as:

$$\hat{\mathbf{D}}(k) = \mathrm{diag}(\mathbf{J}_\Pi(k)\breve{\mathbf{W}}(k)\overset{\circ}{\mathbf{W}}\mathbf{W}_{\mathrm{sp}})^{-1} \tag{32}$$

from which we may obtain:

$$\mathbf{Y}(k,b) = \hat{\mathbf{D}}(k)\mathbf{J}_\Pi(k)\overset{\circ}{\mathbf{Y}}(k,b) \approx \mathbf{S}(k,b), \tag{33}$$

where $\mathbf{S}(k,b)$ represents the source signal as observed at a reference microphone (usually microphone 1). The time-domain signal can then be resynthesized using standard procedures, yielding the separated sources.

Linear Approaches GSC

In this section we shall explore the second class of linear separation algorithms, namely those based on explicit spatial considerations the linearly constrained minimum variance (LCMV) beam-former (Frost, 1972) and its adaptive variant, the generalized sidelobe canceller (GSC) (Griffiths & Jim, 1982).

Figure 2. Amplitude envelope evolution at 1.0 kHz. The x-axis indicates the time frame. Note the similarity between the envelopes of the recovered signal 1 and its approximation using (26).

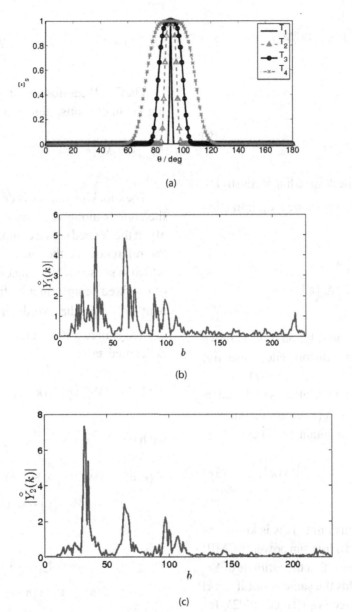

(a)

(b)

(c)

The LCMV Beamformer and the GSC

The LCMV is designed primarily for a single target source, in the presence of directive interferers and noise. Given the *a priori* knowledge of the steering vector[4] $A_q(k)$ for the desired source q, the signal model may be reformulated as:

$$\mathbf{X}(k,b) = \mathbf{A}_q(k)S_q(k,b) + \sum_{q' \neq q}\mathbf{A}_q(k)S_{q'}(k,b) + \mathbf{V}(k,b)$$
$$= \mathbf{A}_q(k)S_q(k,b) + \breve{\mathbf{V}}(k,b),$$

$$(34)$$

where $\breve{\mathbf{V}}(k,b)$ now represents the combined effect of interference and noise. The desired signal may then be enhanced by finding an optimal vector $W_q(k)$ such that:

$$\mathbf{W}_q(k) = \underset{\mathbf{W}(k)}{\mathrm{argmin}}\, \mathbf{W}^H(k)\Psi_{\check{V}\check{V}}(k)\mathbf{W}(k) \qquad (35)$$

subject to

$$\mathbf{W}^H(k)\mathbf{A}_q(k) = \mathrm{G}(k), \qquad (36)$$

where $\mathrm{G}(k) \in \mathbb{C}^{1 \times 1}$ is the desired linear constraint. The solution to this constrained optimization problem is:

$$\mathbf{W}_q(k) = \frac{\mathrm{G}^*(k)\,\Psi_{\check{V}\check{V}}^{-1}\mathbf{A}_q(k)}{\mathbf{A}_q^H(k)\Psi_{\check{V}\check{V}}^{-1}(k)\mathbf{A}_q(k)} \qquad (37)$$

For the case G = 1, the solution is also known as the minimum variance distortionless response (MVDR) beamformer (Cox *et al*, 1987).

In general, however, the statistics of the interference and noise signal $\check{\mathbf{V}}(k,b)$ are not known. An alternative is then to obtain $\mathbf{W}_q(k)$ as:

$$\mathbf{W}_q(k) = \underset{\mathbf{W}(k)}{\mathrm{argmin}}\, \mathbf{W}^H(k)\Psi_{\mathbf{XX}}(k)\mathbf{W}(k), \qquad (38)$$

subject to the same constraint. This is known as the linearly constrained minimum power (LCMP) solution. It is easy to show that the estimate of $\mathbf{W}_q$ using (35) or (38) yields the same result if $\mathbf{A}_q(k)$ is accurately known (see (van Trees, 2002), for example).

The GSC is based on the LCMP principle. However, the system as proposed in (Griffiths & Jim, 1982) optimizes for the elements of $\mathbf{W}(k)$ in an *unconstrained* manner, making the algorithm computationally more efficient. The GSC for a target source q consists of three basic building blocks: the fixed beamformer $\mathbf{W}_{q,\mathrm{d}} \in \mathbb{C}^{M \times 1}$, the blocking matrix $\mathbf{B}_q \in \mathbb{C}^{M \times (M-1)}$, and the adaptive

multi-channel noise canceller $\mathbf{W}_{q,\check{\mathbf{V}}} \in \mathbb{C}^{(M-1) \times 1}$, with:

$$\mathbf{W}_q(k) = \mathbf{W}_{q,\mathrm{d}}(k) - \mathbf{B}_q(k)\mathbf{W}_{q,\check{\mathbf{V}}}(k) \qquad (39)$$

The fixed beamformer is responsible for imposing the linear constraint, and is designed so that:

$$\mathbf{W}_{q,\mathrm{d}}^H(k)\mathbf{A}_q(k) = \mathrm{G}(k) \qquad (40)$$

The blocking matrix is designed to block-out the signals along $\mathbf{A}_q$. Consequently, it does not affect the desired signal component and generates the reference for the spatially correlated noise, which is subsequently cancelled from the output of the fixed beamformer by the adaptive component $\mathbf{W}_{q,\check{\mathbf{V}}}$. In other words, if the estimate of the desired source q (the output of the beamformer) is denoted as

$$Y_q(k,b) = \mathbf{W}_q^H(k)\mathbf{X}(k,b), \qquad (41)$$

we have:

$$\begin{aligned}Y_q(k,b) =\; &\mathbf{W}_{q,\mathrm{d}}^H(k)\mathbf{A}_q\mathbf{S}(k,b)\\ &+ \left(\mathbf{W}_{q,\mathrm{d}}(k) - \mathbf{B}_q(k)\mathbf{W}_{q,\check{\mathbf{V}}}(k)\right)^H \check{\mathbf{V}}(k,b)\end{aligned} \qquad (42)$$

$$\begin{aligned}\mathbf{W}_{q,\check{\mathbf{V}},\mathrm{opt}}(k) &= \underset{\mathbf{W}_{q,\check{\mathbf{V}}}(k)}{\mathrm{argmin}}\, \mathrm{E}\left\{\left|Y_q(k,b)\right|^2\right\}\\ &= \left(\mathbf{B}_q^H(k)\Psi_{\check{V}\check{V}}(k)\mathbf{B}_q(k)\right)^{-1}\mathbf{B}_q^H(k)\Psi_{\check{V}\check{V}}(k)\mathbf{W}_{q,\mathrm{d}}(k)\end{aligned} \qquad (43)$$

The GSC structure of (39) utilizes the canceller $\mathbf{W}_{q,\check{\mathbf{V}}}(k)$ to remove any spatially correlated interference in the beamformed signal $\mathbf{W}_{q,\mathrm{d}}^H(k)\mathbf{X}(k,b)$ on the basis of the noise reference obtained by blocking out the target signal region ($\mathbf{B}^H(k)\mathbf{A}_q(k) = \mathbf{0}$). It is easy now, to see that when $\breve{\mathbf{V}}(k)$ is spatially uncorrelated, i.e., $\Psi_{\breve{\mathbf{V}}\breve{\mathbf{V}}}(k) = \Psi_{\breve{V}\breve{V}}\mathbf{I}$, the canceller is $\mathbf{0}$, and the optimal beamformer in this case is the fixed beamformer satisfying the linear constraint.

Note that in the development from (40) to (43) the propagation vector of the target source is assumed known, allowing us to compute the fixed beamformer and the blocking matrix in advance. Most current applications of GSC to speech are designed for a single target source under this assumption. When these assumptions are violated as, e.g., when $\mathbf{A}_q(k)$ is imperfectly known, the approach suffers from target signal cancellation and corresponding output degradation. To counter this, several safeguards have been proposed in the recent past. These include the robust GSC solution of (Hoshuyama & Sugiyama, 2001), where the noise canceller is constrained to adapt only within the range outside a tolerance region for the target source, preventing target signal cancellation; the robust-GSC (RGSC) approaches of (Herbordt, 2003), which estimates the blocking matrix in a robust manner, when the target source is dominant, preventing target signal cancellation; and the transfer function GSC (TF-GSC) approach of (Gannot *et al*, 2001), where the $\mathbf{A}_q$ in (6) is *estimated* assuming non-stationarity of the target source and stationary background noise. Such approaches belong to the class of 'data-driven' MVDR beamformers. A more recent but essentially similar alternative to the TF-GSC has been proposed in (Chen, Benesty, & Huang, 2008) and is summarized below.

Data-Driven MVDR Beamforming

We shall again consider the narrow band formulation for the multi-channel signal enhancement case as in (34), namely, for microphone m,

$$X_m(k,b) = A_{mq}(k)S_q(k,b) + \breve{V}_m(k,b), \quad (44)$$

We further assume the target source signal is assumed to be uncorrelated with the noise $\breve{V}_m(k,b)$. In the following, the source index and the frequency bin index is dropped for convenience, as the processing is considered to be done for a generic source and independently at each bin. Further, defining $Z_m \overset{\Delta}{=} A_m S$, we may also write (44) compactly as:

$$\mathbf{X} = \mathbf{Z} + \breve{\mathbf{V}}, \quad (45)$$

Now, assuming that there exists a spatial filter $\mathbf{H} \in \mathbb{C}^{M\times 1}$ such that:

$$Z_{m'} = H_{m'}Z_m, \quad (46)$$

then, for signal enhancement, we seek a filter $\mathbf{W}$ such that:

$$\mathbf{W}_{opt} = \underset{\mathbf{W}}{\arg\min}\ \mathrm{E}\left\{\ \left|\mathbf{W}^H\mathbf{X}^2\right|\ \right\} \quad (47)$$

subject to

$$\mathbf{W}^H\mathbf{H} = 1 \quad (48)$$

This constrained optimization leads to the solution:

$$\mathbf{W}_{opt} = \frac{\Psi_{\mathbf{XX}}^{-1}\mathbf{H}}{\mathbf{H}^H\Psi_{\mathbf{XX}}^{-1}\mathbf{H}}. \quad (49)$$

Consider our signal model of (34), modified using the definition of $\mathbf{Z}$ as previously. If we assume that (46) holds, we may write an alternative signal model for the system as:

$$\mathbf{X} = \mathbf{H}Z_m + \breve{\mathbf{V}}, \quad (50)$$

with

$$\Psi_{\mathbf{XX}} = \mathbf{HH}^H \Psi_{Z_m Z_m} + \Psi_{\check{\mathbf{V}}\check{\mathbf{V}}}, \qquad (51)$$

in which case, the solution for the optimal $\mathbf{W}$ from (49) simplifies to

$$\mathbf{W}_{\text{opt}} = \frac{\Psi_{\check{\mathbf{V}}\check{\mathbf{V}}}^{-1} \mathbf{H}}{\mathbf{H}^H \Psi_{\check{\mathbf{V}}\check{\mathbf{V}}}^{-1} \mathbf{H}}. \qquad (52)$$

which form may be recognized as the standard MVDR beamformer, with the target direction vector being estimated by $\mathbf{H}$. The vector $\mathbf{H}$ may also be seen as the *relative transfer function* between the microphones, as in the TF-GSC approach.

Estimation of H: The coefficients $H_{m'}$ indicate the mapping of the target signal component at all microphones m' to that at a specific *reference* microphone m. These coefficients may be estimated in the mean square error sense as:

$$H_{m',\text{opt}} = \operatorname*{argmin}_{H_{m'}} \mathrm{E}\left\{ \left| Z_{m'} - H_{m'} Z_m \right|^2 \right\}, \qquad (53)$$

which leads to the solution

$$H_{m',\text{opt}} = \frac{\Psi_{Z_{m'} Z_m}}{\Psi_{Z_m Z_m}}. \qquad (54)$$

Stacking the results for each $H_{m'}$ into a vectorial form, we obtain:

$$\mathbf{H} = \Psi_{Z_m Z_m}^{-1} \Psi_{\mathbf{Z} Z_m}. \qquad (55)$$

While this approach compensates for irregularities in the knowledge of the true propagation vector, it still requires estimates of $\Psi_{\mathbf{ZZ}}$ and $\Psi_{\check{\mathbf{V}}\check{\mathbf{V}}}$. In (Gannot *et al*, 2001), (Chen *et al*, 2008) the case of a single desired target source enhancement in a *stationary* noise field that is not fully coherent across

the array is considered. Here, the power spectral density of the noise $\Psi_{\check{\mathbf{V}}\check{\mathbf{V}}}$ is estimated by temporal averaging in the noise-only periods. Next, during periods of target signal activity, the power spectral density matrix of the microphone signals $\Psi_{\mathbf{XX}}$ is estimated. From this, and noting that target signal and noise are uncorrelated, we obtain the matrices required for the estimation of $\mathbf{H}$ as:

$$\Psi_{\mathbf{ZZ}} = \Psi_{\mathbf{XX}} - \Psi_{\check{\mathbf{V}}\check{\mathbf{V}}}, \qquad (56)$$

$$\Psi_{\mathbf{Z} Z_m} = \mathrm{E}\{\mathbf{Z} \mathbf{Z}_m^*\} = \Psi_{\mathbf{ZZ}} \mathbf{e}_m, \qquad (57)$$

where $\mathbf{e}_m = [0, \ldots, 0, e_m, 0, \ldots, 0]^T \in \mathbb{R}^{M \times 1}$ is the column selection vector, with only element $e_m = 1$.

Note, however, additional algorithms are required for detecting the noise-only periods. A possible approach is to set a threshold on the spatial coherence function of the microphone signals.

Optimum Multi-Channel Filtering

We shall again consider the narrowband formulation for the multi-channel signal enhancement case as in (45). We further assume the target source signal $A_m(k) S(k, b)$ at any microphone m to be independent of the noise $\check{V}_m(k, b)$ at that microphone.

The traditional multi-channel Wiener filter can be formulated in the following manner: given the microphone signals and knowledge of the target source, the aim is to design a spatial filter $\mathbf{W}_{\text{opt}}$ such that:

$$\mathbf{W}_{\text{opt}} = \operatorname*{argmin}_{\mathbf{W}} \mathrm{E}\{| GS - \mathbf{W}^H \mathbf{X}|^2\}, \qquad (58)$$

where $G = \mathbb{C}^{1 \times 1}$ is an arbitrary, desired response. Optimizing (58) yields:

$$\mathbf{W}_{\text{opt}} = G^* \Psi_{\tilde{\mathbf{V}}\tilde{\mathbf{V}}}^{-1} \Psi_{\mathbf{X}S}, \tag{59}$$

where $\Psi_{\mathbf{X}S} = \mathrm{E}\{\mathbf{X}S^*\}$.

An analysis of this solution is instructive. We begin with writing:

$$\Psi_{\mathbf{XX}} = \mathrm{E}\{\mathbf{XX}^H\} = \mathbf{AA}^H \Psi_{SS} + \Psi_{\tilde{\mathbf{V}}\tilde{\mathbf{V}}}.$$

Then, applying the Woodbury's identity (Woodbury, 1950), we compute the inverse of $\Psi_{\mathbf{XX}}$ as:

$$\Psi_{\mathbf{XX}}^{-1} = \Psi_{\tilde{\mathbf{V}}\tilde{\mathbf{V}}}^{-1} - \Psi_{SS} \frac{\Psi_{\tilde{\mathbf{V}}\tilde{\mathbf{V}}}^{-1} \mathbf{AA}^H \Psi_{\tilde{\mathbf{V}}\tilde{\mathbf{V}}}^{-1}}{(1 + \Psi_{SS} \mathbf{A}^H \Psi_{\tilde{\mathbf{V}}\tilde{\mathbf{V}}}^{-1} \mathbf{A})}. \tag{60}$$

Substituting (60) in (59), and using $\Psi_{\mathbf{X}S} = \Psi_{SS}\mathbf{A}$, we obtain:

$$\begin{aligned}
\mathbf{W}_{\text{opt}} &= G^* \Psi_{SS} \frac{\Psi_{\tilde{\mathbf{V}}\tilde{\mathbf{V}}}^{-1} \mathbf{A}}{(1 + \Psi_{SS} \mathbf{A}^H \Psi_{\tilde{\mathbf{V}}\tilde{\mathbf{V}}}^{-1} \mathbf{A})} \\
&= \underbrace{\frac{G^* \Psi_{\tilde{\mathbf{V}}\tilde{\mathbf{V}}}^{-1} \mathbf{A}}{(\mathbf{A}^H \Psi_{\tilde{\mathbf{V}}\tilde{\mathbf{V}}}^{-1} \mathbf{A})}}_{\text{MVDR}} \underbrace{\frac{\Psi_{SS} \mathbf{A}^H \Psi_{\tilde{\mathbf{V}}\tilde{\mathbf{V}}}^{-1} \mathbf{A}}{(1 + \Psi_{SS} \mathbf{A}^H \Psi_{\tilde{\mathbf{V}}\tilde{\mathbf{V}}}^{-1} \mathbf{A})}}_{\text{post-filter}}.
\end{aligned} \tag{61}$$

Note that the post-filter may be manipulated into a more recognizable form as:

$$\frac{\Psi_{SS} \mathbf{A}^H \Psi_{\tilde{\mathbf{V}}\tilde{\mathbf{V}}}^{-1} \mathbf{A}}{(1 + \Psi_{SS} \mathbf{A}^H \Psi_{\tilde{\mathbf{V}}\tilde{\mathbf{V}}}^{-1} \mathbf{A})} = \frac{\Psi_{SS}}{(\Psi_{SS} + (\mathbf{A}^H \Psi_{\tilde{\mathbf{V}}\tilde{\mathbf{V}}}^{-1} \mathbf{A})^{-1})}, \tag{62}$$

which is readily recognizable as an analogue of the single-channel noise reduction Wiener filter. Thus, we see that the optimum filter for the MMSE estimation in the multi-channel case consists of an MVDR beamformer and a single channel Wiener post-processor. Note that while the MVDR beamformer preserves the signal in the target direction, leading to undistorted response, the

post-filtering introduces target signal distortion. Thus, a multi-channel Wiener filter (MWF), by default, is *not* a distortionless system, and *always* perturbs the target signal when $\left| (\mathbf{A}^H \Psi_{\tilde{\mathbf{V}}\tilde{\mathbf{V}}}^{-1} \mathbf{A})^{-1} \right| > 0$.

This is evident, and has also been pointed out in (Huang *et al*, 2008).

Alternative Implementation

In general the filter developed above is impractical as the source signal is usually not available. For practical purposes the desired signal is chosen to be the *target signal component* at any particular microphone m. In other words, the optimal filter of (58) is modified such that:

$$\mathbf{W}_{\text{opt}} = \underset{\mathbf{W}}{\arg\min}\, \mathrm{E}\left\{ \left| Z_m - \mathbf{W}^H \mathbf{X} \right|^2 \right\}, \tag{63}$$

where $Z_m \triangleq A_m S$ is the target signal component of channel m. We may also pose the cost function for the above optimization in the form:

$$\Theta(\mathbf{W}) = \mathrm{E}\left\{ \left| \mathbf{e}_m^T \mathbf{Z} - \mathbf{W}^H \mathbf{X} \right|^2 \right\}, \tag{64}$$

where $\mathbf{e}_m = [0, \ldots, 0, 1_m, 0, \ldots, 0]^T \in \mathbb{R}^{M \times 1}$ is the selection vector as before, and $\mathbf{Z} = \mathbf{AS}$. Solving the above, we obtain the optimal filter $\mathbf{W}_{\text{opt}}$ as:

$$\begin{aligned}
\mathbf{W}_{\text{opt}} &= \Psi_{\mathbf{XX}}^{-1} \Psi_{\mathbf{XZ}} \mathbf{e}_m \\
&= \Psi_{\mathbf{XX}}^{-1} \Psi_{\mathbf{ZZ}} \mathbf{e}_m
\end{aligned} \tag{65}$$

Under similar assumptions on the speech and noise – as made previously for the derivation of the data-driven MVDR beamformer – this now allows a more practical way to estimate the required quantities: in the noise-only periods, the power spectral density of the noise $\hat{\Psi}_{\tilde{\mathbf{V}}\tilde{\mathbf{V}}}$ is estimated. Next, during periods of target signal activity, the power spectral density matrix of the microphone signals $\hat{\Psi}_{XX}$ is estimated. From this, and noting that target signal and noise are uncorrelated, we obtain an estimate for Ψ_{ZZ} as in (56):

$$\hat{\Psi}_{ZZ} = \hat{\Psi}_{XX} - \hat{\Psi}_{\bar{V}\bar{V}}.$$

Speech Distortion Weighted MWF

From the model in (45) the cost function of (64) is expanded as:

$$
\begin{aligned}
\Theta(\mathbf{W}) &= \mathrm{E}\left\{ \left| Z_m - \mathbf{W}^H \mathbf{x} \right|^2 \right\} \\
&= \mathrm{E}\left\{ \left| \mathbf{e}_m^T \mathbf{Z} - \mathbf{W}^H (\mathbf{Z} + \mathbf{V}) \right|^2 \right\} \\
&= \mathrm{E}\left\{ \left| (\mathbf{e}_m - \mathbf{W})^H \mathbf{Z} - \mathbf{W}^H \mathbf{V} \right|^2 \right\} \\
&= \mathbf{e}_m^T \Psi_{ZZ} \mathbf{e}_m + \mathbf{W}^H \Psi_{XX} \mathbf{W} - \mathbf{W}^H \Psi_{XZ} \mathbf{e}_m - \mathbf{e}_m^T \Psi_{ZX} \mathbf{W} \\
&= \underbrace{\left| A_m \right|^2 \Psi_{SS}}_{\text{desired output}} + \underbrace{\left(\left| \mathbf{W}^H \mathbf{A} \right|^2 - \mathbf{W}^H \mathbf{A}\mathbf{A}^H \mathbf{e}_m - \mathbf{e}_m^T \mathbf{A}\mathbf{A}^H \mathbf{W} \right) \Psi_{SS}}_{\text{speech distortion}} + \underbrace{\mathbf{W}^H \Psi_{\bar{V}\bar{V}} \mathbf{W}}_{\text{noise reduction}}.
\end{aligned}
$$
(66)

The aim now is to optimize the noise reduction, subject to a specified amount of signal distortion (Doclo *et al*, 2005), i.e., we have an optimization of the form:

$$\Theta(\mathbf{W}, \mu) = \frac{1}{\mu} \Psi_{SS} \left| (\mathbf{W} - \mathbf{e}_m)^H \mathbf{A} \right|^2 + \mathbf{W}^H \Psi_{\bar{V}\bar{V}} \mathbf{W}$$

which yields upon optimization

$$\mathbf{W}_{\text{opt}} = \left(\mu \Psi_{\bar{V}\bar{V}} + \mathbf{A}\mathbf{A}^H \Psi_{SS} \right)^{-1} \mathbf{A}\mathbf{A}^H \mathbf{e}_m \Psi_{SS}$$
(67)

In contrast to the MVDR optimization, which is constrained to preserve the target signal in magnitude and phase, the weighted Wiener filter only constrains the *power* of the *distortion*.

Further, expanding (67) into its constituent MVDR and post-filter using the Woodbury's identity, we obtain:

$$\mathbf{W}_{\text{opt}} = \mathbf{W}_{\text{MVDR}} \frac{\Psi_{SS}}{\left(\Psi_{SS} + \mu \left(\mathbf{A}^H \Psi_{\bar{V}\bar{V}}^{-1} \mathbf{A} \right)^{-1} \right)}$$
(68)

with

$$\mathbf{W}_{MVDR} = A_m^* \frac{\Psi_{\bar{V}\bar{V}}^{-1} \mathbf{A}}{\mathbf{A}^H \Psi_{\bar{V}\bar{V}}^{-1} \mathbf{A}}.$$
(69)

for $\mu \to 0$, (68) converges to the MVDR solution. For $\mu = 1$, (68) yields the traditional MWF. In general, $\mu < 1$ preserves the target signal at the cost of lower noise reduction whereas $\mu > 1$ places more emphasis on the noise reduction as compared to signal preservation. An adaptive value for μ, i.e., a higher μ in noise-dominant sections and a lower value in speech-dominant sections can be obtained, for example, by using the speech presence probability as in (Ngo *et al*, 2008).

EXPERIMENTAL EVALUATION

Having presented an overview of the state-of-the-art, we now aim to give the reader an idea of the relative performance (quantitative and qualitative) of representative algorithms from each category. The algorithms selected are presented in Table 2.

The ICA approaches have been selected as the reference for the linear algorithms, as they are *upper* bounded in performance by the adaptive beamforming algorithms based on the GSC or the MWF and their variants[5]. As a result, a comparison of these algorithms with the masking approaches would better illustrate the performance difference between these classes, and selecting any other class of linear algorithms would only increase the difference.

To show the achievable limits of both linear and non-linear approaches, an ideal soft mask (ISM) based approach and an ICA-IDeal algorithm have been added to the field. The ISM uses the

Table 2. Algorithms selected for the comparative evaluation

Non-Linear approaches	Ideal soft mask (ISM) (upper bound, computed using (17), with the *true*, individual source signals at microphone 1), Binary masking (TFM-BM) (Equation (15)), Soft masking (TFM-SM) (Equation(19)),
Linear approaches	ICA-RP (Sawada et al, 2004), beam-initialized ICA (BI-ICA), ICA-ID (upper bound, permutation resolution based on envelope correlation using the true source spectral envelopes as the reference)

true source energy levels on the microphones as input for the mask generation, while the ICA-ID takes the spectral envelopes of the individually recorded sources as a reference to solve the ICA-inherent permutation problem.

We shall evaluate the algorithms on a 2×2 mixing scenario with competing sources. As the aim is to evaluate the separation performance, the background noise is kept to a very low level.

Setup

The sources selected for the tests were drawn from the TIMIT database, and consisted of 5 female and 5 male speakers. Source signals were recorded in the azimuthal range of $\theta \in [0, 180°]$, in steps of $5°$, with $\theta = 90°$ corresponding to the broadside orientation. For each azimuthal position, each test signal was played back individually with the help of loudspeakers (Genelec 2029BR), and recorded by the microphone consisting of 2 Sennheiser KE-4 capsules (omnidirectional) at a sampling rate of f_s = 32kHz. The signals were downsampled offline to 8 kHz for the experiments.

The array and loudspeaker were coplanar, about 1m above the floor. The speaker was at a distance of 1.2m from the center of the microphone pair. The inter-sensor distance was $d = 3$ cm, yielding an upper frequency limit of $(c/2d)$ = 4.25 kHz, beyond which spatial aliasing occurs. The reverberation time for the room in which the recordings were made was $T_{60} = 0.6$s. For the given dimensions of the room (5.7m x 7.4m x 2.4m) and the source-array positioning, we are thus *outside* the critical distance ($d_{crit.} \approx 0.85$m), with almost equal incident signal power from the direct path and the reverberation.

Performance Measures

The instrumental measures for the comparison of the different demixing algorithms are discussed below, along with the rationale behind their choice.

There are two main objective evaluation methods to define the quality of a separated signal, the signal to interference ratio (SIR) and the signal to distortion ratio (SDR). SIR quantifies the interference suppression performance whereas the SDR measures the distortion introduced in the separated target signal, by the separation filter.

Signal to Interference Ratio (SIR)

SIR is measured by the energy ratio of the desired source to the interferers.

$$SIR = 10\log_{10} \frac{\text{Energy}_{\text{target}}}{\text{Energy}_{\text{interferers}}} \quad (70)$$

Assume some algorithm to produce Q separated signals $y_q(n)$ of the sources $s_q(n)$ from M mixtures $x_m(n)$. To evaluate the algorithm by an SIR measure, the focus has to be set on the improvement of the SIR between mixture and separation result. Therefore an *a priori* and an *a posteriori* SIR of source q are introduced in the following. Denote by

$$x_{m|q}(n) = a_{mq}(n) * s_q(n) \quad (71)$$

The received signal at microphone m when only source q is active, with $a_{mq}(n)$ being the corresponding discrete room impulse response. Further, denote

$$y_{q|q'}(n) = \sum W_{q'm}(n)\left(x_{m|q'}(n)\right) \qquad (72)$$

as the output at channel q when only source q' is active (i.e., the cross-talk). The notation $W_{qm}(n)(\bullet)$ indicates that the $W_{mq}(n)$ *operate* on the corresponding input. This notation is used here to take into account possible non-linear, time-variant demixing filters $W_{mq}(n)$. The $W_{qm}(n)$ extract source q from the M mixtures and form the algorithm output for the qth recovered source. Using (71) and (72), the *a priori* (–) and *a posteriori* (+) SIR measures are given by

$$SIR_{m|q}^{(-)} = 10\log_{10} \frac{\sum_n |x_{m|q}(n)|^2}{\sum_n \sum_{q' \neq q} |x_{m|q}(n)|^2}$$

$$SIR_q^{(+)} = 10\log_{10} \frac{\sum_n |y_{q|q}(n)|^2}{\sum_n \sum_{q' \neq q} |y_{q|q'}(n)|^2},$$

$$(73)$$

And the SIR improvement for the signal q is evaluated as

$$\Delta SIR_q = SIR_q^{(+)} - \frac{1}{M}\sum_m SIR_{m|q}^{(-)}. \qquad (74)$$

Note that the $SIR_{m|q}^{(-)}$ is averaged over the M microphones to obtain a non-biased estimate.

Signal to distortion ratio (SDR)

While the perceived degradation of an extracted signal $y_q(n)$ may only be evaluated through listening tests, an instrumental estimate of the signal quality is obtained by the SDR, defined as:

$$SDR = 10\log_{10} \frac{\text{Energy}_{\text{reference source}}}{\text{Energy}_{\text{reference source–filtered source}}}. \qquad (75)$$

The question here is: which signal should be used as a reference? Although taking the original

sources s_q as a reference sounds sensible at a first glance, the drawback is that the room impulse response itself would introduce distortion. Hence, the separately recorded sources $x_{m|q}$ are taken as the reference.

Using the previously introduced signal notation, the time domain version of the SDR can be implemented as

$$SDR_q = 10\log_{10}\left(\frac{1}{M}\sum_m \frac{\sum_n |x_{m|q}(n)|^2}{\sum_n |x_{m|q}(n) - \alpha_{mq} y_{q|q}(n - L_{mq})|^2}\right).$$

$$(76)$$

The real factors α_{mq} and L_{mq} are introduced to make up, respectively, for the amplitude difference and the time shift in the separated signals. L_{mq} is estimated first as:

$$L_{mq} = \underset{L}{\operatorname{argmax}} \frac{1}{N} \Phi_{x_{m|q}y_{q|q}}(L)$$

where

$$\Phi_{x_{m|q}y_{q|q}}(L) = \sum_n x_{m|q}(n) y_{q|q}(n - L).$$

Then amplitudes are then equalized as

$$\alpha_{mq} = \frac{\sum_n |x_{m|q}(n)|^2}{\sum_n |y_{q|q}(n - L_{mq})|^2}. \qquad (77)$$

For a better match, a non-integral shift $L \in R$, obtained from a spline or polynomial interpolation of $\Phi_{x_{m|q}y_{q|q}}(L)$, may be used.

Mixing Process and Analysis Parameters

The mixtures were generated by adding the separately recorded signals $x_m(n)$ at the required azimuth, so that

$$x_m(n) = \sum_q x_{m|q}(n).$$ (78)

Furthermore, the signals were normalized to the same average power before mixing. Thus, SIR$^{(\cdot)}$ is effectively 0 dB.

The analysis parameters for the algorithms are summarized in Table 3.

Instrumental Performance

Figure 3 depicts the performance of the selected algorithms using the two instrumental metrics, for four different spatial separations of the two sources. For each fixed azimuthal separation, the SIR and SDR are averaged over all speaker combinations and spatial constellations, i.e., when $\theta_1 = 30°$, the results are computed for all source position pairs from ($\theta_1 = 0°$, $\theta_2 = 30°$) to ($\theta_1 = 150°$, $\theta_2 = 180°$).

Consider, first, the performance of the non-linear algorithms. The SIR-SDR trade-off based on the thresholds γ_b and γ_s is evident. If the threshold is selected to permit T-F atoms further from a cluster centroid to contribute to that source, the SDR is improved (as fewer T-F atoms are masked out) but SIR reduces. This is clear – the further a T-F atom is from a cluster centroid, the higher the probability that this atom belongs to an interference source and not to the source being extracted. Note, also, that the TFM-SM approach consistently outperforms the approach based on binary masks. This is again expected as the soft mask approach implicitly makes allowances for imperfect disjointness of the spectra. The difference in performance between these two approaches is especially significant at lower inter-source spacings $\Delta\theta$, where the clusters heavily overlap. In such a case, the binary mask, with its winner takes all approach, is not optimal as there is no clear cluster boundary. The performance difference gradually reduces for increasing $\Delta\theta$ because the

Table 3. Analysis parameters for the separation algorithms

Samp. freq.	DFT size	Overlap	Mic. spacing
f_s	K	O	d
(kHz)		(samples)	(cm)
8	512	384	3

clusters become more distinct, and overlap reduces.

Among the linear approaches too we observe this trend of improved separation with increasing $\Delta\theta$. This may be readily explained: for closely spaced sources, steering a sharp null towards the interferer without affecting the target source gain is difficult – especially at low frequencies. As the inter-source distance increases the spatial diversity can be better used. Further, the performance of ICA-ID is better than that of ICA-RP and BI-ICA indicating the lack of complete permutation resolution for small $\Delta\theta$. Here, too, the performance gap reduces with increasing inter-source spacing.

Also, in anticipation of the discussion on post-filtering in the following section, Figure 3 illustrates the performance of the ICA approach enhanced by a post-processor (BI-ICA+post). Note that the post-processor, based on (79) improves the SIR (reduces the interference further) but at the cost of a drop in SDR – indicating again the SIR−SDR trade-off.

A perhaps surprising fact is that the mask-based approaches seem to *outperform* the linear approaches on the instrumental metrics for judiciously selected thresholds. Indeed for a value of $\gamma_s \approx 0.8$ the TFM-SM approach gives the best performance *irrespective* of inter-source spacing, indicating the possibility for an ideal parameter setting for this approach.

As such a behaviour seems contrary to expectations, the performance of these algorithms is next evaluated based on listening tests.

Figure 3. Overall performance for the representative algorithms. The results are averaged for 14 different 2-source combinations, each combination measured over the complete azimuth range keeping Δθ fixed. The multiplicity of the results for the TFM approaches corresponds to different parameter settings

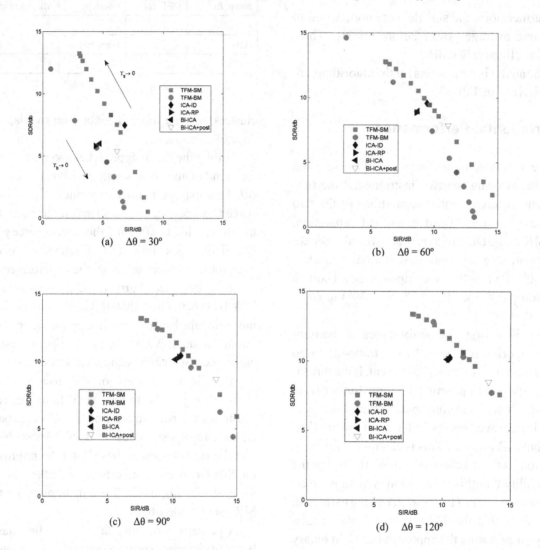

Subjective Performance

Apart from the instrumental quality measurements, listening tests were conducted to rate the perceptive quality of signals separated by the selected algorithms. Subjective evaluation of this kind should give a better indication of the algorithms' performance with respect to potential end-users of such systems. Three evaluation stages were designed to assess different quality

aspects: speech clarity, interference suppression and overall performance.

For the listening tests, a subset of 3 male and 3 female speakers was selected from the previous set, for the two azimuthal spacings of $\Delta\theta = 30°$ and $\Delta\theta = 120°$.

For each test signal, the subjects were presented three different scenarios in which they were told to listen to different aspects of the processed signals. Each scenario was evaluated by a test subject in

Figure 4. MATLAB boxplot for speech clarity evaluation (Scenario 1)

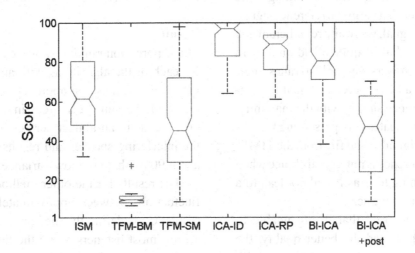

one seating, but in no fixed order. In all, 8 test subjects participated in these experiments. Each subject was an 'expert-listener' and had significant experience with single- and multi-channel speech enhancement algorithms. The results of the listening test are presented subsequently, first in a general fashion, by showing the overall performance graphs for each scenario and each algorithm. Later, the algorithm performance is evaluated separately for the different source positions as this also has an impact on the general performance.

Speech Clarity

Within the first scenario, the listeners were presented a clean, non-processed version of the individually recorded speech signals, without any interfering speaker, as reference for perfect speech clarity. Along with this reference, the seven outputs of the different algorithms were presented, again, with a muted interferer. The task was to rank the signal distortion of each algorithm output on a scale from 1 to 100, where 100 was equivalent to (or better than) the reference (no distortion). A reference for the lower bound was not given.

After ranking each of the algorithm outputs for the first speaker, the scores were saved and the test subject continued with the next signal until each algorithm performance was evaluated on each of the signals.

Results

In terms of speech clarity, the MATLAB boxplot shows the best median results for the ICA-ID method, closely followed by the ICA-RP method, indicating that both methods almost perfectly reconstruct the recorded original signal without adding distortion. These first results show the strong advantages of the linear separation models. Good performance is also achieved by the ISD method and the proposed ICA-MBF approach.

The worst scores go to the binary masking approach (TFM-HD). This reflects the strong distortion introduced by masking the spectrum with binary masks. The scores for the TFM-SD and the ICA+post methods vary heavily with the different listeners and are 'somewhat in the middle' between binary masking and the ICA approaches without postprocessing. The strong variance shows that the test subjects did not disagree if, but rather about 'how much' clarity was lost.

Comments from the listeners included, apart from the hardly audible differences among some signals, the critique that the given reference signal, i.e. the recorded signal, was quite reverberant and therefore perceived as of quite a bad quality. In such a case, the listeners were told to rate signals with an equal or a better perceived quality compared to the reference simply with the maximum score. This also indicates why presenting the raw signal, e.g. the original sound file from the TIMIT database, as a reference is not a good choice when conducting listening tests as it will not lead to a good exploitation of the scale.

Another listener said that, being unable to decide which signal had the better quality, the difference to the reference was evaluated. Still, the relative performance among the algorithms should have not been affected by this behavior.

Interference Suppression

In the second scenario, the listeners were presented the results of the seven algorithms for the separated signals. However, the interfering source was not suppressed anymore. As a reference signal, the corresponding unprocessed mixture was given as the worst case, where particularly no cross-talk suppression is achieved, thus representing the lower bound of the scale, i.e. 1 out of 100 points.

The listeners were told to rate the signals with 100 points if the interferer was completely inaudible.

Results

The suppression ranking shows expected results for each of the algorithms with an exception of the ideal soft masking approach. Using a priori knowledge about the sources in this way obviously leads to an almost perfect suppression of the interfering speaker and results in a score of about 90, with a very low variance.

The results for the other methods show high fluctuations between approximately 20 and 70 points. Considering the median and the average scores, most listeners found the time-frequency masking approaches and the ICA-post approach to suppress the interferer better than the rest. The three `pure ICA' methods, even the ICA-ID with an ideal frequency alignment, lose in this competition, although the distance does not seem to be too large.

The results show the better ability of the non-linear methods to suppress cross-talk in a reverberant environment than the linear methods. The ICA-post seems to benefit from the post-processing stage, as far as the cross-talk suppression is concerned.

Comments from the test subjects included the remark that the given signal was rated better if

Figure 5. MATLAB boxplot for suppression evaluation (Scenario 2)

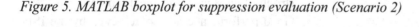

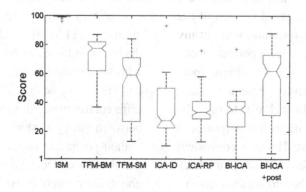

the suppressed voice was less understandable, if there was perceived difference in the volume of the interference compared to a similar test signal.

Overall Quality

In this scenario, the listeners were presented the audio files of the second scenario and asked to evaluate them based on the 1-100 scale. However, this time, no reference was given. Each test subject could freely determine the overall quality of the presented signals, based on his/her gut feeling.

Results

The results for the overall quality ranking speak, again, clearly in favor of the ideal soft masking approach, with a median score of above 80. Its excellent cross-talk suppression ability seems to have a strong influence on the results.

However, suppression was not everything. This is shown by the frequency domain ICA methods which follow with scores ranging in the area of 50 points. Among them, the correctly solved permutation of the ICA-ID is liked most by the listeners, which indicates that the permutation solving in ICA-RP and BI-ICA may still need to be improved.

In terms of preference, the ICA-post method loses out against the linear ICA methods, but still shows better scores than the two purely non-linear masking approaches. Here, the psychoacoustics of the human ear might give an explanation. It seems that the auditory system prefers a non-distorted signal mixture to a distorted signal mixture, even though the interferer is more suppressed in the latter case.

The more unnatural the target signal becomes, the lower the scores are, which is documented by the performance of the two time-frequency masking approaches. Still, the soft masking approach shows a significantly better performance than binary masking, presumably because of the lower target distortion in the separated signal.

Influence of the Azimuthal Spacing

Besides the general performance of the algorithms, the average performance for a fixed azimuthal spacing is of particular interest. For the listening tests, mixtures generated by sound sources at two different distances $\Delta\theta = 120°$ and $\Delta\theta = 30°$ were processed by each of the algorithms and presented to the listeners. The results of the previous section contain an average over these two cases. The evaluation results, for each case separately, are illustrated in Figure 7.

Generally, a direct comparison between the two cases is difficult. For instance, the ISM

Figure 6. MATLAB boxplot for overall quality evaluation (Scenario 3)

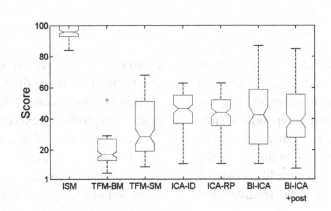

Figure 7. Algorithm performance for different azimuth distances

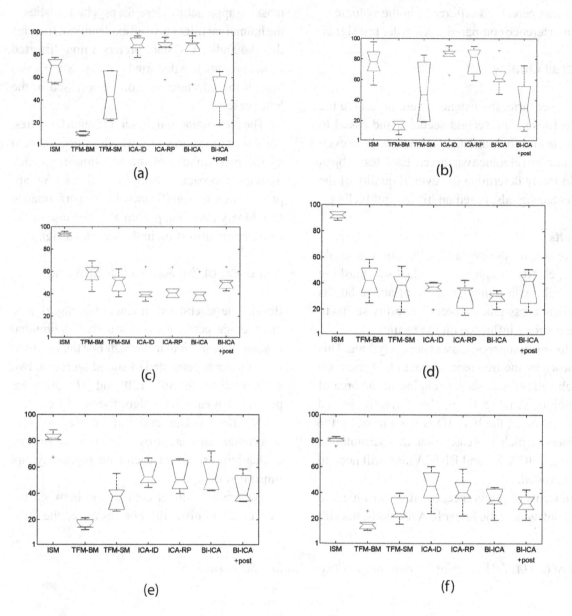

(a)

(b)

(c)

(d)

(e)

(f)

method seems to deliver clearer speech signals when processing sources with a smaller azimuth spacing. Hereby one has to consider, that the listeners have not been able to compare the results for both spacings directly, but rather had to compare the results of each algorithm for one of the spacings only. Therefore, it is quite likely that the listeners just scored each algorithm relative to the

signal which they perceived as the best, regardless of whether a reference file was given.

However, the general performance degradation of all the algorithms – except for the ISM method – when separating mixtures of closely spaced sound sources is clearly visible in the graphs. The main reason for this is the similarity of the room impulse response from two neighboring positions. The (non-ideal) TFM methods have,

Figure 8. Algorithm performance for two different source positions

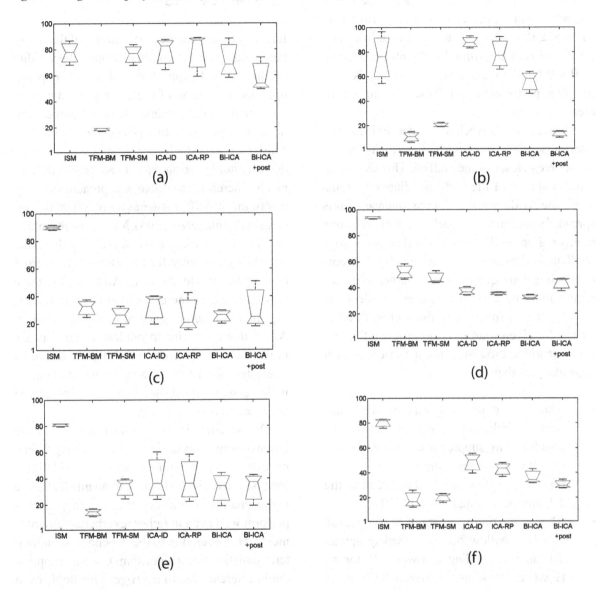

therefore, to distinguish between the sources based on very similar mixing parameters, whereas the linear ICA methods suffer from two facts: modeling the inverses of similar room impulse responses leads to similar demixing vectors and thus to heavy cross-talk of the interfering sources, even for the ICA-ID. Secondly, the use of the null beamformer signals as a means to solve the permutation problem becomes highly difficult, especially for low frequencies.

Influence of Non-Symmetric Source Locations

Another important factor for the performance of the algorithms is the actual positioning of the sources with respect to the broadside location. To illustrate this fact, Figure 8 shows the different performance plots for the separation of the left source at $\theta = 90°$ and the right source at $\theta = 60°$.

Most striking about these plots is the heavy degradation of the perceived speech clarity of the TFM-SD, BI-ICA+post, and, to a certain extent, for the BI-ICA algorithm for $\theta = 60°$ in contrast to $\theta = 90°$. Simultaneously, the cross-talk suppression performance of these algorithms increases.

The reason for this behavior lies in the increased inter-sensor phase smearing between the T-F atoms for sources closer to the endfire. This leads to a broader spread of the corresponding T-F atoms along the $\Delta\tau$ dimension. A consequence of this spread, for the linear approaches, is that the beams in this region (null or reinforcing) are *necessary shallow*. For the non-linear approaches, the corresponding consequence is that a larger tolerance region must be chosen to correctly select the T-F atoms corresponding to the source. In other words, for given sources s_1 closer to endfire and s_2 closer to the broadside, the net effect, for *all* algorithms, is that

- when extracting s_1, s_2 can be well suppressed, indicating a higher SIR for s_1, which is why suppression is better for $\theta = 60°$. But, at the same time, the reconstruction of s_1 suffers due to the spread in the T-F atoms, leading to lower SDR

- when extracting s_2, s_1 cannot be suppressed as well (shallow beams or widely spread T-F atoms) yielding a lower SIR for s_2. However, as source s_2 would be in a region where sharp reinforcing beams can be steered, it suffers from lower distortion (higher SDR), which is why speech clarity is higher for $\theta = 90°$.

This smearing is also dependent upon the amount of reverberation present. Note here that the described algorithm behavior for an 'outer' source compared to an 'inner' source were also observed for other asymmetric mixtures, although it was not explicitly tested in the listening test.

POST-PROCESSING

It is easy to see that the performance of the mask-based algorithms is contingent upon the validity of the disjoint-support model which depends upon the resolution of the T-F representation of the signal. In the presence of reverberation and noise, this representation is smeared in time, as a consequence of which the disjointness assumption does not hold as strongly as in anechoic environments. Therefore, mask-based approaches steadily deteriorate in performance as the reverberation increases (Yilmaz *et al*, 2004). Moreover, the masks generated over the T-F plane are very dynamic, varying significantly, for a single frequency, from one time-frame to the next. Additionally, there may be errors in the estimation of these masks, especially in the presence of background noise. All of this gives rise to random isolated peaks in the masked spectrum, resulting in sinusoidal artefacts of short duration and varying frequencies in the re-synthesized signal, which are perceived as so-called *musical noise*.

On the other hand, as linear algorithms are based on long term statistics, the demixing filters, once estimated, remain constant over a relatively long period of time – leading to no musical noise in the separated signals. Further, such approaches perform well even in rather reverberant environments. However, due to the dependence on long term statistics, linear algorithms can only suppress the interference on an *average*. This holds even for the MWF, as it is based on the *statistics* of the noise and the target. Consequently, interference suppression is obtained to a lesser extent as compared to the mask-based methods.

Thus, neither class of approaches make optimal use of *both* spatial diversity, and the sparsity and disjointness properties peculiar to speech.

To obtain enhanced separation in reverberant environments, the reverberation-robust linear algorithms (ICA, GSC, etc.) are first used to obtain an approximation to the separated signals

Figure 9. Block diagram of the multi-stage separation setup. Such post-processors based on binary masks have been proposed in, e.g., (Kolossa & Orglmeister, 2004) (for various Υ_p). Further improvements to mask-based post-filters include that presented in (Flego et al, 2005) and (Aichner et al, 2006).

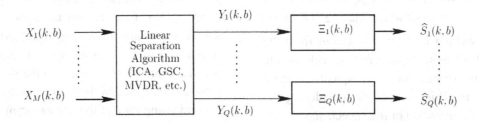

$\left(Y_q(k,b) \approx A_{qq}(k)S_q(k,b)\right)$. Consequently, after this stage we would expect the contribution of $S_q(k,b)$ in $Y_q(k,b)$ to be stronger than its contribution in the other channels $Y_{q'}(k,b)$ $\forall q' \neq q$, as the linear filtering should have attenuated the cross-talk. Next, if we consider the disjointness of the source signals $S_q(k,b)$, we may assume that a particular T-F atom contains at most one source with a considerable amplitude. Thus we may conclude, for instance, when any one recovered signal has more energy than the others at any T-F atom, the corresponding source is dominant for that atom and *appears in the other signals as cross-talk*. We may then define suitable post-processing masks $\Xi_q(k,b)$ to block out such cross-talk. In their simplest form these masks are defined as:

$$\Xi_q(k,b) = \begin{cases} 1 & \Upsilon_p |Y_q(k,b)| > \max_{\forall q' \neq q}\left(|Y_{q'}(k,b)|\right) \\ \Xi_{min} & \text{otherwise} \end{cases}$$

(79)

where $0 < \Upsilon_p \leq 1$ is used to prevent spurious triggering of the masks, and where Ξ_{min} is the maximum suppression allowed. The final, enhanced signals are subsequently obtained as

$$Z_q(k,b) = \Xi_q(k,b)Y_q(k,b),$$ (80)

from which the discrete time signals may be re-synthesized. Such a multi-stage separation setup is illustrated in Figure 9.

Requirements for an Optimal Post-Processing

As mentioned previously, disjointness is affected by room reverberation and the presence of background noise. Thus, while a simple implementation of a post-processing mask as in (79) suppresses the cross-talk, it distorts the target signal and engenders the musical noise phenomenon. This trade-off between cross-talk suppression and signal deterioration is visible in Figure 3 and Figure 4 – 6. One way to avoid this harmonic distortion is to smooth the masks along time and/or frequency. However, simple temporal smoothing delays the response of the masks to speech onsets and smoothing along frequency has the effect of reducing the spectral resolution – smearing the signal across the spectrum. Using *soft* masks, as for example described in the section on mask-based approaches, alleviates this problem by *limiting* the achievable suppression. However, this is at the cost of lower cross-talk suppression as compared to binary masks. This is also evident from the listening tests (compare the soft mask approach with its binary counterpart in Figure 3.

Thus, what we require is a system that can preserve the mask variations due to speech onsets while, at the same time, smooth out the random, unwanted spectral peaks that generate musical noise. In other words, for good cross-talk suppression we require to distinguish between the isolated random peaks in the mask $\Xi_q(k, b)$ on one side, and mask patterns resulting from the spectral structures of the target speech on the other. As we demonstrate subsequently, such a smoothing is achievable when considering the *cepstral* representation of the speech signal.

Mask Smoothing in the Cepstral Domain

As speech signals, in general, have a broad-band envelope, a temporal smoothing should not be applied to the mask when the broad-band structure of the signal changes. Likewise, a change in the fine structure of the spectrum that originates from an onset of voiced speech (pitch harmonics) must also be protected from smoothing effects. Ideally, the smoothing should only affect irregular peaks of short duration. This distinction between the speech related broad-band structures and regular pitch harmonics on one side and the irregular fine-structured artefacts like isolated random peaks on the other is accomplished in the *cepstral* (Oppenheim & Schafer, 1975) domain. As an example, consider a sample 'cepstrogram' representation of one output signal of the ICA algorithm.

Significant in Figure 10 is the large portion of the energy present in the lower cepstral bins. This corresponds to the broadband envelope of the speech signal. We also sporadically see significant energy in a narrow region at higher quefrencies. This indicates the energy corresponding to the pitch harmonics during voiced segments of speech. In this context note also the presence of cross-talk, indicated by the weaker pitch contours. The remaining part of the cepstrogram contains the fine structure of the speech spectrum.

These properties of speech *must* also be reflected in the masks. Consequently, a distinction between the speech related broad-band structures and regular pitch harmonics on one hand and the irregular fine-structured artefacts like isolated random peaks on the other must also be possible for the masks in the cepstral domain allowing for selective smoothing to be carried out.

The cepstral representation of the mask pattern $\Xi_q^C(\ell, b)$ is first obtained as:

$$\Xi_q^C(\ell, b) = \mathrm{DFT}^{-1}\left\{\ln(\Xi_q(k, b))\,|_{k=0,\ ...,\ K-1}\right\}, \quad (81)$$

where ℓ is the quefrency bin index, $\mathrm{DFT}^{-1}\{\cdot\}$ represents the inverse discrete Fourier transform operator, and K is the length of the transform.

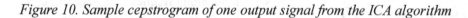

Figure 10. Sample cepstrogram of one output signal from the ICA algorithm

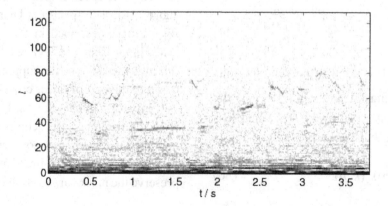

Next a first order, temporal, recursive smoothing is applied to $\Xi_q^C\left(\ell,b\right)$ as:

$$\overline{\Xi}_q^C\left(\ell,b\right) = \eta_\ell \overline{\Xi}_q^C\left(\ell,b-1\right) + (1-\eta_\ell)\Xi_q^C\left(\ell,b\right),$$

(82)

where the smoothing constants η_ℓ are chosen separately for the different quefrency bins ℓ according to:

$$\eta_\ell = \begin{cases} \eta_{env} & \ell \in \{0,...,\ell_{env}\}, \\ \eta_{pitch} & if \quad \ell=\ell_{pitch}, \\ \eta_{peak} & \ell \in \{(\ell_{env}+1),...,K/2\} \setminus \{\ell_{pitch}\} \end{cases}$$

(83)

The rationale behind this choice for η_ℓ is as follows: for the lower bins $\ell \in \{0,...,\ell_{env}\}$, the values of $\Xi_q^C(\ell,b)$ represent the *spectral* envelope of the mask $\Xi_q(k,b)$ (Oppenheim & Schafer, 1975). As speech onsets go along with a sudden rise in the spectral envelope, η_{env} should have a very low value, resulting in a low smoothing, in order not to distort the envelope. Likewise, if ℓ_{pitch} is the quefrency bin that represents the regular structure of the pitch harmonics in $\Xi_q\left(k,b\right)$, we apply a relatively low smoothing η_{pitch} to this bin ($\ell = \ell_{pitch}$). The cepstral bins $\ell \in \{(\ell_{env}+1),...,K/2\} \setminus \{\ell_{pitch}\}$ represent the fine structure of $\Xi_q\left(k,b\right)$ that is not related to the pitch and cover, with high probability, the random unwanted peaks that lead to the harmonic distortion. Therefore, we apply a strong smoothing η_{peak} ($> \eta_{pitch}$) to these coefficients. As the unwanted isolated random peaks represent a sporadic change of the fine structure of $\Xi_q\left(k,b\right)$, and as they last only for a short duration, they are strongly affected by the smoothing (82). Note that this smoothing does not affect the speech information contained in the upper quefrency bins (apart from ℓ_{pitch}) as such information is generally present for

more than one frame and are thus preserved despite the high value of η_{peak}.

We choose ℓ_{pitch} as the cepstral bin that satisfies

$$\ell_{pitch} = \underset{\ell}{\operatorname{argmax}} \ \{\Xi_q^C\left(\ell,b\right) \mid \ell_{low} \leq \ell \leq \ell_{high}\},$$

(84)

which is a well-known method for computing the pitch frequency from a cepstrum (Oppenheim & Schafer, 1975). The search range $\left\{ \ell_{low}, \ell_{high} \right\}$ is selected so that possible pitch frequencies between 70 Hz and 500 Hz may be detected. Although the search in Equation (84) only delivers meaningful results in the presence of voiced speech, the signal energy contained in the bin ℓ_{pitch}, otherwise, is comparably low so that no audible side effects are perceivable from the lesser smoothing $\eta_{pitch} > \eta_{peak}$ of that bin in the absence of voiced speech.

For bins $\ell > K/2$, $\overline{\Xi}_q^C\left(\ell,b\right)$ is determined by the symmetry condition of the DFT: $\overline{\Xi}_q^C(\ell,b) = \overline{\Xi}_q^C(K-\ell,b)$. The final smoothed *spectral* mask is obtained as:

$$\overline{\Xi}_q(k,b) = \exp\left[\operatorname{DFT}\left\{\overline{\Xi}_q^C\left(\ell,b\right) \mid_{\ell=0,...,K-1}\right\}\right],$$

(85)

where the exponential function is applied element-wise. This smoothed mask is then used to obtain the enhanced signal according to (80).

Evaluation and Discussion

The test data used to evaluate the proposed post-processor consists of the individual separated signals obtained using BI-ICA. The separated time-domain signals were segmented into frames of length K and weighted by a Hann window before transformation into the discrete Fourier domain. The overlap between adjacent frames

Table 4. Parameter values for the implemented post-processing system

f_s (kHz)	K	ℓ_{env}	ℓ_{low}	ℓ_{high}	η_{env}	η_{pitch}	η_{peak}	$20\log_{10}(\Upsilon_p)$ (dB)	Ξ_{min}
8	256	8	16	120	0	0.4	0.8	-5	0.1

was set to 50%. Table 4 summarizes the values of the remaining parameters for the system used in the evaluation.

Figure 11. Illustrates the performance of the described post-processing algorithm on a sample mixture. The cross-talk is clearly evident in the separated signals obtained from ICA. Its suppression under a binary mask and the cepstrally-smoothed mask is equally evident. Note the profusion of isolated peaks in Figure 11 (b,e) for the binary mask, and the corresponding version in Figure 11 (c,f), obtained from the proposed approach where the peaks are successfully suppressed. Note also that the proposed approach preserves the speech onsets and the pitch structure in the recovered signals.

(a) Speaker 1: output of the ICA algorithm.
(b) Speaker 1: spectrum after binary masking.
(c) Speaker 1: spectrum after smoothing masks.

(a) Speaker 2: output of the ICA algorithm.
(b) Speaker 2: spectrum after binary masking.
(c) Speaker 2: spectrum after smoothing masks.

The post-processing algorithm was also evaluated via listening tests on eleven test-subjects, encompassing both expert and non-expert listeners. The test set consisted of 24 examples containing mixtures of male-male, male-female and female-female speakers. For each example, the test subject was presented three audio samples – the output of the ICA algorithm (without post processing), the output after post processing the signals obtained from the ICA by the binary masks as in Equation (79) and, finally, the output of the post-processor (the masks of (79), selectively smoothed in the

cepstral domain, as explained in the previous section). The test subject was then asked to select the best of the three for each category:

1. quality of speech of the desired speaker,
2. interference suppression, and
3. overall impression.

The purpose of the listening test was to first confirm that the post-processing using binary masks (79) improved interference suppression and, secondly, to verify that the proposed method improved the masks by removing disturbing musical noise without degrading the high interference suppression, resulting in a better, overall acceptance. The results are presented in Figure 12.

From the listening test results, it is apparent that a post-processing (79) indeed reduces the amount of interference (Figure 12) – indicating that it is useful to implement a mask-based post processor despite the signals being reverberant. This is also in agreement with the results obtained previously (Figure 5). For the evaluation of the quality of speech, most subjects opted for the signal with no post-processing as having the best quality. This is because, due to masking and the threshold γ_p, there is a slight distortion in the post-processed signal spectrum. Note that this originates from the binary mask of (79) and not from the proposed smoothing and could be dealt with by more sophisticated masking approaches. However, the subjects did state that, at times, they found it hard to distinguish between the speech quality afforded by the proposed post-processor and that of ICA. This is reflected in the relatively large number of 'undecided' votes. In terms of overall impression, the proposed method deliv-

Figure 11. Spectra of the recovered signals before and after post-processing. Each row shows the spectrogram for one speaker.

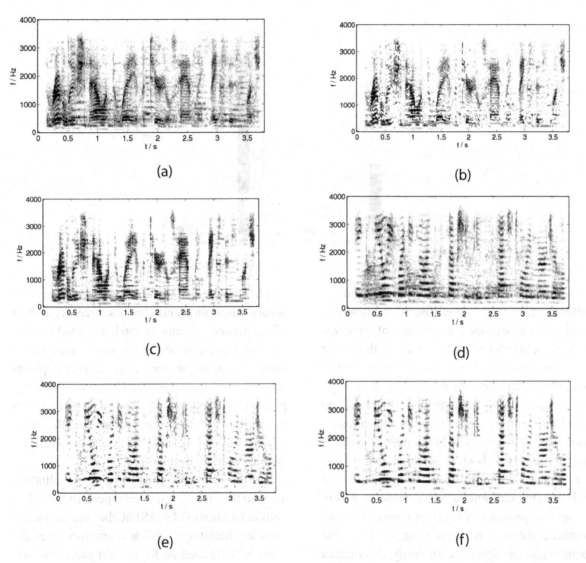

(a)

(b)

(c)

(d)

(e)

(f)

ers the best performance – indicating the merit of the approach.

CONCLUSION

This chapter has attempted to provide an overview of the state-of-the-art in multi-channel source separation. The approaches studied here utilize, variously, the spatial diversity afforded by the sensors and the explicit spatial orientation of the sources; the long-term statistics of the individual source signals; or the disjointness and sparsity of the signal spectra to achieve the goal of separation.

Decomposing speech mixtures into their constituent sources places two competing constraints on the algorithms in terms of performance: the amount of interference suppression and the amount of target signal distortion. In general, the improvement in one metric is usually at the cost

Figure 12. Cumulative results of the listening test in terms of speech quality (Speech), interference suppression (Background) and overall impression (`none' indicates no post-processing)

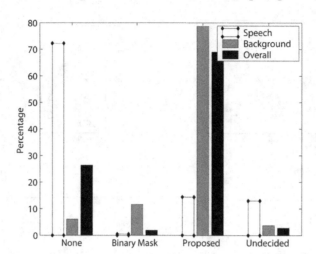

of the other. Linear separation algorithms usually suffer from low target signal distortion. However, as they are based on the minimization of some *statistic* of the interference sources, either the power (e.g., the generalized sidelobe canceller (GSC)) or higher order statistics such as kurtosis (e.g., independent component analysis (ICA) based algorithms), they perform interference cancellation on an *average*. They do not make use of the disjointess of speech within their framework. The consequence is that the interfering sources are audible, although attenuated, especially during the speech pauses of the target source. Usually another constraint on the linear approaches is the requirement of either a completely determined ($M = Q$) or over-determined ($M > Q$) mixtures. This arises from the fact that to steer a spatial null requires a degree of freedom (represented in this case by a microphone). Additionally, batch based linear approaches such as ICA cannot, in general, handle the underdetermined ($M < Q$) case.

Non-linear approaches, on the other hand, can suppress the interfering sources very well, provided that the disjointess condition is met. Additionally, in principle, they do not suffer from any constraints on the number of sensors and sources as compared to the linear approaches, and

can handle the underdetermined case. They can separate an arbitrary number of sources *regardless* of the number of sensors used, provided that the specific representation of the signals considered allows for a unique clustering of the data points belonging to each source. However, these approaches suffer from two drawbacks: they distort the target signal to a larger extent than the linear approaches and they do not utilize the available spatial diversity optimally.

Furthermore, the instrumental evaluation showed that in terms of overall performance, i.e., considering both SIR and SDR, the time-frequency masking methods are able to outperform even the ideal ICA-ID method for certain parameter settings. In fact, TFM-SM with a properly chosen parameter $\gamma_s \approx 0.8$ leads to better results than ICA-ID for inter-source distances $\Delta\theta \geq 60$.

However, such conclusions based only on instrumental measures are misleading. Listening to the processed files reveals the weaknesses of these evaluation criteria: they do not represent the quality perception of a human ear. The human perception, for example, is very sensitive to short, unnatural peaks in the signal that occur, for instance, in non-linear approaches. However, the SDR measure, being an average over the complete signal, is not severely affected by such peaks. This results in the discrepancy between the perceived quality and the instrumental measures.

The listening tests also very well demonstrate the SIR-SDR trade-off: if a (non-ideal) algorithm performs an outstanding separation of the sources, the speech quality of the desired source simultaneously decreases and the other way round.

However, the important question to answer with the listening tests was which degree of quality and suppression is the most agreeable for the listeners. As it seems, the average participant of the tests favors quality over suppression. Presenting a distorted desired signal with lower amount of cross-talk seems unnatural for the human ear. An undistorted target source in combination with an attenuated interferer seems to be more agreeable – even though the absolute volume of the interferer is higher in this case. A possible explanation is that human listeners are far more used to natural signal mixtures with attenuated interferers, e.g. when talking to a specific person in a cocktail party, and are able to do the signal separation part themselves – given a little help from the linear algorithms.

An approach that exploits *both* the spatial diversity and the speech disjointness for source separation has also been studied. This consists, essentially, of a non-linear mask-based approach piggybacked onto the outputs of the linear separation algorithms. Such combinations yield varying results, depending upon their implementation. The post-processor as described here is able to combine the advantages of both classes of approaches, yielding a high interference suppression at the cost of low target signal distortion. This is because the design of the mask and the consequent selective smoothing is motivated by perceptual considerations.

The described post-processor is also simple to implement, requiring little or no statistical information. The listening tests corroborate our conclusions. Note that the selective mask-smoothing method is not restricted to the post-processing for source separation. In general, it lends itself readily as a smoothing approach in cases where the disjointness property of speech is used to compute time and frequency-variant gains for speech enhancement.

As an example, this approach could also be used directly on mask-based separation approaches, or in noise reduction algorithms (Breithaupt *et al*, 2007). However, for the multi-channel algorithms considered in this chapter, it is perhaps wiser to first utilize the spatial diversity by beamforming before utilizing the sparsity property for masking.

REFERENCES

Aichner, R., Zourub, M., Buchner, H., & Kellermann, W. (2006). Residual cross-talk and noise suppression for convolutive blind source separation. In *Proceedings of the annual meeting of the German Acoustical Society (DAGA)*.

Anemüller, J., & Kollmeier, B. (2000). Amplitude modulation decorrelation for convolutive blind source separation. In *Proceedings of the international conference on independent component analysis (ICA)* (pp. 215–220).

Araki, S., Makino, S., Hinamoto, Y., Mukai, R., Nishikawa, T., & Saruwatari, H. (2003). Equivalence between frequency-domain blind source separation and frequency-domain adaptive beamforming for convolutive mixtures. *EURASIP Journal on Applied Signal Processing*, 1157–1166. doi:10.1155/S1110865703305074

Araki, S., Sawada, H., Mukai, R., & Makino, S. (2005). A novel blind source separation method with observation vector clustering. In *Proceedings of the international workshop on acoustic echo and noise control (IWAENC '05)*.

Baumann, W., Kolossa, D., & Orglmeister, R. (2003). Beamforming-based convolutive blind source separation. In *Proceedings of the IEEE international conference on acoustics, speech and signal processing (ICASSP)* (pp. 357–360).

Bofill, P., & Zibulevsky, M. (2000). Blind separation of more sources than mixtures using sparsity of their short-time Fourier transform. In *Proceedings of the international conference on independent component analysis (ICA)*.

Breithaupt, C., Gerkmann, T., & Martin, R. (2007). Cepstral smoothing of spectral filter gains for speech enhancement without musical noise. *IEEE Signal Processing Letters, 14*(12). doi:10.1109/LSP.2007.906208

Buchner, H., Aichner, R., & Kellermann, W. (2004). TRINICON: A versatile framework for multichannel blind signal processing. In *Proceedings of the IEEE international conference on acoustics, speech and signal processing (ICASSP)*.

Cermak, J., Araki, S., Sawada, H., & Makino, S. (2006). Blind speech separation by combining beamformers and a time frequency mask. In *Proceedings of the international workshop on acoustic echo and noise control (IWAENC)*.

Chen, J., Benesty, J., & Huang, Y. (2008). A minimum distortion noise reduction algorithm with multiple microphones. *IEEE Transactions on Audio. Speech and Language Processing, 16*(3), 481–493. doi:10.1109/TASL.2007.914969

Cox, H., Zeskind, R. M., & Owen, M. M. (1987). Robust adaptive beamforming. *IEEE Transactions on Acoustics, Speech, and Signal Processing, 35*(10), 1365–1375. doi:10.1109/TASSP.1987.1165054

Diamantaras, K. I. (2001). Blind source separation using principal component neural networks. In Dorffner, G., Bischof, H., & Hornik, K. (Eds.), *Lecture notes in computer science* (*Vol. 2130*). New York: Springer Verlag.

DiBiase, J. H., Silverman, H. F., & Brandstein, M. S. (2001). Robust localization in reverberant rooms. In Brandstein, M., & Ward, D. (Eds.), *Microphone arrays: Signal processing techniques and applications* (pp. 157–180). Berlin: Springer-Verlag.

Doclo, S., Spriet, A., Wouters, J., & Moonen, M. (2005). Speech distortion weighted multichannel Wiener filtering techniques for noise reduction. In Benesty, J., Makino, S., & Chen, J. (Eds.), *Speech enhancement* (pp. 199–228). New York: Springer Verlag. doi:10.1007/3-540-27489-8_9

Fancourt, C. L., & Parra, L. (2001). The coherence function in blind source separation of convolutive mixtures of non-stationary signals. In *Proceedings of the IEEE international workshop on neural networks for signal processing (NNSP)* (pp. 303–312).

Flego, F., Araki, S., Sawada, H., Nakatani, T., & Makino, S. (2005). Underdetermined blind separation for speech in real environments with F0 adaptive comb filtering. In *Proceedings of the international workshop on acoustic echo and noise control (IWAENC)*.

Frost, O. L. III. (1972). An algorithm for linearly constrained adaptive array processing. *Proceedings of the IEEE, 60*(8), 926–935. doi:10.1109/PROC.1972.8817

Gannot, S., Burshtein, D., & Weinstein, E. (2001). Signal enhancement using beamforming and nonstationarity with applications to speech. *IEEE Transactions on Signal Processing, 49*(8), 1614–1626. doi:10.1109/78.934132

Griffiths, L. J., & Jim, C. W. (1982). An alternative approach to linearly constrained adaptive beamforming. *IEEE Transactions on Antennas and Propagation, AP-30*, 27–34. doi:10.1109/TAP.1982.1142739

Guddeti, R. R., & Mulgrew, B. (2005). Perceptually motivated blind source separation of convolutive audio mixtures with subspace filtering method. In *Proceedings of the international workshop on acoustic echo and noise control (IWAENC)*.

Herbordt, W. (2003). *Combination of robust adaptive beamforming with acoustic echo cancellation for acoustic human/machine interfaces*. Unpublished doctoral dissertation, Friedrich-Alexander-Universität, Erlangen-Nürnberg.

Hoshuyama, O., & Sugiyama, A. (2001). Robust adaptive beamforming. In Brandstein, M., & Ward, D. (Eds.), *Microphone arrays: Signal processing techniques and applications* (pp. 87–109). Berlin: Springer-Verlag.

Huang, Y., Benesty, J., & Chen, J. (2008). Analysis and comparison of multichannel noise reduction methods in a common framework. *IEEE Transactions on Audio. Speech and Language Processing, 16*(5), 957–968. doi:10.1109/TASL.2008.921754

Hyvärinen, A. (1999). Fast and robust fixed-point algorithms for independent component analysis. *IEEE Transactions on Neural Networks, 10*(3), 626–634. doi:10.1109/72.761722

Hyvärinen, A., Karhunen, J., & Oja, E. (2001). *Independent component analysis*. Hoboken, NJ: John Wiley & Sons, Ltd. doi:10.1002/0471221317

Hyvärinen, A., & Oja, E. (1997). A fast fixed-point algorithm for independent component analysis. *Neural Computation, 9*(7), 1483–1492. doi:10.1162/neco.1997.9.7.1483

Hyvärinen, A., & Oja, E. (2000). Independent component analysis: Algorithms and applications. *Neural Networks, 13*(4–5), 411–430. doi:10.1016/S0893-6080(00)00026-5

Ikram, M. Z., & Morgan, D. R. (2002). A beamforming approach to permutation alignment for multichannel frequency-domain blind source separation. In *Proceedings of the IEEE international conference on acoustics, speech and signal processing (ICASSP)* (Vol. 1, pp. 881–884).

Kolossa, D., & Orglmeister, R. (2004). Nonlinear postprocessing for blind speech separation. []. Berlin: Springer Verlag.]. *Lecture Notes in Computer Science, 3195*, 832–839.

Madhu, N. (2002). *Independent component analysis in multiple input multiple output (MIMO) systems*. Unpublished master's thesis, Technische Universität München, Munich, Germany.

Madhu, N., Gückel, A., & Martin, R. (2006). Combined beamforming and frequency domain ICA for source separation. In *Proceedings of the international workshop on acoustic echo and noise control (IWAENC)*.

Madhu, N., & Martin, R. (2008). A scalable framework for multiple speaker localization and tracking. In *Proceedings of the international workshop on acoustic echo and noise control (IWAENC)*. Seattle, USA.

Martin, R. (2004). Speech enhancement using MMSE short time spectral estimation with Gamma distributed speech priors. In *Proceedings of the IEEE international conference on acoustics, speech and signal processing (ICASSP)*.

Matsuoka, K., & Nakashima, S. (2001). Minimal distortion principle for blind source separation. In *Proceedings of the international conference on independent component analysis (ICA)* (pp. 722–727).

Mitianoudis, N., & Davies, M. (2004). Permutation alignment for frequency domain ICA using subspace beamforming. In *Proceedings of the international conference on independent component analysis (ICA)*.

Mukai, R., Sawada, H., Araki, S., & Makino, S. (2005). Real-time blind source separation and DOA estimation using a small 3-D microphone array. In *Proceedings of the international workshop on acoustic echo and noise control (IWAENC)*.

Ngo, K., Spriet, A., Moonen, M., Wouters, J., & Jensen, S. H. (2008). Variable speech distortion weighted multichannel wiener filter based on soft output voice activity detection for noise reduction in hearing aids. In *Proceedings of the international workshop on acoustic echo and noise control (IWAENC)*.

O'Shaughnessy, D. (2000). *Speech communications*. New York: IEEE Press.

Obradovic, D., Madhu, N., Szabo, A., & Wong, C. S. (2004). Independent component analysis for semi-blind signal separation in MIMO mobile frequency selective communication channels. In *Proceedings of the INNS-IEEE international joint conference on neural networks (IJCNN)*.

Oppenheim, A. V., & Schafer, R. W. (1975). *Digital Signal Processing*. Upper Saddle River, NJ: Prentice Hall.

Parra, L., & Alvino, C. V. (2002). Geometric source separation: Merging convolutive source separation with geometric beamforming. *IEEE Transactions on Speech and Audio Processing*, 352–362. doi:10.1109/TSA.2002.803443

Parra, L., & Fancourt, C. (2002). An adaptive beamforming perspective on convolutive blind source separation. In Davis, G. M. (Ed.), *Noise reduction in speech applications* (pp. 361–378). CRC Press.

Porter, J., & Boll, S. (1984). Optimal estimators for spectral restoration of noisy speech. In *Proceedings of the IEEE international conference on acoustics, speech and signal processing (ICASSP)*.

Rickard, S., Balan, R., & Rosca, J. (2001). Real-time time-frequency based blind source separation. In *Proceedings of the international conference on independent component analysis (ICA)*.

Rickard, S., & Yilmaz, Ö. (2002). On the approximate W-Disjoint orthogonality of speech. In *Proceedings of the IEEE international conference on acoustics, speech and signal processing (ICASSP)*.

Roman, N., Wang, D., & Brown, G. (2003). Speech segregation based on sound localization. *The Journal of the Acoustical Society of America*, *114*(4), 2236–2252. doi:10.1121/1.1610463

Rosca, J., Borss, C., & Balan, R. (2004). Generalized sparse signal mixing model and application to noisy blind source separation. In *Proceedings of the IEEE international conference on acoustics, speech and signal processing (ICASSP)*.

Saruwatari, H., Kawamura, T., Nishikawa, T., Lee, A., & Shikano, K. (2006). Blind source separation based on a fast-convergence algorithm combining ICA and beamforming. *IEEE Transactions on Audio. Speech and Language Processing*, *14*, 666–678. doi:10.1109/TSA.2005.855832

Sawada, H., Mukai, R., Araki, S., & Makino, S. (2001). A polar-coordinate based activation function for frequency domain blind source separation. In *Proceedings of the international conference on independent component analysis (ICA)* (pp. 663–668).

Sawada, H., Mukai, R., Araki, S., & Makino, S. (2004). A robust and precise method for solving the permutation problem of frequency-domain blind source separation. *IEEE Transactions on Speech and Audio Processing*, *12*, 530–538. doi:10.1109/TSA.2004.832994

Schmidt, R. O. (1981). *A signal subspace approach to multiple emitter location and spectral estimation*. Unpublished doctoral dissertation, Stanford University.

Servière, C., & Pham, D. T. (2009). Permutation correction in the frequency domain in blind separation of speech mixtures. *EURASIP Journal on Applied Signal Processing* (2006).

Smaragdis, P. (1998). Blind separation of convolved mixtures in the frequency domain. *Neurocomputing*, 21–34. doi:10.1016/S0925-2312(98)00047-2

Strang, G. (1988). *Linear algebra and its applications* (3rd ed.). Belmont, CA: Thompson / Brooks Cole.

Tashev, I., & Acero, A. (2006). Microphone array post-processing using instantaneous direction of arrival. In *Proceedings of the international workshop on acoustic echo and noise control (IWAENC)*.

van Trees, H. L. (2002). *Detection, estimation and modulation theory, part iv*. Hoboken, NJ: John Wiley and Sons.

Vary, P., & Martin, R. (2006). *Digital speech transmission: Enhancement, coding and error concealment*. Hoboken, NJ: John Wiley & Sons, Ltd.doi:10.1002/0470031743

Wang, D. (2008). Time–frequency masking for speech separation and its potential for hearing aid design. *Trends in Amplification*, 332–353. doi:10.1177/1084713808326455

Wang, W., Chambers, J. A., & Sanei, S. (2004). A novel hybrid approach to the permutation problem of frequency domain blind source separation. *In Proceedings of the international conference on independent component analysis (ICA)*.

Woodbury, M. A. (1950). *Inverting modified matrices (Rapport technique No Memorandum Rept. 42)*. Statistical Research Group, Princeton University.

Yilmaz, Ö., Jourjine, A., & Rickard, S. (2000). Blind separation of disjoint orthogonal signals: Demixing N sources from two mixtures. In *Proceedings of the IEEE international conference on acoustics, speech and signal processing (ICASSP)*.

Yilmaz, Ö., Jourjine, A., & Rickard, S. (2004). Blind separation of speech mixtures via time-frequency masking. *IEEE Transactions on Signal Processing, 52*(7). doi:10.1109/TSP.2004.828896

Yoon, B.-J., Tashev, I., & Acero, A. (2007). Robust adaptive beamforming algorithm using instantaneous direction of arrival with enhanced noise suppression capability. In *Proceedings of the IEEE international conference on acoustics, speech and signal processing (ICASSP)*.

ENDNOTES

[1] As a point of note, the signals considered in this work are modelled as realizations of stochastic processes with an underlying probability density function, *a priori* information about which may or may not be available. Thus, when we refer colloquially to signals having a specified distribution, or to signals being uncorrelated or statistically independent, we mean the underlying stochastic processes in the strict sense.

[2] Note that while sparsity in the strict sense implies that most signal components are zero, in the practical sense we take it to indicate that most signal components have a very small value.

[3] Interestingly, as only the derivative is required in the updates, the true non-polynomial form need not necessarily be obtained. This allows for a lot of flexibility in selecting the non-linear function $\mathbf{K}$.

[4] The LCMV and related algorithms were originally formulated for a system containing only a delay, implying that the elements A_{mq} of $\mathbf{A}$ consist simply of a phase shift. However, an extension to a more general propagation matrix is straightforward, and it is this model we imply when we refer to the LCMV and the other algorithms in this category.

[5] Note that the data-driven GSC and its variants are not, *per se*, designed for the competing speaker scenario, requiring stationarity assumptions on the background noise for an adaptive implementation. While these algorithms may, in principle, be configured to work in the competing source environment, such implementation (e.g., Cermak *et al.*, 2006) requires additional constraints on these algorithms in terms of *a priori* knowledge regarding target source activity detection, location. When this knowledge is available, they outperform the ICA based, 'blind' algorithms.

Chapter 10
Audio Source Separation Using Sparse Representations

Andrew Nesbit
Queen Mary University of London, UK

Maria G. Jafari
Queen Mary University of London, UK

Emmanuel Vincent
INRIA, France

Mark D. Plumbley
Queen Mary University of London, UK

ABSTRACT

The authors address the problem of audio source separation, namely, the recovery of audio signals from recordings of mixtures of those signals. The sparse component analysis framework is a powerful method for achieving this. Sparse orthogonal transforms, in which only few transform coefficients differ significantly from zero, are developed; once the signal has been transformed, energy is apportioned from each transform coefficient to each estimated source, and, finally, the signal is reconstructed using the inverse transform. The overriding aim of this chapter is to demonstrate how this framework, as exemplified here by two different decomposition methods which adapt to the signal to represent it sparsely, can be used to solve different problems in different mixing scenarios. To address the instantaneous (neither delays nor echoes) and underdetermined (more sources than mixtures) mixing model, a lapped orthogonal transform is adapted to the signal by selecting a basis from a library of predetermined bases. This method is highly related to the windowing methods used in the MPEG audio coding framework. In considering the anechoic (delays but no echoes) and determined (equal number of sources and mixtures) mixing case, a greedy adaptive transform is used based on orthogonal basis functions that are learned from the observed data, instead of being selected from a predetermined library of bases. This is found to encode the signal characteristics, by introducing a feedback system between the bases and the observed data. Experiments on mixtures of speech and music signals demonstrate that these methods give good signal approximations and separation performance, and indicate promising directions for future research.

DOI: 10.4018/978-1-61520-919-4.ch010

INTRODUCTION

The problem of *audio source separation* involves recovering individual audio *source* signals from a number of observed *mixtures* of those simultaneous audio sources. The observations are often made using microphones in a live recording scenario, or can be taken, for example, as the left and right channels of a stereo audio recording. This is a very challenging and interesting problem, as evidenced by the multitude of techniques and principles used in attempts to solve it. Applications of audio source separation and its underlying principles include audio remixing (Woodruff, Pardo, & Dannenberg, 2006), noise compensation for speech recognition (Benaroya, Bimbot, Gravier, & Gribonval, 2003), and transcription of music (Bertin, Badeau, & Vincent, 2009). The choice of technique used is largely governed by certain constraints on the sources and the mixing process. These include the number of mixture channels, number of sources, nature of the sources (e.g., speech, harmonically related musical tracks, or environmental noise), nature of the mixing process (e.g., live, studio, using microphones, echoic, anechoic, etc), and whether or not the sources are moving in space.

The type of mixing process that generates the observed sources is crucially important for the solution of the separation problem. Typically, we distinguish between *instantaneous*, *anechoic* and *convolutive* mixing. These correspond respectively to the case where the sources are mixed without any delays or echoes, when delays only are present, and when both echoes and delays complicate the mixing. Source separation for the instantaneous mixing case is generally well understood, and satisfactory algorithms have been proposed for a variety of applications. Conversely, the anechoic and convolutive cases present bigger challenges, although they often correspond to more realistic scenarios, particularly for audio mixtures recorded in real environments. Algorithms for audio source separation can also be classified as *blind* or *semi-blind*, depending on whether a priori information

regarding the mixing. Blind methods assume that nothing is known about the mixing, and the separation must be carried out based only on the observed signals. Semi-blind methods incorporate a priori knowledge of the mixing process (Jafari et al., 2006) or the sources' positions (Hesse & James, 2006).

The number of mixture channels relative to the number of sources is also very important in audio source separation. The problem can be *overdetermined*, when more mixtures than sources exist, *determined*, with equal number of mixtures and sources, and *underdetermined*, when we have more sources than mixtures. Since the overdetermined problem can be reduced to a determined problem (Winter, Sawada, & Makino, 2006), only the determined and underdetermined situations have to be considered. The latter is particularly challenging, and conventional separation methods alone cannot be applied. An overview of established, statistically motivated, model-based separation approaches are presented elsewhere in this book (Vincent et al., 2010), which can also serve as an introduction to audio source separation for the non-expert reader. Another useful introduction is the review article by O'Grady, Pearlmutter, & Rickard (2005).

A widely used class of model-based source separation algorithms that exploits the sparsity of the source signals in some time-frequency (TF) transform domain is *sparse component analysis* (SCA). It entails transforming the signals into a domain in which they are *sparse*, estimating the mixing matrix from the transform coefficients, estimating the source representations, and finally, inverting the transform representation of the estimated sources. A *sparse* signal representation is one which conveys the information within the signal using only a few elementary components, denoted as *atoms*, which are selected from a *dictionary* to form a sparse signal decomposition. This often helps to uncover hidden structure in the analysed signal by characterising the original signal using only a small number of large coefficients. The short-time Fourier transform (STFT), for instance, decomposes a time-domain signal using a dictionary of windowed Fourier (complex exponential) atoms, and will reveal the frequency content of the signal even though this might not be evident from the temporal waveform. Fixed-basis transforms such as the STFT or the fixed-basis modified discrete cosine transform (MDCT) are often used in audio (Ravelli & Daudet, 2006). They have the advantageous property of being easily invertible and providing a unique signal representations.

However, transforms based on a fixed dictionary fail to match all signal features present, such as fast-varying transients and slower components (Daudet & Torrésani, 2002), and they are often based on a rigid structure that prevents the compact representation of some signals (Davis, 1994). In response to this, *redundant* or *overcomplete* dictionaries are often used, where the number of atoms is greater than the dimensionality of the signal space. An alternative approach is to construct an orthogonal dictionary directly from the observed data, so that it captures features that are exactly relevant to the analysed signal, and introduces a feedback system between the signal and the dictionary (Górecki & Domanski, 2007). Examples of dictionary learning algorithms include independent component analysis (ICA) (Abdallah & Plumbley, 2004) and K-SVD (Aharon, Elad & Bruckstein, 2006).

In this chapter, SCA for audio source separation is considered under two mixing scenarios, and in each case, a different sparse decomposition technique for SCA is used. The instantaneous, underdetermined problem is addressed using a class of adaptive *lapped orthogonal transforms*, which select from a dictionary of localised cosine basis functions, those which yield an orthogonal, linear transform. There are many possible orthogonal bases to choose from (i.e., the *library* of bases for the entire time-domain signal is large), due to the fact that there are many ways in which the signal may be segmented in time by overlapping

windows. In the conceptual SCA framework, once the mixture signals have been transformed using this method, the sources are estimated by assigning energy from each of the transform domain coefficients to the source estimates (it is assumed here that the mixing matrix is either known, or has been estimated, i.e., the semi-blind case). Finally, the time-domain source estimates are recovered by applying the inverse transform.

We then direct our attention to the anechoic, determined audio source separation problem. We present an orthogonal transform that is used to sparsify the data in the first step of the SCA procedure. The transform is a greedy algorithm which adaptively learns a dictionary from data blocks taken from the observed signal. This maximises the ℓ^2 norm of the data, while minimizing its ℓ^1 norm, hence resulting in a sparse representation for the signal. The transform is forced to be orthogonal by removing all the components lying in the direction of a particular vector (corresponding to the selected data frame) at each iteration. Since the atoms are extracted from the observed data, the greedy adaptive dictionary (GAD) algorithm finds atoms that are directly relevant to the data being analysed. Thus, we apply the transform to the audio source separation problem, within the SCA framework, and compare its performance to that of ICA and K-SVD within the same framework, as presented in (Jafari et al., 2008), and (Jafari & Plumbley, 2008).

SOURCE SEPARATION

The problem of source separation arises when two or more signals (sources) are mixed by passage through an unknown medium, and the objective of source separation algorithms is to recover the original sources from only the available mixtures. We consider the separation of J sources, from an equal number of mixtures, generated according to the anechoic mixing model, defined as (Saab et al, 2005)

$$x_i(n) = \sum_{j=1}^{J} a_{i,j} s_j(n - \tau_{i,j}), \quad i = 1, \ldots, J \quad (1.1)$$

where $x_i(n)$ is the observed mixture, and $a_{i,j}$, and $\tau_{i,j}$ are the real-valued attenuation coefficients ($a_{i,j} > 0$) and time delays relating to the path from source j to mixture i.

In this chapter, we also consider the underdetermined and instantaneous case, where the problem becomes one of estimating $J > 2$ sources when the number of mixture channels is two. Thus, Equation (1.1) becomes

$$x_i(n) = \sum_{j=1}^{J} a_{i,j} s_j(n), \quad i = 1, 2 \quad (1.2)$$

which in matrix can be written as

$$\mathbf{x}(n) = \mathbf{A}\mathbf{s}(n) \quad (1.3)$$

w h e r e $\mathbf{x}(n) = \begin{bmatrix} x_1(n) & x_2(n) \end{bmatrix}^T$ a n d $\mathbf{s}(n) = \begin{bmatrix} s_1(n) & \cdots & s_J(n) \end{bmatrix}^T$ are the mixture and source vectors respectively, $\mathbf{A} = [a_{i,j}]_{2 \times J}$ is the instantaneous mixing matrix with real-valued entries, and the discrete-time index ranges as $0 \leq n < N$, where N is the length of the signal.

Sparse Component Analysis

Sparse component analysis methods, based on the assumption that the source signals are sparse in some transform domain, are frequently applied to source separation, since working with signal representations that do not overlap simplifies the separation problem (Gribonval & Lesage, 2006). Moreover, many approaches to audio source separation based on, for instance, ICA, assume that the number of mixture channels is equal to the number of sources. As this condition is not always satisfied, we look for a different solution.

Generally, the SCA procedure is comprised of the following four conceptual stages.

Firstly, the mixture signals are transformed so that they lie in a domain in which they are sparse; this typically entails the use of orthogonal transforms such as the wavelet transform or MDCT or nonorthogonal transforms such as the STFT, but learned dictionaries are acquiring popularity. Examples of sparsifying transforms based on learned dictionaries are ICA (Jafari et al., 2008), and K-SVD (Aharon, Elad & Bruckstein, 2006). Secondly, the mixing matrix is estimated, typically by clustering coefficients in the sparse transform domain. Thirdly, the sources in the transform domain are estimated by apportioning energy from each source coefficient to the source estimates according to their mixing parameters determined in the previous stage. Finally, the sources are reconstructed by applying the inverse transform.

It should be noted that these four stages are used for conceptualising the SCA procedure, but in practical implementations the various stages might have varying dependencies upon each other.

SPARSE COMPONENT ANALYSIS BASED ON LAPPED ORTHOGONAL TRANSFORMS

Adaptive *lapped orthogonal transforms* (LOTs), which adapt to the time-varying signal structures in the TF domain, have the potential to yield sparser representations and superior performance compared to commonly used transforms such as the STFT or fixed-basis MDCT (Nesbit, Vincent & Plumbley, 2009). This section describes their construction and the way they naturally fit within the SCA framework.

Sparsifying Step Adaptive Lapped Orthogonal Transforms

Adapting a LOT to the mixture channels $x_i(n)$ entails forming an appropriate partition of their

Figure 1. Schematic representation of window denoted by β_k^λ. The partition points are given by n_k and n_{k+1} and the bell parameters by η_k and η_{k+1}.

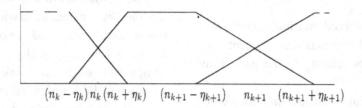

$$(n_k - \eta_k)\ n_k\ (n_k + \eta_k) \qquad (n_{k+1} - \eta_{k+1}) \qquad n_{k+1} \qquad (n_{k+1} + \eta_{k+1})$$

domain $[0,\ldots,N-1]$, that is, a collection of K strictly increasing points n_k such that

$$0 = n_0 < n_1 < \cdots < n_k < \cdots < n_{K-1} = N - 1. \tag{2.1}$$

This segments the domain of $x_i(n)$ into adjacent intervals $\mathcal{I}_k = [n_k, n_{k+1} - 1]$ which should be relatively long over durations which require good frequency resolution, and relatively short over durations requiring good time resolution. It is well known that simply using rectangular windows to divide the signal along its time axis at these points leads to the familiar 'ringing' artifacts at the window boundaries. However, by using a differentiable window of compact support, which does not have such objectionable discontinuities, these border artifacts can be alleviated. In the context of adaptive LOTs, this means that any two adjacent windows will overlap by a certain amount. To specify this amount of overlap, augment the aforementioned partition by associating with each n_k a *bell parameter* η_k, so that the partition becomes a finite set of ordered pairs $\lambda = \{(n_k, \eta_k)\}$ Figure 1 is a schematic representation of the way $x_i(n)$ is windowed with windows $\beta_k^\lambda(n)$ according to some particular partition λ. Each window $\beta_k^\lambda(n)$ is supported in $[n_k - \eta_k, n_{k+1} + \eta_{k+1} - 1]$, thus partly overlapping with its immediately adjacent windows $\beta_{k-1}^\lambda(n)$ and $\beta_{k+1}^\lambda(n)$ by η_k and η_{k+1} points respectively.

These bell parameters η_k are thus subject to the constraint

$$\eta_{k+1} - n_k \geq \eta_{k+1} + \eta_k. \tag{2.2}$$

Note that $\eta_0 = \eta_{K-1} = 0$ and appropriate border modifications need to be made for this special case (Mallat, 1999). For every partition λ we form its associated windows according to the following function:

$$\beta_k^\lambda(n) = \begin{cases} r\left(\dfrac{n - \left(n_k - \frac{1}{2}\right)}{\eta_k}\right) & \text{if } n_k - \eta_k \leq n < n_k + \eta_k, \\[2ex] 1 & \text{if } n_k + \eta_k \leq n < n_{k+1} - \eta_{k+1}, \\[2ex] r\left(\dfrac{\left(n_{k+1} - \frac{1}{2}\right) - n}{\eta_{k+1}}\right) & \text{if } n_{k+1} - \eta_{k+1} \leq n < n_{k+1} + \eta_{k+1}, \\[2ex] 0 & \text{otherwise} \end{cases} \tag{2.3}$$

where the *bell function* $r(t)$ satisfies $r^2(t) + r^2(-t) = 1$ for $-1 \leq t \leq 1$, $r(t) = 0$ for $t < -1$ and $r(t) = 1$ for $t_{>1}$, where t is real-valued and satisfies various differentiability properties (Mallat, 1999). The bell parameters η_k and η_{k+1} determine how quickly the window monotonically rises on its left side and monotonically falls on its right side. Although there are many possible bell functions which satisfy these constraints, in practice we use a sine bell; refer to Mallat (1999) for its definition.

The local cosine basis associated with the interval I_k is then given by modulating $\beta_k^\lambda(n)$ by functions from a cosine-IV basis as follows:

$$\mathcal{B}_k^\lambda = \left\{ \beta_k^\lambda \sqrt{\frac{2}{n_{k+1} - n_k}} \cos\left[\pi\left(m' + \frac{1}{2}\right) \frac{n - (n_k - \frac{1}{2})}{n_{k+1} - n_k} \right] \right\} \tag{2.4}$$

where $m' \in [0, n_{k+1} - n_k - 1]$ is the discrete cosine frequency index. This defines the basis B^λ for the orthogonal LOT, adapted to the partition λ, for the space of signals of length N:

$$B^\lambda = \bigcup_{k=0}^{K-1} \mathcal{B}_k^\lambda. \tag{2.5}$$

Since our aim is to find the *best orthogonal basis* (BOB) of all possibilities, we will consider all admissible partitions $\lambda \in \Lambda$ subject to some relatively lenient constraints, each of which determines a different orthogonal basis. Thus we obtain a *library* of bases for this space of signals of length N:

$$\mathcal{L} = \bigcup_{\lambda \in \Lambda} B^\lambda. \tag{2.6}$$

As such, the union of all bases in the library constitutes an overcomplete dictionary from which we obtain our sparse representation. Each admissible basis $B^\lambda \in \mathcal{L}$ has an associated *cost* of representing a particular signal in that basis, given by an additive cost function. Finding the BOB amounts to minimizing this cost, which, ideally, should maximize the separation performance criterion. Examples of suitable cost functions are the ℓ^1 norm (useful in blind and semi-blind cases), and the *oracle* benchmarking criterion (useful for algorithm evaluation); each of these cost functions is defined and described later in this section, because, in this particular framework for SCA, the computation of the BOB is inti-

mately tied in with estimating the source coefficients.

Given any additive cost function, the BOB is determined by applying one of several partitioning schemes and associated algorithms based on dynamic programming (Huang, Pollak, Bouman, & Do, 2006; Xiong, Ramchandran, Herley, & Orchard, 1997). In previous work (Nesbit, Plumbley, & Vincent, 2009) a *flexible segmentation* (FS) scheme was described, which admits all possible partitions λ with some 'resolution' L, so that if the signal length N is an integral multiple of L, then each partition point can be written as $n_k = cL$ for $c \geq 0$, and where η_k is subject only to the condition (2.2). Provided that both L and N are powers of two, any library L admitted by FS is a superset of the library admitted by the less flexible, *dyadic* partitioning scheme, in which intervals are recursively formed by 'splitting' already existing intervals at their middles (Mallat, 1999). Although FS gives excellent separation results, its library L is very large due to a combinatorial explosion between the range of allowed interval lengths, interval onsets and bell parameters. Therefore, its computation time is impractically high. As we wish to maintain flexible partitioning on the domain of the signal, yet decrease the time required for estimation of $s(n)$, we are motivated by the corresponding ideas from the MPEG-4 AAC audio coding framework (ISO, 2005) and introduce the following 'MPEG-like' partitioning schemes:

- **Long-Short (LS).** We restrict the range of allowable partitions to admit intervals I_k of only two lengths, that is, a *long interval* of length L_L and a *short interval* of length $L_S = L$, where L_L is an integral multiple of L_S, and we admit only bell parameters such that $2\eta_k \in \{L_L, L_S\}$. Apart from this restriction of interval lengths and bell parameters, there are no additional constraints, and LS is otherwise the same as FS.

- **Window Shapes (WS).** This is equivalent to LS with the additional constraint that if I_k is long, then at most one of η_k and η_{k+1} is short. In other words, the four different window shapes admitted (compared to five in LS) correspond to a long window ($2\eta_k = 2\eta_{k+1} = L_L$), a short window ($2\eta_k = 2\eta_{k+1} = L_S$), a long-short *transition window* ($2\eta_{k+1} = L_L, 2\eta_{k+1} = L_S$), and a short-long ($2\eta_{k+1} = L_S, 2\eta_{k+1} = L_L$) transition window in the MPEG-4 framework.

- **Onset Times (OT).** This is equivalent to LS with the additional constraint if any interval I_k is long, then n_k must satisfy $n_k = cL_L$ for some $c = 0, \ldots, \frac{N}{L_L} - 1$.

- **WS/OT.** This scheme imposes both the WS and OT constraints simultaneously.

- **WS/OT/Successive Transitions (WS/OT/ST).** This scheme imposes the WS/OT constraints in addition to disallowing adjacent transition windows, i.e., a transition window must be adjacent to a long window and a short window. This implements the windowing scheme used by MPEG-4, apart from the choice of the bell function $r(t)$.

Even though the sizes of the libraries become significantly smaller as we impose more constraints, we expect that the MPEG-like partitioning schemes are nevertheless sufficiently flexible so that benefits gained in computation time will outweigh any decrease in separation performance.

Estimating the Mixing Matrix

In the SCA framework, the mixing matrix, **A**, is typically estimated by clustering TF coefficients. For example, the method of Bofill (2008) applies a linear, sparsifying transform to each of the mixture channels and selects only those coefficients whose spatial 'direction', given by the ratio of the magnitudes of the two mixture channels at each point in the transform domain, remain constant over time.[1] The idea is that such coefficients are more likely to belong to a single source, and can then be clustered using a weighted histogram to estimate **A**. However, as the description of the particular source separation framework described in this section is more concerned with evaluating the adaptive nature of LOTs, only semi-blind experiments will be performed, and it is assumed that **A** is either already known or has been estimated.

Estimating the Sources and Inverting the Transform

Let $\tilde{\mathbf{x}}(m) = \begin{bmatrix} \tilde{x}_1(m) & \tilde{x}_2(m) \end{bmatrix}^T$ be the vector of a linear, orthogonal, TF transform of each channel of $\mathbf{x}(n)$, and let $\tilde{\mathbf{s}}(m) = \begin{bmatrix} \tilde{s}_1(m) & \cdots & \tilde{s}_J(m) \end{bmatrix}^T$ be the transform of $\mathbf{s}(n)$, where m indexes the coefficients in the TF domain and $0 \leq m < N$. In the present case, the transform used is an LOT, as described above.

In the semi-blind case, by assuming that the source coefficients in the transform domain follow a Laplacian distribution independently and identically for all j and m, the maximum a posteriori estimation of $\mathbf{s}(n)$ is equivalent to minimising the ℓ^1-norm of the sources coefficients given by the following:

$$C\left(\hat{\tilde{\mathbf{S}}}\right) = \sum_{m=0}^{N-1} \sum_{j=1}^{J} \left| \hat{\tilde{s}}_j(m) \right| \tag{2.7}$$

where $\hat{\tilde{\mathbf{S}}}$ is a $J \times N$ matrix of estimated source coefficients in the transform domain (Bofill & Zibulevsky, 2001). The primary implication of this, in the present case where there are two mixture channels, is that exactly two sources are assumed to be active at each m; incidentally, this gives better performance than the simpler *binary masking* case which allows only one active source (Bofill & Zibulevsky, 2001; Yilmaz & Rickard,

2004). Furthermore, it is known that minimising the ℓ^1-norm promotes sparsity of the estimated coefficients; as such, it is an appropriate estimation criterion for this implementation of SCA (Zibulevsky & Pearlmutter, 2001).

The set of both source indices contributing to $\tilde{x}(m)$ is denoted by $\mathcal{J}_m = \{j : \tilde{s}_j(m) \neq 0\}$, and is called the *local activity pattern* at m. Given a particular J_m, (1.3) then reduces to a determined system:

$$\tilde{x}(m) = \mathbf{A}_{\mathcal{J}_m} \tilde{\mathbf{s}}_{\mathcal{J}_m}(m) \qquad (2.9)$$

where $\mathbf{A}_{\mathcal{J}_m}$ is the 2×2 submatrix of $\mathbf{A}$ formed by taking columns $\mathbf{A}_j$, and $\tilde{\mathbf{s}}_{\mathcal{J}_m}(m)$ is the subvector of $\tilde{s}(m)$ formed by taking elements $\tilde{s}_j(m)$, whenever $j \in J_m$. As such the activity patterns need to be estimated according to

$$\widehat{\mathcal{J}}_m^{\text{sb}} = \arg\min_{\mathcal{J}_m} \sum_{j=1}^{J} \left| \hat{\tilde{s}}_j(m) \right| \qquad (2.9)$$

which depends implicitly on the following:

$$\begin{cases} \hat{\tilde{s}}_j(m) = 0 & \text{if } j \notin \mathcal{J}_m, \\ \hat{\tilde{\mathbf{s}}}_{\mathcal{J}_m}(m) = \mathbf{A}_{\mathcal{J}_m}^{-1} \tilde{x}(m) & \text{otherwise} \end{cases} \qquad (2.11)$$

where $\mathbf{A}_{\mathcal{J}_m}^{-1}$ is the matrix inverse of $\mathbf{A}_{\mathcal{J}_m}$ (Gribonval, 2003). Finally, the estimated source vectors in the time domain $\hat{s}(n)$ are recovered by using the inverse transform.

Experiments and Results

We performed two sets of experiments to test our algorithms. Performance is measured through the *signal to distortion ratio* (SDR), which is defined as the following in this section (Vincent, Gribonval, & Plumbley, 2007):

$$\text{SDR [dB]} = 10 \log_{10} \frac{\displaystyle\sum_{n=0}^{N-1} \sum_{j=1}^{J} \left(s_j(n) \right)^2}{\displaystyle\sum_{n=0}^{N-1} \sum_{j=1}^{J} \left(\hat{s}_j(n) - s_j(n) \right)^2}. \qquad (2.11)$$

This particular (yet standard) definition of SDR is chosen for this section because *oracle* source estimation depends on it (see below).

In the first set of experiments, we applied our methods to twenty mixtures in total (ten music mixtures and ten speech mixtures), where each mixture had $J = 3$ sources at a sampling rate of 16 kHz, with a resolution of 16 bits per sample, and length of $N = 2^{18}$ (approx. 11 s). The sources were mixed according to following mixing matrix:

$$\mathbf{A} = \begin{bmatrix} 0.21 & 0.95 & 0.64 \\ 0.98 & 0.32 & 0.77 \end{bmatrix}. \qquad (2.12)$$

For each mixture, we performed semi-blind estimations of $s(n)$ for each of the LS, WS, OT, WS/OT and WS/OT/ST partitioning schemes, with long intervals $L_L = 2^c$, where $c \in \{8, \ldots, 11\}$ (12 ms to 93 ms), and short intervals $L_S = 2^c$ where $c \in \{4, \ldots, 9\}$ (0.73 ms to 23 ms). We exclude all long-short combinations where $L_L \leq L_S$. Results are presented in Table 1, where each entry is the average over the twenty different mixtures corresponding to a particular transform scheme with given block lengths. We also compare the MPEG-like schemes to the baseline fixed basis (FB) transform (where $L_L = L_S$ and $2\eta_k = L_L$ for all k) and find that the maximum average SDR is 12.06 dB at $L_L = L_S = 2^{10}$.

For the results in Table 1, the best average SDR is approximately 12.3 dB for each transform scheme. Admittedly, there is no significant difference in performance between the different segmentation schemes, which indicates that more flexible schemes, e.g., LS, do not offer enough of a performance improvement to justify their

Table 1. Average results for MPEG-like transforms for semi-blind separation on music and speech mixtures. Long and short interval sizes are given by L_L and L_S respectively, and LS, WS, OT, WS/OT and WS/OT/ST correspond to each of the MPEG-like partitioning schemes. The best average SDR for each scheme is highlighted in bold.

Scheme	L_L	L_S					
		2^4	2^5	2^6	2^7	2^8	2^9
LS	2^8	10.45	10.50	10.51	10.55	-	-
	2^9	11.72	11.71	11.72	11.72	11.79	-
	2^{10}	12.14	12.10	12.19	12.16	12.23	12.29
	2^{11}	11.70	11.59	11.73	11.77	11.92	**12.34**
WS	2^8	10.45	10.51	10.52	10.55	-	-
	2^9	11.76	11.71	11.74	11.74	11.80	-
	2^{10}	12.16	12.14	12.18	12.16	12.23	**12.28**
	2^{11}	11.62	11.66	11.69	11.75	11.91	12.22
OT	2^8	10.68	10.66	10.65	10.64	-	-
	2^9	11.83	11.83	11.85	11.85	11.83	-
	2^{10}	12.07	12.07	12.07	12.06	12.15	12.19
	2^{11}	11.65	11.56	11.60	11.61	11.86	**12.29**
WS/OT	2^8	10.68	10.67	10.66	10.64	-	-
	2^9	11.84	11.83	11.85	11.85	11.83	-
	2^{10}	12.07	12.07	12.08	12.08	12.16	12.20
	2^{11}	11.62	11.56	11.59	11.61	11.83	**12.29**
WS/OT/ST	2^8	10.69	10.68	10.67	10.64	-	-
	2^9	11.84	11.84	11.85	11.85	11.85	-
	2^{10}	12.05	12.04	12.06	12.08	12.16	12.21
	2^{11}	11.57	11.52	11.53	11.55	11.77	**12.28**

increased computational burden. Previous results demonstrated oracle performance of approximately 25 dB, but the differences between the two cases are not surprising; in contrast to the semi-blind estimation criterion (ℓ^1-norm), the oracle estimation criterion is optimised for the performance measurement criterion (SDR). The greatest variability in average SDR occurs with changing the long interval length L_L. The SDR improvements in the demonstrated range of 1-2 dB may be significant in high fidelity applications. In each case in Table 1, the best average SDR is achieved at the greatest length for the short intervals ($L_S = 2^9$).

For the second set of experiments, we indicate the performance achievable on particular types of mixtures. We applied the best transform scheme as determined by Table 1 (that is, LS) to each instantaneous mixture in the *dev1* data set of the *Signal Separation Evaluation Campaign* (SiSEC 2008) [2] and present the results in Table 2. Also shown in the Table are *oracle estimation* results, where the L_L and L_S which give best results were determined in previous work (Nesbit, Vincent, & Plumbley, 2009). The aim of oracle estimation is to determine those J_m and $B^\lambda \in \mathcal{L}$ which give the best possible separation performance for every TF index m. This allows us to judge the difficulty of estimating the sources $s(n)$ from a given

Table 2. Results for LS scheme for semi-blind and oracle separation on SiSEC 2008 data

Mixture	J	Semi-blind			Oracle		
		L_L	L_S	Avg SDR [dB]	L_L	L_S	Avg SDR [dB]
3 Female Speakers	3	2^9	2^5	10.35	2^{10}	2^4	24.09
4 Female Speakers	4	2^{11}	2^9	7.04	2^{10}	2^4	18.61
3 Male Speakers	3	2^9	2^9	8.41	2^{10}	2^4	18.56
4 Male Speakers	4	2^{10}	2^9	5.62	2^{10}	2^4	14.37
Music with no drums	3	2^{10}	2^7	16.33	2^{10}	2^4	34.26
Music with drums	3	2^9	2^4	11.95	2^{10}	2^4	28.06

mixture $x(n)$, and to gain insight into the upper performance bounds of our class of separation algorithms (Vincent, Gribonval, & Plumbley, 2007). Oracle results are computed by jointly determining the local activity patterns J_m and the best orthogonal basis $B^\lambda \in \mathcal{L}$ which maximise the SDR. As oracle estimation depends on knowing the reference source signals $s(n)$ and the mixing matrix $\mathbf{A}$ it is intended to be used for algorithm evaluation rather than for practical (semi-)blind separation applications.

In contrast to Table 1, Table 2 shows individual, rather than average, results. Previous oracle results for the LS and WS schemes show that the best average SDR was obtained at the least length for the short intervals ($L_S = 2^4$), where we suggested that a library which allows fine-grained placement of the long windows improves performance (Nesbit, Vincent, & Plumbley, 2009). The current ℓ^1-norm criterion does not lead to such a basis being selected, but a semi-blind criterion which admits such fine-grained placement will be a good step towards closing the performance gap between semi-blind and oracle performance.

SPARSE COMPONENT ANALYSIS BASED ON A LEARNED DICTIONARY

In this section we consider the problem of audio source separation when a set of anechoic mix-

tures generated by the same number of sources are observed. The problem is again considered within the SCA framework, where the dictionary used for the sparsifying transform is now learned from the observed data, rather than selected from a fixed set of pre-existing bases.

Dictionaries that are inferred from the training data have the advantage of being more finely tuned to the data itself. Their main disadvantage is the limit on the size of the dictionary that can be trained, due to the complexity of the training algorithms, and the limit on the size of the signal that can be analysed (Rubinstein, Zibulevsky & Elad, 2009). Two pre-existing dictionary learning methods are the ICA and K-SVD algorithms. The reader is referred to (Abdallah & Plumbley, 2004) and (Aharon, Elad & Bruckstein, 2006), respectively, for more details on these techniques. They were applied to the audio separation problem in (Jafari et al., 2008), and (Jafari & Plumbley, 2008) respectively, and therefore will be used later in comparisons with the separation approach based on the *greedy adaptive dictionary* (GAD) algorithm presented here. In this section, we also summarise the other SCA steps necessary to separate the sources.

Sparsifying Step Learning the Dictionary

We consider a data vector, $\mathbf{x}(n)$, which contains two observed signals. The GAD algorithm is used to find a basis set that encodes both spatial and temporal correlations in the observed data. To do this, the data vector $\mathbf{x}(n)$ is reshaped into a matrix $\mathbf{X}$, such that sample pairs from the former are stacked to form the columns of the latter. Reshaping the input in this fashion allows correlations between microphones and across time to be modelled.

Thus, $\mathbf{x}(n)$ is reshaped into a $P \times Q$ matrix, where successive blocks of $P/2$ sample pairs are taken from the mixture vector, with an overlap of T samples. Then the (p,q)-th element of the matrix $\mathbf{X}$ is given by

$$[\mathbf{X}]_{p,q} = \begin{cases} x_1 \left((q-1)Z + (p+1)/2 \right) & : p \text{ odd} \\ x_2 \left((q-1)Z + p/2 \right) & : p \text{ even} \end{cases}$$

where

$Z = P/2 - T$, and $p \in \{0,...,P-1\}$, and $q \in \{0,...,Q-1\}$.

The q-th column of the newly constructed matrix is represented by the signal block $\mathbf{x}_q = [x_1 \ldots x_P]^T$, with $Q > P$, and the dictionary is learned from the columns of $\mathbf{X}$. Therefore, the sparse representation problem can be stated as follows: given a real valued signal $\mathbf{x}_q = [x_0 \ldots x_{P-1}]^T$, and an orthogonal dictionary D, we seek a decomposition of $\mathbf{x}_q$, such that

$$\mathbf{x}_q = \sum_{m=0}^{N-1} \alpha_q(m)\psi(m), \quad \forall q \in \{0,...,Q-1\}$$

(3.1)

where $\alpha_q(m)$ is the coefficient of expansion relating to the q-th column of $\mathbf{X}$.

Greedy Adaptive Dictionary Algorithm (GAD)

The GAD algorithm is a greedy method that adaptively learns a data dependent dictionary by sequentially extracting the columns of the matrix

$\mathbf{X}$. At each iteration, the column of $\mathbf{X}$ with highest ℓ^2-norm becomes a dictionary element; all the columns of $\mathbf{X}$ are decreased by an appropriate amount, determined by the currently selected atom and the expansion coefficients. As a result, the column corresponding to the current atom is set to zero, thus reducing the space dimension by 1. Then, each atom subsequently extracted is orthogonal to the current atom. Hence, the GAD algorithm yields an orthogonal transform.

At ach iteration, extraction of a new atom depends on finding the column of $\mathbf{X}$ that satisfies:

$$\max_q \frac{\|\mathbf{x}_q\|_2}{\|\mathbf{x}_q\|_1}$$

(3.2)

where $\|\cdot\|_1$ and $\|\cdot\|_2$ denote the ℓ^1- and ℓ^2-norm respectively. Thus at each iteration, the method reduces the energy of the data by a maximum amount, across all frames, while ensuring that the ℓ^1-norm is reduced by a minimum amount. It is interesting to note how the expression in Equation (3.2) relates to the sparsity index ξ for a signal vector s_q, defined in (Tan & Fevotte, 2005) as

$$\xi_q \triangleq \frac{\|s_q\|_1}{\|s_q\|_2}.$$

(3.3)

The sparsity index quantifies the sparsity of a signal, and is such that the smaller ξ_q is, the sparser the vector s_q. Clearly, Equation (3.2) is equivalent to

$$\min_q \xi_q.$$

(3.4)

Thus, by ensuring that the ℓ^1-norm is minimum, the proposed algorithm seeks a sparse dictionary by construction. The proposed sparse adaptive dictionary algorithm solves the maximization problem in Equation (3.2) according to the following steps:

1. Initialisation:
   set $m = 0$;
   ensure that the columns of $\mathbf{X}$ have unit ℓ^1-norm

$$\mathbf{x}'_q = \frac{\mathbf{x}_q}{\|\mathbf{x}_q\|_1} \qquad (3.5)$$

   initialise the residual matrix

$$\mathbf{R}^0 = \mathbf{X}' \qquad (3.6)$$

where $\mathbf{R}(m) = [\mathbf{r}_0(m),...,\mathbf{r}_{Q-1}(m)]$, and $\mathbf{r}_q(m) = [r_0(m)...r_{Q-1}(m)]$ is a residual column vector corresponding to the q-th column of $\mathbf{R}(m)$.

2. Compute the ℓ^2-norm of each frame

$$E(q) = \|\mathbf{r}_q(m)\|_2 = \sum_{q=0}^{Q-1} |\mathbf{r}_q(m)|^2 \qquad (3.7)$$

3. Find the index $\hat{q}$ corresponding to the signal block with largest ℓ^2-norm, $\mathbf{r}_{\hat{q}}(m)$

$$\hat{q} = \arg\max_{q \in \mathbb{Q}}\left(E(q)\right) \qquad (3.8)$$

where $\mathbb{Q} = \{0,...,Q-1\}$ is the set of all indices pointing to the columns of $\mathbf{R}(m)$.

4. Set the m-th dictionary element $\Psi(m)$ to be equal to the signal block with largest ℓ^2-norm $\mathbf{r}_{\hat{q}}(m)$

$$\psi(m) = \frac{\mathbf{r}_{\hat{q}}(m)}{\|\mathbf{r}_{\hat{q}}(m)\|_1} \qquad (3.9)$$

5. For all the columns of the residual matrix $\mathbf{R}(m)$, evaluate the coefficients of expansion $\alpha_q(m)$, given by the inner product between the residual vector $\mathbf{r}_q(m)$, and the atom $\Psi(m)$

$$\alpha_q(m) = \left\langle\mathbf{r}_q(m), \psi(m)\right\rangle, \ \forall q = 0,...,Q-1 \qquad (3.10)$$

6. For all the columns of the residual matrix $\mathbf{R}(m)$, compute the new residual, by removing the component along the chosen atom, for each element q in $\mathbf{r}_q(m)$

$$\mathbf{r}_q(m+1) = \mathbf{r}_q(m) - \frac{\alpha_q(m)}{\left\langle\psi(m),\psi(m)\right\rangle}\psi(m), \ \forall q = 0,...,Q-1 \qquad (3.11)$$

7. Repeat from step 2, until $m = N$-1.

The term in the denominator of $\alpha_q(m) / \left\langle\psi(m),\psi(m)\right\rangle$ in Equation (3.11), is included to ensure that the coefficient of expansion $\alpha_q(m)$ corresponding to the inner product between the selected atom $\Psi(m)$ and the frame of maximum ℓ^2-norm $\mathbf{r}_{\hat{q}}(m)$, is normalised to 1. Then, the corresponding column of the residual matrix $\mathbf{R}(m)$ is set to zero, since the whole atom is removed. This is the step that ensures that the transform is orthogonal. This implies that the inverse transform is evaluated straightforwardly from $\mathbf{X}^L = \mathbf{DY}$, where $\mathbf{X}^L$ is the $L \times L$ matrix which approximates $\mathbf{X}$ using the first L atoms, and $\mathbf{D} = [(\psi(0))^T,...,(\psi(Q-1))^T]$ is the dictionary matrix. The method has the implicit advantage of producing atoms that are directly relevant to the data being analyzed.

Since the algorithm operates upon a stereo signal, whose data samples have been reshaped into the matrix, $\mathbf{X}$, as described earlier, GAD learns a set of stereo atoms, $\psi_{(i)}(m)$, $i = 1, 2$ from the columns of $\mathbf{X}$. For comparison purposes, we also use ICA and K-SVD to construct stereo dictionaries from the data, and apply the remaining SCA steps in all cases, to obtain estimates for the separated sources. The reshaping of the data allows modelling of correlations between the microphones and across time, and therefore the stereo atoms that are learned encode information regarding the mixing process. The clustering approaches outlined below aim at exploiting this property.

Estimating the Mixing Matrix by Clustering the Atom Pairs

It was shown in (Jafari et al., 2008), that the atom pairs encode information regarding the time delays for the two source signals, and therefore the atoms can be clustered according to the time delay existing between the atoms $\psi_{(j)}(m), j = 1,2; m = \{0,...,N-1\}$, in the pair. The time delay, or direction of arrival (DOA), is evaluated according to the generalized cross-correlation with phase transform (GCC-PHAT) algorithm in (Knapp & Carter, 1976).

GCC-PHAT typically results in a function that exhibits a single sharp peak at the lag corresponding to the time delay between the two signals, which is consistent with the learned atom pairs exhibiting a dominant DOA. Thus, we seek to find the delay at which the peak occurs for each atom pair, and use the K-means clustering algorithm on this data, in order to group the atoms. K-means will identify two clusters, whose centers correspond to the time delay for each source $\gamma_j, j = 1,2$. This can then be used to identify those atoms that relate to one source or the other, by finding a set of indices $\gamma_j, j = 1,2$, that map the m-th atom to the source to which it belongs

$$\gamma_j = \{m \mid (Y_j - \Delta) \leq \tau_m \leq (Y_j + \Delta)\}$$

(3.12)

within some threshold Δ of the cluster centroid. We also define a 'discard' cluster

$$\gamma_0 = \{m \mid m \notin \gamma_j, j = 1,2\}$$

(3.13)

for those atoms that will not be associated with any of the j sources.

Estimating the Source and Inverting the Transform

Reconstruction of the source is performed using binary masking, followed by inverting the sparsifying transform. Two mask matrices $\mathbf{H}_j(m), j = 1,2$ are defined as

$$\mathbf{H}_j(m) = \mathrm{diag}(h_j(0),...,h_j(N-1))$$

(3.14)

where

$$h_j(m) = \begin{cases} 1 & \text{if } m \in \gamma_j \\ 0 & \text{otherwise} \end{cases}$$

(3.15)

for $m = 0,...,N-1$. Thus, the diagonal elements of $\mathbf{H}_j(m)$ set to one or zero depending on whether an atom is considered to belong to the j-th source. Then, the estimated image $\hat{\tilde{\mathbf{X}}}_j$ of the j-th source is given by

$$\hat{\tilde{\mathbf{X}}}_j = \mathbf{D}^T \mathbf{H}_j(m) \mathbf{D} \mathbf{X}_j$$

(3.16)

Finally, the vector of images of the j-th source at both microphones is obtained by transforming the matrix $\hat{\tilde{\mathbf{X}}}_j$ back into a vector, to find the source image $\hat{\mathbf{x}}^j(n) = \left[\hat{x}_1^j(n), \hat{x}_2^j(n)\right]^T$. This entails reversing the reshaping process that was carried out on the data before applying the SCA method.

Experimental Results

In this section we compare the GAD, ICA, and K-SVD algorithms, for the analysis of a male speech signal, and in all cases we look for a dictionary containing 512 atoms. The KSVD Matlab Toolbox was used to implement the K-SVD algorithm[3]. The number of nonzero entries T_0 in the coefficient update stage was set to 10.

To determine how sparse the representation obtained with the proposed approach is, we plot the sparsity index for the transform coefficients obtained with the three methods. The sparsity index of a signal γ is defined in Equation (3.3) as $\xi = \| y \|_1 / \| y \|_2$; generally, the lower the sparsity index is, the sparser the signal γ. Figure 2 shows a plot of the sparsity index for the original signal blocks in $\mathbf{X}$, and for the coefficients of expansion obtained with the GAD, ICA and K-SVD algorithms. We can see that the signal transformed with the GAD algorithm is sparser than in the time domain, and than the coefficients obtained with ICA.

K-SVD yields significantly sparser results, thanks to the strong sparsity constraint it imposes. Nonetheless, while such a strong constraint leads to a very sparse signal decomposition, the accuracy of the approximation decreases proportionally with T_0. This can be seen by considering the approximation error $\in$ obtained when the function f is approximated by $\tilde{f}$,

$$\epsilon = \| \tilde{f} - f \|. \qquad (3.17)$$

It was found that for K-SVD with $T_0 = 3$ nonzero entries, $\in = 0.0036$, while with $T_0 = 10$, $\in = 0.0010$, the approximation error becomes almost a third. Therefore, in what follows, we use K-SVD with $T_0 = 10$.

Table 3 shows the approximation error for all algorithms, describing the accuracy of the approximation as the number of atoms used in the signal reconstruction decreases from 512 to 50. The results indicate that the GAD algorithm performs better, while ICA and K-SVD yield signal

Figure 2. Sparsity index for the GAD algorithm, compared to the original signal, and to ICA and K-SVD for every block in the observation matrix. The GAD algorithm consistently achieves a sparser representation than ICA, but not as sparse as K-SVD.

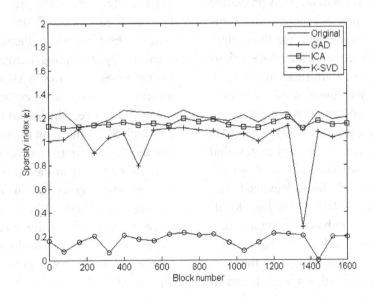

Table 3. Approximation error for the GAD, ICA and K-SVD algorithms. All values are expressed in decibels (dB).

Method	Number of Atoms					
	512	400	300	200	100	50
GAD	0.0000	0.0007	0.0017	0.0028	0.0053	0.0068
ICA	0.0000	0.0022	0.0043	0.0078	0.0122	0.0151
K-SVD	0.0010	0.0052	0.0069	0.0093	0.0103	0.0135

approximations that suffer most from the reduction in number of atoms, with ICA performance suddenly worsening as the number of atoms goes from 200 to 100. This behaviour is a result of the way GAD works. Since the atoms with highest ℓ^2-norm are extracted first, as new atoms are found, they have less information to convey. This, however, is not the case with ICA and K-SVD. Therefore, the GAD algorithm results in good signal approximations even when the number of atoms is reduced.

The three methods were then used to address the audio source separation problem. A stereo mixture was generated when a male and female speech signals were synthetically mixed according to the anechoic mixing model in Equation (1.1), with delays of 7 and -29 samples. Separation was performed with GAD, K-SVD and ICA as the sparsifying transforms in the SCA procedure described earlier. The plots in Figure 3 show some of the atom pairs obtained with the three algorithms. Comparing these, we see that all algorithms extract atoms that capture information unique to the analyzed signal, with the ICA-based method finding atoms that appear to represent very localised and elementary components. The GAD method yields much less elementary atoms, that appear to capture more information about the signal, and which are still fairly localized. The atoms extracted with K-SVD are the least localized, and do not appear to be capturing any particular features of the speech signal, but perhaps more general characteristics. Moreover, the atom pairs obtained with all methods were found to encode how the extracted features are received at the microphone, that is, they capture information about time-delays and amplitude differences.

Figure 4 shows estimates for the time delays, and their histograms, obtained by the three algorithms from all atom pairs. All methods were found to correctly identify the time delays as 7 and -29 samples. Their performance was also evaluated using a slightly modified version of the the signal-to-distortion ratio compared to the previous section, which required that particular definition for oracle estimation of source within the adaptive LOT framework. Here, the modified signal-to-distortion ratio is denoted SDR*, and is combined with two additional separation performance metrics: the *signal-to-interference ratio* (SIR) and *signal-to-artifacts ratio* (SAR) measuring, respectively, the distortion due to interfering sources and the distortion due to artifacts resulting from the separation process itself (Fevotte, Gribonval & Vincent, 2005). Table 4 shows the criteria obtained, where the single figures were obtained by averaging across all sources and microphones. The low SAR and SDR* values indicate that large artifacts are present on the recovered source, which dominate the distortion. The high SIR values, on the other hand, suggest that the desired source can now be heard clearly, or more clearly than the other source. Informal listening tests suggest that in all cases the separation algorithm has the effect of making each source more audible within the mixture, but do not clearly separate them. This indicates that perhaps sparsity alone is not a sufficient criterion for separation.

Figure 3. Examples of the atom pairs learned with the ICA, K-SVD and GAD methods. Within each pair the signals are delayed relative to each other in time.

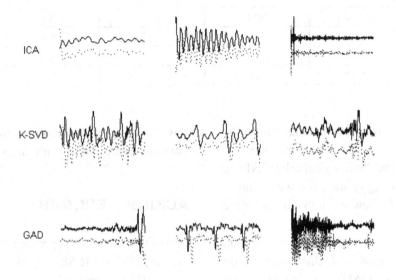

Figure 4. Upper plots: Scatterplots of the estimated time delays for all basis vectors, where the delays between signals within the atoms are apparent. Lower plots: Histograms associated with of the upper plots

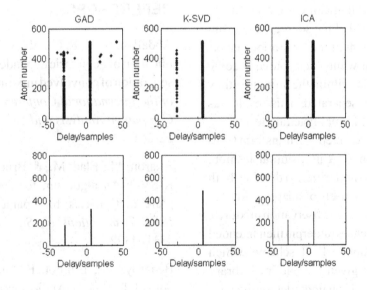

CONCLUSION

In this chapter we have addressed the audio source separation problem within a sparse component analysis (SCA) framework. When the mixing is instantaneous and underdetermined, sparse signal representations are learned with adaptive lapped orthogonal transforms (LOTs). This method demonstrated average SDR performance of 12-13 dB on mixtures of music and speech signals. Further

Table 4. Objective performance of GAD, K-SVD and ICA-based separation algorithms. All values are expressed in decibels (dB).

Method	SDR	SAR	SIR
GAD	3.10	3.07	9.80
ICA	3.73	3.87	8.43
K-SVD	1.31	2.58	7.59

work includes extending this technique from the semi-blind separation case considered here, to the blind situation; preliminary experiments have shown very promising results, and we intend to incorporate that framework into our adaptive transform schemes.

SCA has also been applied to the anechoic, determined mixing problem. In this case, a greedy adaptive dictionary (GAD) learning algorithm was presented, and it was compared to the ICA and K-SVD methods; it was found to give good signal approximations, even as the number of atoms in the reconstructions decreases considerably. The GAD algorithm can correctly identify the directions of arrival of the source signals, but an objective assessment of the separation performance indicated that while each source become more clearly audible within the mixture, they were not completely separated. This result was corroborated by an informal listening test.

Hence, we have presented two transform techniques that fit within SCA in a similar fashion. They have important similarities, in that they both represent the sources sparsely by adapting directly to the estimated sources and observation mixtures. However, their differences underpin their intended applications; the adaptive LOT scheme, which adapts the transform given a predefined library of bases, operates within an underdetermined, instantaneous mixing framework, whereas the GAD algorithm, which adaptively learns the dictionary atoms per se, is intended for the anechoic case. In our future work, we intend to look at the extension of the GAD method to the underdetermined case, and the LOT scheme to anechoic and convolu-

tive mixing problems, and compare directly the performance of the two methods.

ACKNOWLEDGMENT

Part of this work was supported by EPSRC grants GR/S82213/01, GR/S85900/01, EP/E045235/1, & EP/G007144/1, and EU FET-Open project 225913 "SMALL". Part of this work was done when AN was hosted as a visiting researcher at INRIA.

REFERENCES

Abdallah, S. A., & Plumbley, M. D. (2004). Application of geometric dependency analysis to the separation of convolved mixtures. In *Proceedings of the International Conference on Independent Component Analysis and Signal Separation* (pp. 22-24).

Aharon, M., Elad, M., & Bruckstein, A. (2006). K-SVD: An algorithm for designing overcomplete dictionaries for sparse representations. *IEEE Transactions on Signal Processing, 54*, 4311–4322.

Benaroya, L., Bimbot, F., Gravier, G., & Gribonval, R. (2003). Audio source separation with one sensor for robust speech recognition. In *NOLISP-2003*.(paper 030).

Bertin, N., Badeau, R., & Vincent, E. (2009). *Enforcing harmonicity and smoothness in Bayesian non-negative matrix factorization applied to polyphonic music transcription.* (Report No. 2009D006). Paris, France: Telecom ParisTech

Bofill, P. & Zibulevsky, M. (2001). Underdetermined blind source separation using sparse representations. *Signal Processing, 81,* 2353–2362.

Daudet, L., & Torrésani, B. (2002). Hybrid representations for audiophonic signal encoding. *Signal Processing, 82,* 1595–1617.

Davis, G. (1994). *Adaptive nonlinear approximations.* Unpublished doctoral dissertation, New York University.

Fevotte, C., Gribonval, R., & Vincent, E. (2005). *BSS_EVAL Toolbox User Guide* (Technical Report No. 1706).Retrieved from http://www.irisa.fr/metiss/bss_eval/: IRISA.

Górecki, L., & Domanski, M. (2005). Adaptive dictionaries for matching pursuit with separable decompositions. In *Proceedings of the European Signal Processing Conference*(pp.786-790).

Gribonval, R. (2003). Piecewise linear source separation. In Unser, M.A., Aldroubi, A., & Laine, A. F. (Eds.), *Wavelets: Applications in Signal and Image Processing X, Proceedings of SPIE* (pp. 297–310). San Diego, USA: SPIE.

Gribonval, R., & Lesage, S. (2006). A survey of sparse component analysis for blind source separation: principles, perspectives, and new challanges. In *Proceedings of the European Symposium on Artificial Neural Networks* (pp. 323-330).

Hesse, C. W., & James, C. J. (2006). On semi-blind source separation using spatial constraints with applications in EEG analysis. *IEEE Transactions on Bio-Medical Engineering, 53,* 2525–2534.

Huang, Y., Pollak, I., Bouman, C. A., & Do, M. N. (2006). Best basis search in lapped dictionaries. *IEEE Transactions on Signal Processing, 54,* 651–664.

Jafari, M. G., & Plumbley, M. D. (2008). Separation of stereo speech signals based on a sparse dictionary algorithm. In *Proceedings of the European Signal Processing Conference.* (pp.786-790).

Jafari, M. G., Vincent, E., Abdallah, S. A., Plumbley, M. D., & Davies, M. E. (2008). An adaptive stereo basis method for convolutive blind audio source separation. *Neurocomputing, 71,* 2087–2097.

Jafari, M. G., Wang, W., Chambers, J. A., Hoya, T., & Cichocki, A. (2006). Sequential blind source separation based exclusively on second-order statistics developed for a class of periodic signals. *IEEE Transactions on Signal Processing, 54,* 1028–1040.

Knapp, C., & Carter, G. (1976). The generalized correlation method for estimation of time delay. *IEEE Transactions on Acoustic, Speech, and Signal Processing, 24,* 320-327.

Mallat, S. (1999). *A Wavelet Tour of Signal Processing* (2nd ed.). San Diego, CA: Academic Press.

Nesbit, A., Vincent, E., & Plumbley, M. D. (2009). Extension of sparse, adaptive signal decompositions to semi-blind audio source separation. In *Proceedings of the Independent Component Analysis and Signal Separation* (pp. 605-612).

O'Grady, P. D., Pearlmutter, B. A., & Rickard, S. T. (2005). Survery of sparse and non-sparse methods in source separation. *International Journal of Imaging Systems and Technology, 15,* 18–33.

Ravelli, E., & Daudet, L. (2006). Representations of audio signals in overcomplete dictionaries: what is the link between redundancy factor and coding properties? In *Proceedings of the International Conference on Digital Audio effects* (pp. 267-270).

Rubinstein, R., Zibulevsky, M., & Elad, M. (2009Submitted to). *Learning sparse dictionaries for sparse signal representation.* IEEE Transactions on Signal Proceedings.

Saab, R., Yilmaz, O., McKeown, M. J., & Abugharbieh, R. (2005). Underdetermined sparse blind source separation with delays. In *Proceedings of the Workshop on Signal Processing with Adaptive Sparse Structured Representations.*

Tan, V., & Fevotte, C. (2005). A study of the effect of source sparsity for various transforms on blind audio source separation performance. In *Proceedings of the Workshop on Signal Processing*

Vincent, E., Gribonval, R., & Plumbley, M. D. (2007). Oracle estimators for the benchmarking of source separation algorithms. *Signal Processing, 87*, 1933–1950.

Vincent, E., Jafari, M. G., Abdallah, S. A., Plumbley, M. D., & Davies, M. E. (2010). Probabilistic modeling paradigms for audio source separation. In *Machine Audition: Principles, Algorithms and Systems*. Hershey, PA: IGI Global.

Winter, S., Sawada, H., & Makino, S. (2006). Geometrical interpretation of the PCA subspace approach for overdetermined blind source separation. *EURASIP Journal on Applied Signal Processing, 2006*, 176–186.

Woodruff, J., Pardo, B., & Dannenberg, R. (2006). Remixing stereo music with score-informed source separation. In *Proceedings of the Seventh International Conference on Music Information Retrieval* (pp. 314-319).

Xiong, Z., Ramchandran, K., Herley, C., & Orchard, M. T. (1997). Flexible tree-structured signal expansions using time-varying wavelet packets. *IEEE Transactions on Signal Processing, 43*, 333–345.

Yilmaz, Ö., & Rickard, S. (2004). Blind separation of speech mixtures via time-frequency masking. *IEEE Transactions on Signal Processing, 52*, 1830–1847.

Zibulevsky, M., & Pearlmutter, B. A. (2001). Blind source separation by sparse decomposition in a signal dictionary. *Neural Computation, 13*(4), 863–882.

ENDNOTES

[1] Although Bofill (2008) specifically uses the STFT, the mixing matrix estimation algorithm can readily be adapted to use the LOT framework.

[2] Available online at http://sisec.wiki.irisa.fr/tiki-index.php.

[3] The K-SVD Matlab Toolbox is available at http://www.cs.technion.ac.il/~elad/software/

Section 3
Audio Transcription, Mining and Information Retrieval

Chapter 11
Itakura–Saito Nonnegative Factorizations of the Power Spectrogram for Music Signal Decomposition

Cédric Févotte
CNRS LTCI; TELECOM ParisTech, France

ABSTRACT

Nonnegative matrix factorization (NMF) is a popular linear regression technique in the fields of machine learning and signal/image processing. Much research about this topic has been driven by applications in audio. NMF has been for example applied with success to automatic music transcription and audio source separation, where the data is usually taken as the magnitude spectrogram of the sound signal, and the Euclidean distance or Kullback-Leibler divergence are used as measures of fit between the original spectrogram and its approximate factorization. In this chapter the authors give evidence of the relevance of considering factorization of the power spectrogram, with the Itakura-Saito (IS) divergence. Indeed, IS-NMF is shown to be connected to maximum likelihood inference of variance parameters in a well-defined statistical model of superimposed Gaussian components and this model is in turn shown to be well suited to audio. Furthermore, the statistical setting opens doors to Bayesian approaches and to a variety of computational inference techniques. They discuss in particular model order selection strategies and Markov regularization of the activation matrix, to account for time-persistence in audio. This chapter also discusses extensions of NMF to the multichannel case, in both instantaneous or convolutive recordings, possibly underdetermined. The authors present in particular audio source separation results of a real stereo musical excerpt.

DOI: 10.4018/978-1-61520-919-4.ch011

INTRODUCTION

Nonnegative matrix factorization (NMF) is a linear regression technique, employed for non-subtractive, part-based representation of nonnegative data. Given a data matrix $\mathbf{V}$ of dimensions $F \times N$ with nonnegative entries, NMF is the problem of finding a factorization

$$\mathbf{V} \approx \mathbf{WH} \qquad (1)$$

where $\mathbf{W}$ and $\mathbf{H}$ are nonnegative matrices of dimensions $F \times K$ and $K \times N$, respectively. K is usually chosen such that $FK + KN << FN$, hence reducing the data dimension. Early works about NMF include (Paatero, 1997) and (Lee and Seung, 1999), the latter in particular prove very influential. NMF has been applied to diverse problems (such as pattern recognition, clustering, data mining, source separation, collaborative filtering) in many areas (such as text processing, bioinformatics, signal/image processing, finance). Much research about NMF has been driven by applications in audio, namely automatic music transcription (Smaragdis and Brown, 2003; Abdallah and Plumbley, 2004) and source separation (Virtanen, 2007; Smaragdis, 2007), where the data $\mathbf{V}$ is usually taken as the magnitude spectrogram of the audio signal.

Along Vector Quantization (VQ), Principal Component Analysis (PCA) or Independent Component Analysis (ICA), NMF provides an unsupervised linear representation of data, in the sense that a data point $\mathbf{v}_n$ (n^{th} column of $\mathbf{V}$) is approximated as a linear combination of salient features. (see Table 1)

A distinctive feature of NMF with respect to VQ, PCA or ICA is that it keeps $\mathbf{W}$ and $\mathbf{h}_n$ nonnegative, hence improving the interpretability of the learnt dictionary and of the activation coefficients when the data is nonnegative. More precisely, the nonnegativity restriction on $\mathbf{W}$ allows the learnt features to belong to the same space than data, while the nonnegative restriction on $\mathbf{H}$ favors part-based decomposition as subtrac-

Table 1.

$\mathbf{V}_n \approx$	$\mathbf{W}$	$\mathbf{h}_n$
	"explanatory variables"	"regressors",
	"basis", "dictionary",	"expansion coefficients",
	"patterns"	"activation coefficients"

tive combination are forbidden, i.e, the data has to be "assembled" from the elementary building blocks in $\mathbf{W}$. As such, in their seminal paper Lee and Seung (1999) show how parts of faces (noise, eyes, cheeks, etc.) can be learnt from a training set composed of faces, when the bases returned by PCA or VQ are more "holistic" in the sense that each feature attempts to generalize as much as possible the entire dataset. The effect of NMF onto an audio spectrogram is illustrated on Figure 1. It can be seen that the NMF model is well suited to the composite structure of music in the sense that the factorization can be expected to separate mingled patterns in the spectrogram; the patterns may correspond to spectra of elementary musical objects such as notes or percussions or, as we shall see later, higher level structures.

In the literature, the factorization (1) is usually achieved through minimization of a measure of fit defined by

$$D(\mathbf{V} \mid \mathbf{WH}) = \sum_{f=1}^{F} \sum_{n=1}^{N} d([\mathbf{V}]_{fn} \mid [\mathbf{WH}]_{fn}) \qquad (2)$$

where $d(x|y)$ is a scalar cost function, typically a positive function with a single minimum 0 for $x = y$. The minimization, with respect to $\mathbf{W}$ and $\mathbf{H}$, is subject to nonnegativity constraints on the coefficients of both factors. Popular cost functions are the Euclidean distance, here defined as

$$d_{EUC}(x \mid y) = \frac{1}{2}(x - y)^2 \qquad (3)$$

and the (generalized) Kullback-Leibler (KL) divergence, also referred to as I-divergence, defined by

Figure 1. Illustration of the effect of NMF on an audio spectrogram

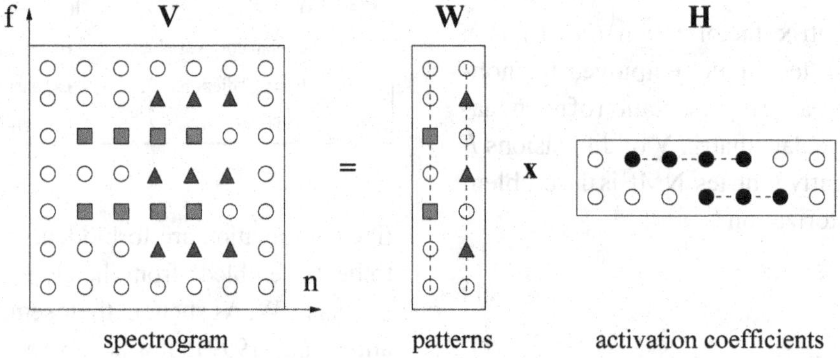

$$d_{KL}(x \mid y) = x \log \frac{x}{y} - x + y. \qquad (4)$$

More general families of cost functions have also been considered for NMF, such as Csiszár and Bregman divergences (Cichocki et al., 2006; Dhillon and Sra, 2005). The choice of the NMF cost function should be driven by the problem setup and type of data, and if a good deal of literature is devoted to improving performance of algorithms given a cost function, little literature has been devoted to how to choose a cost function with respect to a particular type of data and application.

In this chapter we are specifically interested in NMF with the Itakura-Saito (IS) divergence, for its relevance to the decomposition of audio power spectrograms, as we intend to show. The expression of the IS divergence is given by

$$d_{IS}(x \mid y) = \frac{x}{y} - \log \frac{x}{y} - 1 \qquad (5)$$

This divergence was obtained by Itakura and Saito (1968) from the maximum likelihood (ML) estimation of short-time speech spectra under autoregressive modeling. It was presented as "a measure of the goodness of fit between two spectra" and became popular in the speech community during the seventies. It was in particular

praised for the good perceptual properties of the reconstructed signals it led to (Gray et al., 1980).

As we shall see, this divergence has interesting properties. It is in particular scale-invariant, meaning that low energy components of **V** bear the same relative importance as high energy ones. This is relevant to situations in which the coefficients of **V** have a large dynamic range, such as in audio short-term spectra. The IS divergence also leads to desirable statistical interpretations of the NMF problem. Indeed, IS-NMF can be recast as ML estimation of **W** and **H** in a model of superimposed Gaussian components. Equivalently, IS-NMF can be interpreted as ML of **W** and **H** in multiplicative Gamma noise. As will shall see, this statistical framework open doors to Bayesian approaches to NMF, that can account for regularization constraints on either **W** or **H**, model order selection as well as a variety of computational inference techniques.

This chapter is organized as follows. Section "NMF with the Itakura-Saito divergence" is devoted to the general presentation of NMF with the IS divergence. We discuss its scale invariance, its nonconvexity, the latent statistical model and describe algorithms for achieving IS-NMF. Decomposition results of a simple case-study piano sequence are presented; they illustrate the relevance of IS-NMF of the power spectrogram as compared to the more standard approach consisting of KL-NMF of the magnitude spectrogram. Section "Bayesian extensions to Itakura-Saito NMF" describe Bayesian extensions of IS-NMF. We present in particular a model order selection strategy based on *automatic relevance determination* that allows to determine an "efficient" number of components K. We also describe an IS-NMF algorithm with a Markov model for $\mathbf{H}$ that promotes smoothness of the activation coefficients. We also mention advanced computational techniques for NMF, based on Markov chain Monte Carlo (MCMC). While Sections "NMF with the Itakura-Saito divergence" and "Bayesian extensions to Itakura-Saito NMF" inherently assume single-channel data, Section "Multichannel IS-NMF" describes extensions to multichannel data: we present nonnegative *tensor* factorization (NTF) techniques for either instantaneously or convolutively mixed data, that allow joint processing of the channel spectrograms. Finally, last section draws conclusions and perspectives of this work. This chapter intends to describe and discuss in a unified framework parts of recent contributions (Févotte et al., 2009; Ozerov and Févotte, 2010; Tan and Févotte, 2009; Ozerov et al., 2009; Févotte and Cemgil, 2009; Durrieu et al., 2009, 2010).

NMF WITH THE ITAKURA-SAITO DIVERGENCE

This section is devoted to a general presentation of NMF with the IS divergence. In the following, the entries of matrices $\mathbf{V}$, $\mathbf{W}$ and $\mathbf{H}$ are denoted v_{fn}, w_{fk} and h_{kn} respectively. Lower case bold letters will in general denote columns, such that $\mathbf{W} = [\mathbf{w}_1, \ldots, \mathbf{w}_K]$, while lower case plain letters with a single index denote rows, such that $\mathbf{H} = [h_1^T, \ldots, h_K^T]^T$. We also define the matrix, whose entries are denoted $\hat{v}_{fn}$. Where these conventions clash, the intended meaning should be clear from the context.

Properties

Scale Invariance and Nonconvexity

An interesting property of the IS divergence is scale-invariance, i.e,

$$d_{IS}(\lambda x | \lambda y) = d_{IS}(x | y). \tag{6}$$

This property is not shared by the popular Euclidean and KL cost functions. As such we have $d_{EUC}(\lambda x | \lambda y) = \lambda^2 d_{EUC}(x|y)$ and $d_{KL}(\lambda x | \lambda y) = \lambda d_{KL}(x|y)$. The scale invariance means that same relative weight is given to small and large coefficients of $\mathbf{V}$ in cost function (2), in the sense that a bad fit of the factorization for a low-power coefficient v_{fn} will cost as much as a bad fit for a higher power coefficient $v_{f'n'}$. In contrast, factorizations obtained with the Euclidean distance or the KL divergence will rely more heavily on the largest coefficients and less precision is to be expected in the estimation of the low-power components. The scale invariance of the IS divergence is relevant to the decomposition of audio spectra, which typically exhibit exponential power decrease along frequency f and also usually comprise low-power transient components such as note attacks together with higher power components such as tonal parts of sustained notes.

A property shared by the Euclidean and KL costs $d_{EUC}(x|y)$ and $d_{KL}(x|y)$ is convexity with respect to y. This means that in their cases, the cost function $D(\mathbf{V}|\mathbf{WH})$ is at least convex with respect to either $\mathbf{W}$ or $\mathbf{H}$. In contrast, the IS divergence $d_{IS}(x|y)$ is, as a function of y, convex on $(0,2x]$ and concave on $[2x, \infty)$, see Figure 2, which, we observed in practice, makes it more prone to local minima.

Statistical Interpretations

Very interestingly, IS-NMF can be viewed as maximum likelihood estimation of $\mathbf{W}$ and $\mathbf{H}$ in

Figure 2. Euclidean, KL and IS costs d(x|y) as a function of y and for x = 1. The Euclidean and KL divergences are convex on (0, ∞). The IS divergence is convex on (0,2x] and concave on [2x, ∞).

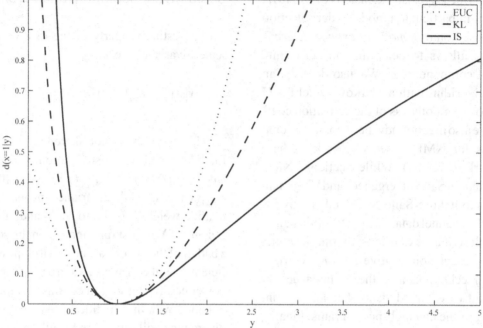

the statistical composite model described next. Let $\mathbf{x}_n \in C^{F \times 1}$ be the STFT at frame n of some time-domain signal x. Consider the generative model defined by, $\forall n = 1,\ldots,N$

$$\mathbf{x}_n = \sum_{k=1}^{K} \mathbf{c}_{k,n} \qquad (7)$$

where $\mathbf{c}_{k,n}$ belongs to $C^{F \times 1}$ and

$$\mathbf{c}_{k,n} \sim \mathcal{N}_c(0, h_{kn} diag(\mathbf{w}_k)), \qquad (8)$$

where $\mathcal{N}_c(\mu, \Sigma)$ denotes the proper multivariate complex Gaussian distribution, defined in Appendix "Standard distributions". The variable $\mathbf{c}_{k,n}$, which we refer to as component in the following, is basically characterized by a spectral signature $\mathbf{w}_k$, amplitude-modulated in time by the frame-dependent coefficient h_{kn}, which accounts for nonstationarity. Assume each component sequence

of frames $\{\mathbf{c}_{k,1},\ldots,\mathbf{c}_{k,N}\}$ to be independently distributed and the components $\mathbf{c}_{1,n},\ldots,\mathbf{c}_{K,n}$ to be mutually independent at each frame. Then, the likelihood criterion to optimize writes

$$C_{ML}(\mathbf{W}, \mathbf{H}) \overset{def}{=} - \log p(\mathbf{X}|\mathbf{W}, \mathbf{H}) \qquad (9)$$

$$= -\sum_{n=1}^{N}\sum_{f=1}^{F} \log \mathcal{N}_c\left(x_{fn} \mid 0, \sum_k w_{fk} h_{kn}\right) \qquad (10)$$

$$\overset{c}{=} -\sum_{n=1}^{N}\sum_{f=1}^{F} d_{IS}\left(| x_{fn} |^2 | \sum_k w_{fk} h_{kn}\right) \qquad (11)$$

where $\overset{c}{=}$ denotes equality up to additive constant terms. Taking $\mathbf{V}$ as the matrix with entries $v_{fn} = |x_{fn}|^2$, ML estimation of $\mathbf{W}$ and $\mathbf{H}$ hence amounts to the NMF $\mathbf{V} \approx \mathbf{WH}$, with the IS divergence.

The generative model (7)-(8) was considered by Benaroya et al. (2003) (2006a) for single-channel audio source separation, but there the dictionary **W** is trained separately with VQ and the link with IS-NMF is not fully exploited. Another equivalent way to look at the statistical structure is to assume that **V** is a noisy observation of $\hat{\mathbf{V}}$, with *multiplicative* independently and identically Gamma distributed noise (with mean 1). This is how Abdallah and Plumbley (2004) derive a "statistically motivated error measure", which coincides with the IS divergence, in the very similar context of nonnegative sparse coding. Parry and Essa (2007) derive a "phase-aware nonnegative spectrogram factorization" method which also amounts to NMF of the power spectogram with the IS divergence, based on a statistical model very similar to (7)-(8). In contrast Euclidean and KL NMF respectively underlay additive Gaussian and Poisson noise, see, e.g., (Févotte and Cemgil, 2009) and below.

Phase and Component Reconstruction

The IS-NMF composite model (7)-(8) sets no informative assumption about the phase of each component; the proper complex Gaussian assumption amounts to modeling the phases as uniform random variables. Given estimates of **W** and **H**, minimum mean square error (MMSE) estimates can be obtained through Wiener filtering, such that

$$\hat{c}_{k,fn} = \frac{w_{fk}h_{kn}}{\sum_{l=1}^{K} w_l h_{l\,n}} x_{fn}. \tag{12}$$

A consequence of Wiener reconstruction is that the phase of all components $\hat{c}_{k,fn}$ is equal to the phase of x_{fn}. Note that with the Wiener gains summing up to 1 for a fixed entry (f,n), the decomposition is conservative, i.e,

$$\mathbf{x}_n = \sum_{k=1}^{K} \hat{\mathbf{c}}_{k,n}. \tag{13}$$

We would like to contrast the IS-NMF model (7)-(8) with the more common approach consisting of factorizing the *magnitude* spectrogram with the KL divergence, see e.g, (Smaragdis and Brown, 2003; Smaragdis, 2007; Virtanen, 2007; Cemgil, 2009). In that case, the assumed latent generative model is

$$\left|\mathbf{x}_n\right| = \sum_{k=1}^{K} \left|\mathbf{c}_{k,n}\right| \tag{14}$$

with

$$\left|c_{k,fn}\right| \sim \mathcal{P}(h_{kn}w_{fk}), \tag{15}$$

where $\mathcal{P}(\lambda)$ denotes the Poisson distribution, defined in Appendix "Standard distributions". The Poisson distribution being closed under summation (like the Gaussian distribution), one obtains $\left|x_{fn}\right| \sim \mathcal{P}(\sum_{k=1}^{K} w_{fk}h_{kn})$ and it can easily be derived that the likelihood $-\log p(|\mathbf{X}| \mid \mathbf{W},\mathbf{H})$ is up to a constant equal to $D_{KL}(|\mathbf{X}| \mid |\mathbf{WH})$. Given estimates of **W** and **H**, MMSE estimates of the magnitude-components are obtained by

$$\widehat{\left|c_{k,fn}\right|} = \frac{w_{fk}h_{kn}}{\sum_{l=1}^{K} w_{fl}h_{l\,n}} \left|x_{fn}\right|. \tag{16}$$

A major difference between the approaches consisting of using KL-NMF on the magnitude spectrogram and IS-NMF on the power spectrogram is that the generative model (14)-(15) implied by the former simply discards the phase of the observation, and of the components. In contrast, the phase is taken into account in the other approach, even though in a noninformative way. When it comes to reconstruct time domain components from Equation (16) through inverse-STFT, it is common practice to set the phase of the individual components to the phase of x_{fn}, i.e,

$$\hat{c}_{k,fn} = \left|\widehat{c_{k,fn}}\right| \arg\left(x_{fn}\right), \tag{17}$$

where arg(x) denotes the phase of complex scalar x. So one can argue that in the end, component estimates have same phase than observation in both cases - but it is important to understand that in the case of IS-NMF of the power spectrogram this is a natural consequence of the modeling, while it is a somehow ad-hoc choice for KL-NMF of the magnitude spectrogram. Another criticism about model (14)-(15) concerns the Poisson modeling of $|c_{kfn}|$, which is formerly only defined for integers and thus impairs rigorous statistical interpretation of KL-NMF on non-countable data such as audio spectra.

Finally, we want to stress that applying IS-NMF to the *power* spectrogram or KL-NMF to the magnitude spectrogram can be motivated by the equivalence with ML estimation of **W** and **H** in an assumed generative model of respectively x_n or $|x_n|$. In contrast applying IS-NMF to the *magnitude* spectrogram, as considered in (Virtanen, 2007), or KL-NMF to the power spectrogram, as considered in (Févotte et al., 2009) pertains to an ad-hoc choice that cannot be motivated by a sound statistical model of the observed data. Then, the results presented in Section "Case study" tend to show that the IS-NMF model (7)-(8) is a more suitable model than the KL-NMF model (14)-(15) because it leads to better decompositions, in the sense that the semantics revealed by the factors **W** and **H** and the reconstructed components is closer to our own comprehension of sound.

Algorithms for IS-NMF

MATLAB implementations of the algorithms described next are available from http://www.tsi.enst.fr/~fevotte.

Multiplicative Updates

A very popular optimization strategy in NMF is based on multiplicative updates. In this iterative scheme **W** and **H** are optimized alternatively. Each matrix is updated through a gradient descent, where the step size is analytically chosen so that the update becomes multiplicative. More precisely, the approach is equivalent to updating each coefficient θ of **W** or **H** by multiplying its value at previous iteration by the ratio of the negative and positive parts of the derivative of the criterion with respect to this parameter, namely $\theta \leftarrow \theta . [\nabla f(\theta)]_- / [\nabla f(\theta)]_+$, where $f(\theta) = [\nabla f(\theta)]_+ - [\nabla f(\theta)]_-$ and the summands are both nonnegative. This ensures nonnegativity of the parameter updates, provided initialization with a nonnegative value. A fixed point θ^* of the algorithm implies either $\nabla f(\theta^*) = 0$ or $\theta^* = 0$. In the IS case, the gradients of $D(\mathbf{V}|\mathbf{WH})$ write

$$\nabla_\mathbf{H} D_{IS}(\mathbf{V} \mid \mathbf{WH}) = \mathbf{W}^T\left((\mathbf{WH})^{[-2]} \cdot (\mathbf{WH} - \mathbf{V})\right) \tag{18}$$

$$\nabla_\mathbf{W} D_{IS}(\mathbf{V} \mid \mathbf{WH}) = \left((\mathbf{WH})^{[-2]} \cdot (\mathbf{WH} - \mathbf{V})\right)\mathbf{H}^T \tag{19}$$

where '.' denotes Hadamard entrywise product and $\mathbf{A}^{[n]}$ denotes the matrix with entries $\left[\mathbf{A}\right]_{ij}^n$. This leads to Algorithm 1, in which $\mathbf{A}/\mathbf{B}$ denotes the matrix $\mathbf{A}.\mathbf{B}^{[-1]}$. This algorithm includes a normalization step at every iteration, which eliminates trivial scale indeterminacies leaving the cost function unchanged. We impose $\|\mathbf{w}_k\|_1 = 1$ and scale h_k accordingly.

The multiplicative approach to NMF was proposed by Lee and Seung (2001) for the Euclidean and KL costs, and the simplicity of the algorithm structure played a key role in the popularization of NMF. Using the convexity of $d_{EUC}(x|y)$ and $d_{KL}(x|y)$ as functions of y, the criterion $D(\mathbf{V}|\mathbf{WH})$ can be shown non-decreasing

Algorithm 1. IS-NMF/MU

> **Input** : nonnegative matrix **V**
> **Output** : nonnegative matrices **W** and **H** such that $\mathbf{V} \approx \mathbf{WH}$
> Initialize **W** and **H** with nonnegative values
> **for** $l = 1 : n_{iter}$ **do**
>
> $\qquad \mathbf{H} \leftarrow \mathbf{H} . \dfrac{\mathbf{W}^T((\mathbf{WH})^{.[-2]}.\mathbf{V})}{\mathbf{W}^T(\mathbf{WH})^{.[-1]}}$
>
> $\qquad \mathbf{W} \leftarrow \mathbf{W} . \dfrac{((\mathbf{WH})^{.[-2]}.\mathbf{V})\mathbf{H}^T}{(\mathbf{WH})^{.[-1]}\mathbf{H}^T}$
>
> $\qquad$ Normalize **W** and **H**
> **end for**

under the multiplicative rules (Lee and Seung, 2001; Kompass, 2007; Févotte and Cemgil, 2009). The proof, based on the introduction of an auxiliary function, does not however hold for the IS divergence because it is not convex, but in practice we always observed monotonicity of the criterion under Algorithm 1.

EM Algorithm

The statistical composite model underlying IS-NMF can readily serve for the construction of an EM algorithm for the maximization of the likelihood of **W** and **H**, or equivalently the minimization of $D_{IS}(\mathbf{V}|\mathbf{WH})$. Denoting $\mathbf{C}_k$ the $F \times N$ matrix with coefficients $c_{k,fn}$ and **C** the tensor with slices $\mathbf{C}_k$, the latent components **C** are a natural choice of complete data. More precisely, each component $\mathbf{C}_k$ can act as a complete data space for the subset of parameters $\theta_k = \{\mathbf{w}_k, h_k\}$. The EM functional to minimize iteratively writes

$$Q^{ML}(\theta \mid \theta') \overset{def}{=} - \int_c \log p(\mathbf{C} \mid \theta) p(\mathbf{C} \mid \mathbf{X}, \theta') d\mathbf{C}. \tag{20}$$

Using conditional independence

$$p(\mathbf{C} \mid \theta) = \prod_k p(\mathbf{C}_k \mid \theta_k) \tag{21}$$

the EM functional can be written

$$Q^{ML}(\theta \mid \theta') = \sum_k Q_k^{ML}(\theta_k \mid \theta'), \tag{22}$$

where

$$Q_k^{ML}(\theta_k \mid \theta') \overset{def}{=} - \int_{\mathbf{C}_k} \log p(\mathbf{C}_k \mid \theta_k) p(\mathbf{C}_k \mid \mathbf{X}, \theta') d\mathbf{C}_k. \tag{23}$$

Finally, under stated independent assumptions the functional is further reduced to

$$Q_k^{ML}(\theta_k \mid \theta') \overset{def}{=} - \sum_{n,f} \int_{C_{k,fn}} \log p(c_{k,fn} \mid \theta_k) p(c_{k,fn} \mid x_{fn}, \theta') dc_{k,fn}. \tag{24}$$

The minus log-likelihood of the complete data writes

$$- \log p(c_{k,fn} \mid \theta_k) \overset{c}{=} \log(w_{fk} h_{kn}) + \frac{|c_{k,fn}|^2}{w_{fk} h_{kn}} \tag{25}$$

and its posterior distribution writes

$$p(c_{k,fn} \mid x_{fn}, \theta) = \mathcal{N}(c_{k,fn} \mid \mu_{k,fn}^{post}, \lambda_{k,fn}^{post}) \tag{26}$$

with

$$\mu_{k,fn}^{post} = \frac{w_{fk} h_{kn}}{\sum_l w_{fl} h_{ln}} x_{fn}, \quad \lambda_{k,fn}^{post} = \frac{w_{fk} h_{kn}}{\sum_l w_{fl} h_{ln}} \sum_{l \neq k} w_{fl} h_{ln}. \tag{27}$$

Plugging equation (25) into Equation (24), computing and solving the gradients $Q_k^{ML}(\mathbf{w}_k, h_k \mid \theta')$ finally leads to

$$h_{kn} = \frac{1}{F} \sum_f \frac{v'_{k,fn}}{w_{fk}} \tag{28}$$

Algorithm 2. IS-NMF/EM

Input : nonnegative matrix **V**
Output : nonnegative matrices **W** and **H** such that $\mathbf{V} \approx \mathbf{WH}$
Initialize **W** and **H** with nonnegative values
for $l = 1 : n_{iter}$ **do**
  for $k = 1 : K$ **do**

    Compute $\mathbf{G}_k = \dfrac{\mathbf{w}_k h_k}{\mathbf{WH}}$ %Wiener gain

    Compute $\mathbf{V}_k = \mathbf{G}_k^{\cdot[2]}.\mathbf{V} + (1 - \mathbf{G}_k).(\mathbf{w}_k h_k)$ % Posterior power of $\mathbf{C}_k$

    $h_k \leftarrow \dfrac{1}{F} (\mathbf{w}_k^{\cdot[-1]})^T \mathbf{V}_k$ % Update row k of **H**

    $\mathbf{w}_k \leftarrow \dfrac{1}{N} \mathbf{V}_k (h_k^{\cdot[-1]})^T$ % Update column k of **W**

    Normalize $\mathbf{w}_k$ and h_k
  end for
end for

% Note that WH needs to be computed only once, at initialization, and be
subsequently updated as $\mathbf{WH} - \mathbf{w}_k^{old} h_k^{old} + \mathbf{w}_k^{new} h_k^{new}$.

$$w_{fk} = \frac{1}{N} \sum_n \frac{v'_{k,fn}}{w_{fk}}, \tag{29}$$

where $v_{k,fn} \overset{def}{=} \left| \mu_{k,fn}^{post} \right|^2 + \lambda_{k,fn}^{post}$ is the posterior power of $c_{k,fn}$ and the apostrophe refers to parameter values from previous iteration. Note that these update equations differ from the multiplicative updates given in Algorithm 1. In practice the subsets θ_k are updated sequentially and the set of all parameters θ is refreshed hereafter, leading to the Space-Alternating Generalized Expectation-Maximization (SAGE) algorithm described in (Févotte et al., 2009). The general EM algorithm is summarized in Algorithm 2 and its convergence to a stationary point of $D_{IS}(\mathbf{V}|\mathbf{WH})$ is granted by property of EM.

Case Study

In this section we wish to establish the relevance of decomposing audio with IS-NMF of the power spectrogram as compared with KL-NMF of the magnitude spectrogram. To that purpose we consider a well structured simple piano sequence. The sequence, played from score given in Figure 3 on a Yamaha DisKlavier MX100A upright piano, was recorded in a small size room by a Schoeps omnidirectional microphone, placed about 15 cm (6 in) above the opened body of the piano. The sequence is composed of 4 notes, played all at once in the first measure and then played by pairs in all possible combinations in the subsequent measures. The 15.6 seconds long recorded signal was downsampled to 22 kHz, yielding $T = 339501$ samples. A STFT **X** of x was computed using a sinebell analysis window of length $L = 1024$ (46 ms) with 50% overlap between two frames, leading to $N = 674$ frames and $F = 513$ frequency bins. The time-domain signal x and its log-power spectrogram are represented on Figure 3.

NMF of the power spectrogram $|\mathbf{X}|^2$ of this piano sequence with various model orders K and with either Euclidean, IS or KL cost function was thoroughly studied in (Févotte et al., 2009). Here, given the fixed number of components $K = 8$, we rather compare the decomposition results of IS-NMF of $|\mathbf{X}|^2$ and KL-NMF of $|\mathbf{X}|$; our motivation is to compare the decomposition results obtained from the two statistical composite models discussed in Section "Phase and component reconstruction", based either on the Poisson modeling of $|\mathbf{c}_{k,n}|$ or the Gaussian modeling of $\mathbf{c}_{k,n}$. In each

Figure 3. Three representations of data; (top): original score, (middle): time-domain recorded signal x, (bottom): log-power spectrogram log $|\mathbf{X}|^2$. The four notes read D_4^b (pitch 61), (pitch 65), A_4^b (pitch 68) and C_5 (pitch 72). They all together form a D^b major seventh chord. In the recorded interpretation the third chord is slightly out of tempo. Figure reproduced from (Févotte et al., 2009).

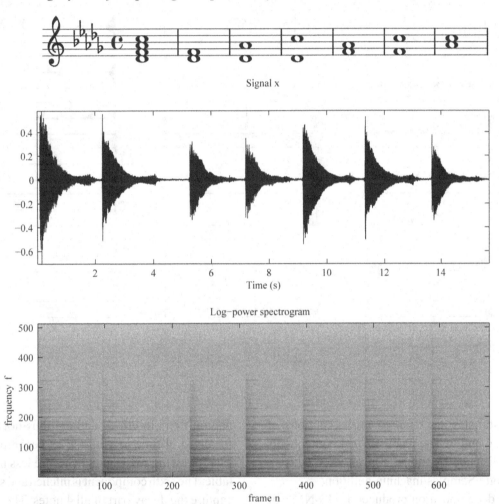

case we run the corresponding multiplicative NMF algorithm for 5000 iterations. To reduce the impact of initialization and the odds of obtaining a local solution, we run the algorithms 10 times in both case, from random nonnegative initializations of $\mathbf{W}$ and $\mathbf{H}$ and select the factorization with lowest final cost value. The learnt factor matrices $\mathbf{W}$ and $\mathbf{H}$ as well as the reconstructed time components $\hat{c}_k(t)$ are shown in Figures 4 and 5; the results are displayed by decreasing variance of $\hat{c}_k(t)$. The

pitch estimator described in (Vincent et al., 2007; Févotte et al., 2009) was applied to the elements of the dictionary in order to inspect correctness of pitch with ground truth. In our implementation the MIDI range was sampled from 20.6 to 108.4 with step 0.2. An arbitrary pitch value of 0 is given to unpitched dictionary elements; as a matter of fact the pitch estimator returns maximum value 108.4 for these elements and the unpitchedness is confirmed by looking at the dictionary and listening to the reconstructed components. The

Figure 4. IS-NMF of $|\mathbf{X}|^2$ with K = 8. Left: columns of $\mathbf{W}$ ($\log_{10}$ scale). Middle: rows of $\mathbf{H}$. Right: Component reconstruction with Equation (12). Pitch estimates: [65.0 68.0 61.0 72.0 0 0 0 0]. Top to down display by decreasing variance of the reconstructed components.

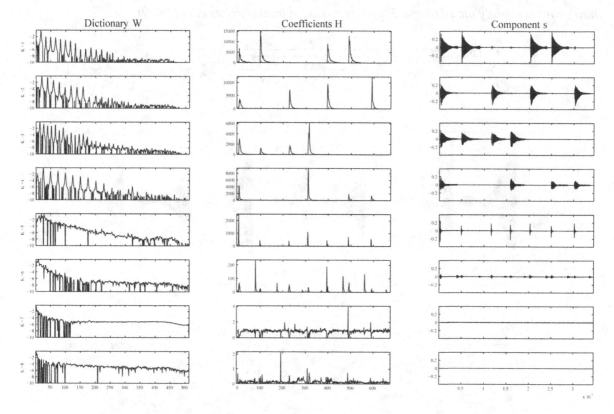

pitch estimates are reported in the captions of Figures 4 and 5. The reconstructed components can be listened to online at http://www.tsi.enst. fr/~fevotte/Samples/machine-audition/.

The decomposition produced by IS-NMF of $|\mathbf{X}|^2$ is as follows. The first four components each capture one of the four notes. The fifth component captures the sound produced by the hammer hitting the strings, the sixth component captures the sound produced by the sustain pedal when it is released, seventh and eighth components contain inaudible residual noise. The pitch estimates perfectly correspond to the ground truth.

The decomposition produced by KL-NMF of $|\mathbf{X}|$ is as follows. The first four components each capture one of the four notes. The fifth component captures both the sound of hammer hits and pedal releases; the hammer hits are followed by an un-

natural tremolo effect, and are thus not as well localized in time as with the IS decomposition. The following two components are less interpretable. The sixth component is pitched and seems to capture the decay part of all 4 notes. The seventh component is made of "breath" sound localized at the hammer hits and pedal release occurrences. The eighth component contains faintly audible residual noise. The pitch estimates of the first four components are close to the ground truth values, but not exactly so.

This experimental study shows that the nature of the decomposition obtained with IS-NMF of the power spectrogram of this well structured example is in accord with our own comprehension of sound. Entities with well-defined semantics emerge from the decomposition (individual notes, hammer hits, pedal releases, residual noise) while

*Figure 5. KL-NMF of |**X**| with K = 8. Left: columns of **W** (log₁₀ scale). Middle: rows of **H**. Right: Component reconstruction with Equation (17). Pitch estimates: [65.2 68.2 61.0 72.2 0 56.2 0 0]. Top to down display by decreasing variance of the reconstructed components.*

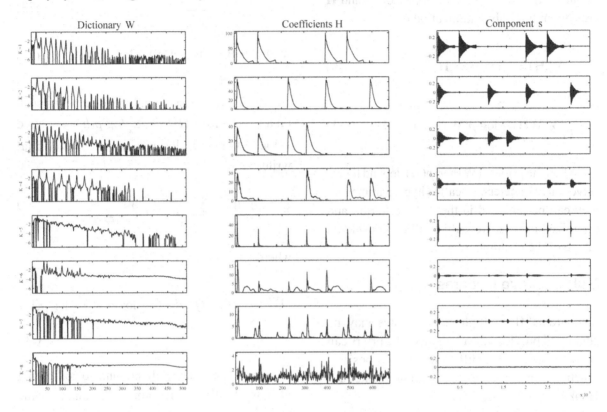

the decomposition obtained from KL-NMF of the magnitude spectrogram is less interpretable from this perspective. More experiments with the same dataset are described in (Févotte et al., 2009) and further illustrate the relevance of the IS-NMF model for sound decomposition.

BAYESIAN EXTENSIONS TO ITAKURA-SAITO NMF

Bayesian NMF

The ML likelihood framework presented above inherently assumes **W** and **H** to be deterministic parameters with no prior information available. In this section we turn to a Bayesian setting where the parameters are given prior distributions $p(\mathbf{W})$ and $p(\mathbf{H})$, reflecting prior beliefs such as smoothness, sparsity, structure, etc. Bayesian inference revolves around the posterior distribution $p(\theta|\mathbf{X})$ of the set of all unknown parameters: information about θ or subsets of θ is inferred from the data through manipulation of the posterior. As such, typical point estimates are the maximum a posteriori (MAP) estimate $\hat{\theta}_{MAP} = \arg\max_{\theta} p(\theta \mid \mathbf{X})$ and the MMSE estimate $\hat{\theta}_{MMSE} = \mathbb{E}\{\theta|\mathbf{X}\} = \int \theta p(\theta|\mathbf{X})d\theta$.

While we present in the following Bayesian extensions of IS-NMF, it is worth mentioning related Bayesian treatments of KL-NMF. In particular sparse priors have been considered in (Shashanka et al., 2008; Cemgil, 2009) and regularization constraints enforcing smoothness of the rows of **H** have been considered in (Virtanen et al., 2008).

MAP Estimation

In our NMF setting, MAP estimates of $\mathbf{W}$ and $\mathbf{H}$ are sought through minimization of

$$C_{MAP}(\mathbf{W},\mathbf{H}) \overset{\text{def}}{=} -\log p(\mathbf{W},\mathbf{H}|\mathbf{X}) \qquad (30)$$

$$\overset{c}{=} D_{IS}(\mathbf{V}|\mathbf{WH}) - \log p(\mathbf{W}) - \log p(\mathbf{H}) \qquad (31)$$

When the priors $p(\mathbf{W})$ and $p(\mathbf{H})$ depend themselves on parameters, so-called hyperparameters, they can be included in the MAP criterion and optimized over as well; this will be considered in one of the examples below.

Multiplicative Updates

Standard NMF multiplicative updates may be attempted provided the gradient of the priors can be expressed as the difference of two positive functions. In that case the resulting updates for $\mathbf{H}$ take the following form

$$\mathbf{H} \leftarrow \mathbf{H}.\frac{[\nabla_{\mathbf{H}} D_{IS}(\mathbf{V}|\mathbf{WH}) - \log p(\mathbf{H})] -}{[\nabla_{\mathbf{H}} D_{IS}(\mathbf{V}|\mathbf{WH}) - \log p(\mathbf{H})] +}$$

$$(32)$$

and similar updates are obtained for $\mathbf{W}$. While this scheme was reported to decrease the MAP criterion for various pairs of cost function and priors, see e.g (Cichocki et al., 2006) and Section "Automatic relevance determination in NMF", there is yet no theoretical guarantee of such a property.

EM Algorithm

In contrast, the structure of the EM algorithm can accommodate MAP estimation, with guaranteed convergence. In the MAP setting, the functional to optimize iteratively writes

$$Q^{MAP}(\boldsymbol{\theta}|\boldsymbol{\theta}') \overset{\text{def}}{=} -\int_C \log p(\boldsymbol{\theta}|\mathbf{C})p(\mathbf{C}|\mathbf{X},\boldsymbol{\theta}')d\,\mathbf{C}$$

$$(33)$$

$$\overset{c}{=} Q^{ML}(\boldsymbol{\theta}|\boldsymbol{\theta}') - \log p(\mathbf{W}) - \log p(\mathbf{H}) \qquad (34)$$

Hence, if we assume independent priors such that $-\log p(\mathbf{H}) = -\Sigma_k \log p(h_k)$ and $-\log p(\mathbf{W}) = -\Sigma_k \log p(\mathbf{w}_k)$, the functional writes

$$Q^{MAP}(\boldsymbol{\theta}|\boldsymbol{\theta}') = \sum_k Q_k^{MAP}(\boldsymbol{\theta}_k|\boldsymbol{\theta}') \qquad (35)$$

where

$$Q_k^{MAP}(\boldsymbol{\theta}_k|\boldsymbol{\theta}') \overset{\text{def}}{=} Q_k^{ML}(\boldsymbol{\theta}|\boldsymbol{\theta}') - \log p(\mathbf{w}_k) - \log p(h_k)$$

$$(36)$$

Hence, the E-step still amounts to computing $Q_k^{ML}(\mathbf{w}_k, h_k|\boldsymbol{\theta}')$, see Equation (23), and only the M-step is changed by the regularization constraints $-\log p(\mathbf{w}_k)$ and $-\log p(h_k)$ which now need to be taken into account. However, the addition of the prior terms may render the M-step more complex, with in some cases no analytical solutions. Hence, a compromise may need to be made between the complexity of the prior structure and the optimization it leads to, so as to keep inference tractable.

Sampling the Posterior Distribution

The above EM algorithm for MAP estimation can be easily adapted so as to produce a MCMC sampling algorithm. Sampling the posterior distribution, i.e, generating realizations of $p(\theta|\mathbf{X})$, is interesting because it yields a more detailed characterization of the posterior distribution than mere point estimates. In particular, confidence intervals and error variances can readily be computed from the samples. In most settings sampling directly from the posterior distribution is difficult and a common strategy consists of producing a Markov chain whose stationary distribution is $p(\theta|\mathbf{X})$, yielding the family of so-called Markov chain Monte Carlo (MCMC) algorithms. Parameter values $\theta^{(l)}$ are generated iteratively according to a Markov chain kernel $Q(\theta|\theta')$ until convergence is achieved. The problem then boils down to how to generate a Markov chain having the desired stationary distribution $p(\theta|\mathbf{X})$.

In our case, a Space Alternating Data Augmentation (SADA) algorithm can readily be employed. SADA is a stochastic variant of SAGE, described in (Doucet et al., 2005). Instead of computing the expectation of the log parameter posterior with respect to the hidden data posterior, SADA generates, at each iteration (l) of the sampler and sequentially over k, a realization $\mathbf{C}_k^{(l)}$ from the (instrumental) distribution $p(\mathbf{C}_k|\mathbf{X},\theta^{(l-1)})$, and then update the parameters by generating a realization $\theta_k^{(l)}$ from $p(\theta_k|\mathbf{C}_k^{(l)})$.

Following a "burn in" period, the realizations of θ obtained from the sampler are drawn from the desired posterior distribution $p(\theta|\mathbf{X})$.

MCMC algorithms are more computationally demanding than their EM counterpart. The cost per iteration of each algorithm may be similar as sampling variables from their conditional posterior (MCMC) is somehow as expensive as computing the value of the mode (EM), provided the distribution is easy to sample. But the convergence of MCMC algorithms is usually attained in many more iterations than EM, as the former thoroughly explores the posterior space while EM points at nearest local minimum. As such, a very important characteristic of MCMC algorithms is that they are theoretically less prone to local convergence: over an infinitely large number of iterations, the MCMC algorithm is guaranteed to explore the full posterior while EM will stay trapped in the nearest local minimum. In practice however, MCMC

convergence may be slow and the sampler may get stuck in local modes. A challenging aspect in the design of MCMC algorithms is to produce samplers that "mix" well, i.e, move fast in the posterior space. Other works related to NMF using MCMC techniques can be found in (Moussaoui et al., 2006; Schmidt et al., 2009; Cemgil, 2009; Févotte and Cemgil, 2009).

Automatic Relevance Determination in NMF

Model Order Selection

A very challenging problem in NMF, as in most decomposition algorithms, is how to determine a suitable number of components K? There might not be a ground truth value, but one would like to at least be able to select an "efficient" or "relevant number". This a model order selection problem. Usual criteria such as the Bayesian information criterion (BIC) or Akaike's criterion (AIC) - see, e.g., (Stoica and Selén, 2004) - cannot be directly applied to NMF, because the number of parameters ($FK + KN$) is not constant with respect to the number of observations N. This feature breaks the validity of the assumptions in which these criteria have been designed. What would be ideally required is ML estimation over $p(\mathbf{V}|\mathbf{W})$ instead of $p(\mathbf{V}|\mathbf{W},\mathbf{H})$, treating $\mathbf{H}$ as a latent variable, like in independent component analysis (MacKay, 1996; Lewicki and Sejnowski, 2000) or in some dictionary learning methods (Kreutz-Delgado et al., 2003). But this is nontrivial as this likelihood function is not always easily computed, in particular in our case.

The Bayesian setting offers ways to handle the model order selection problem. In essence, the BIC and AIC criteria form approximations of the model marginal likelihood. Denoting the model consisting of assuming that the dimensionality of the dictionary $\mathbf{W}$ is K, the marginal likelihood, sometimes also referred to as evidence, writes

$$p(\mathbf{X}|\mathcal{M}_K) = \int_\theta p(\mathbf{X}|\theta, \mathcal{M}_K)p(\theta|\mathcal{M}_K)d\theta \quad (37)$$

Model order selection can be envisaged by computing the marginal likelihood of each considered value of K and then form a decision based on the largest value of $\{p(\mathbf{X}|\mathcal{M}_K)\}_K$. However, for most models the integral involved in Equation (37) is difficult to compute and various approximations or numerical optimization strategies have been considered for this task. One of them, Chib's method (Chib, 1995), allows to compute (37) numerically using the output of a MCMC sampler. This method was in particular considered for KL-NMF in (Cemgil, 2009).

Automatic Relevance Determination

Hence, we now turn to another yet more simpler Bayesian method based on automatic relevance determination (ARD). ARD was introduced by Mackay (1995) in the context of regression to assess a relevant number of explanatory variables. It was then considered by Bishop (1999) to determine an "efficient" number of components in PCA and by Tipping (2001) with similar motives in sparse Bayesian learning. Our idea, originally described in (Tan and Févotte, 2009), is to place priors, dependent on variance-like "relevance" parameters $\boldsymbol{\phi} = [\phi_1,...,\phi_K]$, on both the columns of $\mathbf{W}$ and the rows of $\mathbf{H}$. More precisely, we tie $\mathbf{w}_k$ and h_k together through the following priors:

$$p(\mathbf{w}_k | \phi_k) = \prod_f \mathcal{HN}(w_{fk}|\phi_k), \quad (38)$$

$$p(h_k | \phi_k) = \prod_n \mathcal{HN}(h_{kn}|\phi_k), \quad (39)$$

where $\mathcal{HN}(x,\sigma^2)$ is the half-normal distribution defined in *Appendix A: Standard Distributions*. Note that this prior is not over-constraining the scales, because of the scale indeterminacy between

$\mathbf{w}_k$ and h_k. We also consider a conjugate inverse-Gamma prior $\mathcal{IG}(\phi_k|\alpha,\beta)$ for the relevance parameters, whose influence will be discussed later. Then we seek MAP estimates of $\mathbf{W}$, $\mathbf{H}$ and $\boldsymbol{\phi}$ through minimization of

$$C_{MAP}(\mathbf{W},\mathbf{H},\phi) \overset{def}{=} -\log p(\mathbf{W},\mathbf{H},\phi|\mathbf{V}),$$

$$\overset{c}{=} -\log p(\mathbf{V}|\mathbf{W},\mathbf{H}) - \log p(\mathbf{W}|\phi) - \log p(\mathbf{H}|\phi) - \log p(\phi),$$

$$\overset{c}{=} D_{IS}(\mathbf{V}|\mathbf{WH}) = \sum_k \left[\frac{1}{2}\left(\sum_f w_{fk}^2 + \sum_n h_{kn}^2\right)+\beta\right]\frac{1}{\phi_k} + \left(\frac{F+N}{2}+\alpha+1\right)\log\phi_k \quad (40)$$

As a result of inference, a subset of the relevance parameters ϕ corresponding to irrelevant components is driven to a small lower bound, with the corresponding columns of $\mathbf{W}$ and rows of $\mathbf{H}$ driven to small values, by Equations (38) and (39). The value of the lower bound depends on the hyperparameters α and β, see Algorithm 3, which have to be user-defined. As can be seen from the MAP function given at Equation (40) setting these variables to low values leads to a noninformative prior (i.e, the data is let to speak for itself).

The gradients of cost function (40) leads to

$$\nabla_\mathbf{W} C_{MAP}(\mathbf{W},\mathbf{H},\phi) = ((\mathbf{WH})^{[-2]}.(\mathbf{WH}-\mathbf{V}))\mathbf{H}^T + \mathbf{W}\mathrm{diag}(\phi^{[-1]}), \quad (41)$$

$$\nabla_\mathbf{H} C_{MAP}(\mathbf{W},\mathbf{H},\phi) = \mathbf{W}^T((\mathbf{WH})^{[-2]}\cdot(\mathbf{WH}-\mathbf{V})) + \mathrm{diag}(\phi^{[-1]})\mathbf{H}, \quad (42)$$

$$\nabla_{\phi k} C_{MAP}(\mathbf{W},\mathbf{H},\phi) = -\left[\frac{1}{2}+\left(\sum_f w_{fk}^2+\sum_n h_{kn}^2\right)+\beta\right]\frac{1}{\phi_k^2}+\left(\frac{F+N}{2}+\alpha+1\right)\frac{1}{\phi_k}. \quad (43)$$

and the multiplicative strategy described in Section "MAP estimation" leads to Algorithm 3.

Algorithm 3. Automatic relevance determination for IS-NMF

Input : Nonnegative matrix **V**. fixed hyperparameters α, β
Output : Nonnegative matrices **W** and **H** such that
$\mathbf{V} \approx \hat{\mathbf{V}} = \mathbf{WH}$, nonnegative vector ϕ.
Initialize **W** and **H** with nonnegative values.
for $l = 1 : n_{iter}$ do

$$\mathbf{H} \leftarrow \mathbf{H} . \frac{\mathbf{W}^T((\mathbf{WH})^{.[-2]}.\mathbf{V})}{\mathbf{W}^T(\mathbf{WH})^{.[-1]} + \mathrm{diag}(\phi^{.[-1]})\mathbf{H}}$$

$$\mathbf{W} \leftarrow \mathbf{W} . \frac{((\mathbf{WH})^{.[-2]}.\mathbf{V})\mathbf{H}^T}{(\mathbf{WH})^{.[-1]}\mathbf{H}^T + \mathbf{W}\mathrm{diag}(\phi^{.[-1]})}$$

$$\phi_k \leftarrow \frac{\Sigma_f w_{fk}^2 + \Sigma_n h_{kn}^2 + 2\beta}{F + N + 2(\alpha + 1)}, \quad k = 1,...,K.$$

end for

Results

We applied Algorithm 3 to the piano data considered in Section "Case study". We set the number of iterations to 5000 and as before, in order to marginalize the influence of local minima, we run the ARD algorithm from different random initializations and selected the factorization with lowest final MAP criterion value. We set the initial number of components K to 25 and we set $\alpha = 0$ and $\beta = 0.001$, yielding a rather non-informative prior. The convergence and final values of the relevance parameters ϕ_k are displayed on Figure 6. We see that only 6 components emerge. Inspection of these six components (not shown here) reveals that they essentially correspond to the first six components displayed in Figure 4, i.e, the four notes, hammer hits and pedal releases. We wish to point out that the problem of convergence to a local solution seemed even more severe here, probably due to the large dimension $K = 25$ of the hidden space, and that we experienced numerical difficulties with Algorithm 3 for too low values of β. However the factorizations given by the 10 runs all agreed upon a number of relevant components in the 5-7 range, so that a solution of practical value to avoid the enhanced problem of local convergence can consist in applying the ARD algorithm first, so as to obtain an approximation

of the relevant number of components, and then re-run the straight IS-NMF algorithm (possibly from various initializations) to improve the correctness of the decomposition.

IS-NMF with Markov Prior

If a reasonable amount of literature has been devoted to NMF with sparse constraints (either on **W** or **H**), little literature is dealing with persistence constraints. However if **V** is indexed by time (such as time-frequency spectra), it is expected that $\mathbf{h}_n$ is correlated with $\mathbf{h}_{n-1}$ and this information should be integrated in the NMF model. In (Févotte et al., 2009), we have described a IS-NMF algorithm accounting for Markov structure of the rows of **H**. In this setting the following prior structure is assumed for h_k:

$$p(h_k) = \prod_{n=2}^{N} p(h_{kn} | h_{k(n-1)}) p(h_{k1}), \qquad (44)$$

where the Markov kernel $p(h_{kn} | h_{k(n-1)})$ is a pdf with mode $h_{k(n-1)}$. The motivation behind this prior is to constrain h_{kn} not to differ significantly from its value at entry n-1, hence favoring smoothness of the estimate. A possible pdf choice is, for $n = 2,...,N$,

$$p(h_{kn} | h_{k(n-1)}) = \mathcal{IG}(h_{kn} | \alpha, (\alpha + 1)h_{k(n-1)}) \qquad (45)$$

where $\mathcal{IG}(x | \alpha, \beta)$ is the inverse-Gamma pdf defined in *Appendix A: Standard Distributions*, with mode $\beta/(\alpha+1)$, and variance $\beta^2/[(\alpha-1)^2 (\alpha-2)]$ (for $\alpha > 2$). The prior is constructed so that its mode is obtained for $h_{kn} = h_{k(n-1)}$. α is a shape parameter that controls the sharpness of the prior around its mode. A high value of α will increase sharpness and will thus accentuate smoothness of h_k while a low value of α will render the prior more diffuse and thus less constraining. More details as well as presentation of Gamma Markov chains can be

Figure 6. Values of the relevance parameters $\phi_1, ..., \phi_K$, of the $K = 25$ components, by decreasing order. The six most relevant components correspond to the first six components on Figure 4, but in a different order.

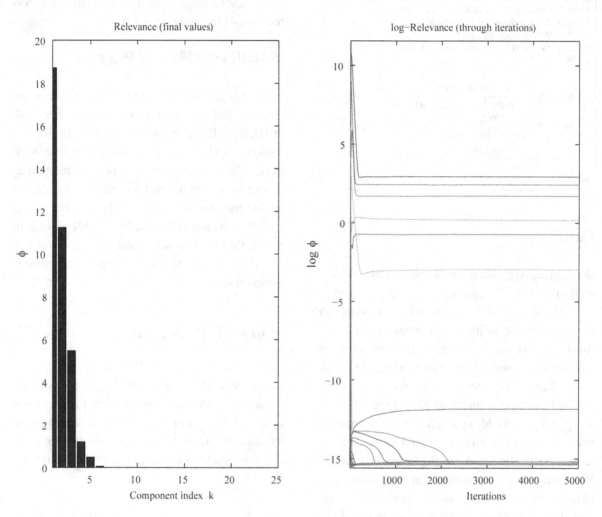

found in (Févotte et al., 2009). In the following, h_{k1} is assigned the scale-invariant Jeffreys non-informative prior $p(h_{k1}) \propto 1/h_{k1}$.

EM Algorithm

Under prior structure (44), the derivative of $Q_k^{MAP}(\mathbf{w}_k, h_k | \theta')$ with respect to h_{kn} writes, $\forall n = 2, ..., N-1,$

$$\nabla_{h_{kn}} Q_k^{MAP}(\mathbf{w}_k, h_k | \theta') =$$
$$\nabla_{h_{kn}} Q_k^{ML}(\mathbf{w}_k, h_k | \theta') - \nabla_{h_{kn}} \log p(h_{k(n+1)} | h_{kn}) - \nabla_{h_{kn}} \log p(h_{kn} | h_{k(n-1)})$$
$$(46)$$

This is shown to be equal to

$$\nabla_{h_{kn}} Q_k^{MAP}(\mathbf{w}_k, h_k | \theta') = \frac{1}{h_{kn}^2}(p_2 h_{kn}^2 + p_1 h_{kn} + p_0)$$
$$(47)$$

where the values of p_0, p_1 and p_2 are given in Table 2. Updating h_{kn} then simply amounts to solving

Table 2. Coefficients of the order 2 polynomial to solve in order to update h_{kn} in Bayesian IS-NMF with an inverse-Gamma Markov chain prior $\hat{h}_{kn}^{ML}$ denotes the ML update, given by Equation (28)

inverse-Gamma Markov chain			
	p_2	p_1	p_0
h_{k1}	$(\alpha+1)/h_{k2}$	$F-\alpha+1$	$-F\hat{h}_{k1}^{ML}$
h_{kn}	$(\alpha+1)/h_{k(n+1)}$	$F+1$	$-F\hat{h}_{k1}^{ML} - (\alpha+1)h_{k(n-1)}$
h_{kN}	0	$F+\alpha+1$	$-F\hat{h}_{kN}^{ML} - (\alpha+1)h_{k(N-1)}$

an order 2 polynomial. The polynomial has only one nonnegative root, given by

$$h_{kn} = \frac{\sqrt{p_1^2 - 4p_2 p_0} - p_1}{2p_2}. \tag{48}$$

The coefficients h_{k1} and h_{kN} at the borders of the Markov chain require specific updates, but they also only require solving polynomials of order either 2 or 1, with coefficients given in Table 2 as well. The overall IS-NMF approach using an inverse-Gamma Markov prior for the rows of **H** is described in Algorithm 4. A MATLAB implementation of this algorithm is available from http://www.tsi.enst.fr/~fevotte.

Results

We applied the previous algorithm with an inverse-Gamma Markov chain prior on the rows of **H**, with $\alpha = 50$, to the piano data presented in Section "Case study". Figure 7 displays on the same graph a zoom on the row h_1 obtained with the multiplicative algorithm (see Figure 4) and with the regularized version. The difference in smoothness is apparent. In (Févotte et al., 2009), both algorithms were considered for the decomposition of a real early jazz music piece and the

regularized version of IS-NMF was shown to lead to source estimates much more pleasant to listen to.

IS-NMF and Beyond

The IS-NMF composite model can be extended in many ways in order to either give a more general model to every component, or singularize a particular component. Recall that model (7) takes the audio data x to be a sum of components each characterized by a spectral signature. This model is well suited for polyphonic music, where each frame is a sum of sounds such as notes. This model may however not be entirely relevant for certain sources, such as voice, either spoken or sung. As a matter of fact, voice is often relegated into a specific component, see, e.g, (Benaroya et al., 2006b; Ozerov et al., 2007; Blouet et al., 2008; Durrieu et al., 2010). Voice is not a sum of elementary components but rather a single component with many states, each representative of an elementary sound (phoneme, note). As such, it is more appropriate to model voice with a mixture of distributions, such as a Gaussian Mixture Model (GMM). A relevant voice + music model is then

$$\mathbf{x}_n = \mathbf{s}_{V,n} + \mathbf{s}_{M,n} \tag{49}$$

where $\mathbf{s}_{V,n}$ stands for the voiced component and $\mathbf{s}_{M,n}$ stands for the musical accompaniment. From there, the accompaniment may be given a IS-NMF model $\{\mathbf{W}^M, \mathbf{H}^M\}$ as of Equations (7)-(8):

$$p(\mathbf{s}_{M,n} \mid \mathbf{W}^M, \mathbf{H}^M) = \mathcal{N}\left(\mathbf{s}_{M,n} \mid 0, \sum_{k=1}^{K} h_{kn}^M \text{diag}(\mathbf{w}_k^M)\right) \tag{50}$$

while the voice component may be given a Gaussian scaled mixture model $\{\mathbf{W}^V, \mathbf{H}^V\}$ (Benaroya et al., 2006b), described by

Algorithm 4. IS-NMF with inverse-Gamma Markov prior for **H**

Input : nonnegative matrix **V**
Output : nonnegative matrices **W** and **H** such that $\mathbf{V} \approx \mathbf{WH}$
Initialize **W** and **H** with nonnegative values
for $l = 1 : n_{iter}$ **do**
  for $k = 1 : K$ **do**

    Compute $\mathbf{G}_k = \dfrac{\mathbf{w}_k h_k}{\mathbf{WH}}$ % Wiener gain
    Compute $\mathbf{V}_k = \mathbf{G}_k^{\cdot[2]}.\mathbf{V} + (1 - \mathbf{G}_k).(\mathbf{w}_k h_k)$ % Posterior power of $\mathbf{C}_k$

    % Update of h_k

    Compute $\hat{h}_k^{ML} = \dfrac{1}{F}(\mathbf{w}_k^{\cdot[-1]})^T \mathbf{V}_k$ % ML estimate of h_k
    for $n = 1 : N$ **do**
      Compute p_0, p_1, p_2 as in Table 2.
      $h_{kn} \leftarrow (\sqrt{p_1^2 - 4p_2 p_0} - p_1)/(2p_2)$ % Smooth ML estimate : MAP estimate of h_k
    end for

    % Update of $\mathbf{w}_k$

    $\mathbf{w}_k \leftarrow \dfrac{1}{N}\mathbf{V}_k(h_k^{\cdot[-1]})^T$ % ML estimate of $\mathbf{w}_k$
    Normalize $\mathbf{w}_k$ and h_k
  end for
end for

% Note that WH needs to be computed only once, at initialization, and be subsequently
updated as $\mathbf{WH} - \mathbf{w}_k^{old}h_k^{old} + \mathbf{w}_k^{new}h_k^{new}$.

$$p(\mathbf{s}_{V,n} \mid \mathbf{W}^V, \mathbf{H}^V) = \sum_{k=1}^{K} \alpha_k \mathcal{N}(\mathbf{s}_{v,n} \mid 0, h_{kn}^V \mathrm{diag}(\mathbf{w}_k^V))$$

(51)

Pay attention that in the accompaniment model a summation occurs on the frame domain, while it occurs on the pdfs of the frames in the voice model. Inference in the model defined by Equations (49), (50) and (51) can be carried with an EM algorithm similar to the one described in Section "Algorithms for IS-NMF", but where the sequence of states of the voice component is added to the complete dataset, as routinely done in EM estimation of GMMs. The resulting algorithm is described in (Ozerov et al., 2009). The latter paper reports speech + music separation results for which both IS-NMF and GSMM are envisaged for modeling the voice component, while the music component is modeled with IS-NMF. A Source to Distortion Ratio improvement is systematically observed with the GSMM model, corroborating the relevance of the latter model for voice.

Note also that pitchness of the voice component (especially when sung) can further be enforced in the model, as proposed in (Durrieu et al., 2009, 2010). This is done through $\mathbf{W}^V$, which is given a excitation/filter model. More precisely, given a fixed dictionary of harmonic combs $\mathbf{E} = \{\mathbf{e}_1,\ldots,\mathbf{e}_M\}$ (the "excitations") and a series of unknown envelopes $\mathbf{F} = \{\mathbf{f}_1,\ldots,\mathbf{f}_Q\}$ (the "filters"), the dictionary $\mathbf{W}^V$ is made of all excitation-filters combinations $\{\mathbf{e}_m.\mathbf{f}_q\}_{q,m}$, mimicking the human voice production system. Note that in that setting, only the spectral envelopes $\mathbf{F}$ are learnt from the data, and not the entire dictionary $\mathbf{W}^V$. Durrieu, Richard, David, and Févotte (2010) describe both EM and multiplicative updates for inference in generative model

Figure 7. Segment of row h_1 (≈ 400 - 650 frame range) as obtained from IS-NMF with the multiplicative nonregularized algorithm (dotted line) and from IS-NMF with a Markov regularization (solid line)

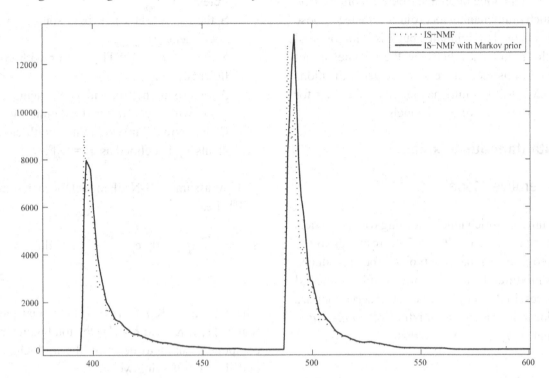

(50),(51),(52) with the latter voice production model. The paper reports in particular excellent voice separation results, some of them available from the Signal Separation Evaluation Campaign (SiSEC 2008) webpage.[1]

Finally, we would like to mention an interesting extension of the plain NMF model that has been considered in the literature, using the Euclidean or KL cost functions, and that could readily be considered with the IS divergence. The NMF model (1) basically assumes that the spectrogram (either in power or in magnitude) is decomposed as a linear combination of elementary patterns $\mathbf{w}_k$. These patterns are in essence a spectral characterization of sound objects with time support equal to the STFT window size. While this simple assumption can lead to satisfying decompositions, as shown in this chapter, a more realistic assumption would consist of assuming that the spectrogram is a linear combination of elementary "patches", i.e, patterns with frame-duration larger than one, or equivalently sound objects with support spread over several STFT windows. This framework was coined "convolutive NMF" in (Smaragdis, 2007) and was shown to adequately learn speech phones from mixtures of speech signals. It was furthermore shown to improve NMF-based onset detection in (Wang et al., 2009).

MULTICHANNEL IS-NMF

The work described in the previous sections inherently assumes the audio data to be single-channel: the spectrogram $\mathbf{V}$ of some unidimensional observation x is computed, factorized and a time-domain decomposition of x is then reconstructed from the factorization. However, most musical data is now available in multichannel format, especially stereo. Each channel is typically a mixture of mutual sources, with different mixing parameters. One approach to the decomposition of such multichannel recordings is to decompose each channel individually, but this is not optimal as the redundancy between the channel is not used. In this section we describe generalizations of NMF to the multichannel case, allowing for joint processing of the channels.

Instantaneous Mixing

Generative Model

Assume a multichannel recording with I channels $\mathbf{x}(t) = [x_1(t),\ldots, x_I(t)]^T$ ($I = 2$ corresponds to the stereo case). The data has typically been produced as a mixture of a certain number of instrumental sources. In the simplest case the observations are a linear instantaneous mixture of *point-source* signals $s_1(t),\ldots, s_J(t)$, such that

$$x_i(t) = \sum_{j=1}^{J} a_{ij} s_j(t), \qquad (52)$$

where the coefficients a_{ij} are real; the instantaneous mixing corresponds to elementary "pan pot" mixing. By linearity of STFT, the multichannel model reads similarly in the time-frequency domain

$$\mathbf{x}_{i,n} = \sum_{j=1}^{J} a_{ij} \mathbf{s}_{j,n}, \qquad (53)$$

where $\mathbf{x}_{i,n}$ and $\mathbf{s}_{j,n}$ denote the complex-valued STFTs of time-domain signals $x_i(t)$ and $s_j(t)$. In the following we note:

- $\mathbf{X}_i$ the $F \times N$ STFT matrix of channel i, with coefficients $\{x_{i,fn}\}_{fn}$,
- $\mathbf{V}_i$ the $F \times N$ power spectrogram matrix of channel i, with coefficients $\{v_{i,fn}\}_{fn}$ defined as $v_{i,fn} = |x_{i,fn}|^2$,

- $\mathbf{X}$ the $I \times F \times N$ STFT tensor with coefficients $\{x_{i,fn}\}_{ifn}$,
- $\mathbf{S}_j$ the $F \times N$ STFT matrix of source j, with coefficients $\{s_{j,fn}\}_{fn}$,
- $\mathbf{S}$ the $J \times F \times N$ STFT tensor with coefficients $\{s_{j,fn}\}_{jfn}$,
- $\mathbf{A}$ the mixing matrix with coefficients $\{a_{ij}\}_{ij}$, and with rows $\{a_i\}_i$ and columns $\{\mathbf{a}_j\}_j$,
- $\mathbf{Q}$ the "power" mixing matrix with coefficients $\{q_{ij}\}_{ij}$ defined as $q_{ij} = |a_{ij}|^2$.

Now assume a IS-NMF model for each source STFT, i.e,

$$\mathbf{s}_{j,n} = \sum_{k \in \mathcal{K}j} \mathbf{c}_{k,n} \text{ with } \mathbf{c}_{k,n} \sim \mathcal{N}_c(0, h_{kn}\text{diag}(\mathbf{w}_k)) \qquad (54)$$

where $\{K_1, \ldots, K_J\}$ denotes a nontrivial partition of $\{1,\ldots,K\}$ and $K \geq J$ is the total number of components used to describe the multichannel data. In the following we note:

- $\mathbf{W}$ and $\mathbf{H}$ the dictionary and activation matrices of sizes, respectively, $F \times K$ and $K \times N$, with coefficients $\{w_{fk}\}$ and $\{h_{kn}\}$ characterizing the components of all sources,
- $\mathbf{W}_j$ and $\mathbf{H}_j$ the dictionary and activation matrices of sizes, respectively, $F \times \#K_j$ and $\#K_j \times N$, with coefficients $\{w_{fk}\}_{f,k \in \mathcal{K}_j}$ and $\{h_{kn}\}_{k \in \mathcal{K}_j, n}$, characterizing the components of source j,
- $\mathbf{C}_k$ the $F \times N$ matrix with coefficients $\{c_{k,fn}\}_{fn}$ and $\mathbf{C}$ the $K \times F \times N$ matrix with coefficients $\{c_{k,fn}\}_{kfn}$.

The task envisaged in this section is the estimation of $\mathbf{W}$, $\mathbf{H}$ and $\mathbf{A}$ from $\mathbf{X}$, and then the reconstruction of the components $\mathbf{C}$ and/or sources $\mathbf{S}$. The problem may be coined "multichannel NMF" because we are attempting to estimate the nonnegative factors $\mathbf{W}_j$ and $\mathbf{H}_j$, but not from the sources themselves (because not available) but from mixtures of these sources. The mixing system is so far assumed linear instantaneous, the convolutive case being addressed in the next section.

Under the assumed models, the expectations of the source and channel power spectrograms are given by

$$E\{|\mathbf{S}_j|^2\} = \mathbf{W}_j \mathbf{H}_j \tag{55}$$

$$E\{|\mathbf{X}_j|^2\} = \sum_j q_{ij} \mathbf{W}_j \mathbf{H}_j \tag{56}$$

$$\stackrel{\text{def}}{=} \mathbf{V}_i \tag{57}$$

Given independence assumptions between all components, the likelihood of each channel writes

$$-\log p(\mathbf{X}_i \mid \mathbf{W}, \mathbf{H}, a_i) \stackrel{c}{=} D_{IS}(\mathbf{V}_i \mid \hat{\mathbf{V}}_i) \tag{58}$$

The approach we propose here to process the channels jointly is to minimize the sum of the individual channel likelihoods, i.e,

$$C(\boldsymbol{\theta}) \stackrel{\text{def}}{=} \sum_i D_{IS}(\mathbf{V}_i \mid \hat{\mathbf{V}}_i) \tag{59}$$

An algorithm based on multiplicative updates for the optimization of this criterion will be described in Section "Convolutive mixing".

Statistical Implications

We stress that the proposed approach is not ML estimation. Indeed our criterion is not equivalent to the full joint likelihood of the observations $-\log p(\mathbf{X}|\boldsymbol{\theta})$, but instead to the sum of the individual likelihoods of each channel $\sum_i -\log p(\mathbf{X}_i|\boldsymbol{\theta})$. Our approach is hence suboptimal, given that the generative data model is true. Optimizing the joint likelihood is somehow more complex than optimizing the mere sum of individual channel likelihoods. A multiplicative algorithm for the latter is described in the next section. An EM algorithm for optimizing the joint likelihood is described in (Ozerov and Févotte, 2010), it is in essence a generalization of the EM algorithm presented at Section "Algorithms for IS-NMF" and is based on same complete dataset **C**. As noted in (Durrieu et al., 2009), $C(\boldsymbol{\theta})$ is actually the real likelihood corresponding to the model where the channel STFTs are assumed mutually independent. To evidence this, note that model (53)-(54) can be rewritten as

$$\mathbf{x}_{i,n} = \sum_{k=1}^{K} a_{ij_k} \mathbf{c}_{k,n} \text{ with } \mathbf{c}_{k,n} \sim \mathcal{N}_c(0, h_{kn} \text{diag}(\mathbf{w}_k)) \tag{60}$$

where j_k indexes the set to which k belongs. Now if we assume that the contributions of component k to each channel is not the exact same signal $\mathbf{c}_{k,n}$ but different realizations $\{\mathbf{c}_{ik,n}\}_{i=1,...I}$ of the same random process $\mathcal{N}_c(0, h_{kn} \text{diag}(\mathbf{w}_k))$, our model writes

$$\mathbf{x}_{i,n} = \sum_{k=1}^{K} a_{ij_k} \mathbf{c}_{ik,n} \text{ with } \mathbf{c}_{ik,n} \sim \mathcal{N}_c(0, h_{kn} \text{diag}(\mathbf{w}_k)) \tag{61}$$

and the joint likelihood is now equivalent to (59).

Optimizing the sum of likelihoods $\sum_i -\log p(\mathbf{X}_i|\boldsymbol{\theta})$ under the assumption that model (60) is true is suboptimal as compared to optimizing the joint likelihood. However, it may be something sensible to do when Equation (60) fails to represent the data correctly, in particular when the point-source assumption fails. See further discussion in (Ozerov and Févotte, 2010).

Reconstruction of Source Images

Given that optimizing $C(\theta)$ is equivalent to maximizing the joint likelihood for model (61), component contributions to each channel may for example be reconstructed via MMSE estimates given by

$$\hat{c}_{ik,n} = \mathrm{E}\{\mathbf{c}_{ik,n}|\mathbf{x}_i,\hat{\theta}\} \tag{62}$$

Under our Gaussian model assumptions this leads to the following Wiener filter

$$\hat{c}_{ik,fn} = \frac{q_{ijk}w_{fk}h_{kn}}{\hat{v}_{i,fn}} x_{i,fn.} \tag{63}$$

Note at this point that though criterion $C(\theta)$ is blind to the sign of a_{ij}, only the modulus of the mixing coefficients intervenes in this component reconstruction formula. The decomposition is conservative in the sense that it satisfies

$$\mathbf{x}_{i,n} = \sum_k \hat{\mathbf{c}}_{ik,n} \tag{64}$$

Inverse-STFT of the $F \times N$ matrices $\{\hat{c}_{ik,fn}\}_{fn}$ for all i and k leads to a set of time-domain component "images" $\{\hat{\mathbf{c}}_1(t),...,\hat{\mathbf{c}}_K(t)\}$, with

$$\hat{\mathbf{c}}_k(t) = \begin{bmatrix} \hat{c}_{1k}(t) \\ \vdots \\ \hat{c}_{Ik}(t) \end{bmatrix} \tag{65}$$

With Equation (64) and with the linearity of the inverse-STFT, the time-domain decomposition is conservative as well, i.e,

$$\mathbf{x}(t) = \sum_k \hat{\mathbf{c}}_k(t) \tag{66}$$

where we recall that $\mathbf{x}(t)$ is the time-domain original multichannel data. Source image estimates may be obtained as

$$\hat{\mathbf{s}}_j(t) = \sum_{k \in \mathcal{K}_j} \hat{\mathbf{c}}_k(t). \tag{67}$$

Note that we are thus not estimating the point-source signal $s_j(t)$ given in Equation (52) but rather yield a "spatial" multichannel image estimate $\hat{s}_j(t)$ reflecting the contribution of $s_j(t)$ to the mix.

Relation to PARAFAC-NTF

Our model has links with the PARAFAC-NTF approach employed in (FitzGerald et al., 2005; Parry and Essa, 2006) for stereo source separation. PARAFAC refers to the parallel factor analysis tensor model which essentially consists of approximating a tensor as a sum of rank-1 tensors, see, e.g, (Bro, 1997). The approximate data structure is

$$\hat{v}_{i,fn}^{NTF} = \sum_k q_{ik}^{NTF} w_{fk} h_{kn}. \tag{68}$$

It is only a sum of $I \times F \times N$ rank-1 tensors and amounts to assuming that the variance model for channel i, $\hat{\mathbf{V}}_i^{NTF} = \left[\hat{v}_{i,fn}^{NTF}\right]_{fn}$, is a linear combination of $F \times N$ time-frequency patterns $\mathbf{w}_k h_k$, where $\mathbf{w}_k$ is column k of $\mathbf{W}$ and h_k is row k of $\mathbf{H}$. It also intrinsically implies a linear instantaneous mixture but requires a post-processing binding step in order to group the K elementary patterns into J sources, based on clustering of the ratios $\{q_{1k}/q_{2k}\}_k$ (in the stereo case). To ease comparison, our model can be rewritten as

$$\hat{v}_{i,fn} = \sum_k q_{ij_k} w_{fk} h_{kn} \tag{69}$$

where we recall that if and only if $k \in K_j$. Hence our model has the merit of imposing that the K mixing proportions $\{q_{ik,f}\}_k$ can only take J possible values out of K, which implies that the clustering of the components is taken care of within the decomposition as opposed to after the decomposition. PARAFAC-NTF is then achieved by minimizing $D(\mathbf{V} \mid \hat{\mathbf{V}})$ using multiplicative updates given in (Welling and Weber, 2001; Shashua and Hazan, 2005).

Convolutive Mixing

Generative Model

The instantaneous model has allowed us to introduce the concepts of multichannel NMF based on simple mixing assumptions. However in practice, most audio recordings involve convolution, i.e,

$$x_i(t) = \sum_j \sum_{\tau=0}^{L} a_{ij}(\tau) s_j(t - \tau) \tag{70}$$

When the convolution length L is "significantly" shorter than the STFT analysis window size the time-domain convolutive mixing can be approximated by linear instantaneous mixing in each frequency band f, i.e

$$x_{i,fn} = \sum_j a_{ij,f} s_{j,fn}, \tag{71}$$

which is to be contrasted with the linear instantaneous mixture of Equation (53), i.e, a_{ij} has been replaced by $a_{ij,f}$. From there, everything described in previous section holds, from source assumptions to inference, given that q_{ij} is everywhere replaced by $q_{ij,f} = |a_{ij,f}|^2$. In the following we note $\mathbf{q}_{ij,f} = [q_{ij,1}, \ldots, q_{ij,F}]^T$ and $\mathbf{Q}_f$ the $I \times J$ matrix with coefficients $\{q_{ij,f}\}_{ij}$. In the convolutive mixture, the variance model for channel i now writes

$$\hat{\mathbf{V}}_i = \sum_j \text{diag}(\mathbf{q}_{ij}) \mathbf{W}_j \mathbf{H}_j \tag{72}$$

and we aim at minimizing criterion (59).

Indeterminacies

Structure (72) suffers from obvious scale and permutation indeterminacies.[2] Regarding scale, let $\theta_1 = \{\{\mathbf{Q}_f\}_f, \{\mathbf{W}_j, \mathbf{H}_j\}_j\}$ be a minimizer of (59) and let $\{\mathbf{D}_f\}_f$ and $\{\mathbf{A}_j\}_j$ be sets of nonnegative diagonal matrices. Then, the set $\theta_2 = \{\{\mathbf{Q}_f \mathbf{D}_f^{-1}\}_f, \{\text{diag}([d_{ij,f}]_f) \mathbf{W}_j \Lambda_j^{-1}\}_{ji}, \{\Lambda_j \mathbf{H}_j\}_j\}$ leads to $v_{i,fn}(\theta_1) = v_{i,fn}(\theta_2)$, hence same criterion value. Similarly, permuted diagonal matrices would also leave the criterion unchanged. In practice, we remove these scale ambiguities by imposing $\sum_i q_{ij,f} = 1$ (and scaling the rows of $\mathbf{W}_j$ accordingly) and then by imposing $\sum_f w_{fk} = 1$ (and scaling the rows of $\mathbf{H}_j$ accordingly). Note again that the indeterminacy on the phase of $a_{ij,f}$ is total.

Multiplicative Updates

Like in the single-channel case we adopt a multiplicative gradient descent approach for minimization of criterion $C(\mathbf{W}, \mathbf{H}, \mathbf{Q})$, which in particular allows to ensure the nonnegativity of all parameters. The following derivatives may be obtained

$$\nabla_{q_{ij,f}} C(\theta) = \sum_{n=1}^{N} \sum_{k \in K_j} w_{fk} h_{kn} d'_{IS}(v_{ifn} \mid \hat{v}_{i,fn}) \tag{73}$$

$$\nabla_{w_{jfk}} C(\theta) = \sum_{i=1}^{I} \sum_{n=1}^{N} q_{ij,f} h_{j,kn} d'_{IS}(v_{i,fn} \mid \hat{v}_{i,fn}) \tag{74}$$

$$\nabla_{h_{jkn}} C(\theta) = \sum_{i=1}^{I} \sum_{f=1}^{F} q_{ij,f} w_{j,fk} d'_{IS}(v_{i,fn} \mid \hat{v}_{i,fn}) \tag{75}$$

Algorithm 5. Mulitichannel IS-NMF

Input : nonnegative tensor **V**
Output : nonnegative matrices **W** and **H**, nonnegative matrix
or tensor **Q**
Initialize **W**, **H**, and **Q** with nonnegative values
for $l = 1 : n_{iter}$ **do**

$$q_{ij} \leftarrow q_{ij} \cdot \frac{[\hat{\mathbf{V}}_i^{-2} \cdot \mathbf{V}_i \cdot (\mathbf{W}_j \mathbf{H}_j)]\mathbf{1}_{N \times 1}}{[\hat{\mathbf{V}}_i^{-1} \cdot (\mathbf{W}_j \mathbf{H}_j)]\mathbf{1}_{N \times 1}}$$

$$\mathbf{W}_j \leftarrow \mathbf{W}_j \cdot \frac{\Sigma_{i=1}^{I} \mathrm{diag}(\mathbf{q}_{ij}) \mathbf{H}_j^{T}}{\Sigma_{i=1}^{I} \mathrm{diag}(\mathbf{q}_{ij}) \hat{\mathbf{V}}_i^{-1} \mathbf{H}_j^{T}}$$

$$\mathbf{H}_j \leftarrow \mathbf{H}_j \cdot \frac{\Sigma_{i=1}^{I} (\mathrm{diag}(\mathbf{q}_{ij}) \mathbf{W}_j)^{T} (\hat{\mathbf{V}}_i^{-2} \cdot \mathbf{V}_i)}{\Sigma_{i=1}^{I} (\mathrm{diag}(\mathbf{q}_{ij}) \mathbf{W}_j)^{T} \hat{\mathbf{V}}_i^{-1}}$$

Normalize **Q**, **W**, and **H**
end for

---

where $d'_{IS}(x \,|\, y) = 1 \,/\, y - x \,/\, y^2$. Separating the positive and negative summands of each equations and rearranging the expressions in a matrix form leads to Algorithm 5, whose convergence was observed in practice. Updates for the linear instantaneous mixing are obtained as a special case, by setting $q_{ij,f} = q_{ij}$ everywhere and using the update

$$q_{ij} \leftarrow q_{ij} \cdot \frac{\mathrm{sum}\left[\hat{\mathbf{V}}_i^{-2} \cdot \mathbf{V}_i \cdot (\mathbf{W}_j \mathbf{H}_j)\right]}{\mathrm{sum}\left[\hat{\mathbf{V}}_i^{-1} \cdot (\mathbf{W}_j \mathbf{H}_j)\right]} \tag{76}$$

where sum[**M**] is the sum of all coefficients in **M**. In the specific linear instantaneous case, multiplicative updates based on Khatri-Rao and contracted tensor products can be exhibited for the whole matrices **Q**, **W**, **H** (instead of individual updates for q_{ij}, $\mathbf{W}_j$, $\mathbf{H}_j$), but are not given here for conciseness. They are similar in form to (Welling and Weber, 2001) and (Shashua and Hazan, 2005) and lead to a faster MATLAB implementation.

Results

We present decomposition results of a real stereo music excerpt taken as the first 24 s of the song *So Much Trouble in the World* by Bob Marley.

The excerpt is composed two guitars, drums & percussions, bass, voice and synthesizer sounds. One guitar plays the off-beat rhythmic component characteristic of reggae and we will refer to it as lead guitar, while we will refer to the other as second guitar. The audio signal is downsampled at 22.05 kHz and a 50% overlap sinebell STFT was computed with window size 92 ms - a rather long window size is here preferable for model (71) to hold. We decomposed the signal with the convolutive NTF method described in previous section, with $J = 4$ sources and only 2 components per source, i.e, $K = 8$. It is clear that such a small number of components is insufficient to capture every elementary object of this rich and diverse audio scene, but we wish to inspect what can our convolutive IS-NTF model learn with such a restricted number of components. We run the algorithm for 1000 iterations (approximatively 30 min with our MATLAB implementation on a Mac 2.6 GHz with 2 Go RAM) and as before we select the solution with minimum cost value from 10 random initializations. The learnt dictionary **W**, coefficients **H** and reconstructed stereo components are displayed on Figure 8. The sound samples can be listened to online at http://www. tsi.enst.fr/~fevotte/Samples/machine-audition/. The MATLAB code of the algorithm is available from the author webpage as well.

Very interestingly the decomposition captures high-level structures from the data in the sense that each of the components captures pieces of a subset of the instrumental sources. The decomposition describes coarsely as follows. The first component contains mainly all of the bass, the bass drum, one part of the second guitar, one sort of the synthesizer sounds. The second and fourth component contains mainly parts of the voice. The fifth component contains mainly the lead guitar and the other part of the second guitar. Finally, the remaining components each capture one of the drum sources. Hence, binding components 1 and 5 mainly provide the bass, guitars and synthesizer part, components 2 and 4 mainly

*Figure 8. Convolutive IS-NTF with K = 8. Left: columns of **W** (log$_{10}$ scale). Middle: rows of **H**. Right: Component reconstructions with equation (63).*

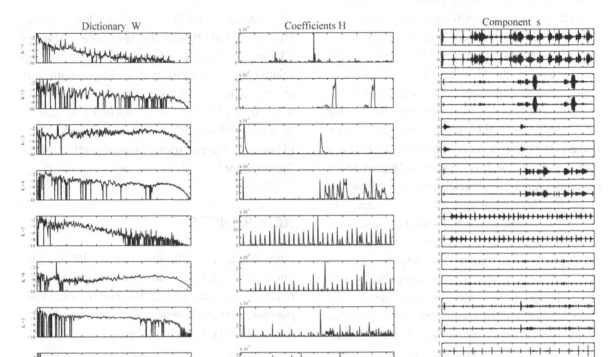

provide the voice and the four remaining components mainly provide the drums. Note the "instrumental sources" resulting from the manual binding of the components belong to different "directional sources" as intended in model (71), showing the limits of the point-source model. The separation between all the instruments can be further improved by allotting more components to each directional source j. We present online separation results obtained with $J = 4$ and 6 component per source, i.e, a total number of $K = 24$ components, that were manually bound into 6 instrumental sources containing respectively the lead guitar, the second guitar, the voice, the bass, the drums and the synthesizer.

CONCLUSION

In this chapter the authors have attempted to show the relevance of using nonnegative factorization of the power spectrogram with the Itakura-Saito divergence, for musical audio decomposition. On the modeling side, they wish to bring out the following three features of IS-NMF: 1) IS-NMF is underlain by a sound statistical model of superimposed Gaussian components, 2) this model is relevant to the representation of audio signals, 3) this model can accommodate regularization constraints and model selection scenarios through Bayesian approaches. The authors compared the decompositions of a well structured piano sequence obtained using IS-NMF of the power spectrogram and using the more common approach of KL-NMF of the magnitude spectrogram. The organization of the decomposition with the former better matches our own comprehension of sound.

In the second part of the paper we described extensions of NMF-based sound decomposition to the multichannel case. NMF-based models usually convey the idea that the dictionary elements should represent low-level elementary objects such as notes. However, experiments on a real stereo musical excerpt showed that, given a small number of components, the model is able to retrieve both low-level objects and higher-level structures encompassing rich and diverse sources.

On the algorithmic part, one of the limitations of the decomposition techniques they described is their sensitivity to local minima, and we found out in practice that the decompositions obtained from the local solutions were semantically not as satisfactory as the "more optimal" ones - this observation also corroborates the relevance of the IS divergence for audio, in the sense that lower cost solutions are better indeed. In order to reduce this problem they systematically ran the algorithms several times from different random solutions, which prove rather satisfactory. However, more advanced MCMC inference strategies have also been mentioned, though they do not give any results at this stage.

The computation times involved by the multiplicative algorithms presented in this paper is fair; though still far from real-time (in the order of 1 min for 1 s of data, to decompose stereo signals sampled at 22 kHz, using a MATLAB implementation on a standard machine) the methods may be used in an off-line setting, typically for sound edition.

Finally, as also discussed in the chapter, the plain IS-NMF model can be sophisticated in many ways, for example to model voice or include explicit pitched structure. The general inference methodology presented in this chapter holds in every case and combinations of various component models are possible, either in the single or multichannel cases.

ACKNOWLEDGMENT

The author would like to acknowledge Nancy Bertin, Raphaël Blouet, Taylan Cemgil, Maurice Charbit and Jean-Louis Durrieu for collaborations related to the content of this chaper, with very special thanks to Alexey Ozerov and Vincent Y. F. Tan. This work was supported in part by project ANR-09-JCJC-0073-01 *TANGERINE* (Theory and applications of nonnegative matrix factorization).

REFERENCES

Abdallah, S. A., & Plumbley, M. D. (2004). Polyphonic transcription by nonnegative sparse coding of power spectra. In *Proc. 5th International Symposium Music Information Retrieval (ISMIR '04)* (pp. 318–325). Barcelona, Spain.

Benaroya, L., Blouet, R., Févotte, C., & Cohen, I. (2006a). Single sensor source separation using multiple window STFT representation. In *Proc. International Workshop on Acoustic Echo and Noise Control (IWAENC '06)*. Paris, France.

Benaroya, L., Gribonval, R., & Bimbot, F. (2003). Non negative sparse representation for Wiener based source separation with a single sensor. In *Proc. IEEE International Conference on Acoustics, Speech and Signal Processing (ICASSP '03)* (pp. 613–616). Hong Kong.

Benaroya, L., Gribonval, R., & Bimbot, F. (2006b). Audio source separation with a single sensor. *IEEE Transactions on Audio, Speech, and Language Processing, 14*(1), 191–199. doi:10.1109/TSA.2005.854110

Bishop, C. M. (1999). Bayesian PCA. In *Advances in neural information processing systems* (pp. 382–388). NIPS.

Blouet, R., Rapaport, G., Cohen, I., & Févotte, C. (2008). Evaluation of several strategies for single sensor speech/music separation. In *Proc. International Conference on Acoustics, Speech and Signal Processing (ICASSP '08)*. Las Vegas, USA.

Bro, R. (1997). PARAFAC. Tutorial and applications. *Chemometrics and Intelligent Laboratory Systems, 38*(2), 149–171. doi:10.1016/S0169-7439(97)00032-4

Cemgil, A. T. (2009). Bayesian inference for non-negative matrix factorisation models. *Computational Intelligence and Neuroscience*, 2009(Article ID 785152), 17 pages. (doi:10.1155/2009/785152)

Chib, S. (1995). Marginal likelihood from the Gibbs output. *Journal of the American Statistical Association, 90*(432), 1995. doi:10.2307/2291521

Cichocki, A., Amari, S.-I., Zdunek, R., Kompass, R., Hori, G., & He, Z. (2006). Extended SMART algorithms for non-negative matrix factorization. In *Proc. International Conference on Artificial Intelligence and Soft Computing (ICAISC '06)* (p. 548-562). Zakopane, Poland.

Dhillon, I. S., & Sra, S. (2005). *Generalized nonnegative matrix approximations with Bregman divergences. Advances in Neural Information Processing Systems*. NIPS.

Doucet, A., Sénécal, S., & Matsui, T. (2005). Space alternating data augmentation: Application to finite mixture of Gaussians and speaker recognition. In *Proc. IEEE International Conference on Acoustics, Speech and Signal Processing (ICASSP '05)* (pp. IV-713 – IV-716). Philadelphia, PA.

Durrieu, J.-L., Ozerov, A., Févotte, C., Richard, G., & David, B. (2009). Main instrument separation from stereophonic audio signals using a source/filter model. In *Proc. 17th European Signal Processing Conference (EUSIPCO '09)* (pp. 15–19). Glasgow, Scotland.

Durrieu, J.-L., Richard, G., David, B., & Févotte, C. (2010). Source/filter model for main melody extraction from polyphonic audio signals. *IEEE Transactions on Audio, Speech, and Language Processing. 3*(3). doi:10.1109/TASL.2010.2041114

Févotte, C., Bertin, N., & Durrieu, J.-L. (2009). Nonnegative matrix factorization with the Itakura-Saito divergence. With application to music analysis. *Neural Computation, 21*(3). doi:10.1162/neco.2008.04-08-771

Févotte, C., & Cemgil, A. T. (2009). Nonnegative matrix factorisations as probabilistic inference in composite models. In *Proc. 17th European Signal Processing Conference (EUSIPCO '09)* (pp. 1913–1917). Glasgow, Scotland.

FitzGerald, D., Cranitch, M., & Coyle, E. (2005). Non-negative tensor factorisation for sound source separation. In *Proc. of the Irish Signals and Systems Conference*. Dublin, Ireland.

Gray, R. M., Buzo, A., Gray, A. H., & Matsuyama, Y. (1980). Distortion measures for speech processing. *IEEE Transactions on Acoustics, Speech, and Signal Processing, 28*(4), 367–376. doi:10.1109/TASSP.1980.1163421

Itakura, F., & Saito, S. (1968). Analysis synthesis telephony based on the maximum likelihood method. In *Proc 6th International Congress on Acoustics* (pp. C-17 – C-20). Tokyo, Japan.

Kompass, R. (2007). A generalized divergence measure for nonnegative matrix factorization. *Neural Computation, 19*(3), 780–791. doi:10.1162/neco.2007.19.3.780

Kreutz-Delgado, K., Murray, J. F., Rao, B. D., Engan, K., Lee, T.-W., & Sejnowski, T. J. (2003). Dictionary learning algorithms for sparse representation. *Neural Computation, 15*(2), 349–396. doi:10.1162/089976603762552951

Laurberg, H., Christensen, M. G., Plumbley, M. D., Hansen, L. K., & Jensen, S. H. (2008). Theorems on positive data: On the uniqueness of NMF. *Computational Intelligence and Neuroscience*, 764206.

Lee, D. D., & Seung, H. S. (1999). Learning the parts of objects with nonnegative matrix factorization. *Nature, 401,* 788–791. doi:10.1038/44565

Lee, D. D., & Seung, H. S. (2001). Algorithms for non-negative matrix factorization . In *Advances in Neural and Information Processing Systems* (pp. 556–562). NIPS.

Lewicki, M. S., & Sejnowski, T. J. (2000). Learning overcomplete representations. *Neural Computation, 12,* 337–365. doi:10.1162/089976600300015826

MacKay, D. (1996). Maximum likelihood and covariant algorithms for independent component analysis. Retrieved from http://www.inference.phy.cam.ac.uk/mackay/ica.pdf. (Unpublished)

Mackay, D. J. C. (1995). Probable networks and plausible predictions – a review of practical Bayesian models for supervised neural networks. *Network (Bristol, England), 6*(3), 469–505. doi:10.1088/0954-898X/6/3/011

Moussaoui, S., Brie, D., Mohammad-Djafari, A., & Carteret, C. (2006). Separation of non-negative mixture of non-negative sources using a Bayesian approach and MCMC sampling. *IEEE Transactions on Signal Processing, 54*(11), 4133–4145. doi:10.1109/TSP.2006.880310

Ozerov, A., & Févotte, C. (2010). (in press). Multichannel nonnegative matrix factorization in convolutive mixtures for audio source separation. *IEEE Transactions on Audio . Speech and Language Processing.* doi:10.1109/TASL.2009.2031510

Ozerov, A., Févotte, C., & Charbit, M. (2009). Factorial scaled hidden markov model for polyphonic audio representation and source separation. In *Proc. IEEE Workshop on Applications of Signal Processing to Audio and Acoustics (WASPAA'09).* Mohonk, NY, USA.

Ozerov, A., Philippe, P., Bimbot, F., & Gribonval, R. (2007). Adaptation of Bayesian models for single channel source separation and its application to voice/music separation in popular songs. *IEEE Transactions on Audio, Speech, and Language Processing, 15*(5), 1564–1578. doi:10.1109/TASL.2007.899291

Paatero, P. (1997). Least squares formulation of robust non-negative factor analysis. *Chemometrics and Intelligent Laboratory Systems, 37*(1), 23–25. doi:10.1016/S0169-7439(96)00044-5

Parry, R. M., & Essa, I. (2007). Phase-aware non-negative spectrogram factorization. In *Proc. International Conference on Independent Component Analysis and Signal Separation (ICA'07)* (pp. 536–543). London, UK.

Parry, R. M., & Essa, I. A. (2006). Estimating the spatial position of spectral components in audio. In *Proc. 6th International Conference on Independent Component Analysis and Blind Signal Separation (ICA'06)* (p. 666-673). Charleston SC, USA.

Schmidt, M. N., Winther, O., & Hansen, L. K. (2009). Bayesian non-negative matrix factorization. In *Proc. 8th International conference on Independent Component Analysis and Signal Separation (ICA'09).* Paraty, Brazil.

Shashanka, M., Raj, B., & Smaragdis, P. (2008). Probabilistic latent variable models as nonnegative factorizations. *Computational Intelligence and Neuroscience*(Article ID 947438, 8 pages). (doi:10.1155/2008/947438)

Shashua, A., & Hazan, T. (2005). Non-negative tensor factorization with applications to statistics and computer vision. In *Proc. 22nd International Conference on Machine Learning* (pp. 792–799). Bonn, Germany: ACM.

Smaragdis, P. (2007). Convolutive speech bases and their application to speech separation. *IEEE Transactions on Audio, Speech, and Language Processing, 15*(1), 1–12. doi:10.1109/TASL.2006.876726

Smaragdis, P., & Brown, J. C. (2003). Non-negative matrix factorization for polyphonic music transcription. In *Proc. IEEE Workshop on Applications of Signal Processing to Audio and Acoustics (WASPAA'03)*. Mohonk, NY, USA.

Stoica, P., & Selén, Y. (2004). Model-order selection: a review of information criterion rules. *IEEE Signal Processing Magazine, 21*(4), 36–47. doi:10.1109/MSP.2004.1311138

Tan, V. Y. F., & Févotte, C. (2009). Automatic relevance determination in nonnegative matrix factorization. In *Proc. Workshop on Signal Processing with Adaptative Sparse Structured Representations (SPARS'09)*. Saint-Malo, France.

Tipping, M. E. (2001). Sparse Bayesian Learning and the relevance vector machine. *Journal of Machine Learning Research, 1*, 211–244. doi:10.1162/15324430152748236

Vincent, E., Bertin, N., & Badeau, R. (2007). Two nonnegative matrix factorization methods for polyphonic pitch transcription . In *Proc. Music Information Retrieval Evaluation eXchange*. MIREX.

Virtanen, T. (2007). Monaural sound source separation by non-negative matrix factorization with temporal continuity and sparseness criteria. *IEEE Transactions on Audio . Speech and Language Processing, 15*(3), 1066–1074. doi:10.1109/TASL.2006.885253

Virtanen, T., Cemgil, A. T., & Godsill, S. (2008). Bayesian extensions to non-negative matrix factorization for audio signal modelling. In *Proc. International Conference on Acoustics, Speech and Signal Processing (ICASSP'08)* (pp. 1825–1828). Las Vegas, Nevada, USA.

Wang, W., Cichocki, A., & Chambers, J. A. (2009). A multiplicative algorithm for convolutive non-negative matrix factorization based on squared Euclidean distance. *IEEE Transactions on Signal Processing, 57*(7), 2858–2864. doi:10.1109/TSP.2009.2016881

Welling, M., & Weber, M. (2001). Positive tensor factorization. *Pattern Recognition Letters, 22*(12), 1255–1261. doi:10.1016/S0167-8655(01)00070-8

ENDNOTES

[1] http://sisec.wiki.irisa.fr/

[2] There might also be other less obvious indeterminacies, such as those inherent to NMF, see, e.g., (Laurberg, Christensen, Plumbley, Hansen, and Jensen, 2008), but this study is here left aside.

APPENDIX A: STANDARD DISTRIBUTIONS

Proper complex Gaussian: $N_c(\mathrm{x} \mid \mu, \Sigma) = \mid \pi \Sigma \mid^{-1} \exp{-(\mathrm{x} - \mu)^H \Sigma^{-1}(\mathrm{x} - \mu)}$

Poisson: $\mathcal{P}(x \mid \lambda) = \exp(-\lambda) \dfrac{\lambda^x}{x!}$

Gamma: $\mathcal{G}(u \mid \alpha, \beta) = \dfrac{\beta^\alpha}{\Gamma(\alpha)} u^{\alpha-1} \exp(-\beta u), u \geq 0$

inverse-Gamma: $\mathcal{IG}(u \mid \alpha, \beta) = \dfrac{\beta^\alpha}{\Gamma(\alpha)} u^{-(\alpha+1)} \exp(-\dfrac{\beta}{u}), u \geq 0$

(The inverse-Gamma distribution is the distribution of $1/X$ when X is Gamma distributed.)

half-normal: $\mathcal{HN}(x \mid \phi) = \left(\dfrac{\pi\phi}{2}\right)^{-\frac{1}{2}} \exp\left(-\dfrac{1}{2}\dfrac{x^2}{\phi}\right)$

(The half-normal distribution is the distribution of $|X|$ when X is normally distributed with mean 0.)

Chapter 12
Music Onset Detection

Ruohua Zhou
Queen Mary University of London, UK

Josh D. Reiss
Queen Mary University of London, UK

ABSTRACT

Music onset detection plays an essential role in music signal processing and has a wide range of applications. This chapter provides a step by step introduction to the design of music onset detection algorithms. The general scheme and commonly-used time-frequency analysis for onset detection are introduced. Many methods are reviewed, and some typical energy-based, phase-based, pitch-based and supervised learning methods are described in detail. The commonly used performance measures, onset annotation software, public database and evaluation methods are introduced. The performance difference between energy-based and pitch-based method is discussed. The future research directions for music onset detection are also described.

INTRODUCTION

The audio signal is often considered to be a succession of the discrete acoustic events. The term music onset detection refers to detection of the instant when a discrete event begins in a music signal. Music onset detection plays an essential role in music signal processing and has a wide range of applications such as automatic music transcription, beat-tracking, tempo identification and music information retrieval.

DOI: 10.4018/978-1-61520-919-4.ch012

Different sound sources (instruments) have different types of onsets that are often classified as "soft" or "hard". The human perception of the onset is usually related to the salient change in the sound's pitch, energy or timbre. Hard onsets are characterized by sudden increases in energy, whereas soft onsets show more gradual change. Hard onsets can be well detected by energy-based approaches, but the detection of soft onsets remains a challenging problem. Let us suppose that a note consists of a transient, followed by a steady-state part, and the onset of the note is at the beginning of the transient. For hard onsets, energy changes

Figure 1. Three stages of music onset detection: time-frequency processing of the audio signal, producing an onset detection function, and using peak-picking to identify onsets

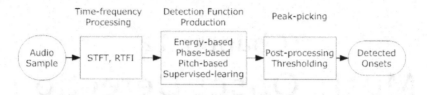

are usually significantly larger in the transients than in the steady-state parts. Conversely, when considering the case of soft onsets, energy changes in the transients and the steady-state parts are comparable, and they do not constitute reliable cues for onset detection any more. Consequently, energy-based approaches fail to correctly detect soft onsets. Stable pitch cues enable to segment a note into a transient and a steady-state part, because the pitch of the steady-state part often remains stable. This fact can be used to develop appropriate pitch-based methods that yield better performances, for the detection of soft onsets, than energy-based methods. However, although many approaches use energy information, only a few pitch-based methods have been proposed in the literature.

We discuss general scheme for onset detection and how to develop an onset detection algorithm step by step. Many existing methods are described, and a few typical methods are to be described in detail. Performance evaluation and future research directions will also be discussed. The organization of this chapter is listed as follows. The ALGO-RITHMS section explains the general scheme for music onset detection and typical algorithms for energy-based, phase-based, pitch-based and supervised learning approaches. In the section on PERFORMANCE EVALUATION, the evaluation of onset detection approaches is discussed, and several established evaluation results are presented. Finally, the section on FURTHER RESEARCH DIRECTIONS discusses possible research directions, inspired by human perception, which could be applied to the field of music onset detection.

ALGORITHMS

General Scheme

Many different onset detection systems have been described in the literature. As shown in Figure 1, they typically consist of three stages; time-frequency processing, detection function generation, and peak-picking (Bello et al., 2005). At first, a music signal is transformed into different frequency bands by using a filter-bank or a spectrogram. For example, the Short Time Fourier Transform (STFT) and the Resonator Time Frequency Image (RTFI) are two useful time-frequency analysis tools for onset detection. Then, the output of the first stage is further processed to generate a detection function at a lower sampling rate. Finally, a peak-picking operation is used to find onset times within the detection function, which is often derived by inspecting the changes in energy, phase, or pitch.

Time-Frequency Processing

Music signals are time-varying, and most of the analysis tasks require a joint time-frequency analysis. One commonly-used time-frequency analysis tool is Short Time Fourier Transform (STFT). The Fourier Transform and its inverse can transform signals between the time and frequency domains. It can make it possible to view the signal characteristics either in time or frequency domain, but not to combine both domains. In order to obtain a joint time-frequency analysis for non-stationary signals, the STFT cuts the time signal into different frames and then perform a Fourier Transform in each frame. The STFT can be defined as follows,

$$STFT(t,\omega) = \int_{-\infty}^{\infty} s(\tau)w(\tau - t)e^{-j\omega\tau}d\tau \qquad (1)$$

The STFT at time t is the Fourier Transform of a local signal, which is obtained by multiplication of a signal $s(t)$ and a short window function $w(\tau - t)$ centered at time t. When moving the window along the signal time axis, we can calculate the STFT at different time instants and obtain a joint time-frequency analysis. The discrete STFT of a signal $s(n)$ can be defined as follows,

$$X_m(n) = \sum_{l=-N/2}^{N/2-1} s(nh + l)w(l)e^{-2j\pi ml} \qquad (2)$$

where $w(l)$ is a N-point window, h is the hop size and m denotes the different frequency bins.

Another useful time-frequency representation for music signal analysis is the Resonator Time Frequency Image (RTFI). To better explain the RTFI, first a frequency-dependent time-frequency (FDTF) analysis is defined as follows:

$$FDTF(t,\omega) = \int_{-\infty}^{\infty} s(\tau)w(\tau - t,\omega)e^{-j\omega(\tau-t)}d\tau \qquad (3)$$

Unlike the STFT, the window function w of the FDTF may depend on the analytical frequency ω. This means that time and frequency resolutions can be changed according to the analytical frequency. At the same time, Equation (3) can also be expressed as convolution:

$$FDTF(t,\omega) = s(t) * I(t,\omega) \qquad (4)$$

where

$$I(t,\omega) = w(-t,\omega)e^{j\omega t} \qquad (5)$$

Equation (3) is more suitable for expressing a transform-based implementation, whereas Equation (4) leads to a straightforward implementation of a filter bank with impulse response functions expressed in Equation (5). On the one hand, we can also group the terms in the STFT definition differently to obtain the filter bank interpretation for STFT. However, there are two main differences between the band-pass filter implementations of STFT and FDTF.

As illustrated in Figure 2, one difference is that, in the implementation of the STFT, the bandwidth of the band-pass filter is kept fixed and independent of its centre frequency ω. Instead, for the FDTF, the bandwidth of the band-pass filter can be changed according to centre frequency ω. Another difference is that, in the implementation of the STFT, the output of every band-pass filter centered at ω is then demodulated to zero frequency. Such a demodulation process does not exist in the implementation of the FDTF.

Computational efficiency and simplicity are the two essential criteria used to select an appropriate filter bank for implementing the FDTF. The order of the filter bank needs to be as small as possible to reduce computational cost. The basic idea behind the filter-bank-based implementation of FDTF is to realize frequency-dependent frequency resolution by possibly varying the filters' bandwidths with their center frequencies. Therefore, the implementing filters must be simple so that their bandwidths can be easily controlled according to their center frequencies. The RTFI selects a first-order complex resonator filter bank to implement a frequency-dependent time-frequency analysis.

The RTFI can be expressed as follows:

$$RTFI(t,\omega) = s(t) * I_R(t,\omega) \qquad (6)$$

$$= r(\omega)\int_{0}^{t} s(\tau)e^{r(\omega)(\tau-t)}e^{-j\omega(\tau-t)}d\tau$$

Figure 2. Filter bank implementation of STFT and FDTF

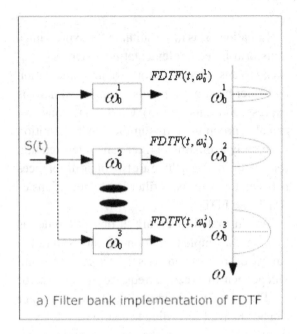

a) Filter bank implementation of FDTF

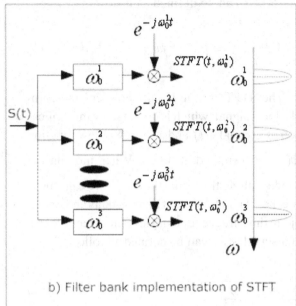

b) Filter bank implementation of STFT

where

$$I_R(t, \omega) = r(\omega)e^{(-r(\omega)+j\omega)t}, \qquad t > 0 \qquad (7)$$

In these equations, I_R denotes the impulse response of the first-order complex resonator filter with oscillation frequency ω. The factor $r(\omega)$ before the integral in Equation (6) is used to normalize the gain of the frequency response when the resonator filter's input frequency is the oscillation frequency. The decay factor r is dependent on the frequency ω and determines the exponent window length and the time resolution. At the same time it also determines the bandwidth (i.e., the frequency resolution). The frequency resolution of time-frequency analysis implemented by the filter bank is defined as the equivalent rectangular bandwidth (ERB) of the implementing filter, according to the following equation:

$$B^{ERB} = \int_0^\infty |H(\omega)|^2 d\omega \qquad (8)$$

where $H(\omega)$ is the frequency response of a band pass filter and the maximum value of $|H(\omega)|$ is normalized at 1 (Hartmann, 1997). The ERB value of the digital filter can be expressed according to angular frequency as follows:

$$B^{ERB}(\omega) = r(\omega)(0.5\pi + \arctan(\frac{\omega}{r(\omega)})) \qquad (9)$$

In most practical cases, the resonator filter exponent factor is nearly zero, so *arctan(ω/r(ω))* can be approximated to 0.5π, and Equation (9) is approximated as follows:

$$B^{ERB}(\omega) \approx r(\omega) \cdot \pi \qquad (10)$$

The resolution B^{ERB} can be set through a map function between the frequency and the exponential decay factor r. For example, a frequency-dependent frequency resolution and corresponding r value can be parameterized as follows:

$$B^{ERB}(\omega) = d + c\omega, \quad d + c > 0, \quad c \geq 0, d \geq 0 \tag{11}$$

$$r(\omega) \approx B^{ERB}(\omega) / \pi = (d + c\omega) / \pi \tag{12}$$

The commonly used frequency resolutions for music analysis are special cases of the parameterized resolutions in Equation(11). When $d=0$, the resolution is constant-Q; when $c=0$, the resolution is uniform; when $d = 24.7 \times 2\pi = 155.2$, $c=0.1079$, the resolution corresponds to the widely-accepted resolution of an auditory filter bank (Moore & Glasberg, 1996).

As the RTFI has a complex spectrum, it can be expressed as follows:

$$RTFI(t,\omega) = A(t,\omega)e^{j\phi(t,\omega)} \tag{13}$$

where $A(t,\omega)$ and $\varphi(t, \omega)$ are real functions.

$$RTFI_{Energy}(t,\omega) = \left|A(t,\omega)\right|^2 \tag{14}$$

It is proposed to use a complex resonator digital filter bank for implementing a discrete RTFI. To reduce the memory usage of storing the RTFI values, the RTFI is separated into different time frames, and the average RTFI value is calculated in each time frame. The average RTFI energy spectrum can be expressed as follows:

$$A(n,\omega_m) = 20\log_{10}(\frac{1}{M}\sum_{l=(n-1)M+1}^{nM}\left|RTFI(l,\omega_m)\right|^2) \tag{15}$$

where n is the index of a frame, M is an integer, and the ratio of M to sampling rate is the duration time of each frame in the average process. $RTFI(l, \omega_m)$ represents the value of the discrete RTFI at sampling point l and frequency ω_m. A detailed description of the discrete RTFI can be found in the references (Zhou, 2006; Zhou & Mattavelli, 2007).

Energy-Based Detection

In early methods, the amplitude envelope of a music signal was used to derive the detection function. The amplitude envelope can be constructed by rectifying and smoothing the signal:

$$C(n) = \sum_{k=-N/2}^{N/2-1} \left|s(n + k)\right| w(k) \tag{16}$$

where $w(k)$ is N-point window. A variation on this is to derive the detection function from local energy, instead of amplitude.

$$E(n) = \sum_{k=-N/2}^{N/2-1} s^2(n + k)w(k) \tag{17}$$

In the simplest case, differences in a signal's amplitude or energy are used to detect note onsets. However, such an approach has been shown to give poor results. Researchers have found it useful to separate the analyzed signal into a number of bands and then detect onsets across the different frequency bands. This constitutes the key element of multi-band processing. For example, Goto utilizes the sudden energy changes to detect onsets in seven different frequency ranges and uses these onsets to track the music beats by a multiagent architecture (Goto, 2001). Klapuri divides the signal into 21 frequency bands by the nearly critical-band filter bank (Klapuri, 1999). Then, he uses amplitude envelopes to find onsets across these frequency bands. Duxbury et al. introduce a hybrid multiband processing approach for onset detection (Duxbury, Sandler and Davies, 2002). In the approach, an energy-based detector is used to detect hard onsets in the upper bands, whereas a frequency based distance measure is utilized in the lower bands to improve the detection of soft onsets. Wang et al. proposes a novel approach based on music spectra magnitude (Wang et al., 2008). They first decompose the music spectra magnitude into linear temporal bases by nonnegative matrix factorization, and then use the linear temporal bases to construct detection functions.

The spectrum is used to measure the energy change in the time-frequency domain. The first-order difference of energy has been utilized to evaluate the energy change and derive a detection function. However, the first-order difference is usually not able to precisely mark onset times. According to psychoacoustic principles, a perceived increase in the signal amplitude is relative to its level. The same amount of increase can be perceived more clearly in a quiet signal (Klapuri, 1999). Consequently, as a refinement, the relative difference can be used to better locate onset times.

For example, when the STFT is selected as the time-frequency processing tool, the spectrum D can be defined as follows,

$$D_m(n) = 20\log_{10}\left(\left|X_m(n)\right|^2\right) - 20\log_{10}\left(\left|X_m(n-1)\right|^2\right)$$

(18)

where $X_m(n)$ is the discrete STFT of the input signal.

The commonly-used energy-based detection methods can be generalized as follows,

$$M(n) = \frac{1}{N}\sum_{m=1}^{N} H(D_m(n))$$

(19)

where $H(x) = (x + \left|x\right|)/2$ is the half-wave rectifier function, N is the total number of frequency bins in the spectrum D, and M is the detection function. The detection function is further smoothed by a moving average filter and a simple peak-picking operation is used to find the note onsets. In the peak-picking operation, only those peaks having values greater than a threshold θ are considered as the onset candidates.

In this paragraph, it is explained that why time-frequency decomposition can greatly improve the energy-based detection methods, and why the positive flux is necessary. In many cases, during the note transition time, the current note may decay and decrease energy, while the new note may begin and increase in energy, and the change in total energy is not noticeable. If the two successive notes have different pitch, then the energy-increasing and energy-decreasing will occur in the different frequency channels after an appropriate time-frequency decomposition. As only the energy-increasing is the useful cue for onset time, energy-decreasing during the decay of the former note should be ruled out. When summing energy change across all frequency channels to derive a detection function, the type of flux is limited to the positive flux. Accordingly, only the energy increase during the onset time of the latter note is considered.

Phase-Based Detection

As opposed to the standard energy-based detection, phase-based detection makes use of the spectral phase information as its source of information. The STFT can also be considered as complex band-bass filter banks with equal bandwidth, and the STFT coefficient $X_m(n)$ denotes the output of the mth filter. In cases where there is only one sinusoid component passing the mth band-pass filter and at the same time this sinusoid component is stable, the output of the mth filter must have a nearly constant frequency. Therefore, the difference between two consecutive unwrapped phase values of $X_m(n)$ must remain nearly constant:

$$\phi_m(n) - \phi_m(n-1) \approx \phi_m(n-1) - \phi_m(n-2)$$

(20)

where $\varphi_m(n)$ is defined as the 2π-upwrapped phase of the STFT coefficient $X_m(n)$. The phase deviation $\Delta\varphi_m(n)$ can also be defined as:

$$\Delta\phi_m(n) = \phi_m(n) - 2\phi_m(n-1) + \phi_m(n-2) \approx 0$$

$$(21)$$

During the steady-state portion of the signal, $\Delta\varphi_m(n)$ is nearly equal to zero. During the transient portion, the frequency of $X_m(n)$ is not constant, and $\Delta\varphi_m(n)$ tends to be large. The analysis can be extended to the distribution of phase deviations of all frequency bins of the STFT (Bello & Sandler, 2003). During the steady-state part of the signal, the distribution is pointed. In the transient part, the corresponding distribution is flat and wide. These observations can be quantified by calculating the inter quartile range and the kurtosis coefficient of the distribution.

Phase-based onset detection has demonstrated better performance in the detection of the soft onset than standard energy-based methods. However, it is susceptible to phase distortion and to phase noise introduced by the phases of low energy components.

Pitch-Based Detection

The approaches that use only energy and/or phase information are not satisfactory for the detection of soft onsets. Pitch-based detection appears as a promising solution for the problem. Pitch-based approaches can use stable pitch cues to segment the analyzed signal into transients and steady-state parts, and then locate onsets only in the transients. A pitch-based onset detection system is described in the reference (Collins, 1999). In the system, an independent constant-Q pitch detector provides pitch tracks that are used to find likely transitions between notes. For the detection of soft onsets, such a system performs better than other state-of-the-art approaches. However, it is designed only for onset detection in monophonic music. As polyphonic pitch estimation remains a largely unsolved problem, this makes it difficult to construct a pitch-based onset detection for polyphonic music. This subsection describes a pitch-based

approach that detects onsets in real polyphonic music (Zhou, Mattavelli and Zoia, 2008).

The monaural music signal is used as the input signal at a sampling rate of 44.1 kHz. The system applies the RTFI as the time-frequency analysis. The center frequencies of the discrete RTFI are set according to a logarithmic scale. The resolution parameters in Equation (11) are set as $d=0$ and $c=0.0058$. The frequency resolution is constant-Q and equal to 0.1 semitones. Ten filters are used to cover the frequency band of one semitone. A total of 960 filters are necessary to cover the analyzed frequency range that extends from 26 Hz to 6.6 kHz. The RTFI energy spectrum is averaged to produce the RTFI average energy spectrum in units of 10ms.

It is well known that the human auditory system reacts with different sensitivities in the different frequency bands. This fact is often described by tracing equal-loudness contours. Jensen suggests a detection function called the perceptual spectral flux (Jensen & Andersen, 2004), in which he weighs the difference frequency bands by the equal-loudness contours. Collins uses the equal-loudness contours to weight the different ERB scale bands and derive another detection function (Collins, 2005a). Considering these works, in the method described here, the average RTFI energy spectrum is transformed following the Robinson and Dadson equal-loudness contours, which have been standardized in the international standard ISO-226. To simplify the transformation, only an equal-loudness contour corresponding to 70 dB is used to adjust the average RTFI energy spectrum. The standard provides equal-loudness contours limited to 29 frequency bins. Then, this contour is used to get the equal-loudness contours of 960 frequency bins by cubic spline interpolation in the logarithmic frequency scale. Let us identify this equal-loudness contour as $Eq(\omega_m)$ in dB. Then, the spectrum Y can be calculated as follows:

$$Y(k, \omega_m) = A(k, \omega_m) - Eq(\omega_m) \qquad (22)$$

where ω_m represents the angular frequency of the mth frequency bin. $A(k, \omega_m)$ denotes the average RTFI energy spectrum that is defined in Equation (15).

The music signal is structured according to notes. It is interesting to observe that an energy spectrum is organized according to note pitches rather than to a single frequency component. Then, the spectrum Y is further recombined to yield the spectrum R according to a simple harmonic grouping principle:

$$R(k, \omega_m) = \frac{1}{5} \sum_{i=1}^{5} Y(k, i \cdot \omega_m) \qquad (23)$$

In practical cases, instead of using Equation (23), the spectrum R can be easily calculated on the logarithmic scale by the following approximation:

$$R(k, \omega_m) \approx \frac{1}{5} \sum_{i=1}^{5} Y(k, \omega_{m+A[i]}) \qquad (24)$$

$$A[5] = [0, 120, 190, 240, 279] \qquad (25)$$

In Equations (24) and (25), $\omega_m = 2\pi \cdot 26 \cdot 2^{m/120}$, m is from 1 to 680 and the corresponding pitch range is 26Hz to 1.32kHz. To reduce noise, a 5×5 mean filter is used for the low-pass filtering of the spectrum R according to the expression:

$$S(k, \omega_m) = \frac{1}{25} \sum_{i=-2}^{2} \sum_{j=-2}^{2} R(k + i, \omega_{m+j}) \qquad (26)$$

To show energy changes more clearly, the spectrum D is calculated by the nth-order difference of spectrum S.

$$D(k, \omega_m) = S(k, \omega_m) - S(k - n, \omega_m) \qquad (27)$$

where the difference order n is set as 3 in a heuristic way.

$$F(k, \omega_m) = S(k, \omega_m) - \max((S(k, \omega_m))_{m=1:N}) \qquad (28)$$

where N is the total number of frequency bins, and spectrum F is the relative measure of the maximum of S.

Finally the spectra D and F together are considered as the input for the second stage of the onset detection algorithms.

The energy-based detection algorithm does not perform well for detecting soft onsets. Consequently, a pitch-based algorithm has been developed to improve detection accuracy of soft onsets. A music signal can be separated into transients and steady-state parts. The basic idea behind the algorithm is to find the steady-state parts by using stable pitch cues and then look backward to locate onset times in the transients by inspecting energy changes.

In most cases, a note has a spectral structure where dominant frequency components are approximately equally spaced. The energy of a note is mainly distributed in the first several harmonic components. Let us suppose that all the energy of a note is distributed in the first 10 harmonic components. For a monophonic note with fundamental frequency ω, usually its spectrum Y (Equation 22) can have peaks $P(\omega, A_1)$, $P(2\omega, A_2)$ ... $P(10\omega, A_{10})$ at the harmonic frequencies. $P(\omega, A)$ denotes the spectral peak that has value A at frequency ω. In most cases, the corresponding spectrum R (Equation 23) presents the strongest spectral peak $P(\omega, (A_1 + A_2 + A_3 + A_4 + A_5)/5)$ at the fundamental frequency of the note. Accordingly, the fundamental frequency of a monophonic note can be estimated by searching for the maximum peak in the note's spectrum R. For a polyphonic note, the predominant pitches can be estimated by searching the spectral peaks that have values approaching or equal to the maximum in spectrum R.

These peaks are near the fundamental frequencies of the note's predominant pitches; hence, the peaks are named "predominant peaks". The spectrum F (Equation 28) is the relative measure of the maximum of R. Consequently, in F, the predominant peaks have values approximately equal to 0 dB. To know how a pitch changes in a music signal, F can be calculated in each short time frame in units of 10ms to get a two-dimensional time-frequency spectrum. Given the time-frequency spectrum F of a signal, if there is always a predominant peak around a frequency ω_{m1} in every time frame of a time span, this means that there is a stable pitch in the time span, and it can be assumed that the time span corresponds to a steady-state part. The time span can be called "steady time span". The images of the time-frequency spectrum are very useful to validate algorithm development by visual inspection. Several different music signals and their spectra have been analyzed during the experimental work. It can be commonly observed that, during the steady-state part of a note, there are always one or more steady time spans, which are located just after the note's onset. Consequently, the steady-state parts of a signal can be found by searching steady time spans in the signal's spectrum F.

The pitch–based algorithm described here consists of two steps:

1) Searching possible note onsets in every frequency channel.
2) Combining the detected onset candidates across all the frequency channels.

In the first step, the algorithm searches for possible pitch onsets in every frequency channel. When searching in a certain frequency channel with frequency ω_{m1}, the detection algorithm tries to find only the onset where the newly occurring pitch rightly has an approximate fundamental frequency ω_{m1}. In each frequency channel with frequency ω_{m1}, the algorithm searches the steady time spans, each of which corresponds to the steady-state part of a note having a predominant pitch with fundamental frequency ω_{m1}. Given a time-frequency spectrum $F(k, \omega_m)$, a time span $T[k1, k2]$ (in units of 10ms) is considered to be steady if it meets the following three conditions:

$$(F(k,\omega_m))_{m=m1,k=k1:k2} > \alpha_1 \tag{29}$$

$$\max((F(k,\omega_m))_{m=m1,k=k1:k2}) > \alpha_2 \tag{30}$$

where α_1 and α_2 are two thresholds.

The third condition is that $Sum(\omega_m)$ has a spectral peak at the frequency ω_{m1},

$$Sum(\omega_m) = \sum_{k=k_1}^{k_2} F(k,\omega_m) \tag{31}$$

The boundary ($k1$ and $k2$) of a time span can be easily determined as follows. $F_t(k)$ is the time-frequency spectrum F in the frequency channel with frequency ω_{m1}.

$$F_t(k) = (F(k,\omega_m))_{m=m1} \tag{32}$$

Then, a two-value function $P(k)$ is defined as:

$$P(k) = \begin{cases} 1, & F_t(k) \geq \alpha_1 \\ 0, & F_t(k) < \alpha_1 \end{cases} \tag{33}$$

$$G(k) = P(k) - P(k-1) \tag{34}$$

where $G(k)$ is the first-order difference of $P(k)$. The beginning of a time span corresponds to the time at which $G(k)$ assumes the value 1 and the end of the time span is the first instant, when $G(k)$ assumes the value -1.

After all the steady time spans have been determined, the algorithm looks backward to locate onsets from the beginning of each steady time span using the spectrum D (Equation 27).

For a steady time span T [k1, k2], the detection algorithm locates the onset time by searching for most noticeable energy-change peak larger than the threshold α_3 in spectrum $(D(k, \omega_m))_{m=m1, k=(k1-30):k1}$. The search is done backward from the beginning of a steady time span, and the searching range is limited inside the 0.3-s window before the steady time span. The time position of this energy-change peak of the spectrum D is considered as a candidate pitch onset.

After all frequency channels have been searched, the pitch onset candidates are found and can be expressed as follows:

$$Onset\_C(k, \omega_m) \geq 0, m=1, 2, 3, ...N, \qquad (35)$$

where k is the index of time frame and N is the total number of the frequency channels.

If $Onset\_C(k, \omega_m)=0$, no onset exists in the kth time frame of the mth frequency channel. If $Onset\_C(k, \omega_m)>0$, there is an onset candidate in the kth time frame of the mth frequency channel, and the value of $Onset\_C(k, \omega_m)$ is set to the value of $D(k, \omega_m)$.

In the second step, the detection algorithm combines the pitch onset candidates across all the frequency channels to generate the detection function as follows,

$$DF(k) = \frac{1}{N} \sum_{m=1}^{N} Onset\_C(k, \omega_m) \qquad (36)$$

The detection function is low-pass filtered by a moving average filter. Then, a peak-picking operation is used to find the onset times. If two onset candidates are neighbors in a 0.05-s time window, then only the onset candidate with the larger value is kept.

A bow violin excerpt is provided to exemplify the specific usage and advantage of the pitch-based algorithm. The example is a slow-attacking violin sound. Very strong vibrations can be observed from its spectrum Y reported in Figure 3. Because of the vibrations, noticeable energy changes also exist in the steady-state parts of the signal. Therefore, the energy changes are not reliable for onset detection in this case. In the energy-based detection function, it is seen that there are many spurious peaks that are, in fact, not related to the true note onsets. Consequently, the energy-based detection algorithm shows very poor performance in this example.

Figure 3. Bow Violin example: adjusted energy spectrum (spectrum Y)

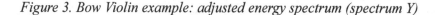

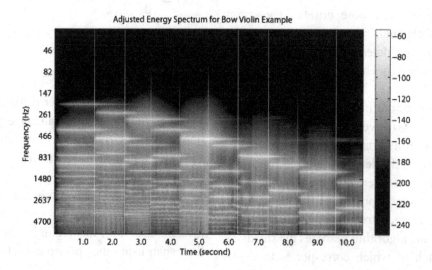

Figure 4 illustrates the spectrum *F* of the example, and the vertical lines in the image denote the positions of the true onsets. It can be clearly observed that there is always at least one steady time span (white spectral line) just behind an onset position. The algorithm searches every frequency channel to find steady time spans, each of which is assumed to correspond to a steady-state part.

For example, steady time spans are searched in frequency channel 294 Hz. As shown in Figure 5,

in the spectrum *F* of this frequency channel, there is a time span *T [244, 320]* (in units of 10 ms). *T* has values larger than the threshold α_2=*-10dB*, and presents its maximum up to 0 dB. There is also a peak rightly at a frequency of 294Hz in the *Sum*^{T} (ω_m), which is obtained by the following expression:

$$Sum^T(\omega_m) = \sum_{k=244}^{320} Fv(k, \omega_m) \qquad (37)$$

Figure 4. Bow Violin example: normal pitch energy spectrum (spectrum F). The vertical lines in the image denote the positions of the true onsets. The Figure is adapted from (Zhou, Mattavelli and Zoia, 2008)

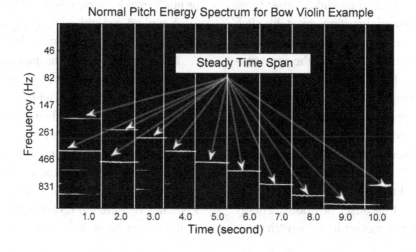

Figure 5. Bow Violin example: search of steady time spans in one frequency channel. The Figure is adapted from (Zhou, Mattavelli and Zoia, 2008)

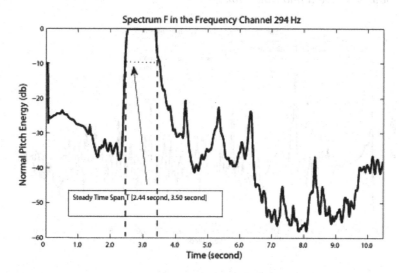

$Fv(k, \omega_m)$ is the time-frequency spectrum F of the bow violin example. T is considered to be a steady time span because it meets the three conditions, which were introduced earlier and used to judge if the time span is steady. Then, the detection algorithm locates the onset position by searching for a noticeable energy change peak larger than the threshold α_3 (in this example, $\alpha_3 = 2$) in the spectrum D of the frequency channel. The searching window is limited inside the 0.3-s window before the steady time span T. As shown in Figure 6, in the spectrum D of the frequency channel 294Hz, a peak with a value larger than the threshold α_3 is positioned near 2.42 s. The time position is considered as a candidate onset time.

Here the pitch-based algorithm uses stable pitch cues to separate the signal into the transients and the steady-state parts, and searches the onset candidates by energy changes only in the transients. So the energy changes caused by the vibrations in steady-steady parts are not considered as detection cues. The dots in Figure 7 denote the detected onset candidates in the different frequency channels by the pitch-based detection algorithm. It can be observed that the onset candidates are nearly around the true onset positions. Finally the detection algorithm combines the pitch onset

candidates across all the frequency channels to get the final result.

Supervised Learning

Some approaches to onset detection are not compatible with the typical procedure described earlier, and they are based on machine learning (Marolt, et al., 1999; Chuan & Elaine, 2008; Davy & Godsill, 2002). Generally speaking, these methods first perform a time-frequency analysis, such as STFT or constant-Q analysis for the music signal. Then, corresponding energy and phase information is used to classify every frame as being onset or non-onset by supervised learning algorithms.

A typical supervised learning method is described as follows (Lacoste & Eck, 2007).

As shown in Figure 8, the method first performs a STFT analysis to produce a spectrogram, which is then used as the input variables to a feed-forward neural network (FNN). The FNN is trained to evaluate how much every spectrogram frame can be classified as being onset. The outputs of the network are then treated with a simple peak-picking algorithm based on a moving average. The FNN has two hidden layers and a single neuron in the output layer. The tanh activation function

Figure 6. Bow Violin example: location of the onset position backward from steady time span. The Figure is adapted from (Zhou, Mattavelli and Zoia, 2008)

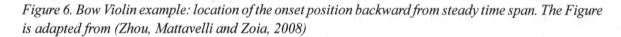
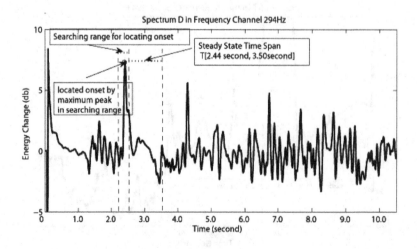

is used for hidden layers, and the logistic sigmoid activation function is selected for the output layer. The conjugate gradient descent is employed as learning function.

Although every spectrogram frame could also be classified as a simple 0 or 1 (onset/nononset), it is more reasonable to use smooth changes to model the transition between onset and nononset. Accordingly, the target trace for every frame can be a combination of the peaked Gaussians, which is centred on the labelled onset time.

$$T(t) = \sum_i \exp(-\frac{(t - \tau_i)^2}{\sigma^2}) \qquad (38)$$

Where $T(t)$ represents the target trace value of the spectrogram frame at the time position of t,

τ_i is the ith labelled onset time and σ is the width of the peak, chosen to be 10 milliseconds. In the training phase, the network produces a predicted value for every time step. As shown in the following equation, the error function is the sum of the squared error over all input patterns.

$$E = \sum_j (T(t_j) - O(t_j))^2 \qquad (39)$$

where $O(t_j)$ represents the output of the neural network for pattern j.

The goal of the neural network is to predict an onset trace at the time of every time step. The input variables to the neural network are selected from the spectrogram of the input signal. The number of input variables should be as small as possible,

Figure 7. Bow Violin example: onset candidates in all the frequency channels. The dots denote the detected onset candidates, the vertical lines are true onsets.

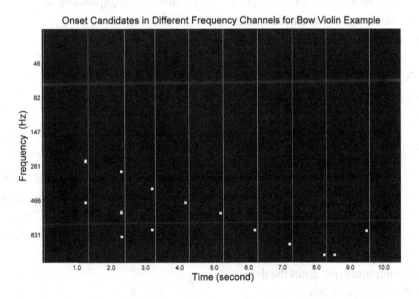

Figure 8. A music onset detection method based on supervised learning

because the large size of input variables makes it very difficult to train the neural network. Accordingly, when predicting an onset trace for a certain frame, it is reasonable that only the spectrogram points near the frame are selected as the input variables. In the method, the input variables are some spectrogram points within a time-frequency window centred on the predicted frame. To reduce the number of input variables, the spectrum points in the input window are randomly sampled both on the time and frequency axis. Uniform sampling is used along frequency axis, and the values along the time axis are sampled according to a normal distribution. More than 200 input variables are sufficient to yield a good result.

The input window has a width of 200 milliseconds. The window height is 90% of the height of the spectrogram. Thus, when moving the input window across the frequency axis, there are multiple similar input windows for the same time step and this will yield a more robust model. Accordingly, the network has multiple predicted values for a single frame, and the multiple values are merged to generate a detection function

Finally, a simple peak picking algorithm is used to find onset times from the detection function. The peak picking algorithm can be expressed as follows.

$$p(t) = d(t) - u(t) \tag{40}$$

where

$$u(t) = g * d(t) \tag{41}$$

where g is the Gaussian filter, d denotes the detection function, and p is the peak trace.

In the peak picking algorithm, a high-pass filter is used to isolate the interesting fast change information from the slow change, which is considered to be not related to onsets. The high pass filter is implemented by subtracting the Gaussian-filtered signal from the original signal. In the final step, in the peak trace p, each peak with a value larger

than threshold K is considered to represent an onset time. The position of the onset is calculated as the centre of mass of all points inside the peak. The optimal threshold K can be selected from training samples.

PERFORMANCE EVALUATION

Performance Measures

To evaluate the detection method, the detected onset times must be compared with the reference ones. For a given reference onset at time t, if there is a detection within a tolerance time-window [t-50ms, t+50ms], it is considered to be a correct detection (CD). If not, there is a false negative (FN). The detections outside all the tolerance windows are counted as false positives (FP). The F-measure, Recall and Precision measures are used to summarize the results. The Precision and Recall can be expressed as:

$$P = \frac{N_{CD}}{N_{CD} + N_{FP}} \tag{42}$$

$$R = \frac{N_{CD}}{N_{CD} + N_{FN}} \tag{43}$$

where N_{CD} is the number of correct detections, N_{FP} is the number of false positives and N_{FN} is the number of false negatives. These two measures can be summarized by the F-measure defined as:

$$F = \frac{2PR}{P + R} \tag{44}$$

Onset Annotation

It is important to construct a reference database with reliable annotated onset times. Onset detection is a subjective task, usually there is no perfect reference for onset times. In most cases, the onset times need to be hand labeled. For percussive onsets, the reference times can be precisely labeled by visualizing the waveform in audio display software. In the spectrogram of the analyzed signal, the concurrent fast energy-increasing of different harmonic components of a music note can be often visualized at the onset time. Accordingly, the spectrogram is also a very useful tool to help annotate the onset times, although it is not very precise. The most precise and flexible method for onset annotation is to listen to signal slice with the support of visualizations.

The Sound Onset Labelizer (SOL) is a free onset annotation software for research purpose (Leveau, Daudet and Richard, 2004). This software provides a user-friendly interface to annotators. Both the waveform and the spectrogram of the analyzed signal can be seen in the screen of the software's GUI. The spectrogram and waveform parts have the same time axis. Using the tool, onset labels can be first annotated in the spectrogram by visual inspection, and then they can be more precisely adjusted by aural feedbacks. More reliable reference onset times can be achieved by cross-validation among the different expert annotators.

As onset annotation is a very time consuming task, it is more efficient to share some public database among different researchers. Leveau et al. provide a reliable public distributed database for onset detection, which contains 17 short music sequences in different music instruments and genres (Leveau, Daudet and Richard, 2004).

The validated onset labels for more than 700 corresponding onsets are also freely distributed.

Performance Comparison and MIREX Evaluation

It is quite difficult to make performance comparison among the different methods for onset detection, because there is a shortage of public database available, and different researchers use different test databases. There is a direct comparison between an energy-based method and a pitch-based one in the literature (Zhou, Mattavelli and Zoia, 2008). Both methods are based on the RTFI time-frequency analysis. The pitch-based method has been described in the above section. The same test dataset was used for the evaluation. The test database contains 30 music sequences of different genres and instruments. In total there are 2543 onsets and more than 15-minutes of time duration. The music files are classified into the following classes: piano, plucked string, sustained string, brass, winds, complex mixes. Here the piano is considered as a single class because most of the piano music contains many hard onsets.

The total test results on the test dataset are summarized in Table 1. The energy-based algorithm performs better than does the pitch-based algorithm on the piano and complex music, which contains several hard onsets. The energy-based detection gains 5.0% for piano music and 8.4% for the complex music. Conversely, the pitch-based

Table 1. Comparison between the energy-based and pitch-based methods

	Piano	Complex Mixes	Plucked String (*Guitar, Violin, Cello*)	Brass (*Trumpet, Horn*)	Winds (*Clarinet, Flute, Oboe*)	Sustained String (Quartet, Violin, Viola)
Average F-Measure (Pitch-based)	92.7%	82.6%	87.6%	93.2%	88.4%	87.0%
Average F-Measure (Energy-based)	97.7%	91.0%	83.6%	87.8%	80.8%	44.1%

detection algorithm performs better in the brass, winds and sustained string, in which note onsets are considered to be softer. For the sustained string, the pitch-based algorithm gains 42.9% and greatly improves the performance from 44.1% to 87.0%. In addition, the pitch-based algorithm gains 5.4%, 7.6% for brass and winds, respectively.

A comparison between the precisions of the pitch-based and energy-based methods is shown in Figure 9. The comparison clearly suggests that the pitch-based method has a much better precision than the energy-based method.

The pitch-based method overperforms the energy-based algorithm for the detection of soft onsets. The reason for improved performance can be explained as follows. Energy-based approaches are based on the assumption that there are relatively more salient energy changes at the onset times than in the steady-state parts. In case of soft onsets, the assumption can not stand. The significant energy changes in the steady-state parts can mislead energy-based approaches and cause many false positives. Conversely, the proposed pitch-based algorithm can first utilize stable pitch cues to separate the music signal into the transients and the steady-state parts, and then find note onsets only in the transients. The

pitch-based algorithm reduces the false positives that are caused by the salient energy changes in the steady-state parts, and greatly improves the onset detection performance of the music signal with many soft onsets. Because of the reduction of false positives, it also gets a better precision.

Similar to pitch-based onset detection, phase-based method has a good performance for the detection of soft onsets. But phase-based detection is very susceptible to phase distortion and to phase noise introduced by the phases of low energy components. Compared to pitch-based detection, phase-based detection shows very low performance for the onset detection in real polyphonic music signal.

Music Information Retrieval Evaluation Exchange (MIREX) provides a formal evaluation framework (MIREX, 2005). From MIREX 2005 to MIREX 2007, several onset detection methods have been evaluated on the same dataset in the audio onset detection task. The test dataset contains 85 music sequences of different genres and instruments. In total there are 14-minutes of time duration. The dataset contains four different classes such as solo drum, solo polyphonic pitched instruments, solo monophonic pitched instruments and complex mixtures. In addition,

Figure 9. Precision comparison of energy-based and pitch-based onset detections

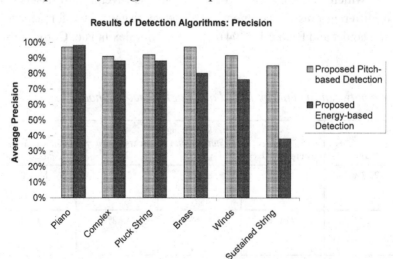

the monophonic pitched instruments class is sub-divided into 5 different subclasses: brass, wind, sustained strings, plucked strings, bars and bells, singing voice.

In the MIREX 2005~2007 onset detection tasks, many methods have been evaluated. Almost all the methods fail to detect onsets in singing voice. This result suggests that it is quite difficult to develop a general onset detection method, which can work well for both singing voice and the other music. Most of the submitted methods are energy-based and show a poor performance on the detection of the classes: solo brass, solo wind, solo sustained string. These classes usually contain a large number of soft onsets. The significant energy changes in the steady-state parts can mislead energy-based approaches and cause many false positives. As explained before, the pitch-based detection can clearly outperform the energy-based detection for the detection of soft onsets. In addition, the phase information is also useful to improve the detection for soft onsets. The Zhou and Reiss method combines the energy-based and pitch-based detection so that the method has much better performance on the solo brass class and solo wind class than other methods (Zhou and Reiss, 2007). The Lee method combines energy and phase information and achieves the best performance on the sustained string class (Lee, Shiu and Kuo, 2007). According to the average F-measure, the overall performance difference between the first four best methods [Zhou and Reiss, 81%; Lee 80%; Lacoste and Eck, 80%; Robel, 80%] is minor (Zhou and Reiss, 2007; Lee, Shiu and Kuo, 2007; Lacoste & Eck, 2005; Robel, 2007).

FUTURE RESEARCH DIRECTIONS

Since the nature of music signals is quite varied, no single method is suitable for all music signals. different detection methods could be used for different types of sound events to achieve better performances (Collins, 2005b; Ricards, 2005). Inspired by the human perceptual system, further improvements may arise by combining multiple simpler methods using a voting mechanism. These improvements could be achieved by developing more efficient classification algorithms capable of assisting music onset detection. The classification algorithms would automatically estimate the dominant onset type for the music signal being analyzed. Then, the adaptive combination of different methods is expected to improve the overall performance. In addition, as the human ear performs much better for onset detection than an automatic detection method, computational auditory models such as a loudness model could also play an important role in the further research.

REFERENCES

Bello, J. P., Daudet, L., Abadia, S., Duxbury, C., Davies, M., & Sandler, M. B. (2005). A tutorial on onset detection in music signals. *IEEE Trans. Speech and Audio Signal Processing, 13,* 1035–1047. doi:10.1109/TSA.2005.851998

Bello, J. P., & Sandler, M. (2003). Phase-based note onset detection for music signals. *Proc. IEEE Int. Conf. Acoustics, Speech, and Signal Processing (ICASSP-03)* (pp.49-52).Hong Kong.

Chuan, C., & Elaine, C. (2008). Audio Onset Detection Using Machine Learning Techniques: The Effect and Applicability of Key and Tempo Information. University of Southern California Computer Science Department Technical Report No. 08-895.

Collins, N. (1999). Using a pitch detector as an onset detector. *Proc. International Conf. On Music Information Retrieval.*

Collins, N. (2005a). A comparison of sound onset detection algorithms with emphasis on psycho-acoustically motivated detection functions. *AES Convention 118.* Barcelona.

Collins, N. (2005b). A change discrimination onset detector with peak scoring peak picker and time domain correction. *MIREX 2005 audio onset detection contest*: Retrieved from http://www.music-ir.org/evaluation/mirex-results/articles/onset/collins.pdf

Davy, M., & Godsill, S. (2002). Detection of abrupt spectral changes using support vector machines an application to audio signal segmentation. In *Proceedings of IEEE International Conference on Acoustics, Speech and Signal Processing (ICASSP'02)*(Vol. 2, pp. 1313-1316). Orlando, Fla, USA.

Duxbury, C., Sandler, M., & Davies, M. (2002). A hybrid approach to musical note onset detection. *Proc. 5th International Conf. Digital Audio Effects (DAFX-02)*. Hamburg, Germany.

Goto, M. (2001). An audio-based real-time beat tracking system for music with or without drumsounds. *Journal of New Music Research, 30*(2), 159–171. doi:10.1076/jnmr.30.2.159.7114

Hartmann, W. M. (1997). *Signals Sound and Sensation*. American Institute of Physics Press.

Jensen, K., & Andersen, T. H. (2004). Causal rhythm grouping. *Proc. 2nd International Symposium on Computer Music Modeling and Retrieval*. Esbjerg, Denmark.

Klapuri, A. (1999). Sound onset detection by applying psychoacoustic knowledge. *Proc. IEEE International Conf. Acoustics, Speech, and Signal Processing (ICASSP-99)*(pp. 3089–3092).

Lacoste, A., & Eck, D. (2005) Onset detection with artificial neural network for MIREX 2005. *MIREX 2005 audio onset detection contest*: Retrieved from http://www.music-ir.org/evaluation/mirex-results/articles/onset/lacoste.pdf

Lacoste, A., & Eck, D. (2007). A supervised classification algorithm for Note Onset Detection. *EURASIP Journal on Advances in Signal Processing* (Article ID 43745),(vol. 2007, 13 pages).

Lee, W., Shiu, Y., & Kuo, C. (2007). Musical onset detection with linear predication and joint features. *MIREX 2007 audio onset detection contest*.Retrieved from http://www.music-ir.org/mirex/2007/abs/OD_lee.pdf

Leveau, P., Daudet, L., & Richard, G. (2004). Methodology and Tools for the evaluation of automatic onset detection algorithms in music. *Proc. 5th International Conf. On Music Information Retrieval*. Barcelona, Spain.

Marolt, M., Kavcic, A., & Privosnik, M. (1999). Neural networks for note onset detection in piano music. *Proc. International Conf. On Computer Music*.

MIREX. (2005), First Annual Music Information Retrieval Evaluation eXchange (MIREX '05). Retrieved from http://www.music-ir.org/mirex2005/index.php/Audio_Onset_Detection.

Moore, B. C. J., & Glasberg, B. R. (1996). A revision of Zwicker's loudness model. *ACTA Acustica, 82*, 335–345.

Ricard, J. (2005). An implementation of multi-band onset detection. *MIREX 2005 audio onset detection contest*. Retrieved from http://www.music-ir.org/evaluation/mirex-results/articles/onset/ricard.pdf

Robel, A. (2007) Onset detection in polyphonic signals by means of transient peak classification. *MIREX 2007 audio onset detection contest*.Retrieved from http://www.music-ir.org/mirex/2007/abs/OD_roebel.pdf

Wang, W., Luo, Y., Chambers, J. A., & Sanei, S. (2008). Note Onset Detection via Nonnegative Factorization of Magnitude Spectrum. *EURASIP Journal on Advances in Signal Processing* vol. 2008, Article ID 231367, 15 pages, 2008. doi:10.1155/2008/231367.

Zhou, R. (2006). Feature Extraction of Musical Content for Automatic Music Transcription. Ph.D. dissertation, Swiss Federal Institute of Technology, Lausanne, Retrieved from http://library.epfl.ch/en/theses/?nr=3638.

Zhou, R. & Mattavelli (2007). A new time-frequency representation for music signal analysis. *Signal Processing and Its Applications, 2007. ISSPA 2007. 9th International Symposium on,* (pp. 1-4).

Zhou, R., Mattavelli, M., & Zoia, G. (2008). Music onset detection based on Resonator Time-frequency Image. *IEEE Trans. Audio. Speech and Language Processing*, 16, 1685–1695. doi:10.1109/TASL.2008.2002042

Zhou, R., & Reiss, J. D. (2007) Music onset detection combining energy-based and pitch-based approaches. *MIREX 2007 audio onset detection contest*: Retrieved from http://www.music-ir.org/mirex2007/abs/OD_zhou.pdf

ADDITIONAL READING

Bello, J. P., Daudet, L., Abadia, S., Duxbury, C., Davies, M., & Sandler, M. B. (2005). A tutorial on onset detection in music signals. *IEEE Trans. Speech and Audio Signal Processing*, 13, 1035–1047. doi:10.1109/TSA.2005.851998

Bello, J. P., Duxbury, C., Davies, M., & Sandler, M. (2004). On the use of phase and energy for musical onset detection in the complex domain. *IEEE Signal Processing Letters*, 11(6), 553–556. doi:10.1109/LSP.2004.827951

Bello, J. P., & Sandler, M. (2003). Phase-based note onset detection for music signals. *Proc. IEEE Int. Conf. Acoustics, Speech, and Signal Processing (ICASSP-03)* (pp. 49-52). Hong Kong.

Chuan, C., & Elaine, C. (2008). Audio Onset Detection Using Machine Learning Techniques: The Effect and Applicability of Key and Tempo Information. University of Southern California Computer Science Department Technical Report No. 08-895.

Chuan, C., & Elaine, C. (2008). Audio Onset Detection Using Machine Learning Techniques: The Effect and Applicability of Key and Tempo Information. University of Southern California Computer Science Department Technical Report No. 08-895.

Collins, N. (1999). Using a pitch detector as an onset detector. *Proc. International Conf. On Music Information Retrieval* Sep.

Collins, N. (2005a). A comparison of sound onset detection algorithms with emphasis on psychoacoustically motivated detection functions. *AES Convention 118,* Barcelona.

Collins, N. (2005b). A change discrimination onset detector with peak scoring peak picker and time domain correction. First Annual Music Information Retrieval Evaluation eXchange (MIREX '05).

Dixon, S. (2006). Onset detection revisited *in Proceedings of the 9th International Conference on Digital Audio Effects* (pp. 133–137).

Duxbury, C., Sandler, M., & Davies, M. (2002). A hybrid approach to musical note onset detection. *Proc. 5th International Conf. Digital Audio Effects (DAFX-02)*. Hamburg, Germany.

Goto, M. (2001). An audio-based real-time beat tracking system for music with or without drum-sounds. *Journal of New Music Research*, 30(2), 159–171. doi:10.1076/jnmr.30.2.159.7114

Hartmann, W. M. (1997). *Signals Sound and Sensation*. American Institute of Physics Press.

Jensen, K., & Andersen, T. H. (2004). Causal rhythm grouping. *Proc. 2ⁿᵈ International Symposium on Computer Music Modeling and Retrieval*. Esbjerg, Denmark.

Klapuri, A. (1999). Sound onset detection by applying psychoacoustic knowledge. *Proc. IEEE International Conf. Acoustics, Speech, and Signal Processing (ICASSP-99)(* pp. 3089–3092).

Lacoste, A., & Eck, D. (2007). A supervised classification algorithm for Note Onset Detection. *EURASIP Journal on Advances in Signal Processing*, vol. 2007, Article ID 43745, 13 pages.

Leveau, P., Daudet, L., & Richard, G. (2004). Methodology and Tools for the evaluation of automatic onset detection algorithms in music. *Proc. 5ᵗʰ International Conf. On Music Information Retrieval*, Barcelona, Spain.

Marolt, M., Kavcic, A., & Privosnik, M. (1999). Neural networks for note onset detection in piano music. *Proc. International Conf. On Computer Music*.

MIREX. (2005). First Annual Music Information Retrieval Evaluation eXchange (MIREX '05). Retrieved from http://www.music-ir.org/mirex2005/index.php/Audio_Onset_Detection

Moore, B. C. J., & Glasberg, B. R. (1996). A revision of Zwicker's loudness model. *ACTA Acustica, 82*, 335–345.

Ricard, J. (2005). *An implementation of multi-band onset detection. First Annual Music Information Retrieval Evaluation eXchange*. MIREX.

Wang, W., Luo, Y., Chambers, J. A., & Sanei, S. (2008). Note Onset Detection via Nonnegative Factorization of Magnitude Spectrum. *EURASIP Journal on Advances in Signal Processing*, vol. 2008, Article ID 231367, 15 pages, 2008. doi:10.1155/2008/231367.

Zhou, R. (2006). Feature Extraction of Musical Content for Automatic Music Transcription. Ph.D. dissertation, Swiss Federal Institute of Technology, Lausanne,Retrieved from http://library.epfl.ch/en/theses/?nr=3638.

Zhou, R. & Mattavelli (2007). A new time-frequency representation for music signal analysis. *Signal Processing and Its Applications, 2007. ISSPA 2007. 9th International Symposium on(* pp. 1-4).

Zhou, R., Mattavelli, M., & Zoia, G. (2008). Music onset detection based on Resonator Time-frequency Image. *IEEE Trans. Audio. Speech and Language Processing, 16*, 1685–1695. doi:10.1109/TASL.2008.2002042

Zhou, R., & Reiss, J. D. (2007) Music onset detection combining energy-based and pitch-based approaches. *MIREX 2007 audio onset detection contest*: Retrieved from http://www.music-ir.org/mirex2007/abs/OD_zhou.pdf

Chapter 13
On the Inherent Segment Length in Music

Kristoffer Jensen
Aalborg University Esbjerg, Denmark

ABSTRACT

In this work, automatic segmentation is done using different original representations of music, corresponding to rhythm, chroma and timbre, and by calculating a shortest path through the selfsimilarity calculated from each time/feature representation. By varying the cost of inserting new segments, shorter segments, corresponding to grouping, or longer, corresponding to form, can be recognized. Each segmentation scale quality is analyzed through the use of the mean silhouette value. This permits automatic segmentation on different time scales and it gives indication on the inherent segment sizes in the music analyzed. Different methods are employed to verify the quality of the inherent segment sizes, by comparing them to the literature (grouping, chunks), by comparing them among themselves, and by measuring the strength of the inherent segment sizes.

INTRODUCTION

Music consists of sounds organized in time. These sounds can be understood from a rhythmic, timbral, or harmonic point of view, and they can be understood on different time scales, going from the very short (note onsets) to the medium (grouping), to the large scale with musical form. Note onsets, grouping and form are common musical terms, which can be compared to different aspects of audition, memory and grouping behavior. These terms can be compared to chunks, riffs, and other temporal segmentation terms currently used in music.

When identifying chunks, riffs, sections, forms, or other structural elements, do they really exist, or does the identification process create them? This work presents a method, based on automatic segmentation, that identifies the inherent structure sizes in music, i.e. gives indications as to what are the optimal segmentation sizes in the music. This work has implications for rhythmical and

DOI: 10.4018/978-1-61520-919-4.ch013

classical music understanding, and processing. Structure is a necessary dimension in most, if not all music, and if this structure should be made visible for any purpose, the methods presented here can help identifying the optimal structure. While this fundamental research gives a method for finding the optimal segment size in music, and results using this method, more work is needed in order to assess the inherent structure with certainty for all music. Until then, research and development of automatic segmentation of music should possibly ascertain the inherent structure in the music genres that is the aim of the work, prior to performing the segmentation.

Any feature, that can be calculated from the acoustics of the music, can be presented in a manner, for instance by taking the time-derivative, so as to give indication of the local changes in the music. Such an existence of a local change is not a guarantee of an inherent structure, however. In order to assess the quality of the segmentation, the relative distance (or any measure of similarity) within a segment should be compared to the distance to the other segments. If the segment is well grouped, and far, in some sense, to the other segments, then it is a good segmentation. A method for assessing the segmentation is the silhouette (Kaufman & Rousseeuw 1990). Given a segmentation, the mean of the silhouette value for all segments is a good measure of the quality of the segmentation. Therefore, if all possible segmentations are calculated, the associated mean silhouette values can be used to ascertain the best, i.e. the inherent structure sizes.

As to the question of which feature is used for temporal perception of music, Scheirer (1998) determined in several analysis by synthesis experiments that rhythm could not be perceived by amplitude alone, but needed some frequency dependent information, which he constructed using six band-pass filters. Several other studies have investigated the influence of timbre on structure. McAuley & Ayala (2002) found that timbre did not affect the recognition of familiar melodies, but that it had importance enough to hurt recognition on non-familiar melodies. McAdams (2002) studied contemporary and tonal music, and found that the orchestration affects the perceived similarity of musical segments strongly in some cases. He also found that musically trained listeners find structure through surface features (linked to the instrumentation) whereas untrained listeners focused on more abstract features (melodic contour, rhythm).

Deliège and Mélen (1997) postulates that music is segmented into sections of varying length using cue abstraction mechanism, and the principle of sameness and difference, and that the organization of the segmentation, reiterated at different hierarchical levels, permits the structure to be grasped. The cues (essentially motifs in classical music, and acoustic, instrumental, or temporal otherwise) act as reference points during long time spans. Deliège and Mélen furthermore illustrate this cue abstraction process through several experiments, finding, among other things, that musicians are more sensitive to structural functions, and that the structuring process is used for remembering, in particular, the first and last segment. In order to ensure that at least part of the full dimensionality of music is taken into account in the work presented here, three different features are used. One feature is believed to be related to tempo and rhythm, and it is called the rhythmogram. Another feature is considered related to the timbre perception, at least the time-varying perceptive spectrum, and it is called the timbregram. Finally, another feature is related to the note values in the music, and it is called chromagram. By using three features with distinctly different content, it is the aim to further assess the results on inherent and optimal segment size presented here.

Segmentation of music is often done for thumbnailing (music summary) purposes. This is supposedly a means for presenting music, prior to selling it, for instance in online stores. Other uses of segmentation are artistic, for instance for live mixing of music, for faster navigation, where the knowledge of structural elements can be used for skipping similar elements, or related to music identification. Finally, segmentation automatic labeling of music can be beneficial for music analysis.

As for the methods for automatic segmentation, Foote (2000) introduced the use of selfsimilarity matrices, by convolving the selfsimilarity matrix with a checker kernel, thus calculating the novelty measure, which gives indications of the degree of novelty over time. Bartsch and Wakefield (2001) used the chroma representation for audio thumbnailing, by selecting the maximum of the time-lag matrix, which is the selfsimilarity matrix filtered along the diagonal in order to reveal similarities along extended regions of the songs. Goto (2003) and Chai & Vercoe (2003) also identify repeating segments using chroma representation, Goto (2003) using a similarity measure of the distance between vectors together with a method for integrating vectors into segments, and Chai & Vercoe (2003) by identifying local minima in the dynamic programming, which is an indicator of repetition of segments. Paulus and Klapuri (2008) in addition use Markov models to assign labels (Chorus/Verse, etc) to the segments.

In this work, focus will be on determining if there exists an inherent segment size in the music. Indeed, most segmentation methods are able to compute segmentation at different time scales, while the chosen segmentation size is left to the application development stage. Knowing the inherent time scale in music is done in the following manner. First, the feature estimation is presented, then the segmentation using dynamic programming is performed for all time scale, then a measure of the quality of the segmentation is calculated, and the peaks of this measure are identified and used as an indicator of the inherent segmentation size. Several methods for assessing the importance of the optimum segment sizes are employed and discussed in the conclusions.

FEATURE ESTIMATION

In order to perform a good segmentation of the songs, a robust feature is needed. Indeed, the feature used for segmentation can change the segmentation result significantly. Three different features are investigated here; the rhythmic feature (the rhythmogram, Jensen 2005) is based on the autocorrelation of the perceptual spectral flux (PSF, Jensen 2005). The PSF has high energy in the time position where perceptually important sound components, such as notes, have been introduced. The timbre feature (the timbregram) is based on the perceptual linear prediction (PLP), a speech front-end (Hermansky 1990), and the harmony feature (the chromagram) is based on the chroma (Bartsch & Wakefield 2001), calculated on the short-time Fourier transform (STFT). The Gaussian weighted spectrogram (GWS) is performed in order to improve resilience to noise and independence on block size for the timbregram and chromagram. A speech front-end, such as the PLP alters the STFT data by scaling the intensity and frequency so that it corresponds to the way the human auditory system perceives sounds. The chroma maps the energy of the FFT into twelve bands, corresponding to the twelve notes of one octave. By using the rhythmic, timbral, and harmonic features to identify the structure of the music, some of the different aspects of music perception are believed to be taken into account. More information of the feature estimation used here can be found in (Jensen 2007).

Rhythmogram

Any model of rhythm should have as basis some kind of feature that reacts to the note onsets. The note onsets mark the main characteristics of the rhythm. In a previous work (Jensen 2005), a large number of features were compared to an annotated database of twelve songs, and the perceptual spectral flux (PSF) was found to perform best. The PSF is calculated with a step size of 10 milliseconds, and the block size of 46 milliseconds. As the spectral flux in the PSF is weighted so as to correspond roughly to the equal loudness contour, both low frequency sounds, such as bass drum, and high frequency sounds, such as hi-hat are equally well taken into account.

This frequency weighting is obtained in this work by a simple equal loudness contour model. The power function is introduced in order to simulate the intensity-loudness power law and reduce the random amplitude variations. These two steps are inspired from the PLP front-end (Hermansky 1990) used in speech recognition. The PSF was compared to other note onset detection features with good results on the percussive case in a recent study (Collins 2005). In order to obtain a more robust rhythm feature, the autocorrelation of the feature is now calculated on overlapping blocks of 8 seconds, with half a second step size (2 Hz feature sample rate). Only the information between zero and two seconds is retained. The autocorrelation is normalized so that the autocorrelation at zero lag equals one. If visualized with lag time on the y-axis, time position on the x-axis, and the autocorrelation values visualized as intensities, it gives a fast overview of the rhythmic evolution of a song. This representation, called rhythmogram (Jensen 2005), provides information about the rhythm and the evolution of the rhythm in time. The autocorrelation has been chosen instead of the fast Fourier transform FFT, for two reasons. First, it is believed to be more in accordance with the human perception of rhythm (Desain 1992), and second, it is believed to be more easily understood visually. The rhythmogram firstly gives information about the tempo of the song, along with the strength of the tempo, and secondly gives information about the time signature, although this information is not always clearly visible.

Timbregram

The timbre is understood here as the spectral estimate and done here using the perceptual linear prediction, PLP (Hermansky 1990). This involves using the bark (Sekey & Hanson 1984) scale, together with an amplitude scaling that gives an approximation of the human auditory system. The PLP is calculated with a block size of approximately 46 milliseconds and with a step size of 10 millisecond. The timbregram is a feature that is believed to capture orchestration of the music, mainly. In the timbregram, information about which instruments are participating in the music at the current time step is given, along with indications of what dynamic level the instruments are played. It represents the perceptual frequency axis in 25 steps. When an instrument is introduced in the music, it is often visible in the timbregram. It can also show the overall frequency content, i.e. older music lacks in bass and treble, pop music generally has energy on all frequencies, while some dance music (techno) only has energy in the treble and bass regions. The timbregram also reveals when sections are repeated, and in particular when sections are climaxed, with stronger instruments throughout. This is reflected with stronger values in the particular bark/time locations.

Chromagram

Note estimation is notoriously error-prone even if a lot of progress is done in the domain currently. There exists one estimate that is robust and related to the note values, the chroma, which is used here. In the chroma, only the relative content of energy in the twelve notes of the octave is found. No information of the octave of the notes is included. The chroma is calculated from the STFT, using a blocksize of 46 milliseconds and a stepsize of 10 milliseconds. The chroma is obtained by summing the energy of all peaks of 12 $\log_2$ of the frequencies having multiples of 12. The chromagram gives information about the note value, without information about the octave. This is a rather good measure of which chords are played, and also of the musical scale and tonality. If several notes are played for a moment, then this is clearly visible in the chromagram. Also when a note is dropped, and another note is instead played more, this is also clearly reflected in the chromagram values.

Gaussian Windowed Spectrogram

If the raw features are used, it has been found that the detailed information sometimes overshadows the long-term changes in the music. If the features are calculated on short segments (10 to 50 milliseconds), they give detailed information in time, too varying to be used in the segmentation method used here. Instead, the features are calculated on a large segment, but localized in time by using the average of many STFT blocks multiplied with a Gaussian. This is called the Gaussian Weighted Spectragram, GWS. Using the GWS, all segments are used at all time steps, but the current block values are weighted higher than the more distant blocks. By averaging, using the Gaussian average, no specific time localization information is obtained of the individual notes or chords, but instead a general value of the time area is given. In this work, the averaging is done corresponding to a −3 dB window of approximately 1 second. After the GWS, the timbregram and chromagram has a stepsize of ½ second.

As an example of the features, the rhythmogram, timbregram and chromagram of August Engkilde – Beautiful Noise (Brumtone, 2008) is shown in Figure 1. All three features seem informative, although they do not give similar information. While the rhythm evolution is illustrated in the rhythmogram, it is the evolution of the timbre that is shown with the timbregram and the evolution of the note values that can be seen in the chromagram. Beautiful Noise is not a typical rhythmic piece of music, as can be seen from the lack of clear rhythm information in large part of the music. While the rhythmogram values are normalized, but instead the low time-lag values are set to zero. As these are also the autocorrelation value, which is by definition set

to one, the relative strength of the higher time-lag correlations are reflected in the rhythmogram. In the case of Beautiful Noise, the very fast, almost vibrating rhythms have very similar repetitions, which are reflected as stronger values in the corresponding time segments in the rhythmogram. The timbregram reveals that this song has energy in two distinct frequency ranges, one low and one high, until almost three minutes. Then the high frequency component (a noise, windy sound) disappears. The timbregram is not normalized, so the crescendos are visible at a little after two minutes, at two and a half minute, and after five minutes. The chromagram is normalized, and reveals a single note played at the time, through this song. It changes from 'G' to 'D#', and back at around one minute, and to other note values elsewhere in the song. Both the rhythmogram, the timbregram, and the chromagram give pertinent information about the evolution in time of the music, and it seems judicious to investigate all three here.

SEGMENTATION

Automatic segmentation using dynamic programming has been proposed previously (Foote 2000, Bartsch & Wakefield 2001, Goto 2003, Chai 2003, Jensen 2005, Jensen et al 2005, Jensen 2007). In an automatic segmentation task, adjacent blocks are grouped together, forming segments. This can for instance correspond to the chorus/verse structure found in most rhythmic music, or to changes in the rhythmic pattern, in the orchestration or in the notes played.

The dynamic programming used here is based on the shortest-path algorithm (Cormen *et al* 2001) and done on self-similarity matrices, created from the original features (rhythm, chroma or timbre, Jensen 2007) by calculating the L2 norm of each time vector compared to all other time vectors, using a sequence of N vectors of each song that should be divided into a number of segments.

Figure 1. Rhythmogram (top), timbregram, and chromagram (bottom) of Beautiful Noise

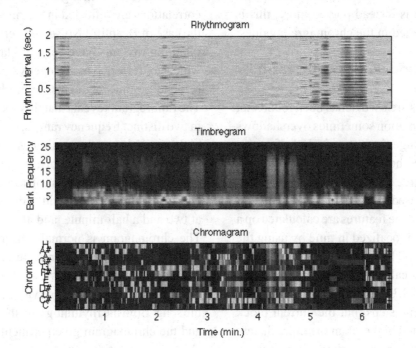

First, let the *cost c(i,j)* of a segment from block *i* to *j* be the weighted sum of the self-similarity and the cost of a new segment be a fixed cost α. Secondly, in order to compute a best possible segmentation, an edge-weighted directed graph *G* is constructed with the set of nodes being all the block of the song. For each possible segment an edge exists. The weight of the edge is *α+c(i, j)*. A path in *G* from node *1* to node *N+1* corresponds to a complete segmentation, where each edge identifies the individual segment. The weight of the path is equal to the total cost of the corresponding segmentation. Therefore, a shortest path (or path with minimum total weight) from node *1* to node *N+1* gives a segmentation with minimum total cost. Such a shortest path can be computed in time $O(N^2)$.

The dynamic programming will cluster the time vectors into segments, as long as the vectors are similar. By varying the insertion cost α of new segments, segment boundaries can be found at different time scales. A low insertion cost will create boundaries corresponding to micro-level chunks, while a high insertion cost will only create few meso-level chunks. Thus, the same segmentation method can create segments of varying size, from short to long, from the grouping to the form of the music. An example of the segmentation is shown in Figure 2 for August Engkilde – Beautiful Noise (Brumtone 2008). As the segment cost (α) is increased, less and less segments are created, which in turn gives longer mean segment lengths.

The comparison of the segmentation done using the method presented here based on the three features rhythmogram, timbregram and chromagram reveals a F1 value of approximately 0.6 (Jensen 2007), corresponding to a matching recall and precision value of 50-70%. The comparison to manual segmentation gives F1 values slightly higher, at approximately 0.7 (Jensen 2007). This is an indication that the manual segmentation is done using different rhythmic, timbral and chroma cues, as the features are better matched to the manual segmentation than among themselves. Therefore,

Figure 2. Segmentation using the timbregram feature for all segment costs for August Engkilde – Beautiful Noise

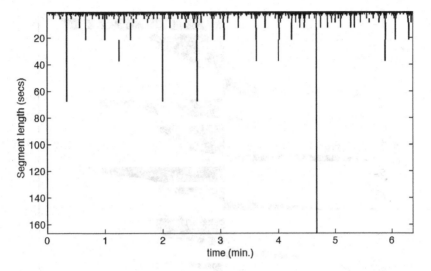

it seems that all features should be employed in a segmentation task. As the final segmentation is not the target goal, this has not been deemed important here.

While many methods for segmentation of music exist, the problem of finding the inherent number of segments still exists. Kuhl related this to the notion of chunks. According to him, the chunk is an important element of music. A chunk is a short segment of a limited number of sound elements; a chunk consists of a beginning, a focal point (peak) and an ending. Kuhl (2007) extends the chunks to include microstructure (below 1/2 sec), mesostructure (chunks, the present, appr. 3-5 secs) and macrostructure (Superchunks, Kuhl and Jensen 2008) (at 30-40 secs).

BEST SEGMENT SIZE

The question investigated here is about whether there exist an inherent segment size in the music, and if so, if it is the same for different music, and if it is related to the chunk theory sizes. This question has been analyzed from different points-of-view

in the literature. Huron (1996) investigated the melodic arch, and found a single arch up to 11 notes melodies, while melodies consisting of 12 or more notes present a double arch. This is, of course, related to the short-time memory theory of 7±2 (Miller 1956), but it does not give information about the time, only the number of notes.

In order to investigate this further, a database of varied music has been collected, and segmented using the shortest-path algorithm with the rhythm, timbre and chroma related parameters. The free variable, α, is varied in order to produce segment sizes between one block to the full song, i.e. all possible segment sizes. The classical way of investigating the clustering quality has to do with comparing the inter distance (the size of each cluster) to the extra distance (the distance between the clusters). Unfortunately, this cannot be computed for the one-cluster solution or the one cluster for each block solution, and it generally produces a 'U'-shape solution, with best values for small or large cluster sizes. A robust estimate of the cluster quality is the silhouette (Kaufman & Rousseeuw 1990), calculated for each observation i as

Figure 3. Silhouette plot for Beautiful Noise. A high positive values indicate that the observation is well clustered, while a large negative values indicate a bad clustering for the observation.

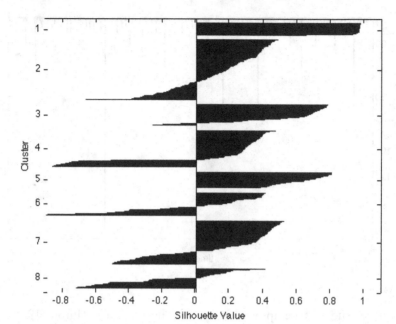

$$s = \frac{b_i - a_i}{\max(a_i, b_i)},\tag{1}$$

where a is the average dissimilarity to all other points in its own cluster and b is the minimum of the average dissimilarities of i to all objects in another cluster. The silhouette value for each observation is always comprised between -1 and 1. If the silhouette value is large, i.e. close to 1, the observation is centered in the cluster, while if the value is low, the observation is also close to other clusters. The silhouette for a clustering solution can be calculated as the average of each observations silhouette value. An example of the silhouette for the segmentation using the timbregram feature of Beautiful Noise is shown in Figure 3. There are eight clusters with an average length of 49 seconds. The average silhouette value is 0.2. Some of the clusters, the first and fifth in particular, have high silhouette values throughout, while some of the others have negative silhouette values for some of the observations of the cluster.

Segmentation Analysis

The mean silhouette value is now calculated for each new segmentation cost in order to analyze the quality of the different segmentations. One silhouette value is retained for each average cluster length, calculated as the total length divided by the number of clusters. An example of the mean silhouette value as a function of average cluster size for Beautiful Noise is shown in Figure 4. The average silhouette is plotted for the rhythmogram, timbregram and chromagram, along with indications of the peaks in each silhouette plot using plus '+' signs. This song has silhouette peaks for different segment lengths, including for the chunk size at approximately 5 seconds, and the superchunk size at approximately 40 seconds. Other optimum chunk sizes are also visible.

Nine songs of classical, pop/rap and jazz genres have been segmented using the rhythmogram, timbregram and chromagram features for varying new segment cost. Each song has a number of silhouette

Figure 4. Mean silhouette value as a function of average segment length for Beautiful Noise. Peaks are indicated with plus '+' signs.

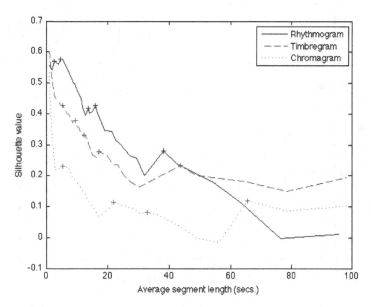

peaks for each feature, giving an indication of the inherent segment size as a function of the average segment length. Visually, the rhythmogram seems to give a better result. To compare to the chunk theory of Kühl (2007), the peaks of the average silhouette values can be identifies as belonging to the range 3-5 seconds, corresponding to the chunk size, and between 30-40 seconds, corresponding to the superchunk size. For the nine songs there has been found 5 (19.23%) chunk matches for rhythmogram, 8 (30.77%) superchunk matches, 4 (8.7%) chunk matches for timbregram, 5 (10.87%) superchunk matches and 2 (9.52%) chunk matches for chromagram, 4 (19.05%) superchunk matches. The rhythmogram performs significantly better than the other features for this particular task. This is also visible, if the mean of the nine songs is calculated and plotted (Figure 5). Indeed, the rhythmogram silhouette plot presents a prominent peak at the chunk level, around 5 second average segment length, and also one peak at approximately 30 seconds average segment length. The timbregram and chromagram has a more 'U' shaped silhouette value, effectively preventing any

silhouette peak at the chunk level. Several other possible peak positions also exist, for instance around 60 seconds, and around 80 seconds.

Another distinction that can be made is between the short-term memory and the long-term memory. Snyder (2000) relates the short-term memory to melodic and rhythmic grouping and situates it between 1/16 second to 8 second, and the long-term memory to musical form, and situates this above 8 seconds. If the question is; what is more prominent, grouping or form, then the study performed here gives indications that form is most prominent, as there is 10 (38.46%), 10 (21.74%) and 4 (19.05%) peaks below 8 seconds (corresponding to grouping) for rhythm, timbre and chroma, respectively. Thus grouping is seemingly more related to rhythm, and less to timbre and chroma.

As to the question of the similarity of the peak position of the silhouette as a function of average segment length, the normalized histogram of the segmentation peaks are calculated, along with a measure of the peakedness of each peak. The normalized histogram gives values of the

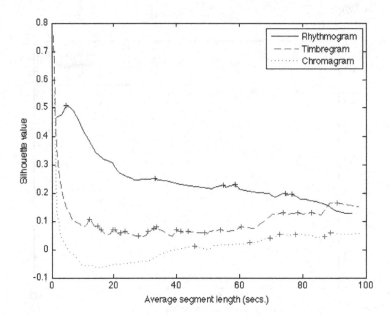

Figure 5. The mean silhouette values for nine songs and rhythmogram, timbregram and chromagram

relative occurrences of different optimal segment lengths. The peakedness is calculated as the relative strength of the peak, divided by the width of the two surrounding samples

$$p = \frac{s_i}{4 \cdot (s_{i-1} + s_{i+1}) \cdot (l_{i+1} - l_{i-1})}, \qquad (2)$$

where s_i is the silhouette value at index i, and l_i is the average length at index i. This normalization by the width is necessary, as the silhouette values are not uniformly sampled along the average segment length axis. In addition, the peak silhouette value is also retained. The silhouette peak distrubution, values and peakedness for nine songs are shown in Figure 6.

There are 26 rhythmogram silhouette peaks, 46 timbregram, and 21 chromagram peaks in all in the nine songs. In the histogram (Figure 6, top), the rhythmogram have an apparent peak at approximately 5, 15, 25, 37, and 55 seconds average segment length, the timbregram has peaks at 10, 30, 45, and 75 seconds, and the chromagram has peaks at 5, 15, 35 and 65 seconds average segment

length. In the peak value subplot (middle), the rhythmogram silhouette values seem higher than the other values. The mean silhouette peak values are 0.45, 0.15, and -0.03, showing a significantly better value for the rhythmogram, and a rather unusable value for the chromagram. As for the peakedness (Figure 6, bottom), the peakedness values are decreasing with the average length of the segments, except for a few peaks with high peakedness values at very high segment lengths. The timbregram has apparently the highest peakedness values, and the chromagram the lowest. The mean of the peakedness is 0.23, 0.64, and 0.17 for rhythmogram, timbregram, and chromagram, respectively. However, the actual peak values are deemed more important, and they are showing the rhythmogram to be the best feature for segmentation.

ACTUAL INHERENT SEGMENT BOUNDARIES

Given the method presented here, it is now possible to identify the optimal segmentation sizes.

Figure 6. Histogram of silhouette peak position (top), the peak silhouette values (middle), and the silhouette peakedness (bottom) as function for average segment length for nine songs. The rhythmogram values are depicted with a '+', the timbregram a 'x', and the chromagram a 'o' in the middle and lower subplot.

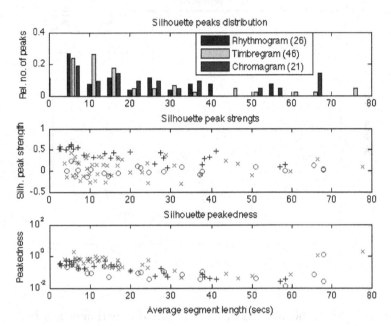

The question is now, what do these sizes represent in the music. As an example, the song Hold On by Jamie Walters (Atlantic 1994) is further investigated. The mean silhouette values as function of average segmentation length for this song is shown in Figure 7. As for the other songs, the rhythmogram mean silhouette values have a rising peak for short average segment lengths, and then decreasing, while both the timbregram and the chromagram-based silhouette values have a 'U'-shape, i.e. the silhouette values decrease to a minimum, and then rise again, with only local maxima. The maxima of silhouette for rhythmogram are found at approximately 4, 11 and 38 seconds, while the timbregram silhouette maxima are found at (0.5), 7, 11, 13, 24 and 66, while for the chromagram, the maxima of the silhouette are found at (0.5), 25 and 68. The (0.5) seconds are the peaks at the cases where all observations have a separate segment (all observations a grouped into individual segments), and thus the average

segment length is equal to the sampling rate of the features.

The musigram plots along with the automatic segmentation boundaries for the same song are found in Figure 8. The rhythmogram is shown in the upper subplot, the timbregram in the middle subplot and the chromagram in the lower subplot. The ensemble is called musigram (Kuhl & Jensen 2008). The rhythmogram reveals alternating sections with more or less strong pulse. The timbregram reveals a weak intro and first sections, a stronger section, which is repeated (1min30, and 2min30), and possibly repeated in a crescendo at 3min10. Similar observations can be made in the chromagram. However, the segmentations found using the automatic segmentation do not necessarily find the same segments, which is possibly impeding on the quality of these experiments. However, it is not believed to be very influential in the results of the experiments.

The average segment lengths for the automatic segmentation boundaries in Figure 8 are 11, 13

Figure 7. Mean silhouette value as a function of average segments length for Hold On – Jamie Walter (1994)

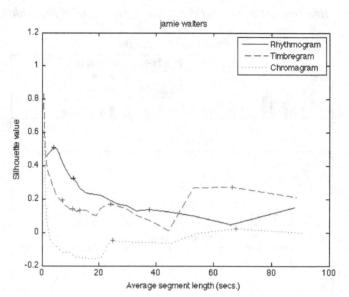

and 25 seconds. It is clear, from the analysis of more songs, that the automatic segmentation gives at the same time shorter and longer segments. For these average segmentation lengths, the rhythmogram gives segment lengths between 5.5 and 27 seconds (standard deviation is 5.35), the timbregram renders segment lengths between 1.5 and 41 (std=9.7 seconds), and the chromagram segment lengths between 12.5 and 56.5 seconds (std=15.81). It is therefore difficult to say whether the optimum segment lengths correspond or not to other theories, such as the chunk theory of Kuhl (2007). However, indications towards such a correspondence is nonetheless observed. First, there is often peaks in the silhouette values for different segment lengths, which corresponds somewhat to the micro, meso and super chunks of Kuhl, which has sizes at 0.5, 3-5 and 30-40 seconds. However, often, the segmentation based on the different features renders different optimal segmentation lengths using the silhouette method.

Album Study

On the question of how reproducible the results of the study of inherent segment sizes in music,

a second experiment has been performed. Are the inherent segment sizes similar across the music genres, or within a music style, or are the inherent segment sizes changing to a degree if there are no systematic values to be found? In order to investigate this further, a full album, The Beatles – Sgt Peppers Lonely Hearts Club Band (Parlophone/Capitol, 1967) has been analyzed in the same manner as above. The three features, rhythmogram, timbregram and chromagram have been calculated from the acoustics of each song of the album, then the automatic segmentation has been done for all possible segment sizes. Finally, the silhouette values have been calculated as a measure of the quality of each segment size. If these silhouette values have peaks on similar segment sizes for the different songs, this is an indication that the inherent segment sizes are similar across this particular album, which can be seen as a sample of a genre. If the silhouette peaks are scattered around, the inherent segment sizes are individual for each song.

In order to investigate this, the relative number of silhouette peaks for different segment sizes has been calculated for the Beatles album, along with

Figure 8. Musigram (rhythmogram (top), timbregram, and chromagram (bottom), along with automatic segmentation boundaries (illustrated with vertical lines) obtained using each feature for Hold On - Jamie Walter (1994)

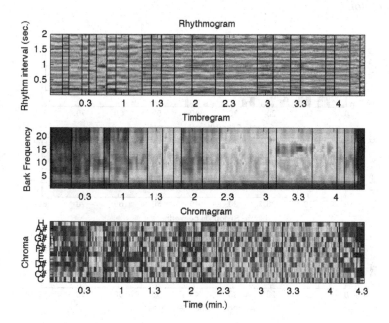

the peak values, and the peakedness values, and are shown in Figure 9.

The timbregram and chromagram always renders a peak at the shortest possible segment size (0.5 second). This has not been taken into account here. When compared with the similar data for the nine songs of varied genres (Figure 6), the differences are seemingly minor. The rhythmogram renders peaks at 5, 25 and 72 seconds, but not at 15 and 37 seconds. The timbregram renders peaks at 5, 25 and 55 seconds, and the chromagram peaks at 10, 25, 400 and 65 seconds. The rhythmogram silhouette peak values are significantly higher than the timbregram values, which are significantly higher than the chromgram values, with average silhouette peak strength of 0.45, 0.15, and -0.03 for rhythmgoram, timbregram and chromagram. As for the nine songs of varying genres, only the rhythmogram has acceptable silhouette values. When analyzing the silhouette peakedness, the same decreasing with average segment length peakedness is observed for the Beatles album as

for the nine songs, along with some high peakedness values for the vey high segment lengths. The mean peakedness values are 0.53, 0.79, and 0.17 for rhythmogram, timbregram, and chromagram, respectively. The timbregram again has the best peakedness, and the chromagram the worst. All in all, however, the rhythmogram performs best, with better silhouette values, and also there is a distinctive grouping of the rhythmogram peaks in Figure 9. This is more visible in the peak values and peakedness subplots, than in the histogram. There is one group consisting of 11 observations between four and six seconds, and one group with five observations between 11 and 13 seconds, and another group with five observations between 23 and 27 seconds. All in all, these three groups account for 21 of the 26 peaks for the rhythmogram.

As for the chunk and superchunk identification, there has been found 10 (38.46%) chunks and 5 (19.23%) superchunk for the rhythmogram, 8 (14.81%) chunk and 5 (9.26%) superchunk for

Figure 9. Histogram of silhouette peaks as a function of average segment lengths for The Beatles - Sgt Peppers Lonely Hearts Club Band (top), and silhouette peakedness values for same (bottom). The rhythmogram values are depicted with a '+', the timbregram a 'x', and the chromagram a 'o' in the middle and lower subplot.

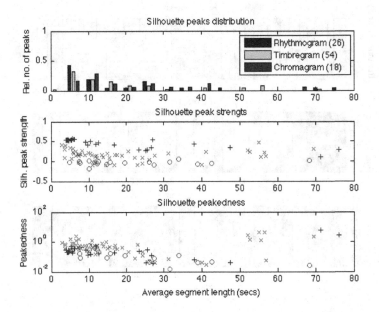

timbregram, and 1 (5.56%) chunk and 6 (33.33%) superchunk for the chromagram.

There has been found 11 (42.31%), 17 (31.48%) and 3 (16.67%) below 8 seconds (grouping) for rhythm, timbre and chroma, respectively. These numbers confirm that the rhythmogram corresponds better to the chunk and grouping theory for the Beatles songs, as it did for the nine songs of varied genres above.

CONCLUSION

Researchers and developers have found an increasing number of reasons for segmenting music into smaller segments, be it for thumbnailing, re-mixing (artistic), identification, playlist generation or other music information retrieval purposes, copyright issues, music analysis purposes, or yet other issues. However, while segmentation can easily be done, a grounded theory of the obtained, or wished for segmentation sizes should be available. This can be found in the music theory, for instance by the grouping theory of Lerdahl & Jackendorff (1973). However, their subdivision into groups of notes (often corresponding to measures) are based on rules, of which one states that groups at the same level have the same duration, which is not found in this work. While they state the rules as *preferences* that can be based on melodic or rhythmic proximity and continuity, it does not seem consistent with the results obtained here. Results from memory research (Snyder 2000) can also be used as the ground reference. Snyder refers to echoic memory (early processes) for event fusion, where fundamental units are formed by comparison with 0.25 seconds, the short-term memory for melodic and rhythmic grouping (by comparison up to 8 seconds), and long-term memory for formal sectioning by comparison up to one hour. Snyder (2000) relates this to the Gestalt theory grouping mechanisms of proximity (events close in time or pitch will be grouped together. Proximity is the primary grouping force at the melodic and rhythmic level (Snyder 2000, p 40). The second factor in grouping is similarity (events judged as similar, mainly with respect to timbre, will be grouped together). A third factor is continuity (events change in the same direction, for instance pitch). These grouping mechanisms give rise to closure, that can operate at the grouping level, or the phrase level, which is the largest group the short-term memory can handle. When several grouping mechanisms occur at the same time, intensification occurs, which gives rise to higher-level grouping. Other higher-level grouping mechanisms are parallelism (repeated smaller groups), or recurrence of pitch. The higher-level grouping demands long-term memory and they operate at a higher level in the brain, as compared to the smaller time-scale grouping. The higher-level grouping is learned while the shorter grouping is not. Snyder (2000) further divides the higher level grouping into the objective set, which is related to a particular music, and the subjective set, which is related to a style of music. Both sets are learned by listening to the music repeatedly. Snyder (2000) also related the shorter grouping to the 7±2 theory (Miller 1956), that states that the short-term memory can remember between five to nine elements.

While the music theory and memory-based research can give grounded results for the segmentation tasks, they are seemingly not giving the full truth. The music theory operated with a constant size of segments, which is not what is observed by automatic segmentation. Obviously, both the music theory and the memory-based grouping are related in many senses, which Snyder (2000) also points out. These works find some of its basis in traditional music theory and solfège. The main problem with these theories is the seemingly lack of emphasis on the actual sound, the timbre, and the performance with respect to timing and dynamics, in particular.

In contrast to these theories, the work presented here only takes into account the acoustics of the music. There is no high-level music theory, and no prior understanding based on the mechanisms of the brain.

Automatic segmentation is performed here by calculating the shortest-path through the selfsimilarity of different audio features, which can be related to rhythm, timbre and chroma. By varying the cost of inserting a new segment, different time scales are created, going from the short (seconds) to the long (up to 100 seconds). The question that is investigated here is whether music has an inherent segment length. Indeed, both music theory and brain research have theories about different time scale, which is visible in the music scores, and in different psycho-physical experiment regarding memory. In order to investigate the inherent time scale in the music, the silhouette values are calculated for all observations (blocks) for each segmentation scale. The mean of the silhouette values is a good measure of the quality of the segmentation. By matching the peaks of the silhouette values to the chunk theory of 3-5 seconds and the superchunk theory of 30-40 seconds, a measure of the inherent segmentation size has been found, together with indications of which feature that permits a better analysis of this. The rhythmogram has the best match for the chunk (19%) and superchunk (31%) levels, respectively for nine songs of varying genres, while a Beatles album gives 38%, and 19% for rhythmogram. In this case, the chromagram has better superchunk result (33%). Visually inspecting the mean silhouette values of nine songs of varying genres further reveals that only the rhythmogram has a peak at the chunk level, while all three features has peaks at the vicinity of the superchunk size of 40 seconds. Most peaks are situated above the average length of eight seconds, which gives indication that form is more prominent than grouping in the songs investigated here. Indications that form is more prominent than grouping (Snyder 2000) is given, along with indications that grouping is more prominent in the rhythmic features than in the timbral or chroma features. Further analysis of the silhouette peaks reveals the systematic occurrences of peaks in several average segment length positions, including short segments around 5 seconds, medium length segments at around 20 seconds, and longer segments. These findings are similar for a collection of nine songs of varying genres, and the Sgt Peppers album of the Beatles. The rhythmogram has systematically larger silhouette values at the peaks, with an average of approximately 0.4, while the timbregram and chromagram have mean silhouette peak values of 0.1 and 0, which is an indication that all observations could just as well belong to another segment than the one they belong to. An analysis of the peakedness of the silhouette peaks reveals that the timbregram produces stronger peaks, and chromagram the weaker peaks. Seemingly, the low length peaks have higher peakedness than the peaks found for longer segments.

While more work is necessary in order to confirm the findings here, several indicative conclusions can nonetheless be drawn; 1) The music investigated here, which is of varying genres, has inherent segment sizes of different length. These inherent segment lengths are found for all songs with relative small variations. 2) The rhythmogram performs best when the found inherent segment lengths are compared to theory, and it is also the only feature that has an acceptable average silhouette peak value.

REFERENCES

Bartsch, M. A. & Wakefield, G.H. (2001). To Catch a Chorus: Using Chroma-Based Representations For Audio Thumbnailing. *Proceedings of the Workshop on Applications of Signal Processing to Audio and Acoustics* (CD). New York: IEEE.

Chai, W., & Vercoe, B. (2003). Music thumbnailing via structural analysis. *Proceedings of ACM Multimedia Conference*. November.

Collins, N. (2005). A comparison of sound onset detection algorithms with emphasis on psychoacoustically motivated detection functions. *Proceedings of AES 118th Convention*, Barcelona, Spain, May.

Cormen, T. H., Stein, C., Rivest, R. L., & Leiserson, C. E. (2001). *Introduction to Algorithms*, (2nd Ed.). Boston: MIT Press. and New York: McGraw-Hill.

Deliege, I., & Melen, P. (1997). Cue abstraction in the representation of musical form. In Deliège, J. Sloboda (Eds). *Perception and cognition of music* (387-412). East Sussex, England: Psychology Press.

Desain, P. (1992). A (de)composable theory of rhythm. *Music Perception, 9*(4), 439–454.

Foote, J. (2000). Automatic Audio Segmentation using a Measure of Audio Novelty. [July.]. *Proceedings of IEEE International Conference on Multimedia and Expo, 1*, 452–455.

Goto, M. (2003). A chorus-section detecting method for musical audio signals. *Proceedings of the IEEE International Conference on Acoustics, Speech, and Signal Processing, 437-440* (April).

Hermansky, H. (1990). Perceptual linear predictive (PLP) analysis of speech. *The Journal of the Acoustical Society of America, 87*(4), 1738–1752. doi:10.1121/1.399423

Huron, D. (1996). The Melodic Arch in Western Folk songs. *Computing in Musicology, 10*, 323.

Jensen, K. (2005). A causal rhythm grouping. Proceedings of 2nd International Symposium on Computer Music Modeling and Retrieval (CMMR '04), Denmark (LNCS, vol. 3310, pp. 83-95)

Jensen, K. (2007). Multiple scale music segmentation using rhythm, timbre and harmony. *EURASIP Journal on Applied Signal Processing, Special issue on Music Information Retrieval Based on Signal Processing*.

Jensen, K., Xu, J., & Zachariasen, M. (2005). Rhythm-based segmentation of Popular Chinese Music. *Proceeding of the ISMIR*. London, UK, (pp.374-380).

Kaufman, L., & Rousseeuw, P. J. (1990). *Finding Groups in Data: An Introduction to Cluster Analysis*. New York: Wiley.

Kühl, O. (2007). *Musical Semantics*. Bern: Peter Lang.

Kuhl, O., & Jensen, K. (2008). *Retrieving and recreating Musical Form. Lectures Notes in Computer Science*. New York: Springer-Verlag.

Lerdahl, F., & Jackendoff, J. (1983). *A Generative Theory of Tonal Music*. Cambridge, MA: MIT Press.

McAdams, S. (2002). Musical similarity and dynamic processing in musical context. *Proceedings of the ISMA* (CD). Mexico City, Mexico.

McAuley, J. D., & Ayala, C. (2002). The effect of timbre on melody recognition by familiarity. *Meeting of the A.S.A.*, Cancun, Mexico (abstract).

Miller, G. (1956). The Magical Number Seven, Plus or Minus Two. *Psychological Review, 63*, 81–97. doi:10.1037/h0043158

Paulus, J., & Klapuri, A. (2008). Labelling the Structural Parts of a Music Piece with Markov Models. *Proceedings of the 2008 Computers in Music Modeling and Retrieval*, (pp.137-147), Copenhagen, Denmark.

Scheirer, E. (1998). Tempo and Beat Analysis of Acoustic Musical Signals. *The Journal of the Acoustical Society of America, 103*(1), 588–601. doi:10.1121/1.421129

Sekey, A., & Hanson, B. A. (1984). Improved 1-bark bandwidth auditory filter. *The Journal of the Acoustical Society of America, 75*(6), 1902–1904. doi:10.1121/1.390954

Snyder, B. (2000). *Music and Memory. An Introduction*. Cambridge, Mass.: The MIT Press.

Chapter 14
Automatic Tagging of Audio:
The State-of-the-Art

Thierry Bertin-Mahieux
Columbia University, USA

Douglas Eck
University of Montreal, Canada

Michael Mandel
University of Montreal, Canada & Columbia University, USA

ABSTRACT

Recently there has been a great deal of attention paid to the automatic prediction of tags for music and audio in general. Social tags are user-generated keywords associated with some resource on the Web. In the case of music, social tags have become an important component of "Web 2.0" recommender systems. There have been many attempts at automatically applying tags to audio for different purposes: database management, music recommendation, improved human-computer interfaces, estimating similarity among songs, and so on. Many published results show that this problem can be tackled using machine learning techniques, however, no method so far has been proven to be particularly suited to the task. First, it seems that no one has yet found an appropriate algorithm to solve this challenge. But second, the task definition itself is problematic. In an effort to better understand the task and also to help new researchers bring their insights to bear on this problem, this chapter provides a review of the state-of-the-art methods for addressing automatic tagging of audio. It is divided in the following sections: goal, framework, audio representation, labeled data, classification, evaluation, and future directions. Such a division helps understand the commonalities and strengths of the different methods that have been proposed.

INTRODUCTION

Many tasks require machines to *hear* in order to accomplish them. In the case of music, we would like computers to help us discover, manage, and describe the many new songs that become available every day. The goal is not necessarily to replace humans: the best description of an album is probably the one of a music expert. That being said, it is now impossible for any group of experts to listen to every piece on the Internet and summarize it in order for others to discover it. For example, let's

DOI: 10.4018/978-1-61520-919-4.ch014

consider an online radio like Pandora (www.pandora.com) or Last.fm (www.last.fm). As a service, they provide listeners with a personal continuous stream of music based on their musical tastes. In order to make recommendations, they rely heavily on collaborative filtering: if a listener liked songs A and B and you liked A, you might like B. Such algorithms have proven to be extremely efficient. However, it leaves two major problems. First, what is often called the cold-start problem, the fact that new items entering the system are not popular, hence never recommended, hence never popular. Secondly, some songs that start as popular end up even more popular because they do get recommended. A machine that could understand music as experts do would improve both situations.

Understanding music is a very general statement. In this work, we are interested in describing music with appropriate tags (or labels, keywords), addressing the previous situation in a natural way. Knowing a set of tags that applies to a song is in itself a description. One can also manage music by grouping pieces that are described in a similar way. Recommendations can also be made from the space of tags, e.g. one can identify that a listener like "rock" music with "female voices". Note that on Pandora and Last.fm, users can already browse music according to tags that were applied by other users. Once again, we do not claim that machines would create better tags than human listeners. Automatically created tags, or *autotags*, are useful for new or unpopular music, as well as for completing the set of tags applied by humans. Describing music with a "bag of words" is the same approach taken by text search engines that describe web pages using the words they contain. With the ability to create an appropriate set of tags that applies to any given audio, we could develop as many tools as Google and Yahoo did for web documents and change the way we handle music.

Many different groups have been trying to predict tags from audio, yet there have been few attempts at uniting the community behind a clear

shared task definition. This was partially addressed at MIREX 2008. MIREX stands for Music Information Retrieval Evaluation eXchange, a set of contests held each year at the International Conference on Music Information Retrieval (ISMIR). Throughout this paper when we refer to a MIREX contest we mean the 2009 audio tag classification task, unless otherwise mentioned. More information can be found at http://www.music-ir.org/mirex/2009/index.php/Main_Page. Though we applaud the hard work of the contest organizers, there is room for improvement. For example, the contest could have been more clearly defined in terms of evaluation and we discuss it later on in this chapter. One goal of our review is to bring together the many proposed evaluation methods and work towards a common framework for evaluation. In addition we hope that this effort will help bring new researchers into this area by offering them a clear set of goals.

Note that the lack of a common goals does not mean that learning tags have been useless so far. For instance, Eck et al. (2008) and Barrington et al. (2009) both showed that automatically generated tags can improve music recommendation. Also, Turnbull et al. (Turnbull, Barrington, Torres & Lanckriet, 2008) explain how to manage a sound effect database using automatic tagging.

This chapter focuses on automatic tagging of music. However, regarding the vast and diverse set of tags that have been used and the absence of prior knowledge assumed on the audio, this work addresses tagging of audio in general. For instance, someone working on a speech versus music classifier should also find the following methods and algorithms interesting.

Human Tags

We presented the goal as finding a set of descriptive tags for given audio frames, but it is important to first understand how humans tag audio. We often call them social tags as they are applied by humans on some collaborative platform, as opposed to tags produced by an automatic tagging algorithm. The different tags obtained are better understood when we know why people tag in the first place. Lamere lists six reasons (Lamere, 2008) that we summarize here:

- **Memory and context:** items are tagged to assist personal retrieval, e.g. having access to all "pop" songs in a database.
- **Task organization:** items are tagged to assist in the organization of music discovery tasks, e.g. tag a new song "check out" or create a future playlist of "emo" artists.
- **Social signaling:** items are tagged as a way for an individual to express their tastes to others, e.g. the use of the tag "seen live".
- **Social contribution:** items are tagged to add to the group knowledge, e.g. a metal fan tagging a song "not metal" if it is not considered truly metal.
- **Play and competition:** items are tagged as part of a game, more details in the Sources of Data section.
- **Opinion expression:** items are tagged to convey an individual's opinion, e.g. the use of the tag "awesome".

The types of tag themselves can be associated with a few categories, see Table 1. Finally, here is specific example of tagging of the band *The Shins* in Table 2.

In this paper, we present how to learn to apply similar tags to audio based on human tagging examples as the ones in Tables 1 and 2. We can already highlight a limitation of automatic tagging systems based on audio, unlike humans they could not learn to apply tags like "seen live" and "love" since there is no correlation with the audio itself. However, tags being categorized as *genre*, *mood*, and *instrumentation* are within an algorithm's reach.

Table 1. Distribution of tag types on Last.fm (in 2007)

Tag Type	Frequency	Examples
Genre	68%	Heavy metal, punk
Locale	12%	French, Seattle, NYC
Mood	5%	Chill, party
Opinion	4%	Love, favorite
Instrumentation	4%	Piano, female vocal
Style	3%	Political, humor
Misc	2%	Coldplay, composers
Personal	1%	Seen live, I own it
Organizational	1%	Check out

Definitions

A tag is a user-generated keyword associated with some resource, in our case audio. In general we tag audio tracks (or segments of a track) but we will also talk about tagging albums or artists by aggregating predictions made over tracks. Tag and label are used interchangeably. Autotag is a short name for a label applied to some audio by an automatic tagging algorithm. We may refer to an automatic tagging algorithm as an autotagger, but we must be careful as that term as been used for a specific algorithm in Bertin-Mahieux et al. (2008).

FRAMEWORK

One goal of this paper is to provide a unified view of all automatic tagging systems for audio that are currently being investigated. These systems can be decomposed into four parts: audio representation, tagging data, machine learning algorithm and evaluation (see Figure 1). Evaluation is included as a full part of the system as it has impact on the way the machine learning algorithm is trained. For instance one might use a different algorithm to train a model evaluated for artist similarity prediction than for precision/recall

Table 2. Top 21 tags applied to The Shins on Last.fm (in 2007)

Tag	Freq	Tag	Freq	Tag	Freq
Indie	2375	The Shins	190	Punk	49
Indie rock	1183	Favorites	138	Chill	45
Indie pop	841	Emo	113	Singer-songwriter	41
Alternative	653	Mellow	85	Garden State	39
Rock	512	Folk	85	Favorite	37
Seen live	298	Alternative rock	83	Electronic	36
Pop	231	Acoustic	54	Love	35

of tag vocabularies. Regarding machine learning algorithms, the term must be understood here in its most general definition, as a function that takes an input and produces an output depending on the input. In the case of automatic tagging, an algorithm can be viewed as a "machine" that takes a piece of audio, and a set of tags, and decides which tags apply and eventually to what degree. Classification can be seen as the case where the degree must be either 0 or 1.

The next sections follow the four parts of the framework. An algorithm can be described by how it deals with each of these parts: what audio features and tagging data it uses, what learning algorithm is used, and how performance is evaluated. Choices for each part can usually be made independently of the choices in the other parts.

AUDIO REPRESENTATION

We briefly discuss the vast area of representing audio, as it is always an issue when applying machine learning techniques to sounds. Let's start by stating the obvious: there is no one single best representation that will work in all cases. Furthermore, it is difficult to know in advance which representation will work with which technique. In this section we present the most typical approach, which is to mix together many representations. We present some specific choices that were made in recent papers on automatic tagging of audio.

Figure 1. Overview of an automatic tagging algorithm for audio

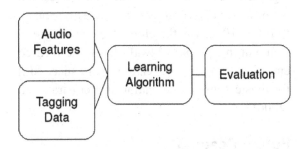

For an introduction to audio features or specific details on the implementations, we refer the reader to the future reading section.

Bag of Frames

The "bag of frames" representation is an analogy to the term "bag of words" in the text search community: to describe a text document, one keeps a vector of word counts from that document, disregarding the order in which the words appeared in that document. In the case of audio, for each "frame", one computes one or many features, which are considered in a collection that ignores their order.

An example of a bag of words setting would be the following approach: for each 100 ms of audio, compute the following features: fourier transform, mel-frequency cepstral coefficients (MFCC), chromagrams, autocorrelation coefficients, delta

MFCC, zero-crossing rate. Each of these features can be seen as a vector of size at least 1, and all are simply concatenated. Another specific example from (Turnbull, Barrington, Torres & Lanckriet, 2008), authors use MFCC, delta-MFCC and delta-delta-MFCC on 10ms-length frames.

In the bag of frames representation, these features are then aggregated over longer durations. One simple aggregation technique is taking the mean and possibly the variance of each dimension of the previously created vectors. This has merit when dealing with frames of length 1 to 10 seconds. The intuition is that, for automatic labeling, the occurrence of an event is of interest but not necessarily its time stamp. A time division up to 100 or 10 ms can therefore be too much precision, but this property always has to be verified empirically. Aggregate features were successful for music genre classification in Bergstra et al. (2006).

Future Reading

A complete description of typical audio features for Music Information Retrieval applications can be found in Aucouturier & Pachet (2003) or Gold & Morgan (1999). A more recent approach is the one of sparse coding, i.e. use representations that better compress the information into a few values. For work on sparse coding in the frequency domain, see Plumbley et al. (2006) and Gardner & Magnasco (2006). For work in the time domain, see (Grosse et al. 2007; Manzagol et al., 2007; Smith & Lewicki, 2006). For commonly used features, one can use the two following toolboxes that are freely available online: MIR toolbox (http://www.jyu.fi//laitokset//en//coe/materials/mirtoolbox) and jAudio (http://jmir.sourceforge.net/jAudio.html). Some companies even offer to analyze audio online and provide you with features, e.g. the Echo Nest (http://www.echonest.com).

OBTAINING LABELED DATA

More specific to our task than representing audio is finding a proper dataset of labeled <audio,tag> pairs. As we explained in the introduction, the tags applied by humans are of great quality. The machine learning assumption is that if we show an algorithm enough examples, the correlation will become clear. However, the following trade-off remains: gathering more examples help, but we usually need to explore less reliable sources to do so. For instance, tags applied by music companies are usually of little value since they are chosen according to commercial interests instead of the music itself. The ultimate goal would be to have a large set of examples that is "clean" at the same time, i.e. that could have been created by a human expert. There have been many attempts to build datasets, and (Turnbull, Barrington & Lanckriet, 2008) presents them as five possible sources. In the following section, we will follow Turnbull et al. and present the first four sources (the fifth one refers to automatic tagging, the purpose of this paper). Then, we discuss the size of the available datasets and their implications. Finally, we briefly present different ways to "clean up" the tagging data and arrange it in either a classification or regression setting for the machine learning algorithm. The number of tags to be learned simultaneously is also problematic.

Sources of Data

We follow (Turnbull, Barrington & Lanckriet, 2008) and present four sources of data.

Survey. Most straightforward and costly method, one can ask people to listen to songs and tag them. One problem usually arises, either the participants are paid, or there are not enough of them. The CAL lab at the University of California in San Diego (UCSD) paid undergraduates to fill out a survey, the resulting dataset CAL500 is available online (Turnbull, Barrington, Torres & Lanckriet, 2007). It consists of tags applied to 500 songs by an average of approximately 3 listeners. The vocabulary (set of possible tags) was fixed by the survey. Later in this section we talk about obtaining tag data from games. This overcomes many of the survey problems, participants fill the survey because of a reward (winning), but the reward is non monetary, hence acquiring data is not as costly.

Social tags. Tags applied by human users. Last.fm is an online radio that enables users to tag an artist, an album, or a song through a web-browser or a donwloaded client. By the beginning of 2007, the database contained a vocabulary of 960,000 free-text tags and millions of songs were annotated. Last.fm data is available through their Audioscrobbler service page (Audioscrobbler). Last.fm, provides the largest freely available collection of tagging data, but other data available from the web exist, including MusicBrainz (http://musicbrainz.org). Last.fm data have been used or described in (Eck et al., 2008; Lamere, 2008; Mandel & Ellis, 2008b).

Game. Different tagging games have been developed by research teams to gather clean data (Kim et al, 2008; Law et al., 2007, Mandel & Ellis, 2007; Turnbull, Liu, Barrington & Lanckriet, 2007). The idea is to give users an incentive to apply appropriate tags to songs or song snippets. For instance, in MajorMiner (Mandel & Ellis, 2007), users get points if they are the first or second person to use a tag on a particular excerpt. This avoids usage of random, unrelated, or mischievous tags. Cheating is always possible, but there are ways to counter it, usually by tracking a user behavior over some time. Data acquired this way are usually very clean, but still many orders of magnitude smaller in size than social tags. The largest game data available has been released by the Magnatagatune team (http://tagatune.org/Datasets.html) and contains tags applied to about 20,000 songs.

Web documents. A fourth idea is to use documents available on the Internet to describe audio. Celma et al. (2006) crawls MP3 blogs to obtain tags. For instance, one could search for words that are more often associated with a particular artist than with an "average artist", and use it as a tag. One can easily gather millions of tags, but the main drawback of this method is the noise in the data. Other approaches include querying search engines (Knees et al., 2008) and mining music websites (Whitman & Ellis, 2004).

Size of Datasets

Following what we saw as the different sources of tagging data, we emphasize the question of the size of the dataset. These days, the choice can be summarized into *small and clean* versus *large and noisy*. A typical small and clean data would come from a game, and a typical large and noisy dataset would be Last.fm data. To help clarify the choice and its implications, let's focus on the two following questions:

- **What is the application?** If the goal is to build a new online music recommender based on tags, the choice is obvious, the data has to be large. No performance obtained on small datasets can be guaranteed in a real life setting of millions of songs. However, if the goal is to classify a set of songs into 10 or 20 categories, it makes sense to learn these categories on very clean, unambiguous data, even if we sacrifice the size.

- **What is the algorithm?** We will discuss in the next section the different algorithms used for automatic tagging, but it is clear that some are more suited than others for a particular size of dataset. Algorithms like the support vector machine (SVM) classifier can be trained well on small datasets, but their training time is on the order of the square of the number of examples. On the other hand, algorithms such as neural networks with stochastic gradient descent can be trained on very large datasets, but can be defeated by too few examples. If a specific algorithm must be used (for research purpose for instance), choosing a proper dataset size is essential.

The authors believe that most of the future applications will rely on large datasets, a trend already seen in image information retrieval, e.g. in (Li et al., 2006). The incredible amount of data should overcome the inherent noise, except for some specific task where the classification is expected to be clear and very accurate. This is rarely the case in real life, a sound can be tagged in various ways, and the tagging can change with context and over time. We encourage new researchers to mine web documents and make extensive use of available datasets like Last.fm. We also hope that in the end, online games will produce larger and more reliable datasets. Magnatagatune (tagatune. org/Magnatagatune.html*),* a recently published tagging dataset of 20.000 audio songs, is a step in the right direction.

Cleanup of Data

Here we mention different heuristics one might want to use to improve tagging data. No dataset coming from the four sources we described can be efficiently used "out of the box". Furthermore, the way the data is prepared has to be consistent with the task at hand, the machine learning algorithm, and the evaluation method. For instance, if a band like *Radiohead* has been tagged ten thousand times more often than others, should the algorithm see ten thousands time more often audio coming from *Radiohead*? Another example, some tags are synonyms, or the negation of one another. Should they be combine into one label, and do we penalize the algorithm during learning if it predicts a synonym instead of the tag it has seen?

The first thing is to select the vocabulary. As we mentioned, Last.fm data has approximately one million different tags. Since it would be unlikely for anyone to try to learn them all, a subset has to be chosen. Eck et al. (2008) simply take the most popular tags (the one applied the most) on Last.fm. It is straightforward, but sometimes misleading. For instance, many listeners tag songs as "favorite" so they can make playlists out of their favorite pieces. Unfortunately, no algorithm should be able to learn such a tag unrelated to the music itself. A better list of tags to be used would be the tags people use to search for music. A user can search for "R&B" music, but he has no reason to search for "favorite" music unless it is his own. The list of tags used for search is therefore cleaner and probably more useful to learn. Another method is also described in the Future reading section.

Another thing to be careful about is popularity bias. Some artist or songs are more popular than others, hence more frequently tagged. Additionally, some tags are more popular than other, hence more frequently applied. This bias appears in data coming from social tags or web documents, and to some extent in games data (tag popularity). Easy examples would be *Radiohead* versus most of the existing artists, and "rock" versus "japanese ska". One can decide to either leave the data as it is, or to try to reduce the bias, usually with the hope of helping the learning algorithm later on. See future readings for pointers.

Organization of Data

We discuss the last two essential choices that must be made: should the data be presented as a classification or regression? Then, should the tags be learned one or many at a time?

A classification implies a set of binary questions: does this tag apply to this audio, yes or no. With a regression, the question becomes: to what degree can this audio be described by this tag? In the real world, there are few cases where a belonging can either be 100% or zero. It is especially true for genre tags for music, where songs never belong to only one. Thus, a regression setting is the natural choice for an automatic tagging algorithm. There are many ways to transform a tagging dataset into a regression dataset. If it comes from a survey, one can take the percentage of people that tagged a song with a particular tag.

There are two major reasons to transform a tagging dataset into a classification dataset: 1) it is easier for a learning algorithm to find a proper class than a proper belonging value, and 2) values one gets for pairs <audio,tag> can be extremely noisy, transforming them into a classification can mitigate the noise. An example where the value <audio,tag> can be too noisy to be used is the CAL500 dataset (Turnbull, Barrington, Torres & Lanckriet, 2007). Most of the songs are listened to by 3 people. If we would take the proportion of listeners that tagged a song "rock" for instance, the numbers could only be 0, 0.33, 0.66 and 1. Obviously, the granularity does not account for real life and the number of listeners is not large enough to be confident in the value. To transform a regression dataset into a classification dataset, we usually use a threshold. In the case of CAL500, the authors suggest that we consider that a tag was applied to a song only if 80% of the listeners agreed. If the amount of data is large enough, e.g. coming from Last.fm or web documents, you can use rankings to determine if a tag applies to some audio or not. Eck et al. (2008) consider that a tag was applied only to the top 10 artists the most related to the tag (according to TFxIDF, described in the next section). The other applications of the tag were ignored or discarded.

Regarding the number of tags to be learned simultaneously, we can safely say that in theory, the more the better. Tags often share mutual information, e.g. the use of the tag "r&b" indicates that the tag "hip hop" will probably be applied as well. Learning a set of tags instead of one enables us to use those correlations in addition to those coming from audio features. That being said, the vocabulary can be a very large set, and can even

grow with time. Not every machine learning algorithm can handle multiple outputs, and the computational complexity often grows accordingly. Another practical restriction is the use of cloud computing: if we learn one tag at a time, one can launch N learning tasks on N processors. Thus, the learning of the whole vocabulary scales inversely with the number of CPUs.

In the literature, Turnbull et al. (2008), Eck et al. (2008), and Mandel & Ellis (2008a) learn tags independently, and Trohidis et al. (2008) learn them simultaneously.

Future Reading

Another method for selecting tags to be learned is described in Torres et al. (2007) and involves Canonical Correlation Analysis (CCA). CCA is especially designed to find dependencies between two datasets living in different but related spaces. The two spaces here are the audio features and the tagging space. The idea is that a tag is meaningful if it is linked to some audio event (seen in the features). From a practical point of view, it amounts to choosing a vocabulary that can probably be learned.

Regarding popularity bias, few papers face this problem directly, mostly because published results often come from small datasets. We mention Eck et al. (2008), which uses term-frequency, inverse document-frequency (TFxIDF) to approach the issue. TFxIDF come from the text search community that deal with documents of different lengths and words used with varying frequency in a particular language. Seeing artists (or songs) as documents and tags applied to them as words of these documents, TFxIDF produces a value of how much a tag is particular to a given artist (or song). This problem could also be seen as bd-matching where we try to associate users to products. Each user has to be associated with b products, and each product associated with d users. The framework fits the popularity bias we face, but its application to tagging data is ongoing research. Huang & Jebara (2007) present a bd-matching implementation example.

Note that the TFxIDF method can be used to get a score in order to transform the data into a regression setting, the value to predict is TFx-IDF's ouput.

MACHINE LEARNING METHODS

The central part of any automatic tagging algorithm is the model that links tags to audio features. Being as general as possible, any method that finds (possibly highly complex) correlations between the two can be seen as a machine learning algorithm and be applied to automatic tagging. Such a large research field is impossible to cover or summarize. We will focus on three algorithms recently used for this task. For a general introduction to the field, or for pointers to other interesting algorithms, see the future reading section.

We split machine learning methods into two classes: classification methods, and regressions and probabilistic methods. This refers to the kind of output the methods learn to produce, and it is a typical division between supervised learning methods. It is appropriate here since, as we saw before, our tagging data can exist as one or the other.

Classification Methods

Support vector machines (SVMs) are one of the most widely used machine learning algorithms, and have been applied in M. Mandel's papers to automatic tagging. Their performance as a classifier has been demonstrated and they can also handle regression, but a concern with it is the training speed, which is of order N^2, N being the number of examples (audio frames here). Mandel & Ellis (2008a) use SVMs in a multiple-instance learning framework (Dietterich et al., 1997) In this framework, supervision for training is provided not at the level of clips, but of at the level of col-

lections of clips (e.g. tracks, albums, or artists), and the classifier's job is to predict whether a classification is relevant to each of the clips in that collection and to clips in a separate test set. For music, if an artist is tagged with "saxophone", some of their clips should contain saxophone, but not necessarily all of them.

Boosting is a meta-algorithm in the sense that it works on top of other learning algorithms. For now on, we discuss boosting single-stumps, i.e. a decision tree with two leaves. Boosting has been used by the Gamme lab at the University of Montreal, first for genre classification (Bergstra et al., 2006), then for automatic tagging (Bertin-Mahieux et al., 2008; Eck et al., 2008; Kegl et al., 2008). In an iterative way, boosting finds the best possible classifier (in the set of all possible single-stumps) and adds it to a "strong classifier". It then reweights the examples so that classifying the hard ones is more rewarding. As single-stumps see only one dimension at a time, the information contained in those dimensions must be highly relevant. Hence, the authors used boosting in conjunction with aggregate features. Boosting training time scales linearly in the number of examples.

Regression and Probabilistic Methods

We already mentioned SVMs and neural networks that have extensions to handle the regression case. It is also the case for k-Nearest Neighbors (kNN), but it has been rarely used in the literature. We now focus our attention on the method used by the CAL group at UCSD (Turnbull, Barrington, Torres & Lanckriet, 2008).

Gaussian mixture is a learning algorithm that models a distribution using gaussians. In our case, audio frames are a point in the features space and we model their position. The assumption is that, if a new point (audio frame) is close in the feature space, it should be tagged the same way. The advantage of the Gaussian mixture model is that it gives a probability, i.e. the probability that a tag X was applied to an audio frame F. Gaussian mixtures are trained using the well-known EM algorithm (Bishop, 2006). Gaussian mixtures are more powerful (in terms of representation capacity) than an algorithm that only classifies because it estimates the likelihood of a data point. The drawback of such methods is that, if the goal is to be discriminative, resources are spent modeling the data. Specifically, if two classes are 99% the same, the generative approach tries to model each class and probably ignores the 1% difference between them, while the discriminative approach focuses on that 1% that is different. Another disadvantage is that training Gaussian mixtures are extremely demanding in computational resources as soon as the number of audio frames get large.

To overcome the computational complexity, Turnbull et al. use the Hierarchical Gaussian mixture model (HGMM), a method introduced for vision in (Vasconcelos, 2001). The idea is to train Gaussian mixtures on a subset of audio frames, for instance all frames from one song. This gives a single Gaussian mixture per song, meaning 500 Gaussian mixtures for the CAL500 dataset. Vasconcelos showed how to approximate all these mixture by a new Gaussian mixture. This divide-and-conquer approach is very efficient.

According to MIREX 2008 results and some comparisons done in (Bertin-Mahieux et al., 2008), HGMM seems the better performing algorithm for automatic tagging of music until MIREX 2009. However, Bertin-Mahieux et al. raise concern about the small size of the datasets that were used for the comparisons as it could favor HGMM.

Future Reading

For a complete introduction to the machine learning field, we refer the reader to (Bishop, 2006) or (Duda et al., 2000).

K-nearest neighbors (KNN) is one of the most simple, and surprisingly effective, machine learning techniques. Due to its simplicity, KNN should be a first comparison again any new tagging algorithm. KNN has been used in (Sordo et al., 2007) to explicitly propagate labels among neighbors, neighbors being derived from audio features. See also (Cano & Koppenberger, 2004).

Trohidis et al. (2008) discuss four algorithms to classify audio into emotions. Three algorithms: binary relevance (BR), label powerset (LP), and random k-labelsets (RAKEL) are taken from their previous work (Tsoumakas et al., 2007) and MLkNN is described in (Zhang & Zhou, 2007). These are interesting methods because they aim at directly predicting a subset of classes. In our audio case, it could mean they build a predictor from a set of audio features to the subset of tags {"rock", "metal", "hardcore"}. These algorithms are clearly of interest, but since their relatively poor results in the MIREX 2008 contest, their application must be refined for audio and automatic tagging in particular.

Neural networks have not been been used in recent papers on automatic tagging of audio, but there is no reason why it would not work efficiently. In particular, it handles multi-label classification and regression cases, and new developments in the field (Bengio et al., 2007) allow the use of very large networks, hence possibly capturing highly complex relations between audio and tags. Neural networks have been used successfully for music genre classification in (Bergstra, 2006)..

Finally, Bergstra (2006) does a review of algorithms that have been used for genre classification and all of them have potential for automatic tagging.

As the size of datasets increases, algorithms need to scale efficiently. Online algorithms are trained by seeing only a few examples at a time, thus avoiding the need of an increasingly large memory. For online learning versions of some of the algorithms we presented, see (Bordes et al., 2005) (SVM), (Bradley & Schapire, 2008) (boosting) and (Declercq & Piater, 2008; Song & Wang, 2005) (gaussian mixture model).

EVALUATION

Evaluation may be the most problematic part of the automatic tagging of audio task. We can be more general and say that the task definition itself is problematic, and that is why the community has not agreed on a set of measure functions. We gave the goal of having a machine that can describe music the same way a human expert would. Thus, the perfect evaluation would be to have human experts grade the quality of the autotags produced by different algorithms. Unfortunately, such an evaluation is often impossible in practice, and other evaluation measures need to be used as an approximation for the judgment of an expert.

We split evaluation measures into three categories: direct measures, indirect measures, and human evaluation. Direct measures are tightly related to the machine learning setting. For instance, classification accuracy for a classification task or mean squared error for a regression task. Indirect measures imply using autotags in a model for another task, and measuring how well the model performs. For instance, what is the quality of recommendations based on autotags? Finally, human evaluations involve humans asserting the quality of the autotags.

Although the separation between the three types of evaluations is not always crisp, it helps questioning the results reported so far in the literature.

Direct Measures

A first measure, especially easy to compute if the problem is posed as a classification, is classification accuracy. It is the percentage of songs that were correctly identified as being tagged or not tagged with a particular label. We often see the two numbers presented separately, as the number of songs tagged and not tagged are usually very unbalanced. Also, for some applications, not predicting a label is not as penalizing as predicting

Figure 2. Formulas for precision and recall

$$precision = \frac{|relevant\ documents| \cap |documents\ retrieved|}{|document\ retrieved|}$$

$$recall = \frac{|relevant\ documents| \cap |documents\ retrieved|}{|relevant\ documents|}$$

a wrong label. Therefore, classification accuracy for positive examples (song being tagged) and negative examples (song not being tagged) should be analyzed independently.

This leads us to precision and recall (Figure 2), a pair of measures that tries to analyze similar aspects but from a retrieval point of view. More specifically, it asks the two questions: when I ask for a song with tag X, how often do I get one correctly? Then, can I get all songs tagged with X? One aspect can be more important than the other depending on the goal. Precision measures how often we tag a song with the correct label. Recall measures the fraction of relevant songs that are correctly identified.

Good recall avoids having an algorithm that never tags anything in order to avoid a mistake. However, if a user is looking for a "rock" song on the internet, he does not care to get billions of them, but the ones he receives should really be "rock", thus precision is predominant.

One usually wants a good combination of both precision and recall. We might also want to compare algorithms according to both, F-measure is the average of precision and recall. Two other methods are presented in the future reading section.

The problem is that all these measures represent slightly different aspects of a good tagging algorithm. We can either select one of them as a community standard and ignore the rest, use a large number of them and get overwhelmed with data (often contradictory), or devise new and more rounded methods of measuring a model's performance. We discuss the latter in the next subsections.

Indirect Measures

We have seen measures that are closely linked to what the algorithm is trained to do, for instance classification accuracy. These are not the only way to state whether our autotagging algorithm produces pertinent labels or not. We can use tags, and autotags, in derivate tasks and see if both perform as well. Eck et al. (2008) use tags to compute a similarity measure between artists and compare it against a ground truth similarity. Note that it is far from obvious how to build a ground truth similarity metric and they actually rely on one that is "good enough", details can be found in their paper. At the end, Eck et al. can claim that autotags do not perform as well as real tags, but clearly better than random. Thus, autotags "have merit". Other derivative tasks can easily be imagined. If one has access to an online radio station like Last.fm, one could look at user satisfaction with their recommendations when they search for a song by tags. Derivative tasks also enable us to add a human in the evaluation loop, and that is what we discuss in the next subsection.

Human Evaluation

The most direct human evaluation is to set up a panel of experts, or simply a large survey of individuals, and ask them to rate how appropriate a tag is for a particular song. If one started from clean data (from a survey for instance), one can hide some entries during the training of our algorithm and then test how likely the test entries are according to our model. However, there is one major limitation with this method. It is quite easy to find positive examples, i.e. a tag that was applied to a song. It is harder to determine that a tag should not have been applied to the song. The test set from a survey data is therefore half complete, and we still need a human to evaluate the output of an automatic tagger.

Here is a specific example of what we just said. Consider the band *U2*. It has obviously been tagged with "rock". Thus, if an algorithm produces that tag for a *U2* song, one can mark that as a success. Next, assume that the algorithm produced the tag "country". This does not fit perfectly the style of *U2*, but it is closer than "rap" for instance. If none of these tags were applied by listeners, both would be penalized the same way. However, a human judge would prefer an algorithm that decides that *U2* is more "country" than "rap". This illustrates the need for a human evaluation.

Setting up a panel to judge algorithms is difficult, as they are required to tag thousands or even millions of songs. A very promising approach, already considered in the section about obtaining labeled data, is to use a game to encourage users to becoming judges. E. Law suggested we modify the Tagatune game for that purpose (Law, 2008). In Tagatune, two players listen to a song simultaneously and the goal is to determine if they are listening to the same one. Players are only allowed to communicate by typing labels which are visible to both of them and must make their decision based on these tags. If an automatic tagging system outputs appropriate tags, it should enable a human partner to decide if he is listening to the same song or not. Hence, the algorithm that yields the best average score for its human partners is considered the most accurate of all models. As we are writing, this evaluation experiment is underway, with many submissions from MIREX 2008 automatic tagging contest (Law et al., 2009).

Concerns about Current Evaluation Methods

Many researchers in the field feel we did not find the proper evaluation methods for automatic tagging, most of these concerns are expressed in (Law, 2008). We try to summarize the main arguments here. Classification accuracy is somewhat irrelevant if the testing data are noisy. One can always argue that, as long as the training and testing data come from the same distribution, the noise becomes part of the task and the evaluation is valid. That being said, when we consider that non only are the data noisy, but they are overwhelmed with negative examples (tag X was not applied to audio frame F), the confidence in the test set gets very low. The *U2* example applies here, the fact that *U2* is tagged neither "country" nor "rap" does not mean that both predictions are equally wrong.

Precision and recall are more relevant to actual applications of an automatic tagger. In particular, for an online radio like Last.fm, it is important to provide a "pop" song or "ska" song to a user that asked for that genre. Precision measures exactly that, and we argue that it is more important than recall in most real-life applications.

All tags are not born equals, and some are more popular than others. Turnbull et al. find that the most useful tags are the one that are neither the most popular nor the most obscure. Thus, we should consider evaluation methods that take the popularity of tags into account, but this is extremely difficult to do. For MIREX 2008, the beta-binomial model (Gelman et al., 2003) was used and one of its properties is to put more weight on tags that are better represented. According to Turnbull et al.'s finding, this can be problematic.

Finally, as we mention before, the size of the datasets is problematic. If the goal is to create a program that can be implemented on a very large scale like the Internet, one needs to measure the performance of algorithms on very large datasets. This has not been the case so far and it is likely to remain a problem for the years to come. Fortunately, indirect and human evaluations like we presented have the potential to circumvent the matter.

Future Reading

Another direct evaluation measure is Area under the Receiver Operating Characteristic curve (AROC). AROC assumes that, for a tag X, you can order songs by how much they should be tagged with X. AROC computation can be found in numerous papers, for instance (Turnbull, Bar-

rington, Torres & Lanckriet, 2008). Many of the concerns expressed above have been explored by the search engine community. We recommend the work of Herlocker et al. for a complete overview (Herlocker et al., 2000; Herlocker et al., 2004).

THREE PUBLISHED IMPLEMENTATIONS

In this section, we present three approaches that have been successfully implemented and published recently. According to the results of the 2008 MIREX contest on automatic tagging, they also appear as the three best performing algorithms. We can therefore consider them as the state-of-the-art and a reference point for future research. Then, we briefly presents the MIREX 2008 results according to one measure, F-measure. The full results are available online and are too detailed to be presented here.

UCSD - CAL

A first successful implementation was done at the University of California in San Diego in the Computer Audition Laboratory (CAL) headed by Professor G. Lanckriet.

The feature they use are MFCC, delta-MFCC and delta-delta-MFCC over frames of approximately 23ms. The tagging data comes from CAL500 dataset. The machine learning algorithm is hierarchical gaussian mixture. Evaluation is done with precision / recall and AROC.

Publications about this work are: (Turnbull, Barrington, Torres & Lanckriet, 2007; Turnbull, Barrington, Torres & Lanckriet, 2008).

Columbia - LabROSA

A second method was developed by M. Mandel at Columbia in the Laboratory for the Recognition and Organization of Sound and Audio (LabROSA) headed by Professor D. Ellis.

The features used are the mean and unwrapped covariance of MFCCs and rhythmic features that measure modulations in a few gross frequency bands. The training data comes from the MajorMiner game. The machine learning algorithm is SVMs. Evaluation is done by measuring the classification accuracy on a test set with the same number of positive and negative examples, ensuring a constant baseline of 50%.

Publications about this work are: (Mandel & Ellis, 2008a; Mandel & Ellis, 2008b).

University of Montreal - GAMME

A third method was investigated at the GAMME laboratory headed by Professor D. Eck and in collaboration with Sun Microsystems (Search Inside the Music project, main researcher was P. Lamere).

The features used are aggregate spectrograms, MFCC and autocorrelation coefficients. The training data comes from Last.fm. The machine learning algorithm is multi-class boosting of single stumps. The evaluations include classification accuracy and artist similarity.

Publications about this work are: (Eck et al., 2007; Eck et al., 2008; Bertin-Mahieux et al., 2008; Kegl et al, 2008).

Results of MIREX 2008 Audio Tag Classification Task

In Table 3 we present the results of MIREX 2008 according to the F-measure. The complete and detailed results are available online. The first three teams are the implementations we presented above. Note that the "Smurf" team is a sort of control submission. The algorithm always tagged any audio with the most popular tags. The number of tags output was previously optimized to maximize the F-measure on a training set similar in size to the one used at MIREX. Also, the entry from G. Peeters was a generic algorithm which was submitted to all MIREX tasks, thus it was not optimized for automatic tagging.

Table 3. Submissions to MIREX 2008 audio tag classification task, teams orderedaccording to F-measure. When a team has multiple entries, only the best entry is reported. For more details, see: http://www.music-ir.org/mirex/2008/

Team	Algorithm
UCSD	HGMM
Columbia	SVM
University of Montreal	Boosting
Smurf	Tag popularity
Geoffrey Peters	ircamclassification (generic)
Trohidis et al.	RAKEL / MLkNN

Note on MIREX 2009 Audio Tag Classification Task

The results for MIREX 2009 were released just before this work went to press. Unfortunately, most of the teams from 2008 did not resubmit, but we can look at the results on the MajorMiner dataset, the same one used in 2008. Summarized results are shown in Table 4.

As we can see from the F-measure, the accuracy of the systems is improving. Lo et al. (2009) used an ensemble classifier, something similar to boosting. Tzanetakis (2009) used two layers of SVM, one to learn each tag independently, and a second to take advantage of the correlations between tags. The detailed results from 2008 and 2009 are available on the MIREX website.

FUTURE RESEARCH DIRECTIONS

Automatic tagging of audio, and automatic tagging of multimedia in general, are active research fields and research directions are numerous. We want to highlight two improvements that we hope to see in the next five years, namely the use of large and scalable algorithms, and the proper handling of sparse coding.

Table 4. Winning entries from MIREX 2008 and MIREX 2009 audio tag classification task, teams ordered according to F-measure on the "major minor" dataset. When a team has multiple entries, only the best entry is reported. For more details, see: http://www.music-ir.org/mirex/2009/

Team	F-measure
Lo et al., Taiwan (2009)	0.31
Tzanetakis, CAN (2009)	0.29
UCSD (2008)	0.28
Columbia (2008)	0.26
University of Montreal (2008)	0.19

The future of audio and machine learning belongs to a fast online learning algorithm. The audio data is accessible, and so is metadata (tags for instance). The possibilities offered by such an amount of information are endless. From a machine learning point of view, we can describe any manifold that holds meaningful information, e.g. the subspace of scary audio sounds. From an industry point of view, we are able to spot any new trends or peculiar taste that might develop among listeners. The only problem is that we cannot currently synthesize so much data. The perfect algorithm should be online because no matter how cheap memory gets, we will never be able to store everything in main memory at once. The perfect algorithm should be fast for obvious reasons, and being online helps. Let us add something there, the perfect algorithm will probably be simple, and its low complexity will be balanced by the quantity of data seen. Low memory usage, fast, and simple, it should be pure gain for developers, and it is made possible by the enormous amounts of data online.

On a more signal processing aspect, we are looking forward to an algorithm that will handle correctly sparse encodings, especially encodings performed in the time domain. As it is convincingly exposed in (Smith & Lewicki, 2005; Smith

& Lewicki, 2006), frame-based audio features have inherent limitations, namely the frequency accuracy / time accuracy trade-off. Note that developing "sparse algorithms" is a general trend in machine learning research in the recent years. The recent work done by Weinstein and Moreno (2007) on audio fingerprinting is a good example of a successful application of sparse coding.

CONCLUSION

We described automatic tagging algorithms for audio as a set of four components, and we presented the state-of-the-art in each of these components. We also presented three successful implementations that have been published and that performed well at MIREX. Finally, we emphasize the current trend toward large-scale data, and explained why algorithms that handle such data should be investigated. In accordance with the goal of this paper, we presented an overview of the existing models and gave the appropriate pointers and references needed by a researcher trying to develop his own approach.

Automatic tagging is a step towards a better understanding of music by machines. One road map to achieve this goal consists of two steps: describing audio with meaningful labels, and using these labels to manage and discover new products. The second step has been intensively developed by web search engines, and it is the greatest incentive to create a good automatic tagging algorithm.

REFERENCES

Andrews, S., Tsochantaridis, I., & Hofmann, T. (2003). Support vector machines for multiple-instance learning. In *Advances in Neural Information Processing Systems 15*. Cambridge, MA: MIT Press.

Aucouturier, J. J., & Pachet, F. (2003). Representing Musical Genre: A State of the Art. *Journal of New Music Research, 32,* 83–93. doi:10.1076/jnmr.32.1.83.16801

Audioscrobbler. *Web Services.* Retrieved from http://www.audioscrobbler.net/~data/webservices/

Barrington, L., Turnbull, D., Yazdani, M., & Lanckriet, G. (2009). Combining audio content and social context for semantic music discovery. In *Proceedings of the 32th annual international ACM SIGIR conference on Research and development in information retrieval, ACM.*

Bengio, Y., Lamblin, P., Popovici, D., & Larochelle, H. (2007). Greedy layer-wise training of deep networks. In *Advances in Neural Information Processing Systems 19* (pp. 153–160). Cambridge, MA: MIT Press.

Bergstra, J. (2006). *Algorithms for classifying recorded music by genre.* Montreal, Canada: University of Montreal.

Bergstra, J., Casagrande, N., Erhan, D., Eck, D., & Kégl, B. (2006). Aggregate Features and AdaBoost for Music Classification. *Machine Learning, 65,* 473–484. doi:10.1007/s10994-006-9019-7

Bertin-Mahieux, T., Eck, D., Maillet, F. & Lamere, P. (2008). Autotagger: a model for Predicting social tags from acoustic features on large music databases. *Journal of New Music Research, special issue: From genres to tags: Music Information Retrieval in the era of folksonomies., 37.*

Bishop, C. (2006). *Pattern Recognition and Machine Learning.* New York: Springer Verlag.

Bordes, A., Ertekin, S., Weston, J., & Bottou, L. (2005). Fast Kernel Classifiers with Online and Active Learning. *Journal of Machine Learning Research, 6,* 1579–1619.

Bradley, J. K., & Schapire, R. (2008). *FilterBoost: Regression and Classification on Large Datasets. Advances in Neural Information Processing Systems 20.* Cambridge, MA: MIT Press.

Cano, P., & Koppenberger, M. (2004). Automatic sound annotation. In *IEEE workshop on Machine Learning for Signal Processing,* 391-400.

Celma, O., Cano, P., & Herrera, P. (2006). Search Sounds: An audio crawler focused on weblogs. In *Proceedings of the 7th International Conference on Music Information Retrieval (ISMIR 2006).*

Declercq, A., & Piater, J. H. (2008). Online Learning of Gaussian Mixture Models - a Two-Level Approach, In *3rd International Conference on Computer Vision Theory and Applications (VISAPP),* 605-611.

Dietterich, T., Lathrop, R., & Lozano-Pérez, T. Solving the multiple instance problem with axis-parallel rectangles, In *Artificial Intelligence, Elsevier Science Publishers Ltd.* (1997), 89, 31-71

Duda, R. O., Hart, P. E., & Stork, D. G. (2000). *Pattern Classification.* New York: Wiley-Interscience Publication.

Eck, D., Bertin-Mahieux, T., & Lamere, P. (2007). Autotagging music using supervised machine learning. In *Proceedings of the 8th International Conference on Music Information Retrieval (ISMIR 2007).*

Eck, D., Lamere, P., Bertin-Mahieux, T., & Green, S. (2008). Automatic generation of social tags for music recommendation. In *Advances in Neural Information Processing Systems 20.* Cambridge, MA: MIT Press.

Garnder, T. J., & Magnasco, M. O. (2006). Sparse time-frequency representations. *Proceedings of the National Academy of Sciences of the United States of America, 103,* 6094–6099. doi:10.1073/pnas.0601707103

Gelman, A., Carlin, J., Stern, H., & Rubin, D. (2003). *Bayesian Data Analysis* (2 Ed.). New York: Chapman & Hall/CRC.

Gold, B., & Morgan, N. (1999). *Speech and Audio Signal Processing: Processing and Perception of Speech and Music*. New York: John Wiley & Sons, Inc.

Grosse, R., Raina, R., Kwong, H., & Ng, A. Y. (2007). Shift-Invariant Sparse Coding for Audio Classification. In *Proceedings of the Twenty-third Conference on Uncertainty in Artificial Intelligence* (2007).

Herlocker, J. L., Konstan, J. A., & Riedl, J. T. (2000). Explaining collaborative filtering recommendations. In *Computer Supported Cooperative Work*, 241-250.

Herlocker, J. L., Konstan, J. A., Terveen, L. G., & Riedl, J. T. (2004). Evaluating collaborative filtering recommender systems. In *ACM Trans. Inf. Syst., ACM Press*, 22, 5-53

Huang, B., & Jebara, T. (2007). Loopy Belief Propagation for Bipartite Maximum Weight b-Matching. In *Artificial Intelligence and Statistics*.

Kégl, B., Bertin-Mahieux, T., & Eck, D. (2008). Metropolis-Hastings sampling in a FilterBoost music classifier. In *ICML Workshop on Music and Machine Learning*.

Kim, Y., Schmidt, E., & Emelle, L. (2008). Moodswings: a collaborative game for music mood label collection. In *Proceedings of the 9th International Conference on Music Information Retrieval (ISMIR 2008)*.

Knees, P., Pohle, T., Schedl, M., Schnitzer, D., & Seyerlehner, K. (2008). A document-centered approach to a natural language music search engine. In *European Conference on Information Retrieval (ECIR)*.

Lamere, P. (2008). Semantic tagging and music information retrieval, In *Journal of New Music Research, special issue: From genres to tags: Music Information Retrieval in the era of folksonomies*.

Law, E. v. Ahn, L., Dannenberg, R. & Crawford, M. (2007). TagATune: a game for music and sound annotation, In *Proceedings of the 8th International Conference on Music Information Retrieval (ISMIR 2007)*.

Law, E. (2008). The problem of accuracy as an evaluation criterion. In *ICML Workshop on Evaluation Methods in Machine Learning*.

Law, E., West, K., Mandel, M., Bay, M., & Downie, S. (2009). Evaluation of algorithms using games: the case of music tagging. In *Proceedings of the 10th International Conference on Music Information Retrieval (ISMIR 2009)*.

Li, X., Chen, L., Zhang, L., Lin, F., & Ma, W.-Y. (2006). Image annotation by large-scale content-based image retrieval. In *MULTIMEDIA '06: Proceedings of the 14th annual ACM international conference on Multimedia*.

Lo, H.-Y., Wang, J.-C., & Wang, H. M. (2009). An ensemble method for MIREX audio tag classificationMusic Information Retrieval Evaluation Exchange (MIREX), Kobe, 2009. Retrieved from http://www.music-ir.org/mirex/2009/

Mandel, M., & Ellis, D. (2007). A web-based game for collecting music metadata. In *Proceedings of the 8th International Conference on Music Information Retrieval (ISMIR 2007)*.

Mandel, M., & Ellis, D. (2008a). Multiple-instance learning for music information retrieval. In *Proceedings of the 9th International Conference on Music Information Retrieval (ISMIR 2008)*.

Mandel, M., & Ellis, D. (2008b). A web-based game for collecting music metadata. In *Journal of New Music Research, special issue: From genres to tags: Music Information Retrieval in the era of folksonomies*.

Manzagol, P.-A., Bertin-Mahieux, T., & Eck, D. (2008). On the use of sparse time relative auditory codes for music. *Proceedings of the 9th International Conference on Music Information Retrieval (ISMIR 2008)*.

Plumbley, M., Abdallah, S., Blumensath, T., & Davies, M. (2006). Sparse representations of polyphonic music. *Signal Processing, 86*, 417–431. doi:10.1016/j.sigpro.2005.06.007

Smith, E., & Lewicki, M. S. (2005). Efficient coding of time-relative structure using spikes. [Boston: MIT Press.]. *Neural Computation, 17*, 19–45. doi:10.1162/0899766052530839

Smith, E., & Lewicki, M. S. (2006). Efficient auditory coding. *Nature, 439*, 978–982. doi:10.1038/nature04485

Song, M., & Wang, H. (2005). Highly efficient incremental estimation of Gaussian mixture models for online data stream clustering. In *Society of Photo-Optical Instrumentation Engineers (SPIE) Conference Series*.

Sordo, M., Laurier, C., & Celma, O. (2007). Annotating music collections: how content-based similarity helps to propagate labels. *In Proceedings of the 8th International Conference on Music Information Retrieval (ISMIR 2007)*.

Torres, D., Turnbull, D., Barrington, L., & Lanckriet, G. (2007). Identifying words that are musically meaningful. In *Proceedings of the 8th International Conference on Music Information Retrieval (ISMIR 2007)*.

Trohidis, K., Tsoumakas, G., Kalliris, G., & Vlahavas, I. (2008). Multi-label classification of music into emotions. In *Proceedings of the 9th International Conference on Music Information Retrieval (ISMIR 2008)*.

Tsoumakas, G., & Vlahavas, I. (2007). Random k-Labelsets: an ensemble method for multilabel classification. In *ECML '07: Proceedings of the 18th European conference on Machine Learning*.

Turnbull, D., Barrington, L., & Lanckriet, G. (2008). Five Approaches to Collecting Tags for Music. In *Proceedings of the 9th International Conference on Music Information Retrieval (ISMIR 2008)*.

Turnbull, D., Barrington, L., Torres, D., & Lanckriet, G. (2007). Towards musical query-by-semantic-description using the CAL500 data set. In *SIGIR '07: Proceedings of the 30th annual international ACM SIGIR conference on Research and development in information retrieval*.

Turnbull, D., Barrington, L., Torres, D., & Lanckriet, G. (2008). Semantic annotation and retrieval of music and sound effects. In *IEEE Transactions on Audio, Speech & Language Processing*, 16.

Turnbull, D., Liu, R., Barrington, L., & Lanckriet, G. (2007). A game-based approach for collecting semantic annotations of music. In *Proceedings of the 8th International Conference on Music Information Retrieval (ISMIR 2007)*.

Tzanetakis, G. (2009). Marsyas submissions to MIREX 2009, in Music Information Retrieval Evaluation Exchange (MIREX), Kobe.Retrieved from http://www.music-ir.org/mirex/2009/

Vasconcelos, N. (2001). Image indexing with mixture hierarchies. In *Proceedings of the 2001 IEEE Computer Society Conference on Computer Vision and Pattern Recognition (CVPR 2001)*.

Weinstein, E., & Moreno, P. (2007). Music Identification with Weighted Finite-State Transducers. In *Proceedings of the IEEE International Conference on Acoustics, Speech, and Signal Processing (ICASSP)*.

Whitman, B., & Ellis, D. (2004). Automatic record reviews. In *Proceedings of the 5th International Conference on Music Information Retrieval (ISMIR 2004)*.

Zhang, M., & Zhou, Z. (2007). ML-KNN: A lazy learning approach to multi-label learning. [Maryland Heights, MO: Elsevier Science Inc.]. *Pattern Recognition, 40,* 2038–2048. doi:10.1016/j.patcog.2006.12.019

KEY TERMS AND DEFINITIONS

Machine Learning: linked to artificial intelligence, machine learning is a science discipline that is concerned with functions that can algorithmically predict an output based on some data.

Social Tags: a user-generated keyword associated with some resource, in our case audio.

Automatic Tagging: the use of a machine learning algorithm to apply a tag to some resource.

Feature: a descriptor of some resource, e.g. beats per minute for a music performance.

Music Information Retrieval Evaluation eXchange (MIREX): a set of contests held each year at the ISMIR conference

Evaluation: in our case, some measure of how well a particular tag applies to some audio.

Recommendation: the process of suggesting a new and relevant resource to some user.

Chapter 15

Instantaneous vs. Convolutive Non–Negative Matrix Factorization:
Models, Algorithms and Applications to Audio Pattern Separation

Wenwu Wang
University of Surrey, UK

ABSTRACT

Non-negative matrix factorization (NMF) is an emerging technique for data analysis and machine learning, which aims to find low-rank representations for non-negative data. Early works in NMF are mainly based on the instantaneous model, i.e. using a single basis matrix to represent the data. Recent works have shown that the instantaneous model may not be satisfactory for many audio application tasks. The convolutive NMF model, which has an advantage of revealing the temporal structure possessed by many signals, has been proposed. This chapter intends to provide a brief overview of the models and algorithms for both the instantaneous and the convolutive NMF, with a focus on the theoretical analysis and performance evaluation of the convolutive NMF algorithms, and their applications to audio pattern separation problems.

INTRODUCTION

Since the seminal paper published in 1999 by Lee and Seung, non-negative matrix factorization (NMF) has attracted tremendous research interests over the last decade. The earliest work in NMF is perhaps by (Paatero, 1997) and is then made popular by Lee and Seung due to their elegant multiplicative algorithms (Lee & Seung, 1999,

Lee & Seung, 2001). The aim of NMF is to look for latent structures or features within a dataset, through the representation of a non-negative data matrix by a product of low rank matrices. It was found in (Lee & Seung, 1999) that NMF results in a "parts" based representation, due to the nonnegative constraint. This is because only additive operations are allowed in the learning process. Although later works in NMF may have mathematical operations that can lead to negative elements within the low-rank matrices, their

DOI: 10.4018/978-1-61520-919-4.ch015

non-negativity can be ensured by a projection operation (Zdenuk & Cichocki, 2007, Soltuz et al, 2008). Another interesting property with the NMF technique is that the decomposed low-rank matrices are usually sparse, and the degree of their sparseness can be explicitly controlled in the algorithm (Hoyer, 2004). Thanks to these promising properties, NMF has been applied to many problems in data analysis, signal processing, computer vision, and patter recognition, see, e.g. (Lee & Seung, 1999, Pauca et al, 2006, Smaragdis & Brown, 2003, Wang & Plumbley, 2005, Parry & Essa, 2007, FitzGerald et al, 2005, Wang et al, 2006, Zou et al, 2008, Wang et al, 2009, Cichocki et al, 2006b).

In machine audition and audio signal processing, NMF has also found applications in, for example, music transcription (Smaragdis & Brown, 2003, Wang et al, 2006) and audio source separation (Wang & Plumbley, 2005, Parry & Essa, 2007, FitzGerald et al, 2005, FitzGerald et al, 2006, Virtanen, 2007, Wang et al, 2009). In these applications, the raw audio data are usually transformed to the frequency domain to generate the spectrogram, i.e. the non-negative data matrix, which is then used as the input to the NMF algorithm. The instantaneous NMF model given in (Lee & Seung, 1999, Lee & Seung, 2001) has been shown to be satisfactory in certain tasks in audio applications provided that the spectral frequencies of the analyzed signal do not change dramatically over time (Smaragdis, 2004, Smaragdis, 2007, Wang, 2007, Wang et al, 2009). However, this is not a case for many realistic audio signals whose frequencies do vary with time. The main limitation with the instantaneous NMF model is that only a single basis function is used, and therefore is not sufficient to capture the temporal dependency of the frequency patterns within the signal. To address this issue, the convolutive NMF (or similar methods called shifted NMF) model has been introduced (Smaragdis, 2004, Smaragdis, 2007, Virtanen, 2007, FitzGerald et al, 2005, Morup et al, 2007, Schmidt & Morup, 2006, O'Grady

& Pearlmutter, 2006, Wang, 2007, Wang et al, 2009). For the convolutive NMF, the data to be analyzed are modelled as a linear combination of shifted matrices, representing the time delays of multiple bases. Several algorithms have been developed based on this model, for example, the Kullback-Leibler (KL) divergence based multiplicative algorithm proposed in (Smaragdis, 2004, Smaragdis, 2007), the squared Euclidean distance based multiplicative algorithm proposed in (Wang, 2007, Wang et al, 2009), the two-dimensional deconvolution algorithms proposed in (Schmidt & Morup, 2006), the logarithmic scaled spectrogram decomposition algorithm in (FitzGerald et al, 2005), and the algorithm based on the constraints of the temporal continuity and sparseness of the signals in (Virtanen, 2007).

This chapter will briefly review the mathematical models for both instantaneous and convolutive NMF, some representative algorithms, and their applications to the machine audition problems, in particular, the problem of audio pattern separation and onset detection. This chapter also aims to serve as complementary material to our previous work in (Wang et al, 2009). To this end, we will provide a theoretical analysis of the convolutive NMF algorithm based on the squared Euclidean distance. These results can be readily extended to the KL divergence based algorithms. Moreover, we will provide several examples in addition to the simulations provided in (Wang et al, 2009). The remainder of the chapter is organised as follows. The next two sections will review the models and the algorithms of instantaneous and convolutive NMF, respectively. Then, we provide the theoretical analysis to the convolutive NMF algorithm based on the squared Euclidean distance. After this, we show some simulations to demonstrate the applicability of the NMF algorithms (both instantaneous and convolutive) to the machine audition problems including audio pattern separation and onset detection. In addition to the performance comparison between the three typical convolutive NMF algorithms, we will further compare their performance based on the relative reconstruction errors and the rejection ratio. Finally, we discuss future research directions in this area.

INSTANTANEOUS NMF

The mathematical model of the instantaneous NMF can be described as follows. Given a non-negative data matrix $\mathbf{X} \in \Re_+^{M \times N}$, find two matrices $\mathbf{W} \in \Re_+^{M \times R}$ and $\mathbf{H} \in \Re_+^{R \times N}$ such that $\mathbf{X} \approx \mathbf{WH}$, where the factorization rank R is generally chosen to be smaller than M(or N), or akin to $(M + N)R < MN$. In other words, NMF aims to map the given data from a higher dimensional space to a lower one. As a result, some redundancies within the data can be reduced and at the same time, some latent features can be extracted. In practice, such data can be an image (Lee & Seung, 1999), the spectrogram of an audio signal (Smaragdis & Brown, 2003), among many others, see e.g. (Berry, 2007) for a recent review. Several cost functions have been used in the literature for finding $\mathbf{W}$ and $\mathbf{H}$, see e.g. (Paatero, 1997, Lee & Seung, 1999, Lee & Seung, 2001, Hoyer, 2004, Cichocki et al, 2006a, Dhillon & Sra, 2006). One frequently used criterion is based on the mean squared reconstruction error defined as follows

$$(\hat{\mathbf{W}}, \hat{\mathbf{H}}) = \arg \min_{\mathbf{W}, \mathbf{H}} \frac{1}{2} \left\| \mathbf{X} - \mathbf{WH} \right\|_F^2 \qquad (1)$$

where $\left\| * \right\|_F$ denotes the Frobenius norm, and $\hat{\mathbf{W}}$ and $\hat{\mathbf{H}}$ are the estimated optimal values of $\mathbf{W}$ and $\mathbf{H}$ (when the algorithm converges). It is also referred to as the squared Euclidean distance based criterion. Another criterion is based on the extended KL divergence,

$$(\hat{\mathbf{W}}, \hat{\mathbf{H}}) = \arg \min_{\mathbf{W}, \mathbf{H}} \sum_{m=1}^{M} \sum_{n=1}^{N} \left\{ \mathbf{X} \bullet \log \left[\frac{\mathbf{X}}{\mathbf{WH}} \right] - \mathbf{X} + \mathbf{WH} \right\} \qquad (2)$$

where $\bullet$ denotes the element-wise multiplication, and the division also operates in element wise. If we denote $\mathbf{WH}$ as $\hat{\mathbf{X}}$, then $\hat{\mathbf{X}}$ is the reconstructed data, which should ideally be equal to $\mathbf{X}$. In practice, as shown in Equation (1) and (2), the difference between $\hat{\mathbf{X}}$ and $\mathbf{X}$ is used to find $\mathbf{W}$ and $\mathbf{H}$.

To optimize the above cost functions, Lee and Seung have proposed simple yet efficient multiplicative algorithms based on the variable step-size normalization of each element of $\mathbf{W}$ and $\mathbf{H}$ (Lee & Seung, 1999, Lee & Seung, 2001), where $\mathbf{W}$ and $\mathbf{H}$ are updated alternately in each iteration, i.e. fixing $\mathbf{W}$, updating $\mathbf{H}$, then fixing $\mathbf{H}$ and updating $\mathbf{W}$. Based on criterion (1), the update equations for $\mathbf{W}$ and $\mathbf{H}$ can be written as

$$\mathbf{H}^{q+1} = \mathbf{H}^q \bullet \frac{(\mathbf{W}^q)^T \mathbf{X}}{(\mathbf{W}^q)^T \mathbf{W}^q \mathbf{H}^q} \qquad (3)$$

$$\mathbf{W}^{q+1} = \mathbf{W}^q \bullet \frac{\mathbf{X}(\mathbf{H}^{q+1})^T}{\mathbf{W}^q \mathbf{H}^{q+1}(\mathbf{H}^{q+1})^T} \qquad (4)$$

where $(*)^T$ denotes matrix transpose and q is the iteration number. Similarly, for criterion (2), we have the following update equations

$$\mathbf{H}^{q+1} = \mathbf{H}^q \bullet \frac{(\mathbf{W}^q)^T \dfrac{\mathbf{X}}{\mathbf{W}^q \mathbf{H}^q}}{(\mathbf{W}^q)^T \mathbf{E}} \qquad (5)$$

$$\mathbf{W}^{q+1} = \mathbf{W}^q \bullet \frac{\dfrac{\mathbf{X}}{\mathbf{W}^q \mathbf{H}^q}(\mathbf{H}^{q+1})^T}{\mathbf{E}(\mathbf{H}^{q+1})^T} \qquad (6)$$

where $\mathbf{E} \in \Re_+^{M \times N}$ is a matrix whose elements are all set to unity.

Since the publication of these multiplicative algorithms, there have been an increasing number of activities in developing new algorithms for NMF. These include using new cost functions (such as Csiszar's divergence, alpha and beta divergence, Cichocki et al, 2006a, Cichocki et al, 2006b, Cichocki et al, 2007), new adaptation algorithms (such as the projected gradient methods, alternating least squares (ALS) method and the conjugate gradient algorithm, Lin, 2007, Zdenuk & Cichocki, 2007, Kim et al, 2007, Wang & Zou, 2008), applying additional constraints (such as sparseness, smoothness, continuity, etc., Hoyer, 2004, Virtanen, 2003, Virtanen, 2007). For a review of recent development on NMF, please refer to e.g. (Albright et al, 2006, Berry et al, 2007).

Here we show the learning rules of ALS algorithm. The ALS method uses the following iterations to update $\mathbf{W}$ and $\mathbf{H}$

$$\mathbf{H}^{q+1} = \left((\mathbf{W}^q)^T \mathbf{W}^q \right)^{-1} (\mathbf{W}^q)^T \mathbf{X} \qquad (7)$$

$$\mathbf{W}^{q+1} = \mathbf{X}(\mathbf{H}^{q+1})^T \left(\mathbf{H}^{q+1}(\mathbf{H}^{q+1})^T \right)^{-1} \qquad (8)$$

The matrix inverse used in above equations may result in negative elements within $\mathbf{W}$ and $\mathbf{H}$. In practice, the negative elements are projected back to the non-negative orthant. It was found in (Soltuz et al, 2009) that the ALS algorithm has fast convergence rate, however, its convergence performance is not consistent. The algorithm suffers from instability and may diverge in practice. To improve its stability, one can combine the multiplicative algorithm due to (Lee & Seung, 2001) with the ALS algorithm, as suggested in (Soltuz et al, 2009). For example, $\mathbf{W}$ and $\mathbf{H}$ can be updated in the following way,

$$\mathbf{H}^{q+1} = \mathbf{H}^q \bullet \frac{(\mathbf{W}^q)^T \mathbf{X}}{(\mathbf{W}^q)^T \mathbf{W}^q \mathbf{H}^q} \qquad (9)$$

$$\mathbf{W}^{q+1} = \mathbf{X}(\mathbf{H}^{q+1})^T \left(\mathbf{H}^{q+1}(\mathbf{H}^{q+1})^T \right)^{-1} \qquad (10)$$

The hybrid algorithm provides a fast convergence rate and at the same time offers good convergence stability. More details of the theoretical and numerical analysis of this algorithm can be found in (Soltuz et al, 2009).

CONVOLUTIVE NMF

The instantaneous NMF has limitations in dealing with many non-stationary signals whose frequencies change dramatically over time, since only a single basis is used in the model. To address this issue, Smaragdis extended the standard (instantaneous) NMF model to the convolutive case (Smaragdis, 2004). Rather than using $\hat{\mathbf{X}} = \mathbf{WH}$, $\hat{\mathbf{X}}$, is represented by a sum of shifted matrix products, i.e.

$$\hat{\mathbf{X}} = \sum_{p=0}^{P-1} \mathbf{W}(p) \overset{p \rightarrow}{\mathbf{H}} \qquad (11)$$

where $\mathbf{W}(p) \in \Re_+^{M \times R}$, $p = 1, \cdots, P-1$, are a set of bases, and $\overset{p \rightarrow}{\mathbf{H}}$ shifts the columns of $\mathbf{H}$ by p spots to the right. Similarly, $\overset{\leftarrow p}{\mathbf{H}}$ shifts the columns of $\mathbf{H}$ by p spots to the left. The shifts are non-circular, which means the elements of the columns shifted in from outside the matrix will be set to zeros (Smaragdis, 2004, Wang, 2007, Wang et al, 2009). For example, suppose

$$\mathbf{H} = \begin{bmatrix} 2 & 1 & 7 \\ 9 & 9 & 3 \\ 4 & 5 & 8 \end{bmatrix}$$

Then

$$
\overset{0\rightarrow}{\mathbf{H}} = \begin{bmatrix} 2 & 1 & 7 \\ 9 & 9 & 3 \\ 4 & 5 & 8 \end{bmatrix}, \quad \overset{1\rightarrow}{\mathbf{H}} = \begin{bmatrix} 0 & 2 & 1 \\ 0 & 9 & 9 \\ 0 & 4 & 5 \end{bmatrix},
$$

$$
\overset{2\rightarrow}{\mathbf{H}} = \begin{bmatrix} 0 & 0 & 2 \\ 0 & 0 & 9 \\ 0 & 0 & 4 \end{bmatrix}, \quad \overset{3\rightarrow}{\mathbf{H}} = \begin{bmatrix} 0 & 0 & 0 \\ 0 & 0 & 0 \\ 0 & 0 & 0 \end{bmatrix}
$$

$$
\overset{\leftarrow 0}{\mathbf{H}} = \begin{bmatrix} 2 & 1 & 7 \\ 9 & 9 & 3 \\ 4 & 5 & 8 \end{bmatrix}, \quad \overset{\leftarrow 1}{\mathbf{H}} = \begin{bmatrix} 1 & 7 & 0 \\ 9 & 3 & 0 \\ 5 & 8 & 0 \end{bmatrix},
$$

$$
\overset{\leftarrow 2}{\mathbf{H}} = \begin{bmatrix} 7 & 0 & 0 \\ 3 & 0 & 0 \\ 8 & 0 & 0 \end{bmatrix}, \quad \overset{\leftarrow 3}{\mathbf{H}} = \begin{bmatrix} 0 & 0 & 0 \\ 0 & 0 & 0 \\ 0 & 0 & 0 \end{bmatrix}
$$

Using the convolutive model (11) and the extended KL divergence based criterion (2), Smaragdis obtained the following multiplicative learning algorithm

$$
\mathbf{H}^{q+1} = \mathbf{H}^q \bullet \frac{(\mathbf{W}^q(p))^T \left(\dfrac{\overset{\leftarrow p}{\mathbf{X}}}{\hat{\mathbf{X}}^q} \right)}{(\mathbf{W}^q(p))^T \bullet} \tag{12}
$$

$$
\mathbf{W}^{q+1}(p) = \mathbf{W}^q(p) \bullet \frac{\left(\dfrac{\mathbf{X}}{\hat{\mathbf{X}}^q} \right) \overset{p\rightarrow}{(\mathbf{H}^{q+1})^T}}{\bullet \, \overset{p\rightarrow}{(\mathbf{H}^{q+1})^T}} \tag{13}
$$

As in our previous work (Wang, 2009), we refer to this algorithm as ConvNMF-KL in this chapter.

Recently, using the same convolutive model (11), we have derived a new algorithm using the squared Euclidean distance based criterion (1), see details in (Wang et al, 2009). In this algorithm, the update equations for $\mathbf{W}(p)$ and $\mathbf{H}$ are given as

$$
\mathbf{W}^{q+1}(p) = \mathbf{W}^q(p) \bullet \frac{\mathbf{X} \overset{p\rightarrow}{\left(\mathbf{H}^q \right)^T}}{\hat{\mathbf{X}}^q \overset{p\rightarrow}{\left(\mathbf{H}^q \right)^T}} \tag{14}
$$

$$
\mathbf{H}^{q+1} = \mathbf{H}^q \bullet \frac{(\mathbf{W}^{q+1}(p))^T \overset{\leftarrow p}{\mathbf{X}}}{(\mathbf{W}^{q+1}(p))^T \overset{\leftarrow p}{\hat{\mathbf{X}}}} \tag{15}
$$

The update Equation (15) may lead to a biased estimate of $\mathbf{H}$. To address this issue, in practice, $\mathbf{H}$ can be further modified as

$$
\mathbf{H}^{q+1} = \frac{1}{P} \sum_{p=0}^{P-1} \left(\mathbf{H}^q \bullet \frac{(\mathbf{W}^{q+1}(p))^T \overset{\leftarrow p}{\mathbf{X}}}{(\mathbf{W}^{q+1}(p))^T \overset{\leftarrow p}{\hat{\mathbf{X}}}} \right) \tag{16}
$$

To improve the computational efficiency of the proposed algorithm, we have introduced a recursive update method for $\hat{\mathbf{X}}$ as follows

$$
\hat{\mathbf{X}}^q = \hat{\mathbf{X}}^q - \mathbf{W}^q(p) \overset{p\rightarrow}{\mathbf{H}^q} + \mathbf{W}^{q+1}(p) \overset{p\rightarrow}{\mathbf{H}^q} \quad (p = 0, \cdots, P-1) \tag{17}
$$

The subtraction used in (17) may result in negative values of the elements in $\hat{\mathbf{X}}^q$. We use the following projection to prevent this

$$
\hat{\mathbf{X}}_{i,j}^q = \max(\varepsilon, \hat{\mathbf{X}}_{i,j}^q) \tag{18}
$$

where $\hat{\mathbf{X}}_{i,j}^q$ is the ij-th element of the matrix $\hat{\mathbf{X}}$ at iteration q, and ε is a floor constant, and typically, we choose $\varepsilon = 10^{-9}$ in our implementations. Same as in our previous work (Wang et al, 2009), we denote the algorithm described above as ConvNMF-ED. The implementation details of ConvNMF-ED can be found in (Wang et al, 2009) and are omitted in this chapter.

It is worth noting that there is another method considering the convolutive model, i.e. SNMF2D developed in (Schmidt & Morup, 2006, Morup & Schmidt, 2006). This algorithm can be regarded as an extension of Smaragdis's work by considering a two-dimensional deconvolution scheme, together with sparseness constraints (Morup & Schmidt, 2006), where both the extended KL divergence and the least squares criterion are considered. For their least square criterion based approach, denoted as SNMF2D-LS in this chapter, the shifted versions of $\mathbf{W}^q$ and $\mathbf{H}^q$ at all time lags $p = 0, \ldots, P - 1$ are used for updating $\mathbf{W}^q(p)$ and $\mathbf{H}^q(p)$, with an individual time lag at each iteration. The update equation for $\mathbf{H}^q$ is given as

$$\mathbf{H}^{q+1} = \mathbf{H}^q \bullet \frac{\left(W^{q+1}(0)\right)^T \overset{\leftarrow p}{\mathbf{X}} + \cdots + \left(W^{q+1}(P-1)\right)^T \overset{\leftarrow p}{\mathbf{X}}}{\left(W^{q+1}(0)\right)^T \overset{\leftarrow p}{\hat{\mathbf{X}}} + \cdots + \left(W^{q+1}(P-1)\right)^T \overset{\leftarrow p}{\hat{\mathbf{X}}}}$$

(19)

The advantage of this formulation is the increased sparseness that may be achieved for the decomposition matrices. For audio pattern separation purpose, however, this representation may break the structure of audio objects which makes event or onset detection directly from $\mathbf{W}^q(p)$ and $\mathbf{H}^q$ even more difficult (Wang et al, 2009). Another issue with this formulation is the over-shifting effect (Wang et al, 2009) where the time-frequency signature in the data has been shifted more than it actually requires in the sense of audio object separation. Also the computational load with the above formulation is higher as compared with the ConvNMF-ED algorithm. In this chapter, as a compliment to the results in (Wang et al, 2009), we will show additional simulations and comparisons between the above methods in the subsequent sections.

As in instantaneous NMF, one can also consider sparseness constraint within the convolutive NMF algorithm. For example, we can enforce sparseness constraint on $\mathbf{H}$ using the following cost function,

$$(\hat{\mathbf{W}}, \hat{\mathbf{H}}) = \arg\min_{\mathbf{W},\mathbf{H}} \left\| \mathbf{X} - \hat{\mathbf{X}} \right\|_F^2 + \lambda \sum_{ij} \mathbf{H}_{ij}$$

(20)

where $\hat{\mathbf{X}}$ takes the form of (11), and λ is a regularization constant which controls the amount of sparseness constraints. To optimize this cost function, we can use the same expression as (14) for the update of $\mathbf{W}(p)$. However, $\mathbf{H}$ needs to be updated as follows (Wang, 2008)

$$\mathbf{H}^{q+1} = \mathbf{H}^q \bullet \frac{\left((W^{q+1}(p))^T \overset{\leftarrow p}{\mathbf{X}} \right)}{\left((W^{q+1}(p))^T \overset{\leftarrow p}{\hat{\mathbf{X}}^q} + \lambda \check{\mathbf{z}} \right)}$$

(21)

CONVERGENCE ANALYSIS OF THE CONVOLUTIVE NMF ALGORITHM

The exact convergence analysis of the proposed algorithm would be difficult. However, the overall performance can be approximated by the key updating Equations (14) and (15). As we know that, when $P = 1$, ConvNMF-ED is approximately equivalent to the instantaneous NMF (i.e. the algorithm based on update Equations (3) and (4)). This implies that we can effectively follow the method used in (Lee & Seung, 2001) for the convergence analysis of the proposed algorithm in terms of (14) and (15). Similarly, we have the following lemma.

Lemma 1: The squared Euclidean distance $\Im$ is non-increasing under the learning rules (14) and (15).

Proof: Suppose $G(\mathbf{w}, \mathbf{w}^q)$ is an auxiliary function for $\Im = \frac{1}{2} \left\| \mathbf{X} - \hat{\mathbf{X}} \right\|_F^2$, then according to (Lee & Seung, 2001), the conditions $G(\mathbf{w}, \mathbf{w}^q) \geq \Im(\mathbf{w})$, $G(\mathbf{w}, \mathbf{w}) = \Im(\mathbf{w})$ should be satisfied, and $\Im$ is non-increasing under the update $\mathbf{w}^{q+1} = \arg\min G(\mathbf{w}, \mathbf{w}^q)$, where $\mathbf{w}$ is a vector derived from the matrix $\mathbf{W}(p)$ by stacking its columns together into one column vector, i.e. the vectorization of matrix $\mathbf{W}(p)$, and q is again the iteration index. Likewise, $\mathbf{w}$ can be replaced by the vector $\mathbf{h}$ in order to prove the convergence property of the learning rule of $\mathbf{H}$, where $\mathbf{h}$ can be obtained in the same way as $\mathbf{w}$ using vectorization. Correspondingly, $\Im$ is represented as a function of $\mathbf{w}$, i.e. $\Im(\mathbf{w})$, instead of $\mathbf{W}(p)$. To proceed the proof, we need the following derivatives, $\dfrac{\partial \hat{\mathbf{X}}_{i,j}}{\partial \mathbf{W}_{m,n}(p)}, \dfrac{\partial \Im}{\partial \mathbf{W}_{m,n}(p)}$, and the components of the Hessian tensor

$$\Pi_{m,n,m',n'}(p) = \frac{\partial^2 \Im}{\partial \mathbf{W}_{m,n}(p)\partial \mathbf{W}_{m',n'}(p)},$$

where the sub-script denotes the specific element of a matrix; for example, $\mathbf{W}_{m,n}(p)$ represents the mn-th element of the matrix $\mathbf{W}(p)$, and the same notation is used for other matrices throughout the chapter.

In terms of Equation (11), we have the following derivative (see the Appendix for its derivation)

$$\frac{\partial \hat{\mathbf{X}}_{i,j}}{\partial \mathbf{W}_{m,n}(p)} = \delta_{i,m} \overset{p\rightarrow}{\mathbf{H}}_{n,j} \qquad (22)$$

where $\delta_{i,m}$ is denoted as

$$\delta_{i,m} = \begin{cases} 1, & i-m \\ 0, & i \neq m \end{cases} \qquad (23)$$

Similary, according to Equation (1) and (22), we have (see the Appendix for details)

$$\frac{\partial \Im}{\partial \mathbf{W}_{m,n}(p)} = \sum_j (\hat{\mathbf{X}}_{m,j} - \mathbf{X}_{m,j}) \overset{p\rightarrow}{\mathbf{H}}_{n,j} \qquad (24)$$

Based on Equations (1) (22) (24), the components of the Hessian tensor $\Pi_{m,n,m',n'}(p)$ can be derived as (refer to the Appendix for details)

$$\Pi_{m,n,m',n'}(p) = \sum_j \delta_{m,m'} \overset{p\rightarrow}{\mathbf{H}}_{n,j} \overset{p\rightarrow}{\mathbf{H}}_{n',j} \qquad (25)$$

Let $\lambda = \{m,n\}$, $\lambda' = \{m',n'\}$, so that the tensor $\Pi_{m,n,m',n'}(p)$ can be compressed as a matrix with elements denoted as $\mathbf{T}_{\lambda,\lambda'}(p)$. With these derivatives, we are now ready for the whole proof using a procedure similar to that in (Lee & Seung, 2001, Morup & Schmidt, 2006). First, we can expand $\Im$ in terms of a second order Taylor series, i.e.

$$\Im(\mathbf{w}) = \Im(\mathbf{w}^q) + (\mathbf{w} - \mathbf{w}^q)\frac{\partial \Im}{\partial \mathbf{W}(p)} + \frac{1}{2}(\mathbf{w} - \mathbf{w}^q)^T \mathbf{T}(\mathbf{w} - \mathbf{w}^q) \qquad (26)$$

Then, let $G(\mathbf{w}, \mathbf{w}^q)$ take the following form

$$G(\mathbf{w}, \mathbf{w}^q) = \Im(\mathbf{w}^q) + (\mathbf{w} - \mathbf{w}^q)\frac{\partial \Im}{\partial \mathbf{W}(p)} + \frac{1}{2}(\mathbf{w} - \mathbf{w}^q)^T \mathbf{K}(\mathbf{w}^q)(\mathbf{w} - \mathbf{w}^q) \qquad (27)$$

where $\mathbf{K}(\mathbf{w}^q)$ is a diagonal matrix defined as

$$\mathbf{K}_{\lambda,\lambda'} = \delta_{\lambda,\lambda'} \frac{(\mathbf{Tw}^q)_\lambda}{(\mathbf{w}^q)_\lambda} \qquad (28)$$

According to the same method as in (Lee & Seung, 2001), it is straightforward to show that

$$(\mathbf{w} - \mathbf{w}^q)(\mathbf{K}(\mathbf{w}^q) - \mathbf{T})(\mathbf{w} - \mathbf{w}^q) \geq 0 \qquad (29)$$

Therefore, we have $G(\mathbf{w}, \mathbf{w}^q) \geq \Im(\mathbf{w})$ in terms of $G(\mathbf{w}, \mathbf{w}^q) - \Im(\mathbf{w})$ computed from Equations (26) (27). It is also straightforward to prove that $G(\mathbf{w}, \mathbf{w}) = \Im(\mathbf{w})$ in terms of Equations (26) and (27). Finally, we need to show that the learning rules (14) were obtained when the gradient of $G(\mathbf{w}, \mathbf{w}^q)$ with respect to $\mathbf{w}$ equals to zero, i.e.

$$\frac{\partial G}{\partial \mathbf{w}} = \frac{\partial G}{\partial \mathbf{W}_{m,n}(p)} = 0 \tag{30}$$

According to Equation (25), we have (see the derivation in the Appendix)

$$(\mathbf{Tw})_{m,n} = \left[\hat{\mathbf{X}} \left(\overset{p\rightarrow}{\mathbf{H}} \right)^T \right]_{m,n} \tag{31}$$

Expanding (30) and incorporating (31), we obtain the following element-wise adaptation equation

$$\mathbf{W}_{m,n}^{q+1}(p) = \mathbf{W}_{m,n}^q(p) - \frac{\mathbf{W}_{m,n}^q(p)}{\sum_j \overset{p\rightarrow}{\mathbf{H}}_{n,j} \hat{\mathbf{X}}_{m,j}} \sum (\hat{\mathbf{X}}_{m,j} - \mathbf{X}_{m,j}) \overset{p\rightarrow}{\mathbf{H}}_{n,j} = \mathbf{W}_{m,n}^q(p) \frac{\left[\mathbf{X} \left(\overset{p\rightarrow}{\mathbf{H}} \right)^T \right]_{m,n}}{\left[\hat{\mathbf{X}} \left(\overset{p\rightarrow}{\mathbf{H}} \right)^T \right]_{m,n}} \tag{32}$$

Apparently, Equation (32) is an element-wise operation of (14). Consequently, $\Im$ is non-increasing under the update (32), as it is obtained by the minimization of $G(\mathbf{w}, \mathbf{w}^q)$. Similarly, $\Im$ is non-increasing under the update Equation (15). This concludes the proof of Lemma 1. Obviously, the distance $\Im$ is invariant under these updates if and only if $\mathbf{W}(p)$ and $\mathbf{H}$ are at a limit point of the distance. However, as in instantaneous NMF, whether any limit point is always stationary remains an open issue, see, e.g. (Lin, 2007) and therefore is an interesting topic for future research.

APPLICATIONS TO AUDIO PATTERN SEPARATION

In this section, we show an example of applying the ConvNMF-ED algorithm to the audio object separation problem using artificially generated audio signals. More application examples to real music audio signals can be found in (Wang, 2007, Wang et al, 2009), and are not included in this chapter. We generate the audio signal in the same way as used in our previous work (Wang, 2007). First, we generated two audio signals, with one containing five repeating patterns whose frequencies changing linearly with time from 320Hz to 270Hz, and the other containing four repeating patterns whose frequencies change linearly from 500Hz to 600Hz. The sampling frequency f_s for both signals is 1500Hz. These two signals were added together to generate a mixture. The length of the signal is 30 seconds. Then, this mixture was transformed into the frequency domain by the procedure described in (Wang et al, 2006, Wang, 2007, Wang et al, 2008, Wang et al, 2009), where the frame length T of the fast Fourier transform (FFT) was set to 2048 samples, i.e., the frequency resolution is approximately 0.73Hz. The signal was segmented by a Hamming window with the window size being set to 600 samples (400ms), and the time shift to 250 samples (approximately 167ms), that is, an overlap between the neighboring frames was used. Each segment was zero-padded to have the same size as T for the FFT operation. The generated matrix $\mathbf{X}$ is visualized in Figure 1. Note that the parameters used for generating $\mathbf{X}$ are identical to those used in (Wang, 2007).

The ConvNMF-ED algorithm was then applied to $\mathbf{X}$. In this algorithm, the factorization rank R was set to two, i.e., exactly the same as the total number of the signals in the mixture. The matrices $\mathbf{W}(p)$ and $\mathbf{H}$ were initialized as the absolute values of random matrices with elements drawn from a standardized Gaussian probability density function. P was set to six (in order for the object to be separated, P should be sufficiently large to cover the length of the object in the signal). All tests were run on a computer whose CPU speed is 1.8GHz. Figure 2 and Figure 3 show $\mathbf{H}^o$ and $\mathbf{W}^o(p)$, i.e. optimal values of $\mathbf{H}$ and $\mathbf{W}(p)$, respectively. It is clear from these figures that the audio objects

Figure 1. The contour plot of the magnitude spectrum matrix $\mathbf{X}$ generated from the artificial audio data

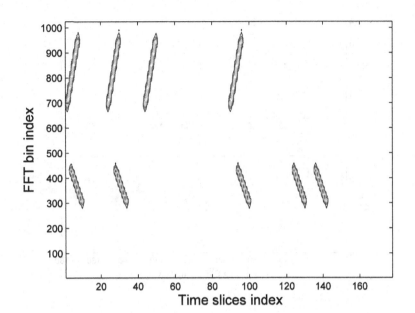

with repeating patterns are successfully separated by the ConvNMF-ED algorithm, with $\mathbf{W}^o(p)$ being the time-frequency representation of the repeating patterns, and $\mathbf{H}^o$ containing the temporal structure of these patterns, i.e., the occurrence time of individual patterns. We should note that the instantaneous NMF described by the learning rules (3) and (4) (as well as (5) and (6)), however, totally fails for separating the audio objects in these tests. ConvNMF-KL offers similar results to ConvNMF-ED, see e.g. (Wang, 2007, Wang et al 2009) for comparisons. We have extensively tested the algorithm for different set-ups of the parameters, including other randomly initialized matrices $\mathbf{W}$ and $\mathbf{H}$, and found similar separation performance.

APPLICATIONS TO MUSIC ONSET DETECTION

Onset detection is an important issue for machine perception of music audio signal. It aims to detect the starting point of a noticeable change in intensity, pitch and timbre of musical sound. It usually involves several steps including preprocessing, construction of detection function and peak picking. We have shown in (Wang et al, 2008) that the linear temporal bases obtained by an NMF algorithm (e.g. Lee & Seung 2001) can be used to construct a detection function. An advantage of constructing the detection function using the NMF bases is that no prior knowledge or statistical information is required. We have demonstrated in (Wang et al, 2006, Wang et al, 2008) that different types of detection functions can be constructed from $\mathbf{H}^o$, including the first-order difference function, the psychoacoustically motivated relative difference function, and the constant-balanced relative difference function. Recently, we have also shown application examples of convolutive NMF algorithms for onset detection, see e.g. (Wang et al, 2009), where we have compared the performance of applying different convolutive NMF algorithms to onset detection. Details of these results can be found in (Wang et al, 2009) and will not be exhaustively repeated in this chapter.

Figure 2. Visualisation of the two rows of matrix $\mathbf{H}^o$ with each row in one sub-plot

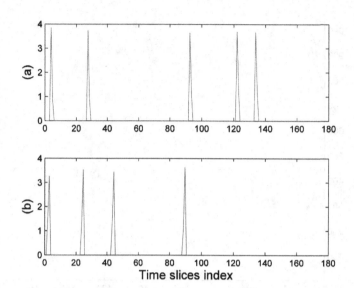

Figure 3. Visualisation of the two columns of all matrices $\mathbf{W}^o(p)$, $p = 0, ..., 5$ as a collection, with each column visualized in one sub-plot

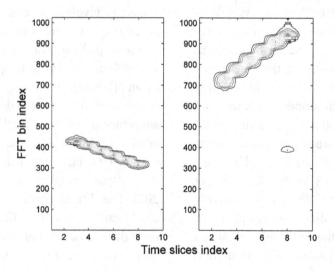

EVALUATIONS OF THE CONVOLUTIVE NMF ALGORITHMS

In this section, we evaluate the performance of the three convolutive NMF algorithms, i.e. ConvNMF-ED, ConvNMF-KL and SNMF2D-LS. In (Wang et al, 2009), we have already evaluated the three algorithms from several aspects including convergence performance, computational efficiency, and note onset detection performance. Here, we intend to provide more evaluation results, some of which are complementary to those given in (Wang et al, 2009). For example, Figure 4 shows a typical convergence curve of the ConvNMF-ED

Figure 4. A typical convergence curve of the ConvNMF-ED algorithm measured by the reconstruction error versus the iteration number, where the reconstruction error is the absolute estimation error of $\hat{\mathbf{X}}$

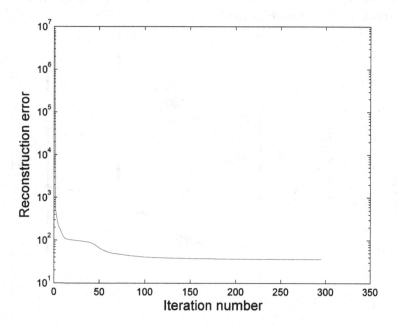

algorithm obtained by a single run of the algorithm with a random initialization, while a comparison of the average convergence performance between the three algorithms is given in (Wang et al, 2009).

Now, we study two more aspects of the three algorithms using the following performance indices. One is the rejection ratio (RR). Let us represent $\hat{\mathbf{X}}$ as the combination of R factorized components, i.e.

$$\hat{\mathbf{X}} = \sum_{i=1}^{R} \hat{\mathbf{X}}(i) \qquad (33)$$

Then, we can define the *RR* as follows

$$RR(\text{dB}) = 10 \log_{10} \left(\sum_{\forall j \neq i} cor\left(\hat{\mathbf{X}}(i), \hat{\mathbf{X}}(j)\right) \right) \qquad (34)$$

where *cor* denotes the correlation. This performance index can measure approximately the ac-

curacy of the separation performance for which a lower value represents a better performance. The other is the relative estimation error (REE),

$$REE(\text{dB}) = 10 \log_{10} \frac{\left\| \mathbf{X} - \hat{\mathbf{X}} \right\|_F}{\left\| \mathbf{X} \right\|_F} \qquad (35)$$

This performance index is less sensitive to the signal dynamics as compared with the absolute estimation error due to the adopted normalization. It measures approximately the accuracy of the factorization and a lower value represents a better performance. We ran ConvNMF-ED, ConvNMF-KL, and SNMF2D-LS for five random tests for each T, where T is the FFT frame size, and was set to be 256, 512, 1024, 2048 and 4096 respectively. Note that the results shown in (Wang et al, 2009) were based on 50 (instead of 5) random tests. The results of these five tests, together with their average are shown in Figure 5 and Figure 6, respectively. Several interesting points can be

Figure 5. The RR comparison between the algorithms ConvNMF-ED (a), ConvNMF-KL (b) and SN-MF2D-LS (c). The FFF frame length T was chosen to be 256, 512, 1024, 2048, and 4096 respectively. For each T, five random tests were performed, and the RR was plotted as the average of the five tests, with individual test results plotted on the error bars.

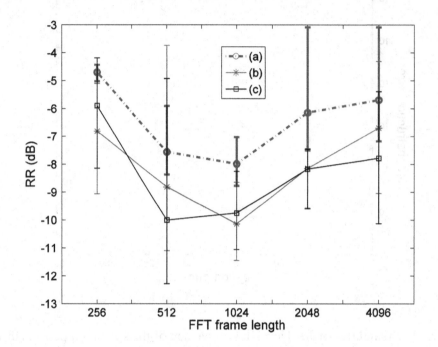

Figure 6. The REE comparison between the algorithms ConvNMF-ED (a), ConvNMF-KL (b) and SNMF2D-LS (c). The FFF frame length T was chosen to be 256, 512, 1024, 2048, and 4096 respectively. For each T, five random tests were performed, and the RR was plotted as the average of the five tests, with individual test results plotted on the error bars.

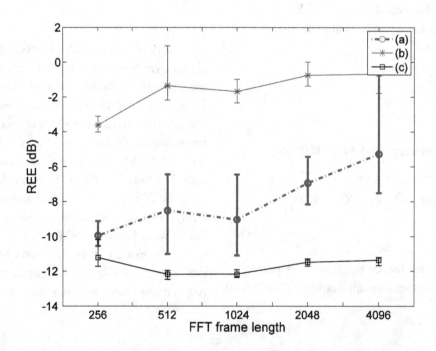

observed from these figures. First, both ConvN-MF-ED and ConvNMF-KL are relatively sensitive to different initializations, which is a common issue for many NMF algorithms and how to find a performance independent initialization method remains an open problem. Second, from the test results, we notice that the algorithm ConvNMF-ED performs approximately equally well as ConvNMF-KL, although it is less accurate in terms of *RR* measurement. This suggests that the KL divergence may be advantageous for the separation of signals in the convolutive case. However, according to the *REE* measurement, ConvNMF-ED performs much better for reconstructing the original data. These observations somehow coincide with the findings for instantaneous NMF algorithms. One thing to note is that *RR* can be informative for the performance evaluation of signal separation. Therefore, SN-MF2D-LS performs best in this experiment from the viewpoint of signal separation. However, it is clear from the results shown in our previous work in (Wang et al, 2009) that note events represented by $\mathbf{W}^o(p)$ and $\mathbf{H}^o$ (optimal values of $\mathbf{W}(p)$ and $\mathbf{H}$) obtained by the SNMF2D-LS algorithm are actually far from similar to the original events (e.g. the onset locations and the time-frequency signatures). This is because $\hat{\mathbf{X}}$ is a convolution of $\mathbf{W}^o(p)$ and $\mathbf{H}^o$, and consequently $\hat{\mathbf{X}}$ remains unchanged if both $\mathbf{W}^o(p)$ and $\mathbf{H}^o$ are over-shifted to the same extent. This implies that even though an algorithm reconstructs $\hat{\mathbf{X}}$ perfectly close to the original data $\mathbf{X}$, the obtained decomposition $\mathbf{W}^o(p)$ and $\mathbf{H}^o$ may not provide a meaningful interpretation to the original data. As a consequence, the *REE* and *RR* reveal only a part of the picture of the behavior of the algorithms.

FUTURE RESEARCH DIRECTIONS

Although NMF has shown to be useful for audio pattern separation (more broadly machine audio perception), there are still many open issues that require more research efforts. One of them is automatic rank selection. The decomposition rank is an important parameter for the application of an NMF algorithm. Its selection affects the results that can be achieved by the NMF algorithm and how the results might be interpreted. The convolutive NMF model involves the multiplications and additions of the multiple delayed components, current algorithms seem to be unsuitable for real-time applications, and more computationally efficient algorithms are required for such an application scenario. Most existing algorithms process the signal as a whole block. This may be a problem for long audio signals, as the generated non-negative matrix from the long signal can be of a high dimension. It is therefore desirable if we could develop adaptive or sequential algorithms to process the signals in shorter blocks and then apply the NMF algorithms for each of these blocks.

REFERENCES

Albright, R. Cox, J., Duling, D., Langville, A. & Meyer, C. (2006). Algorithms, initializations, and convergence for the nonnegative matrix factorization. *NCSU Technical Report Math 81706*.

Berry, M., Browne, M., Langville, M., Pauca, P., & Plemmons, R. (2007). *Algorithms and applications for approximate nonnegative matrix factorization*. Computational Statistics and Data Analysis.

Cichocki, A., Zdunek, R., & Amari, S. (2006a). Csiszar's divergences for non-negative matrix factorization: family of new algorithms. *Spinger Lecture Notes in Computer Science, 3889*, 32–39. doi:10.1007/11679363_5

Cichocki, A., Zdunek, R., & Amari, S. (2006b). New algorithms for non-negative matrix factorization in applications to blind source separation. In *Proc. IEEE Int. Conf. on Acoustics, Speech, and Signal Process.* (Vol. 4, pp. 621-624). Toulouse, France.

Cichocki, A., Zdunek, R., Choi, S., Plemmons, R., & Amari, S. (2007). Non-negative tensor factorization using alfa and beta divergences. *Proc. Int. Conf. on Acoustics, Speech, and Signal Process.* (pp. 1393-1396), Honolulu, Hawaii, USA.

Dhillon, I. S., & Sra, S. (2006). Generalized non-negative matrix approximations with Bregman divergences. In Y. Weiss, B. Schölkopf, and J. Platt, (Eds). *Advances in Neural Information Processing 18* (in Proc. NIPS 2006). Cambridge, MA: MIT Press.

FitzGerald, D., Cranitch, M., & Coyle, E. (2005). Shifted non-negative matrix factorization for sound source separation. In *Proc. IEEE Int. Workshop on Statistical Signal Process.* (pp.1132-1137), Bordeaux, France.

FitzGerald, D., Cranitch, M., & Coyle, E. (2006). Sound source separation using shifted non-negative tensor factorization. In *Proc. IEEE Int. Conf. on Acoust., Speech, and Signal Process.* (Vol. 4, pp. 653-656).

Hoyer, P. O. (2004). Non-negative matrix factorization with sparseness constraints. *Journal of Machine Learning Research, 5*, 1457–1469.

Kim, D., Sra, S., & Dhillon, I. S. (2007). Fast Newton-type methods for the least squares non-negative matrix approximation Problem. In *Proc. of the 6th SIAM Int. Conf. on Data Mining* (pp. 343-354).

Lee, D. D., & Seung, H. S. (1999). Learning the parts of objects by non-negative matrix factorization. *Nature, 401*, 788–791. doi:10.1038/44565

Lee, D. D., & Seung, H. S. (2001). Algorithms for non-negative matrix factorization. *Advances in Neural Information Processing 13* (in Proc. NIPS 2000).Cambridge, MA: MIT Press.

Lin, C.-J. (2007). Projected gradient methods for non-negative matrix factorization. *Neural Computation, 19*, 2756–2779. doi:10.1162/neco.2007.19.10.2756

Morup, M., Madsen, K. H., & Hansen, L. K. (2007). Shifted non-negative matrix factorization. In *Proc. IEEE Int. Workshop on Machine Learning for Signal Process* (pp. 427-432). Maynooth, Ireland.

Morup, M., & Schmidt, M. N. (2006). *Sparse non-negative matrix factor 2D deconvolution. Technical Report.* Technical University of Denmark.

O'Grady, P. D., & Pearlmutter, B. A. (2006). Convolutive non-negative matrix factorisation with a sparseness constraint. In *Proc. IEEE Int. Workshop on Machine Learning for Signal Process* (pp. 427-432), Maynooth, Ireland.

Paatero, P. (1997). Least squares formulation of robust non-negative factor analysis. *Chemometrics and Intelligent Laboratory Systems, 37*, 23–35. doi:10.1016/S0169-7439(96)00044-5

Parry, R. M., & Essa, I. (2007). Incorporating phase information for source separation via spectrogram factorization. In *Proc. IEEE Int. Conf. on Acoust., Speech, and Signal Process.* (Vol. 2, pp. 661-664). Honolulu, Hawaii, USA.

Pauca, V. P., Piper, J., & Plemmons, R. (2006). Non-negative matrix factorization for spectral data analysis. *Linear Algebra and Its Applications, 416*(1), 29–47. doi:10.1016/j.laa.2005.06.025

Schmidt, M. N., & Morup, M. (2006). Nonnegative matrix factor 2D deconvolution for blind single channel source separation. In *Proc. 6th Int. Conf. on Independent Component Analysis and Blind Signal Separation* (pp. 700-707), Charleston, SC, USA.

Smaragdis, P. (2004). Non-negative matrix factor deconvolution, extraction of multiple sound sources from monophonic inputs. In *Proc. 5th Int. Conf. on Independent Component Analysis and Blind Signal Separation* (LNCS 3195, pp.494-499), Granada, Spain.).

Smaragdis, P. (2007). Convolutive speech bases and their application to supervised speech separation. *IEEE Trans. Audio Speech and Language Processing, 15*(1), 1–12. doi:10.1109/TASL.2006.876726

Smaragdis, P., & Brown, J. C. (2003). Nonnegative matrix factorization for polyphonic music transcription. In *IEEE Int. Workshop on Applications of Signal Process. to Audio and Acoustics* (pp. 177-180). New Paltz, NY.

Soltuz, S., Wang, W., & Jackson, P. (2009). A hybrid iterative algorithm for non-negative matrix factorization. In *Proc. IEEE Int. Workshop on Statistical Signal Processing* (pp. 409-412).

Virtanen, T. (2003). Sound source separation using sparse coding with temporal continuity objective. In *Proc. Int. Comput. Music Conf.* (pp. 231-234), Singapore.

Virtanen, T. (2007). Monaural sound source separation by non-negative matrix factorization with temporal continuity and sparseness criterion. *IEEE Trans. Audio, Speech, and Language Processing, 15*(3), 1066–1074. doi:10.1109/TASL.2006.885253

Wang, B., & Plumbley, M. D. (2005). Musical audio stream separation by non-negative matrix factorization. In *Proc. DMRN Summer Conf.* Glasgow, UK

Wang, W. (2007). Squared Euclidean distance based convolutive non-negative matrix factorization with multiplicative learning rules for audio pattern separation. In *Proc. IEEE Int. Symp. on Signal Proces. and Info. Tech.*, Cairo, Egypt.

Wang, W. (2008). Convolutive non-negative sparse coding. In *Proc. International Joint Conference on Neural Networks* (pp. 3681-3684). Hong Kong, China.

Wang, W., Cichocki, A., & Chambers, J. A. (2009). A multiplicative algorithm for convolutive non-negative matrix factorization based on squared Euclidean distance. In *IEEE Trans. on Signal Processing, 57*(7), 2858-2864.

Wang, W., Luo, Y., Sanei, S., & Chambers, J. A. (2006). Non-negative matrix factorization for note onset detection of audio signals. In *Proc. IEEE Int. Workshop on Machine Learning for Signal Process* (pp. 447-452). Maynooth, Ireland.

Wang, W., Luo, Y., Sanei, S., & Chambers, J. A. (2008). Note onset detection via non-negative factorization of magnitude spectrum. In *EURASIP Journal on Advances in Signal Processing* (pp. 447-452).

Wang, W., & Zou, X. (2008). Non-negative matrix factorization based on projected conjugate gradient algorithm. In *Proc. ICA Research Network International Workshop* (pp. 5-8). Liverpool, UK.

Zdenuk, R., & Cichocki, A. (2007). Nonnegative matrix factorization with quadratic programming. *Neurocomputing, 71*, 2309–2320. doi:10.1016/j.neucom.2007.01.013

Zou, X., Wang, W., & Kittler, J. (2008). Non-negative matrix factorization for face illumination analysis. In *Proc. ICA Research Network International Workshop* (pp. 52-55), Liverpool, UK.

APPENDIX A

Derivation of Equation (22)

$$
\begin{aligned}
\frac{\partial \hat{\mathbf{X}}_{i,j}}{\partial \mathbf{W}_{m,n}(p)} &= \frac{\partial \sum_p \sum_d \mathbf{W}_{i,d}(p) \overset{p\rightarrow}{\mathbf{H}}_{d,j}}{\partial \mathbf{W}_{m,n}(p)} \\
&= 0 + \cdots + \frac{\partial \sum_d \mathbf{W}_{i,d}(p) \overset{p\rightarrow}{\mathbf{H}}_{d,j}}{\partial \mathbf{W}_{m,n}(p)} + \cdots + 0 \\
&= \delta_{i,m} \overset{p\rightarrow}{\mathbf{H}}_{n,j}
\end{aligned}
\tag{36}
$$

Derivation of Equation (24)

$$
\begin{aligned}
\frac{\partial \Im}{\partial \mathbf{W}_{m,n}(p)} &= \frac{\partial \sum_i \sum_j (\mathbf{X}_{i,j} - \hat{\mathbf{X}}_{i,j})^2}{\partial \mathbf{W}_{m,n}(p)} \\
&= \sum_i \sum_j (\hat{\mathbf{X}}_{i,j} - \mathbf{X}_{i,j}) \frac{\partial \hat{\mathbf{X}}_{i,j}}{\partial \mathbf{W}_{m,n}(p)} \\
&= \sum_i \sum_j (\hat{\mathbf{X}}_{i,j} - \mathbf{X}_{i,j}) \delta_{i,m} \overset{p\rightarrow}{\mathbf{H}}_{n,j} \\
&= \sum_j (\hat{\mathbf{X}}_{m,j} - \mathbf{X}_{m,j}) \overset{p\rightarrow}{\mathbf{H}}_{n,j}
\end{aligned}
\tag{37}
$$

Derivation of Equation (25)

$$
\begin{aligned}
\Pi_{m,n,m',n'}(p) &= \frac{\partial^2 \Im}{\partial \mathbf{W}_{m,n}(p) \partial \mathbf{W}_{m',n'}(p)} \\
&= \frac{\partial \sum_j (\hat{\mathbf{X}}_{m,j} - \mathbf{X}_{m,j}) \overset{p\rightarrow}{\mathbf{H}}_{n,j}}{\partial \mathbf{W}_{m',n'}(p)} \\
&= \frac{\partial \sum_j \hat{\mathbf{X}}_{m,j} \overset{p\rightarrow}{\mathbf{H}}_{n,j}}{\partial \mathbf{W}_{m',n'}(p)} \\
&= \sum_j \overset{p\rightarrow}{\mathbf{H}}_{n,j} \frac{\partial \hat{\mathbf{X}}_{m,j}}{\partial \mathbf{W}_{m',n'}(p)} \\
&= \sum_j \delta_{m,m'} \overset{p\rightarrow}{\mathbf{H}}_{n,j} \overset{p\rightarrow}{\mathbf{H}}_{n',j}
\end{aligned}
\tag{38}
$$

Derivation of Equation (31)

$$
\begin{aligned}
\left(\Pi\mathbf{w}\right)_{m,n} &= \sum_{m'}\sum_{n'}\sum_{p}\left(\sum_{j}\delta_{m,m'}\overset{p\rightarrow}{\mathbf{H}}_{n,j}\overset{p\rightarrow}{\mathbf{H}}_{n',j}\right)\mathbf{W}_{m',n'}(p) \\
&= \sum_{j}\overset{p\rightarrow}{\mathbf{H}}_{n,j}\sum_{m'}\sum_{n'}\sum_{p}\delta_{m,m'}\mathbf{W}_{m',n'}(p)\overset{p\rightarrow}{\mathbf{H}}_{n',j} \\
&= \sum_{j}\overset{p\rightarrow}{\mathbf{H}}_{n,j}\hat{\mathbf{X}}_{m,j} \\
&= \left(\hat{\mathbf{X}}(\overset{p\rightarrow}{\mathbf{H}})^{T}\right)_{m,n}
\end{aligned}
\tag{39}
$$

Section 4
Audio Cognition, Modeling and Affective Computing

Chapter 16
Musical Information Dynamics as Models of Auditory Anticipation

Shlomo Dubnov
University of California in San Diego, USA

ABSTRACT

This chapter investigates the modeling methods for musical cognition. The author explores possible relations between cognitive measures of musical structure and statistical signal properties that are revealed through information dynamics analysis. The addressed questions include: 1) description of music as an information source, 2) modeling of music–listener relations in terms of communication channel, 3) choice of musical features and dealing with their dependencies, 4) survey of different information measures for description of musical structure and measures of shared information between listener and the music, and 5) suggestion of new approach to characterization of listening experience in terms of different combinations of musical surface and structure expectancies.

GENERAL INTRODUCTION

The research on modeling musical cognition involves multiple perception modalities, with expectancies playing one of the central roles in shaping the experience of musical structure. An idea put forward many years ago by music theorists such as Meyer and Narmour states that listening to music consists of forming expectations and continual fulfillment or denial thereof (Narmour 1990, Meyer 1956). Recently several information

theoretic measures of audio structure have been proposed in attempt to characterize musical contents according to its predictive structure (Dubnov, 2006; Dubnov et al. 2006; Potter et al., 2007; Abdallah and Plumbley 2009). These measures consider statistical relations between past, present and future in signals, such as predictive information that measures the mutual information between limited past and the complete future, information rate that measures information between unlimited past and the immediate present and predictive information rate that tries to combine past and future in view of a known present. Additional

DOI: 10.4018/978-1-61520-919-4.ch016

models of musical expectancy structure build upon short-long term memory neural networks and predictive properties that are local to a single piece versus broader knowledge collected through corpus-based analysis.

The underlying assumption in investigation of Musical Information Dynamics is that the changes in information content, that could be measured in terms of statistical properties such as entropy and mutual information, correlate with musically significant events, which in parallel could be captured by cognitive processes related to music perception and acquired through exposure and learning of regularities present in a corpus of music in a certain style. These models may provide an explanation for the "inverted-U" relationship often found between simple measures of randomness (e.g. entropy rate) and judgments of aesthetic value (Rigau et al.).

In this chapter the authors will explore possible relations between cognitive measures of musical structure and statistical signal properties that are revealed through such information dynamics analysis. The questions they will try to address are: 1) description of music as an information source, 2) modeling of music–listener relations in terms of communication channel, 3) choice of musical features and dealing with dependencies, 4) survey of different information measures for description of musical structure and measures of shared information between listener and the music, and 5) suggestion of new approach to characterization of listening experience in terms of different combinations of musical surface and structure expectancies.

STRUCTURE OF THIS CHAPTER

After a brief introduction to the theories of expectancy in music and some historical as well as modern musicological and computational background, the authors will address the question of modeling music as an information source

and listener as information receiver. From this approach they will develop a model of listening that is based on mutual information between the past and the present called Information Rate (IR) (Dubnov, 2006; Dubnov et al. 2006). This model will be extended to include Predictive Information (PI) (Bialek et al.) and Predictive Information Rate (PIR) (Abdallah and Plumbley, 2009).

The authors introduce a new notion of Information Gap as a measure of the salience of a present musical segment (instance in time) with respect to future and past of a musical signal. This measure combines notions of predictive information with a notion of momentary forgetfulness, determining saliency of the present instance in terms of how detrimental forgetfulness is on the ability to make predictions. They will show that the information gap unites the three notions of information dynamics through simple algebraic relations. Next they will consider application of IR for simple Markov chains (Cover and Thomas, 2006), and consider actual musical data from MIDI representation and cepstral audio features from recordings. Dealing with multiple features requires orthogonalization, which establishes the basis for vector IR.

Information theoretic, statistical or corpus-based approaches rely on adaptive capabilities of the listening apparatus to extract rules from data rather then being pre-wired or explicitly taught through an expert. The authors will discuss the question of symbolic rules versus learning algorithms in the context of neural network model (Potter et al., 2007) that creates melodic pitch expectancies for minimalist music using Short and Long Term models. Short-term affective and long-term cognitive familiarity features will be discussed in relation to spectral feature expectancies and spectral repetitions (Dubnov et al., 2006) for a contemporary large orchestral piece. They will discuss model-based Bayesian approaches to surprise and salience detection in non-musical cases, such as Bayesian surprise in images (Itti and Baldi, 2005).

These experiments suggest that a principled approach is required for combination of expectancies from surface and structural predictions. Surface predictions are finding regularities in the data in a short-term stationary regime using information about the next sample from its immediate past. When used in a sliding window manner, an anticipation profile captures changes in surface expectancy over a complete musical piece. Clustering of musical features over larger periods leads to measure of expectancies for structural repetition. This creates an anticipation profile of expectancies for model change, capturing novelty and surprise in a musical form. The authors will show how both aspects of expectancy can be derived from Information Rate, depending on the underlying assumptions about the type of data distribution (type of musical source) and choice of the listening mechanism that is employed by the listener when creating these expectancies.

EXPECTANCY IN MUSIC

Modeling musical listening in terms of information processing has to deal with modeling of cognitive functions that try to "make sense" of incoming auditory data using various cognitive processes as well as relying on natural and learned schemata (Temperley, 2004; Huron, 2006; Narmour, 1990; Meyer, 1956). One of salient functions is forming anticipations on different time scales and structural levels of music information. The structure of music can be seen as a complex network of short and long-time relations between different music parameters, established through schemata related to repetitions and variations. In order to evoke a musical experience, a listening model needs to be able to recognize and predict such different structures in the audio signal. Moreover, response to music is unique in the sense that in addition to operating on specific perceptual categories such as sense of loudness, pitch, dissonance versus consonance, recognition of rhythm, tonality, and

so on, an important aspect of musical "meaning" is related to the process of activating memories and forming expectations in an attempt to capture temporal structural information in the musical data. So "understanding" music is ultimately linked with a specification of the listening mechanism, such as a computer audition system, that encapsulates a set of listening operations. The process of allocating resources during the listening act considers music itself as an organization of sounds that creates an experience through a process of active listening and appraisal of its own abilities in discovering such organization. Following this line of thought, we distinguish here between two levels of listening: one of forming expectations about the immediate musical events, which, depending on the type of musical representation, could be either notes in a musical score or spectral features in a recording. We will term this type of information as Musical Surface, to distinguish it from Musical Structure or larger musical form that creates a different set of expectations related to likelihood of repetition of larger blocks of sonic materials during a musical piece.

Musical theorists suggest that meaning in music is related to emotions that arise through the process of implication-realization (Narmour 1990). In that sense, past musical material is framing our appraisal of what comes next, such as expecting a resolution after a melodic leap in a musical phrase. These expectations could be "natural", i.e. described by simple mathematical relations, or be learned from cultural conventions, requiring complex syntactic models or be style specific. Going beyond melodic expectations, framing of larger scale expectancy can be established through conventions of style known to the listener through familiarity with typical patterns (schematic expectations), large scale repetition structure typical to certain musical forms, and even expectations framed as recognizable references to other musical works called veridical expectations (Huron, 2006).

Figure 1. Information Dynamics are represented in terms of different mutual information measures between Past, Present and Future

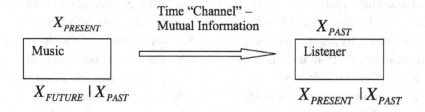

Box 1.

$$IR: \quad I(X_{PRESENT}, X_{PAST}) = H(X_{PRESENT}) - H(X_{PRESENT} \mid X_{PAST})$$

$$PI: \quad I_{pred}(T) = \lim_{T^1 \to \infty} I(X_{FUTURE}(T^1), X_{PAST}(T))$$

$$PIR: \quad I(X_{PRESENT}, X_{FUTURE} \mid X_{PAST}) = H(X_{FUTURE} \mid X_{PAST}) - H(X_{FUTURE} \mid X_{PRESENT}, X_{PAST})$$

Communicative Listening Act

The model of musical listening that we develop comprises of a pair music-listener that are connected through a virtual time-channel where present or next (future) musical observations enter the channel at the transmitter end and the past appears at the receiving end. This model is shown in Figure 1, and is described using the following variables: $X_{PAST}, X_{PRESENT}, X_{FUTURE}$.

The idea is that the receiver (listener) holds some past information that represents both his ability to make predictions based on earlier heard materials belonging to the current musical piece, and possibly employing long term prior musical information acquired through training or exposure to other works in the same genre. Using the past, present and future we define three measures of anticipation: information rate (IR) (Dubnov 2006), predictive information (PI) (Bialek et al. 1999) and predictive information rate (PIR) (Abdallah and Plumbley, 2009) as shown in Box 1.

It should be noted that all three measures use slightly different definitions of what Past, Present

and Future are. In case of IR, the present is a single observation and the past is of arbitrary length, which could be infinite. If we observed samples $x_{[1:n]} = x_1, x_2, ..., x_n$ till the current moment n, then the present is $X_{PRESENT} = x_n$, and the past is $X_{PAST} = x_{[1:n-1]}$. Since the beginning of time can be earlier then the start of the present musical piece, the past can extend to minus infinity. Another extension of IR that will be considered later is allowing a whole buffer of samples to exit in the present. In the case of PI, there is no clear notion of present, or one might say that present is included in the future as its first sample. What is special about PI is that it explicitly defines the duration of the past and the future, where T^1 is the extent of the future and T is the duration of the past, relative to some zero point where the two meet. Since PI was originally defined for continuous time, we will modify it for discrete time and define it as follows. If we assume that the present (zero time) point is n, then the past and future become $X_{PAST}(T) = x_{[n-T:n-1]}$ and

$X_{FUTURE}(T^1) = x_{[n:n+T^1-1]}$.

In the PIR approach, an explicit distinction is made between Past, Present and Future. In this case the definitions of the different random variables become $X_{PAST} = x_{[1:n-1]}$, $X_{PRESENT} = x_n$, and $X_{FUTURE} = x_{[n+1:...]}$. It should be noted that

the durations of the past or future are not defined, leaving it open to interpretation of the reader, or defined according to the specific problem at hand. Let us discuss these three measures in more detail.

In the first approach the past is used to predict the present. In this model there is no further guessing beyond the immediate present sample, and the overall listening act is measured in terms of its average ability to predict this sample given several past samples over some time period. Since the predictability of the present based on the past varies in time, the measure is only segment-wise stationary. Modeling of this situation requires two variables $X_{PRESENT}$ and X_{PAST} that establish a sort of communication channel, where the mutual information between $X_{PRESENT}$ and X_{PAST} represents the amount of information transferred from the past to the present. The listener tries to reduce the uncertainty of $X_{PRESENT}$ by using information in X_{PAST}, and his achievements in doing so are measured in terms of relative reduction in uncertainty, calculated as a difference between the entropy of $X_{PRESENT}$ and conditional entropy of $X_{PRESENT}$ given X_{PAST}. We call this method Information Rate (IR) (Dubnov 2006). It should be noted that in order to account for mutual information between past and the present, the measure takes into account the overall of listener's expectations about the relations between $X_{PRESENT}$ and X_{PAST}. In other words, IR measures

the average reduction of uncertainty regarding the present using the past for all realizations of both, which in practice means that prediction errors are averaged over a larger macro-frame where multiple occurrences of past and present observations are available. The issue concerning the differences between predictions of the future given a particular past and measuring mutual information between all possible realizations of the two will be discussed in the section on PIR, and also in relation to the difference between Bayesian surprise and average Bayesian surprise.

In a second scenario, the listener tries to predict the entire future based on the past. It is a more demanding task since the prediction quickly deteriorates as we try to guess more then just a few next observations. One of the reasons for considering this scenario is that it alleviates the need to define what the present is. In some sense, the future is as long as the correlation between the past and the future allows it to be. Since in principle the uncertainty about a big segment of sound grows proportionally with the size of the segment, it can be shown that this view, called Predictive Information (PI) (Bialek, 1999), actually reveals the so called "intensive" part of the entropy of the available past, where the difference between intensive and extensive quantities is that extensive quantity grows with the size of the system (like mass for instance) while intensive quantity remains constant with size (like heat). So if we write the entropy as a function of time,

$$H(T) = \sum_{\substack{All\ realizations\ of \\ x_1, x_2, ..., x_{n+T-1}}} P(x_{[1:n+T-1]}) \log_2[P(x_{[1:n+T-1]})]$$

then $H(T)$ can be expressed in terms of a combination of extensive and intensive parts as follows $H(T) = H_0 T + H_1(T)$. Using this expression, PI can be written in terms of relation between entropies of the past, present and the combined time interval

Figure 2. PI reveals the intensive part of the entropy by taking the future to infinity. See text for more detail.

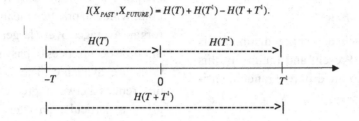

$$I(X_{PAST}, X_{FUTURE}) = H(T) + H(T^1) - H(T + T^1).$$

Box 2.

$$H(X \mid Y) = -\sum_y P(Y)[\sum_x P(X \mid Y = y) \log P(X \mid Y = y)] = E[H(X \mid Y = y)]_{P(Y)}$$

$$I(X_{FUTURE}(T^1), X_{PAST}(T)) = H(T) + H(T^1) - H(T + T^1).$$

Since the intensive part does not grow in time,

$$\lim_{T \to \infty} \frac{H_1(T)}{T} = 0, \text{ for sufficiently long future } T^1$$

the intensive parts of $H(T^1)$ and $H(T + T^1)$ cancel out:

$$I_{pred}(T) = \lim_{T^1 \to \infty} I(X_{FUTURE}(T^1), X_{PAST}(T)) = H_1(T)$$

So by looking into infinite future not only the extensive parts cancel out, but also the intensive parts of the future disappear, leaving only the intensive part related to the past at hand. Looking into larger blocks of future is important in the case of long correlations. In the following we will show that in the case of low order Markov models, predictive information in fact equals information rate, where the present is defined by the size of the memory of the Markov process. PI measure is described in Figure 2.

A third scenario assumes that the present can be distinguished from both the past and the future. In such a case we might think of a listener who holds past instance of music information in his memory. The question now becomes one of measuring information contained in the present segment regarding its ability to predict the entire future, considering that the past is already known. To explain this notion better we would need to use the following relation between relative entropy, also called Kullback-Liebler (KL) distance, and mutual information. Mutual information between two random variables X and Y can be written in terms of KL distance as:

$$I(X, Y) = D[P(X, Y) \| P(X)P(Y)].$$

This can be shown to arise directly from the definitions of KL distance and definitions of entropy and conditional entropy

$$D(X, Y) = \sum P(X) \log \frac{P(X)}{P(Y)},$$

$$H(X) = -\sum P(X) \log P(X),$$

$$H(X \mid Y) = -\sum P(X, Y) \log P(X \mid Y)$$

respectively.

It should be noted that conditional entropy averages log-conditional probability of X given

Box 3.

$$I(X,Y) = D[P(X,Y) \,\|\, P(X)P(Y)] = \sum P(X,Y) \log \frac{P(X,Y)}{P(X)P(Y)} =$$
$$= \sum_y P(Y) \sum_x P(X \mid Y = y) \log \frac{P(X \mid Y = y)}{P(X)} = E\{D[P(X \mid Y = y) \,\|\, P(X)]\}_{P(Y)}$$

Box 4.

$$I(X = x, Y \mid Z = z) = D[P(Y \mid X = x, Z = z) \,\|\, P(Y \mid Z = z)]$$

Box 5.

$$I(X,Y \mid Z) = E\{D[P(Y \mid X = x, Z = z) \,\|\, P(Y \mid Z = z)]\}_{P(X,Z)}$$

Y over both X and Y. If instead of considering every possible event Y we assume a specific outcome $Y = y$, conditional entropy can be considered as averaging of the entropy of X over every outcome of Y (see Box 2). This also allows writing mutual information in terms of averaging of KL between the probability of X for specific outcome of Y and probability of X without seeing that outcome, as shown in Box 3.

This can be extended also for the case of the variables X and Y being conditional on a third variable Z. Assigning times labels to three variables as $X = X_{PRESENT}, Y = X_{FUTURE}, Z = X_{PAST}$, this measure becomes the instantaneous predictive information rate that measures the distortion (in KL sense) between future distribution of observation with or without knowing specific observations of the present X, but with the past Z being known in both cases (see Box 4), PIR, defined as mutual information between present and future given the past, can be obtained by averaging over instanta-

neous predictive information over all possible outcomes of past and present (see Box 5).

It can be shown that in this scenario PIR actually represents a difference between two predictive information situations – one where the past and future are adjacent to each other, and the other where there is a gap between past and future that we call present. By doing so, we realize that PIR is a measure of difference between two types of prediction, one that uses the present and one that skips it to predict the future. We will use a notion of information gap to show how detrimental forgetfulness or absentmindedness of a listener might be on information transmission from past to present. It can be shown that in the case of simple Markov processes, there is a "sweet spot" in terms of correspondence between predictive information rate and the entropy rate of the process, where entropy rate is actually the lower bound on the entropy that exploits all possible knowledge about the process that is available through knowledge of the Markov transition matrix. So in cases where the structure is very loose or very strong, i.e. when entropy rate is close to zero or close to maximum, PIR is low, and a peak occurs at some intermediate values where many but not all continuations are possible for the different steps. The intuition behind this measure is that forgetting one step in such scenario is detrimental in the mid-range, while for totally random or totally predictive processes being absent minded for a moment does not have much effect on the ability to predict the future (zero in one and perfect prediction in the second extreme case).

Informational Aesthetics

Eighty years ago, Birkhoff formalized the notion of beauty by introducing the aesthetic measure (M), defined as the ratio between order and complexity. According to this measure, aesthetic feelings originate from discovery of some harmonious interrelations inside an object, dependent on its initial complexity. He identified three successive phases in the aesthetic experience related to a preliminary effort of attention, which increases proportionally to the object's complexity, and eventually the feeling of value or aesthetic measure coming from this effort through discovery of structures such as harmony, symmetry, or order factors which seems to be necessary for evoking of an aesthetic effect. This measure was later formulated in terms of information theory (Bense 1969) using the notion of compressed versus uncompressed representation. Complexity is measured in terms of uncompressed data size, while order becomes the difference between this and size of data when compression is applied to it. We will modify this idea and replace compression with conditional entropy using past knowledge. In such a case the past is used to "compress" the present, or render it into a more compact representation. This can be written with X representing the present and Z the past or prior knowledge as follows

$$M = \frac{O}{C}$$

$$C : Complexity = H(X)$$

$$O : Order = H(X) - H(X \mid Z)$$

$$M = \frac{H(X) - H(X \mid Z)}{H(X)} = I(X, Z) \,/\, H(X)$$

It is interesting to note that in this information theoretical setting, the order component in aesthetic measure has close resemblance to IR measure of the listening act. In this case the ability to compress the signal is considered as a function of time, where the past is used to discover order in the present. Complexity becomes a measure of entropy without using prediction, and the difference between the two, which is the mutual information between past and present, becomes the measure of order. The complete expression of M includes also a normalization factor that bounds the values of IR to be between zero and one. Simple algebraic manipulation shows that M is one minus the ratio of conditional entropy divided by entropy. So in all respects, the ability to reduce uncertainty about an object using some efficient encoding, such as prediction or employing other rules to discover redundancies can be considered as a measure of the efficiency of the viewing or listening system when it comes do "deal" with a new visual or musical work. How this efficiency is translated into pleasure, aesthetics or some other experiential effect will be a question to be dealt with later.

MUSIC AS AN INFORMATION SOURCE

Dealing with uncertainty and redundancy as musical features requires some sort of statistical approach to describing the music itself. Over the years many attempts were done to capture the structure in music and audio in terms of statistical models. When a sequence of symbols, such as text, music, images, or even genetic codes are considered from an information theoretic point of view, it is assumed that the specific data we observe is only one of many possible realizations that can be produces by that information source. This approach allows description of many variations or families of different sequences through a single statistical model. The idea of looking at a source, rather than a particular sequence characterizes which types of sequences are probable and which are not, or in other words, we care more about what *types* of data are more or less likely to appear rather then any particular realization. For instance, constructing histograms of note appearances in a tonal music can be used to address problems such as key-finding (Temperley, 2004), i.e. the process of inferring the key from a pattern of notes.

To do so, a musical piece, represented in terms of the musical score, is divided into segments, such as individual measures, and the number of pitch-classes (notes "wrapped" inside one octave range) are recorded. These patterns of probability are then compared to some earlier trained distributions of pitch-classes where the tonality is known. The Bayesian approach to key-finding then asks the question of how likely it is for the current empirical distribution of pitches to be generated by one of the known keys. In this respect, a key is considered as a random number generator, absent the notion of time, producing notes so that some are more likely (like the tonic, dominant or subdominant notes) then others, with alterations (nontonal notes) having especially low probability. In order to consider the possibility that the key may change from one segment to the next, an additional probability is given to the likelihood of a key-change, information obtained again through some prior training, sometimes also using musical knowledge about possible chord progressions and modulation represented as a musical grammar. An overall most likely pass through a trellis of possible key probabilities and key-changes can be derived

using dynamic programming approaches, resulting in a profile of most likely key changes over the entire piece. Such Bayesian perspective leads to a simple, elegant, and highly effective model of key-finding process; the same approach can also be extended to other aspects of music perception, such as metrical structure and melodic structure. Bayesian modeling also relates in interesting ways to a number of other musical issues, including musical tension, ambiguity, expectation, and the quantitative description of styles and stylistic differences (Temperley, 2004).

In this respect, Leonard B. Meyer's remarked on the fundamental link between musical style, perception, and probability: "Once a musical style has become part of the habit responses of composers, performers, and practiced listeners it may be regarded as a complex system of probabilities.... Out of such internalized probability systems arise the expectations—the tendencies—upon which musical meaning is built.... The probability relationships embodied in a particular musical style together with the various modes of mental behavior involved in the perception and understanding of the materials of the style constitute the norms of the style" (Meyer, 1957).

Texture Modeling

A more difficult question arises when dealing with natural sounds, such as audio textures, or considering music that has no clear definition of structural categories, such as tonality. Moreover, one might also consider aspects of listening to tonal music in terms of statistics of spectral features without relating it to musical properties such as tonality or rhythm. One such application is Audio Texture modeling (Zhang et al., 2004) that attempts to synthesize long audio stream from an example audio clip. The example clip is first analyzed to extract its basic constituent patterns. An audio stream of arbitrary length is then synthesized by recombination of these patterns as building blocks.

To discover structure one needs to define a distance measure between instances of audio at different times. Recurrence matrix, also known as similarity matrix is a method for showing structural relations in terms of a matrix that shows pair-wise similarity between audio features at all time instances.

Two common methods for constructing similarity matrix are (1) normalized dot product of the feature vectors (Foote 2001), or (2) $e^{-\beta d}$, where d is a distance function and β is a scaling factor that controls how ""fast" increasing distance translates to decreasing similarity.

Figure 3 shows a similarity matrix of an example sound using dot product of cepstral feature vectors of a recording of J.S.Bach Prelude in G major from Book I of the Well Tempered Clavier. The bright red areas in the matrix display correspond to high similarity and dark or blue areas are different. We will use this similarity matrix for partitioning the sound into perceptually similar groups, and will relate it to aspects of information dynamics and perception of familiarity.

Converting similarity matrix S_{ij} into Markov probability matrix is done by assuming that instead of continuing from a current location to the next segment, a jump to another location in the piece is possible if the contents of those target segments are similar (Lu et al. 2002). So instead of a linear progression through the piece, the musical piece is viewed in terms of a generative Markov process where every segment can have multiple next step targets, with probability of jump being proportional to the distance between the next step and all other segments in that piece

This matrix represents statistics of the data in terms of probability of transition from frames i to j. Denoting by X_i the feature vector that summarizes the observations in macro-frame i, we derive probability for transition from frame i to j from similarity matrix as follows

Figure 3. Audio similarity matrix of a recording of Bach's Prelude. The similarity is estimated by taking a dot product between cepstral feature vectors at different times in the musical piece. The red areas correspond to high similarity and blue areas are different

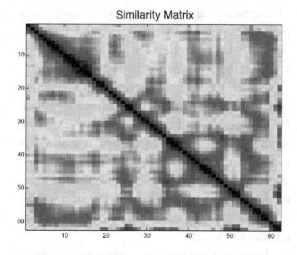

Similarity Matrix

$$P_{ij} = P(j \mid i) = \frac{S(X_{i+1}, X_j)}{\sum\limits_j S(X_{i+1}, X_j)}$$

A stationary vector can be derived through eigenvector analysis of the transition matrix $\mathrm{P} = P_{ij}$, finding a vector $\bar{p}^*$ so that $\bar{p}^* \mathrm{P} = \bar{p}^*$ (Cover and Thomas, 2006). Note that due to the indexing convention chosen for the transition matrix, Markov process operates by left side matrix multiplication. The stationary vector then is a left (row) eigenvector with an eigenvalue that equals to one. The meaning of stationary distribution is that we are looking at a situation where the transitions between the states settle into a "stable" set of probabilities. In terms of information dynamic analysis, we will assume that $\bar{p}^*$ represents the knowledge of the listening system about the musical form. This knowledge will then be used to a form a prior for estimation of structure related expectations. In the following we will use this approach to describe musical from based on similarity between instances of sounds (marco-frames) whose duration is of the order or magnitude of "perceptual present", i.e. between 3 or 7 seconds for short chamber works (solo or small ensemble) and up to 10 or 12 seconds in the case of large scale orchestral works.

Dictionary Based Approaches

Dictionary based models try to address the problem of first-order Markov chains that assume dependence on the last symbol only. Higher-order Markov models assume a longer context, so that generating the next symbol depends on several symbols back into the past. It was shown (Brooks et al, 1993) that at very low orders—such as the second order or so-called bigram—Markov models generate strings that do not recognizably resemble strings in the corpus, while at very high orders, the model simply replicates strings from the corpus. Dictionary-based methods can be used to model the musical (information) source in terms of a lexicon of motifs and their associated prediction probabilities.

To generate new instances (messages), these models "stochastically browse" the prediction tree in the following manner: Given a current context, check if it appears as a motif in the tree. If found, choose the next symbol according to prediction probabilities. If the context is not found, shorten it by removing the oldest (leftmost) symbol and go back to the previous step. By iterating indefinitely, the model is capable of producing a sequence of symbols that presumably corresponds to a new message originating from the same source. In some cases, this procedure might fail to find an appropriate continuation and end up with an empty context, or it might tend to repeat the same sequence over and over again in an infinite loop. The methods for finding such dictionaries include lossless compression methods based on Lempel-Ziv parsing method or lossy methods such as Probabilistic Suffix Trees (Dubnov et al, 2003)

Audio Oracle

Other methods for generalizing an instance of audio into a generative model include the Audio Oracle (AO) (Dubnov et al., 2007) that outputs an automaton that contains pointers to different locations in audio recording that satisfy certain smoothness of continuation and similarity criteria. For synthesis the resulting automaton is loaded into an audio generation module that randomly traverses the automaton outputting a new audio stream by concatenation of audio frames that appear on transitions between AO states. The unique property of the AO is in the construction of a graph that points from every moment in the sound to another moment in that same sound that has the longest common past (common suffix). This assures a sense of continuity and smooth concatenation during synthesis, while creating interesting variations in the output audio stream. AO uses string-matching algorithm known as Factor Oracle (Allauzen et al., 1999; Assayag and Dubnov, 2004), generalizing it to the case of imprecise matching for dealing with sequences of feature vectors rather then exact matching of discrete symbols. In comparison to the Audio Texture method of previous paragraph, AO enjoys from longer overlapping segments between concatenated instances due to its longest common suffix structure. This process was extended to query by example over audio databases by defining a distance measure between AO and new sound. This method has applications to synthesis by using a sound query as a "guideline" for recreating the best matching concatenative synthesis from segments found in a database (Cont et al., 2007). This may lead to new characterization of information dynamics in terms of the ability to predict portions of a new sound by finding best matching segments in a database of prior models.

SURFACE VERSUS STRUCTURE: LONG AND SHORT TERM INFORMATION DYNAMICS

Pearce and Wiggins (2006) evaluate a statistical model of musical pitch perception that predicts the expectation generated by monodic tonal melodies. Their computational system is based on n-gram models commonly used in statistical language modeling (Manning & Schutze, 1999). An n-gram is a sequence of n symbols and an n-gram model is simply a collection of such sequences each of which is associated with a frequency count. During the training of the statistical model, these counts are acquired through an analysis of a corpus of sequences (the training set) in the relevant domain. When the trained model is exposed to a new example, the frequency counts associated with n-grams are used to estimate a probability of the next symbol given the n -1 preceding symbols. The experiments of Pearce and Wiggins were conducted on a set of synthetic examples, comparing statistical prediction to that of listeners who were asked to rate continuation tones following a two-tone context.

A more elaborate application of this approach was done by (Potter et al 2007). Their expectancy model was built from two memory models, one short-term memory (STM) and one long-term memory (LTM). Each model takes as its musical surface sequences of musical notes as written in the score, defined in terms of properties such as onset time, pitch, duration and key. The representation scheme can also express derived features (such as pitch interval) and interactions between features, using the "viewpoint" practice of Conklin and Witten (1995). The LTM was trained on a database of about 900 tonal melodies, while the STM, conversely, had no prior knowledge, and learned dynamically, only from the current piece of music. In this way, the author claim to model "typical human Western musical experience" (LTM) and "on-going listening to unknown music" (STM). The model is applied to study of Philip

Glass' Gradus and Two Pages (both written around 1968), which are monodic and isochronous pieces, the first for solo saxophone and the second for a keyboard (synthesizer). In their paper the authors report a detailed analysis of how the model predictions correspond to musically meaningful events as analyzed by a human expert.

The same Philip Glass works were also analyzed using Markov models and evaluating their performance in terms of predictive-information measures (Abdallah and Plumbley, 2009). The Markov model was learned from the current piece ("on-going listening") with one elaboration that allowed the transition matrix to vary slowly with time in order to track changes in the musical structure. This could be considered as a model where the listener's belief state is represented in terms of a probability distribution over all possible Markov transition matrices, and this belief is slowly updated during the course of listening to the piece. In order to learn the space of Markov models the probability to observe a transition matrix is represented as a product of Dirichlet distributions, one for each column. At each time step, the distribution over the space of transition matrices undergoes two changes – the probabilities slightly broaden to represent a "forgetting" or diffusion process on one hand, and they are also updated to represent more truthfully the next observation. This update for the Dirichlet distribution is done by incrementing by one the Dirichlet parameter corresponding to matrix element (i,j) upon observing a symbol i following symbol j in the data.

In the case of Two Pages, close correspondence is shown between the information measures and the structure of the piece, and in particular, between the six 'most surprising moments' as evaluated by a human expert and so called "model information rate" that measures the relative entropy or Kullback-Liebler (KL) divergence between prior and posterior model distributions $D[P(\theta \mid X = x, Z = z) \| P(\theta \mid Z = z)]$, i.e. the

Figure 4. Spectral representation uses a sliding window to do Fourier analysis over blocks of audio samples, followed by dimension reduction. A feature extraction stage usually follows this step and is not shown in the figure.}

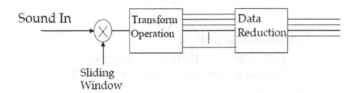

change in the distribution over model parameter space when the present observation X=x has been incorporated into the model. Gradus, which is much less systematically structured than Two Pages did not give such a clear picture. Regarding surface information dynamics, and specifically the predictive information rate, the authors' findings were inconclusive.

INFORMATION DYNAMICS IN AUDIO SIGNALS

In the previous works the methods of information dynamics were applied to symbolic sequences of musical notes, mostly monophonic (one voice). In order to analyze information contents in audio signals several steps need to be done. First features need to be extracted from the audio signal that are both audibly and structurally significant. Second, the statistical model needs to be determined, and finally the amount of fit between the predictions of the model and the actual data need to be determined in order to be able to estimate information dynamics.

Spectral Anticipation

Spectral Anticipation (SA) is a method of Information Rate (IR) analysis of audio recording based on prediction of spectral features. Justification for this choice of features is that spectral information is an important descriptor of the audio contents and that a listening apparatus should be able to recognize, classify or predict spectral properties.

Spectral representation, as shown in Figure 4, is achieved by applying Fourier analysis to blocks of audio samples using a sliding-window that extracts short signal segments (also called frames) from the audio stream. It is often desirable to reduce the amount of information in spectral description so that it captures only essential spectral shapes. In doing so a balanced tradeoff between reducing the dimensionality of data and retaining the information contents can be achieved.

Estimation of IR is done as follows:

- Sound is analyzed and represented in terms of a sequence of N dimensional feature vectors v_t over time

- A block (macro-frame) of features vectors starting at time t and of duration L is selected $v_{[t:t+L-1]}$. This macro frame represents a segment of the original sound in terms of features

- The sequence of feature vectors in a macro-frame is transformed into orthogonal representation using Singular Value Decomposition (SVD) (Cover and Thomas, 2006). This gives a set of approximately independent principal components $u_{[1:L]}$ under Gaussian assumption. In other cases, independent component analysis can be

Figure 5. IR for feature vector is estimated from IR of the individual feature components after an orthogonalization (SVD) procedure that achieves approximate independence transformation

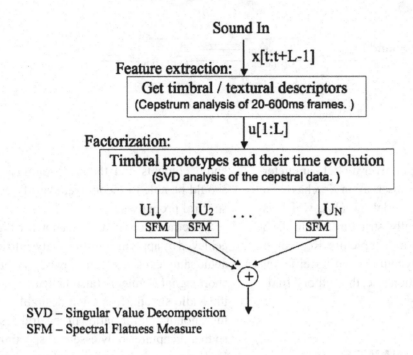

employed instead (Hyvärinen et al., 2001).

- Mutual information between past and present in macro-frame is estimated separately for every component i of the feature vector $\rho[u_{[1:L]}(i)]$. One method of estimation is the spectral flatness measure (Jayant and Noll, 1984; Dubnov, 2004) where each of the N feature components is transformed from being a time sequence of L elements in a macro-frame to a K dimensional spectral magnitude vector U_i, estimated using Welch, Burg or other methods (Cover and Thomas, 2006). It can be shown that spectral flatness can be used as a measure of mutual information between a sample and its past, derived by comparison between signal variance and variance of the prediction error, equivalent also to so called "coding gain" of linear prediction (Jayant and Noll, 1984).

$$e^{-2\rho[u_{[1:L]}(i)]} = \frac{[\prod_{k=1}^{K} U_i(k)]^{1/K}}{\frac{1}{K}\sum_{k=1}^{K} U_i(k)}$$

- The values of mutual information of all elements are summed together to give the overall spectral anticipation (also called vector-IR) measure for that frame

$$\rho(x_{[t:t+L-1]}) = \sum_{i=1}^{N} \rho[u_{[1:L]}(i)]$$

- The process is repeated for the next macro-frame at time $t = t + \Delta$

This process is summarized in Figure 5.

Box 6.

$$I(\theta, X) = KL[P(\theta, X) \| P(\theta)P(X)] = \int P(\theta, X) \log \frac{P(\theta, X)}{P(\theta)P(X)} d\theta dX =$$

$$= \int P(X)P(\theta \mid X) \log \frac{P(\theta \mid X)}{P(\theta)} d\theta dX = \int P(X) \cdot KL[P(\theta \mid X) \| P(\theta)] dX =$$

$$= E\{KL[P(\theta \mid X) \| P(\theta)]\}_{P(X)}$$

Bayesian Surprise and Average Bayesian Surprise

In order to deal with long-term structures we introduce a model parameter space that is parameterized by some variable θ. These parameters are themselves random variables that are distributed over a space of possible parameter values according to a probability function $P(\theta)$. Measuring mutual information between past and present in model space can be done by comparison between a prior distribution over the model parameters that is readily available to the listener before new data arrives (i.e. a model distribution based on the past), and a new model distribution that is inferred using new observations once the new musical data becomes available. Let us denote by $P(\theta)$ the prior (past) distribution and by $P(\theta \mid X)$ an a posteriori distribution that takes into account the data X. It should be noted the variable X denotes a set of observations rather then a single present sample. Since the discussion here is rather general, we abandon the specific separation between past, present and future, and consider X as a generalized notion of present in terms of a block of samples in an analysis window.

The difference between distribution over the space of model parameter after and before specific data was observed can be measured in terms of Kullback-Libler distance $KL[P(\theta \mid X) \| P(\theta)]$ and is termed Bayesian Surprise (Itti and Balidi, 2005).

The difference between KL and IR is that IR measures the information transfer from past to the present in terms of mutual information between present data and prior model, which requires taking into account all possible combinations of model and data. As is shown in the next equation, IR between past model and present data is in fact an average KL over all possible values of the present, (see Box 6) where $P(\theta)$ and $P(X)$ are the marginal distributions of the "old" model parameters and the distribution of "new" data, respectively, and where without loss of generality we assumed a continuous probability distribution function of these variables.

To summarize, the Bayesian approach takes into account the updates of the model distribution space that happen as a result of the arrival of new data without averaging over the chances that this data will appear. This approach requires an online learning of the model parameters, continuously tracking the changes in the "beliefs" about the models.

Spectral Recurrence

A different, though closely related anticipation considers the changes in distribution of the observations that occur due to changes of the underlying models. The idea of a Spectral Recurrence (SR) profile is to be able to summarize the repetition structure into a function of time that indicates how likely an empirical distribution of features in a current frame is in comparison to an overall

Box 7.

$$KL[G(\mu_i, \Sigma_i), G(\mu_j, \Sigma_j)] = \frac{1}{2}\log\left(\frac{|\Sigma_j|}{|\Sigma_i|}\right) + \frac{1}{2}\mathrm{Tr}(\Sigma_i\Sigma_j^{-1}) + \frac{1}{2}(\mu_i - \mu_j)^T\Sigma_j^{-1}(\mu_i - \mu_j) - \frac{N}{2}$$

probability of seeing different realizations of features over the course of a complete musical work.

In order to do so, we start with a pair-wise comparison of feature distributions over some larger segments in time that we call macro-frames. Ideally, we would like to measure these changes in terms of KL distance between empirical distributions, but doing so is impractical since this requires many observations. Instead, one might consider only partial statistics, such as macro-frame centroids or correlation, and compute KL distance between their Gaussian distributions with these statistics (see Box 7).

If covariances are neglected then KL becomes Euclidian distance between the marco-frame centroids. To derive a spectral recurrence profile, we turn the distance matrix into a similarity matrix by using an exponential function $S_{ij} = e^{-\beta d_{ij}}$, where d is a distance function and β is a scaling factor that controls how "fast" increasing distance translates to decreasing similarity, similar to the way it was done for audio texture modeling. Then, after some preprocessing, we use eigenvector analysis of the processed similarity matrix L, known as spectral clustering (von Luxburg, 2007), to reveal data clusters. This clustering method does an embedding of the matrix L in a low dimensional space spanned by its first few eigenvectors. From this embedding cluster centers and their variances can be deduced, so that a new empirical sample can be compared to them.

In practice, it appears that only very few eigenvectors of processed musical self-similarity matrix are non-zero. A particularly simple case is one where the preprocessing consists of normal-

ization of the similarity columns by their sums, notated below as an inverse of a diagonal matrix of these sums, called the rank matrix

$$L = D^{-1}S, \quad D_{ii} = \sum_{j=1}^{N} S_{ij}$$

This effectively turns the similarity matrix into a stochastic or Markov matrix, where the columns describe the probability of transition from a state that is the column index, to next states that are the row indices. This method has great resemblance to the Markov modeling approach of sound texture with one slight difference that a transition between state i and j is based on similarity between actual macro-frames i and j rather then between the next frame i+1 and frame j. In our experience, this distinction makes little difference in the outcomes.

One of the advantages of this simple case is that the eigenvector derived from the analysis of the stochastic matrix already contains the probabilities of appearance of the macro-frames relative to complete musical piece. In other words, the clusters themselves do not need be estimated, and the probability of a frame can be looked up directly from the value of the eigenvector. The disadvantage of this method is that relying on the first eigenvector alone is considered to give poor performance in spectral clustering. Moreover, conceptually, what we have is essentially a fully observed model without any inference of parameters or hidden variables in the usual sense. This would render much of the machinery developed so far unnecessary - a fully observed Markov chain model could be fitted, using the procedure described above to set the transition matrix, and

Figure 6. Recurrence and anticipation profile of an audio recording of Bach's Prelude. See text for more detail.

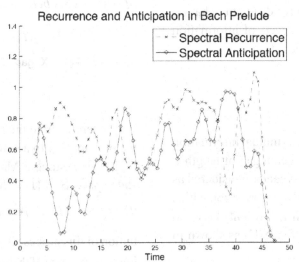

the information rate for the Markov chain can be computed in a straightforward manner, as will be explained in the following.

Let us assume that the listener recognizes and summarizes the types of musical materials that he hears in terms of some parameter θ. This parameter can be as simple as enumeration of the different data types, or as sophisticated as estimation of parameter value in some model parameter space. If the transitions between different parameters obey Markov dynamics, a stationary probability $P^*(\theta)$ of the model parameters can be derived directly from the Markov model. If we assume that at a particular instance in time the listener identifies the musical materials as belonging to some type α, then using the same reasoning as in the case of Bayesian surprise we may consider the KL distance between two probability distributions, one when the parameter is known $P(\theta \mid \alpha) = \delta(\theta - \alpha)$ and a stationary distribution $P^*(\theta)$, as

$$D[\delta(\theta - \alpha) \mid\mid P^*(\theta)] \approx -\log P^*(\alpha)$$

The KL expression then becomes the negative log-likelihood of drawing parameter α from the stationary probability distribution, and it can be interpreted as information dynamics related to listener current choice of α from a set of possible parameters whose dynamics are generated by the Markov process.

Figure 6 shows a stationary distribution vector $P^*(\theta)$, which we call Spectral Recurrence, plotted together with Spectral Anticipation for the Bach Prelude whose recurrence matrix was shown in Figure 3.

Both profiles were derived using cepstrum coefficients as audio features, estimated over a macro-frame of 6 seconds in duration with advance in time of 1.5 seconds (overlap factor 4). The cepstrum coefficients where submitted to IR analysis for each macro frame, resulting in spectral anticipation values for every time step. The recurrence anticipation was obtained from a recurrence matrix, which in turn was estimated from distances between mean cepstral vectors in each macro-frame. The profiles were filtered in order to smooth fluctuations shorter than 5 seconds. The smoothing was done using a linear-phase low pass filter with frequency cutoff at 0.3 of the window advance rate. It is evident from the graphs that both profiles have different behavior as they capture different aspects of information dynamics present in the recording.

INFORMATION GAP

Information gap is defined as mutual information between past and future when a gap of length L exists between the two. This can be considered as a generalization of Predictive Information with a missing segment of length L (present) between past of size T and future of size T', as shown in Figure 7.

From definition of information gap the following information dynamic measure can be derived.

- Predictive information (PI) is equal to information gap with zero gap, i.e. L=0, where the future is taken to infinity.

$$PI = I_{pred}(T) = \lim_{T^1 \to \infty} I_{gap}(T, T^1, 0)$$

- Information Rate (IR) is equal to information gap with zero gap, i.e. L=0, where the future is one time step and the past is taken to infinity.

$$IR = \lim_{T^1 \to \infty} I_{gap}(T, T^1, 0)$$

- Predictive information rate (PIR) is the difference between information gap with L=0 (zero gap) minus information gap with gap of size one (or whatever the size of the present is).

$$PIR = I(X, Y \mid Z) = H(Y \mid Z) - H(Y \mid X, Z)$$
$$= H(Y \mid Z) - H(Y) + H(Y) - H(Y \mid X, Z)$$
$$= -I(Y, Z) + I(Y, \{X, Z\}) = I_{gap}(L=0) - I_{gap}(L=1)$$

Figure 7. Information gap is defined as generalization of Predictive Information so that a gap of size L exists between the past and the future

$$I_{gap}(T, T^1, L) = I(Z, Y)$$

```
-[------- Z --->][<- X (gap of length L) ->](<---- Y ----]---
-T                          0                        T'
```

To demonstrate the usage of information gap we will apply it to a simple Markov case.

Let us assume a Markov chain with a finite state space $S = \{1, ..., N\}$ and transition matrix $P(S_{t+1} = i \mid S_t = j) = a_{ij}$. The stationary distribution of this process is π^a, $\pi^a = a\pi^a$. Calculating the entropies of the stationary distribution and the entropy rate that takes into account the Markov structure gives

$$H(S_t) = H(\pi^a) = \sum_{i=1}^{N} \pi_i^a \log(\pi_i^a)$$
$$H(S_{t+1} \mid S_t) = H_r(a) = -\sum_{i=1}^{N} \pi_i^a \sum_{j=1}^{N} a_{ji} \log(a_{ji})$$

Using these expressions, IR can be simply obtained from the difference between the entropy of the stationary distribution and the entropy rate. Also information gap of size one can be obtained by considering the difference between the stationary entropy and a Markov prediction of two steps into the future, given by the matrix a^2

$$IR = I_{gap}(0) = I(S_{t+1}, S_t) = H(\pi^a) - H_r(a)$$
$$I_{gap}(1) = I(S_{t+1}, S_{t-1}) = H(\pi^a) - H_r(a^2)$$
$$PIR = I(S_t, S_{t+1} \mid S_{t-1}) = I(S_{t+1}, \{S_t, S_{t-1}\}) - I(S_{t+1}, S_{t-1})$$
$$= I_{gap}(0) - I_{gap}(1) = H_r(a^2) - H_r(a)$$

Example: Let us consider a simple Markov case of a circle of values with small probability for deviation from an exact sequence, as described in the graph below. The entropy of this model equals to log(5), while entropy rate for single or two step prediction are close to zero. This results in a process that has maximal IR, since it has big difference between entropy and entropy rate, but close to zero PIR, since one and two step entropy rates are practically zero (Figure 8).

$$H(\pi^a) \approx \log_2(5)$$
$$H_r(a) \approx H_r(a^2) \approx 0$$
$$IR \approx Maximum, PIR \approx 0$$

This example demonstrates the different meaning of IR and PIR, which is related to the difference between two listening scenarios: in the case of IR the listener uses the past to predict the present, and she does it maximally well by capturing the Markov structure that is very predictable. In the PIR scenario the listener is "absent minded" for one instance after having already memorized the past. In such a case a lap in memory does not have a big effect since the sequence is approximately deterministic and can be reliably extrapolated into the future without considering the implications of "now".

RELATIONS BETWEEN DIFFERENT INFORMATION DYNAMICS MEASURES

The characterizations of IR presented above, namely spectral, Bayesian and recurrence anticipations, can be unified under a single formalism that considers anticipation as a sum of different musical information processing functions. In the derivation of the "unified" theory (Dubnov 2008) an algebraic error appears in the sign of one of the information factors, as noted in (Abdallah 2008). The following discussion corrects this error and explains the specific assumptions behind some of the approximations in the unified formalism. The full derivation of this formalism is given in the appendix.

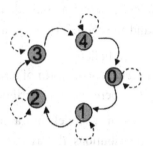

Figure 8. A Markov chain the creates an approximately exact repeating sequence of five states with small chance of repeating a value

Let us assume that the information processing tasks facing the listener are as follows:

1. Constructing a model from a short window (macro-frame) of observations
2. Predicting new observations using that model
3. Changing the "belief" in the current model in view of newly arrived data
4. Comparing the current model to all other models that were constructed during listening to the same piece

Formal modeling of this listening act can be done as follows: considering the space of models in terms of parameterization θ over the distribution of observations, we factor the probability of observations $x_{[1:n]}$ into conditional probability given a model and probability of the model $P(x_{[1:n]}) = \int P(x_{[1:n]} \mid \theta)P(\theta)d\theta$. Using expressions for approximations of entropy in the case of parametric distribution (Bialek et al, 2001), it is shown in the appendix that information rate can be approximated as a sum of several factors

$$\rho(x_{[1:n]}) \approx E[\rho(x_{[1:n]} \mid \theta)]_{P(\theta)} + I(x_n, \theta) - E[D(\theta \| \theta^*)]_{P(\theta)}$$

This formulation accounts for three types of information dynamics:

- IR of the observations given a model $\rho(x_{[1:n]} \mid \theta)$, averaged over all models

- Information between individual observations and the model $I(x_n, \theta)$, also known as averaged belief

- Penalty factor in the form of a KL distance $D(\theta \parallel \theta^*)$ between the distribution of observations in a model and a set of most likely distributions θ^*, averaged over all models

In the second expression an averaging over model parameters occurs by definition of mutual information. It should be noted that in practice such an averaging over the set of all possible models is not preformed and the most likely model at each macro-frame is used. This results in time varying functions or profiles that represent different aspects of information dynamics over time. In such a case the predictions needed for IR are performed using the model for the current macro-frame, and KL distance is estimated between the current model and the set of most likely models over the whole piece. Moreover, in practice the different profiles cannot be added together since they are estimated using different methods and their units of measurement are different. As will be explained below, the second factor of mutual information between individual observations and the model is often neglected. The remaining two factors can be estimated using spectral anticipation and negative of spectral recurrence.

One of the important implications of the above equation is in the realization that several different factors combine together to create overall information dynamic. We will show that important information about musical structure may indeed be derived from various relations between the Spectral Anticipation and Spectral Recurrence factors, as two measures of information dynamics.

Special Cases of the "Unified" IR

Depending upon what aspect of the overall musical information are relevant for the listener different approximations to the unified IR equation can be derived. For instance, if the listener assumes a fixed data model without trying to consider model dynamics or probabilities of model change, only the first factor of the equation remains. Accordingly we call this factor data-IR and estimate it using spectral anticipation.

Alternatively, if a listener disregards prediction aspects of the observations and considers only model aspects of parameter dynamics, we are left with the right side of the equation that contains the KL distance between model distribution functions prior to and after observing the data. We call this term model-IR. It should be also noted that a model parameter is estimated using all available observations and not only the last (present) sample.

Considering the second factor of mutual information between sample and model, and of course depending on the type of musical data, it is likely that a single observation carries little information about the model. In such case the mean Bayesian anticipation factor is approximately zero. On the other extreme, it could be that a single observation carries a lot of information about the model. In such a case mutual information approximately equals the entropy of the model distribution

$$I(x_n, \theta) = H(\theta) - H(\theta \mid x_n) \approx H(\theta)$$

This can also be shown by plugging into the expression of Bayesian anticipation the function $P(\theta \mid x_n) = \delta(\theta - \alpha)$ when an individual sample implies a model parameter α and using the equivalence between distribution of model parameters and probability of observations in this case $\mathrm{Prob}(x_n) \approx P(\alpha)$ (see Box 8).

Box 8.

$$I(x_n, \theta) = E\{D[P(\theta \mid x_n) \mid\mid P(\theta)]\}_{P(x_n)} = E\{D[\delta(\theta - \alpha) \mid\mid P(\theta)]\}_{P(x_n)}$$
$$= E\{-\log P(\alpha)]\}_{P(\alpha)} = H(\alpha)$$

Table 1. Relation between cognitive and signal measures was tested for a large orchestral piece. See text for more details

Cognitive Measure	Signal Measure
Familiarity (Recognition, Categorization)	Long-term Similarity Structure, Repetition Spectral Recurrence)
Emotional Force (Anticipation, Implication-Realization)	Short-term Predictability Structure (Spectral Anticipation)

CONCLUSION: APPLICATIONS OF INFORMATION DYNAMICS

The question of relation between properties of musical works and their perception has attracted many researchers, mostly focusing on direct relationship between acoustical and perceptual features, such as intensity and loudness, relation between frequency contents and perceptions of pitch and tonality, and etc. Researches on emotional response try to relate overall properties such as mode, harmony, tempo, and etc. to primary emotions. These approaches largely disregard aspects of perception that are determined by temporal organization of music. Accordingly, potentially important applications of musical information dynamics arise from its ability to discover temporal information structure of musical data and relate it to dynamically to the act of listening to this data.

A first proof of concept for the use of information dynamics as a predictor of human listening responses was conducted in a large-scale experiment (Dubnov et al., 2006). Spectral Anticipation and Spectral Recurrence profiles were compared to continuous human judgments of Emotional Force and Familiarity when listening to two versions of a large orchestral piece. It was found that the two information profiles explain significant portions (between 20-40 percent) of the corresponding human behavioral responses. The approximate correspondence between signal derived measures and human judgment can be summarized in Table 1.

Due to the difficulty of obtaining large amounts of user judgments, most researches rely on human musical experts in evaluating the results of information dynamics analysis. We already discussed the studies of Philip Glass's Gradus and Two Pages using STM-LTM and Markov models of MIDI or symbolic representations of music (Potter et al 2007, Abdallah and Plumbley, 2009). Those studies indicate that significant correspondence exists between points indicated by an expert as significant or most surprising musical moments and peaks in model-information measures.

Combination of signal and model information measures as a way to detect musical interest points was suggested in (Dubnov 2008). It was shown that musical climax points could be detected consistently for different performances of the same piece by finding a moment that had both high novelty (small probability on the structural level measured in terms of negative quantized SR value) and high surface predictability (predictably structured musical passages that capture high values in quantized SA profile). These results are shown in Figure 9.

Figure 9. Difference between quantized and normalized SA and SR measures lead to detection of a similar climax moment in four different performances of Bach's Prelude No. 2 of Well Tempered Clavier, Book 1. (a) Combined detection function over the whole duration of the prelude for the four performances, (b) Spectral contents of music segments near the detected climax, (c) Musical score of the measures that correspond to the detected climax.

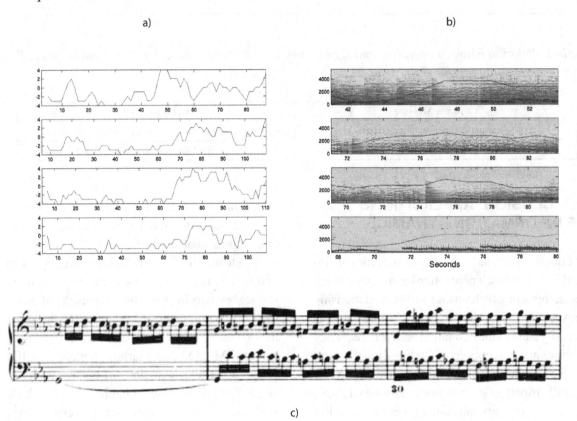

a)

b)

c)

Future Work

Information Dynamics is a promising direction that includes aspects of temporal structure and prior listener knowledge in modeling of the listening experience. It differs from other works on musical perception that are concerned with direct mapping of sound features or their overall statistics to listening experience. The features of information dynamics allow the development of a formal mathematical framework for the manipulation of audio streams by providing alternative structures of manipulation that respect the temporal and probabilistic natures of music more than the usual structures used in audio content analysis applications do.

This formal framework leads to several applicative fields. Applications of information dynamics to automatic structure discovery include segmentation, recognition of auditory scenes in terms of higher-level features, detection of auditory surprise and so on. Information dynamics could be considered as a meta-feature that analysis of audio on a higher semantic level related to musical interest. This will require additional reearch for introducing more features into the analysis, as well as finding ways to combine these features into meaningful musical categories. Such high level labels, performed in temporal manner, will allow variable length content-based matching of audio and will lead to better concatenation type of synthesis that are important for texture synthesis or recombinant music generation. In the context of sound transformations the ability to characterize salient perceptual moments in music may lead to new types of processing, such as content driven analysis-synthesis, or computer-aided human interaction with machine improvisation. Other potential applications of information dynamics include characterization of preferred structures and automated quality assessment, extending the scope of music recommendation systems today that rely on overall listening preference profiles and social filtering.

A promising direction for improving the estimation of information contents in audio comes from new work on music information geometry (Cont, 2008). Information geometry is a recent field of mathematics in particular of statistical inference that studies the notions of probability and information by the way of differential geometry (Amari and Nagaoka, 2000). The notion of Audio Oracle is generalized to include Bregman mutual information between observations and oracle states, thus incorporating data information rate in the process oracle construction. Deriving model information from AO-derived similarity structure is another aspect of this ongoing research.

REFERENCES

Abdallah, S. A. (2008). A critique of Dubnov's 'information rate'. *Technical Report C4DM-TR-08-11* Queen Mary University of London, 2008.

Abdallah, S. A., & Plumbley, M. D. (2009). Information dynamics: patterns of expectation and surprise in the perception of music. *Connection Science*, *21*(2), 89–117. doi:10.1080/09540090902733756

Allauzen, C., Crochemore, M., & Raffinot, M. (1999)., Factor oracle: a new structure for pattern matching. In J. Pavelka, G. Tel & M. Bartosek (Eds)., *Proceedings of SOFSEM'99, Theory and Practice of Informatics (LNCS pp 291-306)*, Milovy, Czech Republic. Berlin: Springer-Verlag.

Amari, S., & Nagaoka, H. (2000). Methods of information geometry, Translations of mathematical monographs. *American Mathematical Society,191*.

Assayag, G., & Dubnov, S. (2004). Using Factor Oracles for Machine Improvisation. [New York: Springer Verlag.]. *Soft Computing*, *8*, 1–7. doi:10.1007/s00500-004-0385-4

Bense, M. (1969). *Einführung in die informationstheoretische Asthetik. Grundlegung und Anwendung in der Texttheorie (Introduction to the Information-theoretical Aesthetics. Foundation and Application to the Text Theory)*. Rowohlt Taschenbuch Verlag.

Bialek, W., Nemenman, I., & Tishby, N. (2001). Predictability, complexity, and learning. *Neural Computation*, *13*, 2409–2463. doi:10.1162/089976601753195969

Birkhoff, G. D. (1933). *Aesthetic Measure*. Cambridge, MA: Harvard Univ. Press.

Brooks, F. Jr (1993). An Experiment in Musical Composition. In Schwanauer, S., & Levitt, D. (Eds.), *Machine Models of Music* (pp. 23–40). Cambridge, MA: MIT Press.

Cont, A. (2008)., Modeling Musical Anticipation: From the time of music to the music of time. (PhD thesis University of Paris 6 (UPMC) and University of California San Diego (UCSD)).See also http://imtr.ircam.fr/index.php/Music_Information_Geometry

Cont, A., Dubnov, S., & Assayag, G. (2007, September) GUIDAGE: A Fast Audio Query Guided Assemblage. In *Proceedings of International Computer Music Conference (ICMC)*.

Cover, T. M., & Thomas, J. A. (2006). *Elements of Information Theory* (2nd ed.). New York: Wiley.

Dubnov, S. (2004). Generalization of Spectral Flatness Measure for Non-Gaussian Linear Processes. *IEEE Signal Processing Letters, 11*(8). doi:10.1109/LSP.2004.831663

Dubnov, S. (2006). Spectral anticipations. *Computer Music Journal, 30*(2), 63–83. doi:10.1162/comj.2006.30.2.63

Dubnov, S. (2008). Unified view of prediction and repetition structure in audio signals with application to interest point detection. *IEEE Transactions on Audio. Speech and Language Processing, 16*(2), 327–337. doi:10.1109/TASL.2007.912378

Dubnov, S. (2009). Information Dynamics and Aspects of Musical Perception. In *Structure of Style*. New York: Springer Verlag.

Dubnov, S., Assayag, G., & Cont, A. (2007- September) Audio Oracle: A New Algorithm for Fast Learning of Audio Structures. *In Proceedings of International Computer Music Conference (ICMC).*

Dubnov, S., Assayag G., Lartillot, O., & Bejerano, G. (2003- August). Using Machine-Learning Methods for Musical Style Modeling. *Computer magazine.*

Dubnov, S., McAdams, S., & Reynolds, R. (2006). Structural and Affective Aspects of Music From Statistical Audio Signal Analysis. *Journal of the American Society for Information Science and Technology, 57*(11), 1526–1536. doi:10.1002/asi.20429

Foote, J., & Cooper, M. (2001). Visualizing musical structure and rhythm via selfsimilarity. In *Proceedings of the International Computer Music Conference* (pp. 419-422).

Huron, D. (2006). *Sweet Anticipation: Music and the Psychology of Expectation.* Boston: MIT Press.

Hyvärinen, A., Karhunen, J., & Oja, E. (2001). *Independent Component Analysis.* New York: John Wiley & Sons. doi:10.1002/0471221317

Itti, L. & Baldi, P. (2005). Bayesian surprise attracts human attention. *In Advances Neural Information Processing Systems (NIPS 2005).*

Jayant, N. S., & Noll, P. (1984). *Digital Coding of Waveforms.* Englewood Cliffs, NJ: Prentice-Hall.

Meyer, L. B. (1956). *Emotion and Meaning in Music.* Chicago: Chicago University Press.

Meyer, L. B. (2001) Music and emotion: Distinctions and uncertainties. In Juslin & Sloboda (Eds.), *Music and Emotion: Theory and Research* (pp. 341–360). Oxford University Press.

Narmour, E. (1990). *The Analysis and Cognition of Basic Melodic Structures: The Implication-Realization Model.* Chicago: University of Chicago Press.

Potter, K., Wiggins, G. A., & Pearce, M. T. (2007). Towards greater objectivity in music theory: Information-dynamic analysis of minimalist music. *Musicae Scientiae, 11*(2), 295–322.

Rigau, J., Feixas, M., & Sbert, M. (2008). *Informational Aesthetics Measures.* IEEE Computer Graphics and Applications.

Temperley, D. (2007). *Music and Probability.* Cambridge, MA: MIT Press.

Von Luxburg, U. (2007). A tutorial on spectral clustering. *Statistics and Computing, 17*(4), 395–416. doi:10.1007/s11222-007-9033-z

Zhang, H-J L. Lu, Wenyin, L. (2004). Audio textures: theory and applications. *IEEE Transactions on Speech and Audio Processing, 12*(2), 156–167. doi:10.1109/TSA.2003.819947

ENDNOTE

[1]   In (Dubnov 2008, eq. 16) there was an error in the sign of the right hand factor (KL distance). Also, as explained in the text, the mutual information between a single sample and the model parameters was neglected, assuming that for most practical cases the model cannot be represented by one sample. Another point worth considering is the relation between the different factors in this equation and the SR and SA estimators presented in this chapter. SA estimator uses spectral flatness measure to estimate IR of the decorrelated (approximately independent) features. This estimation can be also performed by using linear prediction, in which case it is based on the compression gain computed from the ratio of the signal variance and the residual error variance for every feature component. The important point here is that the prediction and the error estimation, or the spectral flatness estimation, are all done over macro-frames, which means that they estimate IR relative to the current empirical distribution. This indeed corresponds to the first factor of the unified IR expression. The second factor can be estimated using average Bayesian surprise that was described in this chapter. To be able to use this method, the definition of IR has to be extended to include more then one sample as the signal present. Doing so requires extending SA to future predictions. The most problematic factor in this equation is the last factor that computes KL distance between the empirical distribution and some other distribution denoted by θ^*. In case when θ^* contains a single peak in model space that is close to the empirical distribution, KL measures model perturbation and is proportional to Fisher information that the observed data carries about a parameter. In case when the distribution of the model space comprises of several peaks, KL distance measures the distance of the empirical distribution to all other most likely distributions. This could be done using spectral clustering method and estimating the cluster parameters by models such as GMM. Currently we use SR as a crude approximation to this process, with reservations that were discussed in the section on Spectral Recurrence.

APPENDIX A

Derivation of the Unified IR Measure

Starting with parameterization of the probability function

$$P(x_{[1:n]}) = \int P(x_{[1:n]} \mid \theta) P(\theta) d\theta$$

we use the approximation (Bialek et al. 2001) to express the probability in terms of a conditional probability relative to an empirical distribution and an expression that measures the distance between this empirical distribution and all other distributions generated by this model space

$$P(x_{[1:n]}) = P(x_{[1:n]} \mid \theta) \int \frac{P(x_{[1:n]} \mid \alpha)}{P(x_{[1:n]} \mid \theta)} P(\alpha) d\alpha = P(x_{[1:n]} \mid \theta) \int e^{-\log\left(\frac{P(x_{[1:n]} \mid \alpha)}{P(x_{[1:n]} \mid \theta)}\right)} P(\alpha) d\alpha$$

$$\approx P(x_{[1:n]} \mid \theta) \int e^{-nD(\theta \| \alpha)} P(\alpha) d\alpha$$

This expression allows writing the entropy of a macro-frame in terms of conditional entropy in a model and log-partition function

$$Z_n(\theta) = \int e^{-nD(\theta \| \alpha)} P(\alpha) d\alpha$$

$$H(x_{[1:n]}) = -\int P(\theta) \int P(x_{[1:n]} \mid \theta) \log[P(x_{[1:n]} \mid \theta)] dx_{[1:n]} d\theta$$

$$-\int P(\theta) \int P(x_{[1:n]} \mid \theta) \cdot \log[\int e^{-\log\left(\frac{P(x_{[1:n]} \mid \alpha)}{P(x_{[1:n]} \mid \theta)}\right)} P(\alpha) d\alpha] dx_{[1:n]} d\theta$$

$$= H(x_{[1:n]} \mid \theta) - E[\log Z_n(\theta)]_{P(\theta)}$$

The entropy of a single observation cannot be approximated in this way, so we express it in terms of conditional entropy and mutual information between the sample and the empirical model

$$H(x_n) = H(x_n \mid \theta) + I(x_n, \theta).$$

Combining these expression into the definition of information rate gives

$$IR(x_{[1:n]}) = H(x_n) + H(x_{[1:n-1]}) - H(x_{[1:n]}) =$$

$$= H(x_n \mid \theta) + I(x_n, \theta) + H(x_{[1:n-1]} \mid \theta) - E[\log Z_{n-1}(\theta)]_{P(\theta)} - H(x_{[1:n]} \mid \theta) + E[\log Z_n(\theta)]_{P(\theta)} =$$

$$= IR(x_{[1:n]} \mid \theta) + I(x_n, \theta) + E[\log \frac{Z_n(\theta)}{Z_{n-1}(\theta)}]_{P(\theta)}$$

This expression can be further simplified if we assume that the space of models comprises of several peaks centered around distinct parameter values. In such case the partition function Zn(θ) can be written through Laplace's method of saddle point approximation in terms of a function proportional to its arguments at extreme values of $\theta = \theta^*$. This allows writing the right hand of previous equation as

$$\log \frac{Z_n(\theta)}{Z_{n-1}(\theta)} \approx -D(\theta, \theta^*)$$

resulting in an expression of information rate

$$IR(x_{[1:n]}) = IR(x_{[1:n]} \mid \theta) + I(x_n, \theta) - E[D(\theta \parallel \theta^*)]_{P(\theta)}$$

Chapter 17
Multimodal Emotion Recognition

Sanaul Haq
University of Surrey, UK

Philip J.B. Jackson
University of Surrey, UK

ABSTRACT

Recent advances in human-computer interaction technology go beyond the successful transfer of data between human and machine by seeking to improve the naturalness and friendliness of user interactions. An important augmentation, and potential source of feedback, comes from recognizing the user's expressed emotion or affect. This chapter presents an overview of research efforts to classify emotion using different modalities: audio, visual and audio-visual combined. Theories of emotion provide a framework for defining emotional categories or classes. The first step, then, in the study of human affect recognition involves the construction of suitable databases. The authors describe fifteen audio, visual and audio-visual data sets, and the types of feature that researchers have used to represent the emotional content. They discuss data-driven methods of feature selection and reduction, which discard noise and irrelevant information to maximize the concentration of useful information. They focus on the popular types of classifier that are used to decide to which emotion class a given example belongs, and methods of fusing information from multiple modalities. Finally, the authors point to some interesting areas for future investigation in this field, and conclude.

INTRODUCTION

Speech is the primary means of communication between human beings in their day-to-day interaction with one another. Speech, if confined in meaning as the explicit verbal content of what is spoken, does not by itself carry all the information that is conveyed during a typical conversation, but is in fact nuanced and supplemented by additional modalities of information, in the form of vocalized emotion, facial expressions, hand gestures and body language. These supplementary sources of information play a vital role in conveying the emotional state of interacting human beings,

DOI: 10.4018/978-1-61520-919-4.ch017

referred to as the "human affective state". The human affective state is an indispensable component of human-human communication. Some human actions are activated by emotional state, while in other cases it enriches human communication. Thus emotions play an important role by allowing people to express themselves beyond the verbal domain.

Most current state-of-the-art human-computer interaction systems are not designed to perceive the human affective state, and as such are only able to deliver or process explicit information (such as the verbal content of speech) and not the more subtle or latent channels of information indicative of human emotion; in effect, the information from the latter sources is lost. There are application domains within existing HCI technology where the ability of a computer to perceive and interpret human emotional state can be regarded as an extremely desirable feature. Consider, for example, that if intelligent automobile systems can sense the driver's emotional state and tune its behavior accordingly, it can react more intelligently in avoiding road accidents. Another example is that of an affect sensing system at a call center for emergency services which can perceive the urgency of the call based on the caller's perceived emotional state, allowing better response to the situation. We can also envision applications in the game and entertainment industries; in fact the ability of computers to interpret and possibly emulate emotion opens up potentially new territories in terms of applications that were previously out of bounds for computers. These considerations have activated investigation in the area of emotion recognition turning it into an independent and growing field of research within the pattern recognition and HCI communities.

There are two main theories that deal with the conceptualization of emotion in psychological research. The research into the structure and description of emotion is very important because it provides information about expressed emotion, and is helpful into affect recognition. Many

psychologists have described emotions in terms of discrete theories (Ortony et al., 1990), which are based on the assumption that there exist some universal basic emotions, although their number and type varies from one theory to another. The most popular example of this description is the classification of basic emotions into anger, disgust, fear, happiness, sadness and surprise. This idea was mainly supported by cross-cultural studies conducted by Ekman (1971, 1994), which showed that emotion perception in different cultures is the same for some basic facial expressions. Most of the recent research in affect recognition, influenced by the discrete emotion theory, has focused on recognizing these basic emotions. The advantage of the discrete approach is that in daily life people normally describe observed emotions in terms of discrete categories, and the labeling scheme based on category is very clear. But the disadvantage is that it is unable to describe the range of emotions which occur in natural communication. There is another theory known as dimensional theory (Russell et al., 1981; Scherer, 2005), which describes emotions in terms of small sets of dimensions rather than discrete categories.

These dimensions include evaluation, activation, control, power, etc. Evaluation and activation are the two main dimensions to describe the main aspects of emotion. The evaluation dimension measures human feeling, from pleasant to unpleasant, while the activation dimension, from active to passive, measure how likely the human is going to take action under the emotional state. The emotion distribution in two dimensions is summarized in Figure 1, which is based on Russell et al. (1981) and Scherer (2005) research.

The first quadrant consists of happiness, pleasure, excitement and satisfaction, the second quadrant consists of anger, disgust, hostile, fear, the third quadrant consists of sad, boredom, shame, depress, and the fourth quadrant consist of relax, content, hope and interest. The point of intersection of the two dimensions represents neutral. The dimensional representation makes it possible for

Figure 1. Distribution of emotion in 2D space based on Russell et al., 1981 and Scherer, 2005 research. The evaluation dimension measures human feeling from pleasant to unpleasant, while the activation dimension measures how likely the human is going to take an action under the emotional state from active to passive. The intersection of the two dimensions provides the neutral state.

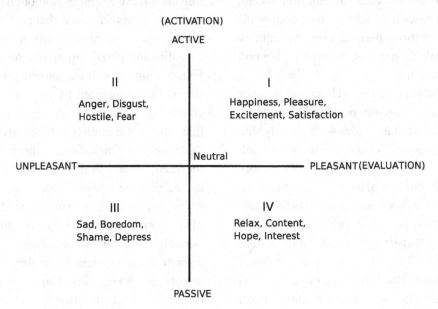

the evaluators to label a range of emotions. In this method, since high dimensional emotional states are projected onto 2D space which result in some loss of information. It becomes difficult to differentiate between some emotions, e.g. anger and fear, while others lie outside 2D Space, e.g. surprise. The evaluators will need training to label the data because this representation is not very clear, e.g. Feeltrace system (Cowie et al., 2000). The results from different raters may be more inconsistent compared to the discrete approach.

The goal of this chapter is to provide a summary of the research work that has been done in the field of human affect recognition by using the audio, visual, and audio-visual information. We first discuss the different types of databases (audio, visual and audio-visual modalities) that have been recorded for the analysis of human affect behavior. The next section explores various kinds of audio and visual features which are investigated by researchers. The feature extraction is followed by feature selection and feature reduction techniques,

which are used to reduce the dimensionality of data for computational efficiency and improved performance. In particular, we present two linear transformations, principal component analysis (PCA) and linear discriminant analysis (LDA). We then describe popular classification strategies, which is followed by fusion techniques, future research directions and the conclusion.

METHODOLOGY

Databases

In order to develop an automatic emotion recognizer, the first requirement is to have sufficient data that spans the variety and range of affective expressions. Spontaneous emotion data are difficult to collect because they are relatively rare, short lived and involve ethical issues. The other problem with these databases is that the data needs to be labeled, which can be expensive, time consuming and error-prone, making it really difficult to analyze the automatic spontaneous emotion recognition. Due to these problems, most of the research in this field is based on acted emotions. The acted databases are recorded by asking the actors or non-actors to express different emotions in front of a recording camera and/or microphone. The recording is performed in a controlled laboratory environment.

It has been found that the acted emotions are different in audio profile, visual appearance and timing from spontaneous emotions. Whissell (1989) concluded that acted emotions in spoken language may differ in timing and choice of words from spontaneous emotions. In the case of facial expressions, differences exist between acted and spontaneous expressions in terms of dynamics and muscle movement (Ekman et al., 2005). Many types of spontaneous smiles, e.g. polite smile, are smaller in amplitude, longer in total duration and slower in onset and offset times than the acted smile (Cohn et al., 2004; Ekman et al., 2005; Valstar et al., 2007). It has been found that spontaneous brow actions are different in morphology and temporal structure from acted brow actions (Valstar et al., 2006). In general, acted emotion expressions are more exaggerated than natural ones, and due to these reasons, a system trained on acted emotion expressions may fail to generalize properly to spontaneously occurring emotions. The other issue is that current emotion recognition systems are evaluated on clear noise free data which has high quality audio and frontal face visual data. However, in natural environment the data may be noisy and the face may not be ideally posed with respect to the camera. There is also a problem of emotion categories; in actual human-computer interaction scenarios the emotions are normally non-basic (Cowie et al., 2005), but still most of the existing emotion recognition systems classify expressions from basic emotion categories.

Despite the existence of differences between acted expressions and natural expressions, databases of acted emotions are still useful and have been recorded for the analysis of emotions. The main advantage to this method is that it allows more control over the design of database. A phonetically balanced set of sentences can be recorded in different emotions, which is difficult to achieve in real environment. Since the acted database is normally recorded in a controlled lab environment, this results in high quality noise-free data.

Emotional behavior databases (audio, visual and audio-visual) have been recorded for investigation of emotion, some natural, while others acted or elicited, as shown in Table 1. Many audio emotional databases have been recorded for the analysis of vocal expressions of emotions. The AIBO database (Batliner et al., 2004) is a natural database which consists of recording from children while interacting with robot. The data consist of 110 dialogues and 29200 words. The emotion categories include anger, bored, emphatic, helpless, ironic, joyful, motherese, reprimanding, rest, surprise and touchy. The data labeling is based on listeners' judgment. The Berlin Database of Emotional Speech (Burkhardt et al., 2005) is a German acted database, which consists of recordings from 10 actors (5 male, 5 female). The data consist of 10 German sentences recorded in anger, boredom, disgust, fear, happiness, sadness and neutral. The final database consists of 493 utterances after listeners' judgment. The Danish Emotional Speech Database (Engberg, 1996) is another audio database recorded from 2 actors and 2 actresses. The recorded data consist of 2 words, 9 sentences and 2 passages, resulting in 10 minutes of audio data. The recorded emotions are anger, happiness, sadness, surprise and neutral. The ISL meeting corpus (Burger et al., 2002) is a natural audio database which consists of recordings from 18 meetings with 5 persons, on average, per meeting. There are three emotion categories: negative, positive and neutral. The data are labeled based on listeners' judgment.

Some facial expressions databases have been recorded for the analysis of facial emotional behavior. The BU-3DFE (Yin et al., 2006) is another

Table 1. Audio and/or Visual Emotional Databases: where A: Audio, V: Visual, AV: Audio-Visual, 6 basic emotions: anger, disgust, fear, happiness, sad, surprise

Database	A/V	Elicitation method	Size	Emotion categories
AIBO database (Batliner et al., 2004)	A	Natural: children interaction with robot	110 dialogues, 29200 words	anger, bored, emphatic, helpless, ironic, joyful, motherese, reprimanding, rest, surprise, touchy
Berlin Database (Burkhardt et al., 2005)	A	Acted	493 sentences; 5 actors & 5 actresses	anger, boredom, disgust, fear, happiness, sadness, neutral
Danish Emotional Speech Database (Engberg, 1996)	A	Acted	10 minutes ; 2 actors & 2 actresses; 2 words, 9 sentences, 2 passages	anger, happiness, sadness, surprise, neutral
ISL meeting corpus (Burger et al., 2002)	A	Natural: meeting corpus	18 meetings; average 5 persons per meeting	negative, positive, neutral
BU-3DFE database (Yin et al., 2006)	V	Acted	100 adults	6 basic emotions with four levels of intensity
Cohn-Kanade database (Kanade et al., 2000)	V	Acted	210 adults; 480 videos	6 basic emotions, Action Units (AUs)
FABO face and body gesture database (Gunes et al., 2006)	V	Acted	23 adults; 210 videos	6 basic emotions, anxiety, boredom, neutral, uncertainty
MMI database (Pantic et al., 2007; Pantic et al., 2005)	V	Acted: static images, and videos in frontal and profile view Natural: Children interacted with a comedian, adults watched emotion inducing videos	Acted: 61 adults Natural: 11 children and 18 adults Total: 1250 videos, 600 static images	6 basic emotions, single Action Unit and multiple Action Units activation
UT Dallas database (O'Toole et al., 2005)	V	Natural: subjects watched emotion inducing videos	229 adults	6 basic emotions, boredom, disbelief, laughter, puzzle
Adult Attachment Interview database (Roisman, 2004)	AV	Natural: subjects were interviewed to describe the childhood experience	60 adults: each interview was 30-60 minutes long	6 basic emotions, contempt, embarrassment, shame, general positive and negative emotions
Belfast database (Douglas-Cowie et al., 2003)	AV	Natural: clips taken from television and realistic interviews with research team	125 subjects; 209 clips from TV and 30 from interviews	Dimensional labeling/categorical labeling
Busso-Narayanan database (Busso et al., 2007)	AV	Acted	612 sentences; an actress	anger, happiness, sadness, neutral
Chen-Huang database (Chen, 2000)	AV	Acted	100 adults; 9900 visual and audio-visual expressions	6 basic emotions, boredom, frustration, interest, puzzle
Haq-Jackson database (Haq & Jackson, 2009)	AV	Acted: emotion stimuli were shown on screen	480 sentences; 4 male subjects	6 basic emotions, neutral
RU-FACS database (Bartlett et al., 2005)	AV	Natural: subjects tried to convince the interviewers about their truth	100 adults	33 Action Units

acted database which consists of 3D range data of 6 basic emotions expressed in four different intensity levels. The data consist of recordings from 100 adults. The Cohn-Kanade facial expression database (Kanade et al., 2000) is a popular acted database of facial expressions, with recordings from 210 adults, in 6 basic emotions and Action Units (AUs). The data is labeled using Facial Action Coding System (FACS). The FABO acted database (Gunes et al., 2006) consists of videos of facial expressions and body gestures from 23 adults in 6 basic emotions along with some non-basic emotions (uncertainty, anxiety, boredom and neutral). The MMI database is a very comprehensive data set of facial behavior (Pantic et al., 2007; Pantic et al., 2005). It consists of facial data for both the acted expressions and spontaneous expressions. The recorded data comprise of both static images and videos, where large parts of the data are recorded in both the frontal and the profile views of the face. For the natural data, children interacted with a comedian, while adults watched emotion-inducing videos. The database consists of 1250 videos and 600 static images in 6 basic emotions, single AU and multiple AUs. The data labeling is done by FACS and observers' judgment. The UT Dallas database (O'Toole et al., 2005) is a natural visual database which is recorded by asking subjects to watch emotion-inducing videos. The database consists of data from 229 adults in 6 basic emotions, along with puzzle, laughter, boredom and disbelief. The data labeling is based on observers' judgment.

Recent work in the field of emotion recognition involves combining the audio and visual modalities to improve the performance of emotion recognition systems. This has resulted in the recording of audio-visual databases, where the facial expressions of the emoting performers are captured simultaneously with speech. The Adult Attachment Interview (AAI) database (Roisman, 2004) is a natural audio-visual database where the subjects are interviewed to describe their childhood experiences. The data consist of recordings from 60 adults and each interview lasts for 30-60 minutes. The database consists of the 6 basic emotions along with embarrassment, contempt, shame, in addition to general kinds of positive and negative emotion. The data labeling is performed by using FACS. The Belfast database (Douglas-Cowie et al., 2003) is another natural audio-visual database which consists of clips taken from television and realistic interviews conducted by a research team. The database consists of data from 125 subjects, which consists of 209 sequences from TV and 30 from interviews.

The data are labeled with both dimensional and categorical approaches using Feeltrace system. The Busso-Narayanan acted database (Busso et al., 2007) consists of recordings from an actress, who is asked to read a phoneme-balanced corpus four times, expressing anger, happiness, sadness and neutral state. A detailed description of the actress' facial expression and rigid head motion are acquired by attaching 102 markers to her face. A VICON motion capture system with three cameras is used to capture the 3D position of each marker. The markers' motion and aligned audio is captured simultaneously in a quiet room. The total data consist of 612 sentences. Chen-Huang audio-visual database (Chen, 2000) is one of the largest acted databases, which consists of acted audio and visual expressions in the 6 basic emotions and 4 cognitive states: boredom, interest, frustration and puzzlement. The database consists of recordings from 100 adults with 9900 visual and audio-visual expressions. Haq & Jackson (2009) recorded an audio-visual database from four English male actors in seven emotions in a controlled environment (see Figure 2). The data are recorded in six basic emotions: anger, disgust, fear, happiness, sadness, surprise and in neutral mode. The database consists of 120 utterances per actor, which resulted in 480 sentences in total. To track the visual features, the actors' face is painted with 60 markers. Recordings consist of 15 phonetically-balanced TIMIT database sentences per emotion: 3 common sentences, 2 emotion specific sentences, and 10 generic sentences that are different for each emotion. The Emotion to be simulated and text prompts are displayed on a monitor in front of the actor during the recordings. The 3dMD dynamic face capture system provided 2D frontal color video and Beyer dynamics microphone signals. The data evaluation is performed by 10 subjects, of which 5 are native English speakers and the remaining subjects lived in UK for more than a year. It has been found in some studies that female experience emotion more intensively than male (Swerts et al., 2008), to avoid

Figure 2. Haq & Jackson (2009) audio-visual emotional database (from left): Displeased (anger, disgust), Excited (happy, surprise), Gloomy (sad, fear), and Neutral (neutral), reproduced from Haq & Jackson (2009).

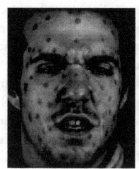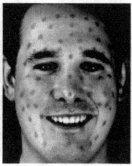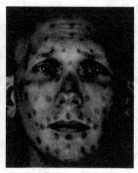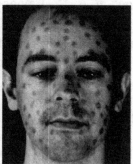

gender biasing half of the evaluators are female. Three types of human evaluation experiments are designed: audio, visual, and audio-visual. Slides are used to show audio, visual and audio-visual clips of each utterance. The data are randomized to remove systematic bias from the responses of human evaluators. For each of the evaluators, a different data set is created by using the Balanced Latin Square method (Edwards, 1962). The portrayed emotion is easier to correctly identify via the visual data alone, compared to the audio data alone, and the overall performance improves by combining the two modalities. The RU-FACS is a natural database (Bartlett et al., 2005) where subjects are tried to convince the interviewers that they are telling the truth. The database consists of data from 100 adults in 33 AUs, and data are labeled by using FACS.

Feature Extraction

It has been found that audio signals follow certain patterns for different kind of emotions. The relationship between audio and emotion is summarized by Cowie et al. (2001). For example anger is characterized by faster speech rate, higher energy and pitch values compared to sadness. The important audio features for emotion recognition are pitch, intensity, duration, spectral energy distribution,

formants, Mel Frequency Cepstral Coefficients (MFCCs), jitter and shimmer. These features are identified as important both at utterance level (Luengo et al., 2005; Ververidis et al., 2005; Vidrascu et al., 2005; Borchert et al., 2005; Haq et al., 2008; Haq & Jackson, 2009) and at frame level (Nogueiras et al., 2001; Lin et al., 2005; Kao et al., 2006; Neilberg et al., 2006).

New research on spontaneous emotion analysis suggests the use of only paralinguistic audio features may not be enough for emotion recognition. It is indicated by Batliner et al. (2003) that the reliability of prosody features for affect recognition degraded in real scenarios. In the initial experiments of Devillers et al. (2006) aimed at recognizing anger, fear, relief and sadness in medical call conversations between humans, it was found that lexical cues performed better than paralinguistic cues. Other studies have been performed to investigate using a combination of acoustic features and linguistic features to improve the performance of audio emotion recognition systems. Litman et al. (2004) and Schuller et al. (2005) used spoken words and acoustic features to recognize emotions. Lee et al. (2005) performed emotion recognition by using prosodic features along with spoken words and information of repetition. Graciarena et al. (2006) combined prosodic, lexical and cepstral features to achieve higher performance. Batliner et al. (2003) used prosodic features, part of speech, dialogue act, repetitions, corrections and syntactic-prosodic boundary to detect the emotions. The role of context information (e.g. subject, gender and turn-level features representing local and global aspects of the dialogue) has also been investigated by Litman et al. (2004) and Forbes-Riley et al. (2004). The above studies showed improvement in performance by using information related to language, discourse and context, but the automatic extraction of these features is a difficult task. First, the automatic speech recognition systems are unable to reliably recognize the verbal content of emotional speech (Athanaselis et al., 2005), and Second, the extraction of semantic discourse information is even more difficult. These features are normally extracted manually or directly from transcripts.

Since facial expressions plays an important role to convey and perceive emotions, most of the vision-based emotion recognition methods focus on the analysis of facial expressions. The machine analysis of facial expression can be divided into two main groups: the recognition of emotions and the recognition of facial muscle actions (facial AUs) (Cohn, 2006; Pantic et al., 2007). The facial AUs are descriptions of facial signals which can be mapped to emotion categories by using high level mapping, like EMFACS and FACSAID (Hager, 2003). The current facial expression based emotion recognition systems use different pattern recognition methods and are based on various 2D spatiotemporal facial features. There are mainly two types of facial features which are used for affect recognition: geometric and appearance features. The examples of geometric features are shape of facial components (eyes, mouth, etc.) and the location of facial salient points (corners of eyes, mouth, etc.). The appearance features represent facial texture which includes wrinkles, bulges, and furrows. The examples of methods based on geometric features are those of Chang et al. (2006), who used shape model defined by 58 facial points, of Pantic et al. (2007, 2006, 2004)

and Valstar et al. (2007, 2006), who used a set of facial points around the mouth, eyes, eyebrows, nose and chin, and of Kotsia et al. (2007), who used the Candide grid. Other examples are the systems developed by Busso et al. (2004), who used 102 facial markers, and by Haq & Jackson (2009), who used 60 frontal face markers. The examples of appearance-feature-based methods are those of Bartlett et al. (2003, 2005, 2006), Littlewort et al. (2007) and Guo et al. (2005), who used Gabor wavelet, Whitehill et al. (2006), who used Haar features, Anderson et al. (2006), who used a holistic spatial ratio face template, and Valstar et al. (2004), who used temporal templates.

It has been suggested in some studies (Pantic et al., 2006), that using both geometric and appearance features may be the best choice for designing an automatic affect recognizer. The examples of hybrid geometric and appearance based features are those of Tian et al. (2005), who used facial component shapes and the transient components (like crow's feet wrinkles and nasal-labial furrows) and that of Zeng et al. (2005), who used 26 facial points around the eyes, eyebrows, and mouth, and the transient features proposed by Tian et al. (2005). A similar method was proposed by Lucey et al. (2007), who used the Active Appearance Model (AAM) to capture the characteristics of facial appearance and shape of facial expressions. Most of the existing 2D feature based methods are suitable for the analysis of facial expressions under small head motions.

There are few studies of automatic facial affect recognition which are based on 3D face models. Cohn et al. (2007) worked on analysis of brow AUs and head movement based on a cylindrical head model (Xiao et al., 2003). Huang and colleagues (Cohen et al., 2003; Sebe et al., 2004; Wen et al., 2003; Zeng et al., 2007) used feature extracted by a 3D face tracker called the Piecewise Bezier Volume Deformation Tracker (Tao et al., 1999). Chang et al. (2005) and Wang et al. (2006) used 3D expression data for facial expression recognition. The progress of the methodology based on 3D face models may be helpful for view-independent facial expression recognition, which is really important in natural settings due to the unconstrained environment.

Feature Selection

Appropriate feature selection is essential for achieving good performance with both global utterance-level and instantaneous frame-level features. This process helps to remove uninformative, redundant or noisy information. In audio-based emotion recognition, Lin and Wei (2005) reported higher recognition rate for 2 prosodic and 3 voice quality instantaneous level features selected by the Sequential Forward Selection (SFS) method from fundamental frequency (f0), energy, formants, MFCCs and Mel sub-band energies features. Kao & Lee (2006) investigated multilevel features for emotion recognition, and found that frame-level features are better than syllable and word-level features. The best performance is achieved with an ensemble of three feature levels. In phoneme based emotion recognition, it is found that some phonemes, particularly semivowels and vowels, are more important than others (Sethu et al., 2008). Schuller et al. (2003) halved the error rate with 20 global pitch and energy features compared to that of 6 instantaneous pitch and energy features.

For Vision-based emotion recognition, Ashraf et al. (2007) used an AAM to decouple shape and appearance parameters from the digitized facial images, to distinguish between pain and no-pain expressions. Bartlett et al. (2005) used Gabor wavelets features for classification of facial expressions and facial Action Units. The feature selection was performed by PCA and AdaBoost before classification. The performance of both LDA and linear kernel SVM classifier was lower without feature selection. The feature selection by PCA improved the performance of LDA classifier but degraded that of SVM classifier. The use of AdaBoost technique for feature selection improved the performance of both classifiers

compared to that of PCA. The AdaBoost feature selection along with SVM classification gave the best results. Gunes et al. (2005) performed visual emotion recognition from face and body. They fused facial expression and body gestures first at feature-level by combining the features from both modalities, and later at decision-level by integrating the outputs of individual systems with suitable criteria. In the feature level fusion, they applied feature selection on combined data with Best-first search method using Weka tool (Witten et al., 2000). The Best-first method can start from an empty set of features and search forward, or start with the full feature set and search backward, or start at any point and search in both directions. The feature-level fusion performed better than decision-level fusion, and the best performance was achieved with 45 features selected out of a pool of 206 features. Valstar et al. (2007) performed experiments to distinguish between posed and spontaneous smiles by fusing head, face and shoulder modalities. They performed fusion at three levels: early, mid-level and late. They used the GentleSVM-Sigmoid classifier for classification, which perform feature selection using GentleBoost and classification using SVM. Whitehill et al. (2006) used Haar features with an AdaBoost classifier to recognize FACS AUs. They compared both the recognition accuracy and processing time of the system with that of Gabor features with SVM classifier. The recognition accuracy of the two systems was comparable, but the AdaBoost classification system was at least 2 orders of magnitude faster than SVM system. They used AdaBoost to select the top 500 Haar features for each AU before classification.

Multi-modal emotion recognition is proposed by Chen et al. (2005). The facial features consisted of 27 features related to eyes, eyebrows, furrows and lips, and the acoustic features consisted of 8 features related to pitch, intensity and spectral energy. The performance of the visual system was better than the audio system, and the overall performance improved for the bimodal system.

Busso et al. (2004) performed emotion recognition using an audio, visual and bimodal system. The audio system used 11 prosodic features selected by the Sequential Backward Selection (SBS) technique, and the visual features were obtained from 102 markers on the face by applying PCA to each of the five parts of face: forehead, eyebrow, low eye, right cheek and left cheek. The visual system performed better than audio system and overall performance improved for the bimodal system. Schuller et al. (2008) reported that emotion recognition in noisy conditions improves with noise and speaker adaptation, and further improvement is achieved with feature selection. The experiments on audio-visual data showed that the performance for both audio and visual features improved with feature selection, and combining the two modalities before feature selection further improved the performance. Haq & Jackson (2009), and Haq et al. (2008) performed feature selection (audio, visual) by Plus *l*-Take Away *r* algorithm (Chen, 1978) based on the Bhattacharyya distance criterion (Campbell, 1997). The algorithm is a combination of SFS and SBS algorithms. The SFS algorithm is a bottom up search method that starts out with an empty feature set, and at each step adds one new feature chosen from a set of candidate features, which performs best in combination with the already chosen features. The problem with the SFS algorithm is that once a feature is added, it cannot be removed. The SBS on the other hand is a top down process. It starts from complete feature set and at each step the worst feature is discarded such that the reduced set gives maximum value of the criterion function. The SBS gives better results but is computationally more complex. Sequential Forward Backward Selection (SFBS) offers benefits of both SFS and SBS, via Plus *l*-Take Away *r* algorithm. At each step, *l* features are added to the current feature set and *r* features are removed. The process continues until the required feature set size is achieved.

Feature Reduction

One of the problems faced by pattern recognition is the dimensionality of data. It is difficult to deal with high dimensional data because it is computationally more expensive. To overcome this problem various techniques have been developed to reduce the dimensionality of data such that most of the useful information is retained. The dimensionality of a feature set can be reduced by using statistical methods to maximize the relevant information preserved. This can be done by applying a linear transformation, Y=WX, where Y is a feature vector in the reduced feature space, X is the original feature vector, and W is the transformation matrix. Principal Component Analysis (PCA) (Shlens, 2005) and Linear Discriminant Analysis (LDA) (Duda et al., 2001) are the examples of such techniques.

Principal Component Analysis

PCA is a simple and non-parametric method to extract useful information from noisy data, and is widely used in statistical analysis of data. PCA is capable of reducing the dimensionality of data to extract the hidden, simple structure of the complex data and remove noise.

The PCA method is described below in detail. Let X be an $m \times n$ matrix, where m is the number of features and n is the number of samples. First, the mean value of each feature is subtracted and each feature is divided by its standard deviation so that each feature variation is contained in the same range, since different types of features have different range of variation. Second, let us define a new mwhere each column of Y has zero mean. It can be shown that

$$Y^T Y = C_X \tag{2}$$

i.e. $Y^T Y$ is equal to covariance of X. The principal components of X are the eigenvectors of C_X. After calculating the *SVD* of Y, the columns of matrix V (eigenvector matrix) contain the eigenvectors of $Y^T Y = C_X$. Thus the columns of V are the principal components of X. Matrix V rotates the row space of matrix Y, therefore it must rotate matrix X.

The *SVD* decomposition of a matrix M is given by equation,

$$M = U\Sigma V^T \qquad (3)$$

Here U and V are orthogonal matrices, where elements of V are the eigenvectors, and U is a set of vectors defined by $\hat{u}_i \equiv \dfrac{1}{\sigma_i} X\hat{v}_i$. The Σ is a

diagonal matrix with rank-ordered set of singular values, $\sigma_1 \geq \sigma_2 \geq ... \geq \sigma_r$. Singular values are positive real and are obtained by taking the square root of eigenvalues of a matrix. Equation (3) states that any arbitrary matrix M can be decomposed into an orthogonal matrix, a diagonal matrix and another orthogonal matrix (or rotation, stretch and another rotation).

The steps for performing PCA can be summarized as follows.

1. Organize the data set as an $m \times n$ matrix, where m is the number of features and n is the number of trials.
2. Subtract off the mean of each feature, or row of matrix X.
3. Calculate the *SVD*.

Linear Discriminant Analysis

LDA is another feature reduction technique, which maximizes the ratio of between-class variance to within-class variance to optimize the separability between classes. The criterion function for the LDA is given by

$$J(\mathbf{W}) = \frac{|\mathbf{W}^T \mathbf{S}_B \mathbf{W}|}{|\mathbf{W}^T \mathbf{S}_W \mathbf{W}|} \qquad (4)$$

where

$$\mathbf{S}_B = \sum_{i=1}^{c} n_i (\mathbf{m}_i - \mathbf{m})(\mathbf{m}_i - \mathbf{m})^T \qquad (5)$$

$$\mathbf{S}_W = \sum_{i=1}^{c} \sum_{\mathbf{x} \in D_i} (\mathbf{x} - \mathbf{m}_i)(\mathbf{x} - \mathbf{m}_i)^T \qquad (6)$$

$$\mathbf{S}_T = \mathbf{S}_W + \mathbf{S}_B \qquad (7)$$

$$\mathbf{S}_T = \sum_{x} (\mathbf{x} - \mathbf{m})(\mathbf{x} - \mathbf{m})^T \qquad (8)$$

where $\mathbf{S}_B$ is between-class scatter, $\mathbf{S}_W$ is within-class scatter, and $\mathbf{S}_T$ is total scatter matrix. The m is the total mean vector, $\mathbf{m}_i$ is the mean vector for class i, and c is the total number of classes. The transformation matrix W in equation (4) maximizes the ratio of between-class variance to the within-class variance.

PCA is non-parametric and the answer is unique and independent of any hypothesis about data probability distribution. These two properties are the weakness as well as strength of PCA. Since it is non-parametric, no prior knowledge can be incorporated and also there is loss of information due to PCA compression. The applicability of PCA is limited by the assumptions made in its derivation, which are linearity, statistical importance of mean and covariance, and that larger variances have important information. To resolve the linearity problem of PCA other non-linear methods, e.g. kernel PCA, have been developed. PCA uses a simple criterion for selection of bases, i.e. it chooses bases that maximize the variance of the observed data points, and consider the new dimensions one at a time. An Independent Component Analysis (ICA) is another technique which uses a finer criterion that looks at the relationship between the projections of data into the new dimensions, and optimizes some criterion based on two or more dimensions at once.

LDA is closely related to PCA in that both are linear feature reduction techniques. The difference is that PCA does not take into account any difference in classes, while the LDA explicitly attempts to model the difference between the classes of data. Some other generalizations of LDA for multiple classes have also been defined to address the problem of heteroscedastic distributions, one such method is Heteroscedastic LDA. The other subspace methods include Factor Analysis (FA), Curvilinear Component Analysis (CCA), Principal Manifold, MLP based method, etc.

To classify among facial expressions, Bartlett et al. (2005) used PCA for feature selection which substantially improved the performance of LDA classifier. Petridis & Pantic (2008) used PCA to reconstruct the positions of 20 facial points for the audio-visual based discrimination between laughter and speech. Busso et al. (2004) used audio and visual information for emotion recognition, and they divided the face into five parts: forehead, eyebrow, low eye, right cheek and left cheek. PCA was applied to each part of the face for dimensionality reduction of facial features (3D markers' coordinate). Haq & Jackson (2009) and Haq et al. (2008) used PCA and LDA to reduce the dimensionality of selected audio and visual features for audio-visual emotion recognition.

Classification

The choice of classifier can also significantly affect the recognition accuracy. In the field of emotion recognition various classifiers have been used, among commonly used approaches are Gaussian Mixture Model (GMM), Hidden Markov Model (HMM), Neural Network (NN), Support Vector Machine (SVM) and AdaBoost.

Gaussian Mixture Model (Bishop, 1995) models the probability density function of observed variables using a multivariate Gaussian mixture density. Given a series of inputs, it refines the weights of each distribution through expectation-maximization algorithms. The Hidden Markov

Model (Young & Woodland, 2009) is a finite set of states, each of which is associated with a probability distribution which is generally multidimensional. The transitions among the states are governed by a set of probabilities known as transition probabilities. In a particular state an outcome or observation can be generated, according to the associated probability distribution. AdaBoost (Adaptive Boosting) (Freund & Schapire, 1999) is a machine learning algorithm, which is used for pattern recognition and feature selection. AdaBoost is adaptive in the sense that subsequent classifiers built by assigning more weights to those samples which are misclassified by the previous classifiers. AdaBoost calls a weak classifier repeatedly in a series of rounds, where weak classifier is the base learning algorithm that can predict better than a chance. For each call a distribution of weights is updated that indicates the importance of examples in the data set for the classification. On each round, the weights of each incorrectly classified example are increased, so that the new classifier is built with more focus on wrongly classified examples.

A Neural Network (Bishop, 1995) consists of units known as neurons, arranged in layers, which convert an input vector into some output. Neural Network consists of three layers: input, hidden and output. Each unit takes an input, applies a function to it and then passes the output on to the next layer. Generally the networks are feed-forward, where a unit feeds its output to all the units on the next layer, but there is no feedback to the previous layer. Weightings are applied to the signals passing from one unit to another, and these weightings are tuned in the training phase to adapt NN to a specific problem. A single sweep forward through the network results in the assignment of a value to each output node, and data is assigned to that class' node which has the highest value. Support Vector Machine (Burges, 1998) performs classification by constructing an N-dimensional hyperplane that optimally separates the data into two categories. Consider that the input data are two sets of vectors in an *n*-dimensional space, an SVM will construct a separating hyperplane in that space such that it maximizes the margin between the two data sets. To calculate the margin, two hyperplanes are constructed, one on each side of the separating hyperplane, which are pushed up against the two data sets. A good separation is achieved by the hyperplane that has the largest distance to the neighboring data points of both classes. When the data points are separated by a nonlinear region, it is difficult to separate them by simply constructing an *N*-dimensional hyperplane. SVM handles this by using a kernel function to map the data onto a high dimensional space where it becomes possible for a hyperplane to do the separation. The different kernel functions of SVM are Linear, Polynomial, Radial Basis Function (RBF) and Sigmoid.

Various results have been reported in emotion recognition literature that uses audio, visual and audio-visual information with these different kinds of classifiers, as shown in Table 2. Borchert et al. (2005) reported an accuracy of 76% with SVM classifier, and 75% with AdaBoost classifier for speaker-dependent case, and 70% with each of the two classifiers for speaker-independent case. The classification was performed for 7 emotions using 63 prosody and quality features. Lin and Wei (2005) achieved recognition rates of 100% with 5-state HMM, 89% with SVM, and 85% with KNN (K=21) for the speaker dependent case using 5 best audio features. There were 5 emotion categories and the extracted audio features were prosody, MFCC, Mel frequency sub-band energies. Luengo et al. (2005) reported 92% recognition rate for SVM classifier compared to 87% for GMM classifier with best six pitch and energy related features. A recognition rate of 98% was achieved for the GMM classifier (512 mixtures) with MFCC features for seven emotions. Schuller et al. (2003) achieved 87% accuracy with 4 components GMM for 7 emotions, compared to 78% with 64-state continuous HMM using pitch and energy related features.

With regard to visual classification, Ashraf et al. (2007) used SVM classifier with several representations from AAM. They were able to achieve an equal error rate of 19% using canonical appearance and shape features to classify between pain and no-pain. Bartlett et al. (2005) used SVM, AdaBoost and LDA with Gabor wavelet features to classify between 7 facial expressions. They were able to achieve 90% accuracy with Ada-Boost, 88% with SVM (linear kernel), 89% with SVM (RBF kernel) without feature selection. The performance improved by using AdaBoost and PCA as feature selection techniques. The best performance was achieved with SVM classifier, and using AdaBoost for feature selection. The recognition rate increased to 93 for SVM (linear and RBF kernel) and for LDA to 88% with AdaBoost feature selection. Gunes et al. (2005) performed affect recognition from face and body by combining the two types of features at feature-level and at decision-level. They used C4.5 decision tree and BayesNet classifiers for classification and Best-first search method for feature selection using Weka tool (Witten et al., 2000). The feature-level fusion performed better than decision-level fusion, and best performance was achieved with BayesNet classifier using 45 features selected out of total 206 combined features. For eight emotion categories, C4.5 decision tree classifier achieved a best performance of 94% with 206 features, and BayesNet classifier achieved a best performance of 96% with 45 selected features. Valstar et al. (2007) fused head, face and shoulder modalities to distinguish between posed and spontaneous smiles. They used GentleSVM-Sigmoid classifier for classification, which perform feature selection using GentleBoost and classification using SVM. Since the output of SVM is not a good measure for the posterior probability of its prediction, they pass the output of SVM to a sigmoid function that is a reasonable measure for the posterior probability. The features were fused at three levels: early, mid-level and late. In late fusion the head, face and shoulder

Table 2. Emotion classification using audio, visual and audio-visual data: where A: Audio, V: Visual, AV: Audio-Visual, MFCC: Mel Frequency Cepstral coefficient, AAM: Active Appearance Model, SVM: Support Vector Machine, GMM: Gaussian Mixture Model, AdaBoost: Adaptive Boosting, HMM: Hidden Markov Model, KNN: K Nearest Neighbor, LDA: Linear Discriminant Analysis, SD: Speaker-Dependent, SI: Speaker-Independent, GI: Gender-Independent.

Reference	Data	Features	Classifier	Test paradigm	Classes	Accuracy
Borchert et al., 2005	A; Berlin Database (Burkhardt et al., 2005); 493 sentences; 5 male, 5 female	Prosody, quality	SVM	Training: 7 speakers data, testing: 3 speakers data	7	70% (SI)
			AdaBoost			70% (SI)
Lin & Wei, 2005	A; DES Database (Engberg, 1996); 10 min; 2 actors & 2 actresses; 2 words, 9 sentences, 2 passages	Prosody, MFCC, Mel freq. sub-band energies	HMM	4-fold leave-one-out cross-validation	5	100% (GI)
		Mel energy spectrum dynamics coefficients	SVM			89% (GI)
			KNN			85% (GI)
Luengo et al., 2005	A; 97 samples per emotion; 21 number, 21 words, 55 sentences; single actress	Prosody	SVM	5-fold leave-one-out cross-validation	7	92% (SD)
			GMM			87% (SD)
		MFCC	GM			98% (SD)
Schuller et al., 2003	A; 5250 phrases in German and English; 5 speakers	Prosody	GMM	Training: 100 utterances per emotion and speaker, testing: 50 utterances per emotion and speaker	7	87% (SD)
			HMM			78% (SD)
Ashraf et al., 2007	V (face); shoulder pain expressions data from 21 subjects	AAM	SVM	Leave-one-subject-out cross-validation	2	Equal Error Rate: 19% (SI)
Bartlett et al., 2005	V (face); Cohn-Kanade database (Kanade et al., 2000); 210 adults; 480 videos	Gabor wavelets	SVM	Leave-one-subject-out cross-validation	7	93% (SI)
			LDA			88% (SI)
Gunes et al., 2005	V (face and body); 206 instances; 3 subjects	Shape features, optical flow	BayesNet	Training: 156 instances, testing: 50 instances	8	96% (SD) (feature-level fusion)
			C4.5 decision tree			94% (SD) (feature-level fusion)
Valstar et al., 2007	V (face, head and shoulder); MMI database (Pantic et al., 2007); 100 videos of posed smile and 102 videos of spontaneous smile	12 facial points, 5 shoulder points, and 6 degrees of freedom of head motion	Gentle SVM-Sigmoid	10-fold cross-validation	2	94% (decision-level fusion)
						89% (feature-level fusion)
						88% (mid-level fusion)
Whitehill et al., 2006	V (face); Cohn-Kanade database (Kanade et al., 2000); 210 adults; 480 videos	Haar features	AdaBoost	Training: 580 images, testing: on all AUs for which at least 40 training images were present; 10-fold cross-validation	11 AUs	92% (SI)
		Gabor features	SVM			91% (SI) (AdaBoost system was at least 2 times faster than SVM system)

continued on following page

Table 2. continued

Reference	Data	Features	Classifier	Test paradigm	Classes	Accuracy
Busso et al., 2004	AV; 612 phonetically balanced sentences; an actress	Prosody, 102 marker points	SVM	Leave-one-out cross-validation	4	71% (A) (SD)
						85% (V) (SD)
						89% (AV fused at feature-level and at decision-level) (SD)
Haq & Jackson, 2009	AV; 480 sentences; four male subjects	Prosody, MFCC, 60 facial marker	Gaussian	4-fold leave-one-out cross-validation	7	56% (A) (SD)
						95% (V) (SD)
						98% (AV fused at decision level) (SD)
					4	69% (A) (SD)
						98% (V) (SD)
						98% (AV fused at decision level) (SD)
Haq, Jackson & Edge, 2008	AV; 120 sentences; a male subject	Prosody, MFCC, 60 facial marker	Gaussian	6-fold leave-one-out cross-validation	7	53% (A) (SD)
						98% (V) (SD)
						98% (AV fused at decision level) (SD)
Pal et al., 2006	AV; Infant's cry face and sound data	Fundamental frequency, first two formants, vertical grey level	Rules, k-means	Not available	5	64% (A)
						74% (V)
						75% (AV fused at decision level)
Schuller et al., 2007	AV; 10.5 hours of spontaneous human-to-human conversation; 11 male and 10 female	Prosody, articulatory, voice quality and linguistic information, AAM, movement activity	SVM	Trainig: 14 subjects, testing: 7 subjects; 3-fold subject independent SCV	3	overall recall: 64% (SI) (audio + activity), (feature-level fusion)
						59% (SI) (audio + AAM)
						42% (SI) (AAM + activity)
Song et al., 2004	AV; 1384 samples	Prosody, 54 facial animation parameters	Tripled HMM	Training; 700 samples, testing: 684 samples	7	85.0% (model-based fusion)
Wang & Guan, 2005	AV; 500 videos; 8 subjects, 6 different languages	Prosody, MFCC, formants, Gabor wavelets	Fisher's LDA	Training: 360 samples, testing: 140 samples	6	82% (SI) (decision-level fusion)
Zeng et al., 2005a	AV; 660 video sequences; 10 male and 10 female subjects	Prosody, motion units	Multi-stream Fused HMM	Leave-one-subject-out cross-validation	11	81% (SI) (model based fusion)

modalities were combined using three criteria: sum, product and weight. The best recognition accuracy of 94% was achieved with late fusion (product). The recognition rates for the early and the mid-level fusions were 89% and 88%. White-

hill et al. (2006) recognized FACS Action Units by using two systems: first, AdaBoost classifier with Haar features, and second, SVM classifier with Gabor features. The AdaBoost system used AdaBoost to select top 500 Haar features for each

AU before classification. For 11 AUs, an average recognition accuracy of 91% was achieved with SVM classifier using Gabor features, and 92% with AdaBoost classifier using Haar features. The recognition accuracy was comparable for both systems, but AdaBoost classifier was at least 2 times faster than SVM classifier.

Busso et al. (2004) performed emotion classification using both audio and visual features. The audio based system used 11 features selected by SBS. The visual based system used facial marker related features by applying PCA to each of the five parts of face: forehead, eyebrow, low eye, right cheek and left cheek. For the bimodal system, the audio and visual information were fused at two different levels: feature-level and decision-level. The SVM classifier was used for classification of 4 emotion categories. The overall recognition rate of audio system was 71%, and of visual system was 85%. The overall performance for the bimodal system improved to 89% for both of the fusion at feature-level and at decision-level. Haq & Jackson (2009) performed audio-visual emotion recognition using an English database from four male speakers. The audio and visual features were fused at decision level for the audio-visual experiments. They performed speaker dependent experiments using a single mixture Gaussian classifier. For seven emotion classes, average recognition rates of 56%, 95% and 98% were achieved for the audio, visual and audio-visual features compared to 67%, 88% and 92% recognition rates of human. For four emotion categories, average recognition rates of 69%, 98% and 98% were achieved for the audio, visual and audio-visual features compared to 76%, 91% and 95% of humans. Haq, Jackson & Edge (2008) performed audio-visual emotion recognition using single subject audio-visual data. Their recognition system was consisted of four stages: feature extraction, feature selection, feature reduction and classification. A single mixture Gaussian classifier was used for classification. In experiments, audio and visual features were combined at four differ-

ent stages: feature level, after feature selection, after feature reduction and at decision level. The fusion at decision level and after feature reduction performed better than the fusion at feature level and after feature selection. A maximum recognition rate of 53% was achieved with audio features alone, 98% with visual features alone, and 98% with audio-visual feature fused at decision level. Emotion recognition from infant facial expressions and cries were investigated by Pal et al. (2006). The facial features were related to eyebrow, mouth and eyes positions. The audio features consisted of fundamental frequency and first two formants. For five classes, the overall accuracy of audio, visual and audio-visual systems were 64%, 74% and 75% respectively. The audio-visual experiments were performed with decision level fusion. Schuller et al. (2007) worked on recognition of three levels of interest in a spontaneous conversation by using the audio-visual information. The audio features consisted of prosody, articulatory, voice quality and linguistic information, and visual features consisted of AAM and movement activity detection which was derived from eye positions. The feature selection was performed for each of the audio and visual features before feature-level fusion and SVM was used for classification. The overall recall for combining the audio and activity features was 64%, for the audio and AAM was 59%, and for the AAM and activity features was 42%. Song et al. (2004) reported 85% accuracy for 7 emotions with tripled HMM classifier using both audio and visual features. The facial feature points were tracked with an AAM based instance which were segmented into two groups: expression and visual speech. For a video frame sequence, express vector stream and visual speech vector stream were generated. The audio feature vector stream was extracted based on low level acoustic features. The three streams were feed to HMM system and higher performance was achieved compared to single modality. Wang and Guan (2005) performed classification experiments using an audio-visual database, which consisted of data from 8 speakers in 6 different languages. The visual features consisted of Gabor wavelets, and audio features were prosody, MFCC and formants. A step wise method based on Mahalanobis distance was used for feature selection. The proposed classification scheme was based on analysis of each individual class and combinations of different classes. An overall accuracy of 82% was achieved over a language and race independent data. Zeng et al. (2005a) used Multi-stream Fused HMM (MFHMM) to detect 11 emotions using both audio and visual information. They used composite facial features, speech energy and pitch as three tightly coupled streams. The MFHMM allows building of an optimal connection among multiple streams based on maximum entropy principle and maximum mutual information criterion. An overall accuracy of 81% was achieved with MFHMM which outperformed face-only HMM, pitch-only HMM, energy-only HMM and independent HMM fusion which assume independence among audio and visual streams.

FUSION TECHNIQUES

Audio-visual emotion recognition is based on three types of fusion techniques: feature-level, decision-level and model-level. Feature-level fusion is performed by combining the features of audio and visual modalities into a single feature vector. Examples of methods based on feature-level fusion are those of Zeng et al. (2005b), Busso et al. (2004), Schuller et al. (2007) and Haq et al. (2008). Feature-level fusion may involve feature selection of individual modalities either before or after combining them. Feature-level fusion has the disadvantage of combining the two different kinds of modalities, which have different time scales and metric levels. The other problem with feature-level fusion is high dimensionality of resulting feature vector, which can degrade the performance of emotion recognition system.

In decision-level fusion, the data from audio and visual modalities are treated independently and the single-modal recognition results are combined at decision level. The results from different modalities are combined by using some criterion (e.g. sum, product, and weighted sum or product). Many researchers have combined audio and visual modalities at decision-level (Busso et al., 2004; Wang et al., 2005; Zeng et al., 2007a; Zeng et al., 2007b; Pal et al., 2006; Petridis et al., 2008; Haq et al., 2008; Haq & Jackson, 2009). Decision-level fusion overcomes the problem of different time scales and metric levels of audio and visual data, plus high dimensionality of the concatenated vector resulted in case of feature-level fusion. Decision-level fusion is based on the assumption that audio and visual data are independent, but in reality humans produce audio and visual expressions in a complementary and redundant manner. The assumption of independence results in loss of mutual correlation information between audio and visual modality.

A model-level fusion technique is proposed by some researchers (Fragopanagos et al., 2005; Zeng et al., 2005a; Sebe et al., 2006; Caridakis et al., 2006; Song et al., 2004) to make use of the correlation between audio and visual information with a relaxed synchronization of the two modalities. Song et al. (2004) used a tripled HMM to model the correlation properties of three component HMMs based on one audio and two visual streams. Zeng et al. (2005a) proposed MFHMM for audio-visual affect recognition. The MFHMM builds an optimal connection between different streams based on maximum entropy and maximum mutual information criterion. Caridakis et al. (2006) and Petridis et al. (2008) proposed neural networks to combine the audio and visual modalities for audio-visual emotion recognition. Sebe et al. (2006) proposed Bayesian network topology to recognize emotions from audio and visual modalities. The Bayesian network topology combines the two modalities in a probabilistic manner.

FUTURE RESEARCH DIRECTIONS

The number of efforts that have been put into improve the automatic emotion recognition have resulted some promising achievements in terms of realistic emotional databases recording, audio and visual modalities analysis, feature extraction, feature selection and fusion of two modalities to improve the classification performance. But there are some potential areas that need to be explored for improvement in automatic emotion recognition systems.

Many audio, visual and audio-visual emotional databases have been recorded for the analysis of emotions, but there is no emotional database which can be used as a benchmark. The emotion research community needs to do collective efforts towards recording a larger emotional database that can be used as a benchmark. Most of the recent methods are developed based on high quality lab recorded data, but for realistic natural environment, methods need to be developed which are robust to arbitrary human movement, occlusion, and noisy conditions. The temporal correlation between audio and visual modalities needs to be explored and techniques need improvement to incorporate temporal behavior of each modality, their correlation and contextual information. The development of various audio-visual fusion techniques to improve the performance of affect recognizers is one of important research areas.

CONCLUSION

The field of emotion recognition has come a long way since its modest beginnings. Significant strides have been made in several areas: acquisition of emotion data for research and experimentation, extraction and selection of feature sets, and techniques of classification. The initial studies on emotion recognition were mostly based on small data sets of acted audio or visual expressions, with the classification categories generally restricted to the six basic emotions. Data were not shared among researchers. Studies on multimodal emotion recognition were rare; most of the studies were based on either audio or visual modality, but not both. Recent studies have progressed to recording large emotional databases (audio, visual and audio-visual) of different kinds (acted, natural), and with a greater number and of emotion categories. Moreover, several audio, visual and audio-visual databases are publicly available for the research. Despite the progress that has been made, there are still some issues related to the emotional data acquisition that need to be addressed. The compilation of naturally-occurring databases is quite a difficult task, it is hard to acquire data in the natural environment, and the databases so obtained are normally unbalanced and the quality of the data is not as good. Although it is comparatively easy to record data in a controlled lab environment, the resulting loss of "naturalness" in the data can have some disadvantages. In addition, some emotions, such as happiness, are relatively easy to induce in a laboratory environment, by showing the subjects some example clips chosen to induce the desired emotion, but other emotions, such as fear, sadness and disgust, pose greater difficulty. Another significant problem with natural databases is that of labeling, which becomes quite difficult for the data that lies outside the range of the six basic emotions. While facial expressions can be labeled using FACS Action Units, which are objective descriptors (that can be used for high-level decision-making processes including emotion recognition), there is no similar coding system available to label emotional audio data. The data recorded is influenced by culture and context (stimuli, data recording environment, and the presence of people), and information about these aspects should be recorded as well. It is proposed that the labeling process can be made more reliable if the data is labeled by many subjects, and the subjects are trained before data labeling. A system designed with this kind of data is expected to be more reliable. Another problem, besides the issue of subjectiveness of human-labeled data mentioned, is that it is very time consuming and expensive to manually label the training data. A possible solution to this problem is to use a semi-supervised method, which involves automatic labeling followed by human labeling. The systems developed by Pantic et al. (2007) and Tian et al. (2005) can recognize the AUs in frontal face images, which can be used for automatic data labeling. Although many efforts have been made in compiling emotional databases, there is a need for more collective effort to develop large and comprehensive emotional databases that can be used as a benchmark for the evaluation of emotion recognition techniques. An example of similar kind of database is that of MMI facial expression database (Pantic et al., 2005; Pantic et al., 2007), which provide easy access and search to the facial images.

Various audio and visual features have been identified as being important for emotion recognition. Some of the important audio features for emotion recognition are pitch, intensity, duration, spectral energy distribution, formants, MFCCs, jitter and shimmer. These features are identified as being significant both at utterance level and at frame level. Some studies showed the improvement in performance by using information related to language, discourse and context. However it is difficult to extract these features automatically: it is difficult to recognize the verbal content of emotional speech, and even harder than that is the problem of extracting semantic discourse information. Vision-based emotion recognition is based primarily on facial expressions, as obviously face plays the most important role in conveying emotions. There are two types of facial features - geometric features and appearance features - which are used for affect recognition. Examples of geometric features are shapes of facial components (eyes, mouth, etc.) and the location of salient facial points (corners of eyes, mouth, etc.). The appearance features represent facial texture which includes wrinkles, bulges, and furrows. Some

studies suggested that using both geometric and appearance features may be the best choice for designing an automatic affect recognizer. There are other studies which are based on 3D face models, and are capable to incorporate head movement in the direction of camera, which is not possible with 2D techniques. Audio and visual features need to be explored that are robust to noise, occlusion and arbitrary human movement. For view-independent facial expression recognition, which is important in natural environments, developments in 3D face modeling techniques may be helpful.

As is true for most classification problems, the performance of emotion recognition system depends on three factors: feature selection, dimensionality reduction and choice of classifier. Feature selection is used to discard uninformative, redundant or noisy information. The process of feature selection improves both classification performance and computational efficiency. Different methods have been used for feature selection, which include SFS, SBS, SFBS, AdaBoost, GentleBoost, PCA, and Best-first search method. In general it is difficult to deal with high-dimensional data and is computationally expensive. To overcome this problem various techniques have been developed to reduce the dimensionality of data, while at the same time retaining the most useful information. The dimensionality of the feature set is reduced by using statistical methods that minimize redundancy and noise while still retaining relevant information. PCA, Kernel PCA, ICA, LDA and Heteroscedastic LDA are the examples of such techniques. In addition to feature selection and feature reduction, the choice of classifier plays an important role in the performance of affect recognizer. In the field of emotion recognition different kind of classifiers have been used among which GMM, HMM, NN, SVM, and AdaBoost being the most common.

The human emotion recognition is a complex problem, and so far many individual efforts have been made to resolve this issue. This is a multidiscipline's problem and in order to truly understand the human affect behavior, researchers from different disciplines, e.g. psychology, linguistic, engineering, computer science and related fields, need to develop a wider network for collective efforts.

ACKNOWLEDGMENT

We are thankful to Kevin Lithgow, James Edge, Joe Kilner, Darren Cosker, Nataliya Nadtoka, Samia Smail, Idayat Salako, Affan Shaukat and Aftab Khan for help with the data capture, evaluation and as subjects, to James Edge for his marker tracker, to Adrian Hilton for use of his equipment, to Akiel Khan and Tim Sheerman-Chase for corrections, and to University of Peshawar, Pakistan for funding.

REFERENCES

Anderson, K., & McOwan, P. W. (2006). A Real-Time Automated System for Recognition of Human Facial Expressions. *IEEE Trans. Systems, Man, and Cybernetics Part B*, *36*(1), 96–105. doi:10.1109/TSMCB.2005.854502

Ashraf, A. B., Lucey, S., Cohn, J. F., Chen, T., Ambadar, Z., Prkachin, K., et al. (2007). The Painful Face: Pain Expression Recognition Using Active Appearance Models. *Proc. Ninth ACM Int'l Conf. Multimodal Interfaces* (pp. 9-14).

Athanaselis, T., Bakamidis, S., Dologlou, I., Cowie, R., Douglas-Cowie, E., & Cox, C. (2005). ASR for Emotional Speech: Clarifying the Issues and Enhancing Performance. *Neural Networks*, *18*, 437–444. doi:10.1016/j.neunet.2005.03.008

Bartlett, M. S., Littlewort, G., Braathen, P., Sejnowski, T. J., & Movellan, J. R. (2003). A Prototype for Automatic Recognition of Spontaneous Facial Actions. *Advances in Neural Information Processing Systems*, *15*, 1271–1278.

Bartlett, M. S., Littlewort, G., Frank, M., et al. (2005). Recognizing Facial Expression: Machine Learning and Application to Spontaneous Behavior. *Proc. IEEE Int'l Conf. Computer Vision and Pattern Recognition* (pp. 568-573).

Bartlett, M. S., Littlewort, G., Frank, M. G., et al. (2006). Fully Automatic Facial Action Recognition in Spontaneous Behavior. *Proc. IEEE Int'l Conf. Automatic Face and Gesture Recognition* (pp. 223-230).

Batliner, A., et al. (2004). You Stupid Tin Box—Children Interacting with the AIBO Robot: A Cross-Linguistic Emotional Speech. *Proc. Fourth Int'l Conf. Language Resources and Evaluation.*

Batliner, A., Fischer, K., Hubera, R., Spilkera, J., & Noth, E. (2003). How to Find Trouble in Communication. *Speech Communication*, *40*, 117–143. doi:10.1016/S0167-6393(02)00079-1

Bishop, C. M. (1995). *Neural Networks for Pattern Recognition*. Oxford University Press.

Borchert, M., & Düsterhöft, A. (2005). Emotions in Speech – Experiments with Prosody and Quality Features in Speech for Use in Categorical and Dimensional Emotion Recognition Environments. *Proc. IEEE Int'l Conf. on Natural Language Processing and Knowledge Engineering* (pp. 147–151).

Burger, S., MacLaren, V., & Yu, H. (2002). The ISL Meeting Corpus: The Impact of Meeting Type on Speech Style. *Proc. Eighth Int'l Conf. Spoken Language Processing.*

Burges, C. J. C. (1998). A Tutorial on Support Vector Machines for Pattern Recognition. *Data Mining and Knowledge Discovery*, *2*, 121–167. doi:10.1023/A:1009715923555

Burkhardt, F., Paeschke, A., Rolfes, M., Sendlmeier, W., & Weiss, B. (2005). *A Database of German Emotional Speech* (pp. 1517–1520). Proc. Interspeech.

Busso, C., Deng, Z., Yildirim, S., Bulut, M., Lee, C. M., Kazemzadeh, A., et al. (2004). Analysis of Emotion Recognition Using Facial Expressions. Speech and Multimodal Information. *Proc. ACM Int'l Conf. Multimodal Interfaces (*pp. 205-211).

Busso, C., & Narayanan, S. S. (2007). Interrelation between Speech and Facial Gestures in Emotional Utterances: A Single Subject Study. *IEEE Trans. on Audio, Speech, and Language Processing, 15*(8), 2331–2347. doi:10.1109/TASL.2007.905145

Campbell, J. (1997). Speaker Recognition: A Tutorial. *Proceedings of the IEEE, 85*(9), 1437–1462. doi:10.1109/5.628714

Caridakis, G., Malatesta, L., Kessous, L., Amir, N., Paouzaiou, A., & Karpouzis, K. (2006). Modeling Naturalistic Affective States via Facial and Vocal Expression Recognition. *Proc. ACM Int'l Conf. Multimodal Interfaces,* (pp. 146-154).

Chang, Y., Hu, C., Feris, R., & Turk, M. (2006). Manifold Based Analysis of Facial Expression. *J. Image and Vision Computing, 24*(6), 605–614. doi:10.1016/j.imavis.2005.08.006

Chang, Y., Vieira, M., Turk, M., & Velho, L. (2005). Automatic 3D Facial Expression Analysis in Videos. *Proc. IEEE Int'l Workshop Analysis and Modeling of Faces and Gestures* (Vol. 3723, pp. 293-307).

Chen, C. (1978). *Pattern Recognition and Signal Processing.* The Netherlands: Sijthoff & Noordoff.

Chen, C., Huang, Y., & Cook, P. (2005). Visual/Acoustic emotion recognition. *Proc. Int'l Conf. on Multimedia & Exp*o (pp. 1468-1471).

Chen, L. S. (2000). *Joint Processing of Audio-Visual Information for the Recognition of Emotional Expressions in Human-Computer Interaction.* (PhD dissertation, Univ. of Illinois, Urbana-Champaign).

Cohen, L., Sebe, N., Garg, A., Chen, L., & Huang, T. (2003). Facial Expression Recognition from Video Sequences: Temporal and Static Modeling. *Computer Vision and Image Understanding, 91*(1-2), 160–187. doi:10.1016/S1077-3142(03)00081-X

Cohn, J. F. (2006). Foundations of Human Computing: Facial Expression and Emotion. *Proc. Eighth ACM Int'l Conf. Multimodal Interfaces,* (pp. 233-238).

Cohn, J. F., Reed, L. I., Ambadar, Z., Xiao, J., & Moriyama, T. (2004). Automatic Analysis and Recognition of Brow Actions and Head Motion in Spontaneous Facial Behavior. *Proc. IEEE Int'l Conf. Systems, Man, and Cybernetics* (vol. 1, pp. 610-616).

Cohn, J. F., & Schmidt, K. L. (2004). The Timing of Facial Motion in Posed and Spontaneous Smiles. *International Journal of Wavelets, Multresolution, and Information Processing, 2,* 1–12. doi:10.1142/S021969130400041X

Cowie, R., Douglas-Cowie, E., et al. (2000). Feeltrace: An Instrument for Recording Perceived Emotion in Real Time. *Proc. ISCA Workshop Speech and Emotion* (pp. 19-24).

Cowie, R., Douglas-Cowie, E., & Cox, C. (2005). Beyond Emotion Archetypes: Databases for Emotion Modeling Using Neural Networks. *Neural Networks, 18,* 371–388. doi:10.1016/j.neunet.2005.03.002

Cowie, R., Douglas-Cowie, E., Tsapatsoulis, N., Votsis, G., Kollias, S., Fellenz, W., & Taylor, J. G. (2001). Emotion Recognition in Human-Computer Interaction. *IEEE Signal Processing Magazine,* 32–80. doi:10.1109/79.911197

Devillers, L. & Vidrascu, L. (2006). Real-Life Emotions Detection with Lexical and Paralinguistic Cues on Human-Human Call Center Dialogs. *Proc. Interspeech,* 801-804.

Douglas-Cowie, E., Campbell, N., Cowie, R., & Roach, P. (2003). Emotional Speech: Towards a New Generation of Database. *Speech Communication, 40*(1/2), 33–60. doi:10.1016/S0167-6393(02)00070-5

Duda, R., Hart, P., & Stork, D. (2001). *Pattern Classification*. New York: John Wiley & Sons, Inc.

Edwards, A. L. (1962). *Experimental Design in Psychological Research*. New York: Holt, Rinehart and Winston.

Ekman, P. (1971). Universal and Cultural Differences in Facial Expressions of Emotion. *Proc. Nebraska Symp. Motivation*, 207-283.

Ekman, P. (1994). Strong Evidence for Universals in Facial Expressions: A Reply to Russell's Mistaken Critique. *Psychological Bulletin, 115*(2), 268–287. doi:10.1037/0033-2909.115.2.268

Ekman, P., & Rosenberg, E. L. (2005). *What the Face Reveals: Basic and Applied Studies of Spontaneous Expression Using the Facial Action Coding System*, (Eds.). Oxford Univ. Press.

Engberg, I. S., & Hansen, A. V. (1996). *Documentation of the Danish Emotional Speech Database (DES)*. Denmark: Aalborg University.

Forbes-Riley, K., & Litman, D. (2004). Predicting Emotion in Spoken Dialogue from Multiple Knowledge Sources. *Proc. Human Language Technology Conf. North Am. Chapter of the Assoc. Computational Linguistics (HLT/NAACL)*.

Fragopanagos, F., & Taylor, J. G. (2005). Emotion Recognition in Human-Computer Interaction. *Neural Networks, 18*, 389–405. doi:10.1016/j.neunet.2005.03.006

Freund, Y., & Schapire, R. E. (1999). A Short Introduction to Boosting. *Journal of Japanese Society for Artificial Intelligence, 14*(5), 771–780.

Graciarena, M., Shriberg, E., Stolcke, A., Enos, F., Hirschberg, J., & Kajarekar, S. (2006). Combining Prosodic, Lexical and Cepstral Systems for Deceptive Speech Detection. *Proc. Int'l Conf. Acoustics, Speech and Signal Processing, 1*, 1033-1036.

Gunes, H., & Piccardi, M. (2005). Affect Recognition from Face and Body: Early Fusion versus Late Fusion. *Proc. IEEE Int'l Conf. Systems, Man, and Cybernetics* (pp. 3437-3443).

Gunes, H., & Piccardi, M. (2006). A Bimodal Face and Body Gesture Database for Automatic Analysis of Human Nonverbal Affective Behavior. *Proc. 18th Int'l Conf. Pattern Recognition, 1*, 1148–1153.

Guo, G., & Dyer, C. R. (2005). Learning from Examples in the Small Sample Case: Face Expression Recognition. *IEEE Trans. Systems, Man, and Cybernetics Part B, 35*(3), 477–488. doi:10.1109/TSMCB.2005.846658

Hager, J. C. (2003). *Date Face*. Retrieved from http://face-and-emotion.com/dataface/general/homepage.jsp

Haq, S., & Jackson, P. J. B. (2009). *Speaker-Dependent Audio-Visual Emotion Recognition*. Proc. Auditory-Visual Speech Processing.

Haq, S., Jackson, P. J. B., & Edge, J. (2008). *Audio-visual feature selection and reduction for emotion Classification* (pp. 185–190). Proc. Auditory-Visual Speech Processing.

Kanade, T., Cohn, J., & Tian, Y. (2000). Comprehensive Database for Facial Expression Analysis, *Proc. IEEE Int'l Conf. Face and Gesture Recognition* (pp. 46-53).

Kao, Y., & Lee, L. (2006). *Feature Analysis for Emotion Recognition from Mandarin Speech Considering the Special Characteristics of Chinese Language* (pp. 1814–1817). Proc. Interspeech.

Kotsia, I., & Pitas, I. (2007). Facial Expression Recognition in Image Sequences Using Geometric Deformation Features and Support Vector Machines. *IEEE Transactions on Image Processing, 16*(1), 172–187. doi:10.1109/TIP.2006.884954

Lee, C. M., & Narayanan, S. S. (2005). Toward Detecting Emotions in Spoken Dialogs. *IEEE Transactions on Speech and Audio Processing, 13*(2), 293–303. doi:10.1109/TSA.2004.838534

Lin, Y., & Wei, G. (2005). Speech Emotion Recognition Based on HMM and SVM. *Proc. 4th Int'l Conf. on Mach. Learn. and Cybernetics* (pp.4898-4901).

Litman, D. J., & Forbes-Riley, K. (2004). Predicting Student Emotions in Computer-Human Tutoring Dialogues. *Proc. 42nd Ann. Meeting of the Assoc. Computational Linguistics.*

Littlewort, G. C., Bartlett, M. S., & Lee, K. (2007). Faces of Pain: Automated Measurement of Spontaneous Facial Expressions of Genuine and Posed Pain, *Proc. Ninth ACM Int'l Conf. Multimodal Interfaces,* pp. 15-21.

Lucey, S., Ashraf, A. B., & Cohn, J. F. (2007). Investigating Spontaneous Facial Action Recognition through AAM Representations of the Face. In Delac, K., & Grgic, M. (Eds.), *Face Recognition* (pp. 275–286). New York: I-Tech Education and Publishing.

Luengo, I., & Navas, E. (2005). *Automatic Emotion Recognition using Prosodic Parameters* (pp. 493–496). Proc. Interspeech.

Neilberg, D., & Elenius, K. (2006). *Emotion Recognition in Spontaneous Speech Using GMMs* (pp. 809–812). Proc. Interspeech.

Nogueiras, A., Moreno, A., Bonafonte, A., & Mariño, J. B. (2001). *Speech Emotion Recognition Using Hidden Markov Models* (pp. 2679–2682). Proc. Eurospeech.

O'Toole, A. J. (2005). A Video Database of Moving Faces and People. *IEEE Transactions on Pattern Analysis and Machine Intelligence, 27*(5), 812–816. doi:10.1109/TPAMI.2005.90

Ortony, A., & Turner, T. J. (1990). What's Basic About Basic Emotions? *Psychological Review, 97*(3), 315–331. doi:10.1037/0033-295X.97.3.315

Pal, P., Iyer, A. N., & Yantorno, R. E. (2006). Emotion Detection from Infant Facial Expressions and Cries, *Proc. IEEE Int'l Conf. Acoustics, Speech and Signal Processing, 2,* 721-724.

Pantic, M., & Bartlett, M. S. (2007). Machine Analysis of Facial Expressions. In Delac, K., & Grgic, M. (Eds.), *Face Recognition* (pp. 377–416). New York: I-Tech Education and Publishing.

Pantic, M., & Patras, I. (2006). Dynamics of Facial Expression: Recognition of Facial Actions and Their Temporal Segments Form Face Profile Image Sequences. *IEEE Trans. Systems, Man, and Cybernetics Part B, 36*(2), 433–449. doi:10.1109/TSMCB.2005.859075

Pantic, M., & Rothkrantz, L. J. M. (2004). Facial Action Recognition for Facial Expression Analysis from Static Face Images. *IEEE Trans. Systems, Man, and Cybernetics Part B, 34*(3), 1449–1461. doi:10.1109/TSMCB.2004.825931

Pantic, M., Valstar, M. F., Rademaker, R., & Maat, L. (2005). Web-Based Database for Facial Expression Analysis. *Proc. 13th ACM Int'l Conf. Multimedia,* (pp. 317-321).

Petridis, S., & Pantic, M. (2008). Audiovisual Discrimination between Laughter and Speech. *IEEE Int'l Conf. Acoustics, Speech, and Signal Processing* (pp. 5117-5120).

Roisman, G. I., Tsai, J. L., & Chiang, K. S. (2004). The Emotional Integration of Childhood Experience: Physiological, Facial Expressive, and Self-Reported Emotional Response during the Adult Attachment Interview. *Developmental Psychology, 40*(5), 776–789. doi:10.1037/0012-1649.40.5.776

Russell, J., Ward, L., & Pratt, G. (1981). Affective Quality Attributed to Environments: A Factor Analytic Study. *Environment and Behavior, 13*(3), 259–288. doi:10.1177/0013916581133001

Scherer, K. (2005). What are emotions? and how can they be measured? *Social Sciences Information. Information Sur les Sciences Sociales, 44*(4), 695–729. doi:10.1177/0539018405058216

Schuller, B., Muller, R., Hornler, B., Hothker, A., Konosu, H., & Rigoll, G. (2007). Audiovisual Recognition of Spontaneous Interest within Conversations *Proc. ACM Int'l Conf. Multimodal Interfaces (* pp. 30-37).

Schuller, B., Rigoll, G., & Lang, M. (2003). Hidden Markov Model-Based Speech Emotion Recognition. *Proc. IEEE Int'l Conf. Acoustics, Speech, and Signal Processing, 2,* 1-4.

Schuller, B., Villar, R. J., Rigoll, G., & Lang, M. (2005). Meta-Classifiers in Acoustic and Linguistic Feature Fusion-Based Affect Recognition. *Proc. IEEE Int'l Conf. Acoustics, Speech, and Signal Processing,* (pp. 325-328).

Schuller, B., & Wimmer, M. (2008). *Detection of security related affect and behavior in passenger Transport* (pp. 265–268). Proc. Interspeech.

Sebe, N., Cohen, I., Gevers, T., & Huang, T. S. (2006). Emotion Recognition Based on Joint Visual and Audio Cues. *Proc. Int'l Conf. Pattern Recognition* (pp. 1136-1139).

Sebe, N., Lew, M. S., Cohen, I., Sun, Y., Gevers, T., & Huang, T. S. (2004). Authentic Facial Expression Analysis. *Proc. IEEE Int'l Conf. Automatic Face and Gesture Recognition.*

Sethu, V., Ambikairajah, E., & Epps, J. (2008). *Phonetic and speaker variations in automatic emotion Classification* (pp. 617–620). Proc. Interspeech.

Shlens, J. (2005). *A Tutorial on Principal Component Analysis.* Systems Neurobiology Laboratory, Salk Institute for Biological Studies, La Jolla.

Song, M., Bu, J., Chen, C., & Li, N. (2004). Audio-Visual-Based Emotion Recognition: A New Approach. *Proc. Int'l Conf. Computer Vision and Pattern Recognition,* (pp. 1020-1025).

Swerts, M., & Krahmer, E. (2008). *Gender-related differences in the production and perception of Emotion* (pp. 334–337). Proc. Interspeech.

Tao, H., & Huang, T. S. (1999). Explanation-Based Facial Motion Tracking Using a Piecewise Bezier Volume Deformation Mode. *Proc. IEEE Int'l Conf. Computer Vision and Pattern Recognition, 1,* 611-617.

Tian, Y. L., Kanade, T., & Cohn, J. F. (2005). Facial Expression Analysis. S.Z. Li and A.K. Jain (Eds.). *Handbook of Face Recognition* (pp. 247-276). New York: Springer.

Valstar, M., Pantic, M., Ambadar, Z., & Cohn, J. F. (2006). Spontaneous versus Posed Facial Behavior: Automatic Analysis of Brow Actions. *Proc. Int'l Conf. Multimodal Interfaces* (pp.162-170).

Valstar, M., Pantic, M., & Patras, I. (2004). Motion History for Facial Action Detection from Face Video. *Proc. IEEE Int'l Conf. Systems, Man, and Cybernetics, 1,* 635-640.

Valstar, M. F., Gunes, H., & Pantic, M. (2007). How to Distinguish Posed from Spontaneous Smiles Using Geometric Features. *Proc. ACM Int'l Conf. Multimodal Interfaces* (pp. 38-45).

Ververidis, D., & Kotropoulos, C. (2005). Emotional speech classification using Gaussian mixture Models. *Proc. ISCAS* (pp. 2871-2874).

Vidrascu, L., & Devillers, L. (2005). *Detection of real-life emotions in call centers* (pp. 1841–1844). Proc. Interspeech.

Wang, J., Yin, L., Wei, X., & Sun, Y. (2006). 3D Facial Expression Recognition Based on Primitive Surface Feature Distribution. *Proc. IEEE Int'l Conf. Computer Vision and Pattern Recognition, 2*, 1399-1406.

Wang, Y., & Guan, L. (2005). Recognizing Human Emotion from Audiovisual Information. *Proc. Int'l Conf. Acoustics, Speech, and Signal Processing* (pp. 1125-1128).

Wen, Z., & Huang, T. S. (2003). Capturing Subtle Facial Motions in 3D Face Tracking. *Proc. Ninth IEEE Int'l Conf. Computer Vision* (pp. 1343-1350).

Whissell, C. M. (1989). The Dictionary of Affect in Language, Emotion: Theory, Research and Experience. In Plutchik, R., & Kellerman, H. (Eds.), *The Measurement of Emotions* (*Vol. 4*, pp. 113–13). Academic Press.

Whitehill, J., & Omlin, C. W. (2006). Haar Features for FACS AU Recognition, *Proc. IEEE Int'l Conf. Automatic Face and Gesture Recognition* (pp. 217-222).

Witten, I. H., & Frank, E. (2000). *Data Mining: Practical machine learning tools with java implementations*. San Francisco: Morgan Kaufmann.

Xiao, J., Moriyama, T., Kanade, T., & Cohn, J. F. (2003). Robust Full-Motion Recovery of Head by Dynamic Templates and Re-Registration Techniques. *International Journal of Imaging Systems and Technology, 13*(1), 85–94. doi:10.1002/ima.10048

Yin, L., Wei, X., Sun, Y., Wang, J., & Rosato, M. J. (2006). A 3D Facial Expression Database for Facial Behavior Research. *Proc. IEEE Int'l Conf. Automatic Face and Gesture Recognition* (pp.211-216).

Young, S., & Woodland, P. (2009). *Hidden Markov Model Toolkit*. Cambridge University Engineering Department (CUED), UK. Online: http://htk.eng.cam.ac.uk/.

Zeng, Z., Fu, Y., Roisman, G. I., Wen, Z., Hu, Y., & Huang, T. S. (2006). Spontaneous Emotional Facial Expression Detection. *J. Multimedia, 1*(5), 1–8.

Zeng, Z., Hu, Y., Roisman, G. I., Wen, Z., Fu, Y., & Huang, T. S. (2007a). Audio-Visual Spontaneous Emotion Recognition. In Huang, T. S., Nijholt, A., Pantic, M., & Pentland, A. (Eds.), *Artificial Intelligence for Human Computing* (pp. 72–90). New York: Springer. doi:10.1007/978-3-540-72348-6_4

Zeng, Z., Tu, J., Liu, M., Huang, T. S., Pianfetti, B., Roth, D., & Levinson, S. (2007b). Audio-Visual Affect Recognition. *IEEE Transactions on Multimedia, 9*(2), 424–428. doi:10.1109/TMM.2006.886310

Zeng, Z., Tu, J., Pianfetti, P., Liu, M., Zhang, T., Zhang, Z., et al. (2005a). Audio-Visual Affect Recognition through Multi-Stream Fused HMM for HCI, *Proc. IEEE Int'l Conf. Computer Vision and Pattern Recognition* (pp. 967-972).

Zeng, Z., Zhang, Z., Pianfetti, B., Tu, J., & Huang, T. S. (2005b). Audio-Visual Affect Recognition in Activation-Evaluation Space. *Proc. 13th ACM Int'l Conf. Multimedia* (pp. 828-831).

Zhang, Y., & Ji, Q. (2005). Active and Dynamic Information Fusion for Facial Expression Understanding from Image Sequences. *IEEE Transactions on Pattern Analysis and Machine Intelligence, 27*(5), 699–714. doi:10.1109/TPAMI.2005.93

ADDITIONAL READING

Since this chapter provides a limited understanding of the human affect recognition, the following list of additional references has been included. Readers are encouraged to refer to these sources which are really important for their personal understanding of the human affect recognition.

Fasel, B., & Luttin, J. (2003). Automatic Facial Expression Analysis: A Survey. *Pattern Recognition, 36*(1), 259–275. doi:10.1016/S0031-3203(02)00052-3

Murrey, I. R., & Arnott, J. L. (1993). Toward the simulation of emotion in synthetic speech: A review of the literature of human vocal emotion. *The Journal of the Acoustical Society of America, 93*(2), 1097–1108. doi:10.1121/1.405558

Oudeyer, P.-Y. (2003). The production and recognition of emotions in speech: features and algorithms. *Int'l J. Human-Computer Studies, 59*, 157–183. doi:10.1016/S1071-5819(02)00141-6

Pantic, M., & Rothkrantz, L. J. M. (2003). Toward an Affect-Sensitive Multimodal Human-Computer Interaction. *Proceedings of the IEEE, 91*(9), 1370–1390. doi:10.1109/JPROC.2003.817122

Zeng, Z., Pantic, M., Roisman, G. I., & Huang, T. S. (2009). A Survey of Affect Recognition Methods: Audio, Visual, and Spontaneous Expressions. *IEEE Transactions on Pattern Analysis and Machine Intelligence, 31*(1), 39–58. doi:10.1109/TPAMI.2008.52

Chapter 18
Machine Audition of Acoustics:
Acoustic Channel Modeling and Room Acoustic Parameter Estimation

Francis F. Li
The University of Salford, UK

Paul Kendrick
The University of Salford, UK

Trevor J. Cox
The University of Salford, UK

ABSTRACT

Propagation of sound from a source to a receiver in an enclosure can be modeled as an acoustic transmission channel. Objective room acoustic parameters are routinely used to quantify properties of such channels in the design and assessment of acoustically critical spaces such as concert halls, theatres and recording studios. Traditionally, room acoustic parameters are measured using artificial probe stimuli such as pseudo random sequences, white noise or sine sweeps. The noisy test signal hinders occupied in-situ measurements. On the other hand, virtually all audio signals acquired by a microphone have undergone a process of acoustic transmission in the first place. Properties of acoustic transmission channels are essential for the design of suitable equalizers to facilitate subsequent machine audition. Motivated by these needs, a number of new methods and algorithms have been developed recently to determine room acoustic parameters using machine audition of naturally occurring sound sources, i.e. speech and music. In particular, reverberation time, early decay time and speech transmission index can be estimated from received speech or music signals using statistical machine learning or maximum likelihood estimation in a semi-blind or blind fashion. Some of these estimation methods can achieve accuracies similar to those of traditional instrument measurements.

DOI: 10.4018/978-1-61520-919-4.ch018

INTRODUCTION

Propagation of sound from a source to a receiver (a listener or a microphone) in an enclosed or semi-enclosed space is subject to multiple reflections and reverberation. This can be viewed as an acoustic transmission channel of sound. Characteristics of acoustic transmission channels are often a part of music enjoyment and a feature of perceived sound. Recordings made in relatively "dry" studios are often processed using artificial reverberation algorithms to achieve preferred artistic effects. Different concert halls have different acoustics; different lecture theatres may show different speech intelligibility. Research into room acoustics over 100 years has accumulated a large knowledgebase of preferred or suitable acoustics of spaces for various purposes in terms of objective acoustic parameters, a set of physical measures of acoustic transmission channels. These parameters are routinely used to quantify acoustics in the design and assessment of acoustically critical spaces such as concert halls, where music needs to be good sounding, lecture theatres, in which speech communication is vital, and transportation hubs where public address broadcast needs to be clearly heard. Objective parameters are traditionally measured using high sound pressure level artificial test signals, which are unacceptable to audiences. For this reason, occupied in-use measurements are rarely carried out even though it is well established that occupancy significantly affects absorption and hence acoustic parameters. It is therefore suggested that the obstacle of obtaining the much sought after occupied data can be circumvented by extracting these parameters from naturally occurring sound sources such as music or speech when the spaces are in use.

On the other hand, machine audition involves predominately digital processing, feature extraction and pattern recognition of acquired acoustic signals. Sources may include but not limited to speech, music and other event sounds. Audio signals are typically picked up by microphones in an enclosure, for example, a room, concert hall, auditorium or recording studio. Sound transmitted from the source to the microphones endures a multiple reflection and reverberation process, i.e. an acoustic transmission channel. Such transmission channels are complicated and may have significant impact on the effectiveness of signal processing algorithms for machine audition purposes. But modeling of the acoustic transmission channel is often neglected, resulting in some algorithms working only under controlled conditions. For example, some automatic speech recognition systems cannot handle speech signals picked up in noisy and reverberant spaces, especially when the microphones are placed at a remote distance from source. An equalization pre-processor would be beneficial. Impulse responses of room acoustic transmission channels are extremely long (hundreds and thousands taps) and non-minimum phase. An exact inverse does not exist. Room acoustic parameters as descriptors of an acoustic transmission channel can therefore provide useful information for the design of equalization algorithms.

Motivated by these needs, the use of machine audition of speech or music to determine acoustic parameters of the channel through which the speech and music have been transmitted has been studied, leading to the development of a number of new algorithms and methods. Reverberation Time (RT) is the most common acoustic parameter used for the assessment in room acoustics. Early Decay Time (EDT) was reported to better correlate with human perception of the reverberation effect and hence has become an ever-popular acoustic parameter. Speech Transmission Index (STI) is an IEC standardized objective parameter for speech intelligibility assessment in a space. These parameters are considered in this chapter. Short-time RMS values of received discrete speech utterances, in particular pronounces digits can be used to determine RT and EDT by statistical machine learning with an Artificial Neural Network

Table 1. Overview of proposed acoustic parameter extraction algorithms

	Machine learning on Envelope	**Machine learning on envelope spectra**	**MLE with a dual decay model**
Source	Speech utterances	Running speech or music	Running speech or music
Parameters	Reverberation parameters only	Reverberation parameters and STI	Reverberation parameters only
Source Dependency	Semi-blind	Semi-blind or blind estimation	Blind

(ANN) (Cox, Li & Darlington, 2001a; Cox & Li, 2001b). STI can be accurately determined from received running speech signals with an envelope spectrum estimator and ANNs (Li & Cox, 2001; Li & Cox, 2003). If the background noise level is reasonably low, RT and EDT can be obtained from running speech in a similar way. Speech stimuli have a limited frequency range and therefore can only be used to determine acoustic parameters from 250 Hz to 4 kHz octave bands effectively. Music is considered to solve the problem, but the uneven spectra of music signals mitigate the accuracy. A note-matching filter bank can be used to circumvent the problem (Kendrick et al., 2006; Kendrick et al., 2008). Envelope spectra are a relatively stable feature of anechoic speech. With the aid of eigenvector as a feature space, blind estimation of STI and RT is possible (Li & Cox, 2007). More accurate bind estimations are achieved with multi-decay model based maximum likelihood estimation (Kendrick et al., 2007). These methods are summarized in Table 1 and will be detailed in subsequent sections following a brief summary of definitions of acoustic parameters.

ACOUSTIC TRANSMISSION CHANNELS AND ACOUSTIC PARAMETERS

Propagation of sound from a source to a receiver is modeled as an acoustic transmission channel. Research into room acoustics suggests that such a channel is fairly linear, and impulse response or transfer function is often used to describe the

sound transmission (Kuttruff, 1991). A received sound signal in a room is the convolution of the source and the impulse response from the source to the receiver,

$$r(t) = s(t) \otimes h(t) \tag{1}$$

where $r(t)$, $s(t)$ and $h(t)$ are the received signal, source signal and impulse response of transmission channel respectively. Room reflection models further suggest that the number of reflections increases rapidly as time elapses. In a diffuse field, temporal density of reflections in a room is given by

$$\frac{dN}{dt} = 4\pi \frac{c^3 t^2}{V} \tag{2}$$

where N, c, t and V are number of reflections, sound speed, time and volume of enclosure respectively, rendering an extraordinarily long mix-phase FIR filter. Hundreds of thousands taps are often needed to accurately represent a room impulse response. Figure 1 (left) shows an example of a fairly short room impulse response. In idealized cases, signal energy vanishes gradually following an exponential trend.

Although the impulse response gives complete information about a sound transmission channel, it can hardly be used as a descriptor or index for perceived acoustics of a space due to its high dimensionality. To quantify the acoustics of a space, acoustic parameters are used. They are purposely-defined objective measures that show

Figure 1. An example of a fairly short simulated room impulse response (left); Difference between RT60 or RT30 on a non-linear (dB scale) decay curve (right) (Figure adapted from Cox, Li and Darlington, 2001a)

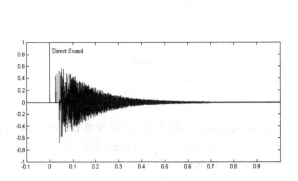

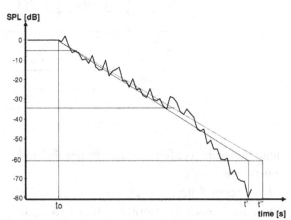

a good correlation with human perception of sound quality or features of acoustics. All objective acoustic parameters can be derived from impulse responses, while some of them can be derived from energy decay curves.

Amongst many objective parameters, reverberation time is the most important and commonly quoted one, because it is strongly correlated to perceived acoustics and is a description of decay rate of sound energy in the space. By definition, reverberation time is referred to as the period of time taken for sound pressure level to decrease by 60 dB within an enclosure after a stationary excitation is switched off abruptly. Reverberation time by this definition is refereed to as RT60. As a modern trend, reverberation time is defined as the 60 dB decay time calculated by a line fit to the portion of the decay curve between -5 and -35 dB. Reverberation time by this definition is denoted as RT30. The use of RT30 avoids the problem of poor signal to noise ratio (SNR) in determining the ending point at −60 dB. However, attentions should be paid to the fact that decay curves of many rooms are not exactly exponential. In the cases of non-exponential decays, RT60 and RT30 become unequal. As shown in Figure 1 (right), the time from t_0 to t' is RT60, while the time from t_0 to

t" is RT30. Another decay time parameter known as Early Decay Time (EDT) is defined as the 60 dB decay time calculated by a line fitting to the 0 to −10 dB portion on the decay curve. When EDT is measured in a completely diffused field, where the decay curve in dB is linear, EDT and RT have the same value. Otherwise, EDT is found to be better correlated with subjective judgment of reverberation than RT30 or RT60. Decay curves can be calculated from the room impulse response using Schroeder's backwards integration method (Schroeder, 1979).

$$\tilde{h}^2(t) = \int_t^\infty h^2(x)dx = \int_0^\infty h^2(x)dx - \int_0^t h^2(x)dx$$
(3)

The ensemble average of all possible decays $\tilde{h}^2(t)$ gives the decay curve, where $h(t)$ is the impose response. It is also worth noting that the rate of sound energy decay in a room is a function of frequency, resulting in different RTs or EDTs in octave bands. It is often required to determine these decay time parameters in octave bands or even 1/3 octave bands. Band-pass filters can be applied to impulse responses before backwards

Table 2. 98 point MTF matrix for STI extraction (Column: 7 octave bands from 125 to 8000Hz; Row: 14 modulation frequencies F from 0.63 to 12.5Hz with 1/3 octave intervals)

	125 Hz	250 Hz	...	4 kHz	8 kHz
0.63 Hz					
0.80 Hz					
...					
10.0 Hz					
12.5 Hz					

integration and curve fitting to determine sub-band acoustic parameters.

For spaces where speech communication is important, Speech Transmission Index (STI) is often used as an objective measure for intelligibility assessment (Houtgast & Steeneken, 1973; Steeneken & Houtgast, 1980; IEC 60268-16:1998, 1998). The rationale of the STI method is that for good speech intelligibility, the envelope of speech signals should be preserved. A transmission channel degrades intelligibility by modifying (smoothening) the envelope of speech signals. The modulation transfer function (MTF) describes such envelope shaping effect and therefore is closely correlated with intelligibility of transmitted speech. A speech spectrum shaped noise carrier $n(t)$ is modulated by a sinusoidal function with a very low frequency (see Table 2)

$$m(t) = \sqrt{1 + m\cos(2\pi Ft)} \qquad (4)$$

to generate a test signal

$$i(t) = n(t) \cdot \sqrt{1 + m\cos(2\pi Ft)} \qquad (5)$$

where F is the modulation frequency and m is the modulation index. The STI method uses the so-formed signals to mimic speech, and identify the envelope shaping effect and additive noise a transmission channel imposes on the signals. To do so, the test signal is applied to the input of a channel under investigation and the output is obtained. The intensity of the excitation and the response can be written as

$$I(t) = I_i[1 + m\cos(2\pi Ft)] \qquad (6)$$

and

$$O(t) = I_o[1 + m_o \cos 2\pi F(t - \phi)] \qquad (7)$$

where m_o is the modulation index of the output intensity function and φ is time delay due to transmission. I_i and I_o are amplitudes of corresponding sinusoidal function (mean intensities). The MFT of a channel is defined as the ratio of m_o to m as a function of modulation frequencies.

$$MTF(F) = \frac{m_o}{m} \qquad (8)$$

The MTF describes envelope shaping and noise injection effects and therefore is closely correlated with intelligibility of transmitted speech. STI is a single index calculated from 98 MTF values at 14 modulation frequencies in seven octave bands as illustrated in Table 2 following 5 steps below:

1. Converting MTF(F) matrix into apparent S/N ratio

$$(S/N)_{app, F} = 10\log(\frac{MFT(F)}{1 - MFT(F)}) \qquad (9)$$

2. Limiting dynamic range to 30 dB

```
if (S/N)app > 15 dB >>
(S/N)app = 15 dB
if (S/N)app < -15 dB >>
(S/N)app= -15 dB
else   (S/N)app=(S/N)app     (10)
```

3. Calculation of mean apparent S/N ratio

$$\overline{(S/N)}_{app} = \frac{1}{14} \sum_{F=0.63}^{12.5} (S/N)_{app}, F \qquad (11)$$

4. Calculation of overall mean apparent S/N by weighting the $(S/N)app,F$ of 7 octave bands

$$\overline{(S/N)}_{app} = \sum w_k \overline{(S/N)}_{app, F} \qquad (12)$$

The values of w_k for the 7 octave bands from 125 Hz to 8 kHz are 0.13, 0.14, 0.11, 0.12, 0.19, 0.17 and 0.14 respectively.

5. Converting to an index ranging from 0 to 1

$$STI = \frac{\overline{(S/N)}_{app} + 15}{30} \qquad (13)$$

If the system is linear, the MTF can alternatively be calculated via the Fourier transform of the squared impulse response according to the following formula under noise free conditions (Schroeder, 1981):

$$MTF(F) = \frac{\left| \int_0^\infty h^2(t)e^{-2\pi jFt}dt \right|}{\int_0^\infty h^2(t)dt} \qquad (14)$$

In the presence of non-trivial ambient noise, the MTF may be determined by the above equation with an additional correction factor:

$$MTF(F) = \frac{\left| \int_0^\infty h^2(t)e^{-2\pi jFt}dt \right|}{\int_0^\infty h^2(t)dt}(1 + 10^{(-S/N)/10})^{-1} \qquad (15)$$

where S/N is the frequency independent signal to noise ratio in dB at listener's location.

It can be seen from the definitions of these room acoustic parameters that extracting room acoustics is a system identification problem in a broad sense or a parameter estimation problem if a decay model is pre-determined. The latter is thought to be more likely to succeed than single channel blind de-convolution to obtain the complete impulse response, because acoustic parameters are dimensionally reduced down to a single value and are often related to energy decay features. In the following sections a number of recently developed algorithms to perform such parameter estimation will be presented and discussed.

EXTRACTION OF REVERBERATION TIME FROM DISCRETE UTTERANCES

Cremer and Müller (1978) discussed the feasibility of extracting reverberation time from live music performances in their classical textbook and postulated that it might be possible to determine the reverberation time from received music signals comprising significant instantaneous energy discrepancies, such as a stop chord followed by a long enough pause for the decay to be measured. Due to the pulsating nature of speech utterance sequences, they are a rich source of instantaneous energy differences; therefore they are also a useful natural sound source for reverberation time estimation. Modeling a speech utterance as a noise burst can shed a light on how speech utterances can be used to determine RTs. When a room is excited by a tone burst or noise burst, the measured short

Figure 2. Exponential build-up and decay of short-time RMS value under noise burst excitation (left); Signatures of anechoic and reverberated speech utterances and their RMS envelopes (normalised amplitude vs time) (Figure adapted from Cox, Li and Darlington, 2001a)

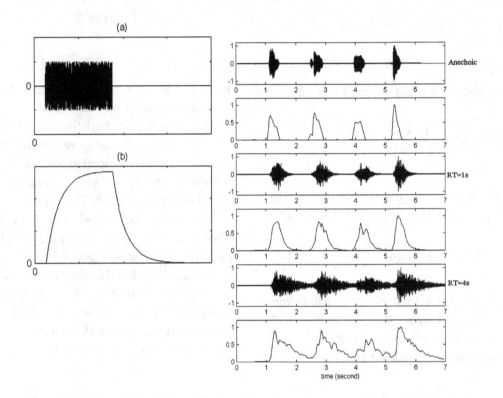

term RMS values of the sound pressure build-up and decay caused by the switch-on and switch-off of the test signal are approximately exponential as illustrated in Figure 2. The exponential decay edge gives information about the reverberation time. In fact reverberation time extraction is simply a problem of estimating the rate of exponential decays.

If Figure 2 (left) was plotted in a logarithmic scale, one could simply perform a straightforward line fitting to determine the RT. Unfortunately, this is an idealized situation. The received signals of speech utterances are much more complicated and noisier than exponentials for a number of reasons: Speech signals are non-stationary stochastic processes, which do not have constant short-term energy like tone bursts. Individual utterances have different build-up and decay

phases. Impulse responses of many rooms are not exactly exponential; impulse responses with two or more decay rates are common due to coupled spaces or non-diffused acoustic fields. A reverberation tail and the next utterance can overlap. Figure 2 (right) shows an anechoic and two reverberated versions of speech utterances "ONE, TWO, THREE, FOUR" read by a narrator and their RMS envelopes. It can be seen from these signatures that the slopes of rise and fall edges are related to reverberation time, the longer the reverberation time the slower the rise and decay in general. But anechoic speech utterances intrinsically have different decay slopes and they are noisy. Estimation of the reverberation time through simple examination of slopes of decay edges (in logarithmic scale) using a straightforward linear regression is simply too inaccurate to be useful.

Figure 3. Neural network system, signal pre-processor and neural network architecture (Figure adapted from Cox, Li and Darlington, 2001a)

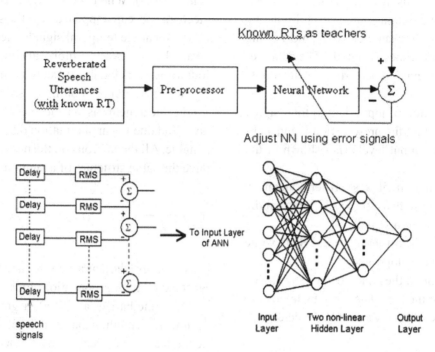

Artificial Neural networks (ANNs) are therefore proposed to accurately extract RTs and EDTs from received signals of pronounced digits (Cox & Li, 2001a). For the algorithm to be useful in room acoustics measurements, the design objective is to reduce estimation errors down to less than 0.1 second or lower than perception limens.

Figure 3 (top) shows a block diagram of the neural network system in its training phase. It follows a typical supervised learning regime. Reverberated speech utterances with known reverberation times are used as training examples. The training examples are pre-processed and conditioned (Figure 3 (bottom, left)) to yield suitable input vectors for the neural network. The ANN outputs and the corresponding true reverberation times (teacher) are compared to obtain the error signal. The training process is to iteratively update the internal synaptic weights of the neural network so that the mean square error between the true and the estimated reverberation times over all the training examples are minimised. In the retrieve

phase, teachers and the network adjustment paths as shown in Figure 3 are removed. Speech utterances as received by a microphone in the space are sent to the trained neural network via the same pre-processor. The trained neural network then gives accurate estimation of reverberation time.

To apply supervised neural network models to a practical problem, it is essential that the training and validation data sets be available. Real room sampling is a convincing way but is almost impossible to obtain the required large data set cross a wide range of RTs. Simulated room impulse responses are used as alternatives. Speech utterances ONE, TWO and THREE are used. The convolution of the anechoic speech utterances and 10,000 simulated room impulse responses with RTs from 0.1 to 5 seconds are performed to generate a large data set. Half of it is used for training, and the other half for validation. Apparently, the ANN is expected to generalize from a limit training set to arbitrary room cases that ANN hasn't seen in the training phase. Generalization is an important concern, and so validation is performed strictly using the data that the ANN hasn't seen in the training phase. In addition, the ANN learns from examples to memorise the feature of stimulus speech signals. The data pre-processor is designed to perform four functions;

1. Normalisation of input data to total signal energy so that the presentation is independent of the input levels (not shown in the diagram),
2. Implementation of a short-term memory mechanism so that a static ANN can handle temporal speech signals,
3. Detection of short-term average RMS value of speech envelope, and
4. Conversion of the input vector to a suitable format for the neural network by taking the difference of two adjacent RMS detectors.

Speech signals are temporal sequences, a multi-tapped delay line with short term RMS value detectors are used to detect the short term average energy changes of the speech signals as illustrated in Figure 3 (left). 2000 point overlapped RMS detectors, providing 10 RMS values per second, are found adequate for speech signals sampled at 16 kHz. This is equivalent to monitoring fluctuations lower than 5 Hz in speech envelope. In this study, unfiltered speech utterances are sent to the above pre-processor. This leads to the wide band reverberation time, which covers the frequency range of speech utterances. For octave band reverberation time extraction, appropriate band-pass filters may be applied to speech signals and related octave band reverberation times used as teacher in the training phase.

A multi-layer feed-forward ANN with two hidden layers of sigmoid neurons as depicted in Figure 3 (bottom, right) is adopted. It has been proven and well known that such networks are effective universal non-linear approximators that can be trained to map arbitrarily complicated non-linear functions, provided that adequate number

of neurons and computing power are used (Cybenco, 1989). When certain short-term memory mechanisms e.g. tapped delay lines, are used, they can handle temporal signals such as speech (Waibel et al., 1989). Empirical comparison has found a network having 40 neurons on input layer, 20 non-linear neurons on the first hidden layer, 5 non-linear neurons on the second non-linear layer and one linear summation output neuron is suitable. All the neurons on the non-linear layers have the same structure of a sigmoid function:

$$y = \frac{1}{1 + e^{-x}} \tag{16}$$

Training of the neural network adopts the popular standard back propagation algorithm (Sanger, 1989; Rumelhart et al.,1986), a gradient-based optimization method that reveals reliable convergence feature, tolerable convergence speed and good generalization capability. For readers who are not familiar with this particular algorithm, a good tutorial and clear explanation can be found in (Kung, 1993). A learning rate (step size) chosen from 0.05 to 0.08 is empirically found suitable for this application. In addition to validating the trained network with the aforementioned validation set. The trained ANN system was also tested using 10 real room sampled impulse responses. This not only further tested the trained network but also validated the simulation algorithm used to generate the training and validation data sets. The errors of neural network estimation over all tests including 10 real room samples (RT from 0.5 to 2.2 seconds) are all within +/- 0.1 second.

As discussed in the previous section, early decay time is another important objective acoustic parameter of acousticians' interest. EDT focuses on the initial 10dB decay period and has been shown to correlate better to subjective response in reverberant fields with continuous signals. The proposed method can also be used to extract EDT from speech utterances in an almost identical way.

The only difference is that the input layer of the neural network needs to be extended to have 60 neurons. This is to ensure the early decay part of the examples is sufficiently sensed. And of course, the true EDT values instead of RTs have to be used as teacher. Testing results show that the maximum error in EDT extraction is 0.06 second.

Generalization to arbitrary discrete utterances was attempted by training the ANN on more speech utterances, but results were not promising. A static neural network with a tapped delay line and RMS detectors simply would be able to handle the complexity of arbitrary speech utterances and determine the reverberation time to the required accuracy. Thus the application of this method is limited to the use of pre-recorded anechoic speech materials as test stimuli. Since the knowledge of speech stimuli is built in the ANN through training, during the measurement, there is no need to monitor the source.

Training the ANN is a one-off process. In the retrieve phase the computational load is very light, RT estimates can be obtained immediately after the recorded speech is played. Rapid assessment is the major advantage of this method when compared with others in subsequent sections.

ESTIMATION OF SPEECH TRANSMISSION INDEX FROM RUNNING SPEECH

STI is a standardized method for the assessment of speech intelligibility of enclosures such as theatres and classrooms (IEC 60268-16:1998, 1998). As summarized in the early part of this chapter, it uses 0.63 Hz - 12.5Hz low frequency sinusoidal modulated noise to simulate speech signals. The modulation transfer function is used to quantify speech envelope shaping and noise interference effects, and thus determines speech intelligibility. If speech signals were truly sinusoidal envelope modulated white noise with equal power per frequency bin, the modulation transfer function

could be easily obtained by subtraction of envelope spectra of received and original speech. For real speech signal this relation become an approximation (Steeneken & Houtgast, 1983; Houtgast & Steeneken, 1972)

$$MTF(F)(dB) \approx Ey(F)(dB) - Ex(F)(dB)$$

$$(17)$$

where $E_X(F)$ and $E_Y(F)$ are the envelope spectra of input and output long-time speech signals of a channel in decibels. The envelope spectra are obtained from squared and low-pass filtered speech signals normalized to total signal energy of the speech excerpt. The envelope spectra are typically obtained from 40-60 seconds speech excerpts to allow statistically meaningful results. Energy of envelope signals lies in a very low frequency band from immediately above DC to about 15 Hz. These frequencies are related to fluctuation of various aspects of running speech as illustrated in Figure 4 (left).

The envelope spectrum subtraction method was validated by empirical results showing that the STI obtained using this approach and the one measured through standard procedure (IEC 60268-16:1998, 1998) have a positive correlation coefficient of 0.971 (Steeneken & Houtgast, 1983). However, both the original paper and the standard pointed out that MTFs obtained from speech envelope subtraction have compromised accuracy. The problem of envelope spectrum subtraction stems from the discrepancy between running speech and low frequency sine wave modulation of speech spectrum shaped noise. Due to the complexity of running speech, an accurate speech model is not available, making it impossible to formulate a precise analytical relationship between the envelope spectra of speech signals and MTFs in a classical sense. Artificial neural network approaches are considered to model such relations through machine learning (Li & Cox, 2001). The proposed neural network model is shown in Fig-

Figure 4. Contributions to speech envelope spectra and representative envelope spectra of running anechoic speech

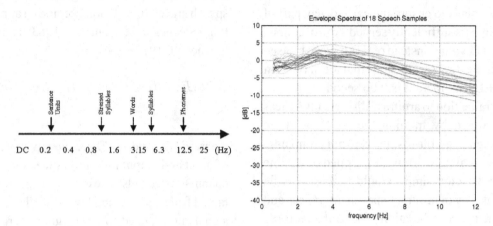

ure 5. It deploys the idea of envelope spectrum subtraction but uses a multi-layer feed-forward network trained by the well-known standard back propagation algorithm to memorize features of speech stimuli and generalize from a large set of impulse responses of different acoustic transmission channels. The trained neural network system can generalize to cases with impulse responses not being included in the training phase and give an estimation accuracy similar to that of the standard method (Typically a better than 0.02 resolution in STI measurements is achievable.). Nevertheless, the model is speech excitation dependent. The information about the speech excitation is built in the network through training. Pre-recorded anechoic speech materials are needed when applying the method in field measurements.

The speech pre-processor is an envelope spectrum analyzer as depicted in Figure 5 (bottom). Running speech signals (60 second excerpts) are band pass filtered obtain signals 7 octave bands as required by the STI method. Speech envelopes are detected using Hilbert transform. For clarity analog format of the equations are given.

$$ev(t) = \sqrt{s^2(t) + s_h^{\;2}(t)} \qquad (18)$$

where $s_h(t)$ is the Hilbert Transform of speech signal *s(t)* defined by

$$s_h(t) = H[s(t)] \equiv \frac{1}{\pi} \int_{-\infty}^{\infty} \frac{s(t - t')}{t'} dt' \qquad (19)$$

Only low frequency contents found in envelope spectra are of room acoustic interest. Envelope signals are lower pass filtered by a 4th order Butterworth filter and resample at 160Hz. The decimated envelope signals are then passed onto an FFT power spectrum estimator to obtain envelope spectra. It is worth noting that the envelope spectra are normalized to average energy of speech signal excerpts, i.e. calibrate the spectrum analyzer so that when a sine wave having a RMS value equal to the mean intensity of the speech signal passes through, 0dB is obtained. The normalization has important practical and physical meanings:

1. Ensuring envelope spectra are not dependent upon input signal levels,
2. Expressing the frequency components of speech envelope with respect to its total (or mean) energy,
3. Reflecting both speech envelope fluctuation and noise level.

Figure 5. System architecture and speech envelope spectrum estimator (Reproduced from Li & Cox 2003)

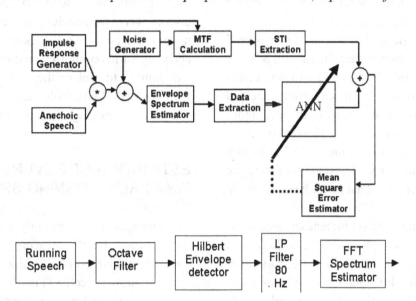

Envelope spectra are frequency domain sampled and fed into the input layer of the neural network. Not surprisingly, the window width and FFT length of the spectrum estimator has a significant impact on obtaining accurate results. According to the standard STI method, 14 data points at central frequencies of 1/3-octave bands from 0.63 Hz to 12.5 Hz are used and find adequate if the system is trained to work with only one pre-recorded particular speech excitation. But for blind estimation, higher frequency resolutions are needed. (Hence the envelope spectra up to 80 Hz are shown in the diagram.)

ANNs are first trained on octave band STI, which is the value obtained following Equations 9 -11 and Equation 13, with the weighting step, i.e. Equation 12, being omitted at this stage. Among various ANNs, non-linear multi-layer feedforward networks trained by back-propagation algorithm as used in the previous section are chosen. It is empirically found that a 14-20-8-1 network performs well over all octave bands. The STI is a normalized index from 0 to 1. A hard limit non-linear neuron at output layer might be used to clamp the output values so that no output can

possibly go beyond the interval of [0 1]. However, it is found that hard limiting the output reduces the back propagation of errors and mitigates the speed of convergence. A linear summation function without non-linear activation function is adopted as the output neuron in the training phase, but output limiting is applied in the retrieve phase. Variable learning rates (step size) are found beneficial in this case. When an output of ANN is beyond the [0 1] interval, larger steps are used to quickly drive the ANN to produce outputs in the [0,1] region. In the final fine tuning period smaller steps are used. No signs of over-training were found before the maximum error in validation tests reduced to below 0.01 STI.

$$\eta = \begin{cases} (1.2 \sim 1.3)\eta & when\ output \notin [0,1] \\ \eta & others \\ (0.3 \sim 0.5)\eta & error \to 0 \end{cases}$$

(20)

14000 simulated impulses responses covering reverberation time from 0.1 to 7 seconds are used and noise added to form the data set. Teacher values are obtained via Schroeder's method according to Equation 15 followed by the standard STI procedures using Equations 9-13.

The STI by definition is considered over 7 octave bands of speech interest. The full STI is a linear combination of STI's in signal octave bands according to Equation 12. This can be implemented with a fixed network structure as shown in Figure 6. Seven neural networks for individual octave bands are training as described in 4.2 to form a bank of neural networks. The outputs of them are processed by the additional linear layer as shown in Figure 6.

The validation data set includes a large number of simulated examples that have not been seen in the training phase and 10 extra real room samples. Results show that the correlation coefficient of the ANN estimated and actual STIs is 0.99987 and maximum prediction error is 0.0181. Therefore, the method offers an alternative to traditional ones to accurately determine STIs in occupied spaces with naturalistic running speech.

Noting that envelope spectra are a relatively stable feature of long-time (40-60 seconds) anechoic speech signals as illustrated in Figure 4 (right), with the intention to achieve blind estimation of STI, training the proposed network with multiple speech excitations was attempted. To obtain the optimal estimation accuracy envelope spectra are taken at 0.5 Hz resolution up to 80Hz

and a 160-40-20-1 network is needed. The training does converge to a relative low mean square error; nonetheless the network does not offer sufficient accuracy (a maximum estimation error of 0.13 was found.) to replace the traditional measurement methods. More sophisticated algorithms are needed to achieve high accuracy blind estimation.

ESTIMATION OF REVERBERATION TIME FROM RUNNING SPEECH

Running speech is apparently a more attractive sound source for the measurement of acoustic parameters. It is therefore considered to extend the above running speech STI method to the extraction of reverberation time. Recall Equation 15: modulation transfer function can be expressed as reverberation and noise terms. If exponential decay is assumed, this can be further written as (Schroeder, 1981)

$$MTF(F) = [1 + (2\pi FRT / 13.8)^2]^{-1/2} \cdot \frac{1}{1 + 10^{(-S/N)/10}}$$

(21)

where F is modulation frequency and RT is reverberation time. It becomes apparent that in noise free cases, the MTF and RT have a nonlinear one-

Figure 6. Combing octave band ANNs to obtain full STI values (Reproduced from Li & Cox 2003)

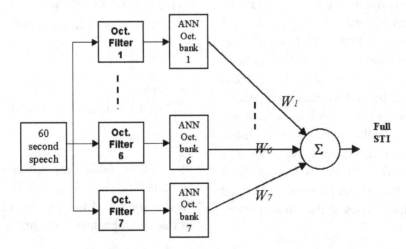

one mapping relation. Therefore the ANN method for STI can be used to extract RTs or EDTs in at least noise free cases. Simulation and validation proved that this would work. If a higher than 45 dB signal to noise ratio is maintained, RT can be accurately determined (error<0.1 second) from running speech using its envelope spectra and proposed machine-learning method (with RT or EDT as teachers in training phase). For more noisy cases, the accuracy will be compromised.

BLIND ESTIMATION USING EIGENVALUES AS A FEATURE SPACE

So far ANN models have developed to accurately extract STIs, RTs, and EDTs from received speech signals. One or one set of ANNs works with a particular speech excitation, as the feature of that particular speech stimulus is built in the ANN through training. This means pre-recorded speech signals have to be used to achieve good accuracy. Feasibility for the above methods to learn from different speech excitations and generalize to arbitrary speech, has been explored but with limited success:- They can provide meaningful estimates but fall short for room acoustics measurement applications. This section looks into the use of an additional feature space for speech excitation to achieve better accuracies in bind estimation.

If the *MTF* can be estimated from the envelope spectra of original and transmitted speech $E_X(F)$ and $E_Y(F)$, *STIs*, and *RTs* can be extracted subsequently. To achieve blind estimation, information about speech stimulus is needed. One possible way to achieve blind estimation is to implement an addition estimator for the $E_X(F)$ from the received speech. It is found that eigenvalues and eigenvectors of the envelope of received speech signals are correlated with reverberation and features of original speech respectively, providing a useful feature space for this application (Li & Cox, 2007).

Figure 7 illustrates eigenvalues and eigenvectors of envelope signals of different speech under diverse reverberation times: 60 second excerpts of 3 different running speech signals (Each row in Figure 7 represents a speech signal.) are convolved with 50 different room impulse responses with RTs from 0.1 to 5s. Envelopes of the reverberated speech signals are estimated, and eigenvalues and vectors of the first principal components of these envelope signals are observed. Figure 7 (left) shows that the principal component eigenvalue of speech envelope monotonically decreases when reverberation time increases. However, the eigenvalues differ when different speech stimuli are used. Figure 7 (right) shows over-plots of the eigenvectors under 50 different RTs. These plots clearly show that individual speech excitations have distinctive eigenvectors. They are robust against RTs of the transmission channel. This means that the eigenvectors are related to the features of anechoic speech and are robust against the channel characteristics, hence providing a useful feature space for speech stimuli. Since principle component eigenvector can be calculated using unsupervised machine learning, this suggests a feasibility of a hybrid ANN model for blind estimation, in which an unsupervised model used to obtain feature space of original speech is added to the supervised models described in previous sections. The hybrid model is illustrated in Figure 8.

The envelope detection and envelope spectrum estimation algorithms are identical to the ones discussed in the previous section. But a higher resolution is needed, from immediately above DC to 25Hz at 0.5 Hz intervals. Eigenvectors of first and second principal components obtained by a Principal Component Analysis (PCA) sub-network from envelope signals and the envelope spectra data are both fed into a supervised neural network. The supervised ANN has distinguishable training and retrieve phases. The PCA subnet is a means to obtain the feature space. So in both training and retrieve phases of the hybrid model,

Figure 7. Eigenvalues and eigenvectors of different speech signal under diverse reverberation times (Reproduced from Li and Cox, 2007)

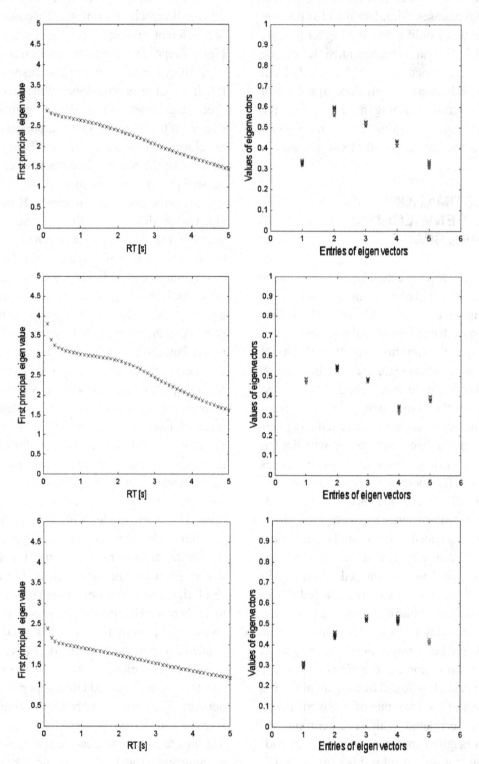

Figure 8. Proposed hybrid model for blind estimation of STI or RT (Reproduced from Li and Cox, 2007)

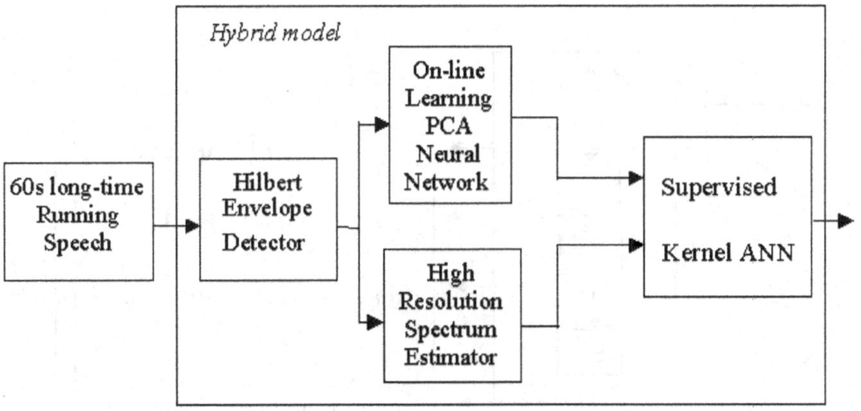

the unsupervised learning to obtain the PCA values is always performed.

The concept of PCA is not new to statisticians and is often used to identify the most representative low dimensional subspaces from a high-dimensional vector space. In statistical signal processing and pattern recognition, the PCA offers an effective method for feature selection. They involve finding the eigenvectors and eigenvalues of the correlation matrix of a data set. The PCA network is a neural computing approach to the PCA problem. A speech envelope signal is a time series. It needs to be converted to correlation matrix before PCA can be performed. An m-tap delay-line and a rectangular window are applied to convert speech envelope signals to a multi-dimensional data space for PCA as depicted in Figure 9. The speech envelope, low-pass filtered at a cut-off frequency of 15Hz and decimated to 40 samples/second, is passed through the delay-line and then windowed to obtain m-dimensional observations. A 125-400ms window is empirically found appropriate. Each column in the data space (reconstruction space) is one observation of the envelope signal. The reconstruction space is used to train a PCA neural network shown in Figure 9.

The PCA network has m inputs and l outputs ($l<m$). The trainable parameters are synaptic weights w_{ij} which connects the ith input to j^{th} neu-ron, where $i=1,2,..m$ and $j=1,2,..l$. The dynamic equation of such a network is

$$y_j(n) = \sum_{i=1}^{m} w_{ji}(n)x_i(n) \qquad (22)$$

and the generalized Hebbian algorithm (GHA) (Sanger, 1989)

$$\Delta w_{ij}(n) = \eta \left[y_j(n)x_i(n) - y_j(n)\sum_{k=1}^{j} w_{ki}(n)y_k(n) \right] \qquad (23)$$

is applied to perform unsupervised learning. The weight w_{ij} of neuron j converges to i^{th} component of the eigenvector related to the jth eigenvalue of the correlation matrix. The outputs are the first l^{th} maximum eigenvalues. The eigenvalues are discarded and the eigenvectors, which are contained in the weights are selected and fed into the supervised final stage.

The final stage of the hybrid model has a supervised ANN kernel. It takes envelope spectra of received speech and the estimated information about envelopes of original speech signals in terms of eigenvectors as inputs and maps these inputs onto STI or RT values. A typical back-propagation network with two layers of hidden neurons and

Figure 9. Converting envelope data to correlation matrix and PCA network (Adapted from Li and Cox, 2007)

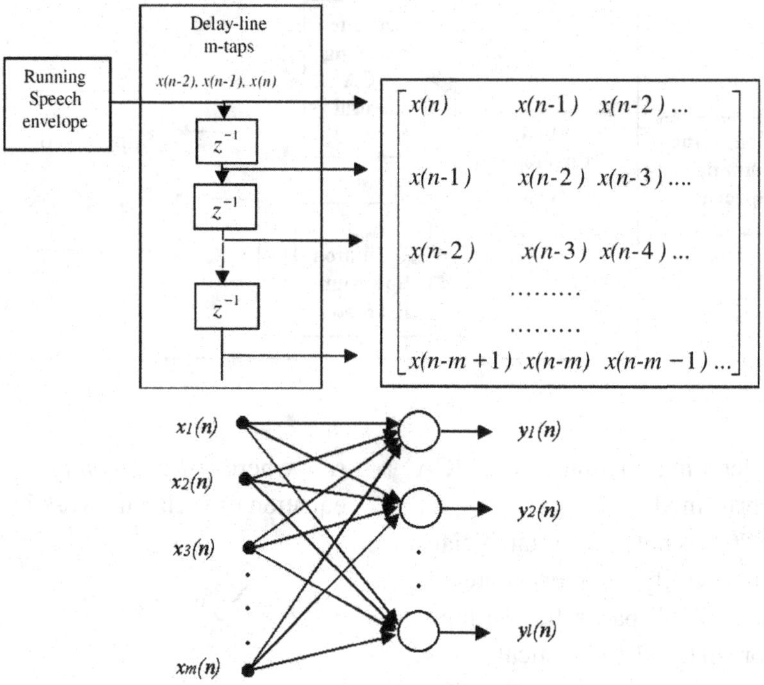

one linear output neuron as used before is again found adequate. The standard neuron model having a linear basis function and sigmoid activation function is used to form the hidden layers. The numbers of neurons on input, non-linear and output layers are 60, 50, 35 and 1 respectively.

The training of the hybrid model follows a typical supervised learning regime. Training and validation examples of received speech are obtained via the convolutions of anechoic speech signals with a large number of impulse responses of transmission channels. The trained hybrid network is tested with acoustic and speech cases not seen in the training phase. The maximum prediction error found in the full range tests was 0.087 for STI extraction. Averaging over a few estimates under different speech stimuli gives improved accuracy.

USING MUSIC AS STIMULI

Speech stimuli have limited frequency contents, and therefore can only be used to determine acoustic parameters in mid octave bands. Experiments show in 250Hz to 4 kHz octave bands, they have sufficient energy and can typically maintain adequate signal to noise ratios for room acoustic parameter extraction in most settings. Music, especially orchestral music is considered as probe stimuli to obtain all octave band room acoustic parameters of music interest. This follows the envelope spectrum based methods outlined above, but the accuracy of estimation in mid-frequency octave bands is not as good as that from speech signals. The spectrum of a speech signal is pretty "full" from 125Hz to about 6300Hz, with no significant discontinuity. Traditional orchestral music, however, follows equal temperament

Figure 10. Envelope spectra for music signals (Reproduced from Kendrick et al., 2006)

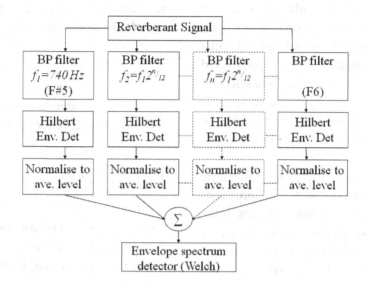

scales. Signal power is centred around discrete frequencies, each related to a note from the scale, and their harmonics. The result is a lack of excitations between notes and uneven spectra biased to particular notes in a piece (major/minor etc). A note matching filter bank is developed to address this issue (Kendrick et al., 2006). For each octave band, the signal is further separated into 12 narrow frequency bands spaced according to the equal temperament scale. Envelope signals for each note are calculated and normalised to the average intensity of that note. Figure 10 gives an example of 12 sub bands within 1kHz octave band. The reverberant signal is passed though the filter bank for 12 notes where the filters' centre frequencies are determined by the equal temperament scale, starting at f#5 ($\approx$740 Hz) in the 1 kHz octave band. Envelope spectrum of the octave band is estimated from the combination of all envelope signals calculated note by note. Thus machine leaning on envelope spectra in room acoustic parameter estimation can be extended to music stimuli. Note matching filters can mitigate the signal to noise ratio problem and help improve estimation accuracy in extracting room acoustic parameters form music signals. After this treatment

over 95% of the reverberation estimates show errors of less than +/-5%, which is generally below human perception limen. It is also worth noting that standard MTF and methods derived around it may not be the best candidate for music stimuli due to non-stationary nature of the signals. Complex Modulation Transfer Function (CMTF) has been previously proposed for music signals. Further work is needed to fully explore the potential of the CMTF in room acoustic parameter estimation.

BLIND ESTIMATION WITH MAXIMUM LIKELIHOOD ESTIMATION

Blind estimation of reverberation time or early decay time can also be achieved using Maximum Likelihood Estimation (MLE) of decay phases found in running speech or music signals based on a suitably chosen decay model. Reverberation time was estimated by performing a maximum likelihood estimation on decays following speech utterances with an exponential decay model (Ratnam et al., 2003). However, the idealised exponential model is based on the assumption of a completely diffused field. Non-exponential or weakly non-exponential decays are commonplace in many rooms. This is why other reverberation parameters, most notably the early decay time, are defined. The single exponential model limits the accuracy of estimation. More sophisticated decay models, signal segmentation and selection can improve the accuracy in blind room acoustic parameter extraction, reducing errors down to below perceptual difference limen (Kendrick et al., 2007).

The MLE is a method used for parametric estimation in statistics. In essence, if there exists a parametric model for a statistical process, in the form of a probability density function f, then the probability that a particular set of parameters θ are the parameters that generated a set of observed data $x_1, x_2, \ldots x_n$ is known as the likelihood L. This is denoted by

$$L(\theta) = f(x_1, x_2 \ldots x_n \mid \theta) \tag{24}$$

An analytic model of an underlying process is first determined and a likelihood function formulated. The parameters that result in a maximum in the likelihood function are, by definition, the most likely parameters that generated the observed set of data. Once the model is chosen and maximum likelihood function formulated, many canned optimization routines can be used to determine the parameter(s) by maximizing the $L(\theta)$.

To succeed, a realistic model for sound pressure decay within a room needs to be defined. One of the problems with previous work (Ratnam et al., 2003) is the assumption that sound energy in acoustic spaces decreases in a purely exponential fashion. It is known that higher order reflections can often decay at different rates than lower order ones because sound fields in rooms are not completely diffuse in most cases. For this reason a new model of sound decay that can account for non-exponential decay curves is proposed.

Let a room impulse response $h[n]$ be modeled as a random Gaussian sequence $r[n]$ modulated by a decaying envelope, $e[n]$.

$$h[n] = e[n]r[n] \tag{25}$$

where n is the sample number. The envelope is represented by a sum of exponentials:

$$e[n] = \sum_{k=1}^{M} \alpha_k a_k^{\ n} \tag{26}$$

where a_k represent decay rates, α_k are weighting factors and M is the number of decays. If two decay rates are chosen, it can be weighted by a single factor.

$$e[n] = \alpha a_1^{\ n} + (1 - \alpha)a_2^{\ n} \tag{27}$$

where a_1 and a_2 represent the two decay rates and α is a weighting factor that changes the level of contribution from each individual decay. This enables the representation of an energy response with a non-uniform decay rate and by changing α the model can adapt to best fit the decay phases. Figure 11 shows the sum of two exponentials models with different decay rates in early and late parts on a decay curve, where the factor α acts to define a knee point where the influence of the two decay rates cross over from a_1 to a_2.

More exponentials, as formulated in Equation 26, can be used to model the decay but at the cost of extra computational overhead when optimizing the likelihood function. However, as the end result of this processing is to calculate reverberation parameters which are necessarily 'averaged' over a considerable amount of the decay, using a great number of exponentials and trying to fit the fine detail of the decay is unnecessary and counter productive. It is empirically found in the current study that the setting with two decay rates is sufficient in vast majority of room cases. The likeli-

Figure 11. A dual exponential decay model can model non-uniform decay, where the faster decaying exponential dominates the early part of the decay curve, and the slower decaying exponential controls the late part of the decay. Decay curves obtained from three different weighting factors are illustrated. (Reproduced from Kendrick et al. 2007)

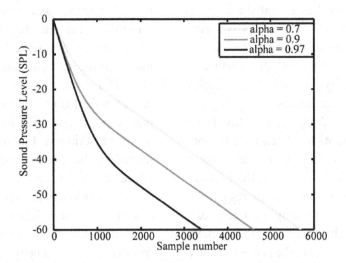

hood of a sequence of independent, identically distributed, Gaussian variables occurring is given by (Weisstein, 2006):

$$L(r,\sigma,\mu) = \prod_{n=0}^{N-1} \frac{1}{\sqrt{2\pi}\sigma} e^{\left(-\frac{(r[n]-\mu)^2}{2\sigma^2}\right)} \qquad (28)$$

where μ is the mean and σ^2 the variance of the Gaussian process. The room impulse response model has no DC component, so $\mu=0$. For the decay phases found in reverberated sounds s, the envelope is of interest. Thus the probability of the sequence, which has a zero mean and is modulated by an envelope e, is given by;

$$L(s;\sigma,e) = \prod_{n=0}^{N-1} \frac{1}{\sqrt{2\pi}e[n]\sigma} e^{\left(-\frac{s[n]^2}{2e[n]^2\sigma^2}\right)} \qquad (29)$$

This can be rearranged to give:

$$L(s,\sigma,e) = e^{\left(\sum_{n=0}^{N-1} \frac{-s[n]^2}{2e[n]^2\sigma^2}\right)} \left(\frac{1}{2\pi\sigma^2}\right)^{N/2} \prod_{n=0}^{N-1} \frac{1}{e[n]} \qquad (30)$$

The proposed decay model Equation 2 is substituted into Equation 30. It is more convenient to work with a logarithmic likelihood function, since the multiplication becomes summation. The log likelihood function is

$$\ln\left\{L(s,\sigma,a_1,a_2,\alpha)\right\} = -\sum_{n=0}^{N-1} \frac{\left[\alpha a_1^n + (1-\alpha)a_2^n\right]^{-2} s[n]^2}{2\sigma^2}$$
$$-\frac{N}{2}\ln(2\pi\sigma^2) - \sum_{n=0}^{N-1} \ln\left[\alpha a_1^n + (1-\alpha)a_2^n\right] \qquad (31)$$

As a Gaussian process has been assumed, maximizing the log likelihood function with respect to the decay parameters α, a_1 and a_2 yields the most likely values for these parameters. This is achieved by minimizing the minus log-likelihood function. Many existing algorithms or canned routines can perform the required optimization. The Sequential

Quadratic Programming (SQP) type of algorithm is found suitable for this application (Fletcher, 2000). Once the parameters in Equation 27 are determined, the decay curve is obtained. Room Acoustic parameters can be calculated according to their standard definitions from the decay curve. In addition to blind estimation, another attractive feature of this new and improved MLE method is its ability to obtain decay curves, which are useful in diagnosing acoustic problems.

The dual decay model MLE method for RT and EDT extractions has been tested rigorously using anechoic speech and music excerpts convolved with 20 real room sampled impulse responses and 100 simulated impulse responses. The method relies on exploiting the free decay phases found in speech or music. Speech signals provide an ideal excitation in the sense that they contain many free decays for analysis. Typically, a 90 second excerpt of running speech from an untrained narrator is sufficient for accurate estimations. When speech stimuli are used, the dual decay MLE algorithm shows reduced prediction errors to below subjective difference limens in most cases, hence providing a useful tool for measuring rooms. But, the limited bandwidth of speech stimulus causes problems at low frequencies. When the algorithm is applied to received orchestral music signals, however, the estimates tend to be less accurate than those obtained from speech. This is not surprising, because music often lacks free decay phases sufficiently long for reverberation time estimation. The accuracy to some extent depends upon the style of music used. Details about estimation errors of speech and music based measurements using the dual decay MLE method can be found in (Kendrick et al., 2007).

CONCLUDING REMARKS

Estimation of acoustic parameters of sound transmission channels via machine audition of transmit-ted speech or music signals has many potential applications. It enables the acquisition of occupied acoustic data of spaces such as concert halls and theatres. It also facilitates in-situ acoustic channel modeling and subsequently provides information for on-line/real time channel equalisation. When blind estimation is applied, a signal pre-processor might be designed to compensate and equalize channel distortions and so improving the performance of further machine auditions such as automated speech recognitions and automated music score transcription. Last but not least, acoustic parameters have been developed and extensively tested over 100 years. It is known that they have good correlation to perceived sound characteristics or acoustic features. To some extent, machine audition to obtain acoustic parameters, might be viewed from a cognitive science perspective as mimicking certain low level of perception using a computer. The work so far has reached the status that decay curves and some major acoustic parameters can be accurately estimated (errors similar or below to human perception limen), with the advance of signal processing techniques, it is hoped that complete impulse responses might be determined in a blind fashion. The use of naturally occurring signals to perform in-situ and non-invasive blind system identification is an interesting area of research not only in acoustics but also in many other scientific and engineering applications.

REFERENCES

Cox, T. J., Li, F., & Darlington, P. (2001a). Extraction of room reverberation time from speech using artificial neural networks. *Journal of AES, 49*(4), 219–230.

Cox, T. J., & Li, F. F. (2001b), Using Artificial Intelligence to Enable Occupied Measurements of Concert Hall Parameters. *Proc. 17th ICA,* 3A.08.05. Italy.

Cremer, L., & Müller, H. Translated by T. Schultz (1978). *Principles and Applications of Room Acoustics, 1*,(p. 194), London: Applied Science.

Cybenco, G. (1989). Approximation by super-positions of a sigmoidal function. *Mathematics of Control, Signals, and Systems, 2*, 303–314. doi:10.1007/BF02551274

Fletcher, R. (2000). *Practical Methods of Optimization*. New York: John Wiley.

Houtgast, T., & Steeneken, H. J. M. (1972). Envelope spectrum and intelligibility of speech in enclosures. *IEEE-AFCRL 1972 Speech Conference Proceedings*(pp. 392-395).

Houtgast, T., & Steeneken, H. J. M. (1973). The modulation transfer function in room acoustics as a predictor of speech intelligibility. *Acustica, 28*, 66–73.

IEC 60268-16:1998 (1998). *Sound system equipment, Part 16: Objective rating of speech intelligibility by speech transmission index.*

Kendrick, P., Cox, T. J., Li, F. F., Zhang, Y., & Chambers, J. A. (2008). Monaural room acoustic parameters from music and speech. *The Journal of the Acoustical Society of America, 124*(1), 278–287. doi:10.1121/1.2931960

Kendrick, P., Cox, T. J., Zhang, Y., Chambers, J. A., & Li, F. F. (2006, May). Room Acoustic Parameter Extraction from Music Signals. *Proc. ICASSP 2006, 5*, DOI: 10.1109/ICASSP.2006.1661397, Kendrick, P., Li, F. F., Cox, T. J., Zhang, Y. & Chambers, J. A. (2007). Blind Estimation of Reverberation Parameters for Non-Diffuse Rooms. *Acta Acustica united with Acustica, 93* (5), 760-770.

Kung, S. Y. (1993). *Digital Neural Network*. Hoboken, NJ: Prentice-Hall.

Kuttruff, H. (1991). *Room Acoustics*. Elsevier Science Publishers Ltd.

Li, F. F., & Cox, T. J. (2001, May). Extraction of Speech Transmission Index from Speech Signals Using Artificial Neural Networks, 110th AES convention (paper 5354). Amsterdam

Li, F. F., & Cox, T. J. (2003). Speech transmission index from running speech: A neural network approach. *The Journal of the Acoustical Society of America, 113*(4), 1999–2008. doi:10.1121/1.1558373

Li, F. F., & Cox, T. J. (2007). A neural network model for speech intelligibility quantification. *J. Applied Soft Computing, 7*(1), 145–155. doi:10.1016/j.asoc.2005.05.002

Polack, J. D., Alrutz, H., & Schroeder, M. R. (1984). The modulation transfer function of music Signals and its Application to reverberation measurement. *Acustica, 54*, 256–265.

Ratnam, R., Jones, D. L., Wheeler, B. C., O'Brien, W. D. Jr, Lansing, C. R., & Feng, A. S. (2003). Blind estimation of reverberation time. *The Journal of the Acoustical Society of America, 114*, 2877–2892. doi:10.1121/1.1616578

Rumelhart, D. E., Hinton, G. E., & Williams, R. J. (1986). Learning internal representations by error propagation. In *Parallel distributed processing: Exploration in the Microstructure of Cognition. 1*, 318-362.Cambridge, MA: MIT Press.

Sanger, T. D. (1989). Optimal unsupervised learning in a single-layer linear feed-forward neural network. *Neural Networks, 12*, 459–473. doi:10.1016/0893-6080(89)90044-0

Schroeder, M. (1981). Modulation Transfer Functions: Definition and Measurement. *Acustica, 49*, 179–182.

Schroeder, M. R. (1979). Integrated impulse method measuring sound decay without impulses. *J. Acoust. Am., 66*(2), 497–500. doi:10.1121/1.383103

Steeneken, H. J. M., & Houtgast, T. (1980). A physical method for measuring speech transmission quality. *The Journal of the Acoustical Society of America, 67*(1), 318–326. doi:10.1121/1.384464

Steeneken, H. J. M., & Houtgast, T. (1983). The temporal envelope spectrum of speech and its significance in room acoustics. *11th ICA conference publication* Paris.

Waibel, A., Hanazawa, T., Hinton, G., Shikano, K., & Lang, K. J. (1989). Phoneme recognition using time-delay neural networks. *IEEE Transactions on Acoustics, Speech, and Signal Processing, 37,* 328–339. doi:10.1109/29.21701

Weisstein, E. (2006). *Wolfram Mathworld*, Eric Weisstein. Retrieved December 2009, from http://mathworld.wolfram.com/

Chapter 19
Neuromorphic Speech Processing:
Objectives and Methods

Pedro Gómez-Vilda
Universidad Politécnica de Madrid, Spain

José Manuel Ferrández-Vicente
Universidad Politécnica de Madrid, Spain

Victoria Rodellar-Biarge
Universidad Politécnica de Madrid, Spain

Roberto Fernández-Baíllo
Universidad Politécnica de Madrid, Spain

Agustín Álvarez-Marquina
Universidad Politécnica de Madrid, Spain

Rafael Martínez-Olalla
Universidad Politécnica de Madrid, Spain

Víctor Nieto-Lluis
Universidad Politécnica de Madrid, Spain

Luis Miguel Mazaira-Fernández
Universidad Politécnica de Madrid, Spain

Cristina Muñoz-Mulas
Universidad Politécnica de Madrid, Spain

ABSTRACT

Current trends in the search for improvements in well-established technologies imitating human abilities, as speech perception, try to find inspiration in the explanation of certain capabilities hidden in the natural system which are not yet well understood. A typical case is that of speech recognition, where the semantic gap going from spectral time-frequency representations to the symbolic translation into phonemes and words, and the construction of morpho-syntactic and semantic structures find many hidden phenomena not well understood yet. The present chapter is intended to explore some of these facts at a simplifying level under two points of view: that of top-down analysis provided from speech perception, and the symmetric from bottom-up synthesis provided by the biological architecture of auditory pathways. An application-driven design of a Neuromorphic Speech Processing Architecture is presented and its performance analyzed. Simulation details provided by a parallel implementation of the architecture in a supercomputer will be also shown and discussed.

DOI: 10.4018/978-1-61520-919-4.ch019

INTRODUCTION

Cognitive Speech Processing is a new concept in which traditional speech processing tasks such as speech recognition, speaker identification, language identification or emotion detection are examined under the point of view of speech processing in the auditory pathways and higher centers to contribute new ideas or paradigms directly inspired in the natural processing, in a first step to better understand how the real system processes speech, and in a second step to improve current processing results. In doing so, a preliminary review of speech processing in the auditory centers is mandatory. This is done under two different points of view: to the light of current knowledge in neurophysiology of the auditory pathways (Physiological Level: PhL) and under the perceptual point of view (Psychoacoustical or Perceptual Level: PsL). This approach is funded in the facts that neurophysiological knowledge is far from being complete, many important questions being still open, and responses are to be complemented from knowledge in the PsL. As the PsL can only reveal observations from the systemic behavioral response, the methodological approach must rely in the formulation of work hypotheses to be contrasted against physiological evidence by means of computer simulations. The general structure of the chapter will respond to this methodological reflection. First most relevant knowledge for the study from well-established facts at the PsL will be reviewed in the section background (sub-section Perceptual Facts), followed by a similar review at the PhL sub-section Neuro-Physiological Facts). This will be followed by the proposition of a bottom-up methodology in section Neuromorphic Speech Processing where a Neuromorphic Hierarchical Architecture for Speech Processing (NHASP) is presented. Results from current simulations will be presented and discussed in the section Some Selected Results. Future research lines will also

be reviewed (section Future Research Directions). The section conclusions will close the work presenting the most relevant reflections derived from the research discussed.

BACKGROUND

The issue of bio-inspired or neuromorphic speech processing has been a matter of discussion since audition started to be studied scientifically (Helmholz, 1885). But it is since mid-twentieth century when the advancement in physiological and psychological studies opened a new door to a set of applications, such as hearing aids and prostheses, which had to rely in a serious systemic comprehension of the processes involved, requiring the formulation and testing of new systemic paradigms (Gold & Pumphrey, 1948, Gold, 1948, Flanagan, 1960a, Flanagan, 1960b). The interest in cochlear modeling (Allen, 1985) produced results as gammatone filters (Katsiamis, 2007) which were directly inspired in the time-frequency filtering capabilities of the Peripheral Auditory System (PAS). Many works were conducted to infer if these methods could be applied in general speech processing (Ghitza, 1988). Part of this research was also applied to the construction of integrated circuits reproducing the behavior of the PAS for intra-cochlear stimulation (López-Poveda, 2001). The proposition of using bio-inspired knowledge in speech processing came as a consequence, which raised immediate answers both in support and in opposition to the underlying idea. This controversy was neatly expressed by Hynek Hermansky (1997) in his famous sentence "Should speech recognizers have ears?" The answer to this important question is given by Hermansky himself: speech perception is very robust to noise, channel distortions, or multiple source effects. Besides, he claimed that bio-inspiration was already present in speech processing in Bark and Mel Scales, equi-loudness curves, Perceptual Linear Predic-

Figure 1. Speech Production Model of G. Fant. The model is explained as a chain of a Source Excitation and a Filter Modulator. Accordingly with the voiced or voiceless nature of speech the excitation may be seen as a pseudo-periodic or harmonic process or as a pseudo-random or noisy one.

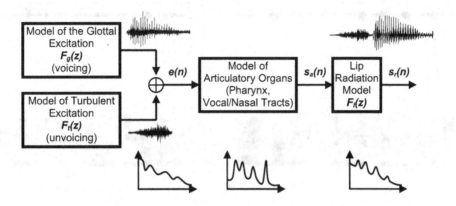

tion (PLP) and RASTA-PLP, etc. To this list MP3 should be also added (Brandenburg & Stoll, 1992). The underlying main question would be why it is necessary to replicate the way the Auditory Pathways and Cortex (AP&C) process speech. The answer to this question is clearly stated by Greenberg & Ainsworth (2004) and can be summarized as follows: classical speech processing is too much based in short-time spectral feature descriptions. Currently specific limits seem to exist in using only that approach. Many researchers feel that time-frequency descriptions, prosody and syllabic nuclei detection inspired in neural processing may offer alternative ways to improve current methods in speech processing. Given the inspired nature of this proposal on the knowledge derived from the neural processing in AP&C, the adequate description for this methodology should be that of Bio-Inspired or Neuromorphic Speech Processing (BINSP). Since Hermansky formulated that question many works have pointed out in the direction of bio-inspiration and improvements in the knowledge of PhL, and PsL have also provided a better background to move towards introducing neuromorphic knowledge in speech processing (Sarpeshkar, 2006).

Perceptual Facts

Speech may be defined as a communication-oriented activity consisting in the production of a sequence of sounds which convey a complex information code derived from language. The production of speech is very well represented by Gunnar Fant's Model as depicted in Figure 1.

The productive process of speech may be induced either by the vibration of the vocal folds (glottal excitation) or by a turbulent excitation regime generated at the constraints of the vocal tract, or by both. The spectral characteristics of both excitation signals are quite different, in the first case being organized as spectral bands at multiples of the fundamental frequency (pitch), or as wide-band colored noise bursts in the second case. The spectral profile of the excitation $e(n)$ is configured by the vocal and nasal tracts, at certain resonant and anti-resonant bands. These may be dynamically modified by the articulation organs, producing a signal $s_a(n)$ which conveys all the characteristics of speech. This signal is radiated mainly through lips and when captured by a microphone results in recorded speech $s_r(n)$.

The description of speech may be given in time by the direct recording of the pressure sound

Figure 2. a) Sentence –She can scoop these things into three red bags, and we will go meet her Wednesday at the train station- by a male speaker. b) FFT spectrogram. c) LPC spectrogram

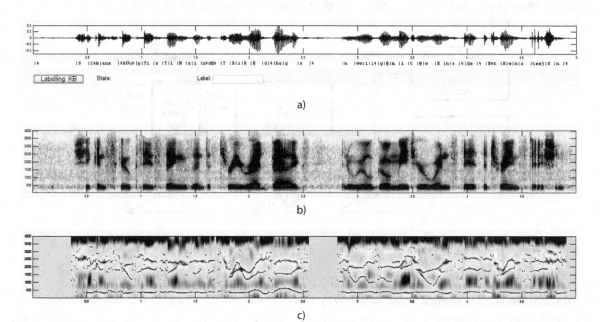

waves captured by the microphone. But much of the clues to perceive speech are coded in the frequency domain. This is why speech is commonly represented in time and frequency plots known as spectrograms. Figure 2 gives an example of two types of spectrogram associated to the wave sound in the time domain corresponding to the sentence –*She can scoop these things into three red bags, and we will go meet her Wednesday at the train station-* as adapted from (SAA, 2009).

The realization of the sentence would correspond to the loose phonetic transcription:

[ʃi:kænz.küu:pði:sθiŋzində.θʃi: ʃɛd.bægs.. nω'ωilgəmi:təʃωɛnz.de.ɛ.tʃens.te:jʃn]

This transcription in the Kirshenbaum Alphabet (KB, 2009) would correspond to:

[Sik&nzkUupDisTiNzind@TRiREd.b&gs.. nw'wilg@mit@RwEnz.deEtRenstejSn]

When observed in the time domain, it may be appreciated that speech is produced as a chain of lumps, which may be compared to beads in a necklace. These show pseudo-periodic spike-like patterns, and correspond mainly to vowel-like bursts. In between, the activity may be residual (background noise) or dominated by less intense sounds (30-50 dB below) which do not show such organized or pseudo-periodic activity. The FFT spectrogram is composed mainly by horizontal bands of energy spaced by a common interval in frequency, which is the fundamental frequency f_0 or pitch. These are known as *harmonics* and convey information about the timbre of speech, which is ultimately related with the speaker's identity as well as with prosody. The LPC spectrogram is composed by pseudo-bands of intensity which sometimes are more or less horizontal, and at times bend in specific patterns. These are known as *formants* and convey information about the coloring of speech, but besides, the three lowest ones contribute important communication or message clues. There are other intervals where speech activity distribution is mainly vertical. These patterns are known as Noise Bursts (NB) and correspond to segments where speech is produced without phonation (voice-less speech). It may be seen that the intervals where formants are present correspond with the segments in time where the pseudo-periodic spike-like activity is also present. The clues which convey the minimum amount of meaning in each part of speech are known as "semantic atoms", or "minimum features" or "information-bearing elements (IBE's)". These can be classified according to the following IBE-taxonomy:

- Inactive intervals
  - ○ Long. If the intervals between speech activity bursts are larger than 50 ms. they are interpreted as speech separating intervals, orthographically represented by commas (,) or periods (.)
  - ○ Short. Below this time silence intervals or activity-reduced intervals are associated to the instants previous to the insertion of stop consonants. Their duration is very important to establish the quality of the stop.
- Active intervals
  - ○ Voiced. When vocal folds are vibrating the FFT spectrogram will show the characteristic harmonic bands. The LPC spectrogram will show the presence of well defined formant bands. These intervals may be further specified as:
    - ▪ Static. The position of the formant changes in less than 10% around an average value within the syllabic interval.
    - ▪ Dynamic. The position of the formant from the starting point to the ending point varies significantly more than 10% within the syllabic interval.
  - ○ Unvoiced. When vocal folds are inactive. The LPC or FFT spectrograms show irregularly distributed broad vertical bands. In whispered speech these may be further specified as:
    - ▪ Static. If the positions of the broad noisy peaks show a stable value according with the above definition.
    - ▪ Dynamic. If the position of the broad noisy peaks vary significantly according with the above definition.

Under the perceptual point of view the most explicit patterns are those associated to vowel-like sounds, as they convey the highest energy in speech. The intervals where formants are more static correspond to vowel-like nuclei. Observe that this definition is broader than the usual division into vowels and consonants. Vowels are those sounds (but not only) encoded as /a, æ, ɛ, e, i, o, ə, u/. But also /l, ʃ, ω, j, m, n, ŋ/ may behave both as vowels or consonants, depending on the preceding or following sounds. For example, /l/ may behave as consonant in –like- broadly produced as /lajk/ or as vowel in –Michael- broadly produced as –majkl-, or /n/ behaving as consonant in –nose- (/nəωs/) or as vowel in –station- (/stejʃn/). For this reason they are quoted as vowel-like sounds. The intervals with less stable formants, or unvoiced, or short inactive, correspond with consonant-like onsets. The sequence of a consonant-like with a vowel-like interval corresponds with the concept of syllable. Another important feature in speech sounds, which is already related with the mentioned ones is the articulation place. This concept is associated to the place(s) where the vocal tract narrows, resulting in strong coloring of the source spectrum by the filter in Fant's Model. Although narrows can occur at almost any place along the vocal tract classically four positions are taken as the most influential under the spectral point of view: (F) front (lips, teeth), (MF) mid-front (alveolus),

(MB) mid-back (pre-post palate), and (B) back (velum). Other important features in the case of vowels are their round or oval characteristic. The following table gives some examples of speech sounds accordingly with the above description:

The International Phonetic Alphabet (IPA, 2009) and the Kirshenbaum Phonetic Alphabet (KB, 2009) have been used alternatively when convenient throughout this paper. Some examples of the features described in the above IBE-taxonomy may be found in Figure 3.

The main IBE's which are to be taken into account under the point of view of articulatory significance are the following: the presence/absence of voicing, the presence of stable formants, the dynamic behavior of unstable formants, the presence of noise bands (vertically distributed), and the duration of silences. Based on this accounting a Generalized Phoneme Structure such as the one in Figure 4 may be proposed.

An example of what is being exposed may be found in Figure 5. The formant positions and trajectories of the four approximants [β, ð, ζ, γ] (front, mid-front, mid-back, back) articulated with vowel [a] are given to illustrate the stable vowel positions and the consonant loci (Sussman, McCaffrey, & Mathews, 1991).

As in a riddle the reader should perceive how these trajectories point to specific vowel triangle positions, and guess where those trajectories are aiming to. It is not difficult to infer that the corresponding loci are related with [ɛ], [ə], and [o], respectively. Some researchers believe that this is the true clue to the articulatory or motor theory which is used by the human auditory perception to model speech variability and to construct the corresponding invariant representation space of phonemes (Greenberg & Ainsworth, 2004). The main difference in the perception of formant positions as vowels or consonants seems to be related to the time the formants remain stable or at least varying below a specific percentage of the average position. Rapid movements between frequencies produce the immediate perception of

consonantal behavior. For example, in the case of [ζ] the transition in the first formant goes from 850 to 400 Hz in about 150 msec, which roughly speaking implies a slope of 3 $Hz.s^{-1}$, whereas the second formant moves from 1300 to 1900 Hz in the same time, implying a slope of 4 $Hz.s^{-1}$. Summarizing, it appears that the following facts convey meaning: the presence of organized doublets of formants are immediately perceived as vowels or vowel-like sounds; the rapid changes in these doublets are immediately perceived as consonants; the presence of broad-band noise-like voiceless bursts associated with rapid formant changes are also perceived as consonants. The degree of closure goes from the most open (vowel-like) through the dynamic (approximants) to the closest (voiceless or stops). The articulation information seems to be strongly tied to the distributions of the first two formants on the vowel triangle, and to the loci theory. Front articulations are associated with a high second formant, back articulations are associated with a low second formant. On its turn close vowels tend to show a low first formant, whereas open vowels tend to show a high first formant. In the sequel the process to detect these features from a neuro-physiological point of view will be reviewed at the light of recent findings.

Neuro-Physiological Facts

The development of speech in humans seems to be based on the creation of Hierarchical Representation Spaces from simple features to complex sounds at the auditory aystem and centers (Rauschecker & Scott, 2009). Representation spaces are specific sets of neural structures specialized in detecting and assigning semantics to the IBE's described before. Specific high-level representation spaces are unique for the human beings, as a consequence of speech development but this fact does not exclude that other lower-level structures may be shared with non-speaking animal species (Suga, 2006). The study of the structure and functionality of these representation spaces (static

Figure 3. Examples studied. From top to bottom: a) First 1-sec segment of the sentence under study, corresponding to the segment: [.Sik&nzkUup]. b) Second segment corresponding to [DisTiNzind@ TRiR]. c) Id. for [Ed.b&gs.nw]. d) Id. for [wilg@mit@RwEnz.d]. e). Id. for [eEtRenstejSn]. Examples of short and long inactive intervals corresponding to [%] can be found in c). An example of a voiced static vowel corresponding to [&] may be found in the same segment. An example of a voiced static wowel-like sound corresponding to [N] may be found in b). An example of a voiced dynamic consonant-like sound corresponding to the first and second [R] may be found in the same segment. Examples of voiced dynamic consonants may be found as [b] in c) or as the second [w] in d). Examples of unvoiced static consonants as [S] may be found in a) and e). An example of an unvoiced dynamic consonant is to be found as the first [t] in e).

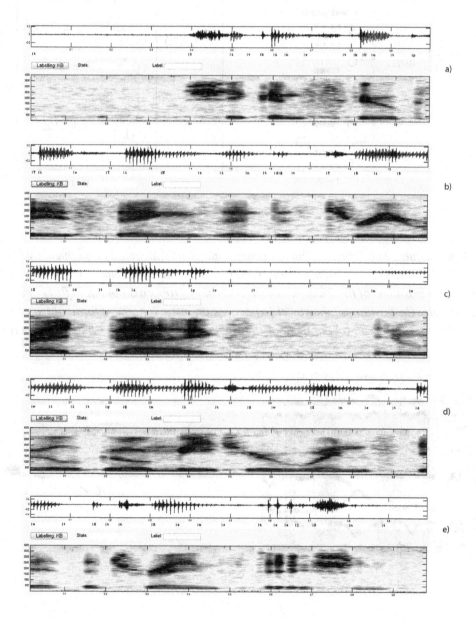

Figure 4. Left. Generalized Phoneme Structure (GPD). Important formant-like bands are F_g (glottal formant, contributed by the source), F_n (nasal formant, present in nasal-like sounds), F_1 and F_2 (message-bearing formants), F_3 and upper formants (related with speaker identity), the loci (L_{11}, L_{21}, L_{24}, L_{25}) pointing to the starting and ending places of the first two formants previous to formant stabilization during the vowel onset time (VOT) and the noise vertical bands or bursts usually referred as 'blips', which may extend in small bands, and can be clearly seen in the two [t] in Figure 3.e. Right: Loci the GPD on the F_2 vs F_1 vowel triangle. White circles indicate the positions of the loci. The dark dot gives the position of the specific vowel modeled (/a/ in the present case).

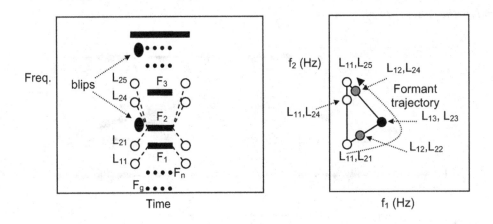

Figure 5. Left: Sequence of formants for the group /aβa:aða:aʑa:aɣa/. The segments where formants are stable (shaded frames) correspond to the vowel nuclei. The complementary in-between segments correspond to the positions of the fricative voiced consonants (approximants). Left: Loci of the GPD on the vowel triangle: the position of the vowel [a] acts as an attractor where formant trajectories depart from and arrive to. Consonant loci of the four approximants are labeled with their respective names.

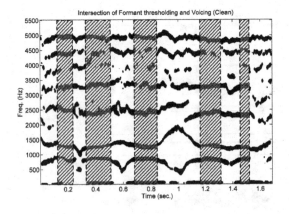

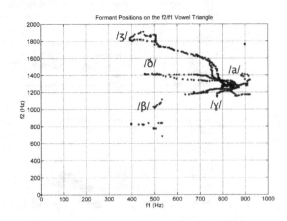

and dynamic) remains incomplete due to the enormous richness of neural phenomena which can be detected in the auditory pathways as revealed from direct measurements. The determination of the specific neural structures involved in speech processing and their precise functionality is one of the most difficult problems faced in the field, as direct in vivo measurements is affected by the highly aggressive nature of the testing techniques, which motivate that most of the neurophysiologic tests have been conducted on animal models (Mendelson & Cynander, 1985), (Rauschecker, Tian, & Hauser, 1995), (Schreiner, 1995), (Secker & Searle, 1990), (Shamma, 1985), (Yin, Ma, El-hilali, Fritz, & Shamma, 2007). Other sources of knowledge are based on indirect evidence from studying perceptual alterations in humans after brain damage, either induced by illness or by external injuries (Ojemann, 1990, 1991, Schreiner, 1995, Corina et al., 2005). Only recently functional magnetic resonance imaging (fMRI) and magneto-encephalography (MEG) have been introduced as real-time introspection tools, although with the limitations in resolution assumed by these promising technologies (FitzGerald, et al., 1997, Buchsbaum, Hickok, & Humphries, 2001, Poeppel, 2003, Gandour, et al., 2007).

With these conditionings in mind a brief review of the most relevant facts in the knowledge of the basic processing functions of specific neural tissue from neurophysiologic evidence are exposed. Needless to say, this overview will not intend to give a complete description of the important time-frequency processing which takes place in the different neural structures (which is still far from being available), but to summarize some of the main phenomena of interest for speech processing under the perceptual point of view: tone intensity and pitch perception, harmonic and formant estimation, noise-like broadband signal perception, amplitude and frequency modulation, vowel onset, sustain and decay detection and its relation to consonant perception, etc. not to speak of sound source location and binaural

hearing, which will not be treated here. The next step to be covered is to disentangle the operation of the auditory pathways under the point of view of speech processing. For such Figure 6, adapted from (Goldstein, 1984) will be taken into account.

The description will start from the point where speech-induced activity in the auditory nerve takes place after time-frequency separation and transduction in the auditory peripheral system (Allen, 2008). Speech processing in the auditory system starts when acoustic signals arrive to the cochlea through the outer and middle ear. Frequency and time separation of signal components is produced in the basilar membrane, along the cochlea (see Figure 6), operating as a filter bank (Allen, 1985). Low frequencies produce maximum excitation in the apical end of the membrane, while high frequencies produce maximum excitation towards the basal area. These locations code different frequency stimuli present in speech inducing the excitation of transducer cells (hair-cells) at different positions along the cochlea which will be responsible for the mechanical to neural transduction process to electrical impulse trains. This results in organized spike-like streams of stimuli coding frequency by place and phase locking, which are transferred from the cochlea to the first relay stage in the Cochlear Nucleus (CN) via the Auditory Nerve (AN) as depicted in Figure 6 (Top). These streams propagate to higher neural centres along auditory nerve fibres, each one being specialized in the transmission of a different characteristic frequency (CF). CF fibres tend to respond to each of the spectral components found in the signal spectrum, although they respond also to nearby tones. An interesting issue is that of the role played by lateral inhibition, which has to see with harmonic and formant detection in the auditory pathways. From the perceptual facts described above it seems clear that speech perception is very much based in formant perception, both static and dynamic. The transition from time-frequency detailed spatiotemporal structure of the responses of the auditory nerve to spe-

Figure 6. Speech Perception Model. Top: Main neural pathways in the peripheral and central auditory centers adapted from (Goldstein, 1984). Bottom: Simplified main structures. The cochlea produces time-frequency organized representations which are conveyed by the auditory nerve to the cochlear nucleus, where certain specialized neurons (Pl: Primary-like, On: Onset, Ch: Chopper, Pb: Pauser) are implied in temporal processing. Binaural information is treated in the Superior Olivar Nucleus, where selective tono-topic units (CF) may be found. Other units specialized in detecting tonal movements (FM), broadband spectral densities (NB) and binaural processing (Bi) are found in the inferior colliculus and the medial geniculate body. The auditory cortex shows columnar layered units (Cl) as well as massively extensive connection units (Ec).

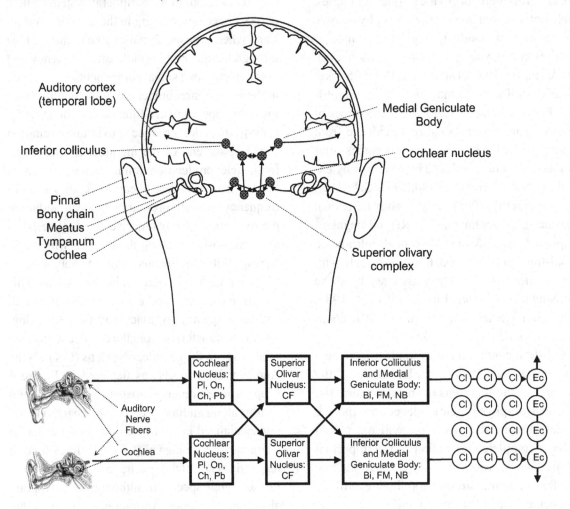

cific CF/CF and FM/FM responses found in the primary auditory cortex (AI) of the moustached bat by Suga (2006) indicates that some powerful mechanism is applied to reduce spike firing rates and the number of fibres conveying information to higher auditory centers, some kind of compression mechanism which acts as a sort of "physiological mpeg" (Brandenburg & Stoll, 1992) in the auditory system. It is believed that the mechanism for this compression coding process is based in "specific lateral inhibition networks which may exist in the anteroventral Cochlear Nucleus (CN), especially involving T-Stellate cells, which exhibit fast inhibitory surrounds and a robust representation of the input spectrum regardless of level" (direct quotation from Shamma, 2001). This belief is also supported by the strong reduction in spike firing rates found in the lower levels of the auditory pathways as compared with the firing rates in the AI areas which suggest the presence of a strong compression mechanism both in the time and in the frequency domain (Greenberg & Ainsworth, 2004). Frequency seems to be also encoded in the inter-peak intervals (phase locking) within each group of CF responses (Shamma, 2001), (Palmer & Shamma, 2004). The firing rate codes the intensity of the stimulus as well. This information flow is transferred to the cochlear nucleus (CN) where different types of neurons specialized in elementary time-space processing are found, some of them segmenting the signals (Cp: chopper units), others detecting stimuli onsets in order to estimate inter-aural differences (On: onset cells), others delaying the information to detect hidden temporal relationships (Pb: pauser units), while others serve as information relay stages (Pl: primary-like units). The CN feeds information to the olivar complex, where sounds are place-located by interaural differences, and to the Inferior Colliculus (IC), which is organized in spherical layers with iso-frequency bands orthogonal to each other. Delay lines of up to 12 msec are found in its structure, their function being related with the detection of temporal elements coded in acoustic signals (CF and FM components). Fibres irradiate from this centre to the thalamus (medial geniculate body) which acts as a relay station (some neurons exhibit delays of a hundred milliseconds), and as a tonotopic mapper of information arriving to cortex, where high level processing takes place. It seems that the neural tissue in the brain is organized as ordered feature maps (Schreiner, 1995) according to this sensory specialization. The specific location of the neural structures in the cortex responsible for speech processing and understanding is not well defined in humans as the subjects of experimentation have been mainly animals, although an enormous progress has been

achieved in the last years (Rauschecker & Scott, 2009). This fact and the need of using anesthesia to record single neuron responses in experimentation animals lacking speech abilities puts some shades to the elaboration of theories on speech processing by the upper auditory system (Ainsworth & Greenberg, 2006). Recently the interest in exploring speech brain centres using nuclear magnetic resonance has experienced a great push forward, many studies using this technique being published, although these do not reach yet the resolution of a single neuron. Nevertheless some findings in neurophysiologic sound perception in animals may give interesting hints on which phenomena of interest for speech processing understanding take place and where and how. For example, certain neurons have been found in the cat's primary auditory cortex (AI) that fire when FM-like frequency transitions are present (FM elements, (Mendelson & Cynander, 1985), while in macaque some neurons respond to specific noise bursts (NB components, Rauschecker, Tian, & Hauser, 1995). In the moustached bat AI neurons have also been found that respond to combinations of two static tones (vowel-like structures) or even to dynamic changes in two tones (Active Voiced Dynamic structures, as were defined above, Suga, 2006). Up to now Suga's work gives one of the most complete descriptions of speech-feature phenomena in AI available, as depicted in a classical sketch reproduced in Figure 7.

In humans, evidence exists of frequency representation maps of this kind near the Heschl circumvolution (Sams & Salmening, 1994) and of a secondary map with word-addressing capabilities (Ojemann, 1990, 1991). From responses registered in humans during reparatory surgery neural centers have been found which seem to be sensitive to the word semantic function (Corina, Gibson, Martin, Poliakov, Brinkley, & Ojemann, 2005). These findings are of most interest for bio-inspired speech processing. A description of the structures involved and their functionality can be found as well in (Ferrández, 1998). As a summary

Figure 7. Functional Organization of the auditory cortex of the moustached bat adapted from (Suga, 2006). The most relevant facts for the present study are the existence of specific areas sensitive to associations of characteristic frequencies (CFi/CFj) and to associations of dynamic frequency modulations (FMi-FMj), which are clear clues of the presence of specific pre-linguistic abstract information processing mechanisms in the bat's auditory cortex.

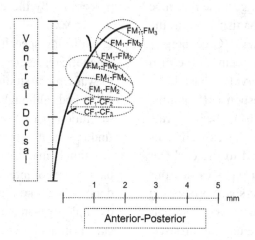

it must be emphasized that the specific processing of speech by the auditory system is based on the detection of stable frequencies, associations of frequencies, onset times, dynamic frequency changes, and tone bursts. At the first hierarchical level CF units are specialized in the detection of single tones associated among themselves or as running streams (Yin, Ma, Elhilali, Fritz, & Shamma, 2007). At a second hierarchical level associations of tones, in many cases separated by large frequency intervals are detected as specific semantic units (vowels being among these). Formant dynamics detection would be based on the capacity of the auditory system of extracting formants and associations between formants from relations among neighbour harmonic positions during short time intervals in using some left hemisphere mechanisms (Poeppel, 2003). Specific sets of neurons are devoted to isolate formants from neighbour harmonic relations using association and lateral inhibition (see Culling & Darwin, 1993). At a higher hierarchical level dynamic changes in harmonics (onset times and slopes) and specific broadband signals present before the

onset time define specific clues to the perception of syllables, seen as associations of consonants and vowels as in C-V structures (other possibilities contemplate tri-phone structures of the kind C-V-C or V-C-V). The perceptual interpretation of such structures is well documented in literature (Weiringen & Pols, 2006).

NEUROMORPHIC SPEECH PROCESSING

Basic Elementary Units

The brief review of the most relevant facts in speech perception and neurophysiologic processing reveal the presence and functionality of specific neurons or small sets of neurons fulfilling specific tasks, which have to be taken into account to emulate or reproduce their features in BINSP, i.e. in the design of specific algorithms or devices implementing or mimicking certain functions in a similar way the auditory pathways and cortex process speech. The most important processing units (Basic Elementary Units: BEU's) revealed of interest for this study are the following:

- Pl: Primary-like. Reproduce the firing stream found at its input as a relay stage.
- On: Onset. Detect the leading edge of a new firing stream or package, discriminating the background firing rate from a new stimulus rate. A variant of this unit is the Pr: Predictor, which is capable of firing when a specific temporal sequence is detected at its input.
- Ch: Chopper. Specialized in dividing a continuous stimulus into slices.
- Pb: Pauser. Act as delay lines, firing sometime after the stimulus onset. Its role may be related with prediction and dynamic tracking.
- CF: Characteristic Frequency. Tonotopically organized, responding to a narrow band of frequencies centred in a specific one.
- FM: Frequency Modulation sensitive. Specialized in detecting changes in frequency, their role is crucial in detecting dynamic speech features.
- NB: Noise Burst sensitive. React to broadband stimuli, as those specific of turbulent noise found in unvoiced fricative consonants.
- Bi: Binaural processors. Specific of binaural hearing by contrasting phase-shifted stimuli. They are found mainly in the inferior colliculus.
- Cl: Columnar. Pyramidal neurons organized linearly in narrow columns through the layers of the auditory cortex. Their function may be related with short-time memory (Mountcastle 1997), they are the object of intense study by Electro-Microscopy (Elston, Benavides-Piccione, & DeFelipe, 2001; Arellano, Benavides-Piccione, DeFelipe, & Yuste, 2007) and High Performance Computing (Friedman, 2009; EFPL, 2009).

- Ec: Extensive Connectors. The outer layers of the auditory cortex seem dominated by extensive connections among distant columns through the tufts of pyramidal neurons.

The Generalized Neuromorphic Computing Unit

The study and functionality of the neuron has been the object of intense study since its first description by Santiago Ramón y Cajal (Ramón y Cajal, 1899-1904). The systemic point of view almost universally admitted nowadays in Artificial Intelligence (although assuming strong simplifications) is due to Warren McCulloch and Walter Pitts (McCulloch & Pitts, 1943) and can be considered as the inspiring starting point to the world of artificial neural networks (Hinton & Anderson, 1989). The morphology and functionality of the units of interest share important features in common: reaction to one or several inputs with an excitatory or inhibitory function which may be based in the model of Donald Hebb (Hebb, 1949 - reprinted 2002); response expressed as a stream of firing spikes within a given time interval delayed with respect to the stimuli (causality); processing time-frequency representations of speech-derived neural activity. Algorithmically a definition of a Generalized Neuromorphic Computing Unit (GNCU) is that of an operator transforming an input representation space mathematically described as a matrix (generalized spectrogram image as the one in Figure 2.c) $X(m,n) \in \mathbf{R}^{mxn}$ to an output representation space $\tilde{X}(m,n) \in \mathbf{R}^{mxn}$ where m and n correspond respectively to the indices of frequency and time accordingly with the following transformation:

$$\tilde{X}(m,n) = F\left\{\sum_{i=-1}^{I}\sum_{j=0}^{J} w_{ij} X(m-i, n-j)\right\}$$

(1)

Figure 8. Top: Structure of a Neuromorphic Generalized Computing Unit. Bottom: image processing templates implementing some simple functions in speech spectrogram processing.

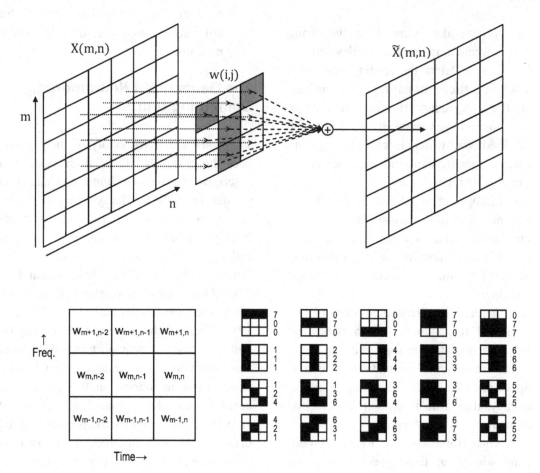

where $w_{ij} \in \boldsymbol{R}^{IxJ}$ is a set of connection weights associated to the inputs (excitatory or inhibitory, depending on their respective value), and $F\{.\}$ is a nonlinear saturation mapping function. The structure and operation of one such GNCU is represented in Figure 8.

Obviously the differences between a BEU of the kind listed above and the GNCU are significant and deserve to be taken into account: BEU's receive discrete spike-like actions which are confined in time accordingly to a specific spike pattern-configuring firing streams. The intensity of the stimulus is defined in the number of spikes received per time unit, and in the time interval between spikes (phase locking). The weights of the excitatory or inhibitory connections are defined in the connection strength from synaptic dynamics, and may be re-inforced or attenuated with time depending on how often stimuli are produced through the same synapse. The response of the BEU is induced if a given threshold is reached, and may consist in the firing of a single spike or a train of them, coding intensity in the number of spikes per time unit and in the interval between spikes. The reception of input and the generation of output streams are asynchronous processes. On its turn the GNCU receives real numbers at a synaptic input, which may be positive or negative, the synaptic weight is expressed also as a real number, the addition of all stimuli is mapped to the output by a non-linear saturating function, which is currently a thresholded sigmoid function, and the response is given also as a real number. The reception of inputs and the generation of outputs are supposed to be regulated by a main timing clock marking the cadence of the time instant n. These important differences should be taken into account when evaluating the results produced by the GNCU's in contrast to that of BEU's. The operation of a BEU is quite similar to that of a pixel template in image processing (Jähne, 2005). This is not a coincidence, as accordingly to the multimodal nature of the brain structures, vision, hearing and somatosensory processing operate on similar physiological and functional grounds (Pascual-Leone & Hamilton, 2001). The number of different functions which may be implemented by the GNCU's is very large, as it may be deducted from examining several 3x3 templates given as examples in Figure 8 (bottom). For instance, the templates in the upper row (700, 070, 007, 770, and 077) are specifically designed to track stable formant positions, and can be considered different variants of CF units. The templates in the second row from left to right (111, 222, 444, 333, and 666) are implementing NB units. The templates 124, 136, 364 and 376 are specialized in detecting descending formants (-fM units), and similarly templates 421, 631, 463 and 673 are designed to detect ascending formants (+fM units). Lateral inhibition is also implementable using these structures, by means of a template defined as:

$$W_{li} = \left[-\frac{1}{2}W_{700} + W_{070} - \frac{1}{2}W_{007} \right] \times W_{444} \quad (2)$$

where W_{700} and W_{007} are the inhibitory masks and W_{070} is the excitatory one. The use of these masks allows a great degree of flexibility to define different excitatory and inhibitory patterns, and is an object of study in itself. Under this point of view the detection of formants in audition is carried out

by similar structures to the ones detecting edges in vision, and both processes can be seen as a part of powerful scene representation coding processes.

A Neuromorphic Hierarchical Architecture for speech processing

From all what has been said up to this point a possible hierarchical structure to implement specific tasks in speech processing can be proposed, by systemic bottom-up synthesis of subtask structures. One such system, which may be described as a neuromorphic hierarchical architecture for speech processing is described in Figure 9 to process the speech trace for a single auditory channel.

The tasks of specific interest in speech processing to be carried out by this architecture are among others:

- Detection of formants by lateral inhibition
- Detection of formant dynamics as ascending or descending segments
- Detection of broad-band turbulent bursts
- Dynamic consonant labeling
- Stable vowel-like phone labeling

These tasks are specifically designed to detect the phone features of interest for a specific speech processing application, as speech recognition for wordspotting (Yu, Chen, Ma, & Seide, 2005). An example of these features is given in Table 2 for a set of consonant phonemes of interest in Spanish (the ones with tighter structure under a descriptive point of view).

This table is directly derived from the features described in Table 1, as O/N is the descriptor of oral or nasal condition, V/U refers to voiced/unvoiced, DC is the degree of closure, AP is the articulation place, O/R is the condition of oval or round. The static or dynamic nature of the consonant is fully extended now in terms of formant dynamics (FM1, FM2, CF and NB). The NHSPA may be seen as different subsystems that are interconnected to process an input audio stream $s(n)$. The

Figure 9. Neuromorphic Hierarchical Speech Processing Architecture for a mono-aural channel

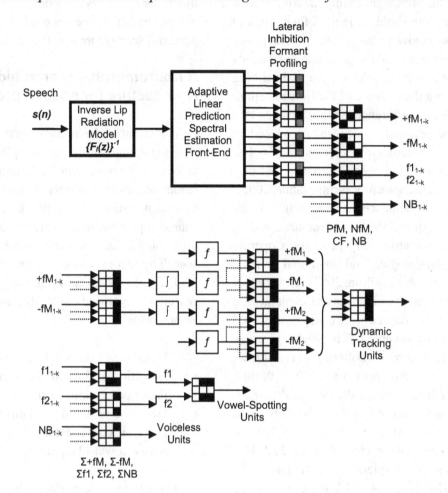

systemic description from top to bottom and left to right is as follows. The first stages consist of a pre-processor to compensate radiation effects and a front-end LPC spectral estimator, which generates a spectrogram. For voicing speech the spectrogram is designed to remove excitation effects, keeping the exclusively the behavior of the vocal tract for a better formant profiling. The pitch and the energy are also evaluated for possible further processing. The estimation is carried out by adaptive algorithms to better track spectral changes. The rest of the structures processing the audio stream are the following:

- LIFP: Lateral Inhibition Formant Profilers, as already described, designed to detect the presence of plausible formants by delineation and prediction; they act as sharp speech compressing coders.

- $+f_{M1-K}$, $-f_{M1-K}$: Positive and Negative Slope Formant Trackers (acting on K neighbor bands) detecting ascending or descending formant activity using masks {124-376} and {421-673}.

- $f1_{1-K}$, $f2_{1-K}$: First and Second Energy Peak Trackers, intended for formant detection mimicking CF neurons, using masks {700-077}.

Table 1. Some speech sounds of interest for the present study: v-voiced, u-unvoiced, s-static, d-dynamic, f-frontal, m-mid, b-back, c-closed, op-open, sc-semiclosed, a-approximant, f-fricative,o-oral, n-nasal

Voicing	Stability	Place	Rounding	Closure	Nasality	IPA	KB	Description
v	s	f	oval	c	o	i	i	Front oval close vowel
v	s	mf	oval	mc	o	e	e	Mid-front oval mid-close vowel
v	s	mf	oval	mo	o	ɛ	E	Mid-front oval mid-open vowel
v	s	m	oval	op	o	æ	&	Central oval open vowel
v	s	m	oval	op	o	a	a	Central oval open vowel
v	s	b	round	mc	o	o	o	Back round mid-close vowel
v	s	b	round	c	o	u	u	Back round close vowel
v	s	b	round	c	o	ũ	U	Back round close vowel
v	s	m	neutral	neutral	o	ə	@	Middle central open vowel
v	d	f	oval	→c	o	j	j	Front oval closing semiconsonant
v	d	b	round	→c	o	ω	w	Back round closing semiconsonant
v	s	mf	-	sc	o	l	l	Alveolar voiced lateral
v	s	m	-	sc	o	ɽ	R	Post-alveolar retroflex voiced lateral
v	d	f	-	s	o	b	b	Bilabial voiced stop
v	d	mf	-	a	o	ð	D	Dental voiced approximant
u	s	mb	-	f	o	ʃ	S	Palatal unvoiced fricative
v	s	f	-	c	n	m	m	Bilabial voiced nasal
v	s	mf	-	c	n	n	n	Alveolar voiced nasal
v	s	b	-	c	n	ŋ	N	Velar voiced nasal

Table 2. Nuclear set of consonant phones shared by the Spanish Dialects

IPA	p	t	c	k	b	d	ĵ	g	f	θ	ʃ	x	β	ð	ζ	γ
KB	p	t	c	k	b	d	J	g	f	T	S	x	B	D	Z	G
O/N	o	o	o	o	o	o	o	o	o	o	o	o	o	o	o	o
V/U	u	u	u	u	v	v	v	v	u	u	u	u	v	v	v	v
DC	s	s	s	s	s	s	s	s	f	f	f	f	f	f	f	f
AP	bl	a	p	v	bl	a	p	v	ld	d	p	v	bl	da	pa	v
O/R	-	-	-	-	-	-	-	-	-	-	-	-	-	-	-	-
FM1	a	a	a	n	a	a	a	n	a	a	a	n	a	a	a	n
FM2	a	n	d	n	a	n	d	n	a	n	d	n	a	n	d	n
CF	-	-	-	-	-	-	-	-	-	-	-	-	-	-	-	-
NB	a	mh	h	ml	-	-	-	-	a	mh	h	ml	-	-	-	-

- Σ+fM, Σ-fM: These are integrators or accumulators working on the inputs of previous Formant Tracker Integration Units on neighbor bands (350-650 Hz for the first formant, or 650-2300 Hz for the second formant).

- $+fM_1$, $-fM_1$, $+fM_2$, $-fM_2$: First and Second Formant Integration Units (positive and negative slopes), estimating the features FM1 and FM2 in Table 2.

- ΣNB: Noise Burst Integration Units ({111-666}) for wide frequency activity detection, as in voiceless consonants.

- VSU: Voiceless Spotting Units. These integrate the outputs of different ΣNB's acting in separate bands to pattern the activity of fricative voiceless consonants.

- WSU: Vowel Spotting Units. These integrate the activity of Σf1 and Σf2 units to detect the presence of vowels and their nature.

- DTU: Dynamic Tracking Units. These integrate the activity of different dynamic trackers on the first two formants to detect consonant dynamic features.

- Vowel spotting. This is a nuclear task in wordspotting, as vowel-like sounds are the "beads-on-a-string" of speech and their detection is of most importance for speech processing (Ainsworth & Greenberg, 2006). Vowel spotting units are based on the band-detected sequences for f1 and f2 and in their reconstruction in a vowel-triangle-like representation space, as this concept has received strong physiological

plausibility. In this task some predictable capabilities found in the columnar structure of the Auditory Cortex will play an essential role.

SOME SELECTED RESULTS

The examination of the capabilities of the NHSPA would take some more space than available. In what follows the emphasis will be placed in showing the detection of some meaningful dynamic features of speech, leaving the interested reader to inspect other related publications (Gómez P., Ferrández, Rodellar, Álvarez, & Mazaira, 2007; Gómez P., et al., 2008; Gómez P., Ferrández, Rodellar, & Fernández, 2009; Gómez P., et al., 2009). Classically to study these features speech segments showing fast formant movements are used. For such a typical example will be shown based on the classical sentence –*Where were you while you were away?*-, phonetically equivalent to [hʷɛˤɷɛˤjuʰɷaeljuʷɛˤaɷɛj] in IPA or to [hwER-weRjuhwaeljuwERawEj] in KB. An example of the LPC spectrogram of the sentence and its corresponding F_2-vs-F1 plot are given in Figure 10.

Figure 10. Left: LPC spectrogram of the sentence –Where were you while you were away?-. Right: Vowel triangle showing the five reference vowels in English framing the formant trajectories of the utterance.

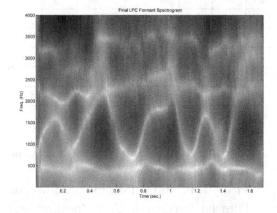
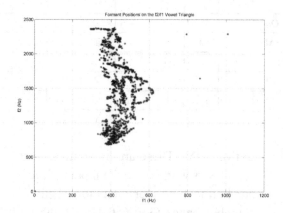

The spectrogram reveals fast up and down movements of formants (especially F_2), confined to a vowel triangle within which formant trajectories smear in time. The modelling of the two first formants by *FM+* and *FM-* units will constitute a specific objective of this study. The details of the architecture used in the study are the following: *M=1024* units are used as characteristic frequency outputs from LPC, defining a resolution in frequency of barely 8 Hz for a sampling frequency of 8000 Hz. These are sampled each 5 msec. to define a stream of approximately 200 spikes per second. The dimensions of the +FM and -FM units are 7x7, which means that the connectivity in frequency extends from +3 to -3 neighbour neurons, whilst the delay lines in the pauser units required for temporal organization of the stimuli go from 0 to 30 msec. As the frequency distribution is linear, the number of channels integrated for the first formant (350-650 Hz) is around 38, whereas for the second formant (700-2300) is around 204.

The templates in the figure above show the activity of the set of 204 FM neurons tracking the fast movements of the second formant (top). In the bottom section the activity at the synaptic input of the integrating units (Σ+fM, Σ-fM) may be appreciated. The granular or spike-like activity may be seen. Usually a coincidence of 2-4 spikes at a time from different neighbor units may be received, which are integrated and thresholded over a short time period to determine the discharge of the integrating unit.

Figure 12 (top) reproduces the behaviour of a Second-Formant Energy Peak Tracking Unit (positive slope) on the output of LIFP neurons, integrating the activity of up 204 units, most of which are not firing simultaneously. A correspondence among the firing histograms and the positive slopes of the second formant is clearly appreciated. This activity is integrated ($\int$) and thresholded by a saturation function (*f*) to produce the plots in Figure 12 (middle). Finally in the bottom template

Figure 11. FM Unit firing. Top: Activity of $+f_{M700-2300}$ Units coding the band of the second formant F_2. Bottom: Activity of Second Formant Integration Units (positive slope $+fM_2$)

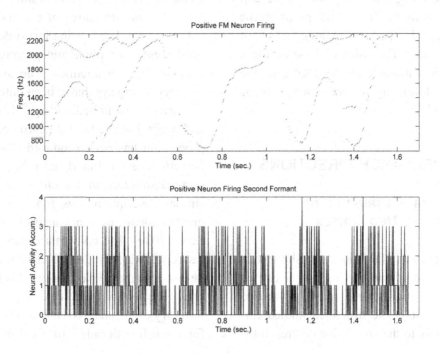

Figure 12. Top: Output of Activity at the output of LIFP Units in the band of the second formant. Middle: Output of the Second Formant Integration Unit +fM2 reproducing the positive slope intervals in the second formant. Bottom: Value of the slope detected on the given interval.

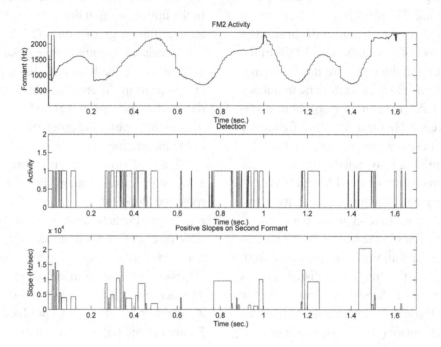

of the figure the values of the different intervals detected with positive slope and the value of the average slope are given. These values are calculated integrating the firing histograms on the interval detected by the specific Integration Unit ($+fM_2$ in this case). The utility of these results is to be found in automatic phonetic labeling the speech trace, following feature descriptions as the one in Table 2.

FUTURE RESEARCH DIRECTIONS

The Columnar Organization of the Auditory Neo-Cortex

Through the present work it has been shown that formant-based speech processing may be carried by well-known bio-inspired mask processors (CF and FM units). The structures studied correspond roughly to the processing centres in the olivar nucleus and the inferior colliculus. The study of short-time memory-like structures found in the upper levels of the brain, and especially the columnar structures of the auditory cortex (Mountcastle, 1997) using low order predictors, fundamental for phonemic parsing deserve an extensive further attention. The lower and mid auditory pathways have been intensively and extensively researched, and a good deal of helpful and useful knowledge for neuromorphic speech processing has been produced (Palmer, 2004). Nevertheless the functional role played by the cortical structure in speech processing lacks a similar description, this functionality being a great challenge even nowadays (Rauschecker & Scott, 2009). The columnar organization of the neocortex was first described by Rafael Lorente de No (Lorente de No, 1949). This scientist was one of the most outstanding disciples of Santiago Ramón y Cajal, and lived and worked in the USA for some five decades till his death in Tucson,

AZ in 1990. It seems that Vernon Mouncastle contrasted carefully his studies against those of Lorente de No as he personally puts it that way: "Whatever the interdigitated pattern may be, the results do suggest that a single or a small group of thalamocortical fibers entering the cortex must be activated by a single mode of peripheral stimulation, and in turn activate a narrow vertical column of cells. This fits closely with the anatomical evidence on cortical organization given by Lorente de No, to which further reference will be made." (Mountcastle, 1957). Now the main underlying question is: Why cortical columnar organization is believed to be important for speech processing by Higher auditory pathways? There are some interesting answers which can only be formulated as hypotheses to be ratified by further research. On one side it is clear that short memory plays an essential role in phone time organization and parsing. Besides, when the fine structure of time alignment is studied in language parsing it becomes obvious that phone features are not synchronously represented at the cortical level: experience as well as pathology brings observation into light, many phenomena related with language disorders apparently being induced by these facts. Phonemic parsing demands specific resources for feature storage and time accounting in order to produce meaningful word definitions. This parsing demands besides a back-and-forth re-framing of the input information chain being processed. Under this point of view a parsing analysis line would be the systemic counterpart of a micro column. In the general strategy applied by the human auditory system, it would be plausible that single fibres would activate instead of whole fibre bundles using wisely the lateral inhibition mechanisms applied in a greedy strategy to save power consumption and preserve cells from exhaustion. Simple neural circuits already described by Ramón y Cajal (1899-1904) would play a crucial role in parsing "already learned" patterns previously consolidated by Hebbian Plasticity (Hebb, 1949 - reprinted 2002). Short-time pat-

tern analysis would use other greedy strategies, as compression of time-extended easy-to-learn patterns into simple impulse responses. This would be in agreement with the observation of Greenberg (2004) that "most auditory cortical neurons respond at very low discharge rates, typically less than 10 spikes/s" while the discharge rates in the auditory thalamic pathways arriving to auditory cortex are almost two orders of magnitude more intense. In this sense some kind of functionality could be inferred related mainly with the short memory capability of bidirectional linear structures reproducing cortical columns, essential for the parsing of phonetic sounds leading to the emergence of the word as a semantic unit. This idea was discussed in a recent paper (Gómez, et. al., 2009) and can be summarized as in Figure 13.

The functionality of these structures is being brought forth to light nowadays, some neural circuits being studied in depth. The research proposed in here is in the same line as the general exposition in the present work: to infer plausible functional subsystems and to implement them using the GNCU before exposed. The simulation of different cortical structures emulating the low-level grammatical functions of speech processing will demand large networks and enormous computing power. The planification of the research is as follows:

- Process a large database to extract the main phonetic and phonemic features of a target language
- Parameterize the database in formant-based patterns
- Detect the dynamics of formant-based features by simple CF and FM neuron functional prototypes (following Suga's behavioral description)
- Propose different structures of autoregressive nature to implement 6-level neocortex columns as:
  - Linear predictive automatae
  - Lattice-like double-column automatae

Figure 13. The columnar organization of the neocortex. Top Left: Columns are parallel structures normal to the outer cortical boundary grouping bundles of layered pyramidal neurons (Top Right, from an original drawing by Ramón y Cajal) with intense vertical interconnections and dense outer connections to a basal switching network, represented schematically in the highlight. Bottom: At least two pyramidal neurons(a and c) and an interneuron (b, or short axon neuron, with inhibitory properties) may interlock in a latch-like structure capable of storing specific temporal patterns using properties of functional predictors. Delays and excitatory-inhibitory connections are cumbersome to implement specific functions for time-pattern detection tasks, as counters, sequence detectors, and parsers. This structure would be compliant with Greenberg's observation. The pattern characterization would be encoded in the relative synaptic strengths w_{ac} and w_{bc}.

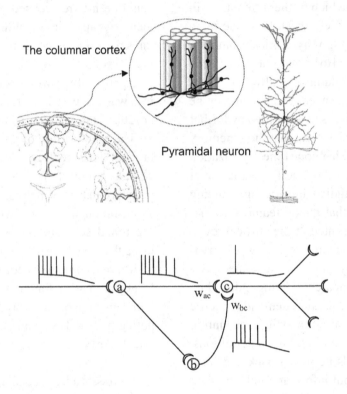

- Create massively parallel structures and simulate their behaviour in real time in terms of the following functionalities:
  - Capability to store and retrieve demi- and tri-phone structures
  - Capability to extend the storage and retrieval to larger word units
  - Capability to express simple synctactic relations among word units
  - Capability of replication and association of different semantic levels associated to word units
  - Capability of visualize temporal differences in the establishment demi-phoneme temporal precedences and time alignment of syntactic relations

The number of structures to be simulated and visualized would comprise one tenth the dimensional order of the auditory nerve. The columnar structure would require the simulation of at least 400.000 microcolumns. This research is to be conducted in the CeSViMa -Supercomputing and Visualization Center of Madrid- in collaboration with Cajal Blue Brain Project (Cajal Blue Brain Project, 2009).

CONCLUSION

Through the present chapter the possibility of exploiting the knowledge of brain structure neurophysiology and functionality for processing speech in dedicated computing structures was explored. For such, a review of perceptual and physiological facts was presented. Based on this review a generalized processing unit (artificial neuron) was proposed. This generalized unit could be used in a bottom-up construction process to define a hierarchical architecture for speech processing. Some specific functions of this structure were tested on real speech to examine the capabilities of the system in detecting the dynamics of speech formants. The results show that formants can be reliably detected and tracked using these simple neuromorphic structures. This opens the possibility to extend neuromorphic mimicking to other structures of the higher auditory centers, as the primary auditory cortex. The study of simple structures to emulate short-time parsing of dynamic features in the construction of representation spaces for specific speech phones is proposed as a future development. The use of massive computing power for the definition of a parallel simulation framework is a direct consequence to solve the strong computing demands of such a research program.

ACKNOWLEDGMENT

This work is being funded by grants TIC2003-08756, TEC2006-12887-C02-00 from the Ministry of Education and Science, CCG06-UPM/ TIC-0028 from CAM/UPM, and by project HESPERIA (http.//www.proyecto-hesperia.org) from the Programme CENIT, CDTI, Ministry of Industry, Spain.

REFERENCES

Ainsworth, W. A., & Greenberg, S. (2006). *Auditory Processing of Speech. En S. G. Ainsworth, Listening to Speech: An Auditory Perspective* (pp. 3–17). Mahwah, NJ: Lawrence Erlbaum Ass. Pub.

Allen, J. B. (1985). Cochlear Modeling. *IEEE ASSP Magazine*, 3–29. doi:10.1109/MASSP.1985.1163723

Allen, J. B. (2008). Nonlinear Cochlear Signal Processing and Masking in Speech Perception. In Benesty, M. M. J. (Ed.), *Springer Handbook of Speech Processing*. Berlin: Springer Verlag. doi:10.1007/978-3-540-49127-9_3

Arellano, J. I., Benavides-Piccione, R., DeFelipe, J., & Yuste, R. (2007). Ultrastructure of dendritic spines: correlation between synaptic and spine morphologies. *Frontiers in Neuroscience*, *1*(1), 131–143. doi:10.3389/neuro.01.1.1.010.2007

Brandenburg, K., & Popp, H. (June de 2000). An introduction to MPEG Layer 3. *EBU Technical Review*, 1-15.

Brandenburg, K., & Stoll, G. (1992). The ISO/MPEG-Audio Codec: A Generic Standard for Coding of High Quality Digital Audio. Vienna.

Buchsbaum, B. R., Hickok, G., & Humphries, C. (2001). Role of left posterior superior temporal gyrus in phonological processing for speech perception and production. *Cognitive Science*, *25*, 663–678. doi:10.1207/s15516709cog2505_2

Cajal Blue Brain Project. (2009, 4 2). Retrieved 5 15, 2009, from http://cajalbbp.cesvima.upm.es/

Corina, D. P., Gibson, E. K., Martin, R., Poliakov, A., Brinkley, J., & Ojemann, G. A. (2005). Dissociation of Action and Object Naming: Evidence from Cortical Stimulation Mapping. *Human Brain Mapping, 24*, 1–10. doi:10.1002/hbm.20063

Culling, J. F., & Darwin, C. J. (1993). Perceptual separation of simultaneous vowels: Within and across-formant grouping by F0. *The Journal of the Acoustical Society of America, 93*, 3454–3467. doi:10.1121/1.405675

EFPL. (2009). *Blue Brain Project.* Retrieved May 23, 2009, from http://bluebrain.epfl.ch/

Elston, G. N., Benavides-Piccione, R., & DeFelipe, J. (2001). The pyramidal cell in cognition: a comparative study in man and monkey. *The Journal of Neuroscience, 21*, 1–5.

Ferrández, J. M. (1998). *Study and Realization of a Bioinspired Hierarchical Architecture for Speech Recognition.* Madrid: Universidad Politécnica de Madrid (PhD Thesis in Spanish).

FitzGerald, D. B., Cosgrove, G. R., Ronner, S., Jiang, H., Buchbinder, B. R., & Belliveau, J. W. (1997). Location of Language in the Cortex: A Comparison between Functional MR Imaging and Electrocortical Stimulation. *American Society of Neuroradiology, 18*, 1529–1539.

Flanagan, J. L. (1960a). Models for approximating basilar membrane displacement. *The Journal of the Acoustical Society of America, 32*(7), 937. doi:10.1121/1.1936560

Friedman, R. (2009). Reverse Engineering the Brain. *Biomedical Cumputation Review, Spring*, 10-17.

Gandour, J., Tong, Y., Talavage, T., Wong, D., Dzemidzic, M., & Xu, Y. (2007). Neural Basis of First and Second Language Processing of Sentence-Level Linguistic Prosody. *Human Brain Mapping, 28*, 94–108. doi:10.1002/hbm.20255

Ghitza, O. (1988). Temporal non-place information in the auditory-nerve firing patterns as a front-end for speech recognition in a noisy environment. *Journal of Phonetics, 20*, 109–123.

Gold, T. (1948b). Hearing II: The physical basis of the action of the cochlea. *Proceedings of the Royal Society of London. Series B. Biological Sciences, 135*(881), 492–498. doi:10.1098/rspb.1948.0025

Gold, T., & Pumphrey, R. J. (1948a). Hearing I: The cochlea as a frequency analyzer. *Proceedings of the Royal Society of London. Series B. Biological Sciences, 135*(881), 462–491. doi:10.1098/rspb.1948.0024

Goldstein, B. (1984). *Sensation and Perception.* Belmont, CA: Wadsworth Publ.

Gómez, P., Ferrández, J. M., Rodellar, V., Álvarez, A., & Mazaira, L. M. (2007). A Bio-inspired Architecture for Cognitive Audio. *Lecture Notes in Computer Science, 4527*, 132–142. doi:10.1007/978-3-540-73053-8_14

Gómez, P., Ferrández, J. M., Rodellar, V., Álvarez, A., Mazaira, L. M., & Martínez, R. (2009). *Detection of Speech Dynamics by Neuromorphic Units. Proc. of the IWINAC09, LNCS 5602* (pp. 67–78). Santiago de Compostela, Spain: Springer.

Gómez, P., Ferrández, J. M., Rodellar, V., & Fernández, R. (2009). Time-frequency Representations in Speech Perception. *Neurocomputing*, 820–830.

Gómez, P., Ferrández, J. M., Rodellar, V., Martínez, R., Muñoz, C., & Alvarez, A. (2008). *Bio-inspired Dynamic Formant Tracking for Phonetic Labelling. V Jornadas en Tecnología del Habla* (pp. 33–36). Bilbao, Spain: University of the Basque Country.

Greenberg, S., & Ainsworth, W. A. (2004). Speech Processing in the Auditory System: An Overview. In Greenberg, W. A. S. (Ed.), *Speech Processing in the Auditory System* (pp. 1–62). New York: Springer. doi:10.1007/0-387-21575-1_1

Hawkins, J., & Blakeslee, S. (2004). *On Intelligence*. New York: Times Books.

Hebb, D. O. (1949 - reprinted 2002). *The Organization of Behavior*. New York: Wiley Interscience.

Helmholz, H. (1885). *On the Sensations of Tone as a Physiological Basis for the Theory of Music*. London, UK: Longmans.

Hermansky, H. (1997). Should Recognizers Have Ears? *ESCA-NATO Tutorial and Research Workshop on Robust Speech Recognition for Unknown Communication Channels*, (págs. 1-10). Pont-à-Mousson, France.

Hinton, G. E., & Anderson, J. A. (1989). *Parallel Models of Associative Memory*. Hillsdale, NJ: Lawrence Erlbaum Ass. Pub.

IPA. (2009). Retrieved May 21, 2009, from IPA: http://www.arts.gla.ac.uk/IPA/ipachart.html

Jähne, B. (2005). *Digital Image Processing*. Berlin: Springer.

Katsiamis, A. G., Drakakis, E. M., & Lyon, R. F. (2007). Practical Gammatone-Like Filters for Auditory Processing. *EURASIP Journal on Audio, Speech and Music Processing*, 2-15.

KB. (2009). Retrieved 5 21, 2009, from http://www.kirshenbaum.net/IPA/ascii-ipa.pdf

López-Poveda, E. A. (2001). A human nonlinear cochlear filterbank. *The Journal of the Acoustical Society of America, 110*(6), 3107–3118. doi:10.1121/1.1416197

Lorente de No, R. (1949). Cerebral cortex: architecture, intracortical connections, motor projections. En J. F. Fulton, *Physiology of the Nervous System* (págs. 288-330). Oxford: Oxford University Press.

McCulloch, W., & Pitts, W. (1943). A logical calculus of ideas immanent in nervous activity. *The Bulletin of Mathematical Biophysics, 5*, 115–133. doi:10.1007/BF02478259

Mendelson, J. R., & Cynander, M. S. (1985). Sensitivity of Cat Primary Auditory Cortex (AI) Neurons to the Direction and Rate of Frequency Modulation. *Brain Research, 327*, 331–335. doi:10.1016/0006-8993(85)91530-6

Mountcastle, V. B. (1957). Modality and Topographic Properties of Single Neurons of Cat's Somatic Sensory Cortex. *Journal of Neurophysiology, 20*, 408–454.

Mountcastle, V. B. (1997). The Columnar Organization of the Neocortex. *Brain*, 701–722. doi:10.1093/brain/120.4.701

O'Shaughnessy, D. (2000). *Speech Communication*. Park Avenue, NY: IEEE Press.

Ojemann, G. A. (1990). Organization of language cortex derived from investigation during neurosurgery. *Seminars in Neuroscience, 2*, 297–305.

Ojemann, G. A. (1991). Cortical Organization of Language. *The Journal of Neuroscience, 11*(8), 2281–2287.

Palmer, A., & Shamma, S. (2004). Physiological Representation of Speech. En S. A. Greenberg, *Speech Processing in the Auditory System* (págs. 163-230). New York: Springer.

Pascual-Leone, A., & Hamilton, R. (2001). The metamodal organization of the brain. *Progress in Brain Research, 134*, 427–445. doi:10.1016/S0079-6123(01)34028-1

Poeppel, D. (2003). The analysis of speech in different temporal integration windows: Cerebral lateralization as asymmetric sampling in time. *Speech Communication, 41*, 245–255. doi:10.1016/S0167-6393(02)00107-3

Ramón y Cajal, S. (1899-1904). *Textura del Sistema Nervioso del Hombre y de los Vertebrados (reprinted in English as: Histology of the Nervous System of Man and Vertebrates, Oxford University Press, 1995)*. Madrid: Imprenta y Librería de Nicolás Moya.

Rauschecker, J. P., & Scott, S. K. (2009). Maps and streams in the auditory cortex: nonhuman primates illuminate human speech processing. *Nature Neuroscience, 12*(6), 718–724. doi:10.1038/nn.2331

Rauschecker, J. P., Tian, B., & Hauser, M. (1995). Processing of Complex Sounds in the Macaque Nonprimary Auditory Cortex. *Science, 268,* 111–114. doi:10.1126/science.7701330

SAA. (2009). Retrieved May 21, 2009, from http://accent.gmu.edu

Sams, M., & Salmening, R. (1994). Evidence of sharp frequency tuning in human auditory cortex. *Hearing Research, 75,* 67–74. doi:10.1016/0378-5955(94)90057-4

Sarpeshkar, R. (2006). Brain power: borrowing from biology makes for low-power computing. *IEEE Spectrum, 43*(5), 24–29. doi:10.1109/MSPEC.2006.1628504

Schreiner, C. E. (1995). Order and Disorder in Auditory Cortical Maps. *Current Opinion in Neurobiology, 5,* 489–496. doi:10.1016/0959-4388(95)80010-7

Secker, H., & Searle, C. (1990). Time Domain Analysis of Auditory-Nerve Fibers Firing Rates. *The Journal of the Acoustical Society of America, 88,* 1427–1436. doi:10.1121/1.399719

Shamma, S. (1985). Speech processing in the auditory system II: lateral inhibition and central processing of speech evoked activity in the auditory nerve. *The Journal of the Acoustical Society of America, 78,* 1622–1632. doi:10.1121/1.392800

Shamma, S. (2001). On the role of space and time auditory processing. *Trends in Cognitive Sciences, 5*(8), 340–348. doi:10.1016/S1364-6613(00)01704-6

Suga, N. (2006). *Basic Acoustic Patterns and Neural Mechanisms Shared by Humans and Animals for Auditory Perception. En S. G. Ainsworth, Listening to Speech: An Auditory Perspective* (pp. 159–181). Mahwah, NJ: Lawrence Erlbaum Associates, Pub.

Sussman, H. M., McCaffrey, H. A., & Mathews, S. A. (1991). An Investigation of Locus Equations as a Source of Relational Invariance for Stop Place Categorization. *The Journal of the Acoustical Society of America, 90,* 1309–1325. doi:10.1121/1.401923

Weiringen, A. v., & Pols, L. (2006). *Perception of Highly Dynamic Properties in Speech. En S. G. Ainsworth. Listening to Speech: An Auditory Perspective* (pp. 21–38). Mahwah, NJ: Lawrence Erlbaum Ass. Pub.

Yin, P., Ma, L., Elhilali, M., Fritz, J., & Shamma, S. (2007). *Primary Auditory Cortical Resoponses while Attending to Different Streams. En B. K. al. Hearing: From Sensory Processing to Perception* (pp. 257–265). Heidelberg: Springer.

Yu, P., Chen, K., Ma, C., & Seide, F. (2005). Vocabulary-independent indexing of spontaneous speech. *IEEE Transactions on Speech and Audio Processing, 7*(5), 635–643.

ADDITIONAL READING

Allen, J. (1995). *Natural Language Understanding.* Redwood City, CA: Benjamin Cummings Pub. Co.

Amit, D. J. (1989). *Modeling Brain Function.* Cambridge, MA: Cambridge University Press.

Benesty, M. M. J. (2008). *Springer Handbook of Speech Processing.* Berlin: Springer Verlag. doi:10.1007/978-3-540-49127-9

Dayan, P., & Abbott, L. F. (2005). *Theoretical Neuroscience: Computational and Mathematical Modeling of Neural Systems*. Cambridge, MA: The MIT Press.

Deller, J., Proakis, J. G., & Hansen, J. H. L. (1993). *Discrete-Time Processing of Speech Signals*. New York: McMillan Pub. Co.

Hawkins, J., & Blakeslee, S. (2004). *On Intelligence*. New York: Times Books.

Huang, X., Acero, A., & Hon, H. W. (2001). *Spoken Language Processing*. Upper Saddle River, NJ: Prentice-Hall.

Kollmeier, B. (2007). *Hearing - From Sensory Processing to Perception*. Berlin: Springer. doi:10.1007/978-3-540-73009-5

Minsky, M. L., & Papert, S. A. (1990). *Perceptrons* (4th ed.). Cambridge, MA: The MIT Press.

O'Shaughnessy, D. (2000). *Speech Communication*. Park Avenue, NY: IEEE Press.

Siegel, A., & Sapru, H. N. (2007). *Essential Neuroscience*. Baltimore: Lippincott W&W.

Wang, D., & Brown, G. J. (2006). *Computational Auditory Scene Analysis*. Piscataway, NJ: IEEE Press.

Zigmond, M. J. (1999). *Fundamental Neuroscience*. San Diego, CA: Academic Press.

KEY TERMS AND DEFINITIONS

PhL: Physiological Level, descriptions are given in terms of observable biological structures and biochemical and electrical behavior.

PsL: Psychoacoustical Level, descriptions are given in terms observable perceptual behavior of stimulus-response.

Neuromorphic: A device or algorithm which is intended to behave or approximate the behavior of a neurologic structure under certain conditions.

Bio-inspired: A device or algorithm which processes information in a similar way as a biological system does.

NHASP: Neuromorphic Hierarchical Architecture for Speech Processing.

PAS: Peripheral Auditory System, composed by the outer, middle and inner ears, including the Cochlea and the Vestibular System, ending in the Auditory Nerve.

AI: Primary Auditory Cortex, part of the temporal cortex where pathways from the auditory thalamus connect.

AP&C: Auditory Pathways and Cortex. The complete Auditory System, including the PAS and the Primary and Secondary Auditory Cortices.

BINSP: Bio-Inspired or Neuromorphic Speech Processing. Speech processing methods and devices based on neuromorphic or bio-inspired principles.

FFT: Fast Fourier Transform

LPC: Linear Predictive Coding

IBE: Information-Bearing Elements. Elementary features conveying simple information clues of phonemic interest.

IPA: International Phonetic Alphabet

KB: Kirshenbaum Alphabet

AN: Auditory Nerve

CF: Characteristic Frequency Unit

NB: Noise Burst Unit

FM: Frequency Modulation Unit

CN: Cochlear Nuclei

C-V: Consonant-Vowel dyphone

V-C-V: Vowel-Consonant-Vowel triphone

BEU: Basic Elementary Unit

GNCU: Generalized Neuromorphic Computing Unit

LIFP: Lateral Inhibition Formant Profiler

474

Compilation of References

Abdallah, S. A., & Plumbley, M. D. (2009). Information dynamics: patterns of expectation and surprise in the perception of music. *Connection Science, 21*(2), 89–117. doi:10.1080/09540090902733756

Abdallah, S. A. (2008). A critique of Dubnov's 'information rate'. *Technical Report C4DM-TR-08-11* Queen Mary University of London, 2008.

Abdallah, S. A., & Plumbley, M. D. (2004). Application of geometric dependency analysis to the separation of convolved mixtures. In *Proceedings of the International Conference on Independent Component Analysis and Signal Separation* (pp. 22-24).

Abdallah, S. A., & Plumbley, M. D. (2004). Polyphonic transcription by nonnegative sparse coding of power spectra. In *Proc. 5th International Symposium Music Information Retrieval (ISMIR'04)* (pp. 318–325). Barcelona, Spain.

Aharon, M., Elad, M., & Bruckstein, A. (2006). K-SVD: An algorithm for designing overcomplete dictionaries for sparse representations. *IEEE Transactions on Signal Processing, 54*, 4311–4322.

Ahissar, M., & Hochstein, S. (2004). The reverse hierarchy theory of visual perceptual learning. *Trends in Cognitive Sciences, 8*(10), 457–464. doi:10.1016/j.tics.2004.08.011

Aichner, R., Zourub, M., Buchner, H., & Kellermann, W. (2006). Residual cross-talk and noise suppression for convolutive blind source separation. In *Proceedings of the annual meeting of the German Acoustical Society (DAGA)*.

Ainhoren, Y., Engelberg, S., & Friedman, S. (2008). *The cocktail party problem*. IEEE Instrumentation and Measurement Magazine.

Ainsworth, W. A., & Greenberg, S. (2006). *Auditory Processing of Speech. En S. G. Ainsworth, Listening to Speech: An Auditory Perspective* (pp. 3–17). Mahwah, NJ: Lawrence Erlbaum Ass. Pub.

Albright, R. Cox, J., Duling, D., Langville, A. & Meyer, C. (2006). Algorithms, initializations, and convergence for the nonnegative matrix factorization. *NCSU Technical Report Math 81706.*

Alghassi, H., Tafazoli, S., & Lawrence, P. (2006). The audio surveillance eye. In *IEEE International Conference on Video and Signal Based Surveillance.* Washington, DC, USA.

Allauzen, C., Crochemore, M., & Raffinot, M. (1999)., Factor oracle: a new structure for pattern matching. In J. Pavelka, G. Tel & M. Bartosek (Eds)., *Proceedings of SOFSEM'99, Theory and Practice of Informatics (LNCS pp 291-306)*, Milovy, Czech Republic. Berlin: Springer-Verlag.

Allen, J. (1994). How do humans process and recognize speech? *Speech and Audio Processing, 2*(4), 567–577. doi:10.1109/89.326615

Allen, J. B. (1985). Cochlear Modeling. *IEEE ASSP Magazine*, 3–29. doi:10.1109/MASSP.1985.1163723

Allen, J. B. (2008). Nonlinear Cochlear Signal Processing and Masking in Speech Perception. In Benesty, M. M. J. (Ed.), *Springer Handbook of Speech Processing*. Berlin: Springer Verlag. doi:10.1007/978-3-540-49127-9_3

Allen, J. & Berkley, D. (1979). Image method for efficiently simulating small-room acoustics, *J. of the Acoustical Soc. Am.* (pp. 943-950), 65(4).

Alvarez, G., & Oliva, A. (2008). The representation of simple ensemble visual features outside the focus of attention. *Psychological Science, 19*(4), 392–398. doi:10.1111/j.1467-9280.2008.02098.x

Amari, S., & Nagaoka, H. (2000). Methods of information geometry, Translations of mathematical monographs. *American Mathematical Society, 191.*

Amari, S., Douglas, S. C., Cichocki, A., & Wang, H. H. (1997). Multichannel blind deconvolution and equalization using the natural gradient, *in Proc. IEEE Workshop Signal Process* (pp. 101–104).

Anderson, K., & McOwan, P. W. (2006). A Real-Time Automated System for Recognition of Human Facial Expressions. *IEEE Trans. Systems, Man, and Cybernetics Part B, 36*(1), 96–105. doi:10.1109/TSMCB.2005.854502

Andrews, S., Tsochantaridis, I., & Hofmann, T. (2003). Support vector machines for multiple-instance learning. In *Advances in Neural Information Processing Systems 15*. Cambridge, MA: MIT Press.

Andringa, T. C., & Niessen, M. E. (2006). *Real World Sound Recognition, a Recipe. Learning the Semantics of Audio Signals*. Athens, Greece: LSAS.

Andringa, T. C. (2002). Continuity Preserving Signal Processing. *Dissertations University of Groningen,* http://dissertations.ub.rug.nl/FILES/faculties/science/2001/t.c.andringa/thesis.pdf.

Andringa, T. C. (2008). The texture of natural sounds. *Proceedings of Acoustics '08, Paris* (pp. 3141-3146).

Anemüller, J., & Kollmeier, B. (2000). Amplitude modulation decorrelation for convolutive blind source separation. In *Proceedings of the international conference on independent component analysis (ICA)* (pp. 215–220).

Araki, S., Makino, S., Sawada, H., & Mukai, R. (2005). Reducing musical noise by a fine-shift overlap-add method applied to source separation using a time-frequency mask. *In Proc. IEEE International Conference Acoustics, Speech. Signal Processing, 3*, 81–84.

Araki, S., Mukai, R., Makino, S., & Saruwatari, H. (2003). The fundamental limitation of frequency domain blind source separation for convolutive mixture of speech. *IEEE Transactions on Speech and Audio Processing, 11*, 109–116. doi:10.1109/TSA.2003.809193

Araki, S., Sawada, H., Mukai, R., & Makino, S. (2007). Underdetermined blind sparse source separation for arbitrarily arranged multiple sources. In *EURASIP Journal App* (*Vol. 87*, pp. 1833–1847). Signal Process.

Araki, S., Makino, S., Hinamoto, Y., Mukai, R., Nishikawa, T., & Saruwatari, H. (2003). Equivalence between frequency domain blind source separation and frequency domain adaptive beamforming for convolutive mixtures. *EURASIP Journal on Applied Signal Processing,* (11): 1157–1166. doi:10.1155/S1110865703305074

Araki, S., Makino, S., Sawada, H., & Mukai, R. (2004). Underdetermined blind separation of convolutive mixtures of speech with directivity pattern based mask and ICA. *In Proc. 5th International Conference Independent Component Anal. Blind Signal Separation* (pp. 898–905).

Araki, S., Sawada, H., Mukai, R., & Makino, S. (2005). A novel blind source separation method with observation vector clustering. In *Proceedings of the international workshop on acoustic echo and noise control (IWAENC '05)*.

Arberet, S., Ozerov, A., Gribonval, R., & Bimbot, F. (2009). Blind spectral-GMM estimation for underdetermined instantaneous audio source separation. In *Proceedings of the 8th International Conference on Independent Component Analysis and Signal Separation* (p. 751-758).

Arellano, J. I., Benavides-Piccione, R., DeFelipe, J., & Yuste, R. (2007). Ultrastructure of dendritic spines: correlation between synaptic and spine morphologies. *Frontiers in Neuroscience, 1*(1), 131–143. doi:10.3389/neuro.01.1.1.010.2007

Ariely, D. (2001). Seeing Sets: Representation by Statistical Properties. *Psychological Science, 12*(2), 157–162. doi:10.1111/1467-9280.00327

Arons, B. (1992). A review of the cocktail party effect. *Journal of the American Voice I/O Society, 12*, 35-50

Ashraf, A. B., Lucey, S., Cohn, J. F., Chen, T., Ambadar, Z., Prkachin, K., et al. (2007). The Painful Face: Pain Expression Recognition Using Active Appearance Models. *Proc. Ninth ACM Int'l Conf. Multimodal Interfaces* (pp. 9-14).

Assayag, G., & Dubnov, S. (2004). Using Factor Oracles for Machine Improvisation. [New York: Springer Verlag.]. *Soft Computing, 8*, 1–7. doi:10.1007/s00500-004-0385-4

Athanaselis, T., Bakamidis, S., Dologlou, I., Cowie, R., Douglas-Cowie, E., & Cox, C. (2005). ASR for Emotional Speech: Clarifying the Issues and Enhancing Performance. *Neural Networks, 18*, 437–444. doi:10.1016/j.neunet.2005.03.008

Attias, H. (2003). New EM algorithms for source separation and deconvolution with a microphone array. In *Proceedings of the 2003 IEEE International Conference on Acoustics, Speech and Signal Processing* (p. V-297-300).

Aucouturier, J.-J., Defreville, B., & Pachet, F. (2007). The bag-of-frames approach to audio pattern recognition: A sufficient model for urban soundscapes but not for polyphonic music. *The Journal of the Acoustical Society of America, 122*, 881–891. doi:10.1121/1.2750160

Aucouturier, J.-J., & Pachet, F. (2004). Improving timbre similarity: How high is the sky? *Journal of Negative Results in Speech and Audio Sciences, 1*(1).

Aucouturier, J. J., & Pachet, F. (2003). Representing Musical Genre: A State of the Art. *Journal of New Music Research, 32*, 83–93. doi:10.1076/jnmr.32.1.83.16801

Audioscrobbler. *Web Services.* Retrieved from http://www.audioscrobbler.net/~data/webservices/

Bach, F., & Jordan, M. I. (2004). Blind one-microphone speech separation: A spectral learning approach. In *Proc. Neural Information Processing Systems* (NIPS), Vancouver, Canada.

Back, A. D., & Tosi, A. C. (1994). Blind deconvolution of signals using a complex recurrent network. In *Proc. IEEE Workshop Neural Networks Signal Process.* (pp. 565–574).

Balakrishnan, V. K. (1997). *Graph Theory* (1st ed.). New York: McGraw-Hill.

Barabell, A. (1983). *Improving* the resolution performance of eigenstructure-based direction-finding algorithms (Vol. 8*). Paper presented at the IEEE International Conference on Acoustics, Speech, and Signal Processing.* Boston, USA.

Barker, J. (2006). Robust automatic speech recognition. In Wang, D., & Brown, G. J. (Eds.), *Computational auditory scene analysis: Principles, algorithms, and applications* (pp. 297–350). Hoboken, NJ: Wiley-IEEE Press.

Barrington, L., Turnbull, D., Yazdani, M., & Lanckriet, G. (2009). Combining audio content and social context for semantic music discovery. In *Proceedings of the 32th annual international ACM SIGIR conference on Research and development in information retrieval, ACM.*

Bartlett, M. S., Littlewort, G., Braathen, P., Sejnowski, T. J., & Movellan, J. R. (2003). A Prototype for Automatic Recognition of Spontaneous Facial Actions. *Advances in Neural Information Processing Systems, 15*, 1271–1278.

Bartlett, M. S., Littlewort, G., Frank, M. G., et al. (2006). Fully Automatic Facial Action Recognition in Spontaneous Behavior. *Proc. IEEE Int'l Conf. Automatic Face and Gesture Recognition* (pp. 223-230).

Bartlett, M. S., Littlewort, G., Frank, M., et al. (2005). Recognizing Facial Expression: Machine Learning and Application to Spontaneous Behavior. *Proc. IEEE Int'l Conf. Computer Vision and Pattern Recognition* (pp. 568-573).

Bartsch, M. A. & Wakefield, G.H. (2001). To Catch a Chorus: Using Chroma-Based Representations For Audio Thumbnailing. *Proceedings of the Workshop on Applications of Signal Processing to Audio and Acoustics* (CD). New York: IEEE.

Batliner, A., Fischer, K., Hubera, R., Spilkera, J., & Noth, E. (2003). How to Find Trouble in Communication. *Speech Communication, 40*, 117–143. doi:10.1016/S0167-6393(02)00079-1

Batliner, A., et al. (2004). You Stupid Tin Box—Children Interacting with the AIBO Robot: A Cross-Linguistic Emotional Speech. *Proc. Fourth Int'l Conf. Language Resources and Evaluation.*

Baumann, W., Kolossa, D., & Orglmeister, R. (2003). Beamforming-based convolutive blind source separation. In *Proceedings of the IEEE international conference on acoustics, speech and signal processing (ICASSP)* (pp. 357–360).

Beal, M. J., Attias, H., & Jojic, N. (2002). Audio-video sensor fusion with probabilistic graphical models. *In Proceedings of the 7th European conference on computer vision (pp. 736–752).* London, UK: Springer-Verlag.

Bello, J., Daudet, L., Abdallah, S., Duxbury, C., Davies, M., & Sandler, M. (2005). A tutorial on onset detection in music signals. *IEEE Transactions on Speech and Audio Processing, 13*(5), 1035–1047. doi:10.1109/TSA.2005.851998

Bello, J. P., & Sandler, M. (2003). Phase-based note onset detection for music signals. *Proc. IEEE Int. Conf. Acoustics, Speech, and Signal Processing (ICASSP-03)* (pp.49-52).Hong Kong.

Belloni, F., Richter, A., & Koivunen, V. (2007). DoA estimation via manifold separation for arbitrary array structures. *IEEE Transactions on Signal Processing, 55*(10), 4800–4810. doi:10.1109/TSP.2007.896115

Belouchrani, A., Abed-Mariam, K., Amin, M. G., & Zoubir, A. (2004). Blind source separation of nonstationary signals. *IEEE Signal Processing Letters,* (7): 605–608. doi:10.1109/LSP.2004.830119

Benaroya, L., Bimbot, F., & Gribonval, R. (2006). Audio source separation with a single sensor. *IEEE Transactions on Audio. Speech and Language Processing, 14*(1), 191–199. doi:10.1109/TSA.2005.854110

Benaroya, L., Bimbot, F., Gravier, G., & Gribonval, R. (2003). Audio source separation with one sensor for robust speech recognition. In *NOLISP-2003.*(paper 030).

Benaroya, L., Gribonval, R., & Bimbot, F. (2003). Non negative sparse representation for Wiener based source separation with a single sensor. In *Proc. IEEE International Conference on Acoustics, Speech and Signal Processing (ICASSP'03)* (pp. 613–616). Hong Kong.

Benaroya, L., McDonagh, L., Bimbot, F., & Gribonval, R. (2003). Non negative sparse representation for Wiener based source separation with a single sensor. In *Proceedings of the 2003 IEEE International Conference on Acoustics, Speech and Signal Processing* (p. VI-613-616).

Benesty, J. (2000). *Adaptive* eigenvalue decomposition algorithm for passive acoustic source localization. *The Journal of the Acoustical Society of America, 107*(1), 384–391. doi:10.1121/1.428310

Benesty, J., Huang, Y., & Chen, J. (2007). Time delay estimation via minimum entropy. *Signal Processing Letters, IEEE, 14*(3), 157–160. doi:10.1109/LSP.2006.884038

Bengio, Y., Lamblin, P., Popovici, D., & Larochelle, H. (2007). Greedy layer-wise training of deep networks. In *Advances in Neural Information Processing Systems 19* (pp. 153–160). Cambridge, MA: MIT Press.

Bense, M. (1969). *Einführung in die informationstheoretische Asthetik. Grundlegung und Anwendung in der Texttheorie (Introduction to the Information-theoretical Aesthetics. Foundation and Application to the Text Theory).* Rowohlt Taschenbuch Verlag.

Bergstra, J. (2006). *Algorithms for classifying recorded music by genre.* Montreal, Canada: University of Montreal.

Bergstra, J., Casagrande, N., Erhan, D., Eck, D., & Kégl, B. (2006). Aggregate Features and AdaBoost for Music Classification. *Machine Learning, 65,* 473–484. doi:10.1007/s10994-006-9019-7

Berkhout, A. J., de Vries, D., & Sonke, J. J. (1997). Array technology for acoustic wave field analysis in enclosures. *The Journal of the Acoustical Society of America, 102*(5), 2757–2770. doi:10.1121/1.420330

Berry, M., Browne, M., Langville, M., Pauca, P., & Plemmons, R. (2007). *Algorithms and applications for approximate nonnegative matrix factorization.* Computational Statistics and Data Analysis.

Bertin, N., Badeau, R., & Vincent, E. (2009). *Enforcing harmonicity and smoothness in Bayesian non-negative matrix factorization applied to polyphonic music transcription.* (Report No. 2009D006). Paris, France: Telecom ParisTech

Bertin-Mahieux, T., Eck, D., Maillet, F. & Lamere, P. (2008). Autotagger: a model for Predicting social tags from acoustic features on large music databases. *Journal of New Music Research, special issue: From genres to tags: Music Information Retrieval in the era of folksonomies., 37.*

Bialek, W., Nemenman, I., & Tishby, N. (2001). Predictability, complexity, and learning. *Neural Computation, 13,* 2409–2463. doi:10.1162/089976601753195969

Birkhoff, G. D. (1933). *Aesthetic Measure.* Cambridge, MA: Harvard Univ. Press.

Bishop, C. (2003). *Neural networks for pattern recognition.* Oxford, UK: Oxford University Press.

Bishop, C. M. (1999). Bayesian PCA. In *Advances in neural information processing systems* (pp. 382–388). NIPS.

Bishop, C. (2006). *Pattern Recognition and Machine Learning*. New York: Springer Verlag.

Bishop, C. M. (1995). *Neural Networks for Pattern Recognition*. Oxford University Press.

Blauert, J. (1983). *Spatial hearing: The psychophysics of human sound localization* (rev. Ed.). Cambridge, MA: MIT Press.

Blauert, J. (1997). *Spatial hearing: The psychophysics of human sound localization*. Cambridge, MA: MIT Press.

Blouet, R., Rapaport, G., Cohen, I., & Févotte, C. (2008). Evaluation of several strategies for single sensor speech/music separation. In *Proc. International Conference on Acoustics, Speech and Signal Processing (ICASSP '08)*. Las Vegas, USA.

Blumensath, T., & Davies, M. E. (2006). Sparse and shift-invariant representations of music. *IEEE Transactions on Audio. Speech and Language Processing, 14*(1), 50–57. doi:10.1109/TSA.2005.860346

Blumensath, T., & Davies, M. (2007). Compressed sensing and source separation. In *International Conference on Independent Component Anal and Blind Source Separation*.

Bofill, P., & Zibulevsky, M. (2001). Underdetermined blind source separation using sparse representations. *Signal Processing*, 2353–2362. doi:10.1016/S0165-1684(01)00120-7

Bofill, P., & Zibulevsky, M. (2000). Blind separation of more sources than mixtures using sparsity of their short-time Fourier transform. In *Proceedings of the international conference on independent component analysis (ICA)*.

Borchert, M., & Düsterhöft, A. (2005). Emotions in Speech – Experiments with Prosody and Quality Features in Speech for Use in Categorical and Dimensional Emotion Recognition Environments. *Proc. IEEE Int'l Conf. on Natural Language Processing and Knowledge Engineering* (pp. 147–151).

Bordes, A., Ertekin, S., Weston, J., & Bottou, L. (2005). Fast Kernel Classifiers with Online and Active Learning. *Journal of Machine Learning Research, 6*, 1579–1619.

Bradley, J. K., & Schapire, R. (2008). *FilterBoost: Regression and Classification on Large Datasets. Advances in Neural Information Processing Systems 20*. Cambridge, MA: MIT Press.

Brandenburg, K., & Popp, H. (June de 2000). An introduction to MPEG Layer 3. *EBU Technical Review*, 1-15.

Brandenburg, K., & Stoll, G. (1992). The ISO/MPEG-Audio Codec: A Generic Standard for Coding of High Quality Digital Audio. Vienna.

Brandstein, M. S., Adcock, J. E., & Silverman, H. F. (1997, January). A closed-form location estimator for use with room environment microphone arrays. *IEEE Transactions on Speech and Audio Processing, 5*(1), 45–50. doi:10.1109/89.554268

Brandstein, M. S., & Silverman, H. F. (1997, April). A practical methodology for speech source localization with microphone arrays. Journal of Computer. *Speech and Language, 11*(2), 91–126. doi:10.1006/csla.1996.0024

Bregman, A. (1990). *Auditory Scene Analysis: The Perceptual Organization of Sound*. Cambridge, MA: MIT Press.

Breithaupt, C., Gerkmann, T., & Martin, R. (2007). Cepstral smoothing of spectral filter gains for speech enhancement without musical noise. *IEEE Signal Processing Letters, 14*(12). doi:10.1109/LSP.2007.906208

Bro, R. (1997). PARAFAC. Tutorial and applications. *Chemometrics and Intelligent Laboratory Systems, 38*(2), 149–171. doi:10.1016/S0169-7439(97)00032-4

Bro, R. (1997). Multi-way analysis in the food industry: Models, algorithms and applications. *PhD thesis, University of Amsterdam, and Royal Veterinary and Agricultural University*.

Bronkhorst, A. (2000). The cocktail party phenomenon: A review of research on speech intelligibility in multiple talker condition. *Acoustica, 86*, 117–128.

Brooks, F. Jr (1993). An Experiment in Musical Composition. In Schwanauer, S., & Levitt, D. (Eds.), *Machine Models of Music* (pp. 23–40). Cambridge, MA: MIT Press.

Brown, G. J., & Cooke, M. (1994). Computational auditory scene analysis. *Computer Speech & Language, 8*(4), 297–336. doi:10.1006/csla.1994.1016

Buchner, H., Aichner, R., & Kellermann, W. (2004). Blind source separation for convolutive mixtures: A unified treatment. In Huang, Y., & Benesty, J. (Eds.), *Audio Signal Process. for Next-Generation Multimedia Communication Systems* (pp. 255–293). Boston, Dordrecht, London: Kluwer Academic Publishers. doi:10.1007/1-4020-7769-6_10

Buchner, H., Aichner, R., & Kellermann, W. (2004). TRINICON: A versatile framework for multichannel blind signal processing. In *Proceedings of the IEEE international conference on acoustics, speech and signal processing (ICASSP).*

Buchner, H., Aichner, R., Stenglein, J., Teutsch, H., & Kellennann, W. (2005). Simultaneous localization of multiple sound sources using blind adaptive MIMO filtering (Vol. 3). *Paper presented at the IEEE International Conference on Acoustics, Speech and Signal Processing.*

Buchsbaum, B. R., Hickok, G., & Humphries, C. (2001). Role of left posterior superior temporal gyrus in phonological processing for speech perception and production. *Cognitive Science, 25*, 663–678. doi:10.1207/s15516709cog2505_2

Burger, S., MacLaren, V., & Yu, H. (2002). The ISL Meeting Corpus: The Impact of Meeting Type on Speech Style. *Proc. Eighth Int'l Conf. Spoken Language Processing.*

Burges, C. J. C. (1998). A Tutorial on Support Vector Machines for Pattern Recognition. *Data Mining and Knowledge Discovery, 2*, 121–167. doi:10.1023/A:1009715923555

Burkhardt, F., Paeschke, A., Rolfes, M., Sendlmeier, W., & Weiss, B. (2005). *A Database of German Emotional Speech* (pp. 1517–1520). Proc. Interspeech.

Burred, J. J., & Sikora, T. (2007). Monaural source separation from musical mixtures based on time-frequency timbre models. In *International Conference on Music Information Retrieval* (ISMIR 2007), Vienna, Austria.

Burred, J. J., R¨obel, A., & Rodet, X. (2006). An accurate timbre model for musical instruments and its application to classification. In *Proc. Workshop on Learning the Semantics of Audio Signals*, Athens, Greece.

Busso, C., & Narayanan, S. S. (2007). Interrelation between Speech and Facial Gestures in Emotional Utterances: A Single Subject Study. *IEEE Trans. on Audio, Speech, and Language Processing, 15*(8), 2331–2347. doi:10.1109/TASL.2007.905145

Busso, C., Deng, Z., Yildirim, S., Bulut, M., Lee, C. M., Kazemzadeh, A., et al. (2004). Analysis of Emotion Recognition Using Facial Expressions. Speech and Multimodal Information. *Proc. ACM Int'l Conf. Multimodal Interfaces (*pp. 205-211).

Cai, R., Lu, L., Hanjalic, A., Zhang, H., & Cai, L.-H. (2006). A flexible framework for key audio effects detection and auditory context inference. *IEEE Transactions on Audio. Speech and Language Processing, 14*(3), 1026–1039. doi:10.1109/TSA.2005.857575

Cai, R., Lu, L., & Hanjalic, A. (2005). Unsupervised content discovery in composite audio. In *Proc. ACM Multimedia.*

Cajal Blue Brain Project. (2009, 4 2). Retrieved 5 15, 2009, from http://cajalbbp.cesvima.upm.es/

Campbell, J. (1997). Speaker Recognition: A Tutorial. *Proceedings of the IEEE, 85*(9), 1437–1462. doi:10.1109/5.628714

Candès, E. (2006). Compressive sampling. In *Proceedings of the International Congress of Mathematics.* Madrid, Spain. Candès, E. & Romberg, J. Sparsity and incoherence in compressive sampling. *Inverse Prob. 23*(3), 969–985

Candès, E. J., & Wakin, M. B. (2008). An introduction to compressive sampling. In *IEEE Signal Process Magazine.* (21).

Cano, P., & Koppenberger, M. (2004). Automatic sound annotation. In *IEEE workshop on Machine Learning for Signal Processing*, 391-400.

Cano, P., Koppenberger, M., Groux, S., Ricard, J., Wack, N., & Herrera, P. (2004). Nearest-neighbor generic sound classification with a wordnet-based taxonomy. In *116th Convention of the Audio Engineering Society.*

Cardoso, J.-F. (1998). Multidimensional independent component analysis. In *Proceedings of the 1998 IEEE International Conference on Acoustics, Speech and Signal Processing* (p. IV-1941-1944).

Cardoso, J.-F. (2001). The three easy routes to independent component analysis; contrasts and geometry. In *Proceedings of the 3rd International Conference on Independent Component Analysis and Blind Signal Separation* (p. 1-6).

Caridakis, G., Malatesta, L., Kessous, L., Amir, N., Paouzaiou, A., & Karpouzis, K. (2006). Modeling Naturalistic Affective States via Facial and Vocal Expression Recognition. *Proc. ACM Int'l Conf. Multimodal Interfaces*, (pp. 146-154).

Carol, J. D., & Chang, J. (1970). Analysis of individual differences in multidimensional scaling via an N-way generalization of 'Eckart-Young' decomposition. *Psychometrika, 35*, 283–319. doi:10.1007/BF02310791

Cartwright-Finch, U., & Lavie, N. (2007). The role of perceptual load in inattentional blindness. *Cognition, 102*, 321–340. doi:10.1016/j.cognition.2006.01.002

Celma, O., Cano, P., & Herrera, P. (2006). Search Sounds: An audio crawler focused on weblogs. In *Proceedings of the 7th International Conference on Music Information Retrieval (ISMIR 2006)*.

Cemgil, A. T., Févotte, C., & Godsill, S. J. (2007). Variational and stochastic inference for Bayesian source separation. *Digital Signal Processing, 17*(5), 891–913. doi:10.1016/j.dsp.2007.03.008

Cemgil, A. T. (2009). Bayesian inference for nonnegative matrix factorisation models. *Computational Intelligence and Neuroscience*, 2009(Article ID 785152), 17 pages. (doi:10.1155/2009/785152)

Cermak, J., Araki, S., Sawada, H., & Makino, S. (2006). Blind speech separation by combining beamformers and a time frequency mask. In *Proceedings of the international workshop on acoustic echo and noise control (IWAENC)*.

Chai, W., & Vercoe, B. (2003). Music thumbnailing via structural analysis. *Proceedings of ACM Multimedia Conference*. November.

Champagne, B., Bedard, S., & Stephenne, A. (1996). Performance of time-delay estimation in the presence of room reverberation. *IEEE Transactions on Speech and Audio Processing, 4*(2), 148–152. doi:10.1109/89.486067

Chang, Y., Hu, C., Feris, R., & Turk, M. (2006). Manifold Based Analysis of Facial Expression. *J. Image and Vision Computing, 24*(6), 605–614. doi:10.1016/j.imavis.2005.08.006

Chang, Y., Vieira, M., Turk, M., & Velho, L. (2005). Automatic 3D Facial Expression Analysis in Videos. *Proc. IEEE Int'l Workshop Analysis and Modeling of Faces and Gestures* (Vol. 3723, pp. 293-307).

Chen, S., Donoho, D., & Saunders, M. (1998). Atomic decomposition by basis pursuit. *SIAM Journal on Scientific Computing, 20*, 33–61. doi:10.1137/S1064827596304010

Chen, J., Benesty, J., & Huang, Y. (2003). Robust time delay estimation exploiting redundancy among multiple microphones. *IEEE Transactions on Speech and Audio Processing, 11*(6), 549–557. doi:10.1109/TSA.2003.818025

Chen, J., Benesty, J., & Huang, Y. (2008). A minimum distortion noise reduction algorithm with multiple microphones. *IEEE Transactions on Audio. Speech and Language Processing, 16*(3), 481–493. doi:10.1109/TASL.2007.914969

Chen, C. (1978). *Pattern Recognition and Signal Processing*. The Netherlands: Sijthoff & Noordoff.

Chen, C., Huang, Y., & Cook, P. (2005). Visual/Acoustic emotion recognition. *Proc. Int'l Conf. on Multimedia & Expo* (pp. 1468-1471).

Chen, L. S. (2000). *Joint Processing of Audio-Visual Information for the Recognition of Emotional Expressions in Human-Computer Interaction*. (PhD dissertation, Univ. of Illinois, Urbana-Champaign).

Cheng, C., & Wakefield, G. (1999). Introduction to head-related transfer functions (HRTFs): Representations of HRTF's in time, frequency, and space. *Presented at the 107th AES Convention*, preprint 5026. New York.

Cherkani, N., & Deville, Y. (1999). Self adaptive separation of convolutively mixed signals with a recursive structure, Part 1: stability analysis and optimisation of asymptotic behaviour. *Signal Processing, 73*(3), 225–254. doi:10.1016/S0165-1684(98)00195-9

Cherry, E. C. (1953). Some experiments on the recognition of speech, with one and with two ears. *The Journal of the Acoustical Society of America, 25*, 975–979. doi:10.1121/1.1907229

Cherry, C., & Taylor, W. (1954). Some further experiments upon the recognition of speech, with one and with two ears. *The Journal of the Acoustical Society of America, 26*, 554–559. doi:10.1121/1.1907373

Chib, S. (1995). Marginal likelihood from the Gibbs output. *Journal of the American Statistical Association, 90*(432), 1995. doi:10.2307/2291521

Chu, S., Narayanan, S., & Kuo, C.-C. J. (2009). Environmental sound recognition with time-frequency audio features. *IEEE Transactions on Audio. Speech and Language Processing, 17*(6), 1142–1158. doi:10.1109/TASL.2009.2017438

Chu, S., Narayanan, S., & Kuo, C.-C. J. (2008). Environmental sound recognition using mp-based features. In *IEEE International Conference on Acoustics, Speech, and Signal Processing*. Washington, DC: IEEE.

Chu, S., Narayanan, S., & Kuo, C.-C. J. (2009) A Semi-Supervised Learning Approach to Online Audio Background Detection. In *IEEE International Conference on Acoustics, Speech, and Signal Processing*. Washington, DC: IEEE.

Chu, S., Narayanan, S., Kuo, C.-C. J., & Mataric, M. (2006). Where am I? scene recognition for mobile robots using audio features. In *IEEE International Conference on Multimedia and Expo*. Washington, DC: IEEE.

Chuan, C., & Elaine, C. (2008). Audio Onset Detection Using Machine Learning Techniques: The Effect and Applicability of Key and Tempo Information. University of Southern California Computer Science Department Technical Report No. 08-895.

Cichocki, A., & Amari, S. (2002). *Adaptive Blind Signal and Image Processing: Learning Algorithms and Applications*. John Wiley. doi:10.1002/0470845899

Cichocki, A., Zdunek, R., Phan, A. H., & Amari, S. (2009). *Nonnegative Matrix and Tensor Factorizations: Applications to Exploratory Multi-way Data Analysis and Blind Source Separation*. Hoboken, NJ: John Wiley & Sons.

Cichocki, A., Zdunek, R., & Amari, S. (2006a). Csiszar's divergences for non-negative matrix factorization: family of new algorithms. *Spinger Lecture Notes in Computer Science, 3889*, 32–39. doi:10.1007/11679363_5

Cichocki, A., Amari, S.-I., Zdunek, R., Kompass, R., Hori, G., & He, Z. (2006). Extended SMART algorithms for non-negative matrix factorization. In *Proc. International Conference on Artificial Intelligence and Soft Computing (ICAISC'06)* (p. 548-562). Zakopane, Poland.

Cichocki, A., Zdunek, R., & Amari, S. (2006). New algorithms for non-negative matrix factorization in applications to blind source separation. In *Proc. ICASSP* (Vol. 5, pp. 621–624) Toulouse, France.

Cichocki, A., Zdunek, R., Choi, S., Plemmons, R., & Amari, S. (2007). Non-negative tensor factorization using alfa and beta divergences. *Proc. Int. Conf. on Acoustics, Speech, and Signal Process.* (pp. 1393-1396), Honolulu, Hawaii, USA.

Cirillo, L., & Zoubir, A. (2005). On blind separation of nonstationary signals. *Proc. of the 8th Symp. On Signal Processing and its Applications (ISSPA).* Sydney, Australia.

Cohen, L. (1995). *Time frequency analysis, Prentice Hall Signal Processing Series*. Upper Saddle River, NJ: Prentice Hall.

Cohen, L., Sebe, N., Garg, A., Chen, L., & Huang, T. (2003). Facial Expression Recognition from Video Sequences: Temporal and Static Modeling. *Computer Vision and Image Understanding, 91*(1-2), 160–187. doi:10.1016/S1077-3142(03)00081-X

Cohn, J. F., & Schmidt, K. L. (2004). The Timing of Facial Motion in Posed and Spontaneous Smiles. *International Journal of Wavelets, Multiresolution, and Information Processing, 2*, 1–12. doi:10.1142/S021969130400041X

Cohn, J. F. (2006). Foundations of Human Computing: Facial Expression and Emotion. *Proc. Eighth ACM Int'l Conf. Multimodal Interfaces,* (pp. 233-238).

Cohn, J. F., Reed, L. I., Ambadar, Z., Xiao, J., & Moriyama, T. (2004). Automatic Analysis and Recognition of Brow Actions and Head Motion in Spontaneous Facial Behavior. *Proc. IEEE Int'l Conf. Systems, Man, and Cybernetics* (vol. 1, pp. 610-616).

Collins, N. (1999). Using a pitch detector as an onset detector. *Proc. International Conf. On Music Information Retrieval.*

Collins, N. (2005). A comparison of sound onset detection algorithms with emphasis on psychoacoustically motivated detection functions. *Proceedings of AES 118th Convention*, Barcelona, Spain, May.

Cont, A. (2008)., Modeling Musical Anticipation: From the time of music to the music of time. (PhD thesis University of Paris 6 (UPMC) and University of California San Diego (UCSD)).See also http://imtr.ircam.fr/index. php/Music_Information_Geometry

Cont, A., Dubnov, S., & Assayag, G. (2007, September) GUIDAGE: A Fast Audio Query Guided Assemblage. In *Proceedings of International Computer Music Conference (ICMC).*

Cooke, M., & Ellis, D. (2001). The auditory organization of speech and other sources in listeners and computational models. *Speech Communication, 35,* 141–177. doi:10.1016/S0167-6393(00)00078-9

Cooke, M. P. (Dec 2002). Computational Auditory Scene Analysis in Listeners and Machines, *Tutorial at NIPS2002,* Vancouver, Canada.

Corina, D. P., Gibson, E. K., Martin, R., Poliakov, A., Brinkley, J., & Ojemann, G. A. (2005). Dissociation of Action and Object Naming: Evidence from Cortical Stimulation Mapping. *Human Brain Mapping, 24,* 1–10. doi:10.1002/hbm.20063

Cormen, T. H., Stein, C., Rivest, R. L., & Leiserson, C. E. (2001). *Introduction to Algorithms,*(2nd Ed.). Boston: MIT Press. and New York: McGraw-Hill.

Cover, T. M., & Thomas, J. A. (2006). *Elements of Information Theory* (2nd ed.). New York: Wiley.

Cowie, R., Douglas-Cowie, E., & Cox, C. (2005). Beyond Emotion Archetypes: Databases for Emotion Modeling Using Neural Networks. *Neural Networks, 18,* 371–388. doi:10.1016/j.neunet.2005.03.002

Cowie, R., Douglas-Cowie, E., Tsapatsoulis, N., Votsis, G., Kollias, S., Fellenz, W., & Taylor, J. G. (2001). Emotion Recognition in Human-Computer Interaction. *IEEE Signal Processing Magazine,* 32–80. doi:10.1109/79.911197

Cowie, R., Douglas-Cowie, E., et al. (2000). Feeltrace: An Instrument for Recording Perceived Emotion in Real Time. *Proc. ISCA Workshop Speech and Emotion* (pp. 19-24).

Cowling, M., & Sitte, R. (2003). Comparison of techniques for environmental sound recognition. *Pattern Recognition Letters, 24,* 2895–2907. doi:10.1016/S0167-8655(03)00147-8

Cowling, M., & Sitte, R. (2000). Sound identification and direction detection in Matlab for surveillance applications. *Paper presented at the Matlab Users Conference.* Melbourne, Australia.

Cox, H., Zeskind, R. M., & Owen, M. M. (1987). Robust adaptive beamforming. *IEEE Transactions on Acoustics, Speech, and Signal Processing, 35*(10), 1365–1375. doi:10.1109/TASSP.1987.1165054

Cox, T. J., Li, F., & Darlington, P. (2001a). Extraction of room reverberation time from speech using artificial neural networks. *Journal of AES, 49*(4), 219–230.

Cox, T. J., & Li, F. F. (2001b), Using Artificial Intelligence to Enable Occupied Measurements of Concert Hall Parameters. *Proc. 17th ICA,* 3A.08.05. Italy.

Cremer, L., & Müller, H. Translated by T. Schultz (1978). *Principles and Applications of Room Acoustics, 1,*(p. 194), London: Applied Science.

Crow, G., Rupert, A. L., & Moushegian, G. (1978). Phase locking in monaural and binaural medullary neurons: Implications for binaural phenomena. *The Journal of the Acoustical Society of America, 64*(2), 493–501. doi:10.1121/1.381999

Culling, J. F., & Darwin, C. J. (1993). Perceptual separation of simultaneous vowels: Within and across-formant grouping by F0. *The Journal of the Acoustical Society of America, 93,* 3454–3467. doi:10.1121/1.405675

Cusack, R., Deeks, J., Aikman, G., & Carlyon, R. (2004). Effects of location, frequency region, and time course of selective attention on auditory scene analysis. *Journal of Experimental Psychology. Human Perception and Performance, 30*(4), 643–656. doi:10.1037/0096-1523.30.4.643

Cybenco, G. (1989). Approximation by superpositions of a sigmoidal function. *Mathematics of Control, Signals, and Systems, 2,* 303–314. doi:10.1007/BF02551274

Daudet, L., & Torrésani, B. (2002). Hybrid representations for audiophonic signal encoding. *Signal Processing, 82*, 1595–1617.

Daudet, L. (2006). A review on techniques for the extraction of transients in musical signals (LNCS). In Kronland-Martinet, R., Voinier, T., & Ystad, S. (Eds.), *Springer-Verlag Berlin Heidelberg, Jan 2006.*

Davies, M., & Mitianoudis, N. (2004, Aug). A simple mixture model for sparse overcomplete ICA. *IEE Proceedings. Vision Image and Signal Processing, 151*(1), 35–43. doi:10.1049/ip-vis:20040304

Davies, M., & Daudet, L. (2006). Sparse audio representations using the mclt. *Signal Processing, 86*(3), 457–470. doi:10.1016/j.sigpro.2005.05.024

Davis, G. (1994). *Adaptive nonlinear approximations.* Unpublished doctoral dissertation, New York University.

Davy, M., & Godsill, S. (2002). Detection of abrupt spectral changes using support vector machines an application to audio signal segmentation. In *Proceedings of IEEE International Conference on Acoustics, Speech and Signal Processing (ICASSP '02)*(Vol. 2, pp. 1313-1316). Orlando, Fla, USA.

Declercq, A., & Piater, J. H. (2008). Online Learning of Gaussian Mixture Models - a Two-Level Approach, In *3rd International Conference on Computer Vision Theory and Applications (VISAPP)*, 605-611.

Dehaene, S., Changeux, J., Naccache, L., & Sackur, J. (2006). Conscious, preconscious, and subliminal processing: a testable taxonomy. *Trends in Cognitive Sciences, 10*(5), 204–211. doi:10.1016/j.tics.2006.03.007

Deliege, I., & Melen, P. (1997). Cue abstraction in the representation of musical form. In Deliège, J. Sloboda (Eds). *Perception and cognition of music(*387-412).East Sussex, England: Psychology Press.

Dempster, A. P., Laird, N. M., & Rubin, D. B. (1977). Maximum-likelihood from incomplete data via the EM algorithm. *Journal of the Royal Statistical Society. Series B. Methodological, 39*(1), 1–38.

Deng, L., & O'Shaughnessy, D. (2003). *Speech processing: A dynamic and optimization-oriented approach, ser. signal processing and communications.* London: Marcel Dekker, Taylor & Francis.

Desain, P. (1992). A (de)composable theory of rhythm. *Music Perception, 9*(4), 439–454.

Desloge, J. G., Rabinowitz, W. M., & Zurek, P. M. (1997). Microphone-array hearing aids with binaural output - Part I: Fixed-processing systems. *IEEE Transactions on Speech and Audio Processing, 5*(5), 529–542. doi:10.1109/89.641298

Devillers, L. & Vidrascu, L. (2006). Real-Life Emotions Detection with Lexical and Paralinguistic Cues on Human-Human Call Center Dialogs. *Proc. Interspeech,* 801-804.

Dhillon, I. S., & Sra, S. (2005). *Generalized nonnegative matrix approximations with Bregman divergences. Advances in Neural Information Processing Systems.* NIPS.

Dhillon, I. S., & Sra, S. (2006). Generalized non-negative matrix approximations with Bregman divergences. In Y. Weiss, B. Schölkopf, and J. Platt, (Eds). *Advances in Neural Information Processing 18* (in Proc. NIPS 2006). Cambridge, MA: MIT Press.

Di Claudio, E., Parisi, R., & Orlandi, G. (2000). Multi-source localization in reverberant environments by root-MUSIC and clustering (Vol. 2). *Paper presented at the IEEE International Conference on Acoustics, Speech and Signal Processing.*

Diamantaras, K. I. (2001). Blind source separation using principal component neural networks. In Dorffner, G., Bischof, H., & Hornik, K. (Eds.), *Lecture notes in computer science (Vol. 2130).* New York: Springer Verlag.

DiBiase, J. H., Silverman, H. F., & Brandstein, M. S. (2001). Robust localization in reverberant rooms. In Brandstein, M. S., & Ward, D. (Eds.), *Microphone arrays signal processing techniques and applications* (pp. 159–160). Berlin: Springer-Verlag.

Dietterich, T., Lathrop, R., & Lozano-Pérez, T. Solving the multiple instance problem with axis-parallel rectangles, In *Artificial Intelligence, Elsevier Science Publishers Ltd.* (1997), 89, 31-71

Dixon, S. (2006). Onset detection revisited. In *Proc. International Conference on Digital Audio Effects* (DAFx), Montreal, Canada.

Doclo, S., Spriet, A., Wouters, J., & Moonen, M. (2005). Speech distortion weighted multichannel Wiener filtering techniques for noise reduction. In Benesty, J., Makino, S., & Chen, J. (Eds.), *Speech enhancement* (pp. 199–228). New York: Springer Verlag. doi:10.1007/3-540-27489-8_9

Donoho, D. (2006). Compressed sensing. *IEEE Transactions on Information Theory, 52*(4), 1289–1306. doi:10.1109/TIT.2006.871582

Doucet, A., Sénécal, S., & Matsui, T. (2005). Space alternating data augmentation: Application to finite mixture of Gaussians and speaker recognition. In *Proc. IEEE International Conference on Acoustics, Speech and Signal Processing (ICASSP '05)* (pp. IV-713 – IV-716). Philadelphia, PA.

Douglas, S., Sawada, H., & Makino, S. (2005, Jan). Natural gradient multichannel blind deconvolution and speech separation using causal FIR filters. *IEEE Transactions on Speech and Audio Processing, 13*(1), 92–104. doi:10.1109/TSA.2004.838538

Douglas, S. C., & Sun, X. (2002). Convolutive blind separation of speech mixtures using the natural gradient. *Speech Communication, 39*, 65–78. doi:10.1016/S0167-6393(02)00059-6

Douglas-Cowie, E., Campbell, N., Cowie, R., & Roach, P. (2003). Emotional Speech: Towards a New Generation of Database. *Speech Communication, 40*(1/2), 33–60. doi:10.1016/S0167-6393(02)00070-5

Dubnov, S. (2004). Generalization of Spectral Flatness Measure for Non-Gaussian Linear Processes. *IEEE Signal Processing Letters, 11*(8). doi:10.1109/LSP.2004.831663

Dubnov, S. (2006). Spectral anticipations. *Computer Music Journal, 30*(2), 63–83. doi:10.1162/comj.2006.30.2.63

Dubnov, S. (2008). Unified view of prediction and repetition structure in audio signals with application to interest point detection. *IEEE Transactions on Audio. Speech and Language Processing, 16*(2), 327–337. doi:10.1109/TASL.2007.912378

Dubnov, S. (2009). Information Dynamics and Aspects of Musical Perception. In *Structure of Style*. New York: Springer Verlag.

Dubnov, S., McAdams, S., & Reynolds, R. (2006). Structural and Affective Aspects of Music From Statistical Audio Signal Analysis. *Journal of the American Society for Information Science and Technology, 57*(11), 1526–1536. doi:10.1002/asi.20429

Dubnov, S., & Appel, T. (2004). Audio segmentation by singular value clustering. In *Proc. International Computer Music Conference* (ICMC).

Dubnov, S., Assayag G., Lartillot, O., & Bejerano, G. (2003- August). Using Machine-Learning Methods for Musical Style Modeling. *Computer magazine*.

Dubnov, S., Assayag, G., & Cont, A. (2007- September) Audio Oracle: A New Algorithm for Fast Learning of Audio Structures. *In Proceedings of International Computer Music Conference (ICMC)*.

Duda, R. O., Hart, P. E., & Stork, D. G. (2000). *Pattern Classification* (2nd ed.). New York: Wiley-Interscience.

Duong, N. Q. K., Vincent, E., & Gribonval, R. (2009). Spatial covariance models for under-determined reverberant audio source separation. In *Proceedings of the 2009 IEEE Workshop on Applications of Signal Processing to Audio and Acoustics* (p. 129-132).

Durrieu, J.-L., Richard, G., David, B., & Févotte, C. (2010). (To appear). Source/filter model for main melody extraction from polyphonic audio signals. *IEEE Transactions on Audio, Speech, and Language Processing*. doi:10.1109/TASL.2010.2041114

Durrieu, J.-L., Ozerov, A., Févotte, C., Richard, G., & David, B. (2009). Main instrument separation from stereophonic audio signals using a source/filter model. In *Proc. 17th European Signal Processing Conference (EUSIPCO '09)* (pp. 15–19). Glasgow, Scotland.

Duxbury, C., Sandler, M., & Davies, M. (2002). A hybrid approach to musical note onset detection. *Proc. 5th International Conf. Digital Audio Effects (DAFX-02)*. Hamburg, Germany.

Ebenezer, S., Papandreou-Suppappola, A., & Suppappola, S. (2004). Classification of acoustic emissions using modified matching pursuit. *EURASIP Journal on Applied Signal Processing, 347–357*. doi:10.1155/S1110865704311029

Eck, D., Lamere, P., Bertin-Mahieux, T., & Green, S. (2008). Automatic generation of social tags for music recommendation. In *Advances in Neural Information Processing Systems 20*. Cambridge, MA: MIT Press.

Eck, D., Bertin-Mahieux, T., & Lamere, P. (2007). Autotagging music using supervised machine learning. In *Proceedings of the 8th International Conference on Music Information Retrieval (ISMIR 2007)*.

Edwards, A. L. (1962). *Experimental Design in Psychological Research*. New York: Holt, Rinehart and Winston.

EFPL. (2009). *Blue Brain Project*. Retrieved May 23, 2009, from http://bluebrain.epfl.ch/

Ekman, P. (1994). Strong Evidence for Universals in Facial Expressions: A Reply to Russell's Mistaken Critique. *Psychological Bulletin, 115*(2), 268–287. doi:10.1037/0033-2909.115.2.268

Ekman, P. (1971). Universal and Cultural Differences in Facial Expressions of Emotion. *Proc. Nebraska Symp. Motivation, 207-283*.

Ekman, P., & Rosenberg, E. L. (2005). *What the Face Reveals: Basic and Applied Studies of Spontaneous Expression Using the Facial Action Coding System*,(Eds.). Oxford Univ. Press.

El Chami, Z., Pham, D. T., Servière, C., & Guerin, A. (2008). A new model-based underdetermined source separation. In *Proceedings of the 11th International Workshop on Acoustic Echo and Noise Control* (paper ID 9061).

Elko, G. W., Pardo, F., Lopez, D., Bishop, D., & Gammel, P. (2003, October). Surface-micromachined MEMS microphone. *Paper presented at the AES 115th Convention*. New York.

Ellis, D. (1996). *Prediction-driven computational auditory scene analysis*. Unpublished doctoral dissertation, MIT Department of Electrical Engineering and Computer Science, MIT, Cambridge.

Ellis, D. (2001). Detecting alarm sounds. In *Workshop Consistent and Reliable Acoustic Cues*.

Ellis, D. P. W. (2006). Model-based scene analysis. In *Computational Auditory Scene Analysis: Principles, Algorithms, and Applications* (p. 115–146). Wiley/IEEE Press.

Ellis, D., & Lee, K. (2004). Minimal-impact audio-based personal archives. In *Workshop on Continuous Archival and Retrieval of Personal Experiences*.

Elston, G. N., Benavides-Piccione, R., & DeFelipe, J. (2001). The pyramidal cell in cognition: a comparative study in man and monkey. *The Journal of Neuroscience, 21*, 1–5.

Engberg, I. S., & Hansen, A. V. (1996). *Documentation of the Danish Emotional Speech Database (DES)*. Denmark: Aalborg University.

Eronen, A., Peltonen, V., Tuomi, J., Klapuri, A., Fagerlund, S., & Sorsa, T. (2006). Audio-based context recognition. *IEEE Transactions on Audio. Speech and Language Processing, 14*, 321–329. doi:10.1109/TSA.2005.854103

Essid, S., Richard, G., & David, B. (2005). Instrument recognition in polyphonic music. In *Proc. IEEE International Conference on Acoustics, Speech, and Signal Processing* (ICASSP), Philadelphia, USA.

Fahy, F. J. (1995). *Sound intensity* (2nd ed.). London: E&FN SPON.

Faller, C., & Merimaa, J. (2004). Source localization in complex listening situations: Selection of binaural cues based on interaural coherence. *The Journal of the Acoustical Society of America, 116*(5), 3075–3089. doi:10.1121/1.1791872

Fallon, M. F., Godsill, S. J., & Blake, A. (2006). Joint acoustic source location and orientation estimation using sequential Monte Carlo. In *Proceedings of the 9th International Conference on Digital Audio Effects* (p. 203-208).

Fancourt, C. L., & Parra, L. (2001). The coherence function in blind source separation of convolutive mixtures of non-stationary signals. In *Proceedings of the IEEE international workshop on neural networks for signal processing (NNSP)* (pp. 303–312).

Feng, A. S., & Ratnam, R. (2000). Neural basis of hearing in real-world situations. *Annual Review of Psychology, 51*, 699–725. doi:10.1146/annurev.psych.51.1.699

Ferrández, J. M. (1998). *Study and Realization of a Bio-inspired Hierarchical Architecture for Speech Recognition.* Madrid: Universidad Politécnica de Madrid (PhD Thesis in Spanish).

Févotte, C., Bertin, N., & Durrieu, J.-L. (2009). Nonnegative matrix factorization with the Itakura-Saito divergence. With application to music analysis. *Neural Computation, 21*(3). doi:10.1162/neco.2008.04-08-771

Févotte, C., & Cardoso, J.-F. (2005). Maximum likelihood approach for blind audio source separation using time-frequency Gaussian models. In *Proceedings of the 2005 IEEE Workshop on Applications of Signal Processing to Audio and Acoustics* (p. 78–81).

Févotte, C., & Cemgil, A. T. (2009). Nonnegative matrix factorisations as probabilistic inference in composite models. In *Proc. 17th European Signal Processing Conference (EUSIPCO'09)* (pp. 1913–1917). Glasgow, Scotland.

Fevotte, C., & Godsill, S. (2005). A bayesian approach for blind separation of sparse sources, In *IEEE Transactions on Speech and Audio Processing.* Washington D.C.

Fevotte, C., Gribonval, R., & Vincent, E. (2005). *BSS_EVAL Toolbox User Guide* (Technical Report No. 1706). Retrieved from http://www.irisa.fr/metiss/bss_eval/: IRISA.

Field, A. S., & Graupe, D. (1991). Topographic component (parallel factor) analysis of multichannel evoked potentials: practical issues in trilinear spatiotemporal decomposition. *Brain Topography, 3*, 407–423. doi:10.1007/BF01129000

Fisher, R., Perkins, S., Walker, A., & Wolfart, E. (2003). *Roberts cross edge detector.* Image Processing Learning Resources.

FitzGerald, D. B., Cosgrove, G. R., Ronner, S., Jiang, H., Buchbinder, B. R., & Belliveau, J. W. (1997). Location of Language in the Cortex: A Comparison between Functional MR Imaging and Electrocortical Stimulation. *American Society of Neuroradiology, 18*, 1529–1539.

FitzGerald, D., Cranitch, M., & Coyle, E. (2005). Nonnegative tensor factorisation for sound source separation. In *Proc. of the Irish Signals and Systems Conference.* Dublin, Ireland.

FitzGerald, D., Cranitch, M., & Coyle, E. (2005). Shifted non-negative matrix factorization for sound source separation. In *Proc. IEEE Int. Workshop on Statistical Signal Process.* (pp.1132-1137), Bordeaux, France.

FitzGerald, D., Cranitch, M., & Coyle, E. (2006) Sound source separation using shifted non-negative tensor factorization. In *Proc. IEEE Int. Conf. on Acoust., Speech, and Signal Process., 5*, 653-656.

Flego, F., Araki, S., Sawada, H., Nakatani, T., & Makino, S. (2005). Underdetermined blind separation for speech in real environments with F0 adaptive comb filtering. In *Proceedings of the international workshop on acoustic echo and noise control (IWAENC).*

Fletcher, R. (2000). *Practical Methods of Optimization.* New York: John Wiley.

Foote, J. (2000). Automatic Audio Segmentation using a Measure of Audio Novelty. [July.]. *Proceedings of IEEE International Conference on Multimedia and Expo, 1*, 452–455.

Foote, J., & Cooper, M. (2001). Visualizing musical structure and rhythm via selfsimilarity. In *Proceedings of the International Computer Music Conference* (pp. 419-422).

Forbes-Riley, K., & Litman, D. (2004). Predicting Emotion in Spoken Dialogue from Multiple Knowledge Sources. *Proc. Human Language Technology Conf. North Am. Chapter of the Assoc. Computational Linguistics (HLT/NAACL).*

Fragopanagos, F., & Taylor, J. G. (2005). Emotion Recognition in Human-Computer Interaction. *Neural Networks, 18*, 389–405. doi:10.1016/j.neunet.2005.03.006

Freund, Y., & Schapire, R. E. (1999). A Short Introduction to Boosting. *Journal of Japanese Society for Artificial Intelligence, 14*(5), 771–780.

Friedman, R. (2009). Reverse Engineering the Brain. *Biomedical Cumputation Review, Spring*, 10-17.

Frost, O. L. III. (1972). An algorithm for linearly constrained adaptive array processing. *Proceedings of the IEEE, 60*(8), 926–935. doi:10.1109/PROC.1972.8817

Gandour, J., Tong, Y., Talavage, T., Wong, D., Dzemidzic, M., & Xu, Y. (2007). Neural Basis of First and Second Language Processing of Sentence-Level Linguistic Prosody. *Human Brain Mapping, 28*, 94–108. doi:10.1002/hbm.20255

Gannot, S., Burshtein, D., & Weinstein, E. (2001). Signal enhancement using beamforming and nonstationarity with applications to speech. *IEEE Transactions on Signal Processing, 49*(8), 1614–1626. doi:10.1109/78.934132

Garnder, T. J., & Magnasco, M. O. (2006). Sparse time-frequency representations. *Proceedings of the National Academy of Sciences of the United States of America, 103*, 6094–6099. doi:10.1073/pnas.0601707103

Gatica-Perez, D., Lathoud, G., Odobez, J.-M., & McCowan, I. (2007). Audiovisual probabilistic tracking of multiple speakers in meetings. *IEEE Transactions on Audio, Speech, and Language Processing, 15*(2), 601–616. doi:10.1109/TASL.2006.881678

Gaver, W. (1993). What in the World Do We Hear?: An Ecological Approach to Auditory Event Perception. *Ecological Psychology, 5*(1), 1–29. doi:10.1207/s15326969eco0501_1

Gelman, A., Carlin, J. B., Stern, H. S., & Rubin, D. B. (2003). *Bayesian Data Analysis* (2nd ed.). Chapman & Hall/CRC.

Gerzon, M. (1975). *The* design of precisely coincident microphone arrays for stereo and surround sound. *Presented at the 50th AES Convention.* London, UK.

Ghitza, O. (1988). Temporal non-place information in the auditory-nerve firing patterns as a front-end for speech recognition in a noisy environment. *Journal of Phonetics, 20*, 109–123.

Gold, B., & Morgan, N. (1999). *Speech and Audio Signal Processing: Processing and Perception of Speech and Music.* New York: John Wiley & Sons, Inc.

Gold, T., & Pumphrey, R. J. (1948a). Hearing I: The cochlea as a frequency analyzer. *Proceedings of the Royal Society of London. Series B. Biological Sciences, 135*(881), 462–491. doi:10.1098/rspb.1948.0024

Goldstein, B. (1984). *Sensation and Perception.* Belmont, CA: Wadsworth Publ.

Golub, G., & Loan, C. (1996). *Matrix computations* (3rd ed.). Baltimore, MD: John Hopkins University Press.

Gómez, P., Ferrández, J. M., Rodellar, V., Álvarez, A., & Mazaira, L. M. (2007). A Bio-inspired Architecture for Cognitive Audio. *Lecture Notes in Computer Science, 4527*, 132–142. doi:10.1007/978-3-540-73053-8_14

Gómez, P., Ferrández, J. M., Rodellar, V., Álvarez, A., Mazaira, L. M., & Martínez, R. (2009). *Detection of Speech Dynamics by Neuromorphic Units. Proc. of the IWINAC09, LNCS 5602* (pp. 67–78). Santiago de Compostela, Spain: Springer.

Gómez, P., Ferrández, J. M., Rodellar, V., & Fernández, R. (2009). Time-frequency Representations in Speech Perception. *Neurocomputing*, 820–830.

Gómez, P., Ferrández, J. M., Rodellar, V., Martínez, R., Muñoz, C., & Alvarez, A. (2008). *Bio-inspired Dynamic Formant Tracking for Phonetic Labelling. V Jornadas en Tecnología del Habla* (pp. 33–36). Bilbao, Spain: University of the Basque Country.

Gopher and Iani. (2002). Attention. Encyclopedia of Cognitive Science L. Nadel (Ed). (pp. 220-226).

Górecki, L., & Domanski, M. (2005). Adaptive dictionaries for matching pursuit with separable decompositions. In *Proceedings of the European Signal Processing Conference* (pp. 786-790).

Goto, M. (2001). An audio-based real-time beat tracking system for music with or without drum-sounds. *Journal of New Music Research, 30*(2), 159–171. doi:10.1076/jnmr.30.2.159.7114

Goto, M. (2003). A chorus-section detecting method for musical audio signals. *Proceedings of the IEEE International Conference on Acoustics, Speech, and Signal Processing, 437-440*(April).

Goto, M., Hashiguchi, H., Nishimura, T., & Oka, R. (2003). RWC music database: Music genre database and musical instrument sound database. In *Proc. International Conference on Music Information Retrieval* (ISMIR) (pp. 229–230).

Gouyon, F. (2005). A computational approach to rhythm description — Audio features for the computation of rhythm periodicity functions and their use in tempo induction and music content processing. *Phd thesis*, Universitat Pompeu Fabra, Barcelona, Spain.

Gover, B. N., Ryan, J. G., & Stinson, M. R. (2002). Microphone array measurement system for analysis of directional and spatial variations of sound fields. *The Journal of the Acoustical Society of America, 112*(5), 1980–1991. doi:10.1121/1.1508782

Gowreesunker, B. V., & Tewfik, A. H. (2007). Two improved sparse decomposition methods for blind source separation. In *Proceedings of the 7th International Conference on Independent Component Analysis and Signal Separation* (p. 365-372).

Graciarena, M., Shriberg, E., Stolcke, A., Enos, F., Hirschberg, J., & Kajarekar, S. (2006). Combining Prosodic, Lexical and Cepstral Systems for Deceptive Speech Detection. *Proc. Int'l Conf. Acoustics, Speech and Signal Processing, 1*, 1033-1036.

Gray, R. M., Buzo, A., Gray, A. H., & Matsuyama, Y. (1980). Distortion measures for speech processing. *IEEE Transactions on Acoustics, Speech, and Signal Processing, 28*(4), 367–376. doi:10.1109/TASSP.1980.1163421

Greenberg, S., & Ainsworth, W. A. (2004). Speech Processing in the Auditory System: An Overview. In Greenberg, W. A. S. (Ed.), *Speech Processing in the Auditory System* (pp. 1–62). New York: Springer. doi:10.1007/0-387-21575-1_1

Gribonval, R., & Bacry, E. (2003). Harmonic decomposition of audio signals with matching pursuit. *IEEE Transactions on Signal Processing, 51*, 101–111. doi:10.1109/TSP.2002.806592

Gribonval, R. (2003). Piecewise linear source separation. In Unser, M. A., Aldroubi, A., & Laine, A. F. (Eds.), *Wavelets: Applications in Signal and Image Processing X, Proceedings of SPIE* (pp. 297–310). San Diego, USA: SPIE.

Gribonval, R., & Lesage, S. (2006). A survey of sparse component analysis for blind source sep-

Griffiths, L. J., & Jim, C. W. (1982). An alternative approach to linearly constrained adaptive beamforming. *IEEE Transactions on Antennas and Propagation, AP-30*, 27–34. doi:10.1109/TAP.1982.1142739

Grosse, R., Raina, R., Kwong, H., & Ng, A. Y. (2007). Shift-Invariant Sparse Coding for Audio Classification. In *Proceedings of the Twenty-third Conference on Uncertainty in Artificial Intelligence*(2007).

Guddeti, R. R., & Mulgrew, B. (2005). Perceptually motivated blind source separation of convolutive audio mixtures with subspace filtering method. In *Proceedings of the international workshop on acoustic echo and noise control (IWAENC)*.

Günel, B., Hacıhabiboğlu, H., & Kondoz, A. M. (2007, July). Wavelet-packet based passive analysis of sound fields using a coincident microphone array. *Applied Acoustics, 68*(7), 778–796. doi:10.1016/j.apacoust.2006.04.008

Günel, B., Hacıhabiboğlu, H., & Kondoz, A. M. (2008, May). Acoustic source separation of convolutive mixtures based on intensity vector statistics. *IEEE Transactions on Audio, Speech, and Language Processing, 16*(4), 748–756. doi:10.1109/TASL.2008.918967

Günel, B., Hacıhabiboğlu, H., & Kondoz, A. M. (2009, April). Intensity vector direction exploitation for exhaustive blind source separation of convolutive mixtures. *Paper presented at the IEEE International Conference on Acoustics.* Taipei, Taiwan.

Gunes, H., & Piccardi, M. (2006). A Bimodal Face and Body Gesture Database for Automatic Analysis of Human Nonverbal Affective Behavior. *Proc. 18th Int'l Conf. Pattern Recognition, 1*, 1148–1153.

Gunes, H., & Piccardi, M. (2005). Affect Recognition from Face and Body: Early Fusion versus Late Fusion. *Proc. IEEE Int'l Conf. Systems, Man, and Cybernetics* (pp. 3437-3443).

Guo, G., & Dyer, C. R. (2005). Learning from Examples in the Small Sample Case: Face Expression Recognition. *IEEE Trans. Systems, Man, and Cybernetics Part B, 35*(3), 477–488. doi:10.1109/TSMCB.2005.846658

Gustafsson, T., Rao, B. D., & Trivedi, M. (2003). Source localization in reverberant environments: modeling and statistical analysis. *IEEE Transactions on Speech and Audio Processing, 11*(6), 791–803. doi:10.1109/TSA.2003.818027

Gygi, B., Kidd, G. R., & Watson, C. S. (2004). Spectral-temporal factors in the identification of environmental sounds. *The Journal of the Acoustical Society of America, 115*(3), 1252–1265. doi:10.1121/1.1635840

Gygi, B., Kidd, G., & Watson, C. (2007). *Similarity and categorization of environmental sounds*. Perception & Psychophysics.

Hacıhabiboğlu, H., Günel, B., & Cvetković, Z. (2010, February). Simulation of directional microphones in digital waveguide mesh-based models of room acoustics. *IEEE Transactions on Audio. Speech and Language Processing, 18*(2), 213–223. doi:10.1109/TASL.2009.2025100

Hacıhabiboğlu, H., Günel, B., & Kondoz, A. M. (2008). On the accuracy of first-order numerical derivatives in multidimensional digital waveguide mesh topologies. *IEEE Signal Processing Letters, 15*, 9–12. doi:10.1109/LSP.2007.911162

Hager, J. C. (2003). *Date Face*. Retrieved from http://face-and-emotion.com/dataface/general/homepage.jsp

Hall, D. E. (2001). *Musical Acoustics* (3rd ed.). Florence, Kentucky: Brooks Cole.

Haq, S., & Jackson, P. J. B. (2009). *Speaker-Dependent Audio-Visual Emotion Recognition*. Proc. Auditory-Visual Speech Processing.

Haq, S., Jackson, P. J. B., & Edge, J. (2008). *Audio-visual feature selection and reduction for emotion Classification* (pp. 185–190). Proc. Auditory-Visual Speech Processing.

Harding, S., Cooke, M., & Konig, P. (2007). Auditory gist perception: an alternative to attentional selection of auditory streams? *In Lecture Notes in Computer Science: Attention in Cognitive Systems.* [Springer-Verlag Berlin Heidelberg.]. *Theories and Systems from an Interdisciplinary Viewpoint, 4840*, 399–416. doi:10.1007/978-3-540-77343-6_26

Härmä, A., McKinney, M., & Skowronek, J. (2005). Automatic surveillance of the acoustic activity in our living environment. In *IEEE International Conference on Multimedia and Expo*.

Harshman, R. A. (1970). Foundation of the PARAFAC: models and conditions for an 'explanatory' multi-modal factor analysis. *UCLA Work. Pap. Phon., 16*, 1–84.

Harshman, R. A. (1972). *UCLA Working Papers. Phonet, 22*, 111.

Hartley, R., & Zisserman, A. (2001). *Multiple View Geometry in Computer Vision*. Cambridge University Press.

Hartmann, W. M. (1998). *Signals, Sound, and Sensation.* AIP Press - Springer.

Hartmann, W. M. (1983). Localization of sound in rooms. *The Journal of the Acoustical Society of America, 74*(5), 1380–1391. Retrieved from http://link.aip.org/link/?JAS/74/1380/1. doi:10.1121/1.390163

Hartmann, W. M. (1997). *Signals Sound and Sensation.* American Institute of Physics Press.

Hawkins, J., & Blakeslee, S. (2004). *On Intelligence*. New York: Times Books.

Haykin, S., & Chen, Z. (2005). The Cocktail Party Problem. *Neural Computation, 17*, 1875–1902. doi:10.1162/0899766054322964

Haykin, S., Principe, J. C., Sejnowski, T. J., & McWhirter, J. (2007). *New Directions in Statistical Signal Processing: From Systems to Brain*. Cambridge, Massachusetts London: The MIT Press.

Haykin, S. (1996). *Adaptive filter theory* (3rd ed.). Englewood Cliffs, NJ, USA: Prentice Hall.

Hebb, D. O. (1949 - reprinted 2002). *The Organization of Behavior.* New York: Wiley Interscience.

Helmholz, H. (1885). *On the Sensations of Tone as a Physiological Basis for the Theory of Music*. London, UK: Longmans.

Herault, J., & Jutten, C. (1986). Space or time adaptive signal processing by neural models. *Proc. AIP Conf., Neural Network for Computing, American Institute of physics* (pp. 206-211).

Herbordt, W. (2003). *Combination of robust adaptive beamforming with acoustic echo cancellation for acoustic human/machine interfaces*. Unpublished doctoral dissertation, Friedrich-Alexander-Universität, Erlangen-Nürnberg.

Herlocker, J. L., Konstan, J. A., & Riedl, J. T. (2000). Explaining collaborative filtering recommendations. In *Computer Supported Cooperative Work*, 241-250.

Herlocker, J. L., Konstan, J. A., Terveen, L. G., & Riedl, J. T. (2004). Evaluating collaborative filtering recommender systems. In *ACM Trans. Inf. Syst., ACM Press*, 22, 5-53

Hermansky, H. (1990). Perceptual linear predictive (PLP) analysis of speech. *The Journal of the Acoustical Society of America*, *87*(4), 1738–1752. doi:10.1121/1.399423

Hermansky, H. (1997). Should Recognizers Have Ears? *ESCA-NATO Tutorial and Research Workshop on Robust Speech Recognition for Unknown Communication Channels*, (págs. 1-10). Pont-à-Mousson, France.

Herrera, P., Peeters, P., & Dubnov, S. G. (2003). Automatic classification of musical instrument sounds. *Journal of New Music Research*, *32*(1), 3–22. doi:10.1076/jnmr.32.1.3.16798

Hesse, C. W., & James, C. J. (2006). On semi-blind source separation using spatial constraints with applications in EEG analysis. *IEEE Transactions on Bio-Medical Engineering*, *53*, 2525–2534.

Hild-II. K. E., Erdogmus, D. & Principe, J. C. (2002). *Blind source extraction of time-varying, instantaneous mixtures using an on-line algorithm*. Proc. IEEE ICASSP, Orlando, Florida, USA.

Hinton, G. E., & Anderson, J. A. (1989). *Parallel Models of Associative Memory*. Hillsdale, NJ: Lawrence Erlbaum Ass. Pub.

Hoshuyama, O., & Sugiyama, A. (2001). Robust adaptive beamforming. In Brandstein, M., & Ward, D. (Eds.), *Microphone arrays: Signal processing techniques and applications* (pp. 87–109). Berlin: Springer-Verlag.

Houtgast, T., & Steeneken, H. J. M. (1973). The modulation transfer function in room acoustics as a predictor of speech intelligibility. *Acustica*, *28*, 66–73.

Houtgast, T., & Steeneken, H. J. M. (1972). Envelope spectrum and intelligibility of speech in enclosures. *IEEE-AFCRL 1972 Speech Conference Proceedings* (pp. 392-395).

Hoyer, P. O. (2004). Non-negative matrix factorization with sparseness constraints. *Journal of Machine Learning Research*, *5*, 1457–1469.

Hu, J.-S., & Liu, W.-H. (2009). Location classification of nonstationary sound sources using binaural room distribution patterns. *IEEE Transactions on Audio, Speech, and Language Processing*, *17*(4), 682–692. doi:10.1109/TASL.2008.2011528

Hu, G., & Wang, D. (2006). An auditory scene analysis approach to monaural speech segregation. *Topics in acoustic echo and noise control* (pp. 485-515).

Huang, J., Ohnishi, N., & Sugie, N. (1995). A biomimetic system for localization and separation of multiple sound sources. *IEEE Transactions on Instrumentation and Measurement*, *44*(3), 733–738. doi:10.1109/19.387320

Huang, J., Ohnishi, N., & Sugie, N. (1997). Building ears for robots: Sound localization and separation. *Artificial Life and Robotics*, *1*(4), 157–163. doi:10.1007/BF02471133

Huang, Y., Benesty, J., & Chen, J. (2008). Analysis and comparison of multichannel noise reduction methods in a common framework. *IEEE Transactions on Audio. Speech and Language Processing*, *16*(5), 957–968. doi:10.1109/TASL.2008.921754

Huang, Y., Pollak, I., Bouman, C. A., & Do, M. N. (2006). Best basis search in lapped dictionaries. *IEEE Transactions on Signal Processing*, *54*, 651–664.

Huang, B., & Jebara, T. (2007). Loopy Belief Propagation for Bipartite Maximum Weight b-Matching. In *Artificial Intelligence and Statistics*.

Huang, Y., Benestry, J., & Elko, G. W. (1999, March). Adaptive eigenvalue decomposition algorithm for realtime acoustic source localization system. *Paper presented at the IEEE International Conference on Acoustics*. Phoenix, Arizona.

Huggett, S., & Jordan, D. (2001). *A topological aperitif*. London, UK: Springer-Verlag.

Huron, D. (1996). The Melodic Arch in Western Folk songs. *Computing in Musicology*, *10*, 323.

Huron, D. (2006). *Sweet Anticipation: Music and the Psychology of Expectation*. Boston: MIT Press.

HyvÄarinen. A., Karhunen, J. & Oja, E. (2001). *Independent Component Analysis*. New York: Wiley.

Hyvarinen, A., Karhunen, J., & Oja, E. (2001). *Independent Component Analysis*. John Wiley and Sons. doi:10.1002/0471221317

Hyvärinen, A. (1999). Fast and robust fixed-point algorithms for independent component analysis. *IEEE Transactions on Neural Networks, 10*(3), 626–634. doi:10.1109/72.761722

Hyvärinen, A., Karhunen, J., & Oja, E. (2001). *Independent component analysis*. Hoboken, NJ: John Wiley & Sons, Ltd.doi:10.1002/0471221317

Hyvärinen, A., & Oja, E. (1997). A fast fixed-point algorithm for independent component analysis. *Neural Computation, 9*(7), 1483–1492. doi:10.1162/neco.1997.9.7.1483

Hyvärinen, A., & Oja, E. (2000). Independent component analysis: Algorithms and applications. *Neural Networks, 13*(4–5), 411–430. doi:10.1016/S0893-6080(00)00026-5

Hyvärinen, A., Karhunen, J., & Oja, E. (2001). *Independent Component Analysis*. New York: John Wiley & Sons. doi:10.1002/0471221317

Ichir, M. H. & Djafari, A. M. (Jul 2006). Hidden markov models for wavelet based blind source separation, *IEEE Transaction on Image Process.* (pp. 1887–1899), vol. 15.

IEC 60268-16:1998 (1998). *Sound system equipment, Part 16: Objective rating of speech intelligibility by speech transmission index.*

IEEE Transactions on Acoustic, Speech, and Signal Processing, 24, 320-327.

Ikram, M. Z., & Morgan, D. R. (2002). A beamforming approach to permutation alignment for multichannel frequency-domain blind source separation. In *Proceedings of the IEEE international conference on acoustics, speech and signal processing (ICASSP)* (Vol. 1, pp. 881–884).

Ikram, M., & Morgan, D. (2000). Exploring permutation inconsistancy in blind separation of speech signals in a reverberant environment. *Proc. of IEEE Conf. on Acoustic, Speech, and Signal Processing (ICASSP)*. Turkey.

IPA. (2009). Retrieved May 21, 2009, from IPA: http://www.arts.gla.ac.uk/IPA/ipachart.html

Irino, T., & Patterson, R. D. (1997). A time-domain, level-dependent auditory filter: The gammachirp. *The Journal of the Acoustical Society of America, 101*(1), 412–419. doi:10.1121/1.417975

Itakura, F., & Saito, S. (1968). Analysis synthesis telephony based on the maximum likelihood method. In *Proc 6th International Congress on Acoustics* (pp. C-17 – C-20). Tokyo, Japan.

Ito, M., Maruyoshi, M., Kawamoto, M., Mukai, T., & Ohnishi, N. (2002). Effectiveness of directional microphones and utilization of source arriving directions in source separation. *Paper presented at 9th International Conference on Neural Information Processing. Singapore.*

Itti, L. & Baldi, P. (2005). Bayesian surprise attracts human attention. *In Advances Neural Information Processing Systems (NIPS 2005).*

Izumi, Y., Ono, N., & Sagayama, S. (2007). Sparseness-based 2ch BSS using the EM algorithm in reverberant environment. In *Proceedings of the 2007 IEEE Workshop on Applications of Signal Processing to Audio and Acoustics* (p. 147-150).

Jafari, M. G., Vincent, E., Abdallah, S. A., Plumbley, M. D., & Davies, M. E. (2008). An adaptive stereo basis method for convolutive blind audio source separation. *Neurocomputing, 71,* 2087–2097.

Jafari, M. G., Wang, W., Chambers, J. A., Hoya, T., & Cichocki, A. (2006). Sequential blind source separation based exclusively on second-order statistics developed for a class of periodic signals. *IEEE Transactions on Signal Processing, 54,* 1028–1040.

Jafari, M. G., & Plumbley, M. D. (2008). Separation of stereo speech signals based on a sparse dictionary algorithm. In *Proceedings of the European Signal Processing Conference.* (pp.786-790).

Jähne, B. (2005). *Digital Image Processing*. Berlin: Springer.

Jan, T. U., Wang, W., & Wang, D. L. (2010). A multistage approach to blind separation of convolutive speech mixtures. In *IEEE Trans.* Audio Speech and Language Processing.

Jan, T. U., Wang, W., & Wang, D. L. (2009). A multistage approach for blind separation of convolutive speech mixtures. In *Proc ICASSP* (pp. 1713-1716). Taiwan.

Jang, G.-J., & Lee, T.-W. (2004). A maximum likelihood approach to single-channel source separation. *Journal of Machine Learning Research, 4*(7-8), 1365–1392. doi:10.1162/jmlr.2003.4.7-8.1365

Jayant, N. S., & Noll, P. (1984). *Digital Coding of Waveforms*. Englewood Cliffs, NJ: Prentice-Hall.

Jensen, K. (2005). A causal rhythm grouping. Proceedings of 2nd International Symposium on Computer Music Modeling and Retrieval (CMMR '04),Denmark (LNCS, vol. 3310, pp. 83-95)

Jensen, K. (2007). Multiple scale music segmentation using rhythm, timbre and harmony. *EURASIP Journal on Applied Signal Processing, Special issue on Music Information Retrieval Based on Signal Processing*.

Jensen, K., & Andersen, T. H. (2004). Causal rhythm grouping. *Proc. 2ⁿᵈ International Symposium on Computer Music Modeling and Retrieval*. Esbjerg, Denmark.

Jensen, K., Xu, J., & Zachariasen, M. (2005). Rhythm-based segmentation of Popular Chinese Music. *Proceeding of the ISMIR*. London, UK, (pp.374-380).

John, H., & Wendy, H. (2001). *Speech synthesis and recognition* (2nd ed.). London: Taylor & Francis.

Jourjine, A., Rickard, S., & Yılmaz, O". (2000). Blind separation of disjoint orthogonal signals: demixing N sources from 2 mixtures. In *Proc. ICASSP* (Vol. 5, pp. 2985–8). Turkey.

Junqua, J. C., & Haton, J. P. (1995). *Robustness in Automatic Speech Recognition: Fundamentals and Applications*. London: Kluwer Academic Publishers.

Jurjine, A. Rickard, S. & Yilmaz, O. (2000). Blind separation of disjoint orthogonal signals: demixing N sources from 2 mixtures. *Proc. of IEEE Conf. on Acoustic, Speech, and Signal Processing (ICASSP), 4*, 2985-2988.

Kanade, T., Cohn, J., & Tian, Y. (2000). Comprehensive Database for Facial Expression Analysis, *Proc. IEEE Int'l Conf. Face and Gesture Recognition* (pp. 46-53).

Kao, Y., & Lee, L. (2006). *Feature Analysis for Emotion Recognition from Mandarin Speech Considering the Special Characteristics of Chinese Language* (pp. 1814–1817). Proc. Interspeech.

Kashino, K., & Murase, H. (1999). A sound source identification system for ensemble music based on template adaptation and music stream extraction. *Speech Communication, 27*, 337–349. doi:10.1016/S0167-6393(98)00078-8

Kates, J. M. (1998). Signal processing for hearing aids. In Kahrs, M., & Brandenburg, K. (Eds.), *Applications of digital signal processing to audio and acoustics* (pp. 235–277). Norwell, MA: Kluwer.

Katsiamis, A. G., Drakakis, E. M., & Lyon, R. F. (2007). Practical Gammatone-Like Filters for Auditory Processing. *EURASIP Journal on Audio, Speech and Music Processing*, 2-15.

Kaufman, L., & Rousseeuw, P. J. (1990). *Finding Groups in Data: An Introduction to Cluster Analysis*. New York: Wiley.

Kégl, B., Bertin-Mahieux, T., & Eck, D. (2008). Metropolis-Hastings sampling in a FilterBoost music classifier. In *ICML Workshop on Music and Machine Learning*.

Kendrick, P., Cox, T. J., Li, F. F., Zhang, Y., & Chambers, J. A. (2008). Monaural room acoustic parameters from music and speech. *The Journal of the Acoustical Society of America, 124*(1), 278–287. doi:10.1121/1.2931960

Kendrick, P., Cox, T. J., Zhang, Y., Chambers, J. A., & Li, F. F. (2006, May). Room Acoustic Parameter Extraction from Music Signals. *Proc. ICASSP 2006, 5*, DOI: 10.1109/ICASSP.2006.1661397, Kendrick, P., Li, F. F., Cox, T. J., Zhang, Y. & Chambers, J. A. (2007). Blind Estimation of Reverberation Parameters for Non-Diffuse Rooms. *Acta Acustica united with Acustica, 93* (5), 760-770.

Kiers, H. A. L., Ten Berge, J. M. F., & Bro, R. (1999). PARAFAC2 – Part 1. A direct fitting algorithm for PARAFAC2 model. *Journal of Chemometrics, 13*, 275–294. doi:10.1002/(SICI)1099-128X(199905/08)13:3/4<275::AID-CEM543>3.0.CO;2-B

Kim, D., Sra, S., & Dhillon, I. S. (2007). Fast Newton-type methods for the least squares nonnegative matrix approximation Problem. In *Proc. of the 6th SIAM Int. Conf. on Data Mining* (pp. 343-354).

Kim, Y., Schmidt, E., & Emelle, L. (2008). Moodswings: a collaborative game for music mood label collection. In *Proceedings of the 9th International Conference on Music Information Retrieval (ISMIR 2008)*.

Klapuri, A. P. (2004). Automatic music transcription as we know it today. *Journal of New Music Research, 33*(3), 269–282. doi:10.1080/0929821042000317840

Klapuri, A. (1999). Sound onset detection by applying psychoacoustic knowledge. *Proc. IEEE International Conf. Acoustics, Speech, and Signal Processing (ICASSP-99)* (pp. 3089–3092).

Knapp, C. H., & Carter, G. C. (1976). The generalized correlation method for the estimation of time delay. *IEEE Transactions on Acoustics, Speech, and Signal Processing, 24*(4), 320–327. doi:10.1109/TASSP.1976.1162830

Knees, P., Pohle, T., Schedl, M., Schnitzer, D., & Seyerlehner, K. (2008). A document-centered approach to a natural language music search engine. In *European Conference on Information Retrieval (ECIR)*.

Knudsen, E. (2007). Fundamental Components of Attention. *Annual Review of Neuroscience, 30*, 57–78. doi:10.1146/annurev.neuro.30.051606.094256

Koch, C., & Tsuchiya, N. (2007). Attention and consciousness: two distinct brain processes. *Trends in Cognitive Sciences, 11*(1), 16–22. doi:10.1016/j.tics.2006.10.012

Kocinski, J. (2008). Speech intelligibility improvement using convolutive blind source separation assisted by denoising algorithms. In *EURASIP Journal. Speech Communication, 50*, 29–37. doi:10.1016/j.specom.2007.06.003

Kolossa, D., & Orglmeister, R. (2004). Nonlinear postprocessing for blind speech separation. []. Berlin: Springer Verlag.]. *Lecture Notes in Computer Science, 3195*, 832–839.

Kompass, R. (2007). A generalized divergence measure fon nonnegative matrix factorization. *Neural Computation, 19*(3), 780–791. doi:10.1162/neco.2007.19.3.780

Kostek, B. (2004). Musical instrument classification and duet analysis employing music information retrieval techniques. *Proceedings of the IEEE, 92*(4), 712–729. doi:10.1109/JPROC.2004.825903

Kotsia, I., & Pitas, I. (2007). Facial Expression Recognition in Image Sequences Using Geometric Deformation Features and Support Vector Machines. *IEEE Transactions on Image Processing, 16*(1), 172–187. doi:10.1109/TIP.2006.884954

Koutras, A., Dermatas, E., & Kokkinakis, G. (2000). *Blind source separation of moving speakers in real reverberant environment.* Proc. IEEE ICASSP, 1133–1136.

Kreutz-Delgado, K., Murray, J. F., Rao, B. D., Engan, K., Lee, T.-W., & Sejnowski, T. J. (2003). Dictionary learning algorithms for sparse representation. *Neural Computation, 15*(2), 349–396. doi:10.1162/089976603762552951

Krijnders, J.D., Niessen, M.E. & Andringa, T.C. (2010). Sound event identification through expectancy-based evaluation of signal-driven hypotheses. Accepted for publication in Pattern Recognition Letters.

Kristjánsson, T. T., Hershey, J. R., Olsen, P. A., Rennie, S. J., & Gopinath, R. A. (2006). Super-human multi-talker speech recognition: The IBM 2006 speech separation challenge system. In *Proceedings of the 9th International Conference on Spoken Language Processing* (p. 97-100).

Kuhl, O., & Jensen, K. (2008). *Retrieving and recreating Musical Form. Lectures Notes in Computer Science.* New York: Springer-Verlag.

Kühl, O. (2007). *Musical Semantics.* Bern: Peter Lang.

Kung, S. Y. (1993). *Digital Neural Network.* Hoboken, NJ: Prentice-Hall.

Kuttruff, H. (1991). *Room Acoustics.* Elsevier Science Publishers Ltd.

Lacoste, A., & Eck, D. (2005) Onset detection with artificial neural network for MIREX 2005. *MIREX 2005 audio onset detection contest*: Retrieved from http://www.music-ir.org/evaluation/mirex-results/articles/onset/lacoste.pdf

Lacoste, A., & Eck, D. (2007). A supervised classification algorithm for Note Onset Detection. *EURASIP Journal on Advances in Signal Processing* (Article ID 43745),(vol. 2007, 13 pages).

Lagrange, M., & Marchand, S. (2007). Estimating the instantaneous frequency of sinusoidal components using phase-based methods. *Journal of the Audio Engineering Society. Audio Engineering Society, 55*(5), 385–399.

Lagrange, M., Marchand, S., & Rault, J. (2007). *Enhancing the tracking of partials for the sinusoidal modeling of polyphonic sounds.* IEEE Transactions on Acoustics, Speech and Signal Processing.

Lagrange, M., & Tzanetakis, G. (2007). Sound source tracking and formation using normalized cuts. In *Proc. IEEE International Conference on Acoustics, Speech, and Signal Processing* (ICASSP), Honolulu, USA.

Lagrange, M., Murdoch, J., & Tzanetakis, G. (2006). Temporal constraints for sound source formation using the normalized cut. In Proc. *Neural Information Processing Systems Workshop* (NIPS), Whistler, BC, Canada.

Lambert, R. H., & Bell, A. J. (1997). Blind separation of multiple speakers in a multipath environment. In *Proc. IEEE International Conference Acoustics, Speech Signal Process.* (pp. 423–426).

Lamere, P. (2008). Semantic tagging and music information retrieval, In *Journal of New Music Research, special issue: From genres to tags: Music Information Retrieval in the era of folksonomies.*

Laurberg, H., Christensen, M. G., Plumbley, M. D., Hansen, L. K., & Jensen, S. H. (2008). *Theorems on positive data: on the uniqueness of NMF.* Computational Intelligence and Neuroscience.

Law, E. (2008). The problem of accuracy as an evaluation criterion. In *ICML Workshop on Evaluation Methods in Machine Learning.*

Law, E. v. Ahn, L., Dannenberg, R. & Crawford, M. (2007). TagATune: a game for music and sound annotation, In *Proceedings of the 8th International Conference on Music Information Retrieval (ISMIR 2007).*

Law, E., West, K., Mandel, M., Bay, M., & Downie, S. (2009). Evaluation of algorithms using games: the case of music tagging. In *Proceedings of the 10th International Conference on Music Information Retrieval (ISMIR 2009).*

Lee, D. D., & Seung, H. S. (2001). *Algorithms for non-negative matrix factorization. Advances in neural information processing* (pp. 556–562). Cambridge, MA: MIT Press.

Lee, T. W. (1998). *Independent Component Anal: Theory and Applications.* London: Kluwer Academic Publishers.

Lee, I., Kim, T., & Lee, T.-W. (2007). Independent vector analysis for convolutive blind speech separation. In *Blind speech separation* (pp. 169–192). New York: Springer. doi:10.1007/978-1-4020-6479-1_6

Lee, D. D., & Seung, H. S. (1999). Learning the parts of objects with nonnegative matrix factorization. *Nature, 401,* 788–791. doi:10.1038/44565

Lee, D. D., & Seung, H. S. (2001). Algorithms for non-negative matrix factorization. In *Advances in Neural and Information Processing Systems* (pp. 556–562). NIPS.

Lee, C. M., & Narayanan, S. S. (2005). Toward Detecting Emotions in Spoken Dialogs. *IEEE Transactions on Speech and Audio Processing, 13*(2), 293–303. doi:10.1109/TSA.2004.838534

Lee,. Y. & Yoo, S. I. (2002). *An elliptical boundary modal for skin color detection.* Proc. Imaging Science, Systems, and Technology.

Lee, I. (2009). Permutation correction in blind source separation using sliding subband likelihood function. In *Proceedings of the 8th International Conference on Independent Component Analysis and Signal Separation* (p. 767-774).

Lee, T. W., Bell, A. J., & Orglmeister, R. (1997). Blind source separation of real world signals. In *Proc. IEEE International Conference Neural Networks* (pp. 2129–2135).

Lee, W., Shiu, Y., & Kuo, C. (2007). Musical onset detection with linear predication and joint features. *MIREX 2007 audio onset detection contest.* Retrieved from http://www.music-ir.org/mirex/2007/abs/OD_lee.pdf

Lerdahl, F., & Jackendoff, J. (1983). *A Generative Theory of Tonal Music.* Cambridge, MA: MIT Press.

Leveau, P., Daudet, L., & Richard, G. (2004). Methodology and Tools for the evaluation of automatic onset detection algorithms in music. *Proc. 5th International Conf. On Music Information Retrieval.* Barcelona, Spain.

Lewicki, M. S., & Sejnowski, T. J. (2000). Learning overcomplete representations. *Neural Computation, 12,* 337–365. doi:10.1162/089976600300015826

Li, Y., & Wang, D. (2007). Separation of singing voice from music accompaniement for monaural recordings. *IEEE Transactions on Audio, Speech, and Language Processing, 15*(4), 1475–1487. doi:10.1109/TASL.2006.889789

Li, Y., Amari, S., Cichocki, A., Ho, D. W. C., & Shengli, X. (2006). Underdetermined blind source separation based on sparse representation. *IEEE Transactions on Signal Processing, 54*(2), 423–437. doi:10.1109/TSP.2005.861743

Li, F. F., & Cox, T. J. (2003). Speech transmission index from running speech: A neural network approach. *The Journal of the Acoustical Society of America, 113*(4), 1999–2008. doi:10.1121/1.1558373

Li, F. F., & Cox, T. J. (2007). A neural network model for speech intelligibility quantification. *J. Applied Soft Computing, 7*(1), 145–155. doi:10.1016/j.asoc.2005.05.002

Li, F. F., & Cox, T. J. (2001, May). Extraction of Speech Transmission Index from Speech Signals Using Artificial Neural Networks, 110th AES convention (paper 5354). Amsterdam

Li, X., Chen, L., Zhang, L., Lin, F., & Ma, W.-Y. (2006). Image annotation by large-scale content-based image retrieval. In *MULTIMEDIA '06: Proceedings of the 14th annual ACM international conference on Multimedia*.

Lin, C.-J. (2007). Projected gradient methods for nonnegative matrix factorization. *Neural Computation, 19*, 2756–2779. doi:10.1162/neco.2007.19.10.2756

Lin, Y., & Wei, G. (2005). Speech Emotion Recognition Based on HMM and SVM. *Proc. 4th Int'l Conf. on Mach. Learn. and Cybernetics* (pp.4898-4901).

Lippmann, R. P. (1997). Speech recognition by machines and humans. *Speech Communication, 22*, 1–15. doi:10.1016/S0167-6393(97)00021-6

Litman, D. J., & Forbes-Riley, K. (2004). Predicting Student Emotions in Computer-Human Tutoring Dialogues. *Proc. 42nd Ann. Meeting of the Assoc. Computational Linguistics.*

Littlewort, G. C., Bartlett, M. S., & Lee, K. (2007). Faces of Pain: Automated Measurement of Spontaneous Facial Expressions of Genuine and Posed Pain, *Proc. Ninth ACM Int'l Conf. Multimodal Interfaces,* pp. 15-21.

Liu, P., & Meng, M.-H. (2007). A bio-inspired robotic sound localization method. *Paper presented at IEEE/ASME International Conference on Advanced Intelligent Mechatronics.*

Livshin, A., & Rodet, X. (2004). Musical instrument identification in continuous recordings. In *Proc. International Conference on Digital Audio Effects* (DAFx), Naples, Italy.

Livshin, A., & Rodet, X. (2006). The importance of the non-harmonic residual for automatic musical instrument recognition of pitched instruments. In *Proc. 120th Convention of the Audio Engineering Society,* Paris.

Lo, H.-Y., Wang, J.-C., & Wang, H. M. (2009). An ensemble method for MIREX audio tag classificationMusic Information Retrieval Evaluation Exchange (MIREX), Kobe, 2009. Retrieved from http://www.music-ir.org/mirex/2009/

López-Poveda, E. A. (2001). A human nonlinear cochlear filterbank. *The Journal of the Acoustical Society of America, 110*(6), 3107–3118. doi:10.1121/1.1416197

Lorente de No, R. (1949). Cerebral cortex: architecture, intracortical connections, motor projections. En J. F. Fulton, *Physiology of the Nervous System* (págs. 288-330). Oxford: Oxford University Press.

Lorenzelli, F., Wang, A., & Yo, K. (1996). Broadband array processing using subband techniques. *Paper presented at the IEEE International Conference on Acoustics, Speech and Signal Processing.* Atlanta, GA USA.

Lucey, S., Ashraf, A. B., & Cohn, J. F. (2007). Investigating Spontaneous Facial Action Recognition through AAM Representations of the Face. In Delac, K., & Grgic, M. (Eds.), *Face Recognition* (pp. 275–286). New York: I-Tech Education and Publishing.

Luengo, I., & Navas, E. (2005). *Automatic Emotion Recognition using Prosodic Parameters* (pp. 493–496). Proc. Interspeech.

Luo, Y., Chambers, J., Lambotharan, S., & Proudler, I. (2006). Exploitation of source non-stationarity in underdetermined blind source separation with advanced clustering techniques. *IEEE Transactions on Signal Processing, 54*(6), 2198–2212. doi:10.1109/TSP.2006.873367

Mack, A. (2003). Inattentional blindness: Looking without seeing. *Current Directions in Psychological Science, 12*(5), 180–184. doi:10.1111/1467-8721.01256

Mackay, D. J. C. (1995). Probable networks and plausible predictions – a review of practical Bayesian models for supervised neural networks. *Network (Bristol, England), 6*(3), 469–505. doi:10.1088/0954-898X/6/3/011

MacKay, D. (1996). Maximum likelihood and covariant algorithms for independent component analysis. Retrieved from http://www.inference.phy.cam.ac.uk/mackay/ica.pdf. (Unpublished)

Madhu, N. (2002). *Independent component analysis in multiple input multiple output (MIMO) systems.* Unpublished master's thesis, Technische Universität München, Munich, Germany.

Madhu, N., & Martin, R. (2008). A scalable framework for multiple speaker localization and tracking. In *Proceedings of the international workshop on acoustic echo and noise control (IWAENC).* Seattle, USA.

Madhu, N., Breithaupt, C., & Martin, R. (2008). Temporal smoothing of spectral masks in the cepstral domain for speech separation. In *Proc. ICASSP* (pp. 45–48).

Madhu, N., Gückel, A., & Martin, R. (2006). Combined beamforming and frequency domain ICA for source separation. In *Proceedings of the international workshop on acoustic echo and noise control (IWAENC).*

Maganti, H. K., Gatica-Perez, D. & McCowan, I. (2007). Speech enhancement and recognition in meetings with an audio-visual sensor array. *IEEE Trans. on Audio, Speech and Language processing, 15*(8), 2257–2269.

Makino, S., Sawada, H., Mukai, R., & Araki, S. (2005). Blind source separation of convolutive mixtures of speech in frequency domain. In *IEICE Trans. Fundamentals. E (Norwalk, Conn.), 88-A*(7), 1640–1655.

Makino, S., Lee, T.-W., & Sawada, H. (Eds.). (2007). *Blind Speech Separation.* New York: Springer.

Makous, J. C., & Middlebrooks, J. C. (1990). Two-dimensional sound localization by human listeners. *The Journal of the Acoustical Society of America, 87*(5), 2188–2200. doi:10.1121/1.399186

Malkin, R., & Waibel, A. (2005). Classifying user environment for mobile applications using linear autoencoding of ambient audio. In *IEEE International Conference on Acoustics, Speech, and Signal Processing.*

Mallat, S., & Zhang, Z. (1993). Matching pursuits with time-frequency dictionaries. *IEEE Transactions on Signal Processing, 41,* 3397–3415. doi:10.1109/78.258082

Mallat, S. (1999). *A Wavelet Tour of Signal Processing* (2nd ed.). San Diego, CA: Academic Press.

Mandel, M. I., Ellis, D. P. W., & Jebara, T. (2007). An EM algorithm for localizing multiple sound sources in reverberant environments. *Advances in Neural Information Processing Systems, 19,* 953–960.

Mandel, M., & Ellis, D. (2007). A web-based game for collecting music metadata. In *Proceedings of the 8th International Conference on Music Information Retrieval (ISMIR 2007).*

Mango, K. N. (1991). *Hearing loss.* New York: Franklin Watts.

Manzagol, P.-A., Bertin-Mahieux, T., & Eck, D. (2008). On the use of sparse time relative auditory codes for music. *Proceedings of the 9th International Conference on Music Information Retrieval (ISMIR 2008).*

Marchand, S., & Lagrange, M. (2006). On the equivalence of phase-based methods for the estimation of instantaneous frequency. In *Proc. European Conference on Signal Processing* (EUSIPCO).

Mardia, K. V., & Jupp, P. (1999). *Directional statistics.* London, New York: Wiley. doi:10.1002/9780470316979

Marolt, M., Kavcic, A., & Privosnik, M. (1999). Neural networks for note onset detection in piano music. *Proc. International Conf. On Computer Music.*

Marr, D. (1982). *Vision.* New York: Henry Holt and Co., Inc.

Martin, R. (2004). Speech enhancement using MMSE short time spectral estimation with Gamma distributed speech priors. In *Proceedings of the IEEE international conference on acoustics, speech and signal processing (ICASSP).*

Martins, L. G. (2009). A Computational Framework For Sound Segregation in Music Signals. *PhD. thesis,* Faculdade de Engenharia da Universidade do Porto (FEUP).

Martins, L. G., Burred, J. J., Tzanetakis, G., & Lagrange, M. (2007). Polyphonic instrument recognition using spectral clustering. In *Proc. International Conference on Music Information Retrieval* (ISMIR), Vienna, Austria.

Matsuoka, K., & Nakashima, S. (2001). Minimal distortion principle for blind source separation. In *Proceedings of the international conference on independent component analysis (ICA)* (pp. 722–727).

McAdams, S., & Bigand, E. (Eds.). (1993). *Thinking in Sound*. Oxford University Press.

McAdams, S. (2002). Musical similarity and dynamic processing in musical context. *Proceedings of the ISMA* (CD). Mexico City, Mexico.

McAulay, R., & Quatieri, T. (1986). Speech analysis/synthesis based on a sinusoidal representation. *IEEE Transactions on Acoustics, Speech, and Signal Processing, 34*(4), 744–754. doi:10.1109/TASSP.1986.1164910

McAuley, J. D., & Ayala, C. (2002). The effect of timbre on melody recognition by familiarity. *Meeting of the A.S.A.*, Cancun, Mexico (abstract).

McCulloch, W., & Pitts, W. (1943). A logical calculus of ideas immanent in nervous activity. *The Bulletin of Mathematical Biophysics, 5*, 115–133. doi:10.1007/BF02478259

Mendelson, J. R., & Cynander, M. S. (1985). Sensitivity of Cat Primary Auditory Cortex (AI) Neurons to the Direction and Rate of Frequency Modulation. *Brain Research, 327*, 331–335. doi:10.1016/0006-8993(85)91530-6

Merimaa, J., & Pulkki, V. (2005). Spatial impulse response rendering I: Analysis and synthesis. *Journal of the Audio Engineering Society. Audio Engineering Society, 53*(12), 1115–1127.

Merimaa, J., Lokki, T., Peltonen, T., & Karjalainen, M. (2001). Measurement, analysis, and visualisation of directional room responses. *Presented at the 111th AES Convention, preprint 5449.* New York, NY, USA.

Meyer, L. B. (1956). *Emotion and Meaning in Music.* Chicago: Chicago University Press.

Meyer, J., & Agnello, T. (2003). Spherical microphone array for spatial sound recording. *Presented at the 115th AES Convention, preprint 5975.* New York.

Meyer, L. B. (2001) Music and emotion: Distinctions and uncertainties. In Juslin & Sloboda (Eds.), *Music and Emotion: Theory and Research* (pp. 341–360). Oxford University Press.

Miller, G. (1956). The Magical Number Seven, Plus or Minus Two. *Psychological Review, 63*, 81–97. doi:10.1037/h0043158

Mills, A. W. (1958). On the minimum audible angle. *The Journal of the Acoustical Society of America, 30*, 237–246. doi:10.1121/1.1909553

MIREX. (2005), First Annual Music Information Retrieval Evaluation eXchange (MIREX '05). Retrieved from http://www.music-ir.org/mirex2005/index.php/Audio_Onset_Detection.

Mitianondis, N. & Davies, M. (2002). Audio source separation: solutions and problems. *International Journal of Adaptive Control and Signal Process.* (pp. 1–6).

Mitianoudis, N., & Davies, M. E. (2003). Audio source separation of convolutive mixtures. *IEEE Transactions on Speech and Audio Processing, 11*(5), 489–497. doi:10.1109/TSA.2003.815820

Mitianoudis, N., & Davies, M. (2004). Permutation alignment for frequency domain ICA using subspace beamforming method. *Paper presented at the International Conference on Independent Component Analysis and Blind Signal Separation.* Granada, Spain.

Miwakeichi, F., Martinez-Montes, E., Valdes-Sosa, P. A., Nishiyama, N., Mizuhara, H., & Yamaguchi, Y. (2004). Decomposing EEG data into space-time-frequency components using parallel factor analysis. *NeuroImage, 22*, 1035–1045. doi:10.1016/j.neuroimage.2004.03.039

Möcks, J. (1988). Decomposing event-related potentials: a new topographic components model. *Biological Psychology, 26*, 199–215. doi:10.1016/0301-0511(88)90020-8

Mokios, K. N., Potamianos, A., & Sidiropoulos, N. D. (2008). On the effectiveness of PARAFAC-based estimation for blind speech separation. *Proc. of IEEE Conf. on Acoustic, Speech, and Signal Processing (ICASSP)* (pp. 153-156).

Mokios, K. N., Sidiropoulos, N. D., & Potamianos, A. (2006). Blind speech separation using PARAFAC analysis and integer least squares. *Proc. of IEEE Conf. on Acoustic, Speech, and Signal Processing (ICASSP)* (Vol. 4, pp73-76).

Moncrieff, S., Venkatesh, S., & West, G. (2007). On-line audio background determination on-line audio background determination for complex audio environments. *ACM Transactions on Multimedia Computing, Communications, and Applications, 3*, 1–30.

Moore, B. C. J., & Glasberg, B. R. (1996). A revision of Zwicker's loudness model. *ACTA Acustica, 82*, 335–345.

Morup, M., & Schmidt, M. N. (2006). *Sparse non-negative matrix factor 2D deconvolution. Technical Report.* Technical University of Denmark.

Mørup, M., Hansen, L. K., Herrmann, C. S., Parnas, J., & Arnfred, S. M. (2006). Parallel factor analysis as an exploratory tool for wavelet transformed event-related EEG. *NeuroImage, 29*(3), 938–947. doi:10.1016/j.neuroimage.2005.08.005

Morup, M., Madsen, K. H., & Hansen, L. K. (2007). Shifted non-negative matrix factorization. In *Proc. IEEE Int. Workshop on Machine Learning for Signal Process* (pp. 427-432). Maynooth, Ireland.

Mountcastle, V. B. (1957). Modality and Topographic Properties of Single Neurons of Cat's Somatic Sensory Cortex. *Journal of Neurophysiology, 20*, 408–454.

Mountcastle, V. B. (1997). The Columnar Organization of the Neocortex. *Brain*, 701–722. doi:10.1093/brain/120.4.701

Moussaoui, S., Brie, D., Mohammad-Djafari, A., & Carteret, C. (2006). Separation of non-negative mixture of non-negative sources using a Bayesian approach and MCMC sampling. *IEEE Transactions on Signal Processing, 54*(11), 4133–4145. doi:10.1109/TSP.2006.880310

Mukai, R., Sawada, H., Araki, S., & Makino, S. (2004). Blind source separation for moving speech signals using blockwise ICA and residual crosstalk subtraction. *IEICE Transactions on Fundamentals of Electronics, Communications and Computer Sciences. E (Norwalk, Conn.), 87-A*(8), 1941–1948.

Mukai, R., Sawada, H., Araki, S., & Makino, S. (2003). *Robust real-time blind source separation for moving speakers in a room.* Proc. IEEE ICASSP, Hong Kong.

Mukai, R., Sawada, H., Araki, S., & Makino, S. (2004) Frequency domain blind source separation for many speech signals. In *Proc. International Conference Independent Component Anal* (pp. 461-469).

Mukai, R., Sawada, H., Araki, S., & Makino, S. (2005). Real-time blind source separation and DOA estimation using a small 3-D microphone array. In *Proceedings of the international workshop on acoustic echo and noise control (IWAENC).*

Murata, N., Ikeda, S., & Ziehe, A. (2001, Oct). An approach to blind source separation based on temporal structure of speech signals. *Neuro Comput, 41*(1-4), 1–24.

Murata, N., Ikeda, S., & Ziehe, A. (2001). An approach to blind source separation based on temporal structure of speech signals. *Neurocomputing, 41*, 1–4. doi:10.1016/S0925-2312(00)00345-3

Nábělek, A. K., & Robinson, P. K. (1982). Monaural and binaural speech perception in reverberation for listeners of various ages. *The Journal of the Acoustical Society of America, 71*(5), 1242–1248. doi:10.1121/1.387773

Nakadai, K., Okuno, H. G., & Kitano, H. (2002). Real-time sound source localization and separation for robot audition. *Paper presented at the IEEE International Conference on Spoken Language Processing.*

Naqvi, S. M., Zhang, Y., & Chambers, J. A. (2008). *A multimodal approach for frequency domain blind source separation for moving sources in a room.* Proc. IAPR CIP2008, Santorini, Greece.

Naqvi, S. M., Zhang, Y., & Chambers, J. A. (2009). Multimodal blind source separation for moving sources. In *Proc ICASSP* (pp. 125-128), Taiwan.

Naqvi, S. M., Zhang, Y., Tsalaile, T., Sanei, S., & Chambers, J. A. (2008). *A multimodal approach for frequency domain independent component analysis with geometrically-based initialization.* Proc. EUSIPCO, Lausanne, Switzerland.

Narmour, E. (1990). *The Analysis and Cognition of Basic Melodic Structures: The Implication-Realization Model.* Chicago: University of Chicago Press.

Naumann, J. J. (2003). MEMS (Microelectromechanical systems) audio devices - dreams and realities. *Paper presented at the AES 115th Convention.* New York, USA.

Navon, D. (1977). Forest before trees: The precedence of global features in visual perception. *Cognitive Psychology, 9,* 353–383. doi:10.1016/0010-0285(77)90012-3

Neff, R., & Zakhor, A. (1997). Very low bit rate video coding based on matching pursuits. *IEEE Transactions on Circuits and Systems for Video Technology, 7,* 158–171. doi:10.1109/76.554427

Neilberg, D., & Elenius, K. (2006). *Emotion Recognition in Spontaneous Speech Using GMMs* (pp. 809–812). Proc. Interspeech.

Nesbit, A., Vincent, E., & Plumbley, M. D. (2009). Extension of sparse, adaptive signal decompositions to semi-blind audio source separation. In *Proceedings of the 8th International Conference on Independent Component Analysis and Signal Separation* (p. 605-612).

Nesta, F., Omologo, M., & Svaizer, P. (2008). Separating short signals in highly reverberant environment by a recursive frequency-domain BSS. In *Proceedings of the 2008 IEEE Joint Workshop on Hands-free Speech Communication and Microphone Arrays* (p. 232-235).

Neti, C., Young, E. D., & Schneider, M. H. (1992). Neural network models of sound localization based on directional filtering by the pinna. *The Journal of the Acoustical Society of America, 92*(6), 3140–3156. doi:10.1121/1.404210

Ngo, K., Spriet, A., Moonen, M., Wouters, J., & Jensen, S. H. (2008). Variable speech distortion weighted multichannel wiener filter based on soft output voice activity detection for noise reduction in hearing aids. In *Proceedings of the international workshop on acoustic echo and noise control (IWAENC).*

Nickel, R. M., & Iyer, A. N. (2006). A novel approach to automated source separation in multispeaker environments. In *Proc. IEEE ICASSP* (pp. 629–632).

Nigam, K., McCallum, A., Thrun, S., & Mitchell, T. (2000). Text classification from labeled and unlabeled documents using EM. *Machine Learning, 39,* 103–134. doi:10.1023/A:1007692713085

Nishiura, T., Yamada, T., Nakamura, S., & Shikano, K. (2000). Localization of multiple sound sources based on a CSP analysis with a microphone array (Vol. 2). *Paper presented at the IEEE International Conference on Acoustics, Speech and Signal Processing.*

Nix, J., & Hohmann, V. (2007). Combined estimation of spectral envelopes and sound source direction of concurrent voices by multidimensional statistical filtering. *IEEE Transactions on Audio. Speech and Language Processing, 15*(3), 995–1008. doi:10.1109/TASL.2006.889788

Nocedal, J., & Wright, S. J. (2006). *Numerical Optimization* (2nd ed.). New York: Springer.

Nogueiras, A., Moreno, A., Bonafonte, A., & Mariño, J. B. (2001). *Speech Emotion Recognition Using Hidden Markov Models* (pp. 2679–2682). Proc. Eurospeech.

O'Grady, P. D., Pearlmutter, B. A., & Rickard, S. T. (2005). Survery of sparse and non-sparse methods in source separation. *International Journal of Imaging Systems and Technology, 15,* 18–33.

O'Grady, P. D., & Pearlmutter, B. A. (2006). Convolutive non-negative matrix factorisation with a sparseness constraint. In *Proc. IEEE Int. Workshop on Machine Learning for Signal Process* (pp. 427-432), Maynooth, Ireland.

O'Shaughnessy, D. (2000). *Speech communications.* New York: IEEE Press.

O'Shaughnessy, D. (2000). Speech communications-human and machin (2nd Ed.) In *Institute of electrical and electronic engineers.* New York.

Obradovic, D., Madhu, N., Szabo, A., & Wong, C. S. (2004). Independent component analysis for semi-blind signal separation in MIMO mobile frequency selective communication channels. In *Proceedings of the INNS-IEEE international joint conference on neural networks (IJCNN).*

O'Grady, P. D., & Pearlmutter, B. A. (2008). The LOST algorithm: finding lines and separating speech mixtures. *EURASIP Journal on Advances in Signal Processing, 2008*, 784296. doi:10.1155/2008/784296

Ojemann, G. A. (1990). Organization of language cortex derived from investigation during neurosurgery. *Seminars in Neuroscience, 2*, 297–305.

Ojemann, G. A. (1991). Cortical Organization of Language. *The Journal of Neuroscience, 11*(8), 2281–2287.

Okubo, H., Otani, M., Ikezawa, R., Komiyama, S., & Nakabayashi, K. (2001). A system for measuring the directional room acoustical parameters. *Applied Acoustics, 62*, 203–215. doi:10.1016/S0003-682X(00)00056-6

Oliva, A. (2005). *Gist of a scene* (pp. 251–256). Neurobiology of Attention.

Olsson, R. K., & Hansen, L. K. (2006). Blind separation of more sources than sensors in convolutive mixtures. In *Proc. IEEE ICASSP* (pp. 657–660).

Omologo, M., & Svaizer, P. (1994). Acoustic event localization using a crosspower-spectrum phase based technique. *Paper presented at the IEEE International Conference on Acoustics, Speech and Signal Processing.* Adelaide, Australia.

Oppenheim, A. V., & Schafer, R. W. (1975). *Digital Signal Processing.* New Jersey: Prentice Hall.

Ortony, A., & Turner, T. J. (1990). What's Basic About Basic Emotions? *Psychological Review, 97*(3), 315–331. doi:10.1037/0033-295X.97.3.315

O'Shaughnessy, D. (2008). Invited paper: Automatic speech recognition: History, methods and challenges. *Pattern Recognition, 41*, 2965–2979. doi:10.1016/j.patcog.2008.05.008

O'Shaughnessy, D. (2000). *Speech Communication.* Park Avenue, NY: IEEE Press.

O'Toole, A. J. (2005). A Video Database of Moving Faces and People. *IEEE Transactions on Pattern Analysis and Machine Intelligence, 27*(5), 812–816. doi:10.1109/TPAMI.2005.90

Ozerov, A., Philippe, P., Bimbot, F., & Gribonval, R. (2007). Adaptation of Bayesian models for single-channel source separation and its application to voice/music separation in popular songs. *IEEE Transactions on Audio. Speech and Language Processing, 15*(5), 1564–1578. doi:10.1109/TASL.2007.899291

Ozerov, A., & Févotte, C. (2010). (in press). Multichannel nonnegative matrix factorization in convolutive mixtures for audio source separation. *IEEE Transactions on Audio. Speech and Language Processing.* doi:10.1109/TASL.2009.2031510

Ozerov, A., & Févotte, C. (2009). Multichannel nonnegative matrix factorization in convolutive mixtures. With application to blind audio source separation. In *Proceedings of the 2009 IEEE International Conference on Acoustics, Speech and Signal Processing* (p. 3137-3140).

Ozerov, A., Févotte, C., & Charbit, M. (2009). Factorial scaled hidden markov model for polyphonic audio representation and source separation. In *Proc. IEEE Workshop on Applications of Signal Processing to Audio and Acoustics (WASPAA'09).* Mohonk, NY, USA.

Paatero, P. (1997). Least squares formulation of robust non-negative factor analysis. *Chemometrics and Intelligent Laboratory Systems, 37*(1), 23–25. doi:10.1016/S0169-7439(96)00044-5

Pachet, F., & Cazaly, D. (2000). A classification of musical genre. In *Proc. RIAO Content-Based Multimedia Information Access Conference.*

Pal, P., Iyer, A. N., & Yantorno, R. E. (2006). Emotion Detection from Infant Facial Expressions and Cries, *Proc. IEEE Int'l Conf. Acoustics, Speech and Signal Processing, 2*, 721-724.

Palmer, A., & Shamma, S. (2004). Physiological Representation of Speech. En S. A. Greenberg, *Speech Processing in the Auditory System* (págs. 163-230). New York: Springer.

Pantic, M., & Patras, I. (2006). Dynamics of Facial Expression: Recognition of Facial Actions and Their Temporal Segments Form Face Profile Image Sequences. *IEEE Trans. Systems, Man, and Cybernetics Part B, 36*(2), 433–449. doi:10.1109/TSMCB.2005.859075

Pantic, M., & Rothkrantz, L. J. M. (2004). Facial Action Recognition for Facial Expression Analysis from Static Face Images. *IEEE Trans. Systems, Man, and Cybernetics Part B, 34*(3), 1449–1461. doi:10.1109/TSMCB.2004.825931

Pantic, M., & Bartlett, M. S. (2007). Machine Analysis of Facial Expressions. In Delac, K., & Grgic, M. (Eds.), *Face Recognition* (pp. 377–416). New York: I-Tech Education and Publishing.

Pantic, M., Valstar, M. F., Rademaker, R., & Maat, L. (2005). Web-Based Database for Facial Expression Analysis. *Proc. 13th ACM Int'l Conf. Multimedia,* (pp. 317-321).

Parra, L., & Spence, C. (2000). Convolutive blind separation of non stationary sources. *IEEE Transactions on Speech and Audio Processing, 8,* 320–327. doi:10.1109/89.841214

Parra, L. C., & Alvino, C. V. (2002). Geometric source separation: Merging convolutive source separation with geometric beamforming. *IEEE Transactions on Speech and Audio Processing, 10*(6), 352–362. doi:10.1109/TSA.2002.803443

Parra, L., & Fancourt, C. (2002). An adaptive beamforming perspective on convolutive blind source separation. In Davis, G. M. (Ed.), *Noise reduction in speech applications* (pp. 361–378). CRC Press.

Parra, L., Spence, C., Sajda, P., Ziehe, A., & Muller, K. R. (2000). Unmixing hyperspectral data. *Advances in Neural Information Processing, 13,* 942-948. Boston: MIT Press.

Parry, R. M., & Essa, I. (2007). Incorporating phase information for source separation via spectrogram factorization. In *Proc. IEEE Int. Conf. on Acoust., Speech, and Signal Process.* (Vol. 2, pp. 661-664). Honolulu, Hawaii, USA.

Parry, R. M., & Essa, I. (2007). Phase-aware non-negative spectrogram factorization. In *Proc. International Conference on Independent Component Analysis and Signal Separation (ICA'07)* (pp. 536–543). London, UK.

Parry, R. M., & Essa, I. A. (2006). Estimating the spatial position of spectral components in audio. In *Proc. 6th International Conference on Independent Component Analysis and Blind Signal Separation (ICA'06)* (p. 666-673). Charleston SC, USA.

Pascual-Leone, A., & Hamilton, R. (2001). The metamodal organization of the brain. *Progress in Brain Research, 134,* 427–445. doi:10.1016/S0079-6123(01)34028-1

Pauca, V. P., Piper, J., & Plemmons, R. (2006). Non-negative matrix factorization for spectral data analysis. *Linear Algebra and Its Applications, 416*(1), 29–47. doi:10.1016/j.laa.2005.06.025

Paulus, J., & Klapuri, A. (2008). Labelling the Structural Parts of a Music Piece with Markov Models. *Proceedings of the 2008 Computers in Music Modeling and Retrieval,* (pp.137-147), Copenhagen, Denmark.

Pearlmutter, B. A., & Zador, A. M. (2004). Monaural source separation using spectral cues. In *Proc. ICA 2004* (pp. 478–485).

Pedersen, M. S., Wang, D. L., Larsen, J., & Kjems, U. (2008). Two-microphone separation of speech mixtures. *IEEE Transactions on Neural Networks, 19,* 475–492. doi:10.1109/TNN.2007.911740

Pederson, M. S., Larsen, J., Kjems, U., & Parra, L. (C:\Program Files\Canon\ZoomBrowser EX\Image Library One\2009_11_242007). A survey of convolutive blind source separation methods. Springer Handbook on Speech Processing and Speech Communication.

Peltonen, V. (2001). *Computational auditory scene recognition.* Master's thesis, Tampere University of Technology, Finland.

Pesquet, J. Chen, B. & Petropulu, A. P. (2001). Frequency-domain contrast functions for separation of convolutive mixtures. *Proc. of the IEEE International Conference on Acoustics, Speech, and Signal Processing (ICASSP)* (pp. 2765-2768).

Peterson, J. M., & Kadambe, S. (2003). A probabilistic approach for blind source separation of underdetermined convolutive mixtures. In *Proceedings of the 2003 IEEE International Conference on Acoustics, Speech and Signal Processing* (p. VI-581-584).

Petridis, S., & Pantic, M. (2008). Audiovisual Discrimination between Laughter and Speech. *IEEE Int'l Conf. Acoustics, Speech, and Signal Processing* (pp. 5117-5120).

Pham, D.-T., Servière, C., & Boumaraf, H. (2003). Blind separation of speech mixtures based on nonstationarity. In *Proceedings of the 7ᵗʰ International Symposium on Signal Processing and its Applications* (p. II–73–76).

Platt, C., & Faggin, F. (1992). Networks for the separation of sources that are superimposed and delayed. *Advances in Neural Information Processing, 4*, 730-737. San Francisco: Morgan Kaufmann.

Plumbley, M., Abdallah, S., Blumensath, T., & Davies, M. (2006). Sparse representations of polyphonic music. *Signal Processing, 86*, 417–431. doi:10.1016/j.sigpro.2005.06.007

Poeppel, D. (2003). The analysis of speech in different temporal integration windows: Cerebral lateralization as asymmetric sampling in time. *Speech Communication, 41*, 245–255. doi:10.1016/S0167-6393(02)00107-3

Polack, J. D., Alrutz, H., & Schroeder, M. R. (1984). The modulation transfer function of music Signals and its Application to reverberation measurement. *Acustica, 54*, 256–265.

Porter, J., & Boll, S. (1984). Optimal estimators for spectral restoration of noisy speech. In *Proceedings of the IEEE international conference on acoustics, speech and signal processing (ICASSP)*.

Potter, M. (1976). Short-term conceptual memory for pictures. *Journal of Experimental Psychology. Human Learning and Memory, 2*(5), 509–522. doi:10.1037/0278-7393.2.5.509

Potter, K., Wiggins, G. A., & Pearce, M. T. (2007). Towards greater objectivity in music theory: Information-dynamic analysis of minimalist music. *Musicae Scientiae, 11*(2), 295–322.

Pridham, R. G., & Mucci, R. A. (1979). Digital interpolation beamforming for lowpass and bandpass signals. *Proceedings of the IEEE, 67*(6), 904–919. doi:10.1109/PROC.1979.11354

Prieto, R. E., & Jinachitra, P. (2005). *Blind source separation for time-variant mixing systems using piecewise linear approximations*. Proc. IEEE ICASSP, 301–304.

Puckette, M. S., & Brown, J. C. (1998). Accuracy of frequency estimates using the phase vocoder. *IEEE Transactions on Audio and Speech Processing, 6*(2).

Puigt, M., Vincent, E., & Deville, Y. (2009). Validity of the independence assumption for the separation of instantaneous and convolutive mixtures of speech and music sources. In *Proceedings of the 8ᵗʰ International Conference on Independent Component Analysis and Signal Separation* (p. 613-620).

Rabinkin, D. V., Renomeron, R. J., Dahl, A., French, J. C., Flanagan, J. L., & Bianch, M. H. (1996). A DSP implementation of source location using microphone arrays. In *Advanced signal processing algorithms, architectures, and implementations VI* (*Vol. 2846*, pp. 88–99). Denver, Colorado: SPIE.

Radfar, M. H., & Dansereau, R. M. (2007). Single channel speech separation using soft mask filtering. In *IEEE Trans. on Audio* (*Vol. 15*, pp. 2299–2310). Speech and Language Process.

Radfar, M. H., Dansereau, R. M., & Sayadiyan, A. (2006). Performance evaluation of three features for model-based single channel speech separation problem. In *Interspeech 2006, International Conference Spoken Language Process.* (ICSLP06), Pittsburgh, PA, (pp. 2610–2613).

Rakerd, B., & Hartmann, W. M. (1985). Localization of sound in rooms II: The effects of a single reflecting surface. *The Journal of the Acoustical Society of America, 78*(2), 524–533. doi:10.1121/1.392474

Rakerd, B., & Hartmann, W. M. (1986). Localization of sound in rooms, III: Onset and duration effects. *The Journal of the Acoustical Society of America, 80*(6), 1695–1706. doi:10.1121/1.394282

Ramón y Cajal, S. (1899-1904). *Textura del Sistema Nervioso del Hombre y de los Vertebrados (reprinted in English as: Histology of the Nervous System of Man and Vertebrates, Oxford University Press, 1995)*. Madrid: Imprenta y Librería de Nicolás Moya.

Rao, B., & Hari, K. (1989). Performance analysis of root-music. *IEEE Transactions on Acoustics, Speech, and Signal Processing, 37*(12), 1939–1949. doi:10.1109/29.45540

Ratnam, R., Jones, D. L., Wheeler, B. C., O'Brien, W. D. Jr, Lansing, C. R., & Feng, A. S. (2003). Blind estimation of reverberation time. *The Journal of the Acoustical Society of America, 114*, 2877–2892. doi:10.1121/1.1616578

Rauschecker, J. P., & Scott, S. K. (2009). Maps and streams in the auditory cortex: nonhuman primates illuminate human speech processing. *Nature Neuroscience, 12*(6), 718–724. doi:10.1038/nn.2331

Rauschecker, J. P., Tian, B., & Hauser, M. (1995). Processing of Complex Sounds in the Macaque Nonprimary Auditory Cortex. *Science, 268*, 111–114. doi:10.1126/science.7701330

Ravelli, E., & Daudet, L. (2006). Representations of audio signals in overcomplete dictionaries: what is the link between redundancy factor and coding properties? In *Proceedings of the International Conference on Digital Audio effects* (pp. 267-270).

Rayleigh, L. (1907). On our perception of sound direction. *Philosophical Magazine, 13*, 214–232.

Rennie, S. J., Hershey, J. R., & Olsen, P. A. (2008). Efficient model-based speech separation and denoising using non-negative subspace analysis. In *Proceedings of the 2008 IEEE International Conference on Acoustics, Speech and Signal Processing* (p. 1833-1836).

Ricard, J. (2005). An implementation of multi-band onset detection. *MIREX 2005 audio onset detection contest.* Retrieved from http://www.music-ir.org/evaluation/mirex-results/articles/onset/ricard.pdf

Rickard, S., & Yilmaz, Ö. (2002). On the approximate W-Disjoint orthogonality of speech. In *Proceedings of the IEEE international conference on acoustics, speech and signal processing (ICASSP).*

Rickard, S., Balan, R., & Rosca, J. (2001). Real-time time-frequency based blind source separation. In *Proceedings of the international conference on independent component analysis (ICA).*

Rigau, J., Feixas, M., & Sbert, M. (2008). *Informational Aesthetics Measures.* IEEE Computer Graphics and Applications.

Ristic, B., Arulampalam, S., & Gordon, N. (2004). *Beyond the Kalman Filter: Particle Filter for Tracking Applications.* Boston, London: Artech House Publishers.

Robel, A. (2007) Onset detection in polyphonic signals by means of transient peak classification. *MIREX 2007 audio onset detection contest.* Retrieved from http://www.music-ir.org/mirex/2007/abs/OD_roebel.pdf

Roberts, S., & Everson, R. (2001). *Independent Component Analysis.* Cambridge, England: Cambridge University Press.

Roisman, G. I., Tsai, J. L., & Chiang, K. S. (2004). The Emotional Integration of Childhood Experience: Physiological, Facial Expressive, and Self-Reported Emotional Response during the Adult Attachment Interview. *Developmental Psychology, 40*(5), 776–789. doi:10.1037/0012-1649.40.5.776

Roman, N., & Wang, D. L. (2008). Binaural tracking of multiple moving sources. *IEEE Transactions on Audio. Speech and Language Processing, 16*(4), 728–739. doi:10.1109/TASL.2008.918978

Roman, N., Wang, D., & Brown, G. (2003). Speech segregation based on sound localization. *The Journal of the Acoustical Society of America, 114*(4), 2236–2252. doi:10.1121/1.1610463

Rong, Y., Vorobyov, S. A., Gershman, A. B., & Sidiropoulos, N. D. (2005). Blind Spatial Signature Estimation via Time-Varying User Power Loading and Parallel Factor Analysis. *IEEE Transactions on Signal Processing, 53*, 1697–1710. doi:10.1109/TSP.2005.845441

Rosca, J., Borss, C., & Balan, R. (2004). Generalized sparse signal mixing model and application to noisy blind source separation. In *Proceedings of the IEEE international conference on acoustics, speech and signal processing (ICASSP).*

Rosch, E., Mervis, C., Gray, W., Johnson, D., & Boyes-Braem, P. (1976). Basic objects in natural categories. *Cognitive Psychology, 8*(3), 382–439. doi:10.1016/0010-0285(76)90013-X

Rosenthal, D. F., & Okuno, H. G. (1998). *Computational Auditory Scene Analysis.* Mahwah, NJ: Lawrence Erlbaum.

Roweis, S. T. (2001). One microphone source separation. *Advances in Neural Information Processing Systems*, *13*, 793–799.

Roy, R., & Kailath, T. (1989). *ESPRIT*-estimation of signal parameters via rotational invariance techniques. *IEEE Transactions on Acoustics, Speech, and Signal Processing*, *37*(7), 984–995. doi:10.1109/29.32276

Rubinstein, R., Zibulevsky, M., & Elad, M. (2009Submitted to). *Learning sparse dictionaries for sparse signal representation*. IEEE Transactions on Signal Proceedings.

Rubsamen, M., & Gershman, A. (2009). Direction-of-arrival estimation for nonuniform sensor arrays: From manifold separation to Fourier domain music methods. *IEEE Transactions on Signal Processing*, *57*(2), 588–599. doi:10.1109/TSP.2008.2008560

Rumelhart, D. E., Hinton, G. E., & Williams, R. J. (1986). Learning internal representations by error propagation. In *Parallel distributed processing: Exploration in the Microstructure of Cognition*. 1, 318-362. Cambridge, MA: MIT Press.

Russell, J., Ward, L., & Pratt, G. (1981). Affective Quality Attributed to Environments: A Factor Analytic Study. *Environment and Behavior*, *13*(3), 259–288. doi:10.1177/0013916581133001

SAA. (2009). Retrieved May 21, 2009, from http://accent.gmu.edu

Saab, R., Yilmaz, O., McKeown, M. J., & Abugharbieh, R. (2005). Underdetermined sparse blind

Sams, M., & Salmening, R. (1994). Evidence of sharp frequency tuning in human auditory cortex. *Hearing Research*, *75*, 67–74. doi:10.1016/0378-5955(94)90057-4

Sanei, S., & Chambers, J. (2007). *EEG Signal Processing*. Hoboken, NJ: John Wiley & Sons.

Sanei, S., Naqvi, S. M., Chambers, J. A., & Hicks, Y. (2007). *A geometrically constrained multimodal approach for convolutive blind source separation*. Proc. IEEE ICASSP, 969–972.

Sanger, T. D. (1989). Optimal unsupervised learning in a single-layer linear feed-forward neural network. *Neural Networks*, *12*, 459–473. doi:10.1016/0893-6080(89)90044-0

Sarpeshkar, R. (2006). Brain power: borrowing from biology makes for low-power computing. *IEEE Spectrum*, *43*(5), 24–29. doi:10.1109/MSPEC.2006.1628504

Saruwatari, H., Kawamura, T., Nishikawa, T., Lee, A., & Shikano, K. (2006). Blind source separation based on a fast-convergence algorithm combining ICA and beamforming. *IEEE Trans on Audio. Speech and Language Processing*, *14*, 666–678. doi:10.1109/TSA.2005.855832

Sawada, H., Mukai, R., Araki, S., & Makino, S. (2004). A robust and precise method for solving the permutation problem of frequency domain blind source separation. *IEEE Transactions on Speech and Audio Processing*, *12*, 530–538. doi:10.1109/TSA.2004.832994

Sawada, H., Araki, S., Mukai, R., & Makino, S. (2007). Grouping separated frequency components with estimating propagation model parameters in frequency-domain blind source separation. *IEEE Transactions on Audio. Speech and Language Processing*, *15*(5), 1592–1604. doi:10.1109/TASL.2007.899218

Sawada, H., Mukai, R., Araki, S., & Makino, S. (2001). A polar-coordinate based activation function for frequency domain blind source separation. In *Proceedings of the international conference on independent component analysis (ICA)* (pp. 663–668).

Sawada, H., Mukai, R., Araki, S., & Makino, S. (2003). Polar coordinate based nonlinear function for frequency-domain blind source separation. In *IEICE Transactions Fundamentals*, E86 (3), 590–596.

Scharnhorst, K. (2001). Angles in complex vector spaces. *Acta Applicandae Mathematicae*, *69*(1), 95–103. doi:10.1023/A:1012692601098

Scheirer, E. (1998). Tempo and Beat Analysis of Acoustic Musical Signals. *The Journal of the Acoustical Society of America*, *103*(1), 588–601. doi:10.1121/1.421129

Scheirer, E. D. (2000). Music-Listening Systems. *Phd thesis*, Massachusetts Institute of Technology (MIT).

Scherer, K. (2005). What are emotions? and how can they be measured? *Social Sciences Information. Information Sur les Sciences Sociales*, *44*(4), 695–729. doi:10.1177/0539018405058216

Schmidt, M. N., & Laurberg, H. (2008). *Nonnegative matrix factorization with Gaussian process priors*. Computational Intelligence and Neuroscience.

Schmidt, M. N., & Olsson, R. K. (2006). *Single-channel speech separation using sparse non-negative matrix factorization*. Interspeech.

Schmidt, R. O. (1986, March). Multiple emitter location and signal parameter estimation. *IEEE Transactions on Antennas and Propagation, 34*(3), 276–280. doi:10.1109/TAP.1986.1143830

Schmidt, M. N., & Morup, M. (2006). Nonnegative matrix factor 2D deconvolution for blind single channel source separation. In *Proc. 6th Int. Conf. on Independent Component Analysis and Blind Signal Separation* (pp. 700-707), Charleston, SC, USA.

Schmidt, M. N., & Olsson, R. K. (2007). Linear regression on sparse features for single-channel speech separation. In *Proceedings of the 2007 IEEE Workshop on Applications of Signal Processing to Audio and Acoustics* (p. 26-29).

Schmidt, M. N., Winther, O., & Hansen, L. K. (2009). Bayesian non-negative matrix factorization. In *Proc. 8th International conference on Independent Component Analysis and Signal Separation (ICA'09)*. Paraty, Brazil.

Schmidt, R. O. (1981). *A signal subspace approach to multiple emitter location and spectral estimation.* Unpublished doctoral dissertation, Stanford University.

Schobben, L., & Sommen, W. (2002). A frequency domain blind signal separation method based on decorrelation. *IEEE Transactions on Signal Processing, 50*(8), 1855–1865. doi:10.1109/TSP.2002.800417

Schreiner, C. E. (1995). Order and Disorder in Auditory Cortical Maps. *Current Opinion in Neurobiology, 5*, 489–496. doi:10.1016/0959-4388(95)80010-7

Schroeder, M. (1981). Modulation Transfer Functions: Definition and Measurement. *Acustica, 49*, 179–182.

Schroeder, M. R. (1979). Integrated impulse method measuring sound decay without impulses. *J. Acoust. Am., 66*(2), 497–500. doi:10.1121/1.383103

Schuller, B., & Wimmer, M. (2008). *Detection of security related affect and behavior in passenger Transport* (pp. 265–268). Proc. Interspeech.

Schuller, B., Muller, R., Hornler, B., Hothker, A., Konosu, H., & Rigoll, G. (2007). Audiovisual Recognition of Spontaneous Interest within Conversations *Proc. ACM Int'l Conf. Multimodal Interfaces (* pp. 30-37).

Schuller, B., Rigoll, G., & Lang, M. (2003). Hidden Markov Model-Based Speech Emotion Recognition. *Proc. IEEE Int'l Conf. Acoustics, Speech, and Signal Processing, 2*, 1-4.

Schuller, B., Villar, R. J., Rigoll, G., & Lang, M. (2005). Meta-Classifiers in Acoustic and Linguistic Feature Fusion-Based Affect Recognition. *Proc. IEEE Int'l Conf. Acoustics, Speech, and Signal Processing,* (pp. 325-328).

Schyns, P., & Oliva, A. (1994). Evidence for Time-and Spatial-Scale-Dependent Scene Recognition. *Psychological Science, 5*(4), 195–200. doi:10.1111/j.1467-9280.1994.tb00500.x

Sebe, N., Cohen, I., Gevers, T., & Huang, T. S. (2006). Emotion Recognition Based on Joint Visual and Audio Cues. *Proc. Int'l Conf. Pattern Recognition* (pp. 1136-1139).

Sebe, N., Lew, M. S., Cohen, I., Sun, Y., Gevers, T., & Huang, T. S. (2004). Authentic Facial Expression Analysis. *Proc. IEEE Int'l Conf. Automatic Face and Gesture Recognition.*

Secker, H., & Searle, C. (1990). Time Domain Analysis of Auditory-Nerve Fibers Firing Rates. *The Journal of the Acoustical Society of America, 88*, 1427–1436. doi:10.1121/1.399719

Sekey, A., & Hanson, B. A. (1984). Improved 1-bark bandwidth auditory filter. *The Journal of the Acoustical Society of America, 75*(6), 1902–1904. doi:10.1121/1.390954

Sekiguchi, K., Kimura, S., & Hanyuu, T. (1992). Analysis of sound field on spatial information using a four-channel microphone system based on regular tetrahedron peak point method. *Applied Acoustics, 37*(4), 305–323. doi:10.1016/0003-682X(92)90017-M

Serra, X. (1989). A System for Sound Analysis/Transformation/Synthesis based on a Deterministic plus Stochastic Decomposition. *Phd thesis*, Stanford University.

Servière, C., & Pham, D. T. (2009). Permutation correction in the frequency domain in blind separation of speech mixtures. *EURASIP Journal on Applied Signal Processing* (2006).

Sethu, V., Ambikairajah, E., & Epps, J. (2008). *Phonetic and speaker variations in automatic emotion Classification* (pp. 617–620). Proc. Interspeech.

Shamma, S. (1985). Speech processing in the auditory system II: lateral inhibition and central processing of speech evoked activity in the auditory nerve. *The Journal of the Acoustical Society of America, 78,* 1622–1632. doi:10.1121/1.392800

Shamma, S. (2001). On the role of space and time auditory processing. *Trends in Cognitive Sciences, 5*(8), 340–348. doi:10.1016/S1364-6613(00)01704-6

Shashanka, M., Raj, B., & Smaragdis, P. (2008). Probabilistic latent variable models as nonnegative factorizations. *Computational Intelligence and Neuroscience*(Article ID 947438, 8 pages). (doi:10.1155/2008/947438)

Shashua, A., & Hazan, T. (2005). Non-negative tensor factorization with applications to statistics and computer vision. In *Proc. 22nd International Conference on Machine Learning* (pp. 792 – 799). Bonn, Germany: ACM.

Shi, J., & Malik, J. (2000). Normalized cuts and image segmentation. *IEEE Transactions on Pattern Analysis and Machine Intelligence, 22*(8), 888–905. doi:10.1109/34.868688

Shilling, R. D., & Shinn-Cunningham, B. (2000). *Virtual auditory displays. In virtual environments handbook.* New York: Lawrence Erlbaum, Associates.

Shinn-Cunningham, B. G. (2000). Learning reverberation: Considerations for spatial auditory displays. *Presented at the International Conference on Auditory Display.* Atlanta, GA.

Shlens, J. (2005). *A Tutorial on Principal Component Analysis.* Systems Neurobiology Laboratory, Salk Institute for Biological Studies, La Jolla.

Shneiderman, B., & Aris, A. (2006). Network visualization by semantic substrates. *IEEE Transactions on Visualization and Computer Graphics, 12*(5). doi:10.1109/TVCG.2006.166

Slaney, M. (1998). A Critique of Pure Audition, Chapter 3. *Computational Auditory Scene Analysis.* Lawrence Erlbaum Associates, Inc.

Smaragdis, P., & Boufounos, P. (2007). Position and trajectory learning for microphone arrays. *IEEE Transactions on Audio. Speech and Language Processing, 15*(1), 358–368. doi:10.1109/TASL.2006.876758

Smaragdis, P. (1998). Blind separation of convolved mixtures in the frequency domain. *Neurocomputing, 22*(1-3), 21–34. doi:10.1016/S0925-2312(98)00047-2

Smaragdis, P. (2007). Convolutive speech bases and their application to supervised speech separation. *IEEE Transactions on Audio. Speech and Language Processing, 15*(1), 1–12. doi:10.1109/TASL.2006.876726

Smaragdis, P. (2004). Non-negative matrix factor deconvolution, extraction of multiple sound sources from monophonic inputs. In *Proc. 5th Int. Conf. on Independent Component Analysis and Blind Signal Separation* (LNCS 3195, pp.494-499), Granada, Spain.).

Smaragdis, P., & Brown, J. C. (2003). Nonnegative matrix factorization for polyphonic music transcription. In *IEEE Int. Workshop on Applications of Signal Process. to Audio and Acoustics* (pp. 177-180). New Paltz, NY.

Smith, E., & Lewicki, M. (2006). Efficient auditory coding. *Nature, 439*(23), 978–982. doi:10.1038/nature04485

Smith, E., & Lewicki, M. S. (2005). Efficient coding of time-relative structure using spikes. [Boston: MIT Press.]. *Neural Computation, 17,* 19–45. doi:10.1162/0899766052530839

Snyder, B. (2000). *Music and Memory. An Introduction.* Cambridge, Mass.: The MIT Press.

Soltuz, S., Wang, W., & Jackson, P. (2009). A hybrid iterative algorithm for non-negative matrix factorization. In *Proc. IEEE Int. Workshop on Statistical Signal Processing* (pp. 409-412).

Song, M., & Wang, H. (2005). Highly efficient incremental estimation of Gaussian mixture models for online data stream clustering. In *Society of Photo-Optical Instrumentation Engineers (SPIE) Conference Series.*

Song, M., Bu, J., Chen, C., & Li, N. (2004). Audio-Visual-Based Emotion Recognition: A New Approach. *Proc. Int'l Conf. Computer Vision and Pattern Recognition,* (pp. 1020-1025).

Soon, V. C., Tong, L., Huang, Y. F., & Liu, R. (1993). A robust method for wideband signal separation. In *Proc. IEEE International Symposium Circuits Systems* (Vol.1, pp. 703–706).

Sordo, M., Laurier, C., & Celma, O. (2007). Annotating music collections: how content-based similarity helps to propagate labels. *In Proceedings of the 8th International Conference on Music Information Retrieval (ISMIR 2007).*

Sound Ideas. (n.d.). *The BBC sound effects library - original series.* Retrieved from http://www.sound-ideas.com/bbc.html

Srinivasan, S., Samuelsson, J., & Kleijn, W. B. (2006). Codebook driven short-term predictor parameter estimation for speech enhancement. *IEEE Transactions on Audio. Speech and Language Processing, 14*(1), 163–176. doi:10.1109/TSA.2005.854113

Srinivasan, S. H. (2004). Auditory blobs. In *Proc. IEEE International Conference on Acoustics, Speech, and Signal Processing* (ICASSP), Montreal, Canada (Vol. 4, pp. 313–316).

Srinivasan, S. H., & Kankanhalli, M. S. (2003). Harmonicity and dynamics based audio separation. In *Proc. IEEE International Conference on Acoustics, Speech, and Signal Processing* (ICASSP), volume 5, pages v–640 – v–643, Hong Kong, China.

Stauffer, C., & Grimson, W. (1999). *Adaptive background mixture models for real-time tracking.* IEEE Computer Vision and Pattern Recognition.

Steeneken, H. J. M., & Houtgast, T. (1980). A physical method for measuring speech transmission quality. *The Journal of the Acoustical Society of America, 67*(1), 318–326. doi:10.1121/1.384464

Steeneken, H. J. M., & Houtgast, T. (1983). The temporal envelope spectrum of speech and its significance in room acoustics. *11th ICA conference publication* Paris.

Stoica, P., & Selén, Y. (2004). Model-order selection: a review of information criterion rules. *IEEE Signal Processing Magazine, 21*(4), 36–47. doi:10.1109/MSP.2004.1311138

Strang, G. (1988). *Linear algebra and its applications* (3rd ed.). Belmont, CA: Thompson / Brooks Cole.

Sturim, D. E., Brandstein, M. S., & Silverman, H. F. (1997). Tracking multiple talkers using microphone-array measurements. *Paper presented at the IEEE International Conference on Acoustics, Speech and Signal Processing.* Munich, Germany.

Suga, N. (2006). *Basic Acoustic Patterns and Neural Mechanisms Shared by Humans and Animals for Auditory Perception. En S. G. Ainsworth, Listening to Speech: An Auditory Perspective* (pp. 159–181). Mahwah, NJ: Lawrence Erlbaum Associates, Pub.

Supper, B., Brookes, T., & Rumsey, F. (2006). An auditory onset detection algorithm for improved automatic source localization. *IEEE Transactions on Audio, Speech, and Language Processing, 14*(3), 1008–1017. doi:10.1109/TSA.2005.857787

Sussman, H. M., McCaffrey, H. A., & Mathews, S. A. (1991). An Investigation of Locus Equations as a Source of Relational Invariance for Stop Place Categorization. *The Journal of the Acoustical Society of America, 90,* 1309–1325. doi:10.1121/1.401923

Svaizer, P., Matassoni, M., & Omologo, M. (1997). Acoustic source location in a three-dimensional space using crosspower spectrum phase. *Paper presented at the IEEE International Conference on Acoustics, Speech and Signal Processing.* Munich, Germany.

Swerts, M., & Krahmer, E. (2008). *Gender-related differences in the production and perception of Emotion* (pp. 334–337). Proc. Interspeech.

Takigawa, I., Kudo, M., Nakamura, A., & Toyama, J. (2004). On the minimum l_1-norm signal recovery in underdetermined source separation. *Proc. of 5th Int. Conf. on Independent Component Analysis* (pp. 22-24).

Tan, V. Y. F., & Févotte, C. (2009). Automatic relevance determination in nonnegative matrix factorization. In *Proc. Workshop on Signal Processing with Adaptive Sparse Structured Representations (SPARS'09).* Saint-Malo, France.

Tan, V., & Fevotte, C. (2005). A study of the effect of source sparsity for various transforms on

Tao, H., & Huang, T. S. (1999). Explanation-Based Facial Motion Tracking Using a Piecewise Bezier Volume Deformation Mode. *Proc. IEEE Int'l Conf. Computer Vision and Pattern Recognition, 1*, 611-617.

Tashev, I., & Acero, A. (2006). Microphone array post-processing using instantaneous direction of arrival. In *Proceedings of the international workshop on acoustic echo and noise control (IWAENC).*

Temperley, D. (2007). *Music and Probability.* Cambridge, MA: MIT Press.

Tian, Y. L., Kanade, T., & Cohn, J. F. (2005). Facial Expression Analysis. S.Z. Li and A.K. Jain (Eds.). *Handbook of Face Recognition* (pp. 247-276). New York: Springer.

Tipping, M. E. (2001). Sparse Bayesian Learning and the relevance vector machine. *Journal of Machine Learning Research, 1*, 211–244. doi:10.1162/15324430152748236

Todros, K., & Tabrikian, J. (2004) Blind separation of non stationary and non gaussian independent sources. In *Proc. IEEE Convention of Electrical and Electronics in Israel.*

Torkkola, K. (1996). Blind separation of convolved sources based on information maximization. *Proc. IEEE workshop on Neural Networks and Signal Processing (NNSP)*(pp. 315-323).

Torralba, A., & Oliva, A. (2003). Statistics of natural image categories. *Network (Bristol, England), 14*, 391–412. doi:10.1088/0954-898X/14/3/302

Torres, D., Turnbull, D., Barrington, L., & Lanckriet, G. (2007). Identifying words that are musically meaningful. In *Proceedings of the 8th International Conference on Music Information Retrieval (ISMIR 2007).*

Trohidis, K., Tsoumakas, G., Kalliris, G., & Vlahavas, I. (2008). Multi-label classification of music into emotions. In *Proceedings of the 9th International Conference on Music Information Retrieval (ISMIR 2008).*

Tsai, R. Y. (1987). A versatile camera calibration technique for high-accuracy 3d machine vision metrology using off-the-shelf tv cameras and lenses. *IEEE Journal on Robotics and Automation, RA-3*(4), 323–344. doi:10.1109/JRA.1987.1087109

Tsalaile, T., Naqvi, S. M., Nazarpour, K., Sanei, S., & Chambers, J. A. (2008). *Blind source extraction of heart sound signals from lung sound recordings exploiting periodicity of the heart sound.* Proc. IEEE ICASSP, Las Vegas, USA.

Tsoumakas, G., & Vlahavas, I. (2007). Random k-Label-sets: an ensemble method for multilabel classification. In *ECML '07: Proceedings of the 18th European conference on Machine Learning.*

Turnbull, D., Barrington, L., & Lanckriet, G. (2008). Five Approaches to Collecting Tags for Music. In *Proceedings of the 9th International Conference on Music Information Retrieval (ISMIR 2008).*

Turnbull, D., Barrington, L., Torres, D., & Lanckriet, G. (2007). Towards musical query-by-semantic-description using the CAL500 data set. In *SIGIR '07: Proceedings of the 30th annual international ACM SIGIR conference on Research and development in information retrieval.*

Turnbull, D., Barrington, L., Torres, D., & Lanckriet, G. (2008). Semantic annotation and retrieval of music and sound effects. In *IEEE Transactions on Audio, Speech & Language Processing, 16.*

Turnbull, D., Liu, R., Barrington, L., & Lanckriet, G. (2007). A game-based approach for collecting semantic annotations of music. In *Proceedings of the 8th International Conference on Music Information Retrieval (ISMIR 2007).*

Tzanetakis, G., & Cook, P. (2002). Musical genre classification of audio signals. *IEEE Transactions on Speech and Audio Processing, 10*, 293–302. doi:10.1109/TSA.2002.800560

Tzanetakis, G., & Cook. P. Musical Genre Classification of Audio Signals *IEEE Transactions on Acoustics, Speech and Signal Processing, 10*(5), pp. 293-302, 2002.

Tzanetakis, G. (2002). Manipulation, Analysis and Retrieval Systems for Audio Signals. *Phd thesis*, Princeton University.

Tzanetakis, G. (2008). Marsyas: a case study in implementing Music Information Retrieval Systems, pages 31–49. *Intelligent Music Information Systems: Tools and Methodologies. Information Science Reference.* ISBN 978-1-59904-663-1.

Tzanetakis, G. (2009). Marsyas submissions to MIREX 2009, in Music Information Retrieval Evaluation Exchange (MIREX), Kobe.Retrieved from http://www.music-ir.org/mirex/2009/

Tzanetakis, G., & Cook, P. (2000). Marsyas: a framework for audio analysis. *Organized Sound, 4*(3).

Tzanetakis, G., Castillo, C., Jones, R., Martins, L. G., Teixeira, L. F., & Lagrange, M. (2008). Interoperability and the marsyas 0.2 runtime. In *Proc. International Computer Music Conference* (ICMC), Belfast, Northern Ireland.

Umapathy, K., Krishnan, S., & Jimaa, S. (2005). Multigroup classification of audio signals using time-frequency parameters. *IEEE Transactions on Multimedia, 7,* 308–315. doi:10.1109/TMM.2005.843363

University of Sheffield, Department of Computer Science. (2007). *Auditory scene analysis: Listening to several things at once.* Retrived on June 27,2009 from http://www.dcs.shef.ac.uk/spandh/research/asa.html

Valenzise, G., Gerosa, L., Tagliasacchi, M., Antonacci, F., & Sarti, A. (2007,). Scream and gunshot detection and localization for audio-surveillance systems. *Paper presented at the IEEE Conference on Advanced Video and Signal Based Surveillance.*

Valstar, M. F., Gunes, H., & Pantic, M. (2007). How to Distinguish Posed from Spontaneous Smiles Using Geometric Features. *Proc. ACM Int'l Conf. Multimodal Interfaces* (pp. 38-45).

Valstar, M., Pantic, M., & Patras, I. (2004). Motion History for Facial Action Detection from Face Video. *Proc. IEEE Int'l Conf. Systems, Man, and Cybernetics, 1,* 635-640.

Valstar, M., Pantic, M., Ambadar, Z., & Cohn, J. F. (2006). Spontaneous versus Posed Facial Behavior: Automatic Analysis of Brow Actions. *Proc. Int'l Conf. Multimodal Interfaces* (pp.162-170).

Van Hengel, P. W. J., & Andringa, T. C. (2007). Verbal aggression detection in complex social environments. In *IEEE Conference on Advanced Video and Signal Based Surveillance* (pp. 15-20).

van Trees, H. L. (2002). *Optimum array processing.* Hoboken, NJ: Wiley. doi:10.1002/0471221104

van Trees, H. L. (2002). *Detection, estimation and modulation theory, part iv.* Hoboken, NJ: John Wiley and Sons.

Varma, K. (2002). Time-delay-estimate based direction-of-arrival estimation for speech in reverberant environments. *Unpublished doctoral dissertation, Department of Electrical and Computer Engineering, Virginia Polytechnic Institute and State University.* Blacksburg, VA.

Vary, P., & Martin, R. (2006). *Digital speech transmission: Enhancement, coding and error concealment.* Hoboken, NJ: John Wiley & Sons, Ltd.doi:10.1002/0470031743

Vasconcelos, N. (2001). Image indexing with mixture hierarchies. In *Proceedings of the 2001 IEEE Computer Society Conference on Computer Vision and Pattern Recognition (CVPR 2001).*

Veen, B. D. V., & Buckley, K. M. (1988). Beamforming: A versatile approach to spatial filtering. *IEEE ASSP Magazine,* 4–21. doi:10.1109/53.665

Ververidis, D., & Kotropoulos, C. (2005). Emotional speech classification using Gaussian mixture Models. *Proc. ISCAS* (pp. 2871-2874).

Vidrascu, L., & Devillers, L. (2005). *Detection of real-life emotions in call centers* (pp. 1841–1844). Proc. Interspeech.

Vielva, L., Erdogmus, D., Pantaleon, C., Santamaria, I., Pereda, J., & Principe, J. C. (2002). Underdetermined blind source separation in a time-varying environment. *Proc. of IEEE Conf. On Acoustic, Speech, and Signal Processing (ICASSP)*(Vol. 3, pp. 3049-3052).

Vincent, E. (2006). Musical source separation using time-frequency source priors. *IEEE Transactions on Audio, Speech and Language Processing, 14*(1), 91–98. doi:10.1109/TSA.2005.860342

Vincent, E., Gribonval, R., & Plumbley, M. D. (2007). Oracle estimators for the benchmarking of source separation algorithms. *Signal Processing, 87,* 1933–1950.

Vincent, E., Jafari, M. G., Abdallah, S. A., Plumbley, M. D., & Davies, M. E. (2010). Probabilistic modeling paradigms for audio source separation. In *Machine Audition: Principles, Algorithms and Systems.* Hershey, PA: IGI Global.

Vincent, E., Bertin, N., & Badeau, R. (2007). Two non-negative matrix factorization methods for polyphonic pitch transcription. In *Proc. Music Information Retrieval Evaluation eXchange*. MIREX.

Vincent, E. (2007). Complex nonconvex lp norm minimization for underdetermined source separation. In *Proceedings of the 7th International Conference on Independent Component Analysis and Signal Separation* (p. 430–437).

Virtanen, T. (2007). Monaural sound source separation by non-negative matrix factorization with temporal continuity and sparseness criteria. *IEEE Transactions on Audio. Speech and Language Processing, 15*(3), 1066–1074. doi:10.1109/TASL.2006.885253

Virtanen, T. (2003). Sound source separation using sparse coding with temporal continuity objective. In *Proc. Int. Comput. Music Conf.* (pp. 231-234), Singapore.

Virtanen, T., & Cemgil, A. T. (2009). Mixtures of gamma priors for non-negative matrix factorization based speech separation. In *Proceedings of the 8th International Conference on Independent Component Analysis and Signal Separation* (p. 646-653).

Virtanen, T., & Klapuri, A. (2000). Separation of harmonic sound sources using sinusoidal modeling. In *Proc. IEEE International Conference on Acoustics, Speech, and Signal Processing* (ICASSP), Istanbul, Turkey.

Virtanen, T., Cemgil, A. T., & Godsill, S. (2008). Bayesian extensions to non-negative matrix factorization for audio signal modelling. In *Proc. International Conference on Acoustics, Speech and Signal Processing (ICASSP '08)* (pp. 1825–1828). Las Vegas, Nevada, USA.

von Luxburg, U. (2007). A tutorial on spectral clustering. *Statistics and Computing, 17*(4), 395–416. doi:10.1007/s11222-007-9033-z

Waibel, A., Hanazawa, T., Hinton, G., Shikano, K., & Lang, K. J. (1989). Phoneme recognition using time-delay neural networks. *IEEE Transactions on Acoustics, Speech, and Signal Processing, 37*, 328–339. doi:10.1109/29.21701

Wang, D. L., & Brown, G. J. (1999, May). Separation of speech from interfering sounds based on oscillatory correlation. *IEEE Transactions on Neural Networks, 10*, 684–697. doi:10.1109/72.761727

Wang, D. L., & Brown, G. J. (2006). *Computational Auditory Scene Analysis: Principles, Algorithms, and Applications*. Hoboken, NJ: Wiley/IEEE Press.

Wang, W., Cichocki, A., & Chambers, J. A. (2009). A multiplicative algorithm for convolutive non-negative matrix factorization based on squared Euclidean distance. In *IEEE Trans* (pp. 447–452). On Signal Processing.

Wang, W., Sanei, S., & Chambers, J. A. (2005). Penalty function-based joint diagnolization approach for convolutive blind separation of nonstationary sources. *IEEE Transactions on Signal Processing, 53*, 1654–1669. doi:10.1109/TSP.2005.845433

Wang, W., Sanei, S., & Chambers, J. A. (2005). Penalty function based joint diagonalization approach for convolutive blind separation of nonstationary sources. *IEEE Transactions on Signal Processing, 53*(5), 1654–1669. doi:10.1109/TSP.2005.845433

Wang, W., Cichocki, A., & Chambers, J. A. (2009). A multiplicative algorithm for convolutive nonnegative matrix factorization based on squared Euclidean distance. *IEEE Transactions on Signal Processing, 57*(7), 2858–2864. doi:10.1109/TSP.2009.2016881

Wang, W., Cichocki, A., & Chambers, J. A. (2009). A multiplicative algorithm for convolutive non-negative matrix factorization based on squared Euclidean distance. In *IEEE Trans* (pp. 447–452). On Signal Processing.

Wang, D. L. (2005). On ideal binary mask as the computational goal of auditory scene analysis. In Divenyi, P. (Ed.), *Speech Separation by Humans and Machines* (pp. 181–197). Norwell, MA: Kluwer Academic. doi:10.1007/0-387-22794-6_12

Wang, B., & Plumbley, M. D. (2005). Musical audio stream separation by non-negative matrix factorization. In *Proc. DMRN Summer Conf.* Glasgow, UK

Wang, J., Yin, L., Wei, X., & Sun, Y. (2006). 3D Facial Expression Recognition Based on Primitive Surface Feature Distribution. *Proc. IEEE Int'l Conf. Computer Vision and Pattern Recognition, 2*, 1399-1406.

Wang, W. (2007). Squared Euclidean distance based convolutive non-negative matrix factorization with multiplicative learning rules for audio pattern separation. In *Proc. IEEE Int. Symp. on Signal Proces. and Info. Tech.* Cairo, Egypt.

Wang, W. (2008). Convolutive non-negative sparse coding. In *Proc. International Joint Conference on Neural Networks* (pp. 3681-3684).Hong Kong, China.

Wang, W., & Zou, X. (2008). Non-negative matrix factorization based on projected conjugate gradient algorithm. In *Proc. ICA Research Network International Workshop* (pp. 5-8). Liverpool, UK.

Wang, W., Chambers, J. A., & Sanei, S. (2004). A novel hybrid approach to the permutation problem of frequency domain blind source separation. *In Proceedings of the international conference on independent component analysis (ICA).*

Wang, W., Luo, Y., Sanei, S., & Chambers, J. A. (2006). Non-negative matrix factorization for note onset detection of audio signals. In *Proc. IEEE Int. Workshop on Machine Learning for Signal Process* (pp. 447-452). Maynooth, Ireland.

Wang, W., Luo, Y., Sanei, S., & Chambers, J. A. (2008). Note onset detection via non-negative factorization of magnitude spectrum, In *EURASIP Journal on Advances in Signal Processing* (pp. 447-452).

Wang, Y., & Guan, L. (2005). Recognizing Human Emotion from Audiovisual Information. *Proc. Int'l Conf. Acoustics, Speech, and Signal Processing* (pp. 1125-1128).

Ward, D., Lehmann, E., & Williamson, R. (2003). Particle filtering algorithms for tracking an acoustic source in a reverberant environment. *IEEE Transactions on Speech and Audio Processing, 11*(6), 826–836. doi:10.1109/TSA.2003.818112

Weinstein, E., & Moreno, P. (2007). Music Identification with Weighted Finite-State Transducers. In *Proceedings of the IEEE International Conference on Acoustics, Speech, and Signal Processing (ICASSP).*

Weiringen, A. v., & Pols, L. (2006). *Perception of Highly Dynamic Properties in Speech. En S. G. Ainsworth. Listening to Speech: An Auditory Perspective* (pp. 21–38). Mahwah, NJ: Lawrence Erlbaum Ass. Pub.

Weiss, R. J., & Ellis, D. P. W. (in press). Speech separation using speaker-adapted eigenvoice speech models. *Computer Speech & Language.*

Weiss, R. J., Mandel, M. M., & Ellis, D. P. W. (2008). Source separation based on binaural cues and source model constraints. In *Proceedings of the 10th ISCA Interspeech Conference* (pp. 419–422).

Weisstein, E. (2006). *Wolfram Mathworld*, Eric Weisstein. Retrieved December 2009, from http://mathworld.wolfram.com/

Welker, D. P., Greenberg, J. E., Desloge, J. G., & Zurek, P. M. (1997). Microphone-array hearing aids with binaural output Part II: A two-microphone adaptive system. *IEEE Transactions on Speech and Audio Processing, 5*(6), 543–551. doi:10.1109/89.641299

Welling, M., & Weber, M. (2001). Positive tensor factorization. *Pattern Recognition Letters, 22*(12), 1255–1261. doi:10.1016/S0167-8655(01)00070-8

Wen, Z., & Huang, T. S. (2003). Capturing Subtle Facial Motions in 3D Face Tracking. *Proc. Ninth IEEE Int'l Conf. Computer Vision* (pp. 1343-1350).

Whalen, P. J., Rauch, S. L., & Etcoff, N. L. (1998). Masked presentations of emotional facial expressions modulate amygdala activity without explicit knowledge. *The Journal of Neuroscience, 18*(1), 411–418.

Whissell, C. M. (1989). The Dictionary of Affect in Language, Emotion: Theory, Research and Experience. In Plutchik, R., & Kellerman, H. (Eds.), *The Measurement of Emotions* (*Vol. 4*, pp. 113–13). Academic Press.

Whitehill, J., & Omlin, C. W. (2006). Haar Features for FACS AU Recognition, *Proc. IEEE Int'l Conf. Automatic Face and Gesture Recognition* (pp. 217-222).

Whitman, B., & Ellis, D. (2004). Automatic record reviews. In *Proceedings of the 5th International Conference on Music Information Retrieval (ISMIR 2004).*

Widrow, B. (2001). A microphone array for hearing aids. *IEEE Circuits and Systems Magazine, 1*(2), 26–32. doi:10.1109/7384.938976

Wilson, K., & Darrell, T. (2006). Learning a precedence effect-like weighting function for the generalized cross-correlation framework. *IEEE Transactions on Audio, Speech, and Language Processing, 14*(6), 2156–2164. doi:10.1109/TASL.2006.872601

Winn, J., & Bishop, C. M. (2005). Variational message passing. *Journal of Machine Learning Research, 6,* 661–694.

Winter, S., Kellermann, W., Sawada, H., & Makino, S. (2007). MAP-based underdetermined blind source separation of convolutive mixtures by hierarchical clustering and l1-norm minimization. *EURASIP Journal on Advances in Signal Processing, 2007,* 24717. doi:10.1155/2007/24717

Winter, S., Sawada, H., & Makino, S. (2006). Geometrical interpretation of the PCA subspace approach for overdetermined blind source separation. *EURASIP Journal on Applied Signal Processing, 2006,* 176–186.

Witten, I. H., & Frank, E. (2000). *Data Mining: Practical machine learning tools with java implementations.* San Francisco: Morgan Kaufmann.

Woodbury, M. A. (1950). *Inverting modified matrices (Rapport technique No Memorandum Rept. 42).* Statistical Research Group, Princeton University.

Woodruff, J., Pardo, B., & Dannenberg, R. (2006). Remixing stereo music with score-informed source separation. In *Proceedings of the Seventh International Conference on Music Information Retrieval* (pp. 314-319).

Wu, M., & Wang, D. L. (2006). A two-stage algorithm for one-microphone reverberant speech enhancement. In *IEEE Transaction on Audio, Speech, and Language Process, 14.*

Wu, X., Ren, T., & Liu, L. (2004). Sound source localization based on directivity of MEMS microphones (Vol. 3). *Paper presented at the 7th International Conference on Solid-State and Integrated Circuits Technology.*

Xiao, J., Moriyama, T., Kanade, T., & Cohn, J. F. (2003). Robust Full-Motion Recovery of Head by Dynamic Templates and Re-Registration Techniques. *International Journal of Imaging Systems and Technology, 13*(1), 85–94. doi:10.1002/ima.10048

Xiong, Z., Ramchandran, K., Herley, C., & Orchard, M. T. (1997). Flexible tree-structured signal expansions using time-varying wavelet packets. *IEEE Transactions on Signal Processing, 43,* 333–345.

Xu, T., & Wang, W. (2009). A compressed sensing approach for underdetermined blind audio source separation with sparse representations. In *Proc. IEEE Int. Workshop on Statistical Signal Processing.* (pp. 493-496). Cardiff, UK.

Xu, T., & Wang, W. (2010). A block-based compressed sensing method for underdetermined blind speech separation incorporating binary mask. In *Proc. IEEE Int. Conf. on Acoustics, Speech and Signal Processing.* Texas, USA.

Yegnanarayana, B., & Murthy, P. S. (2000, May). Enhancement of reverberant speech using LP residual signal. *IEEE Transactions on Speech and Audio Processing, 8*(3), 267–281. doi:10.1109/89.841209

Yeh, W., & Barsalou, L. (2006). The situated nature of concepts. *The American Journal of Psychology, 119*(3), 349–384. doi:10.2307/20445349

Yilmaz, O., & Rickard, S. (2004). Blind separation of speech mixtures via time-frequency masking. *IEEE Transactions on Signal Processing, 52*(7), 1830–1847. doi:10.1109/TSP.2004.828896

Yilmaz, Ö., Jourjine, A., & Rickard, S. (2000). Blind separation of disjoint orthogonal signals: Demixing N sources from two mixtures. In *Proceedings of the IEEE international conference on acoustics, speech and signal processing (ICASSP).*

Yin, P., Ma, L., Elhilali, M., Fritz, J., & Shamma, S. (2007). *Primary Auditory Cortical Resoponses while Attending to Different Streams. En B. K. al. Hearing: From Sensory Processing to Perception* (pp. 257–265). Heidelberg: Springer.

Yin, L., Wei, X., Sun, Y., Wang, J., & Rosato, M. J. (2006). A 3D Facial Expression Database for Facial Behavior Research. *Proc. IEEE Int'l Conf. Automatic Face and Gesture Recognition*(pp.211-216).

Yoon, B.-J., Tashev, I., & Acero, A. (2007). Robust adaptive beamforming algorithm using instantaneous direction of arrival with enhanced noise suppression capability. In *Proceedings of the IEEE international conference on acoustics, speech and signal processing (ICASSP).*

Yost, W. A. (2000). *Fundamentals of hearing: An introduction* (4th ed.). San Diego: Academic Press.

Yost, W. A. (1997). The cocktail party problem: Forty years later. In Gilkey, R., & Anderson, T. (Eds.), *Binaural and spatial hearing in real and virtual environments* (pp. 329–348). Ahwah, NJ: Erlbaum.

Young, S., & Bloothooft, G. (Eds.). (1997). *Corpus-Based Methods in Language and Speech Processing. Text, Speech and Language Technology*. Dordrecht, Netherlands: Kluwer.

Young, S., & Woodland, P. (2009). *Hidden Markov Model Toolkit*. Cambridge University Engineering Department (CUED), UK. Online: http://htk.eng.cam.ac.uk/.

Yu, P., Chen, K., Ma, C., & Seide, F. (2005). Vocabulary-independent indexing of spontaneous speech. *IEEE Transactions on Speech and Audio Processing, 7*(5), 635–643.

Zdenuk, R., & Cichocki, A. (2007). Nonnegative matrix factorization with quadratic programming. *Neurocomputing, 71*, 2309–2320. doi:10.1016/j.neucom.2007.01.013

Zeng, Z., Fu, Y., Roisman, G. I., Wen, Z., Hu, Y., & Huang, T. S. (2006). Spontaneous Emotional Facial Expression Detection. *J. Multimedia, 1*(5), 1–8.

Zhang, T., & Kuo, C.-C. J. (2001). Audio content analysis for online audiovisual data segmentation and classification. *IEEE Transactions on Speech and Audio Processing, 9*, 441–457. doi:10.1109/89.917689

Zhang, M., & Zhou, Z. (2007). ML-KNN: A lazy learning approach to multi-label learning. [Maryland Heights, MO: Elsevier Science Inc.]. *Pattern Recognition, 40*, 2038–2048. doi:10.1016/j.patcog.2006.12.019

Zhang, H-J L. Lu, Wenyin, L. (2004). Audio textures: theory and applications. *IEEE Transactions on Speech and Audio Processing, 12*(2), 156–167. doi:10.1109/TSA.2003.819947

Zhang, Y., & Ji, Q. (2005). Active and Dynamic Information Fusion for Facial Expression Understanding from Image Sequences. *IEEE Transactions on Pattern Analysis and Machine Intelligence, 27*(5), 699–714. doi:10.1109/TPAMI.2005.93

Zhou, R., Mattavelli, M., & Zoia, G. (2008). Music onset detection based on Resonator Time-frequency Image. *IEEE Trans. Audio. Speech and Language Processing, 16*, 1685–1695. doi:10.1109/TASL.2008.2002042

Zhou, R. & Mattavelli (2007). A new time-frequency representation for music signal analysis. *Signal Processing and Its Applications, 2007. ISSPA 2007. 9th International Symposium on, (*pp. 1-4).

Zhou, R. (2006). Feature Extraction of Musical Content for Automatic Music Transcription. Ph.D. dissertation, Swiss Federal Institute of Technology, Lausanne, Retrieved from http://library.epfl.ch/en/theses/?nr=3638.

Zhou, R., & Reiss, J. D. (2007) Music onset detection combining energy-based and pitch-based approaches. *MIREX 2007 audio onset detection contest*: Retrieved from http://www.music-ir.org/mirex2007/abs/OD_zhou.pdf

Zibulevsky, M., & Bofill, P. (2001). Underdetermined blind source separation using sparse representations. *Signal Processing, 81*(11), 2353–2362. doi:10.1016/S0165-1684(01)00120-7

Zibulevsky, M., & Pearlmutter, B. A. (2001). Blind source separation by sparse decomposition in a signal dictionary. *Neural Computation, 13*(4), 863–882. doi:10.1162/089976601300014385

Zibulevsky, M., Pearlmutter, B. A., Bofill, P., & Kisilev, P. (2001). Blind source separation by sparse decomposition in a signal dictionary. In *Independent Component Analysis: Principles and Practice* (p. 181-208). Cambridge, MA: Cambridge Press.

Zotkin, D., & Duraiswami, R. (2004, September). Accelerated speech source localization via a hierarchical search of steered response power. *IEEE Transactions on Speech and Audio Processing, 12*(5), 499–508. doi:10.1109/TSA.2004.832990

Zou, X., Wang, W., & Kittler, J. (2008). Non-negative matrix factorization for face illumination analysis. In *Proc. ICA Research Network International Workshop* (pp. 52-55), Liverpool, UK.

Zwicker, E., & Fastl, H. (1999). *Psychoacoustics: Facts and models* (2nd ed.). Berlin, Germany: Springer.

About the Contributors

Wenwu Wang is a Lecturer at Centre for Vision Speech and Signal Processing, University of Surrey, where he joined since May 2007. Prior to this, he was a Postdoctoral Research Associate at King's College London (from May 2002 to December 2003) and Cardiff University (from January 2004 to April 2005). He also worked in UK industry, first as a DSP Engineer at Tao Group Ltd (now Antix Labs Ltd) (from May 2005 to August 2006), then as an R&D engineer at Creative Labs (from September 2006 to April 2007). During spring 2008, he has been a visiting scholar at the Perception and Neurodynamics Lab and the Center for Cognitive Science, The Ohio State University. He is part of the MOD University Defense Research Centre in Signal Processing. He obtained the PhD degree in April 2002 from Harbin Engineering University, China. His research interests include blind signal processing, audio-visual signal processing, machine learning and perception, and machine audition (listening). He is a member of the IEEE, and belongs to the IEEE Signal Processing, and Circuits and Systems Societies.

* * *

Bahador Makki Abadi received his B.Sc. degree in electrical engineering from Shiraz University, Shiraz, IRAN and M.Sc. degrees in Biomedical engineering from Amirkabir University, Tehran, IRAN, in 1997 and 2000, respectively. For his current PhD studies in Biomedical Signal Processing within the Centre of Digital Signal Processing, Cardiff University, he has been awarded an overseas research scholarship. His current research interests include Tensor Factorization, Blind Source Separation, with major applications in Biomedical Signal processing.

Samer A. Abdallah received the B.A. degree in natural sciences from Cambridge University, Cambridge, U.K., in 1994, after which he spent three years working in industry. He then received the M.Sc. and Ph.D. degrees from King's College London, London, U.K., in 1998 and 2003, respectively. He is now a postdoctoral Researcher at the Centre for Digital Music, Queen Mary, University of London. His research interests include music perception, unsupervised learning and information theory.

Agustín Alvarez-Marquina obtained a MSc and a PhD in Computer Science in 1993 and 1998 respectively from Universidad Politécnica de Madrid. He was enroled as Research Assistant at Universidad Politécnica de Madrid since 1994 through 1999 when he obtained a position as Assistant Teacher at Universidad Rey Juan Carlos of Madrid. In 2003 he obtained an Associate Professorship at Universidad Politécnica de Madrid where he teaches Computer Architecture and Technology and Speech Processing.

His research interests concentrate in Speaker Identification and Speech Enhancement. He is author of 30 papers in journals and book chapters and 120 papers in major conferences and indexed publications.

Tjeerd C. Andringa is Associate Professor in Auditory Cognition at department of Artificial Intelligence at the University of Groningen, The Netherlands, and senior researcher at the INnovation Center for Advanced Sensor and Sensor Systems, INCAS3. After a master in solid-state physics he helped to start a university programme in Artificial Intelligence and Cognitive Systems. This has now become a successful and rapidly growing research institute. He has founded Sound Intelligence, the company that commercializes the first sound recognition system for a nontrivial target, verbal aggression, in unconstrained social setting. Currently, Andringa shapes and manages the soundscape activities of INCAS3. Currently he focuses on sound recognition in unconstrained acoustic environments and the relation between listeners and their sonic environment.

Jonathon A. Chambers holds the Chair of Communications and Signal Processing and leads the Advanced Signal Processing Group, containing six academic and more than thirty research staff, within the Communications Division, Department of Electronic and Electrical Engineering, Loughborough University. He also serves as the Deputy Head Research of the Department. He was awarded the first QinetiQ Visiting Fellowship in 2007 for his outstanding contributions to the field of adaptive signal processing and his successful interaction with the signal processing team at QinetiQ Malvern. He has been working in the area of signal processing and its applications in telecommunications for more than 20 years and has written/co-written two books and more than 300 articles in refereed conferences and journals. He has steered 47 students to PhD graduation and is currently supervising/co-supervising more than 10 postgraduate researchers in communications signal processing. Many of these students are applying advanced signal processing techniques to signal separation problems. He has served as an associate editor for IEEE Trans. Signal Processing for two terms, is currently serving on the IEEE Technical Committee on Signal Processing Theory and Methods. He was the technical chair of the IEEE Workshop on Statistical Signal Processing 2009 and is the co-technical chair of the IEEE flagship conference ICASSP 2011.

Selina Chu received her B.S. degree in the Department of Electrical Engineering from California State Polytechnic University, Pomona and M.S. degree in the Department of Computer Science from University of California, Irvine, in 2000 and 2002, respectively. From 2002 to 2003, she was with IBM T. J. Watson Research Center. Since 2003, she has been a Ph.D. student in the Department of Computer Science at the University of Southern California (USC). She was also a member of the Technical Staff at AT&T Labs-Research in Florham Park, NJ for two summers in 1998 and 2000. Currently, she is a member of the Speech Analysis and Interpretation Lab (SAIL) and also the Multimedia Communications Lab. Her recent work has been in the areas of general unstructured audio. Her general research interests include audio signal processing, machine learning, data mining, and pattern recognition.

Trevor Cox is Professor of Acoustics at the University of Salford, President-Elect of the Institute of Acoustics and a Senior Media Fellow for the Engineering and Physical Sciences Research Council (EPSRC). Professor Trevor Cox is a recognized international expert in room acoustics. His diffuser designs can be found in listening rooms, concert halls and studios worldwide. Trevor's work spans across disciplines, from psychology and social science through to engineering and applied computational physics. Professor Cox has been an investigator on an EPSRC project on environmental conditions in 24 hours cities and he directed the EPSRC Ideas Factory, A Noisy Future? He is making two programmes for the BBC World Service on city soundscapes in 2009. He was awarded the Tyndall medal by the Institute of Acoustics.

Mike E. Davies received the B.A. (Hons.) degree in Engineering from Cambridge University, Cambridge, U.K., in 1989 and the Ph.D. degree in nonlinear dynamics and signal processing from University College London, London (UCL), U.K., in 1993. Mike Davies was awarded a Royal Society Research Fellowship in 1993. He currently holds the Jeffrey Collins SFC funded chair in Signal and Image Processing at the University of Edinburgh and is the Director of the Joint Institute in Signal and Image Processing, part of the Edinburgh Research Partnership. He is currently pursuing a programme of research in the application of sparse representations to signal processing. Most recently his research has concentrated on the emerging field of compressed sensing.

Shlomo Dubnov is an Associate Professor in music technology at UCSD. Prior to this he served as a researcher in Institute for Research and Coordination of Acoustics and Music (IRCAM) in Paris and was a senior lecturer in department of communication systems engineering in Ben-Gurion University in Israel. He holds PhD in Computer Science from Hebrew University, MSc in EE from Israel Institute of Technology (Technion) and B.Mus in music composition from Rubin Academy in Jerusalem. His works on poly-spectral analysis of musical timbre, machine improvisation and learning of musical style are widely acknowledged by the computer music community and are implemented in music retrieval and computer improvisation systems. Dubnov served as co-PI in several projects dealing with semantic analysis of audio. Currently he is co-editing a book on "The Structure of Style: algorithmic approaches to understanding manner and meaning" and is working on a large multimedia production that revives through technology the Talmudic tradition of commentary and debate.

Douglas Eck is an Associate professor of computer science at the Université de Montréal and a member of the music neuroscience group BRAMS (Brain Music and Sound) at and the music technology group CIRMMT at McGill. His area of expertise is machine learning with special focus on music, motion and multimedia.

Roberto Fernández-Baíllo obtained a BS in Speech Therapy and a MD degree in 2003 and 2009 from Universidad Complutense de Madrid respectively. Since 2004 he was enroled at the Grupo de Informática Aplicada al Procesado de Señal e Imagen as Speech Researcher. His research is concentrated in Voice Pathology Detection and Rehabilitation, Speech Processing for Forensic Applications. He is author of 10 papers in journals and book chapters, 40 papers in major conferences and indexed publications.

José M. Ferrández-Vicente received an MSc and a PhD in Computer Science in 1993 and 1998 respectively from Universidad Politécnica de Madrid. He was enroled in Universidad Miguel Hernández of Elche, Spain, as Assistant Professor since 1999 to 2002, when he obtained a nomination as Associate Professor at Universidad Politécnica de Cartagena, Spain, where he teaches Computer Architecture and Technology and Biomedical Instrumentation. His research interests concentrate in Biosignals and Biosystems, Artificial Vision, Brain-Silicon Interfaces. He has published 20 papers in journals and book chapters and 100 papers in major conferences and indexed publications.

Cédric Févotte obtained the State Engineering degree and the MSc degree in Control and Computer Science from the École Centrale de Nantes (France) in 2000, and then the PhD degree in 2003. From Nov. 2003 to Mar. 2006, he was a research associate with the Signal Processing Laboratory at University of Cambridge (UK), working on Bayesian approaches to audio signal processing tasks such as audio source separation, denoising and feature extraction. From May 2006 to Feb. 2007, he was a research engineer with the start-up company Mist-Technologies (Paris), working on mono/stereo to 5.1 surround sound upmix solutions. In Mar. 2007, he joined TELECOM ParisTech, first as a research associate and then as a CNRS tenured research scientist in Nov. 2007. His research interests generally concern statistical signal signal processing and unsupervised machine learning with audio applications.

Pedro Gómez-Vilda received an MSc in Electrical Engineering in 1978 and a PhD in Computer Science in 1983 from Universidad Politécnica de Madrid. He was enroled in the National Nuclear Energy Council during 1976 to 1977 and as a development engineer in a communications company during 1977 and 1978. In 1978 he joined Universidad Politécnica de Madrid as Grading Assistant and started working in his PhD Thesis on Auditory Processing. During 1981 and 1982 he was on leave to spend a term at the University of Maryland with a Fulbright scholarship to complete his PhD Thesis. In 1983 he was enroled at Universidad Politécnica de Madrid as Associate Professor. In 1988 he obtained full professorship at the same University. His teaching is related with Physical and Technological Fundamentals of Computer Science, VLSI Technology, Speech Processing and Speaker Identification. His research is concentrated in Speech Processing, Forensic Voice Identification, Voice Pathology Detection and Signal Processing for Functional Genomics. He is author of 50 papers in journals and book chapters, 200 papers in major conferences and indexed publications and advisor of 13 PhD Thesis in Speech and Signal Processing.

André Gückel holds a Diplom (German equivalent of a Masters) in Electrical Engineering from Technische Universität Braunschweig in Braunschweig, Germany. In his Diplom thesis, which was conducted in collaboration with the Ruhr-Universität Bochum, he investigated and evaluated different multi-channel algorithms for separating speech sources in various acoustic environments. Since then, he has worked on porting low-level audio signal processing algorithms to handsets for Philips and NXP Semiconductors. He can currently be found at Dolby Laboratories in Nürnberg, Germany implementing and optimizing transform-based audio codecs for embedded platforms.

Banu Günel is a senior research associate at the Centre for Communication Systems Research (CCSR) at the University of Surrey, UK. She holds a Ph.D. degree in Computer Science from Queen's University Belfast, U.K., M.Sc. degree in communication systems and signal processing from University of Bristol, U.K. and B.Sc. degree in electrical and electronic engineering from the Middle East Technical University, Turkey. Her research interests include microphone array signal processing, spatial audio capturing and rendering, psychoacoustics, human computer interferences, augmented and virtual reality. She has published several journal and conference papers on the use of compact microphone arrays for source localisation and separation and has a patent on the relevant technology.

Hüseyin Hacıhabiboğlu is a research associate at the Centre for Digital Signal Processing Research (CDSPR), Division of Engineering, King's College London, U.K. He holds a Ph.D. degree in Computer Science from Queens University Belfast, U.K., M.Sc. degree on electrical and electronic engineering from University of Bristol, U.K., and B.Sc . degree on electrical and electronic engineering from Middle

East Technical University, Ankara, Turkey. His research interests include audio signal processing, room acoustics modeling and simulation, game audio, multichannel audio systems, psychoacoustics of spatial hearing, and microphone array processing. He has authored and co-authored more than 25 journal and conference publications in the audio and acoustical signal processing areas and has a patent on acoustic source separation.

Sanaul Haq received the B.Sc. in electrical engineering from N.W.F.P. University of Engineering and Technology, Pakistan, in 2002. He worked in the Telecom industry for more than 3 years on broadband data communication systems, where he was involved in commissioning of Lucent Technologies and Agilent Technologies broadband equipments. He is currently pursuing his PhD in multimodal emotion recognition at Centre for Vision, Speech and Signal Processing, University of Surrey, UK. His main areas of research are pattern recognition and multimodal emotion recognition. He has published two papers in International Conference on Auditory-Visual Speech Processing. He has presented his research on multimodal emotion recognition in one-day technical meetings, including UK Speech, and Facial Analysis and Animation.

Philip Jackson holds an MA from Cambridge University and PhD from the University of Southampton, UK. He has worked in industry on world-leading active noise cancellation technology, at the University of Birmingham as a postdoctoral researcher, and joined the University of Surrey as faculty member in 2002, where he heads the machine audition group. His research output from BALTHASAR, DANSA, Dynamic Faces and QESTRAL projects shows a record of achievement, rated outstanding by funding body EPSRC. Several US and UK patents have been filed with industrial support from BBC and Bang & Olufsen. Current interests include production and perception of voiced fricatives, models of speech articulation and multimodal recognition of expressed emotions. He has published over 40 scientific papers in high-quality academic journals and conference proceedings, and reviews for JASA, IEEE Signal Processing Letters, Computer Speech and Language, Interspeech and ICASSP.

Maria G. Jafari received the M.Eng. (Hons.) degree in electrical and electronic engineering from Imperial College London, U.K., in 1999. The same year, she began the Ph.D. degree study in blind source separation, which she completed at King's College London, U.K., in 2003. Following a year as a Research Associate at King's College London, working on the application of blind source separation to brain science, she joined the Centre for Digital Music at Queen Mary University of London in 2004, where she is currently a Research Assistant. Her research focuses on the application of sparse decompositions and dictionary learning methods to audio and biomedical problems, including source separation and denoising.

TariqUllah Jan received the B.Sc in Electrical and Electronic Engineering from NWFP University of Engineering & Technology Peshawar, Pakistan in 2002, and is currently pursuing his PhD degree in blind source separation and signal processing at the Centre for Vision, Speech and Signal Processing, University of Surrey, UK. In 2003 and 2004, he was a faculty member at COMSATS Institute of IT Abbotabad. Since 2005, he has been with the Department of Electrical and Electronic Engineering at NWFP University of Engineering & Technology Peshawar, Pakistan as a lecturer. His research interests include machine learning and speech processing.

Kristoffer Jensen obtained his Masters degree in 1988 in Computer Science at the Technical University of Lund, Sweden, and a D.E.A in Signal Processing in 1989 at the ENSEEIHT, Toulouse, France. His Ph.D. was delivered and defended in 1999 at the Department of Computer Science, University of Copenhagen, Denmark, treating signal processing applied to music with a physical and perceptual pointof-view. This mainly involved classification, and modeling of musical sounds. Kristoffer Jensen has been involved in synthesizers for children, state of the art next generation effect processors, and signal processing in music informatics. His current research topic is signal processing with musical applications, and related fields, including perception, psychoacoustics, physical models and expression of music. Kristoffer Jensen has chaired 3 major conferences, been the editor of 6 books and conference proceedings, and he currently holds a position at the Software and Media Technology Department, Aalborg University Esbjerg as Associate Professor.

Paul Kendrick received a B.Eng. degree in electronic engineering from the University of Manchester, Manchester, UK, in 2001 and a Master's degree in audio acoustics from the University of Salford, Salford, UK, in 2003. He began working as a research assistant in the acoustics research centre at the University of Salford in 2003 and was awarded a Ph.D. in room acoustics in 2009. Currently he is a postdoctoral research assistant at the University of Salford working in the field of signal processing for acoustic wind speed profiling. He is also active in the areas of blind room acoustic parameter measurement and helicopter noise. His research interests include blind room acoustic parameter measurement, acoustic wind speed profiling, atmospheric sound propagation, digital signal processing, room acoustics, helicopter noise, blind source separation, audio for the hearing impaired and broadcast audio.

C.-C. Jay Kuo received the Ph.D. degree from the Massachusetts Institute of Technology in 1987. He is presently Director of the Signal and Image Processing Institute and Professor of Electrical Engineering at the University of Southern California. His research interests are in the areas of digital video analysis and modeling, multimedia data compression, communication and networking. Dr. Kuo has guided 96 students to their Ph.D. degrees and supervised 20 postdoctoral fellows. He is co-author of 160 journal papers, 780 conference papers and 9 books. Dr. Kuo is a Fellow of IEEE and SPIE. He is co-Editor-in-Chief for the Journal of Visual Communication and Image Representation and has served as Editor for 10 other journals. He received the National Science Foundation Young Investigator Award and Presidential Faculty Fellow Award in 1992 and 1993, respectively. He was an IEEE Signal Processing Society Distinguished Lecturer in 2006, a recipient of the Okawa Foundation Research Grant in 2007, and the recipient of the Electronic Imaging Scientist of the Year Award in 2010.

Mathieu Lagrange is a CNRS researcher at the Institut de Recherche et Coordination Acoustique Musique (IRCAM), Paris, France. He obtained his Ph.D. degree in 2004 at the Laboratoire Bordelais de Recherche en Informatique (LaBRI), Bordeaux, France. After two post-doctoral fellowships respectively at the University of Victoria, BC, Canada and at the University of McGill, Montreal, QC, Canada where he studied model based approaches for the processing of musical and environmental sounds, he joined Telecom ParisTech, Paris, France as a Research Assistant in 2008. He is now with the Analysis/Synthesis team of IRCAM where his research focuses on structured modeling of audio signals applied to the indexing, browsing, and retrieval of multimedia.

Francis Li is Senior Lecturer in Acoustic Signal Processing and Audio Informatics at Salford University. Over 20 years, Francis has accumulated a broad spectrum of expertise and research interests including room acoustics, digital signal processing, multimedia computing, artificial intelligence, soft-computing applied to audio signal processing, data and voice communications, speech technology, software engineering, instrumentation, and control theory, but his major and long-standing research interest centres on the use of intelligent computation and modern signal processing techniques to solve acoustics and audio related problems. He is currently active in the fields of blind acoustic parameter estimation and system identification, in-situ measurement of acoustic parameters with naturalistic sources and synthesised music, acoustic phonetics of speech signals in different communication settings, robust methods for speech intelligibility assessment, and signal processing for ambisonic and interactive audio.

Nilesh Madhu has a PhD in Electrical Engineering from the Ruhr-Universität Bochum, Germany. His research interests lie in the fields of single- and multi-channel statistical signal processing. He has considerable expertise in developing and implementing algorithms for acoustic source localisation, source separation and acoustic echo control. Apart from research, he enjoys any teaching opportunities that come his way. During his stay as a researcher at the Institute of Communications Acoustics, Ruhr-Universität Bochum, he has also been glad to supervise many graduate theses, both at the bachelor's and at the master's level. He is currently a post-doctoral fellow at the Katholieke Universiteit Leuven, Belgium, under the EU project AUDIS (Digital Signal Processing in Audiology).

Thierry Bertin-Mahieux received the B.S. in Mathematics in 2006 and the M.S. in Computer Science in 2009 from the Université de Montréal, Canada. He is currently pursuing a Ph.D. degree in Electrical Engineering at Columbia University, New York, NY. He is a Natural Science and Engineering Research Council of Canada (NSERC) postgraduate scholarship holder and was a MSTA fellow in 2008-2009 in the computer science department at Columbia University. He joined the Laboratory for Recognition and Organization of Speech and Audio (LabROSA) in 2009 and is supervised by professor Daniel P.W. Ellis. Before coming to Columbia, he worked on machine learning and music information retrieval at the LISA laboratory at the Université de Montréal.

Michael I. Mandel received the B.S. degree in Computer Science from the Massachusetts Institute of Technology, Cambridge, MA, in 2004 and the M.S. degree in 2006 and the Ph.D. degree with distinction in 2009 both in Electrical Engineering from Columbia University, New York, NY. He is currently a postdoctoral researcher at the Université de Montréal in the Laboratoire d?Informatique des Systèmes Adaptatifs in the Département d'informatique et de recherche opérationnelle. He has published on sound source separation, music similarity, and music recommendation. His research uses machine learning to model sound perception and understanding and to help people find music.

Rafael Martínez-Olalla got a MSc in Electrical Engineering in 1994 and a PhD in Computer Science in 2003 from Universidad Politécnica de Madrid. He served as Assistant Teacher in Universidad Alfonso X of Madrid in 1998. In 1999 he was enroled as Assistant Teacher at the Electrical Engineering School of Universidad Politécnica de Madrid. He obtained a position as Associate Professor in 2009 to teach Computer Architecture and Technology and Speech Processing at Universidad Politécnica de Madrid. His research interests concentrate in Identification, Speech Enhancement, Pattern Recognition.

He is author of 30 papers in journals and book chapters, 120 papers in major conferences and indexed publications.

Luis Gustavo Martins is a full time professor at the Sound and Image Department of the School of Arts of the Portuguese Catholic University, Porto, Portugal. He obtained the M.Sc. degree in electrical and computer engineering from the University of Porto, Porto, Portugal in 2002, on the topic of polyphonic music transcription. In 2009 he completed his Ph.D. degree in electrical and computer engineering at the University of Porto, in the topic of segregation of sound events in music signals. Until 2008 he hold a researcher position at the Multimedia and Telecommunications Unit of INESC Porto, where he carried out research on the areas of software development, signal processing, machine learning, and audio content analysis. He is currently a researcher at the Research Center for Science and Technology in Art (CITAR), Porto, Portugal. His research is mostly on Audio Content Analysis, being actively involved in the Marsyas open source software framework.

Luis M. Mazaira-Fernández obtained a MSc in Computer Science from Universidad Politécnica de Madrid in 2004. In 2005 he obtained a position as Assistant Teacher at Universidad Politécnica de Madrid to teach Physical and Technological Fundamentals of Computer Science, Computer Architecture and Technology and Operating Systems. His research interests concentrate in Speaker Identification in which field he is currently working for the preparation of a PhD Thesis. He is author of 5 papers in journals and book chapters, 25 papers in major conferences and indexed publications.

Cristina Muñoz-Mulas obtained a MSc in Computer Science from Universidad Rey Juan Carlos of Madrid in 2006. She joined the Grupo de Informática Aplicada al Procesado de Señal e Imagen of Universidad Politécnica de Madrid in 2007 as Research Assistant where she is currently developing her PhD Thesis in Speaker Identification. She is author of 2 papers in journals and book chapters, 15 papers in major conferences and indexed publications.

Syed M. R. Naqvi was born in Sargodha Pakistan in 1975. He obtained his first class B.Eng. degree in 2001 from IIEE NED University of Engineering and Technology Karachi, Pakistan. He worked in the field of research and development from 2001 to 2005 in Pakistan. He was awarded PhD degree from Loughborough University in 2009. Currently he is Postdoctoral Research Associate in Loughborough University, UK. His research interests are in audiovisual speech processing, blind source separation, non-linear filtering and data fusion.

Shrikanth (Shri) Narayanan is Andrew J. Viterbi Professor of Engineering at the University of Southern California (USC), and holds appointments as Professor of Electrical Engineering and jointly as Professor in Computer Science, Linguistics and Psychology. Prior to USC he was with AT&T Bell Labs and AT&T Research. His research focuses on human-centered information processing and communication technologies. Shri Narayanan is an Editor for the Computer Speech and Language Journal and an Associate Editor for the IEEE Transactions on Multimedia and the Journal of the Acoustical Society of America. He was previously an Associate Editor of the IEEE Transactions of Speech and Audio Processing and the IEEE Signal Processing Magazine. Shri Narayanan is a Fellow of the Acoustical Society of America, a Fellow of IEEE, and a recipient of several paper awards including a 2005

Best Paper award from the IEEE Signal Processing society. He has published over 350 papers and has seven granted U.S. patents.

Andrew Nesbit completed the B.Sc. and B.E. degrees at the University of Melbourne, Australia, in 2003, where he majored in applied mathematics and software engineering. He was awarded a Ph.D. from Queen Mary University of London in 2008 for work on audio source separation. Since then, he has been a Research Assistant at the Centre for Digital Music at Queen Mary. Current research interests include source separation and sparse representations of audio, and their applications in digital music technology. Other interests and past research include work on speech recognition, music information retrieval and digital media formats.

Víctor Nieto-Lluis obtained a MSc in Mechanical Engineering in 1975 from Universidad Cujae of Havana, Cuba, and a PhD in Computer Science from Universidad Politécnica de Madrid in 1992. From 1975 to 1983 he worked as Management Engineer at the Transportation Ministry in Cuba. Since 1983 he joined Universidad Politécnica de Madrid as Assistant Teacher in Physics. He obtained a position as Associate Professor in 2000 for teaching Physical and Technological Fundamentals of Computer Science, Computer Architecture and Technology, Speech Processing. His research interests are concentrated in Speech Processing and Data Bases. He is author of 35 papers in journals and book chapters, 100 papers in major conferences and indexed publications.

Mark D. Plumbley received the B.A. (Hons.) degree in electrical sciences in 1984 from the University of Cambridge, Cambridge, U.K., and the Ph.D. degree in neural networks in 1991, also from the University of Cambridge. From 1991 to 2001 he was a Lecturer at King's College London. He moved to Queen Mary University of London in 2002, helping to establish the Centre for Digital Music, and where he is now Professor of Machine Learning and Signal Processing and an EPSRC Leadership Fellow. His research focuses on the automatic analysis of music and other audio sounds, including automatic music transcription, beat tracking, and audio source separation, and with interest in the use of techniques such as independent component analysis (ICA) and sparse representations. Prof. Plumbley chairs the ICA Steering Committee, and is an Associate Editor for the IEEE Transactions on Neural Networks.

Joshua D. Reiss (member IEEE, AES) was born in 1971, and is a Senior Lecturer with the Centre for Digital Music in the School of Electronic Engineering and Computer Science at Queen Mary, University of London. He has bachelor's degrees in both Physics and Mathematics, and received his PhD in physics from the Georgia Institute of Technology, specializing in the analysis of chaotic time series. In June of 2000, he accepted a research position in the Audio Signal Processing research lab at King's College, London, and moved to Queen Mary in 2001. He made the transition from chaos theory to audio and musical signal processing through his work on sigma delta modulators, which has lead to a nomination for a best paper award from the IEEE, as well as a UK patent. He has also investigated proper use of audio formats in music retrieval systems, the evaluation of music information retrieval systems, applications of signal processing to analysis of non-western music, time series analysis of musical signals, digital audio effects and satellite navigation systems. His current primary focus of research, which ties together many of the above topics, is on the use of state-of-the-art signal processing techniques for professional sound engineering.

Victoria Rodellar-Biarge received a MSc and a PhD in Computer Science from Universidad Politécnica de Madrid in 1976 and 1983 respectively. She was enroled as Assistant Teacher since 1976 through 1986 in the Computer Science School at Universidad Politécnica de Madrid where she taught Electronics and Digital Systems. During 1981 and 1982 she was on leave to spend a term at the University of Maryland with a Fulbright scholarship to complete his PhD Thesis. In 1987 she got an Associate Professorship at Universidad Politécnica de Madrid, teaching Computer Technology and Hardware-Software Co-Design. Her research interests are focussed in Auditory Perception, High-Level Description Languates, Neuromorphic Signal Processing. She is author of 40 papers in journals and book chapters, 150 papers in major conferences and indexed publications and has served as Advisor of 6 PhD Theses in High-Level Description Languages, Computer Arithmetics, Field-Programmable Gate Arrays.

Saeid Sanei received his PhD from Imperial College London in Biomedical Signal Processing in 1991. He worked as an academic in Iran, Singapore, and currently in the Centre of Digital Signal Processing, Cardiff University, UK. He has published approximately 200 papers in peer reviewed journals, mainly in IEEE Transactions, and prestigious conference proceedings. He has authored the unique monogram EEG Signal Processing published by Wiley in 2007. He is well known within Signal Processing and Biomedical Engineering communities. As his significant international contributions, He chaired IEEE 15th International Workshop on Statistical Signal Processing (SSP2009) in Cardiff, organized 15th International Conference on Digital Signal Processing (DSP2007) in Cardiff, and co-organised many other scientific events worldwide. I have been serving as Associate Editor of IEEE Signal Processing Letters and Associate Editor of the EURASIP Journal of Computational Intelligence and Neuroscience. He has supervised more than 24 PhD students and co-supervised many others.

George Tzanetakis is an Assistant Professor in the Department of Computer Science with cross-listed appointments in ECE and Music at the University of Victoria. He received his PhD in Computer Science at Princeton University in 2002 and was a Post-Doctoral fellow at Carnegie Mellon University in 2002-2003. His research spans all stages of audio content analysis such as feature extraction, segmentation, classification with specific emphasis on music information retrieval. He is also the primary designer and developer of Marsyas an open source framework for audio processing with specific emphasis on music information retrieval applications. His pioneering work on musical genre classification received a IEEE signal processing society young author award and is frequently cited. More recently he has been exploring new interfaces for musical expression, music robotics, computational ethnomusicology, and computer-assisted music instrument tutoring. These interdisciplinary activities combine ideas from signal processing, perception, machine learning, sensors, actuators and human-computer interaction with the connecting theme of making computers better understand music to create more effective interactions with musicians and listeners.

Emmanuel Vincent received the mathematics degree of the École Normale Supérieure, Paris, France, in 2001 and the Ph.D. degree in acoustics, signal processing and computer science applied to music from the University of Paris-VI Pierre et Marie Curie, Paris, in 2004. From 2004 to 2006, he was a Research Assistant with the Centre for Digital Music at Queen Mary, University of London, London, U.K.. He is now a permanent researcher with the French National Institute for Research in Computer Science and Control (INRIA). His research focuses on probabilistic modeling of audio signals applied to blind source separation, content description and object coding of musical audio.

Miao Yu was born in China in 1986. He obtained his BSc degree in 2003 from Shandong University of Science and Technology China. He also obtained first-class masters degree in 2008 with the best student award from Department of Electrical and Electrical Engineering Loughborough University, where, he is currently PhD student and the topic of his research is on fallen body detection by using audio and video information.

Yonggang Zhang was born in China in 1981. He obtained his BSc degree and MSc degree in 2002 and 2004 respectively from Harbin Engineering University, Harbin, Heilongjiang, China. He was subsequently awarded his PhD degree in Digital Signal Processing in 2007 from Cardiff University, Cardiff, UK. He worked in Loughborough University, UK in 2008 as a Research Associate. Currently he is a lecture of Harbin Engineering University, China. His research interests are in areas of signal processing, data fusion and inertial technology.

Ruohua Zhou received his B.S. degree from Electronics Engineering Department of Beijing Institute of Technology, China, in 1994; his M.S. degree in engineering in microelectronics and semiconductor devices from Chinese Academy of Sciences, Microelectronics R&D Center, Beijing, in 1997; and Ph.D. degree on feature extraction of musical content for automatic music transcription from the Signal Processing Institute of Swiss Federal Institute of Technology, Lausanne, in 2006. During 2007-2009, he was a postdoctoral researcher in the Centre for Digital Music at Queen Mary— University of London. Currently, he is an associate researcher (associate professor) in Thinkit Speech Lab, Institute of Acoustics, Chinese Academy of Sciences. His research interest is mainly focused on the feature extraction of music signal, and its applications to music information retrieval.

Index